EXPLORE & APPLY

Students taking their first course in economics face the hurdle of learning a new language that includes many new terms and concepts and a new way of making decisions and analyzing world events. To promote learning and critical thinking rather than memorizing, Ayers and Collinge have created a special section in each chapter entitled *Explore & Apply.* These sections achieve four goals:

1. Grab students' attention by presenting real-world domestic, international, and technology-related issues such as the impact of the war on terrorism on the economy, the role of technology in growth, and the problems Russia has encountered in transitioning toward a free market system.

A quote and photo capture reader interest.

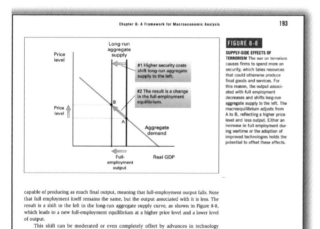

8.4 CLASSICAL VERSUS KEYNESIAN—THE GREAT DEBATE

This chapter started with reference to the Great Depression, which was ended by World War II and the massive government spending associated with it. Keynesian analysis was thought to have been proven correct. As President Richard Nixon phrased it in 1972, "We are all Keynesians, now." However, just as Nixon was proclaiming that Keynes had won, the economics profession was focusing in a more classical direction. It began to emphasize its microeconomic foundations, such as incentives facing individuals and firms that can influence the performance of the overall economy.

Economic analysis influences people's politics and vice versa. For example, political liberals often adopt Keynesian policy prescriptions. The reason is presumably not because most liberals have studied the economy in detail and are convinced of the validity of the Keynesian economic model. More likely, political liberals tend to believe that an activist government can be a powerful force for good in the world. Keynesian economics calls for government to be just such a force. It provides justification for a large government, but leaves open specific categories of spending.

A similar analysis applies to political conservatives, who tend to adhere to a classical perspective on the economy. Conservatives usually distrust big government, preferring instead a more laissez faire approach. Classical analysis suggests that much government action does more harm than good to the macroeconomy, which is in keeping with the conservative perspective.

While some controversy in macroeconomics is positive, concerning factual issues of cause and effect, most disagreement among macroeconomists is normative. For example, modern Keynesian models incorporate classical analysis of the long run. What makes these economists and their models Keynesian is that they discount the significance of the long run, preferring instead to emphasize practical issues in the workplace that inhibit adjustments to full employment. Thus, the disagreement between modern Keynesians and classical economists often boils down to the degrees to which they are willing to trade off short-and long-run objectives.

8.5 FIGHTING TERRORISM—WHAT PRICE DOES THE ECONOMY PAY?

"The world is not ending."

—**New York Mayor Rudy Giuliani after the September 11 terrorist attack**

On September 11, 2001, hijackers turned four passenger airliners into terrorist bombs, demolishing the World Trade Center skyscrapers in New York City and destroying a portion of the Pentagon in Washington, D.C. One of the hijacked planes crashed in rural Pennsylvania. About three thousand people lost their lives from these attacks. Immediately, before any more hijackings could be committed, the U.S. Federal Aviation Authority grounded all planes until security could be tightened. It was only when expensive and time-consuming security measures were in place that planes resumed flying. The country prepared for war, the war against terrorism.

No one could know at the time just what would lie ahead. One thing was certain, however, and that was the addition of tighter security throughout the country. The added security measures meant that it became more expensive to do business. The security industry prospered, as demand and prices went up in that line of business. However, numerous other industries suffered as they faced higher costs of production and slower deliveries of their raw materials.

The added costs for security services cause an increase in the real costs of producing the final goods and services recorded in GDP. The economy's limited resources are thus not

FIGURE 8-8

SUPPLY-SIDE EFFECTS OF TERRORISM The war on terrorism causes firms to spend more on security, which takes resources that could otherwise produce final goods and services. For this reason, the output associated with full employment decreases and shifts long-run aggregate supply to the left. The macroequilibrium adjusts from A to B, reflecting a higher price level and less output. Either an increase in full employment during wartime or the adoption of improved technologies holds the potential to offset these effects.

capable of producing as much final output, meaning that full-employment output falls. Note that full employment itself remains the same, but the output associated with it is less. The result is a shift to the left in the long-run aggregate supply curve, as shown in Figure 8-8, which leads to a new full-employment equilibrium at a higher price level and a lower level of output.

This shift can be moderated or even completely offset by advances in technology that increase productivity. For example, advances in monitoring and scanning cameras can reduce the need for security personnel, freeing them up to be productive in other ways. More generally, technology is applied to the workplace in order to increase productivity. To the extent it does so, the effect is to increase full-employment output and shift aggregate supply to the right, which is exactly opposite to the changes shown in Figure 8-8.

Other influences might also shift aggregate supply to the right. Looking back to World War II, we find that patriotism led to far more hours of work from the general population than was the norm either before or after the war. In effect, wartime full employment was higher than peacetime full employment. Taken by itself, the result was an increase in long-run aggregate supply.

HOW TERRORISM AFFECTS DEMAND

The 2001 terrorist attacks also had a significant effect on the demand side of the economy. The shock and uncertainty caused businesses to postpone new investment and consumers to postpone new purchases. For a while, it seemed everyone was hanging tight to their money and not allowing it to circulate as rapidly as it previously had. Airlines, hotels, amusement parks, and cruise ships all begged for customers. Some went bankrupt. Hundreds of thousands of Americans lost their jobs and millions more worried about their job security. The result was a leftward shift in aggregate demand. In other words, for any given price level, less output was demanded, as shown in Figure 8-9.

2. Encourage students to apply economic concepts to policy issues. The *Explore & Apply* sections apply the concepts of the chapter to real-world policy debates.

Policy issue is highlighted.

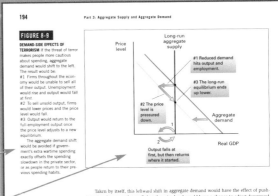

FIGURE 8-9

DEMAND-SIDE EFFECTS OF TERRORISM If the threat of terror makes people more cautious about spending, aggregate demand would shift to the left. The result would be:
#1 Firms throughout the economy would be unable to sell all of their output. Unemployment would rise and output would fall at first.
#2 To sell unsold output, firms would lower prices and the price level would fall.
#3 Output would return to the full-employment output once the price level adjusts to a new equilibrium.
The aggregate demand shift would be avoided if government's extra wartime spending exactly offsets the spending slowdown in the private sector, or as people return to their previous spending habits.

Taken by itself, this leftward shift in aggregate demand would have the effect of pushing prices lower, as shown. Before the price level would have a chance to adjust downward, output would fall and unemployment would rise. Were aggregate demand and aggregate supply both shifting left simultaneously, however, their influences would tend to offset each other in regard to price. Therefore, only output would fall.

There was considerable question following the September 2001 attacks as to how long it would take for consumers to resume their former patterns of spending. The answer was significant in terms of what the government should do. In particular, the government was not only spending additional money to combat the terrorists, but was also taking actions to lower borrowing costs and increase the amount of money circulating in the economy. The idea was to offset any drop in aggregate demand.

While intended to merely offset a drop in aggregate demand, such government actions ran the risk of going too far and actually increasing aggregate demand above what it had been before, particularly once the initial fears subsided and people returned to more normal spending patterns. If aggregate demand were to increase, demand-side inflation would be the result, as shown in Figure 8-10(a). Figure 8-10(b) shows how the situation could easily get out of hand, with demand-side inflation adding to supply-side inflation, causing the economy to move from point A to point B, and on to point C in the figure. This situation is stagflation, in which output falls even as prices rise.

In response to the war against terrorism, there are also additional real and important macroeconomic consequences that lie hidden beneath the surface of the aggregate-demand/aggregate-supply model. For example, for the purposes of this model, it does not matter whether GDP is composed of military spending that we wish was unnecessary or spending on consumer goods and services that would be the alternative in peacetime. It matters to our standard of living, but we do not see these things in the aggregate economic analysis.

> **Dynamic graphs and captions illustrate the policy issue being discussed in the narrative.**

3. Promote critical thinking with *Thinking Critically* questions that push students to use economic reasoning to consider more than one side of a familiar policy debate.

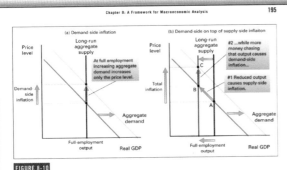

FIGURE 8-10

A DOUBLE DOSE OF INFLATION As shown in (a), demand-side inflation could occur if government spending rises dramatically. Higher government spending could reflect the costs of fighting a war or merely the costs of tax and spending programs intended to prevent or offset an economic downturn. As shown in (b), the demand-side inflation might come in addition to the initial supply-side inflation caused by the higher costs of security and transportation.

1. Identify some additional effects of the war on terrorism that would shift aggregate supply or aggregate demand.

2. What could cause wartime full employment to exceed peacetime full employment? Give some examples from the United States' actual wartime experience.

THINKING CRITICALLY

Visit www.prenhall.com/ayers for updates and web exercises on this Explore & Apply topic.

SUMMARY AND LEARNING OBJECTIVES

1. **Contrast the perspectives of classical economists to those of Keynesians.**
   - When the economy's resources are fully employed, the economy has attained full-employment output, also called full-employment GDP. Actual GDP could be at, above, or below the full-employment level of GDP.
   - The book *The General Theory of Employment, Interest, and Money* (1936) by John Maynard Keynes revolutionized economics and launched the new field

   of macroeconomics. Keynes distinguished between the short run and the long run, observing that "In the long run we are all dead." Keynesian economics takes a short-run perspective. Keynes' goal was to further the understanding of why the economies of the world remained mired in the Great Depression of the 1930s.
   - Classical economics emphasizes the long run. It has achieved a resurgence of interest as the Great Depression recedes further into the past.

---

4. Expand teaching materials and opportunities. The book's Companion Website, **www.prenhall.com/ayers**, includes updates on each *Explore & Apply.* This will save professors many hours of research time finding current topics for their lectures. A custom-filmed video series supports and extends on *Explore & Apply* topics.

> *Thinking Critically* **questions push students to use economic reasoning to consider more than one side of a familiar policy debate.**

The following is a list of the *Explore & Apply* topics. The video icon identifies those *Explore & Apply* topics supported by Prentice Hall's custom-filmed Video Series. The series includes interviews with economists, other professionals, and students who express their viewpoints concerning topics close to home, and by extension, examine current policy issues.

MACROECONOMICS

Explore & Apply

PRENTICE HALL SERIES IN ECONOMICS

Adams/Brock
The Structure of American Industry, Tenth Edition

Ayers/Collinge
Economics: Explore & Apply

Ayers/Collinge
Macroeconomics: Explore & Apply

Ayers/Collinge
Microeconomics: Explore & Apply

Blanchard
Macroeconomics, Third Edition

Blau/Ferber/Winkler
The Economics of Women, Men, and Work, Fourth Edition

Boardman/Greenberg/Vining/Weimer
Cost Benefit Analysis: Concepts and Practice,
Second Edition

Bogart
The Economics of Cities and Suburbs

Case/Fair
Principles of Economics, Updated Sixth Edition

Case/Fair
Principles of Macroeconomics, Updated Sixth Edition

Case/Fair
Principles of Microeconomics, Sixth Edition

Caves
American Industry: Structure, Conduct, Performance,
Seventh Edition

Colander/Gamber
Macroeconomics

Collinge/Ayers
Economics by Design: Principles and Issues, Second Edition

DiPasquale/Wheaton
Urban Economics and Real Estate Markets

Eaton/Eaton/Allen
Microeconomics, Fifth Edition

Folland/Goodman/Stano
Economics of Health and Health Care, Third Edition

Fort
Sports Economics

Froyen
Macroeconomics: Theories and Policies, Seventh Edition

Greene
Econometric Analysis, Fifth Edition

Heilbroner/Milberg
The Making of Economic Society, Eleventh Edition

Hess
Using Mathematics in Economic Analysis

Heyne/Boettke/Prychitko
The Economic Way of Thinking, Tenth Edition

Keat/Young
Managerial Economics, Fourth Edition

Lynn
*Economic Development: Theory and Practice
for a Divided World*

Mathis/Koscianski
Microeconomic Theory: An Integrated Approach

Milgrom/Roberts
Economics, Organization, and Management

O'Sullivan/Sheffrin
Economics: Principles and Tools, Third Edition

O'Sullivan/Sheffrin
Macroeconomics: Principles and Tools, Third Edition

O'Sullivan/Sheffrin
Microeconomics: Principles and Tools, Third Edition

O'Sullivan/Sheffrin
Survey of Economics: Principles and Tools

Petersen/Lewis
Managerial Economics, Fifth Edition

Pindyck/Rubinfeld
Microeconomics, Fifth Edition

Reynolds/Masters/Moser
Labor Economics and Labor Relations, Eleventh Edition

Roberts
The Choice: A Fable of Free Trade and Protectionism,
Revised Edition

Schiller
The Economics of Poverty and Discrimination,
Eighth Edition

Weidenbaum
Business and Government in the Global Marketplace,
Sixth Edition

MACROECONOMICS

EXPLORE
&
APPLY

RONALD M. AYERS
University of Texas at San Antonio

ROBERT A. COLLINGE
University of Texas at San Antonio

Prentice Hall

Upper Saddle River, New Jersey 07458

Library of Congress Cataloging-in-Publication Data

Ayers, Ronald M.
  Macroeconomics : explore & apply / Ronald Ayers, Robert Collinge.
    p. cm.
  Also issued simultaneously as part of the author's Economics.
  Includes bibliographical references and index.
  ISBN 0-13-016422-4
  1. Macroeconomics. I. Collinge, Robert A. II. Ayers, Ronald M. Economics. III. Title.

HB 172.5 .A926 2004
339--dc21

2002042543

Executive Editor: Rod Banister
Editor-in-Chief: P. J. Boardman
Senior Development Editor: Lena Buonanno
Director of Development: Steve Deitmer
Managing Editor: Gladys Soto
Assistant Editor: Marie McHale
Editorial Assistant: Joy Golden
Project Manager, Media: Victoria Anderson
Executive Marketing Manager: Kathleen McLellan
Marketing Assistant: Christopher Bath
Managing Editor (Production): Cynthia Regan
Production Editor: Michael Reynolds
Production Assistant: Joe DeProspero
Permissions Supervisor: Suzanne Grappi
Associate Director, Manufacturing: Vinnie Scelta
Production Manager: Arnold Vila
Design Manager: Maria Lange
Art Director: Steve Frim
Interior Design: Karen Quigley
Cover Design: Kathryn Foot
Cover Illustration/Photo: Boby Model/National Geographic/Getty Images
Manager, Print Production: Christy Mahon
Composition: Carlisle Publishers Services
Full-Service Project Management: Carlisle Publishers Services
Printer/Binder: R.R. Donnelley/Willard

Credits and acknowledgments borrowed from other sources and reproduced, with permission, in this textbook appear on appropriate page within text (or on page 443).

Pearson Education LTD.
Pearson Education Australia PTY, Limited
Pearson Education Singapore, Pte. Ltd
Pearson Education North Asia Ltd
Pearson Education, Canada, Ltd
Pearson Educación de Mexico, S.A. de C.V.
Pearson Education–Japan
Pearson Education Malaysia, Pte. Ltd

10 9 8 7 6 5 4 3 2
ISBN 0-13-016422-4

To my former professors
–Ron

To Mary
–Bob

ABOUT THE AUTHORS

RONALD M. AYERS

Ronald Ayers is Associate Professor of Economics and Director of the Teaching and Learning Center at the University of Texas, San Antonio. He teaches principles of microeconomics and macroeconomics, as well as the university's core curriculum course in political economy and various field courses, including labor economics, money and banking, and industrial organization. His classes have ranged from small honors sections to lecture sections of 300.

After receiving Bachelor's and Master's degrees from the University of New Orleans, he subsequently received his Ph.D. in economics from Tulane University. Earlier in his career, Dr. Ayers served as a faculty member at Loyola University (New Orleans), Ohio State University, and Texas A & M University. He has also worked as a consultant for the City of San Antonio and several private consulting firms and attorneys. In recent years he was awarded the President's Distinguished Achievement Award for Core Curriculum Teaching, the College of Business Teaching Award, and the U.T. System Chancellor's Council Teaching Award. He also was named a Senior Fellow, Texas Higher Education Coordinating Board, in 2000. In 2001–2002, Professor Ayers was elected to serve as the Chair of the University's Faculty Senate.

Dr. Ayers has published chapters in *Putting the Invisible Hand to Work: Concepts and Models for Service-Learning in Economics* (University of Michigan Press) and *U.S.-Mexican Economic Relations: Prospects and Problems* (Praeger Publishing Company). In addition, he has published articles in many different journals, including the *National Social Science Journal,* and the *Journal of Urban and Regional Information Systems.* Along with Robert Collinge, Professor Ayers has written *Economics by Design: Principles and Issues,* forthcoming in its third edition. When he is not pursuing his interest in how people learn, Dr. Ayers enjoys spending time with his dogs, collecting books, and tinkering.

ROBERT A. COLLINGE

Robert Collinge is Professor of Economics at the University of Texas, San Antonio. Among other courses at the graduate and undergraduate levels, Dr. Collinge has taught micro principles, macro principles, or the combined survey/issues class in each of his 16 years at UTSA. In the last few years, Professor Collinge has twice been awarded his University President's Outstanding Achievement Award, once for overall teaching and once for teaching at the core curriculum level. Most recently, he has received his College's Combined Teaching, Research, and Service Excellence Award. Along with Ronald Ayers, Professor Collinge co-directed his University's Center for Economic Education.

After undergraduate studies at the State University of New York at Buffalo, Bob enrolled at the University of Maryland at College Park, where he went on to receive his B.A., M.A., and Ph.D. degrees. In 1982, he joined the Economics faculty at the University of Louisville. To gain experience outside of academia, Dr. Collinge worked in Washington, D.C., first as a Visiting Economist with the U.S. International Trade Commission, and then as an Economist in the Policy Analysis Department of the American Petroleum Institute.

Professor Collinge's research focuses on the design and analysis of public policies, such as his recent articles in the *Journal of Environmental Economics and Management* and the *Canadian Journal of Economics.* He has contributed to an array of other books and journals, including *The Economic Journal, The Journal of Public Economics,* and *World Development.* Professor Collinge currently serves as a member of the editorial board of *Public Works Management and Policy.* In his free time, Bob enjoys hiking through the woods near his Texas Hill Country home.

BRIEF CONTENTS

CONTENTS

A BOOK FOR TODAY'S STUDENTS

Taking your first course in economics can be like finding yourself in a foreign country where you do not know the language. You want the freedom to explore various interesting spots, but you cannot read the street signs for direction and you struggle when trying to communicate with the locals. There may be several different, exciting paths you can choose, but you are not sure which is best. To get your bearings in the country and reach your destinations, you need to learn something about the country's language.

Students in a principles of economics course face many of the same challenges as a wandering traveler. They have registered for the course, but they face the hurdle of learning a new language that includes many new terms and concepts. They also face the challenge of learning how to read and interpret graphs. *Macroeconomics: Explore & Apply* was written to help students learn the language of economics. We engage students with familiar real-world examples and applications that bring economics to life. Our goal is to encourage students to apply the concepts they learn in this book to personal, business, and social issues that will face them long after their economics course is over. We teach students how to analyze events in the world around them and draw their own conclusions. To achieve our goal, we implement three key tools:

1. Real-world applications
2. Sound pedagogy
3. Straightforward presentation

REAL-WORLD APPLICATIONS

Principles of economics is often a required course for a variety of majors, since its subject matter relates to so many of life's issues: Should I stay in school, or quit and get a full-time job? Which major should I select? Why does the Federal Reserve's monetary policy matter? To help students find the answers to such questions and fulfill the purpose of this course, we emphasize both economic tools and the application of those tools. Many of our applications deal with recent events that underscore the importance of economics, such as: the rise in government spending because of the war on terrorism; budget deficits and the size of the national debt; and the effect of immigration on a nation's economy. Such economic issues make it all the more important for students to understand the market economy and the principles that underlie effective public policy.

Explore & Apply

We continually motivate learning and retention of concepts with examples and brief applications throughout this book. Additionally, each chapter concludes with an in-depth *Explore & Apply* section that drives students to use the economic principles they have just learned. Each *Explore & Apply* looks at a current issue and places the student in the position of analyzing the issue using the economic tools presented in the chapter. Whether in class or over coffee, debating these policy issues can be both interesting and instructive. The result is that students retain the concepts and are ready to apply them to the many additional issues they will encounter beyond the confines of this textbook and the course.

The *Explore & Apply* sections include domestic and international topics, with several interweaving technology-related issues. Sample topics include:

- What has motivated China to transition toward a market economy?
- Why does Congress knowingly use an inaccurate forecasting method?
- How do we pay for homeland security?
- Is there a "new economy" that enhances economic growth?

Each *Explore & Apply* includes two *Thinking Critically* questions that promote economic reasoning and encourage students to debate a policy issue. A compass icon, located in the chapter-opening learning objectives and various places in the chapter, identifies material and questions related to the *Explore & Apply* sections. Below are excerpts of narrative, a graph, and questions from the Chapter 3 *Explore & Apply*.

To keep the *Explore & Apply* sections up-to-date and to strengthen class discussions, we offer two kinds of web support materials at www.prenhall.com/ayers:

1. Updates on each *Explore & Apply* section and supporting exercises.

2. Six custom-filmed videos that further explore the issues at hand. Current statistical information and interviews with professionals and students highlight the various viewpoints on each policy issue. Tips on how to use these videos appear in the book's Instructor's Manual.

3.4 DEMANDING BETTER SCHOOLS, SUPPLYING BETTER SCHOOLS

Some people know the importance of education because they have it. I know the importance of education because I didn't.

—Frederick Douglass, ex-slave and abolitionist

"Our schools must be improved!" From kindergarten through the twelfth grade, the education of America's youth is a top concern of both the president and parents. There is less concern, however, about improving colleges; the reasons relate to demand and supply.

College students shoulder the high cost of college, with cost playing a major role in college choice. Consistent with the law of demand, the lower the price of a college education, *ceteris paribus*, the greater the number of students who will apply and the more education they will choose. To promote college education, government offers tax deductions, subsidies, and financial aid that in effect lowers its price.

High school seniors choose among a varied assortment of colleges. In lower grades, however, there is normally a powerful financial incentive to choose only the government-provided local public school. The reason is that taxpayer financing makes those schools free to the student.

Free public schooling was established in the nineteenth century to promote equal opportunity—an equal start in life. However, public schools are not all the same, and the gap between the best and the worst is not likely to close on its own. Schools in wealthy neighborhoods often spend more per pupil than schools in poor ones. Some schools are bureaucratic, inefficient, and ineffective, while others have strong academic reputations. Inefficient

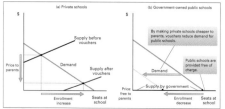

FIGURE 3-13

EFFECTS OF SCHOOL VOUCHERS Vouchers lower the price of private schooling, which increases the quantity demanded. The effect in the market for public schooling, a substitute, is to decrease demand and enrollments. Vouchers increase competition among schools, providing them with the incentive to provide the best value for money spent on education.

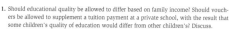

1. Should educational quality be allowed to differ based on family income? Should vouchers be allowed to supplement a tuition payment at a private school, with the result that some children's quality of education would differ from other children's? Discuss.

2. *Myra:* I think voucher amounts should vary with household income. The more income, the less help—it's only fair.
Fred: I think education should be free for everyone. Your income shouldn't have anything to do with how much voucher power you have.

Evaluate Myra's and Fred's ideas. If a voucher plan is to be used, should the voucher amount depend upon a person's income?

Visit www.prenhall.com/ayers for updates and web exercises on this Explore & Apply topic.

THINKING CRITICALLY

PEDAGOGY

Our pedagogical features support our goal of helping students learn the language of economics and apply what they have learned.

- **Learning Objectives.** Each chapter opens with a list of objectives that establishes the goals and organization of the chapter. We repeat these learning objectives and use them as an organizational tool for the end-of-chapter summary. The linking of the learning objectives and summary provides students with a helpful and coherent way to review the concepts in each chapter. One learning objective per chapter supports the *Explore & Apply* section.

- **Snapshots.** Students retain economic concepts best when they see how these concepts relate to their immediate world. We include three Snapshots in each chapter to reinforce key concepts that have been presented. ———→

- **QuickChecks.** Three or more questions with answers interspersed throughout each chapter allow students to check their knowledge of key concepts before moving on. ————→

- **Margin Definitions.** This running glossary allows students to check their understanding of key terms.

- **Graphs.** Reading and interpreting graphs is a key part of understanding economic concepts. Colors are used consistently in the graphs to reinforce key concepts. For example, the supply and aggregate supply curves are red, the demand and aggregate demand curves are blue, and shifts in curves are shown with a different shade. Call-out boxes are inserted into the graphs to help students interpret them. Graph captions are clear and self-contained so that students can understand how and why curves are shifting.

- **Extensive Array of End-of-Chapter Pedagogy.** Each chapter ends with a wide array of summary and self-test materials that appeal to a variety of teaching and learning styles:

  Summary and Learning Objectives summarize the key points of the chapter and tie those points back to the learning objectives that opened the chapter.

  Key Terms List gives students an opportunity to review the concepts they have learned in the chapter. A page reference is included next to each term so that students can easily locate the definitions.

  Test Yourself questions in true/false and multiple-choice formats give students self-assessment opportunities and support the *Explore & Apply* section. Solutions appear at the end of the book.

  Questions and Problems are annotated by topic. The annotation appears before each question and problem so that instructors can easily make assignment choices. Solutions to even-numbered items appear in the back of the book. All solutions appear in the instructor's manual.

  Web Support Materials encourage students to visit www.prenhall.com/ayers to access more self-test quizzes, Exploring the Web exercises, news articles, and much more.

SNAPSHOT **COMPETING WITH COMPARATIVE ADVANTAGE**

Many great athletes are multitalented, possessing strength, speed, and muscle coordination that dwarf that of the general population. These qualities are needed for success in a variety of sports, yet few athletes play more than one sport professionally, even though they might be able to do so. Simply look at the sports pages. Venus Williams makes headlines by swinging a tennis racket, while Tiger Woods swings a golf club and Barry Bonds swings a bat. Their choices tell the rest of us about their comparative advantages.

The best teams exploit the comparative advantages of their players. Each player has a job to do and specializes in doing it well. Whatever the sport, owners and fans expect this principle of comparative advantage to be followed and demand coaches who will best exploit the talents of their players. But even the best coaches can err, as when Cleveland Indians' baseball coach Tris Speaker said in 1921, "Babe Ruth made a great mistake when he gave up pitching. Working once a week, he might have lasted a long time and become a great star." ◄

QUICKCHECK

List three cases in which shifts in demand and/or supply would result in a lower price and a greater quantity.

Answer: One case occurs when supply shifts to the right and demand does not change. A second case is when supply and demand both shift to the right, but the shift in supply is larger. A third case is when supply shifts right and demand shifts left, with the shift in supply being larger than the shift in demand. These cases are shown in Figures 3-10 (case 1), 3–11(b), and 3–12, respectively.

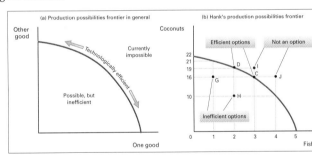

FIGURE 2-3

POSSIBILITIES FOR EFFICIENCY All points on the production possibilities frontier are output combinations that are technologically efficient and feasible, as shown in (a). Points within the production possibilities frontier are also feasible, but are not efficient. Points outside the frontier cannot be reached with current resources and technology.

For example, (b) shows Hank's production possibilities on Castaway Island. On this graph, point G represents 16 coconuts and 1 fish. That combination of outputs is possible, but Hank could do better at point D by producing 19 coconuts and 2 fish. Likewise, point C is more efficient than point H. Both C and D are efficient in a technological sense, meaning that at either point, Hank cannot produce more of one good without giving up some of the other. Hank would like to achieve points I or J, but does not have the resources and technology to do so.

STRAIGHTFORWARD PRESENTATION

One of the most frequent complaints about many existing textbooks is that they offer more material than can be covered adequately during the term. *Macroeconomics: Explore & Apply* responds to this concern by covering essential concepts without bogging down the reader in too much detail. The book accomplishes this objective by emphasizing the intuition of economic concepts and focusing on those topics that are at the heart of economics. The result is a 17-chapter book that can easily be read and taught from, with an ample, but not excessive amount of material.

MACROECONOMICS ORGANIZATION

Macroeconomics: Explore & Apply is flexible enough to be used by those who favor a short-run emphasis or a long-run emphasis. For example, we have isolated the income–expenditure model in Chapter 10, "Aggregate Expenditures," so that instructors who do not use this model can easily skip the chapter without loss of continuity. Please see the *Alternative Sequences* chart on the final preface page xxx.

Part 1, "A Journey Through the Economy" (Chapters 1–4), covers the goals of economics, various economic systems, production possibilities, comparative advantage, demand and supply, market efficiency, and price controls.

Part 2, "Monitoring the Macroeconomy" (Chapters 5–7), covers GDP measurement, inflation, and unemployment.

In *Part 3,* "Aggregate Supply and Aggregate Demand" (Chapters 8–10), Chapter 8 introduces the two primary schools of macro thought, associating Keynes with short-run analysis and classical with long-run analysis. The model of aggregate supply and aggregate demand is then introduced as a framework for analysis. To keep matters from becoming too complex, only the long-run aggregate supply curve is introduced in this chapter. Chapter 9 builds upon chapter 8 by introducing the short-run aggregate supply curve and the issues involved in short-run analysis. Chapter 9 emphasizes how short-run and long-run aggregate supply relate to each other and to aggregate demand. Issues of deficits, debt, and other aspects of fiscal policy are introduced in this framework. Chapter 10 further elaborates upon the model of aggregate supply and aggregate demand by examining the Keynesian aggregate expenditures model that underlies the aggregate demand curve.

Part 4, "Incentives for Productivity" (Chapters 11–12), covers issues related to implementing fiscal policy and how incentives for growth are strongly influenced by the specifics of government fiscal policy design.

Part 5, "Money in the Macroeconomy" (Chapters 13–14), covers money, the Fed, and the logic behind Fed policy actions. These topics are positioned so as not to disrupt the step-by-step building process formed in Chapters 8 through 12.

THE GLOBAL ECONOMY

Whether it be economic incentives in China, the multinational nature of the work force, or treaties on the global environment, international economic issues are integrated throughout the book. Furthermore, they appear in many of the *Explore & Apply* sections, Snapshots, and comparative tables and figures. *Part 6* concludes the book by looking at the global marketplace and issues of trade and development. In Chapter 15, "Into the International Marketplace," and Chapter 16, "Policy Toward Trade," we examine the balance of payments, exchange rates, free-trade agreements, and arguments for trade restrictions. In Chapter 17, "Economic Development," we study the forces that can lead some countries to develop strong economies and other countries to stagnate.

CURRENCY AND ACCURACY

At all times, we strive for currency of content. Graphs and tables include the most recent data available. Throughout the book, we apply economic analysis to genuinely current issues—the ones that appear in headlines today and promise to continue making headlines in years to come. We will also keep the *Explore & Apply* sections current via the book's web site.

Macroeconomics: Explore & Apply was developed based on our forty years' combined experience teaching the principles of economics course, as well as the input of more than 100 economics professors. We realize the extreme importance of accurate graphs, equations, questions and problems, and solutions. To ensure the highest level of accuracy, we carefully and painstakingly evaluated each chapter and also formed an *Accuracy Review Board* of four economics professors who checked every word, number, equation, and figure in the book. The board members were Paul Comolli, University of Kansas; Barry Kotlove, Edmonds Community College; Matthew Marlin, Duquesne University; and Garvin Smith, Daytona Beach Community College.

The supplement package was checked for accuracy by Warren Bilotta, Louisiana State University, Alexandria; Jack Bucco, Austin Community College; Ronald Elkins, Central Washington University; Jeff Holt, Tulsa Community College; and John C. Wassom, Western Kentucky University.

SUPPLEMENTS ADVISOR AND COORDINATOR

We understand how important it is for instructors to have a supplement package that is comprehensive, coordinated with the main text, and easy to use. Professor Mary Lesser of Iona College, who has taught the principles of economics course for 20 years, served as the advisor and coordinator for the extensive print and technology supplement package that accompanies *Macroeconomics: Explore & Apply*. Professor Lesser ensured that each supplement, including the test banks, instructor's manual, study guide, and PowerPoint presentations met the highest standards of quality. Her script ideas and overall direction on the *Explore & Apply* custom-video series helped the film crew focus on topics that resonate with today's students. She also helped develop many of the media supplements, including the *Explore & Apply* Active Book.

PRINT SUPPLEMENTS

Macroeconomics: Explore & Apply has a comprehensive supplements package that is coordinated with the main text through the numbering system of the headings in each chapter. The major sections of the chapters are numbered (1.1, 1.2, 1.3, and so on), and that numbering system is used consistently in the supplements to make it more convenient and flexible for instructors to develop their course assignments.

Study Guide

The authors have personally prepared the comprehensive study guide that accompanies the text. Tied directly to sections of the text, the study guide enhances and reinforces economic concepts for increased student comprehension. Each chapter of the study guide includes approximately 90 questions. Each chapter features the following elements:

- **Chapter Reviews.** A comprehensive summary of the key concepts of the chapter, including the *Explore & Apply* sections.
- **Study Checks.** These problems are included throughout the Chapter Review for quick practice with the concepts just covered.

- **Self-Tests.** 25 true/false/explain, 25 fill in the blanks, and 25 multiple choice, questions give students an opportunity to test their knowledge.
- **Grasping the Graphs.** This section provides students with practice in labeling and analyzing key graphs from the book.
- **Solutions.** Detailed answers to all study guide questions.

Instructor's Manual

The instructor's manual, written by Rose LaMont of Modesto Junior College, provides the following teaching support materials:

- **Summaries**
- **Detailed Chapter Outlines** integrating the following:

  Key terminology
  Topics for Class Discussion that feature real-world ideas that appeal to students and help instructors explore and reinforce the concepts in the text.
  Teaching Tips that help the instructor coordinate the text and its online offerings and present the *Explore & Apply* sections.

- **Extended Applications** that help make economics relevant to students.
- **Experiments and Exercises** to use in the classroom.
- **Sample Syllabi**
- **Solutions** to all problems in the book.
- **Video Guide** to help integrate the *Explore & Apply* videos into the classroom.

Test Banks

Two test banks were prepared by Richard Gosselin of Houston Community College and Scott Hunt of Columbus State Community College. The test banks include *over 5,000 questions,* organized by chapter section. Each question is keyed by degree of difficulty as easy, moderate, or difficult. Easy questions involve straightforward recall of information in the text. *Moderate* questions require some analysis on the student's part. *Difficult* questions usually entail more complex analysis. To help instructors select questions quickly and efficiently, we have used the skill descriptors of fact, definition, conceptual, and analytical. A question labeled *fact* tests a student's knowledge of factual information presented in the text. A *definition* question asks the student to define an economic term or concept. *Conceptual* questions test a student's understanding of a concept. *Analytical* questions require the student to apply an analytical procedure to answer the question.

The test banks includes questions with tables that provide students with the numbers that they need to solve for numerical answers. It also contains questions based on the graphs that appear in the book. The questions ask students to interpret the information presented in the graph. There are also many questions in the test banks that require students to sketch out a graph on their own and interpret curve movements. Test bank questions also support the *Explore & Apply* sections.

Color Transparencies

All figures and tables from the text are reproduced as full-page, four-color acetates.

INTERNET RESOURCES

Prentice Hall's Internet Resources provide students with a variety of interactive graphing and self-assessment tools. It also supplies numerous current news articles and supporting exercises.

Companion Website http://www.prenhall.com/ayers

The Companion Website connects students to *Current Events* economics articles in the news, *Explore & Apply* updates, Exploring the Web exercises and activities, and Practice Quizzes that include many graphs from the text. The Practice Quizzes were prepared by Fernando Quijano and Yvonn Quijano. These quizzes provide immediate feedback for correct and incorrect answers, and let students e-mail results to their professors.

For Instructors

- **Syllabus Manager.** This feature allows instructors to enhance their lectures with all the resources available with this text. Instructors can post their own syllabus and link to any of the material on the site.
- **Downloadable Supplements.** These features allow instructors to access the book's PowerPoint Presentation and instructor's manual. Please contact your Prentice Hall sales representative for password information.

Companion Website PLUS for Instructors and Students

Available by using the access code packaged with every new text, Companion Website PLUS uses all of the content of the Companion Website listed above and the following other interactive resources:

- **Active Graphs.** Forty-two Active Graphs supports key graphs in the text. These JAVA applications invite students to change the value of variables and curves and see the effects in the movement of the graph.
- **Smart Graphs.** Eighteen Smart Graphs ask students to modify graphs based on an economic scenario and questions. Students receive an instant response detailing how they should have changed the graph.
- **Animated Graphing Tutorial with Audio.** Guides the student through a multimedia version of Chapter 1 Appendix: "Working with Graphs and Data."
- **Egraph and Graphing Questions.** This electronic graphing tool allows students to create precise, colorful graphs, using Flash technology. Students can e-mail these graphs to their professor or print and save them. To apply this technology, we have included *Graphing Questions* that require students to analyze information gathered on the Web, then create graphs using the Graphing Tool. Complete answers, with graphs, are included. The *Graphing Questions* were prepared by Leonie L. Stone of the State University of New York, Geneseo.
- *Explore & Apply* **Video Series.** A series of six custom-filmed videos support the *Explore & Apply* sections. The videos dig deeper into the issue presented in each chapter and highlight various viewpoints of the policy issue being discussed. The series includes interviews with professionals and students. A guide to using the videos is included in the Instructor's Manual and provides summaries, lecture tips, discussion questions, and exercises.

ONLINE COURSE OFFERINGS

To accommodate various teaching styles, we offer a complete range of technology-support materials.

WebCT

Developed by educators, WebCT provides faculty with easy-to-use Internet tools to create online courses. Prentice Hall provides content and enhanced features to help instructors create a complete online course. Online courses are free when shrinkwrapped with the text and contain the online study guide and all test questions from the test item files. Please visit our web site at www.prenhall.com/webct for more information or contact your local Prentice Hall sales representative.

www.blackboard.com

Blackboard

Easy to use, Blackboard's simple templates and tools make it easy to create, manage, and use online course materials. Prentice Hall provides content, and instructors can create online courses using the Blackboard tools, which include design, communications, testing, and course management tools. Please visit our web site at www.prenhall.com/blackboard for more information.

CourseCompass

CourseCompass

This customizable, interactive online course-management tool, powered by Blackboard, provides the most intuitive teaching and learning environment available. Instructors can communicate with students, distribute course material, and access student progress online. For further information, please visit our web site at http://www.prenhall.com/coursecompass or contact your Prentice Hall sales representative.

TECHNOLOGY SUPPLEMENTS FOR THE INSTRUCTOR

The following technology supplements are designed to make teaching and testing easy.

TestGen-EQ Test-Generating Software

The test banks appear in print and as computer files that may be used with the TestGen-EQ test-generating software. This computerized package allows instructors to customize classroom tests. Instructors may edit, add, or delete questions from the test banks; edit existing graphics and create new graphics; analyze test results; and organize a database of tests and student results. This new software allows for flexibility and ease of use. It provides many options for organizing and displaying tests, along with a search and sort feature. *Macroeconomics: Explore & Apply* is supported by two test-item files with over 5,000 questions. These test-item files are described in detail under the "Print Supplements" section of this preface.

PowerPoint Lecture Presentation

The PowerPoint presentation, by Paul Harris of Camden County College, offer summaries and reinforcement of key text material. Many graphs "build" over a sequencing of slides so that students may see the step-by-step process of economic analysis. Instructors can create full-color, professional-looking presentations and customized handouts for students. The PowerPoint Presentation is included in the Instructor's Resource CD-ROM and are downloadable from www.prenhall.com/ayers.

Explore & Apply Videos on VHS Cassette

A series of six custom-filmed videos support the *Explore & Apply* sections. The videos dig deeper into the issue presented in each chapter and highlight various viewpoints of the policy issue being discussed. The series includes interviews with professionals and students. A guide to using the videos is included in the Instructor's Manual, which provides summaries, lecture tips, discussion questions, and exercises. The videos are available to instructors on VHS cassette and on the Instructor's Resource CD-ROM. They will also be posted on the book's web site at www.prenhall.com/ayers.

Instructor's Resource CD-ROM

The Instructor's Resource CD-ROM allows instructors to easily access and edit the Instructor's Manual, test banks, and PowerPoint Presentations. The *Explore & Apply* custom videos are also included.

SUBSCRIPTIONS: *WALL STREET JOURNAL, FINANCIAL TIMES,* AND *ECONOMIST.COM*

Analyzing current events is an important skill for economic students to develop. To sharpen this skill and further support the book's theme of exploration and application, Prentice Hall offers you and your students three *news subscription* offers:

The Wall Street Journal Print and Interactive Editions Subscription

Prentice Hall has formed a strategic alliance with the *Wall Street Journal,* the most respected and trusted daily source for information on business and economics. For a small additional charge, Prentice Hall offers your students a ten-week subscription to the *Wall Street Journal* print edition and the *Wall Street Journal* Interactive Edition. Upon adoption of a special book with the subscription package, professors will receive a free one-year subscription of the print and interactive versions as well as weekly subject-specific *Wall Street Journal* educators' lesson plans.

The Financial Times

We are pleased to announce a special partnership with *The Financial Times.* For a small additional charge, Prentice Hall offers your students a fifteen-week subscription to *The Financial Times.* Upon adoption of a special book with the subscription package, professors will receive a free one-year subscription. Please contact your Prentice Hall representative for details and ordering information.

Economist.com

Through a special arrangement with *Economist.com,* Prentice Hall offers your students a twelve-week subscription to *Economist.com* for a small additional charge. Upon adoption of a special book with the subscription package, professors will receive a free six-month subscription. Please contact your Prentice Hall representative for further details and ordering information.

ACKNOWLEDGMENTS

We would like to start by expressing our hearty thanks to Rod Banister, Executive Editor, and Lena Buonanno, Senior Developmental Editor, for their ceaseless commitment to quality. Mike Reynolds, Production Editor, skillfully managed all phases of the production process and ensured a quality product. The extensive print and technology supplements that accompany this book are the result of the dedication of Gladys Soto, Managing Editor; Marie McHale, Assistant Editor; Victoria Anderson, Media Project Manager; and Lisa Amato and Joy Golden, Editorial Assistants. Kathleen McLellan, Executive Marketing Manager, and David Theisen, National Sales Director for Key Markets, provided recommendations through various phases of the book development and created an innovative marketing strategy. Abby Reip, our photoresearcher, located the dynamic and effective photographs that appear in each chapter. Along with the rest of the team at Prentice Hall, their hard work and vision were instrumental in achieving the finished products we have been discussing in this preface.

In addition to having the expertise of the Prentice Hall staff, we benefited from the expertise of numerous professors who teach the principles of economics course. We extend our special thanks and appreciation to Mary Lesser of Iona College, for her careful attention to the extensive supplement package.

Special thanks also go to the members of our *Accuracy Review Board,* who, as mentioned earlier, helped us identify and correct accuracy issues: Paul Comolli, University of Kansas; Barry Kotlove, Edmonds Community College; Matthew Marlin, Duquesne University; and Garvin Smith, Daytona Beach Community College.

We owe a debt of gratitude to our talented and dedicated supplement authors: Andrew Dane of Angelo State University, Richard Gosselin of Houston Community College, Paul Harris of Camden County College, Scott Hunt of Columbus State Community College, Rose LaMont of Modesto Junior College, Peter Mavrokordatos of Tarrant County College, Leonie L. Stone, State University of New York, Geneseo, and Kathy Wilson of Kent State University.

We also owe a great deal to the many reviewers and focus-group participants who assisted us in developing this book. The following professors provided us with thoughtful recommendations and constructive criticism:

Cinda Adams, Chattanooga State Technical Community College
Christie Agioutanti, City University of New York, Baruch
Carlos Aguilar, El Paso Community College
Uzo Agulefo, North Lake College
Ercument G. Aksoy, Los Angeles Valley College
Frank Albritton, Seminole Community College
Newton E. Aldridge, Hinds Community College
Khalid Al-Hmoud, Texas Tech University
Farhad Ameen, SUNY, Westchester Community College
Len Anyanwu, Union County College
Hamid Azari-Rad, State University of New York, New Paltz
Mina N. Baliamoune, University of North Florida
Getachew Begashaw, William Rainey Harper College
Adolfo Benavides, Texas A&M University, Corpus Christi
Victor Brajer, California State University at Fullerton
Fenton L. Broadhead, Brigham Young University, Idaho
Kathleen K. Bromley, Monroe Community College
Jack A. Bucco, Austin Community College

Melvin C. Burton, Jr., J. Sargeant Reynolds Community College
Regina Cassady, Valencia Community College
Chandana Chakraborty, Montclair State University
Marc C. Chopin, Louisiana Tech University
Pam Coates, San Diego Mesa College
John P. Cochran, Metropolitan State College of Denver
Paul Comolli, University of Kansas
Bienvenido S. Cortes, Pittsburg State University
Chandrea Thomas Crowe-Hopkins, College of Lake County
Rosa Lea Danielson, College of DuPage
Irma T. de Alonso, Florida International University
Amrik Singh Dua, Mount San Antonio College
Rex Edwards, Moorpark College
Michael D. Everett, East Tennessee State University
William George Feipel, Illinois Central College
Clara V. P. Ford, Northern Virginia Community College
Kirk D. Gifford, Ricks College
Lynde O. Gilliam, Metropolitan State College of Denver

Michael G. Goode, Central Piedmont Community College

Richard Gosselin, Houston Community College

John W. Graham, Rutgers University

Julie Granthen, Oakland Community College

Chiara Gratton-Lavoie, California State University at Fullerton

Mehdi Haririan, Bloomsburg University

Paul C. Harris, Jr., Camden County College

Victor Heltzer, Middlesex County College

Michael G. Heslop, Northern Virginia Community College

Rick L. Hirschi, Brigham Young University, Idaho

James H. Holcomb, University of Texas, El Paso

Norman Hollingsworth, Georgia Perimeter College

Jeff Holt, Tulsa Community College

R. Bradley Hoppes, Southwest Missouri State University

Yu Hsing, Southwestern Louisiana University

Safiul Huda, Community College of Rhode Island

Scott Hunt, Columbus State Community College

Paul E. Jorgensen, Linn-Benton Community College

Thomas Kemp, Tarrant County College, Northwest Campus

Jenni Kim, Pasadena City College

Marcelle Anne Kinney, Brevard Community College

Barry Kotlove, Edmonds Community College

Louis H. Kuhn, Edison Community College

Rose LaMont, Modesto Junior College

Phillip Letting, Harrisburg Area Community College

Kenneth E. Long, New River Community College

Kjartan T. Magnusson, Salt Lake Community College

Matthew Marlin, Duquesne University

Pete Mavrokordatos, Tarrant County College

Diana McCoy, Truckee Meadows Community College

Erika Weis McGrath, Golden Gate University

Saul Mekies, Kirkwood Community College

Barbara Moore, University of Central Florida

Francis Mummery, Fullterton College

John Nader, Grand Valley State University

Kelly Noonan, Rider University

Alex Obiya, San Diego City College

Charles C. Okeke, College of Southern Nevada

Shawn Osell, Anoka-Ramsey Community College, Augsburg College

Charles Parker, Wayne State College

Elizabeth Patch, Broome Community College

Michael C. Petrowsky, Glendale Community College

Marilyn Pugh, Prince George's Community College

Fernando Quijano, Dickinson State University

Robert Reichenbach, Miami Dade Community College

Charles A. Reichheld, III, Cuyahoga Community College

Teresa Riley, Youngstown State University

Fred D. Robertson, Hinds Community College

Larry Lynn Ross, University of Alaska, Anchorage

Sara Saderion, Houston Community College

Ramazans Sari, Texas Tech University

Reza Sepassi, McLennan Community College

Peter Mark Shaw, Tidewater Community College

William L. Sherrill, Tidewater Community College

Ken Slaysman, York College of Pennsylvania

Garvin Smith, Daytona Beach Community College

Noel S. Smith, Palm Beach Community College

David Sollars, Auburn University

Leonie L. Stone, State University of New York, Geneseo

James L. Swofford, University of South Alabama

Lea Templer, College of the Canyons

J. Ross Thomas, Albuquerque Technical and Vocational Institute

Donna Thompson, Brookdale Community College

Anthony Uremovic, Joliet Junior College

Abu Wahid, Tennessee State University

Chester G. T. Waters, Durham Technical Community College

Paul R. Watro, Jefferson Community College

Mark A. Wilkening, Blinn College

We also wish to thank the many students at the University of Texas, San Antonio, who class tested the manuscript in various stages. They provided us with inspiration and were a great source of feedback.

We welcome comments about the book. Please write to us c/o Economics Editor, Prentice Hall Higher Education Division, One Lake Street, Upper Saddle River, NJ 07458.

Ronald M. Ayers

Robert A. Collinge

Save a Tree!

Many of the components of the teaching and learning package are available in electronic format. Disk-based and web-based supplements conserve paper and allow you to select and print only the material you plan to use. For more information, please ask your Prentice Hall sales representative.

ALTERNATIVE SEQUENCES

LONG-RUN EARLY	SHORT-RUN EARLY

MACROECONOMICS

EXPLORE & APPLY

CHAPTER 1

THE ECONOMIC PERSPECTIVE

A LOOK AHEAD

Choosing the right mix of government and free enterprise involves questions of economics, philosophy, and politics. Economic incentives can lead to the success or downfall of political systems. As discussed in the Explore & Apply section in this chapter, China's leaders recognized the importance of incentives. They shifted the country's policies away from government directive in order to draw upon the incentives found in a dynamic market economy.

Any country's economic system reflects its choices about how to organize economic activity. Scarce resources and unlimited wants force us to make choices, whether they be the grand choices we make as a nation or the personal choices we make in everyday living. Economics examines how to make choices well. This chapter sweeps across the economic landscape to provide the context for our choices.

LEARNING OBJECTIVES

Understanding Chapter 1 will enable you to:
1. **Describe how scarce resources and unlimited wants lead to the study of economics.**
2. **Distinguish between microeconomics and macroeconomics.**
3. **Identify three basic questions that all economies must answer.**
4. **Recognize the strengths of the marketplace and motivations for government involvement.**
5. **Understand what a model is and why models are best kept simple.**
6. **Explain why incentives are important for economic prosperity.**

$\mathscr{E}$XPLORE
&
$\mathscr{A}$PPLY

Economics *studies the allocation of limited resources in response to unlimited wants.*

1.1 SCARCE RESOURCES, UNLIMITED WANTS

scarcity a situation in which there are too few resources to meet all human wants.

Economics is about choice. We are forced to choose because of **scarcity,** which means that society does not have enough resources to produce all the goods and services we want to consume. Both individually and as a society, we seek to choose wisely.

Securing the most value from limited resources is the objective of economic choice. At a personal level, we each have our own economy. We have limited income to spend on the many things we want. For this reason, we might forgo the new Porsche automobile we've long dreamed of in order to pay tuition at Highbrow College. Usually, however, resource scarcity does not force us into all-or-nothing decisions. We might be able to purchase a used Dodge Neon and still afford tuition at Home State University.

MAKING DECISIONS AT THE MARGIN

the margin the cutoff point; decision making at the margin refers to deciding on one more or one less of something.

When something is scarce, we must choose. We commonly make choices at **the margin,** meaning incrementally—in small steps. Decision making at the margin is about the choice of a little more of this and a little less of that. It's about weighing and balancing the benefits and costs of alternatives. Table 1-1 provides examples of choices facing a consumer, a business, and a government. Each choice is considered at the margin and is phrased as a question. In the study of economics, questions will often be posed in this manner in order to emphasize the marginal nature of many decisions.

RESOURCE ALLOCATION AND SCARCITY

It is not a scarcity of money that is at the root of economics. Scarce resources lead to scarce goods, whether or not money is involved. To illustrate that point, consider what would happen if everything were declared to be "free." Supermarkets, department stores, discount stores, and other retailers would quickly be picked bare. People would complain that they did not take home everything they wanted or that they arrived too late to obtain anything at all. This is often what happens during humanitarian relief efforts, in which food and other

TABLE 1-1   EXAMPLES OF CHOICES AT THE MARGIN

Choices Facing a Consumer:
- Should I eat the last slice of pizza?
- What is the best use of the next hour of my time?
- How should I spend the last dollar in my pocket?

Choices Facing a Business:
- Should revenues be used to hire another worker or to upgrade the office computer system?
- Should one more entree be added to a restaurant's menu? Should one be deleted?
- Should the restaurant stay open an hour later, or close an hour earlier?

Choices Facing Government:
- Should we add another freeway exit ramp?
- Should a new elementary school be built?
- How badly does the city need another water treatment plant?

aid is distributed from the back of a truck. The result seen in Somalia and other recipient countries is that the fastest and strongest, rather than the neediest, get the goods. Free distribution is not an economical way to allocate scarce resources and the goods and services they produce.

Resource allocation refers to the uses to which resources are put. How resources are used depends partly upon *technology*, which refers to the techniques of production. When new technologies are created, the results can include new ways of doing things, new product choices, and new uses for resources. For example, the development of the Internet meant that existing television cables could also be used to deliver web sites to home computers.

When society makes choices about what will be produced, it is also choosing its allocation of resources. The choices can literally be a matter of life and death, such as involving a nation's healthcare system. In wealthier nations, it might seem as if scarcity of resources doesn't apply, and that more and better healthcare could be provided for all, apparently without giving up anything else. But since more healthcare requires a greater number of doctors and nurses, where would they come from? Some people who otherwise would have sought careers in engineering, teaching, business, and other fields would have to obtain their degrees in medicine. As a consequence, there would be less *output* of goods and services elsewhere in the economy. The consequences of resource scarcity cannot be avoided.

STUDENTS OF ECONOMICS—ALWAYS EXPLORING, ALWAYS APPLYING

SNAPSHOT

"Let's explore that mountain pass!" shouts the hiker. "Let's explore the financing options," suggests the car dealer to the customer. "Let's explore the possibility of sending astronauts to Mars," argues the scientist. Like these three, everyone is an explorer. We think through our possibilities in life, and that is exploration.

Exploring can involve web surfing, visiting a bookstore, or mingling with one another. It expands our knowledge and experience, which we can then apply in order to make better choices. For example, our explorations can lead to writing a better term paper, finding a good book, making new friends, or other applications.

Students of economics are most assuredly explorers. As a student, you explore the principles and issues of economics, then apply what you learned from your explorations. You apply economics to choosing a career, a mate, a senator, and what to eat for breakfast. The exploration of economics and its application to life's choices are found throughout this book. The Explore & Apply section that precedes each chapter summary offers the opportunity to dig deeper into an issue. Like Daniel Boone, Ponce de León, and John Glenn, you are now a pioneer on a journey of discovery. ◀

QUICKCHECK

Would $2 million satisfy all of your wants?

Answer: It would be quite difficult to discover someone with $2 million who would decline to accept a third million. Even billionaires would accept another billion, if only to better endow their trust funds. Unless you would actually decline to accept that third million, then $2 million does not satisfy all of your wants. Essentially, your wants are unlimited.

1.2 SURVEYING THE ECONOMIC LANDSCAPE

We have seen that economics applies to a vast expanse of choices. To make progress in the study of economics, it is useful to narrow our field of vision by dividing economics into two broad categories: microeconomics and macroeconomics.

MICROECONOMICS—COMPONENTS OF THE ECONOMY

microeconomics analyzes the individual components of the economy, such as the choices made by people, firms, and industries.

Microeconomics studies the individual parts of the economy. It looks at the choices of individuals in their roles as consumers and as workers. It also includes the choices of businesses—*firms*—which are the companies that produce goods and services as their outputs. Microeconomics also studies the industries within which firms operate, where an *industry* is composed of firms producing similar outputs. For example, the airline industry includes United Airlines, American Airlines, Southwest Airlines, and many other airlines.

Microeconomics revolves around the interaction of consumers and producers in markets. Markets can take physical, electronic, or other forms. The common characteristic of all markets is that they make possible the voluntary exchange of resources, goods, and services. Market prices serve as the signals that guide the allocation of resources. Participants in the economy make choices based upon the *incentives* provided by the prices they face, meaning that these prices motivate their actions.

Microeconomic applications affect our lives each day. Suppose you decide to go on vacation. What will be your destination? Will you use the services of a travel agent? At which hotel will you stay? If you decide to fly, which airline will you choose? Is the fare lower if you purchase tickets in advance? Why do many airlines reduce the fare if you stay over a Saturday night? How are ticket prices related to government regulation of the airlines? Should government regulate airplane noise? If so, how? As you can see, the list of microeconomic questions is long. Answering them requires us to know the prices of the various alternatives.

MACROECONOMICS—THE BIG PICTURE

macroeconomics analyzes economic aggregates, such as aggregate employment, output, growth, and inflation.

Macroeconomics looks at the big picture. It concentrates on the analysis of economic *aggregates,* total values that describe the economy as a whole. The most important aggregate is *gross domestic product (GDP),* which measures the market value of a country's aggregate output—the market value of the goods and services that a country produces in one year. Macroeconomic issues are often raised in the news. Employment, economic growth, interest rates, inflation, and the federal budget are examples of macroeconomic issues. These issues reflect the macroeconomic goals that each country sets for itself. Widely accepted goals include a high rate of economic growth, low inflation, and high employment.

Macroeconomics was first considered a separate field of study following the 1936 publication of *The General Theory of Employment, Interest, and Money* by British economist John Maynard Keynes [1883–1946]. Keynes suggested macroeconomic answers to the problems of the Great Depression, answers that seemed lacking in the microeconomic mainstream of economic thought. The writings of Keynes and his followers so influenced the economics profession that for three decades after the publication of *The General Theory,* macroeconomics and *Keynesian* economics were virtually one and the same. Today, Keynesian economics is still prominent, but other macro analysis is also held in high regard.

QUICKCHECK

Pose three questions illustrating microeconomic issues and another three questions illustrating macroeconomic issues.

Answer: The micro questions you ask should be related to an individual, firm, or industry. There are many possible questions. Examples are: Why is the price of a Lexus greater than that of a Toyota? Why do some firms advertise? What do I want for lunch? Your macro questions should be related to issues of the whole economy. Examples are: What is the cause of inflation? Why is there unemployment? What causes an economy to grow?

1.3 THREE BASIC QUESTIONS: WHAT, HOW, AND FOR WHOM?

Every economy must answer three basic economic questions:

1. **What?** What goods and services will be produced and offered for sale and in what quantities? The latest fashions, CDs from established pop stars, medical services, fast food, and countless other items are produced by our economy. What is the reason that these goods are produced, while other items, such as vinyl records and 8-track tapes, are not?

2. **How?** How will goods and services be produced? There are numerous production techniques available. Some methods of production use simple hand tools and much labor. Other production methods employ machines or computers in combination with labor. For example, a shirt could be sewn by hand with no more than a needle and thread. However, most shirts are sewn with a sewing machine that saves on the use of labor. How are these decisions made, and what motivates the development of new and better ways of doing things?

3. **For whom?** Who will consume the goods and services that are produced? People who live on Poverty Row consume less than those who live on Park Avenue, so income matters in the distribution of goods and services. But what determines income? If a family's income is small, should income be redistributed from others who are wealthier? What problems does redistribution cause?

When it comes to deciding what, how, and for whom, society must choose among three kinds of *economic systems.* Government might make the decisions. If so, the economy is termed **command and control.** Alternatively, government might stay out of the picture and allow economic choices to be made entirely in the marketplace. In that case, the economy is characterized by laissez-faire free markets, also termed laissez-faire capitalism. *Laissez faire* means "let it be." **Free markets** are free from government intervention and characterized by freedom of choice in both production and consumption. Free markets are associated with capitalism, in which resources are privately owned.

In practice, all countries have **mixed economies,** meaning that they choose a combination of markets and government. Different countries choose different combinations, with some leaning toward command and control, and others toward laissez faire. The exact mix is influenced by custom, tradition, religion, political ideology, and other factors. Figure 1-1 illustrates this spectrum of choice.

command and control government decrees that direct economic activity.

free markets the collective decisions of individual buyers and sellers that, taken together, determine what outputs are produced, how those outputs are produced, and who receives the outputs; free markets depend on private property and free choice.

mixed economies the mixture of free-market and command-and-control methods of resource allocation that characterize modern economies.

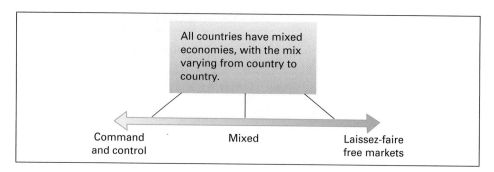

FIGURE 1-1

THE SPECTRUM OF ECONOMIC SYSTEMS Command and control involves government allocation of resources. Laissez faire is characterized by private resource allocation. In reality, all countries have mixed economies, with the mix varying from country to country.

All countries have mixed economies, with the mix varying from country to country.

Command and control   Mixed   Laissez-faire free markets

THE GOALS OF EQUITY AND EFFICIENCY

equity fairness.

There are two primary economic objectives to guide countries in choosing how much government to mix with free markets. The first objective is *equity*, which refers to fairness. While we often intuitively sense what is fair, the concept of equity is difficult to pin down. There are commonly accepted principles of equity that apply in certain circumstances, such as in discussions about taxation and government spending. However, equity is ultimately a matter of personal perception. Well-meaning people can reasonably disagree about what is equitable, and their views cannot be proved or disproved.

efficiency means that resources are used in ways that provide the most value; implies that no one can be made better off without someone else becoming worse off.

The second economic objective is *efficiency*, sometimes called economic efficiency, which means that resources are used in ways that provide the most value—that maximize the size of the economic pie. Efficiency means that no one can be made better off without someone else becoming worse off. Efficiency has both a technological and allocative component, defined as follows.

technological efficiency the greatest quantity of output for given inputs; likewise, for any given output, requires the least-cost production technique.

- **Technological efficiency** implies getting the greatest quantity of output from the resources that are being used. Conversely, for any given output, technological efficiency requires that a least-cost production technique must be chosen.

allocative efficiency involves choosing the most valuable mix of outputs to produce.

- **Allocative efficiency** involves choosing the most valuable mix of outputs to produce. For example, the economy might be able to produce the largest number of toothpicks from the resources at its disposal. That choice would be technologically efficient. However, if the economy produces nothing but toothpicks, consumers would not be getting the greatest value from the economy's resources. The economy would be allocatively inefficient, because the wrong mix of goods would have been chosen.

There is frequently a tradeoff between efficiency and equity, meaning that more equity may result in less efficiency. Likewise, less equity may result in greater efficiency. For example, many people believe that, for the sake of more equity, tax systems should be something like Robin Hood—taxes should take from the rich and give to the poor. However, as taxes paid by the rich rise, their incentives to work and invest can be expected to fall because the rich get to keep less of their earnings. Thus, the more redistributional the tax system, the less productive the economy is likely to be. The economic pie may be divided more equitably, but its size would be diminished.

To see the difficulty in identifying equity and the tradeoff between efficiency and equity, suppose that on the first day of class your instructor reads the following grade policy: "The final grades of all students who have earned an *A* or *B* will be reduced by enough points to bring each of them down to a *C*. The points taken away from them will be distributed among the students who earn a *D* or *F* so that they also receive a *C*." Your instructor supports the equity of this policy by arguing that it recognizes the many differences in learning abilities and opportunities. Perhaps you would agree that the policy is fair. Perhaps you would disagree. In either case, though, the policy is likely to reduce the number of high grades available for redistribution. In an effort to promote equity, this instructor's policy changes students' incentives to work hard for excellence.

COMMAND AND CONTROL—WHO NEEDS MARKETS?

The marketplace seems cluttered with choices. Wouldn't it be better to do away with seemingly unnecessary variety, skip all the advertising, and just have government direct the economy for the good of us all? Throughout history, many countries have embraced economic systems that promised to eliminate the perceived disorder of the marketplace. Often, these efforts have involved government *central planning* that sets production plans for most goods, which are produced by government-owned state enterprises.

Even the most well-meaning central planners cannot know our desires as well as we can know them ourselves. Moreover, nothing ensures that only the most well-meaning central planners will rise to the top. Even if they do, they face difficulties in motivating actual producers to do their bidding. For example, if the government plan assigns farmers production quotas measured by the ton, farmers will seek to maximize the weight of their crops and ignore their quality. The result of command-and-control methods is often inefficiency, in which resources are squandered on the production of the wrong goods and services or wasted through use of the wrong production techniques.

Centrally planned economies must also match production to consumption. If production fails to match their plans, then the government may be forced to ration goods and services. Government *rationing* occurs when consumers are permitted to buy only limited amounts of the goods they want. Rationing has been adopted in the United States, but on a temporary basis and with mixed results. For example, gasoline, tires, sugar, meat, and other essentials were rationed during World War II. When the war emergency was over, rationing was quickly ended by popular demand.

THE INVISIBLE HAND—WHO NEEDS GOVERNMENT?

Is it not something of a mystery that goods and services are regularly offered for sale in quantities that satisfy the wants of consumers? After all, there is no commander-in-chief ordering an army of workers to bring those goods to market. In the *Wealth of Nations,* published in 1776, Scottish philosopher–economist Adam Smith explained this puzzle. Smith described how the **invisible hand** of the marketplace leads the economy to produce an efficient variety of goods and services, with efficient production methods as well. Guided by this invisible hand, producers acting in their own self-interests provide consumers with greater value than even the most well-intentioned of governments.

invisible hand the idea that self-interest and competition promotes economic efficiency without any need for action by government.

The reasoning behind the invisible hand is straightforward. To prosper in the marketplace, producers must provide customers with goods and services that they value. Those producers who are best at doing so thrive. Those who pick the wrong goods and services to produce, or who produce them in an inferior manner, lose out. For this reason, an essential ingredient of the invisible hand is *competition,* which pits rival firms against one another in a contest to win the favor of consumers.

Free markets offer people opportunity—the opportunity to get ahead or to fall behind. The market rewards people who use their abilities to satisfy their fellow citizens, so long as that satisfaction is embodied in a good or service that can be sold in the marketplace. As the saying goes, "Build a better mousetrap, and the world will beat a path to your door."

All participants in a market economy, including consumers, businesses, investors, and workers, make choices on the basis of information conveyed by market prices. The use of prices to answer the three basic questions—what, how, and for whom—characterizes *the price system.* **Prices provide information about scarcity.** For example, you could probably not afford to hire your friend's favorite rock star to perform at her birthday party. The scarce talents of superstars generally command a price that only a very large audience can pay. Responding to this market price, superstars would skip the birthday party in favor of the concert. More generally, **it is the price system that allocates resources in a market economy to their highest-valued uses.**

Price changes lead to changes in both consumer and firm behavior. Following the onset of relatively low gasoline prices in the 1980s, consumers moved up—literally—to gas-guzzling sport-utility vehicles and pickup trucks, with some even sporting monstrous V–10 engines. Light-truck divisions at automakers became profit centers, while companies that relied heavily upon the manufacturing of small cars suffered. However, during times when gasoline prices spike upward to significantly higher levels, just the opposite occurs. Those are the times that small car dealers prosper while the owners of pickups and SUVs are left to their regrets at the gas pump.

Guided by market prices, free-market choices lead the economy toward allocative efficiency. The preferences of consumers dictate answers to the "what" question. Competition provides the incentive for firms to choose least-cost production techniques, thus answering the "how" question. The "for whom" question is answered when people offer their labor and other resources in the marketplace—their incomes reflect the value of these resources to others.

MIXING GOVERNMENT WITH THE MARKETPLACE

For various reasons, markets sometimes fail to achieve efficiency. And when it comes to equity, markets seem amoral—sometimes fair and sometimes not. Markets seem fair in rewarding those who work instead of lying on the beach all day, but can seem unfair in the opportunities presented to one person relative to another. So government steps in to correct the inefficiencies and remedy the inequities that would arise in the laissez-faire marketplace.

Some of the most efficient public policies do not abandon markets. Rather, markets can often be steered back on course with public policies that are minimally disruptive to the workings of the invisible hand, while avoiding the inefficiencies of command and control. For example, government took action against Microsoft in order to increase competition in the marketplace, not to replace it with government planning. Likewise, some of the best pollution-control policies are those that change incentives in the marketplace rather than dictate exactly what firms should do.

The distribution of income in the free marketplace rewards those who provide the most value to others. To some extent this arrangement seems fair. To some extent, it does not. For example, through no fault of their own, some people are incapable of providing much of value in the marketplace. This situation could be due to physical impairment or the lack of opportunity to acquire knowledge and skills. The result is poverty. Government attempts to promote greater equity by redistributing income and by providing social services. For example, welfare programs and public housing are government actions that are rooted in the concerns about equity.

Sorting out when government intervention is helpful and how it might best be done is probably the most challenging task facing a nation and one that different countries answer in different ways. The result is that all economies combine government action and the marketplace. Some economies, such as that of Cuba, lie toward the command-and-control end of the spectrum. Others place greater reliance upon the marketplace, but still retain a role for government.

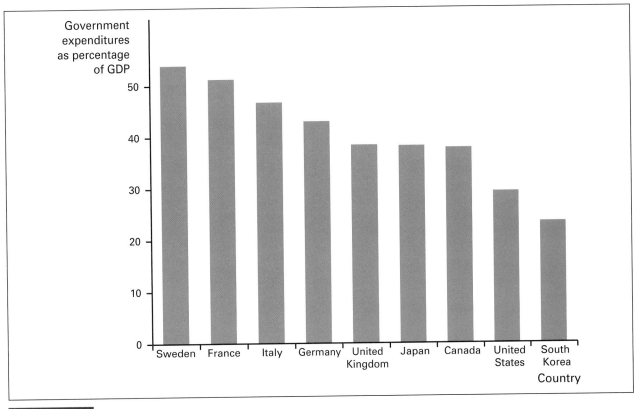

FIGURE 1-2

GOVERNMENT EXPENDITURES AS A PERCENTAGE OF GROSS DOMESTIC PRODUCT (GDP), SELECTED COUNTRIES As evident from the data, countries choose widely varying mixes of government and the market economy. For example, while government expenditures account for more than half of Sweden's GDP, they make up less than a quarter of South Korea's GDP.

Source: 2001 Statistical Abstract of the U.S., Table 1347. Data are for 2000.

Figure 1-2 sheds light on the economic significance of government in selected countries. Specifically, the figure shows the fraction of total economic activity (measured by GDP) directly accounted for by government in each country. In effect, the figure shows the cost of government as a percentage of aggregate output. Government's role in the economy is usually greater when the percentage is higher. The data in the figure understate the economic significance of government to the extent that the costs of complying with government regulations are paid for by firms and individuals rather than government.

Unlike in the nineteenth and early twentieth century, the United States can no longer lay claim to having a nearly pure laissez-faire free-market economy. The transition to a larger, activist government has occurred in response to a public perception that government policy provides the only means for correcting inequities and other problems in the marketplace. At the other extreme, few governments still promote central planning because widespread use of command and control in the formerly communist countries was associated with economic stagnation, leaving their citizens with relatively low living standards. China has been quite successful in creating a vibrant market sector that coexists along with state enterprises. Table 1-2 summarizes briefly the key differences between laissez-faire economies, command-and-control economies, and mixed economies.

TABLE 1-2   A BRIEF COMPARISON OF BASIC ECONOMIC SYSTEMS

	LAISSEZ FAIRE	MIXED ECONOMY	COMMAND AND CONTROL
Key Characteristics	Limited role for government implies a small government with few powers. Low taxes. Private property.	Significant role for government. Taxes take a significant portion of national output. Most production of goods and services occurs in the private sector, but there are many regulations and some government production.	Government ownership of property and government directives control the production of goods and services.
Organizing Principle	Invisible hand guides free markets.	Mix of free markets and command and control. Emphasis upon markets relative to government varies from country to country.	Central planning of the economy by government.
Daily Life	Large degree of personal freedom. Most goods and services provided by the private sector, including such essentials as food and education. Market prices and market wages.	Moderate limits on personal freedom because of government regulation and taxation. A few essential goods (education, for example) provided by government, while others (such as food) provided by the private sector. Market prices, with the possibility of some government price controls. Minimum wage laws and a small degree of other government control of wages.	Severe limits on personal freedom due to government control of the economy. Most goods provided by government. Prices set by government rather than the market. Government-set wages.
Countries Where Applied	None, although the United States, Australia, and some other countries value laissez faire in principle.	All countries, including China, Russia, and other countries in transition away from command and control.	None entirely. Cuba and North Korea come the closest.

S N A P S H O T   **INTERTWINING ECONOMIC AND POLITICAL PHILOSOPHIES**

Bigger or smaller government? An economic stimulus package? Lower taxes? More money for homeland defense? These questions are all answered in the political process. Yet their content is most decidedly economics!

During the eighteenth and nineteenth centuries, economics was called *political economy*. The term *political economy* makes clear that politics and economics intertwine. Even today, some refer to economics as political economy when they want to emphasize the close ties between economics and public policy. ◄

1.4 ECONOMIC ANALYSIS

The practice of economics involves analysis and problem solving. Sometimes these problems force us to think in terms of value judgments; sometimes they are factual. For example, which of many candidates for liver transplants will receive them? The answer involves a value judgment as to what criteria should be used to allocate scarce transplants. It also involves facts, such as what the possibilities are. Then, we apply logic to solve the problem of how best to meet our objectives with our possibilities.

Care must be taken to avoid faulty reasoning that leads to false conclusions. An example is the *fallacy of composition*. This error in reasoning occurs when it is assumed that what is true at the micro level must also be true at the macro level. In other words, the fallacy of composition involves the observation of a truth about some individual component of the economy accompanied by the assumption that this truth will also apply to the economy at large.

Changes in income can illustrate the fallacy of composition. For example, you would probably consider yourself better off if your income were to double, since that would allow you to purchase twice as much as before. However, to then generalize and think that everyone would be better off if everyone's income doubled would be to commit the fallacy of composition. There would be an important fact missing in that generalization. Specifically, while a change in your personal income would not affect prices, a change in everybody's income would. If prices also doubled, people would be no better off than they had been.

POSITIVE AND NORMATIVE ECONOMICS

Economic pronouncements are in abundant supply from an array of sources. Media commentators, politicians, ordinary citizens, and many economists are often quite eager to share their thoughts. How can we make sense of this mishmash of opinions? Is it truly nothing but opinion?

With some sorting, unsupported opinions can be separated from thoughtful analysis. A good start distinguishes between normative and positive economic statements. **Normative** statements have to do with behavioral norms, which are judgments as to what is good or bad. Examples of normative statements often include "ought" or "should" in them. They imply that something deserves to happen, such as: "The federal government ought to balance its budget."

Positive statements have to do with fact. They may involve current, historical, or even future fact. Positive statements concern what is, was, or will be. The accuracy of positive statements can be checked against facts, although verifying predictions about the future will have to wait until that future arrives. Sometimes it is also hard to judge the accuracy of a statement, although in principle it could be done. For example, "A balanced federal budget will lead to lower interest rates" is a positive statement that would be difficult to verify. Positive economic statements are not necessarily true. However, factual evidence may be introduced to support or refute any positive economic statement. Professional economists generally deal in positive economics, although they might assume some basic normative goals, such as goals of efficiency and equity. Table 1-3 provides examples of positive and normative statements, categorized by whether the subject matter is microeconomics or macroeconomics.

Both positive and normative economics rely upon theory, which is organized thought aimed at answering specific questions. Theories can be tested by logic and, for positive economic theories, by data. Theories are first tested for their internal logic. Does a theory make

normative having to do with behavioral norms, which are judgments as to what is good or bad.

positive having to do with what is, was, or will be.

TABLE 1-3 CATEGORIZING ECONOMIC STATEMENTS

	MACROECONOMICS	MICROECONOMICS
Positive	The unemployment rate is rising.	People are eating so much chicken that I'll lose my job at the beef-packing plant.
	Inflation is lower today than it was twenty-five years ago.	DVD players are cheaper today than when they were first introduced.
Normative	The unemployment rate is too high.	People should eat more chicken.
	There's no need to worry about inflation.	DVD players are too expensive.

sense? Sometimes the testing stops there. When feasible, theories are tested by collecting facts to see whether the facts are consistent with the theory. Testing of theories allows us to judge their value, so that the results become more than mere opinion or idle speculation.

For example, consider an economic problem facing Dr. Joan Parker, president of Carbound College. President Parker has commissioned a survey that reveals that the average Carbound College student spends twenty minutes per day driving around looking for a parking space. Conversations with students lead President Parker to theorize that students will be willing to pay an additional $30 per year in parking fees to cut their search time down to five minutes. Based on past construction costs, the president also theorizes that the required number of parking places could be added for less than this amount. President Parker's theorizing is positive because it is about fact—the benefits and costs of more parking spaces. Before authorizing new parking lot construction, though, the president might be well advised to collect additional data that might more fully indicate if the theory is correct. In the process, President Parker is practicing economics.

ECONOMIC MODELING: THE ROUTE TO HIGHER-LEVEL UNDERSTANDING

models simplified versions of reality that emphasize features central to answering the questions we ask of them.

Economics, like other academic fields such as physics, psychology, and political science, makes extensive use of models. A **model** is a simplification of reality that emphasizes features essential to answering the questions we ask of it. A roadmap is a familiar model. A section of a roadmap is seen in Figure 1-3. In this model the wide red lines that designate interstate highways let us know of major high-speed routes. The circles and yellow splotches show us the locations of towns and larger cities. If our goal is high-speed driving, we want the map kept simple, since we need to read it quickly.

Economic models remove unneeded detail, keeping only features that are essential. Similarly, a roadmap eliminates many features of the terrain, such as trees, houses, and hills. That lack of detail would be inappropriate if the map is for surveying or hiking. For driving, though, including those details would reduce the map's usefulness. A good model need not be totally realistic, even in the features it does include. After all, from a helicopter we would not actually find huge red lines connecting black circles and yellow splotches. The roadmap is merely representative, as a good model should be.

QUICKCHECK

Categorize the statements below as normative or positive. Explain your reasoning.

    a. The federal government collects more tax revenue than any state government.

    b. After the tornado hit Central City, Uncle Sam moved too slowly in providing aid.

Answers:

    a. Positive. The statement can be checked for its factual accuracy.

    b. Normative. The statement implies that the government should have moved more quickly, without telling us what is meant by too slowly. A positive version of the statement might read as follows: "After the tornado hit Central City, it took two weeks for aid to reach the stricken population. Officials predict a quicker response to future disasters."

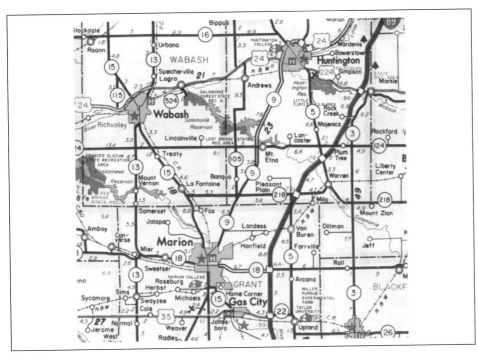

FIGURE 1-3

A FAMILIAR MODEL A roadmap is a model. The map is a simplification of reality that retains the features of the landscape that are most important to travelers.

Keep in mind a guiding principle when producing a model. This principle is termed *Occam's razor,* formulated by the fourteenth-century English philosopher William of Occam. Occam argued that reasoning is improved by focusing one's thinking on the most essential elements of an issue. He suggested using a figurative razor to cut away the unnecessary elements from analysis. Occam's razor increases the likelihood that modeling will lead to correct conclusions when the principle is applied correctly.

To keep models simple, economists make *assumptions,* meaning that they act as though certain things are true without proving them to in fact be true. One common assumption is termed *ceteris paribus,* which is Latin for holding all else constant. The assumption of *ceteris paribus* allows us to look at one thing at a time. For example, when President Parker was considering whether to add to student parking spaces, the *ceteris paribus* condition in her model might be that student enrollments and driving habits stay unchanged. Effects of changes in student enrollments or driving habits could then be looked at separately.

Economists develop models to explain the choices people make and the consequences of those choices. Economic models may be presented in words, as graphs, or using mathematical equations. If you lack experience in working with graphs you should study the appendix to this chapter, since you will encounter numerous graphical models throughout this book.

MODELS—FROM EINSTEIN'S MIND TO YOURS

SNAPSHOT

The renowned physicist Albert Einstein (1879–1955) was in the business of modeling. The most famous model to come from his mind, summarized in the equation $e = mc^2$, provided key insights that led scientists to the ability to split the atom. It is not only economists and physicists that model, however. Psychologists tell us that all of us walk around with models of life in mind.

Take your model of learning. How do you perceive the learning process? A simple model holds that the job of the instructor is to fill your mind with knowledge. In this model you are a passive recipient of facts, figures, and principles. Students whose internal learning model is similar to this one often fail to prosper academically because some important elements of the learning process have been omitted. Remember, Occam's razor tells us to omit

only the nonessential elements from models. As Einstein told us, "Everything should be made as simple as possible, but not simpler."

A more sophisticated learning model allows for the student to interact with the instructor, the material, and other students. Key elements of this model involve setting aside time to reflect on the material, to ask questions, and to work with others. Which model is yours? ◄

1.5 FROM MAO TO NOW—MARKET INCENTIVES TAKE HOLD IN CHINA

For much of the twentieth century, the idea of a command-and-control economy had deep, widespread appeal. Many people believed that the unemployment, inflation, depressions, and other problems faced by mixed economies could be avoided through central planning. Charismatic national leaders came into power that century offering to implement command-and-control principles. Lenin in Russia, Mussolini in Italy, Hitler in Germany, Mao Tse-Tung in China, and Ho Chi Minh in Vietnam are the best known.

For one reason or another, all these countries have turned away from command and control. Consider China. Chinese civilization is one of the oldest on the planet. Its history is one of extremes, both good and bad. In the mid-to-late twentieth century, that extreme was bad. Faced with grinding poverty and stagnation after the death of Mao, the Chinese leaders decided that a larger role for markets was the only thing that could save their country. Let's look at why China needed to be saved.

Like the former Soviet Union and other communist countries, the People's Republic of China was guided by the philosophy of the controversial nineteenth–century theorist, Karl Marx. Marx had a simple maxim: "From each according to his ability, to each according to his need." This idea was used to justify a strong central government that would allocate resources according to the communist idea of equity. That idea focused on equal outcomes rather than equal opportunities. Equality would be achieved by government ownership of resources and central planning of the economy.

Marx's idea was not easy to put into practice. What does a person need? A chicken in every pot? Rice and beans? A glass of wine and a loaf of bread? We each have different ideas when it comes to fulfilling our personal needs. People want more, and yet make do with little. How is a government to know what people want? The result is that Marxist governments expounded a philosophy of *egalitarianism,* in which everyone would get identical access to everything from soap to medical care.

Unfortunately for an economy, egalitarianism provides little incentive for people to be productive. If a country's government distributes the same amount of goods and services to everyone, its people are not motivated to work their hardest and do their best. In this system, smart people act stupid. There is no incentive to do otherwise. Indeed, the smarter you act, the more that might be expected of you and the more risks you run. Great efforts were made in China under Chairman Mao to submerge individual identity into a collective mentality that always put the needs of the state before the needs of the individual. Egalitarianism went so far as to see that everyone—men, women, and children—wore the same "uniform," which consisted of denim pants and jacket topped with a small-billed denim military-style cap.

With central planners attempting to direct the "what," "how," and "for whom" of production, bad choices were made and resources were squandered. Everyone had a job, but productivity and purchasing power lagged badly behind the West. China, already the most populous nation on earth, faced a population explosion that promised to lead to mass starvation and unrest unless the economy could be made to perform. Thus, the turn to the market. Table 1-4 shows selected key events in the economic transition from command and control to the market, a transition that is still occurring.

TABLE 1-4	SELECTED MILESTONES IN CHINA'S TRANSITION TOWARD A MIXED ECONOMY

YEAR	EVENT
1978	Transition from a planned to a market-oriented economy begins.
1979–1983	Collective farming is replaced by "household responsibility system" of individual farms.
1980	Special economic zones are created to experiment with market reforms.
1986	Foreign investment law is passed.
1988	Enterprise law allows for the existence of privately owned stock companies.
1990	Chinese stock markets are established.
1993	Modern corporate system at state-owned enterprises is introduced.
1994	China allows the exchange value of its currency to be set on world markets, reflecting the common practice of market economies.
1999	China's economy becomes the world's second largest, behind only that of the United States.
2001	Price controls on key items are lifted as China is admitted as a member of the World Trade Organization.

Source: As ranked by the *International Monetary Fund's* purchasing power parity index.

THE ROLE OF GOVERNMENT IN A MARKET ECONOMY

The advantage of a market economy is that the marketplace rewards those producers best able to offer goods and services of value to others. The better a person is at providing things of value to others, the more will be that person's income. Those who fail to provide value, and their employees, will experience unemployment. In this way, each person has an incentive to develop his or her productive potential to the maximum of his or her abilities. The marketplace rewards ability and industriousness with more income. That seems fair, to some extent.

A problem arises when, through no fault of their own, people do not all have the same potential. Furthermore, people may develop their potentials in ways that seem productive at the time, but turn out not to be. For example, elevator operators found their skills obsolete when the ingenuity of manufacturers created automatic push-button elevators. That example reflects the changing opportunities in society, but hardly seems fair to many of the people whose livelihoods are involved. In other cases people find themselves with disabilities that prevent them from reaching their full potential to provide for others. This situation does not mean that they are worth any less as humans, although they tend to earn less income than people without disabilities. Again, that does not seem fair.

Enter government, with its power to tax. Specifically, government redistributes wealth by imposing taxes that take wealth from those who can afford to give and that give to those in need. Taken to an extreme, this redistribution of wealth would eliminate incentives for individuals to behave more productively and lead to stagnation. Therefore, in taxing, government must weigh the tradeoff between equity and incentives for efficiency. In the case of China this has meant the willingness to keep taxes relatively low and tolerate inequality in income and wealth. While the majority of its citizenry remain poor, other Chinese have been allowed to become millionaires, with all the trappings of wealth. This change has generated great controversy in China, with many older citizens seeking a return to the former ways of the country.

In China, Russia, and other transition economies in Eastern Europe and elsewhere, the urge to impose new government regulations as a response to every problem must be tempting. The invisible hand is just that, invisible. For this reason, it is often not well understood, at least until people have a chance to observe it in action. What the mix of markets and government ultimately chosen by China will look like is anyone's guess. What we can say is that China seems to have learned the value of mixing incentives into the recipe for its economy.

*T*HINKING
*C*RITICALLY

1. *Jesse:* I like the idea of a strong central government. We need freedom and opportunity within limits, where government keeps us from going too far.
   Lee: When people harm others or take their property, then government needs to intervene. Otherwise, government should keep out, since it's just one group imposing its version of morality on everybody else.
   This exchange illustrates that the mixed economy involves much more than the magnitude of taxes and government regulation. What are some other points of contention in how "free" free markets should be?

2. Some people think that the more democratic a country, the greater reliance it will place upon free markets. Do you think this is true? Explain.

 Visit **www.prenhall.com/ayers** for updates and web exercises on this Explore & Apply topic.

SUMMARY AND LEARNING OBJECTIVES

1. **Describe how scarce resources and unlimited wants lead to the study of economics.**
   - Economics is the study of how to allocate scarce resources to satisfy unlimited wants. Scarcity forces people to make choices, both individually and collectively.
   - Economic choices are often made at the margin, meaning in increments rather than all or nothing. The choices made by individuals, businesses, and government determine the economy's allocation of resources.

2. **Distinguish between microeconomics and macroeconomics.**
   - Economic issues can be classified as falling within microeconomics or macroeconomics. Microeconomics deals with the individual parts of the economy, such as consumers or firms. Macroeconomics looks at the big picture, including gross domestic product, unemployment, inflation, money, and interest rates.

3. **Identify three basic questions that all economies must answer.**
   - The three basic economic questions are what, how, and for whom. The *what* question refers to the choice of goods and services produced. The *how* question is about the choice of production methods. The *for whom* question relates to who receives the output the economy produces.

   - To answer the three questions, countries choose a mix of laissez faire and command and control. The result is that all countries have mixed economies, with the mix varying from country to country.

4. **Recognize the strengths of the marketplace and motivations for government involvement.**
   - In making decisions about the choice of system, countries can be guided by two economic objectives: equity and efficiency. Equity refers to fairness; efficiency to getting the most value from economic resources. Efficiency is of two types: allocative and technological. The first refers to producing the highest-valued mix outputs; the second to producing any particular output in the least-costly way.
   - In a free-market economy resources are allocated as if, in Adam Smith's famous phrase, by an invisible hand. A laissez-faire or hands-off policy by government means that market prices guide the allocation of resources.
   - When the market fails to achieve efficiency, government tends to take action. Government action is also directed toward equity issues. Such government actions include the government provision of goods and services.

5. Understand what a model is and why models are best kept simple.

- Sound logic is essential to proper economic analysis. Care must be taken to avoid the fallacy of composition, which is the error of assuming that what is true for the part is true for the whole.
- Economic analysis can involve normative or positive statements. Normative economics involves value judgments about whether something is good or bad. Positive economics concerns facts.
- Economic analysis is practiced using models, often expressed with graphs. Occam's razor suggests that models ought to be stripped down to their necessary elements. They should be as simple as possible, while still conveying the essence of an issue.

6. Explain why incentives are important for economic prosperity.

- Egalitarianism was a key feature of the economy in China under Chairman Mao. That economy was also characterized by central planning, which led to the inefficient use of resources. For this reason, China's leaders introduced market incentives. How much government to mix with the private marketplace is a choice that each country must make. Care must be taken that incentives are sufficient to promote productivity.

KEY TERMS

economics, 2
scarcity, 2
the margin, 2
microeconomics, 4
macroeconomics, 4
command and control, 5

free markets, 5
mixed economies, 5
equity, 6
efficiency, 6
technological efficiency, 6
allocative efficiency, 6

invisible hand, 7
normative, 11
positive, 11
models, 12

TEST YOURSELF

TRUE OR FALSE

1. The problem of resource scarcity has been solved in recent years through advances in technology.
2. Industry studies are examples of macroeconomic analysis.
3. The tradeoff between efficiency and equity means that increases in efficiency will often be accompanied by less equity.
4. Adam Smith's concept of the invisible hand is that the free marketplace functions better when the hand of government guides it.
5. Occam's razor is a principle that is used in the drawing of roadmaps.

MULTIPLE CHOICE

6. Economics is primarily the study of
   a. stocks and bonds.
   b. allocating limited resources to meet unlimited wants.
   c. methods to eliminate scarcity.
   d. why consumers want what they do.

7. Making decisions at the margin is about
   a. all-or-nothing choices.
   b. choices involving money.
   c. incremental choices.
   d. normative economics.
8. Macroeconomics looks at
   a. the "big picture."
   b. only the government portion of the economy.
   c. only the business portion of the economy.
   d. the behavior of individuals, but not of firms.
9. Which of the following is the best example of microeconomics?
   a. A study of new automobile prices.
   b. Evaluation of the Federal budget.
   c. A statement about what ought to be.
   d. A history of U.S. inflation.

10. The three basic questions an economy must answer are
    a. why produce; how much to produce; who to produce it?
    b. what to produce; how to produce it; who to consume it?
    c. what to produce; why produce; how to produce?
    d. when to produce; how to produce; what to produce?
11. Command-and-control economies are characterized by
    a. reliance upon free markets.
    b. adherence to the principles of capitalism.
    c. economic freedom.
    d. government decision making.
12. Laissez faire is the term for
    a. the philosophy that hard work is bad for a person.
    b. government command-and-control policies.
    c. let it be.
    d. a partnership between government and business.
13. Which of the following is NOT an advantage of market allocation of resources over central government allocation of resources?
    a. Markets distribute income in the most equitable manner possible.
    b. Market prices allocate resources to their highest-valued uses.
    c. People out for their own self-interest in the marketplace have more incentive to provide products of value to others than would government bureaucrats.
    d. Competition among firms causes products to be produced in the most technologically efficient manner.
14. In a capitalist economy, economic activities are coordinated by
    a. tradition.
    b. prices.
    c. government.
    d. business firms.
15. The concept of a mixed economy refers to a mixture of
    a. positive and normative economics.
    b. microeconomics and macroeconomics.
    c. government and free markets.
    d. command with control.

16. Efficiency means
    a. resources are distributed in a fair manner.
    b. all material wants are satisfied.
    c. no one can be made better off, except at someone else's expense.
    d. technology does not change.
17. The idea that the economy should produce its outputs with the least costly combinations of inputs is known as
    a. allocative efficiency.
    b. technological efficiency.
    c. economic efficiency.
    d. equity.
18. The invisible hand of the marketplace refers to the tendency for
    a. government to control the economy behind the scenes.
    b. pollution and other side effects of market activities to harm the economy.
    c. producers to conspire with each other, so as to get as much money as possible out of consumers' pockets.
    d. sellers out for their own self-interests to provide the most valuable assortment of products at the lowest possible prices.
19. Which of the following is the best example of a positive economic statement?
    a. New York should repeal its income tax.
    b. An increase in the minimum wage is likely to increase unemployment.
    c. It is unfair to subsidize farmers.
    d. The price of gasoline is just fine!
20. In response to the inefficient use of resources in China in the days of Mao Tse-Tung, recent Chinese policy has emphasized
    a. egalitarianism.
    b. central planning.
    c. free Internet access.
    d. market incentives.

QUESTIONS AND PROBLEMS

1. *[scarcity]* Describe how scarcity affects the following decision makers:
    a. the president of the United States.
    b. a business executive.
    c. a city manager.
    d. the mother of a baby.
2. *[the margin]* Think back over all the decisions you have made in the last twenty-four hours. Select a few of the clearest examples of decisions made at the margin.

3. *[resource allocation]* Explain how the economy's resource allocation depends in a small way upon the choices you make. For example, how does your choice of going to college affect the economy's resource allocation?
4. *[microeconomics versus macroeconomics]* Identify each of the following topics and issues according to whether they are more appropriate to the study of microeconomics or macroeconomics.

a. the U.S. unemployment rate.

b. electricity prices.

c. gross domestic product.

d. money.

e. advertising by the tobacco industry.

5. *[three economic questions]* List and briefly explain the three economic questions that every economy must answer.

6. *[economic systems]* What are the three types of economic systems? Which of these best describes the economic systems of Canada, the United States, and Western Europe? Discuss the characteristics of this type of economic system.

7. *[equity and efficiency]* Each of the following situations describes an aspect of the issues of equity or efficiency. Identify each situation, according to whether it relates to equity, technological efficiency, or allocative efficiency. Explain why you chose the answers you did.

    a. Jane, a supervisor at the Built-Rite construction company, is concerned because her company does not offer health insurance to its part-time employees, while full-time employees are covered.

    b. Ted, the owner of Ted's Automotive, a small automobile repair shop, has rearranged the layout of the tools and equipment in the shop in order to service more customers each week.

    c. Juanita, a professor of economics at Home State University, is pondering whether to curve the grades on the last test her students took.

    d. Jason, the president of a medium-sized company producing shoes, has decided to stop producing the model #102 running shoe because of a lack of sales.

    e. Ramiro, the owner–manager of BookMax, a chain of discount book stores, has decided to install a $1,000,000 automated shipping system to more quickly and accurately respond to orders that are placed by customers on its web site.

8. *[tradeoffs]* Explain why there could be a tradeoff between efficiency and equity, using taxation as an example.

9. *[role of prices]* During World War II, sugar, gasoline, meat, and other goods were rationed by the U.S. government. Families were issued ration cards that allowed them to buy a government–determined quantity of rationed goods. Why would the government bypass the free market in time of war? Is government rationing, rather than rationing by price, a good idea? How does government rationing affect the allocation of resources?

10. *[role of prices]* If farmers stopped farming or transportation workers quit shipping the food that farmers grow, we might wake up one morning to discover our cupboards bare. Why don't we lose sleep over that possibility? What causes food and other goods to appear in stores?

11. *[mixed economy]* Explain how choices made between government's spending of taxpayer money, or taxpayers spending that money themselves, affect the allocation of society's resources.

12. *[political economy]* Why is economics sometimes called political economy? Explain.

13. *[fallacy of composition]* Ralph the theater manager knows that he can walk from a first row seat to the rear exit in fifteen seconds. When the fire marshal asked Ralph how long it would take his customers to leave the theater in the event of a fire, Ralph responded that it would take fifteen seconds. What flaw in Ralph's reasoning has caused him to commit the fallacy of composition?

14. *[positive versus normative economics]* Why is the statement "Movies today are too violent" a normative statement? Convert the statement into a positive statement. Is your positive statement true? What sort of evidence could be used to establish the truth or falsity of the statement you wrote?

15. *[economic models]* Generally speaking, what is the purpose of an economic model? What guidance does Occam's razor give in creating models? Why do economists make assumptions in developing models? What does the assumption of *ceteris paribus* mean?

16. *[economic models]* Suppose that a college president is developing a model that the administrator hopes will explain how much students will be willing to pay for additional campus parking. Briefly comment on how each of the following might influence student willingness to pay.

    a. Class schedules.

    b. Available bus service.

    c. Students' incomes.

 Visit **www.prenhall.com/ayers** for Exploring the Web exercises and additional self-test quizzes.

WORKING WITH GRAPHS AND DATA

Economists draw graphs in order to clarify thoughts and show economic relationships in a way that can be more easily understood than with words alone. Graphs that present factual information are often drawn as line graphs, bar charts, and pie charts, all of which are seen in this book.

Other graphs represent economic models and contain lines that are referred to as curves. As you read this book, you should study each graph and read its caption. The horizontal line is commonly called the *X* axis and the vertical line the *Y* axis, with the specific labels of the axes varying from graph to graph, depending on what the graph is modeling. Pay attention to both labels and to what the graph is trying to tell you.

When it comes to graphs of models, you will understand the graph better if you can draw it yourself. If you are able to visualize economic relationships graphically, can put an explanation of the graph into your own words, and can draw the graph, you will greatly increase your understanding of economic concepts.

MODELS: DIRECT VERSUS INVERSE RELATIONSHIPS

Each axis of the graph of a model is labeled with the name of a variable, where a variable refers to the name of anything that can change. For example, the price of a pound of tomatoes is a variable because the price could be any of many different values. The price can change with the passage of time. Likewise, the quantity of tomatoes sold is a variable because the quantity sold can change from one time period to the next.

Within the axes, a relationship between two variables is shown by a curve—a line. Some graphs will have more than one curve in them. Other graphs will only show one curve.

Curves that slope upward to the right show a *direct relationship,* also termed a *positive relationship,* between the variables. Curves that slope downward to the right show an *inverse relationship,* also termed a *negative relationship.*

An example will help. Suppose we are interested in the relationship between the average annual quantity of umbrellas sold and the average annual quantity of rainfall, measured in inches. Hypothetical data for these variables in five communities are given in Figure 1A-1.

The relationship between rainfall and umbrella sales is clearly positive, because increases in rainfall are associated with a greater number of umbrellas sold. In Figure 1A-1, the data on the left are plotted in the graph on the right, with rainfall measured on the horizontal axis (the axis that goes left to right) and umbrella sales on the vertical axis (the axis that goes up and

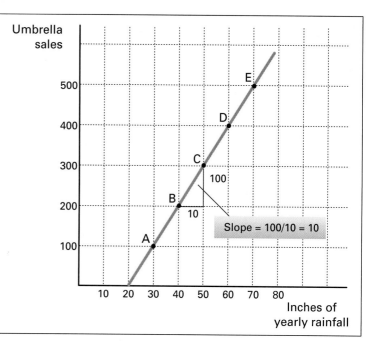

Hypothetical data on yearly rainfall and umbrella sales			
Data point	Community	Yearly rainfall	Umbrella sales
A	Center City	30 inches	100 units
B	Moose Haven	40 inches	200 units
C	Blountville	50 inches	300 units
D	Houckton	60 inches	400 units
E	Echo Ridge	70 inches	500 units

FIGURE 1A-1

A POSITIVE SLOPE A curve that slopes upward to the right illustrates a positive relationship between two variables, also called a direct relationship. The slope of the curve in this figure is positive and constant, equaling 10.

down). A curve is drawn through the plot of data points. The curve slopes upward to the right, again confirming the direct relationship between the two variables.

In contrast, the graph in Figure 1A-2 shows a curve that slopes downward to the right, indicating an inverse relationship between variables. The axes are labeled to show the relationship between the sales of woolen coats, measured on the vertical axis, and the average January temperature, measured on the horizontal axis, in five cities. A greater quantity of coats are sold when temperatures are lower. The data that are plotted in Figure 1A-2 are observable in the table on the left side.

THE SLOPE OF A CURVE

The slope of a curve is measured by the amount of change in the variable on the vertical axis divided by the amount of change in the variable on the horizontal axis. Slope is sometimes referred to as the "rise over the run." In Figure 1A-1, the slope of the curve equals 100 (the rise, or vertical change) divided by 10 (the run, or horizontal change), which equals 10:

Slope = (change in variable on vertical axis)/(change in variable on horizontal axis)
= rise/run
= 100/10 = 10

Applying the definition of slope to Figure 1A-2, the slope of the curve in Figure 1A-2 equals −10, a negative value because the vertical change involves a decrease. Downward sloping curves always have a negative value for their slope.

Straight lines are linear and always have a constant slope. This means that if you know the slope between any two points on the line, you know the slope everywhere on the line. Thus, in Figure 1A-1 the slope equals 10 all along the curve and in Figure 1A-2 the slope equals −10 everywhere on that curve.

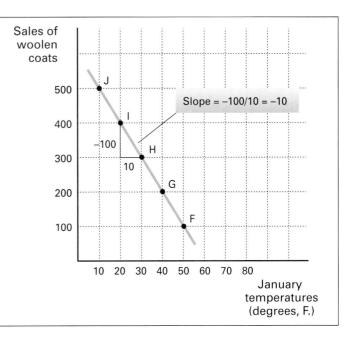

Hypothetical data on sales of woolen coats and average January temperatures			
Data point	City	Coat sales	Average January temperature
F	Tropical city	100 units	50 degrees
G	North town	200 units	40 degrees
H	Snowbound	300 units	30 degrees
I	Cold city	400 units	20 degrees
J	Arctica	500 units	10 degrees

FIGURE 1A-2

A NEGATIVE SLOPE A curve that slopes downward illustrates a negative relationship between two variables, also called an inverse relationship. The slope of the curve shown is negative and constant, equaling -10.

The slope of a nonlinear curve changes from one point to the next on the curve. In Figure 1A-3 graphs (a) and (b) both show curves that have a positive slope. However, the slope becomes decreasingly positive in (a), but increasingly positive in (b). Graphs (c) and (d) show curves with negative slopes. In (c), the slope becomes decreasingly negative, while the slope becomes increasingly negative in (d). Figure 1A-3 illustrates another point about graphs. Notice that these graphs do not have numbers. Graphs of models will often be presented this way when the numbers are less important than the type of relationship between the variables.

Many economic relationships are portrayed as linear. This convention simplifies the analysis, in keeping with the principle of Occam's razor, and allows us to focus our attention on the analysis rather than the shape of the curve. When curves are drawn as nonlinear, the nonlinearity will typically be important to the analysis.

Merely glancing at a curve is often revealing. When the curve slopes upward to the right, you know that it has a positive slope and thus shows a direct relationship between the variables on the axes. Likewise, when the curve slopes downward to the right, it has a negative slope that portrays an inverse relationship between the variables.

The slope of a curve provides information at the margin. The downward sloping curve in Figure 1A-4 shows the incremental spending by the customers of a restaurant in response to additional hours of operation. Note that the slope of the curve equals -25, because incremental customer spending decreases by $25 every additional hour the restaurant remains open. The owners of the restaurant could use this information, in conjunction with data relating to the cost of staying open, to reach a decision about how long to stay open.

SHIFTS AND INTERSECTION POINTS

A change in the relationship between two variables is indicated by a shift in a curve. For example, suppose that umbrellas become a fashion accessory to be carried even when it is

FIGURE 1A-3

NONLINEAR RELATIONSHIPS The graphs in parts (a) through (d) show nonlinear relationships since the curves in the graphs are not straight lines. The two axes are labeled X and Y, which can represent any two variables. The slopes are:
(a) becoming decreasingly positive as X increases,
(b) becoming increasingly positive as X increases,
(c) becoming decreasingly negative as X increases,
(d) becoming increasingly negative as X increases.

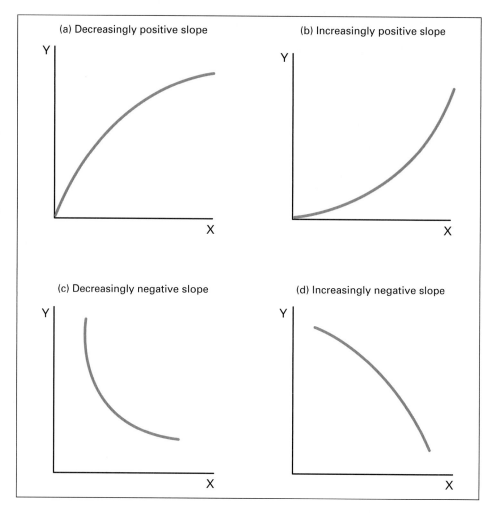

FIGURE 1A-4

INFORMATION AT THE MARGIN Incremental spending by customers at this restaurant decreases as it stays open longer. The slope shown equals −25, which means that the additional spending by restaurant customers decreases by $25 with each passing hour.

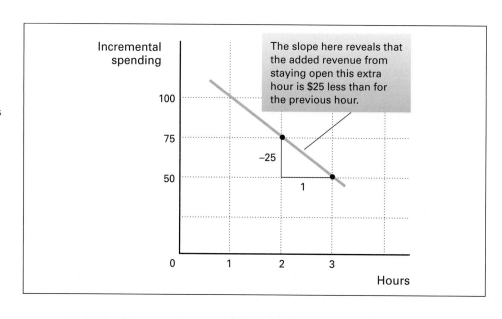

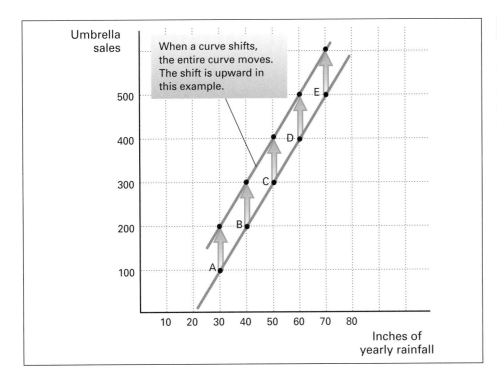

Umbrella sales

When a curve shifts, the entire curve moves. The shift is upward in this example.

Inches of yearly rainfall

FIGURE 1A-5

A SHIFT IN A CURVE When a curve changes position, we say there has been a shift in the curve. A shift represents a new relationship between the variables. This curve shifts upward because umbrellas have become more popular. The shift indicates that 100 additional umbrellas will be sold for each level of rainfall.

not raining. The curve shown in Figure 1A-5 would shift up. In this example, the sales of umbrellas increase by 100 units in each community. If the popularity of umbrellas fades, the curve would shift back down. The student should also be aware that **there is a difference between a shift in a curve and a movement along a curve.** A change in the amount of rainfall will cause a movement along the curve, as in moving from one point to another in Figure 1A-5. For example, the original curve in Figure 1A-5 shows that umbrella sales would increase from 100 to 200 units if rainfall increased from thirty inches to forty inches a year. That increase in sales is a movement along the curve. The increase in umbrella sales from 100 to 200 units would also occur if rainfall stayed at thirty inches a year, but the curve shifted upward, as shown in Figure 1A-5. This time the increase in sales is associated with a shift in the curve, not a movement along it.

Some graphs show two different relationships between the variables on the axes. Each relationship will be illustrated by its own curve. You have just seen this possibility illustrated by a shift in a curve. However, another case involves two relationships that are independent of each other. An example of this possibility occurs when two curves intersect (cross each other). When two curves intersect, the intersection point will sometimes be of particular interest. **At the intersection point the values of each variable will be identical for both relationships—both curves.** Their values are equal only at that point. For example, Figure 1A-6 shows two curves, one that slopes upward and one that slopes downward. The two curves intersect at a point, labeled *A* in the figure. The figure shows that at the intersection point the *X* value is 2 and is the same on both curves. The *Y* value is 75 and is also the same on both curves.

TIME-SERIES AND CROSS-SECTIONAL DATA

Numerical data are important in economic analysis. Data can be presented in a table or a graph. In general, graphs of data are preferred to tables when the details of the data are less

FIGURE 1A-6

AN INTERSECTION POINT At the intersection point of two curves, their values are identical. Point *A* shows a value of 2 for variable *X* and 75 for variable *Y*. Only at that point does curve 1 equal curve 2.

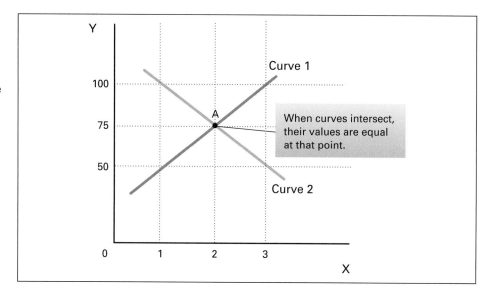

important than the general pattern, since general patterns are more easily ascertained by looking at a graph than at a table.

Time-series data show the values of a variable as time passes. Economists utilize time-series data when changes in the value of a variable over time are the focus of interest. The number of people employed in the United States for each year between 1979 and 2001 is an example of time-series data, as shown by the line chart in Figure 1A-7. Notice that these data could have been presented in a table, but that a table would require more careful study than the graph. The graph easily reveals that the trend in employment was up, since in most years employment increased. Employment moved down, against the trend, in 1982, 1991, and 2001 because of economic slowdowns in those years.

Cross-sectional data are fixed at a moment in time, but vary in some other way. In other words, cross-sectional data change because of some cause that is unrelated to the passage of time. The 2000 unemployment rate for the United States, Canada, Japan, France, Germany, Italy, and the United Kingdom is an example of cross-sectional data. These data are shown in Figure 1A-8 (see page 28) as a bar chart. The bar chart shown would be useful to an economist studying differences in country unemployment rates in the year cited.

SOURCES OF ECONOMIC DATA

Economic research utilizes data in order to identify problems and issues, and to provide evidence about the causes of economic phenomena. Much of the numerical data economists use is collected by various levels of government. Important nongovernmental sources of data include industry trade associations, the United Nations, the Organization for European Community Development (OECD), the International Monetary Fund (IMF), World Bank, Standard and Poor's, Moody's, and Robert Morris Associates.

A short list of useful sources of data follows:

- *Economic Report of the President.* Annual. Roughly one-third of the book is a compilation of numerous data tables selected from among those issued by government agencies. The text is written by the President's Council of Economic Advisers, and provides a professional assessment of the performance of the economy. Written to be understood by the

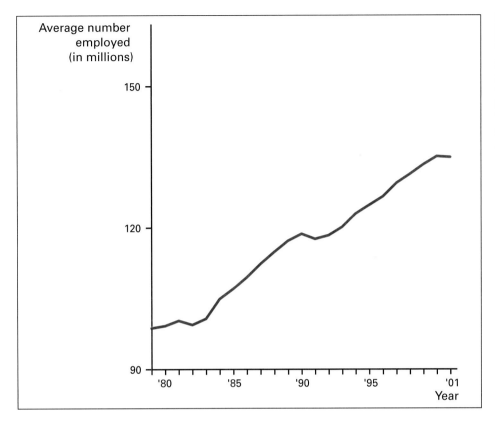

FIGURE 1A-7

TIME-SERIES DATA: NUMBER EMPLOYED The yearly average number of people employed in the United States since 1979 is an example of time-series data. Time-series data show how something changes with time.

Source: Federal Reserve Bank of Dallas on-line data base.

general public, the Economic Report is probably the best place for both novices and experts to start a general search for data about the U.S. economy.

- *International Financial Statistics.* Monthly. Published by the International Monetary Fund in English and other languages, the book presents several hundred large pages of finely printed economic data on the world at large, and on specific countries throughout the world. The focus is on the financial side of economic activity, such as inflation, interest rates, government budgets, and exchange rates. There is also data on a variety of nonfinancial features of world economies, such as the composition of exports and imports. To promote easy access, the IMF also provides a CD-ROM version.

- *Federal Reserve Bulletin.* Monthly. The user will find extensive data on money, banking, interest rates, and finance, along with news relating to the financial environment. Also featured are articles that analyze economic developments. Articles are written to be accessible to the general reader.

- *Survey of Current Business.* Quarterly. This publication of the U.S. Department of Commerce offers a rich source of data on business conditions.

- *City and County Data Book.* Annual. What is the population of your hometown? What is the average age of its residents? Average income? This data source provides information about the economies of U.S. cities and counties.

- *Statistical Abstract of the U.S.* Annual. This source contains hundreds of data tables, packed full of facts about the United States.

- **The Internet.** The Internet has marked a huge change in the way data are retrieved. There are numerous sites offering economic data. Some data sets are free; others are not. For example, the *Economic Report of the President* is freely available on-line, as are many other data sets from the federal government.

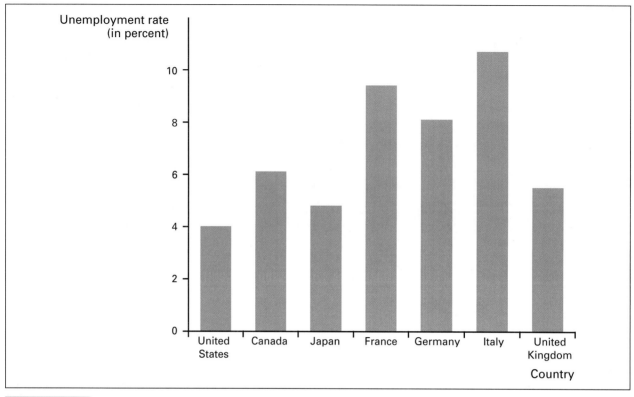

FIGURE 1A-8

CROSS-SECTIONAL DATA: COUNTRY UNEMPLOYMENT RATES The average unemployment rate in each of
several countries is an example of cross-sectional data. These data are not time-series data, because
they are for a single year, 2000.

Source: 2002 Economic Report of the President, Table B-109. Data for Italy and the United Kingdom are preliminary
figures. All figures are for unemployment as a percent of the civilian labor force.

EXERCISES

1. Consider the relationship between a college student's grade in a course and the amount
of time spent studying. Draw a graph with the vertical axis labeled "grade" and the horizontal axis labeled "time spent studying" that shows the general relationship you
would expect between these variables. Do you think the relationship would necessarily
be linear? What factors other than study time would affect the grades of college students? How would changes in these other factors shift the curve in the graph you have
drawn?

2. Gross domestic product data for the imaginary country of Janica are as follows: 1998
GDP = $175 billion; 1999 GDP = $145 billion; 2000 GDP = $164 billion; 2001 GDP =
$200 billion; 2002 GDP = $215 billion. Plot the GDP data on a graph in which the vertical axis measures GDP and the horizontal axis years. Connect the data plots to create a
line graph.

CHAPTER 2

PRODUCTION AND TRADE

A LOOK AHEAD

What does the word *model* bring to mind? A fashion model? A model airplane? A model citizen? In this chapter, we will model the essence of economics—scarcity and choice. While models are designed with different purposes in mind, the economic model shares a common trait with other models. That trait is a studied simplicity that highlights the features of greatest significance.

The basic model of economics developed in this chapter extends from our daily routines as individuals to the grand plans of our society—from our choice of occupations to the rise and fall of nations. For example, the twentieth century has been dubbed "America's century" to reflect the strengths of the U.S. economy in providing for its citizens and in defeating its adversaries. In the Explore & Apply section that concludes this chapter, we will discover how economics helps us better understand those victories. As we journey through the twenty-first century, we will encounter new and sometimes fearsome choices. Economic models can help us to recognize our options so that we will choose well.

LEARNING OBJECTIVES

Understanding Chapter 2 will enable you to:
1. **Analyze tradeoffs facing both individuals and countries.**
2. **Categorize the types of resources an economy possesses.**
3. **Model a country's production possibilities, and how these possibilities respond to technological development.**
4. **Describe how economies can grow faster if they are willing to cut back on current consumption.**
5. **Visualize the flow of goods and services, resources, and money in the economy.**
6. **Explain how people and countries gain from trade by specializing according to comparative advantage.**
7. **Convey how economic strength can lead to victory, sometimes without a fight.**

Explore & Apply

29

2.1 SCARCITY AND CHOICE

There is no such thing as a free lunch.

Economics exists because resources are scarce relative to our wants. Scarcity means we have to make choices. Take lunchtime for example. Suppose your school cafeteria holds a Student Appreciation Day and offers a free sandwich buffet between noon and 1:00 next Thursday. Would you go? Your decision depends upon opportunity costs.

OPPORTUNITY COSTS

opportunity costs the value of the best alternative opportunity forgone.

Opportunity costs represent the value of forgone alternatives. Specifically, the opportunity cost of an action is the value of the single most highly valued alternative choice that has been forgone. Perhaps you contemplate how good the cafeteria's sandwiches are, relative to other things you could eat. You might also consider how pleasant the surroundings are, relative to other lunch spots. You would also want to check your calendar—your time may be needed for something of higher priority, such as studying for an exam. If you choose to eat the cafeteria's sandwiches, you must give up the value of the best alternative way to spend that time. While no money is taken, the lunch is in reality far from free.

The money you pay for an item could have alternatively been spent on something else. The value of the best alternative use of that money is an opportunity cost, but not usually the only opportunity cost. The value of forgone alternative uses of time or other nonmonetary resources must also be included. To compute your own opportunity cost of going to college, for example, you must compute what you would be doing if you were not in school. Would you be working? Then the cost of a semester is tuition plus the forgone earnings from the job you would have had. Maybe you would have been spending all of your time at the beach. That, too, has an opportunity cost. Only you can know how high it is, because only you can know what value you receive from lying in the sun and listening to the surf.

SNAPSHOT   ## "THE GRASS IS ALWAYS GREENER ...

... on the other side of the fence," the saying goes. Take marriage, for example. How many married men and women do not catch themselves envying the freedom of their single friends—freedom to meet new people and do what they want, when they want to do it? How many of those single friends do not look back with envy of their own, seeing the warmth and security of sharing one's life with someone special? Oh, those opportunity costs! We cannot have it all! ◀

RESOURCES

Resources are combined to produce outputs of goods and services. *Inputs* is another name for resources, which are usually divided into the categories of land, labor, capital, and entrepreneurship. We refer to the ability of a resource to produce output as that resource's *productivity.*

land natural resources in their natural states.

Land refers to all natural resources in their natural states. These gifts of nature include such things as minerals, water, and soil. Neither motor oil nor gasoline would fall under the category of land. Rather, they are products that use land as an input. The crude oil from which the motor oil and gasoline were derived is land.

labor the human capacity to work.

Labor refers to people's capacity to work. It ignores the increased labor productivity from acquired skills and the development of peoples' abilities, which constitute **human capital.** Human capital is a special case of an economy's third resource, capital.

human capital acquired skills and abilities embodied within a person.

Just before leaving office in 2001, President Clinton designated as parkland millions of acres of land owned by the federal government. Since the government already owned the land, is it true that there were no opportunity costs to the president's decision?

Answer: No. Although the government did not have to spend money to acquire the land, there were still opportunity costs. For one, national parklands are restricted in terms of their uses. Thus, mineral exploration is curtailed. Ranchers are also not allowed to graze their animals in national parks. By converting the land into a park, the federal government gave up the opportunity of selling it. These opportunity costs are difficult to estimate, but are real nonetheless. The opportunity costs account for the public protests that accompanied the president's action.

Capital is anything that is produced in order to increase productivity in the future. Along with human capital, there is also *physical capital,* which includes buildings, machinery, and other equipment. For example, a college education adds to human capital, and the classroom in which that education was obtained is physical capital. The classroom aids in the production of an education, and the education aids in productivity in the workplace.

capital anything that is produced in order to increase productivity in the future; includes human capital and physical capital.

Caution: The definition of capital used in economics differs from that used in finance. Financial capital refers to financial instruments, such as stocks, bonds, and money.

Entrepreneurship is taking personal initiative to combine resources in productive ways. Rather than accepting jobs where orders are handed down from above, entrepreneurs blaze new trails in the world of commerce. If you start your own business, you are an entrepreneur. Entrepreneurs take risks, but have the potential to become the economy's movers and shakers. Countries tap the creative potential of entrepreneurship in order to improve the value they get from other resources. In the process, the entrepreneurs themselves are sometimes handsomely rewarded.

entrepreneurship personal initiative to combine resources in productive ways; involves risk.

The possibilities for combining an economy's resources depend upon technology. **Technology** refers to possible techniques of production. Technological advances both improve the selection of goods and services and the manner in which we can produce them. As technologies change, the relative values of various resources also change. For example, natural harbors declined in significance in response to the technology of air transportation. While the value of land around harbors diminished, air travel increased the importance of other resources, such as the human capital needed to pilot the planes.

technology possible techniques of production.

2.2 PRODUCTION POSSIBILITIES

Land, labor, capital, and entrepreneurship combine in various ways to produce the output of various goods and services. This section examines the output opportunities these combinations allow and the resulting choices that all economies must make.

MODELING SCARCITY AND CHOICE

Recall that a model is a simplification of reality. Following the principle of keeping a model simple, a good model emphasizes only those features pertinent to solving the problem at

production possibilities frontier
a model that shows the various combinations of two goods the economy is capable of producing.

hand. This section models the essence of economics, which is scarcity and choice. An economy's scarce resources limit its options, so it must make choices about what to produce. We can model these options, and possibilities for choice among them, with a production possibilities frontier.

The **production possibilities frontier** illustrates scarcity and choice by assuming that only two goods can be produced. This simplification is appropriate, because understanding choice between any two goods allows the understanding of choice between each good and any other. It is termed a *frontier* because it represents the limits of output possibilities, given current resources and technology. Frontiers of knowledge and capability are made to be expanded, and the production possibilities frontier is no exception. Over time, as people and firms accumulate more resources and learn new production techniques, the production possibilities frontier will expand.

Consider the fictional economy of Castaway Island, inhabited exclusively by a castaway named Hank. Hank has the island to himself, and it provides for all his material needs. Still, he must spend time gathering food to eat. His options are to catch fish or harvest coconuts. He values both of these foods in his diet and can spend up to eight hours a day to obtain them. Figure 2-1 illustrates a production possibilities frontier for Hank's economy.

The graph of production possibilities in Figure 2-1 reveals the same information as the table, but does so in a visual way that can be interpreted at a glance. Each row of the table corresponds to a point on the graph. For example, the combination of three fish and sixteen coconuts can be read from the third line of the table or seen as point *C* on the graph.

Relationships among data are more readily apparent in the graph than in the table in Figure 2-1. For example, a basic message of the production possibilities frontier is that the more fish Hank catches, the fewer coconuts he can collect. A glance at the graph reveals this relationship. The inverse relationship between fish and coconuts illustrates the opportunity cost of Hank using his limited resource, time.

The opportunity cost of more fish is the number of coconuts forgone. The table in Figure 2-2 shows these opportunity costs. Since we are showing the opportunity cost of more fish, Figure 2-2 rearranges the rows in Figure 2-1 to start with row F, which corresponds to zero fish.

As Hank increases his catch from zero fish (row F in the table) to a maximum of five fish (row A), we see the number of coconuts he collects drop at an increasing rate. In other words, the opportunity cost of the first fish is only one coconut. The opportunity cost of two fish is giving up three coconuts. Then opportunity costs really jump. The opportunity cost of four fish is 12 coconuts, which is quadruple the opportunity cost of two fish. Five fish

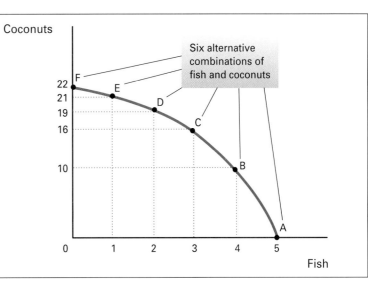

Production possibilities frontier on Castaway Island		
Data point	Fish caught per day	Coconuts collected per day
A	5	0
B	4	10
C	3	16
D	2	19
E	1	21
F	0	22

FIGURE 2-1

THE PRODUCTION POSSIBILITIES FRONTIER ON CASTAWAY ISLAND The production possibilities frontier is a curve that illustrates an economy's options from which to choose. If Hank devotes all of his labor to collecting coconuts, he will have 22 coconuts but no fish, as shown by point *F*. Alternatively, he could catch one fish and still have 21 coconuts, as shown by point *E*. Points *A, B, C,* and *D* on the production possibilities frontier illustrate other possible combinations of the two goods.

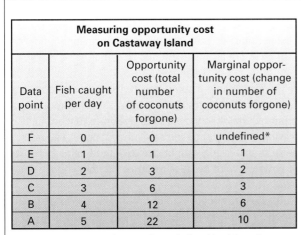

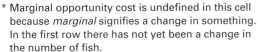

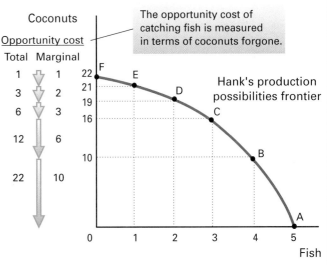

Measuring opportunity cost on Castaway Island			
Data point	Fish caught per day	Opportunity cost (total number of coconuts forgone)	Marginal opportunity cost (change in number of coconuts forgone)
F	0	0	undefined*
E	1	1	1
D	2	3	2
C	3	6	3
B	4	12	6
A	5	22	10

* Marginal opportunity cost is undefined in this cell because *marginal* signifies a change in something. In the first row there has not yet been a change in the number of fish.

FIGURE 2-2

MEASURING OPPORTUNITY COST ON CASTAWAY ISLAND The opportunity cost of fish can be measured at the margin or in total. The marginal opportunity cost is measured one fish at a time. The first fish costs one coconut, the second costs another two coconuts, and so forth. The total opportunity cost is the sum of the marginal opportunity costs, as shown on the left. For example, the total opportunity cost of two fish is three coconuts.

carry an opportunity cost of 22 coconuts, meaning that Hank must give up all coconuts if he wants to catch five fish.

The final column in Figure 2-2 shows *marginal opportunity cost,* which is the additional opportunity cost from catching one more fish. In economics, marginal means incremental—referring to one additional unit of a good or service. For example, you can see that the marginal opportunity cost of the second fish equals 2, computed as the difference between the opportunity cost of two fish and one fish. Similarly, the marginal opportunity cost of the fifth fish equals 10, which is the difference between the opportunity cost of four fish and five fish. The graph in Figure 2-2 duplicates the graph in Figure 2-1, except that Figure 2-2 shows the marginal and total opportunity costs.

law of increasing cost the rise in the marginal opportunity cost of producing a good as more of that good is produced.

The numbers in Figure 2-2 illustrate a principle known as the **law of increasing cost,** which states that as an economy adds to its production of any one good, the marginal opportunity cost of that good will rise. The reason is that resources are often specialized, being more suitable to producing one output than another output. So to increase the output of a good, the most appropriate resources are used first, followed by resources that are increasingly less appropriate for producing that good.

Because marginal opportunity cost increases as output increases, the production possibilities frontier is bowed outward, meaning that its slope becomes increasingly negative. In contrast, if marginal opportunity cost were constant, the production possibilities frontier would be a straight line with a constant downward slope. To understand the law of increasing cost and why the production possibilities frontier is bowed outward in Hank's case, consider the choices he must make.

Each daylight hour, Hank has to choose between fishing and gathering coconuts. The most productive fishing occurs at certain hours of the day when the fish are biting. While all hours are equally well suited to gathering coconuts, Hank knows that the number of coconuts gathered per hour declines as he spends more hours per day gathering, because he gathers the most accessible coconuts first. Knocking a few hours off of coconut gathering allows Hank to fish when the fishing is best and comes at a cost of relatively few coconuts forgone. Adding more hours to his fishing time leads to less and less incremental productivity in fishing and takes away increasingly more productive hours in gathering. The result is the law of increasing cost.

Like Hank, economies are forced to make choices about how to use scarce resources. In producing any good *X*, an economy first uses resources that are best suited to producing *X*. If the economy keeps adding to the production of good *X*, it uses resources that are increasingly less well suited to *X,* but increasingly better suited to some other good, *Y.* The result is that the production of good *Y* drops at an increasingly rapid rate as *X* production increases. The production possibilities frontier bows outward because resources are not equally suited to the production of different goods.

For instance, classrooms are well suited to producing education, but not to producing automobiles. Resources are often specialized to perform limited tasks: fish hooks are great for fishing, cooktops for cooking, coal mines for mining coal, and so on. They can sometimes be used for other purposes, but will not be as productive in these uses. For example, coal mines are fine places to grow mushrooms and have led to commercial production under such brand names as Moonlight Mushrooms. However, until the coal seams are fully mined, the coal output is likely to be of higher value.

Figure 2-3(a) shows a production possibilities frontier without numbers, since the idea of a production possibilities frontier transcends any particular numbers. If you have trouble with a graph without numbers, however, just put in some illustrative numbers as is done in Figure 2-3(b). All points within or along the production possibilities frontier are feasible combinations of two goods. For the economy to reach that frontier, it must use all of its resources. It must also use these resources efficiently in the technological sense of getting

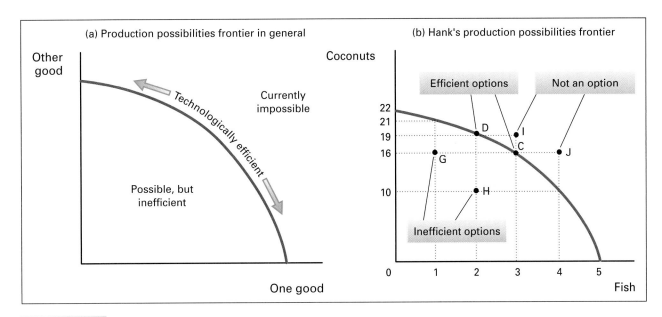

FIGURE 2-3

POSSIBILITIES FOR EFFICIENCY All points on the production possibilities frontier are output combinations that are technologically efficient and feasible, as shown in (a). Points within the production possibilities frontier are also feasible, but are not efficient. Points outside the frontier cannot be reached with current resources and technology.

For example, (b) shows Hank's production possibilities on Castaway Island. On this graph, point *G* represents 16 coconuts and 1 fish. That combination of outputs is possible, but Hank could do better at point *D* by producing 19 coconuts and 2 fish. Likewise, point *C* is more efficient than point *H*. Both *C* and *D* are efficient in a technological sense, meaning that at either point, Hank cannot produce more of one good without giving up some of the other. Hank would like to achieve points *I* or *J*, but does not have the resources and technology to do so.

the most output for given inputs. Otherwise, the economy would be inefficient and at a point inside the frontier. In short, **any point along the production possibilities frontier is a technologically efficient combination of outputs.** Points inside the frontier are inefficient and points outside the frontier are currently unattainable.

Recall from Chapter 1 that, while *technological efficiency* is part of economic efficiency, there is also another part, *allocative efficiency.* Allocative efficiency implies a specific point on the production possibilities frontier that is the most valuable combination of outputs. In general, **there will be only one point on the production possibilities frontier that is allocatively efficient,** and we cannot know what it is by sight. However, the invisible hand of the market economy will tend to lead the economy to that point on the production possibilities frontier that is the allocatively efficient combination of outputs. In Hank's case, his preferences for fish vis à vis coconuts will guide his use of time so that he picks the combination of fish and coconuts that provide him with the most satisfaction.

ECONOMIC GROWTH AND TECHNOLOGICAL CHANGE

Land, labor, capital, and entrepreneurship—these are the resources available to the economy. Production possibilities will depend on how much of each resource the economy has and on the technology that is available to make use of those resources. As resources increase

Are all points along a production possibilities frontier equally efficient? Is an economy indifferent among them?

Answer: All points on the production possibilities frontier are technologically efficient, meaning that it is impossible to produce more of one good without giving up some of the other. However, while technological efficiency is necessary for overall economic efficiency, so too is allocative efficiency, which identifies the specific point on the production possibilities frontier that is the most valuable combination of outputs. Not all points on the production possibilities frontier are allocatively efficient, meaning there is a point that will be preferred over others since it best reflects wants.

economic growth the ability of the economy to produce more or better output.

or technology improves, production possibilities grow and the economy's entire production possibilities frontier shifts outward, as shown in Figure 2-4(a). **When the production possibilities frontier shifts outward, the economy experiences economic growth.** Economic growth occurs when the economy uses expanded production possibilities to produce an output of greater value. In the event of natural disasters, the exhaustion of natural resources, or anything else that causes an economy's resource base to shrink, the country's production possibilities will also shrink, which would lead to negative economic growth. Figure 2-4(b) illustrates negative economic growth as a shift inward of the production possibilities frontier.

Let's return to the economy of Castaway Island for examples of positive and negative growth. Hank might find some netting that has washed ashore that he can use to catch fish or to collect the coconuts as they fall to the ground. The netting is capital that allows him to catch more fish and to collect more coconuts per hour. This shifts Hank's production possi-

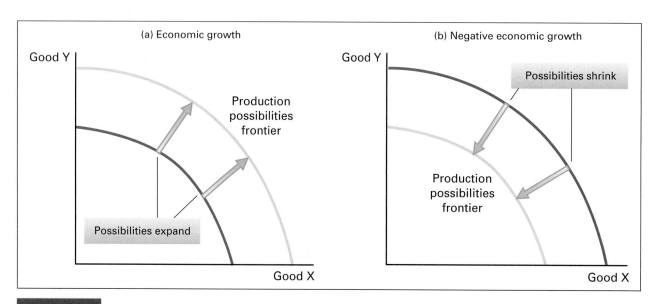

FIGURE 2-4

ECONOMIC GROWTH Economic growth shifts the production possibilities frontier outward, as shown in (a). More resources or improved technology have this effect. Negative economic growth, seen in (b), is associated with a shift inward in the frontier. Negative growth can be caused by the destruction of resources, such as from natural disasters or warfare.

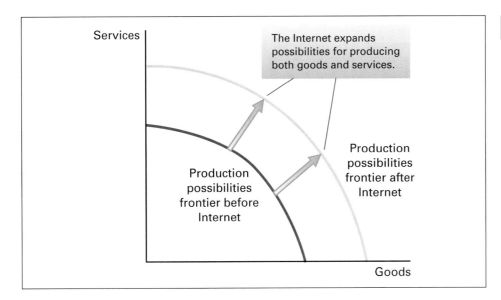

FIGURE 2-5

ECONOMIC GROWTH FROM THE INTERNET The efficiencies brought about by the Internet shift the production possibilities frontier outward. The equipment that allows this flow is capital, and includes such things as fiber optic cables and personal computers.

bilities frontier outward. Alternatively, were Hank to overfish and a coconut blight to strike, fewer fish and coconuts would be available. His production possibilities frontier would shift inward.

Closer to home, the Internet has improved information flows and allowed more efficient choice. The result is that the economy is able to obtain more output from its scarce resources. The Internet is at least partly capital because it was produced in order to make information flow easier, which can increase the production of other goods and services. It includes such components as the computer and modem from which you connect, the lines upon which the data travel, and the routers and switches that direct that data to the right places. Adding this Internet capital to the economy causes the production possibilities frontier to shift outward, as shown in Figure 2-5.

MODELING GROWTH—IMPOVERISHED COUNTRIES FACE A DIFFICULT TRADEOFF

It takes capital to make use of technological change and increase labor productivity. Since capital represents output that is produced now for the purpose of increasing productivity later, the creation of capital comes at the expense of current consumption. This choice can be illustrated with the production possibilities frontier, as shown in Figure 2-6.

For example, at point *A* the economy is devoting nearly all of its resources to producing goods for current consumption. The result is that the amount of capital it possesses decreases over time, because of equipment wearing out, buildings falling into disrepair, and other forms of *depreciation*. With its economy producing too little new capital to offset depreciation of existing capital, the production possibilities frontier shifts inward. Point *B*, in contrast, trades off some current consumption for significantly more production of capital, more than enough to offset depreciation. The result is that the production possibilities frontier shifts out over time.

When an economy is characterized by widespread poverty, the route to economic growth involves particularly tough tradeoffs. For countries to reduce poverty, they must channel resources into amassing capital. Those resources are taken away from the production of goods that meet current needs, such as food and housing. Yet Bangladesh, Somalia, and other countries that can ill afford to sacrifice current consumption are the ones most in need of the economic growth that such a sacrifice would bring.

CAPITAL'S ROLE IN GROWTH

Sacrificing current consumption in favor of producing more capital hastens economic growth, but may be painful in the present. For example, choosing point *B* provides the capital needed to expand production possibilities over time. In contrast, choosing point *A* allows for more current consumption, but shrinks the production possibilities frontier over time. This is because not enough new capital is produced to offset the depreciation of existing capital.

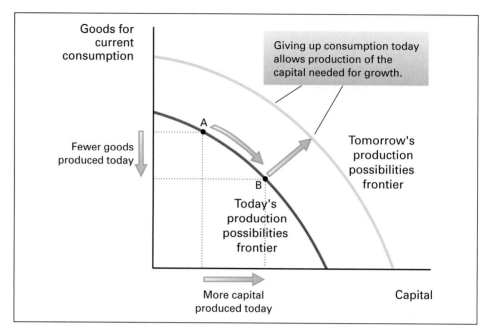

SNAPSHOT   **JAPANESE RICE FOR NORTH KOREAN ROCKETS**

Was it a test missile or a satellite launch vehicle that North Korea fired in the direction of Japan? Either way, the Japanese were not amused by this unexpected projectile hurtling their way late in the summer of 1998. In response, Japan was quick to cut off its food aid to North Korea. After all, it was the food aid that allowed North Korea the luxury of devoting resources to developing its expertise in rocketry. Food aid from Japan was meant to help the North Koreans survive, not to allow them to reallocate their resources toward financing investment in new, threatening capabilities, now thought to include nuclear weapons. ◀

GENERAL AND SPECIALIZED GROWTH

Technological change can increase productivity across a broad range of industries, as with the better information flows made possible by modern computers and telecommunications. Oftentimes, however, technological change is specific to an industry. For example, an advance in biotechnology might improve cucumber yields but have no effect on the steel industry.

Figure 2-7 illustrates the difference between general growth and specialized growth, where the economy starts from the original production possibilities frontier. In the case of general growth, productivity in both the pretzel and pumpkin industries increases. In the case of specialized growth, productivity increases in only one industry.

The production possibilities frontiers in the graph labeled Specialized Growth in Figure 2-7(b) indicate technological improvement in only the pretzel industry. To see why growth occurred in the pretzel industry but not the pumpkin industry, consider the output of each good separately when none of the other is produced. When no pretzels are produced, the technological change has not affected the production possibility for pumpkins, because the point on the vertical axis is the same as before. However, when no pumpkins are produced, the technological change has allowed an increase in the possible output of pretzels. We know this because the intercept on the horizontal axis has moved to the right. Whatever that maximum quantity of pretzels had been, it is now higher. **Specialized growth thus pivots**

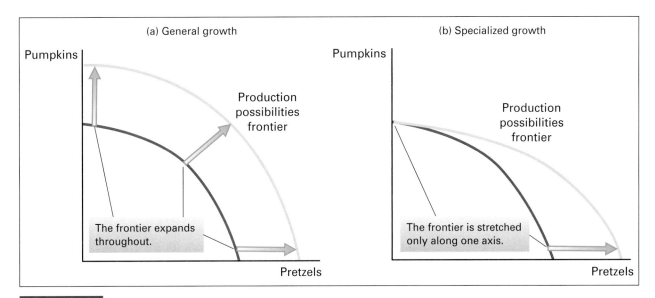

FIGURE 2-7

GENERAL AND SPECIALIZED GROWTH Broad-reaching technological change brings general growth, which shifts the entire production possibilities frontier (ppf) outward as shown in part (a). Specialized technological change brings specialized growth, which causes the production possibilities frontier to expand in the direction of the industry to which the new technology applies. In part (b), that industry is pretzels.

the production possibilities frontier in the direction of more output in the industry affected by the technological change.

In summary:

- The production possibilities frontier shows how much of one good can be produced for any feasible amount of another good.
- If an economy is on its frontier, the opportunity cost of producing more of one good is less of the other good.
- The production possibilities frontier is bowed outward, consistent with the law of increasing cost, which notes the increasing marginal opportunity cost of additional output.
- Every point along the production possibilities frontier is technologically efficient.
- Points inside the frontier imply some unemployed or misallocated resources and are thus inefficient.
- Points outside the frontier are unattainable with current resources and technology.
- Economies grow by acquiring resources or better technology, which shifts the frontier outward.
- If the economy acquires resources that are specialized in the production of a certain good, the production possibilities frontier expands outward in the direction of more of that good.

2.3 THE CIRCULAR FLOW OF ECONOMIC ACTIVITY

Production possibilities frontiers are about *possibilities*. What a market economy will actually choose to produce is decided through the interaction of consumers and businesses. In effect, consumers vote with their money for the assortment of goods and services that is offered. **Money** is a medium of exchange, meaning that it facilitates the exchange of goods and services. Without money, people would be forced to exchange goods directly, a situation

money a medium of exchange that removes the need for barter; also a measure of value and a way to store value over time.

FIGURE 2-8

THE CIRCULAR FLOW OF ECONOMIC ACTIVITY The sale of goods and services by business firms occurs in the output market, while the purchase of resources by firms occurs in the input market. The circular flow model shows that household income depends on the sale of resources, as seen by the arrows that pass through the input market along the bottom of the flow. The arrows through the output market indicate that household spending determines outputs. Taxes, regulations, and other government actions will influence both markets.

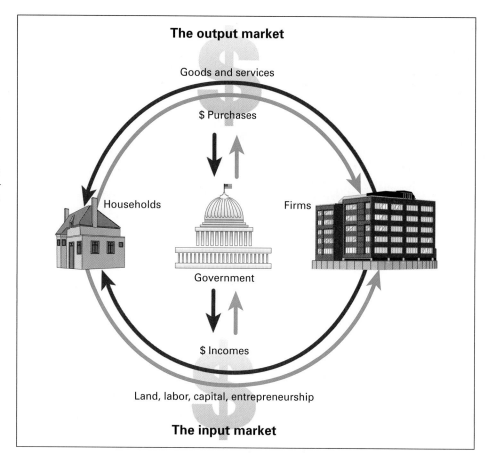

barter the exchange of goods and services directly for one another, without the use of money.

circular flow a model of the economy that depicts how the flow of money facilitates a counterflow of resources, goods, and services in the input and output markets.

output market the market where goods and services are bought and sold.

input market the market where resources are bought and sold.

known as **barter.** Barter would be very difficult in a complicated economy. For example, to buy a mystery novel, you would have to provide something the bookseller would want in return. What do you have? Would you offer a chicken? What if the bookseller is in the mood for Buffalo wings? Money comes to the rescue—it greases the wheels of commerce.

Many things have served as money through the years. In prisoner-of-war camps during World War II, cigarettes served as money. Traditionally, gold, silver, and other scarce metals have been considered money, since they are inherently scarce and relatively easy to transport in the form of coins. Paper is even easier to transport, which is why it is the most common form of money in use today. However, for paper or anything else to be used as money, its quantity must be limited, which is why counterfeiting is illegal. Government must also be careful about printing too much currency if it wishes its currency to retain value as money.

Figure 2-8 illustrates the **circular flow** of economic activity, a model that depicts how markets use the medium of money to determine what goods and services are produced and who gets to buy them. The top part of the diagram illustrates the **output market** in which businesses sell goods and services to consumers. The actual assortment of goods and services is determined by how much households are willing to pay relative to business firms' production costs.

The bottom part of the diagram shows the **input market,** which illustrates that households supply the resources of land, labor, capital, and entrepreneurship. All of these resources are ultimately owned by people, who make up households. The sale of resources to business firms provides the income that households use to buy products. Since people own businesses, business profits also belong to households. For this reason, the circular flow of inputs and outputs is maintained by a counterflow of dollars.

Through taxation, regulation, and production, government influences the mix of goods that is produced and the manner in which resources are used. The circular flow diagram could be expanded to include foreign commerce, banking, or other economic details, but can become complex and difficult to interpret.

2.4 EXPANDING CONSUMPTION POSSIBILITIES THROUGH TRADE

For their own self-interest, economies engage in trade with other economies. This is true for national economies, regional economies, local economies, and even personal economies. For example, we each have our own production possibilities. Yet, if we each had to rely upon our own production possibilities frontier and could not trade, we would be hard-pressed to live as well as Hank the castaway. Instead, we trade with one another. We trade our labor services for income to let us buy what we want. We trade so that we can consume more quantity and variety than we could produce on our own. Cities, states, and countries trade among themselves for the same reasons individuals trade with one another.

People specialize in their jobs according to their interests and opportunities. They then use the income they earn in order to purchase goods and services. Note that this is a two-part decision. First people decide what to produce; then they decide what to consume. The economies of countries engaged in international trade operate the same way.

SPECIALIZATION ACCORDING TO COMPARATIVE ADVANTAGE— THE BASIS FOR TRADE

In order to gain from trade, an economy must *specialize* according to its **comparative advantage. An economy has a comparative advantage in producing a good if it can produce that good at a lower opportunity cost than could other economies.** This means the economy chooses to produce those things it does well relative to other things it could be doing. Contrary to popular belief, trade is not based on **absolute advantage,** which refers to the ability to produce something with fewer resources than could others. **To gain from trade, specialize according to comparative advantage, whether or not you have any absolute advantage.**

> **comparative advantage** the ability to produce a good at a lower opportunity cost (other goods forgone) than others could do.

> **absolute advantage** the ability to produce a good with fewer resources than other producers.

The principle of comparative advantage holds even in our imaginary wanderings through space, as illustrated in the Star Trek series that got its start in the 1960s. One of the early mainstays was the pointy-eared science officer named Mr. Spock. With his mental prowess and physical strength, Spock had an absolute advantage in performing a variety of tasks. For example, he might have been a master at quickly cleaning the passageways of the *Starship Enterprise.* However, he did not spend his time mopping the floors because, as Spock would say, "That would be illogical!" It would waste his time.

Logic suggests making the most productive use of our time. We don't have time to do everything, something today's college students know well. College students follow their comparative advantages and specialize when selecting their majors and careers. For example, Michael Jordan selected economics as his major and basketball as his career. With his physical prowess and mental savvy, he could have excelled at other majors or other careers. But he had to make a choice. He chose basketball, where he could dazzle. He tried baseball for a time, but quickly returned to his area of relative strength.

Even if a person cannot do anything well, he or she can still do some things relatively better than other things. It might take Doug longer to mow yards than it would take other people. Yet, if that is what Doug could do best, he would mow yards. Other people would be delighted to hire him because he would charge them less than the opportunity cost of their own time were they to do the mowing themselves. Michael Jordan might hire him. It would be irrelevant whether Michael could mow his own lawn faster. The opportunity cost of his time would be too high.

These lessons apply to any economy, whether the economy is that of an individual or that of a country. Countries gain from trade whether or not they have an absolute advantage in anything. The country can start off rich or poor and still gain from trade. While a country is constrained to produce along or inside its production possibilities frontier, it can exchange some of its own output for the output of other countries. Goods and services a country sells to other countries are termed **exports.** Exports are traded for **imports,** which are goods and services a country buys from other countries. **Through trade, a country can consume a combination of goods and services that lies outside its production possibilities frontier, meaning that the country's consumption possibilities will exceed its production possibilities.**

exports goods and services a country sells to other countries.

imports goods and services a country buys from other countries.

International trade is more important to small countries than to large countries. This is because the larger the country, the more opportunities there are to specialize internally. For example, the United States produces potatoes in Maine and Idaho for sale throughout the other states. Likewise, Michigan specializes in automobile production, Texas in oil and gas production, and so forth. If the United States were broken into fifty different countries, this trade among states would all be international. As it is, the tremendous diversity of resources found within the United States leads it to have one of the smallest proportions of international trade relative to its output of any country in the world. Figure 2-9 shows the proportion of various countries' exports relative to their outputs. The smaller the country, typically, the higher that ratio is, and the more it gains from trade. These gains occur because smaller countries would be hard pressed to produce the variety of goods and services that are available through trade.

Economists rarely compute the goods in which countries have their comparative advantages. Rather, markets do that quite effectively on their own. If a country has a comparative advantage in producing certain goods, it can produce those goods cheaply, relative to the other goods that it could produce. Those goods in which it has a comparative advantage will be the goods it can offer at the best prices in the international marketplace. Thus, without any economic research, economies engaging in international trade naturally tend to export those goods for which they have a comparative advantage and import the rest.

COMPUTING COMPARATIVE ADVANTAGE

Although people and countries act according to comparative advantage whether or not they sit down to compute it, a hypothetical computation helps to clarify its meaning. Consider a model involving two countries, Japan and England, that can each produce only computer memory chips and oil. Assume that all computer memory chips are interchangeable and that oil is also identical. The productivity of workers is shown in Table 2-1. Note that in this example Japan's workers are more productive at both producing oil and manufacturing computer chips, meaning that Japan has an absolute advantage in both computer chips and oil production. However, because a worker cannot do two things at one time, countries must allocate each worker to producing either one good or the other. To maximize its gains from trade, each country chooses to produce according to its comparative advantage.

The key to computing comparative advantage is to measure opportunity cost. In this case, the choices are simple. To produce computer chips, a country must allocate labor away from oil production and thus forgo some oil. Likewise, to produce oil, a country must forgo computer chips. Thus, the opportunity cost of computer chips is the oil forgone, and the opportunity cost of oil is the computer chips forgone. We can use some simple algebra to compute the opportunity cost of a single barrel of oil or computer chip, so as to allow comparison of opportunity costs between countries. Applying this math to Table 2-1 yields the

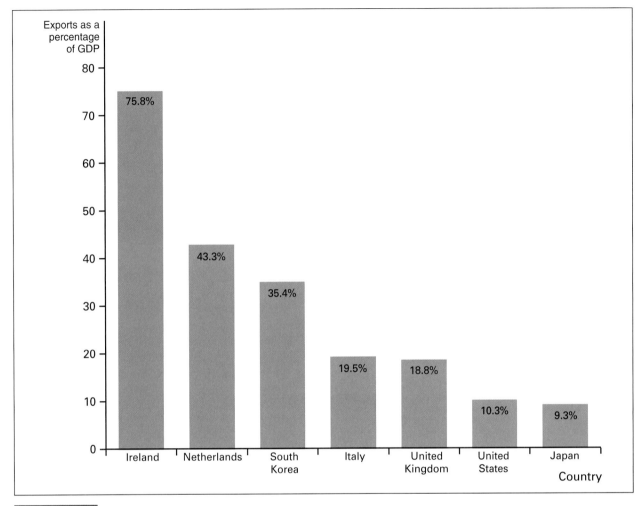

FIGURE 2-9

EXPORTS AS A PERCENTAGE OF GROSS DOMESTIC PRODUCT Countries with larger economies usually export a smaller percentage of their output than do countries with smaller economies. The United States and Japan are two of the world's largest economies and both export a relatively small percentage of their output.

Sources: 2001 Statistical Abstract of the U.S. Percentages compiled from 1999 data in Table Nos. 1340 and 1386. U.S. percentage compiled from Tables B–1 and B–106 in *2002 Economic Report of the President.*

TABLE 2-1   PRODUCTIVITY PER WORKER IN JAPAN AND ENGLAND

COUNTRY	COMPUTER MEMORY CHIPS	BARRELS OF OIL
Japan	10 units per day	4 per day
England	5 units per day	3 per day

TABLE 2-2 COMPUTING OPPORTUNITY COST AND COMPARATIVE ADVANTAGE

PRODUCT LOCATION	OPPORTUNITY COST	OPPORTUNITY COST PER UNIT
Computer chips in Japan	of 10 chips is 4 barrels	2/5 barrel of oil = .4 barrels*
Computer chips in England	of 5 chips is 3 barrels	3/5 barrel of oil = .6 barrels
Oil in Japan	of 4 barrels is 10 chips	5/2 computer chips = 2.5 chips
Oil in England	of 3 barrels is 5 chips	5/3 computer chips = 1.67 chips**

*Lower opportunity cost per unit of computer chips implies comparative advantage in Japan.
**Lower opportunity cost per unit of barrels of oil implies comparative advantage in England.

results shown in Table 2-2. By specializing according to this comparative advantage, countries will gain the most from trade.

In Japan, we see that making a computer chip requires giving up the ability to produce 2/5 or .4 barrels of oil, while in England the computer chip costs 3/5 or .6 barrels of oil. Since Japan has a lower opportunity cost of producing the computer chips, it is said to have a comparative advantage in computer chips. Verify for yourself that England has a comparative advantage in oil.

SNAPSHOT **COMPETING WITH COMPARATIVE ADVANTAGE**

Many great athletes are multitalented, possessing strength, speed, and muscle coordination that dwarf that of the general population. These qualities are needed for success in a variety of sports, yet few athletes play more than one sport professionally, even though they might be able to do so. Simply look at the sports pages. Venus Williams makes headlines by swinging a tennis racket, while Tiger Woods swings a golf club and Barry Bonds swings a bat. Their choices tell the rest of us about their comparative advantages.

The best teams exploit the comparative advantages of their players. Each player has a job to do and specializes in doing it well. Whatever the sport, owners and fans expect this principle of comparative advantage to be followed and demand coaches who will best exploit the talents of their players. But even the best coaches can err, as when Cleveland Indians' baseball coach Tris Speaker said in 1921, "Babe Ruth made a great mistake when he gave up pitching. Working once a week, he might have lasted a long time and become a great star." ◀

Explore & Apply

2.5 GUNS AND BUTTER—VICTORY FROM A STRONG ECONOMY

"We will bury you."
    —*Nikita Khrushchev, Soviet Premier, speaking to the United Nations in 1960*

"I pledge allegiance to the flag of the United States of America ...."
    —*Sergei Khrushchev, son of Nikita Khrushchev, taking oath of citizenship in 1999*

On December 7, 1941, the Empire of Japan attacked Pearl Harbor and drew the United States into World War II. As President Roosevelt reported the next day, that attack also caused "severe damage" to American military capabilities. At the time, Japanese military might extended through much of the Far East, and Nazi Germany controlled most of Europe. Yet,

the United States was able to quickly convert many civilian industries to military production and play a pivotal role in defeating both the Nazis and the Japanese three and a half years later. The world marveled at the ability of the U.S. economy to accomplish this feat. The United States had not sought war, but nonetheless proved able to win.

Nearly five decades later, the United States economy was again able to defeat a foreign adversary that had engaged it in a "cold war." This time, the adversary was the Union of Soviet Socialist Republics, a country armed to the teeth and openly hostile to the United States. Yet, when the United States decided to strengthen its armed forces in the 1980s, the Soviet Union struggled so hard to keep pace that it impoverished its own people and lost its will to exist. The Soviet Union was formally dissolved in 1991 without a shot being fired, breaking up into several different countries, including Russia. That's the best kind of victory, unlike, in the words of Ronald Reagan, "The bloody futility of two World Wars, Korea, Vietnam and the Persian Gulf."

Now, as we seek to surmount the unfolding terrorist threats of the twenty-first century, the lessons of America's twentieth-century success can help guide our way. How has the United States been able to maintain prosperity during peacetime and yet still have the wherewithal to be victorious in wartime? The secret has been the vibrancy of a strong U.S. economy, meaning that the United States has been able to maintain production possibilities that exceed those of its adversaries.

Figure 2-10(b) depicts the production possibilities frontier for a country with a strong economy, such as the United States in the 1980s, and another production possibilities frontier for an adversary with a weak economy, such as the Soviet Union in the 1980s. The axes of the production possibilities frontier are labeled *guns* and *butter*, where guns represents military output and butter represents output for civilian consumption. In Figure 2-10(a), the Soviet Union is shown to be producing more guns in the 1970s than produced in the United States. However, because of its strong economy, the United States could increase its production of guns to exceed that of the Soviet Union and still have more butter for its civilians. When the Soviets tried to match U.S. spending on guns in the 1980s, their production of butter fell so low that the Soviet people were forced to endure severe hardships. The result is shown in Figure 2-10(b).

HOW EFFICIENCY LEADS TO GROWTH

To maintain a strong economy, a country must use its existing resources and technology efficiently. As shown in Figure 2-11, moving from an inefficient economy to an efficient economy allows the production of both more guns and more butter. The economy must use the right people and the right capital to produce the right goods in the right way. By producing more in the present, the economy also has more ability to put aside some current consumption of guns and butter in favor of investing in new capital and better technology that will allow production possibilities to grow over time. In other words, the more efficient an economy is in the present, the more ability it will have to expand its production possibilities for the future, as shown by the long arrow in Figure 2-11.

The United States has been able to use its production possibilities with relative efficiency and achieve significant economic growth over time by relying in large measure upon the marketplace to allocate resources. The lure of profit in the market economy has motivated people and companies to look for the most valuable products to produce, keep costs as low as possible, and invest in new capital that expands the country's production possibilities frontier. These actions constitute the invisible hand of the marketplace that motivates individuals out for their own self-interests to best serve the needs of others.

While there are exceptions in which either markets or government policies have failed to achieve efficiency, it is its reliance upon a market economy that has generally allowed the United States to prosper relative to its adversaries with more centralized economies. In contrast, as former Soviet Premier Mikhail Gorbachev told Columbia University students in

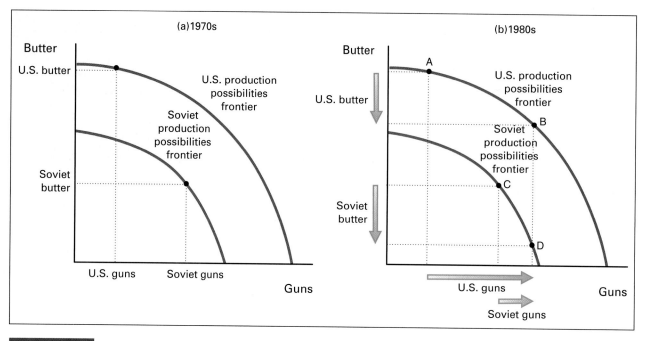

FIGURE 2-10

GUNS AND BUTTER In the 1970s, the Soviets are seen in (a) to devote more resources to their military (guns) than did the United States, even though production possibilities for the Soviets were less. The result was a lower standard of living in the Soviet Union (less butter). In the 1980s as shown in (b), the Soviets decided to match what was by then a higher U.S. output of guns. This reduced still further the already meager Soviet output of butter, resulting in a standard of living that the Soviet people would not accept. In 1991, the Soviet Union dissolved itself in favor of market-oriented economies that chose fewer guns and more butter.

FIGURE 2-11

SHAPING THE FUTURE Today's choices shape future possibilities. Increasing efficiency within the economy, such as moving from point *A* to point *B,* allows the production of both more guns and more butter. In addition, a more efficient economy has more possibilities for growth over time, which would shift the production possibilities frontier outward.

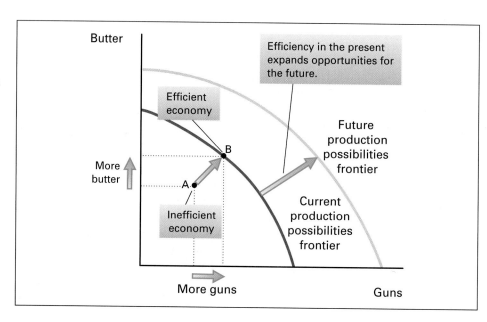

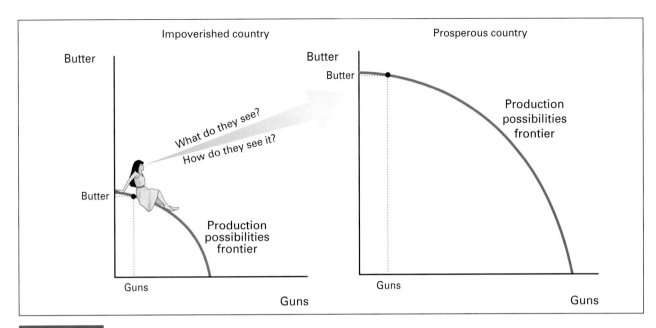

FIGURE 2-12

LOOKING TOWARD PROSPERITY Will impoverished countries choose to emulate prosperous countries and follow their path to success? Such a path would be one of peace and mutual self-interest. Alternatively, the view from below could be one of resentment, providing a spawning ground for ongoing conflict.

March 2002, the Soviets had created an "unreal system" of "pure propaganda." In that system, the ruling politicians "were discussing the problem of toothpaste, the problem of detergent, and they had to create a commission of the Politburo to make sure that women have pantyhose."

The twentieth century has not always brought victory to the United States or other prosperous countries. As the United States learned in Cuba and Vietnam, citizens of impoverished countries can be stubborn adversaries when their patriotic zeal is aroused. Why not peace, with its promise of prosperity?

Whether the world in the twenty-first century sees economic victory or the impoverishment of warfare might hinge in part upon attitudes. Are people of impoverished nations inspired to replicate for themselves the success of the United States and other developed countries? Or is that prosperity seen as out of reach and the source of resentment and ongoing conflict? While economic analysis can help frame the questions, such as in the manner of Figure 2-12, only time will reveal the answers.

1. While it clearly helped the United States in World War II and in the Cold War against communism, does a strong economy do any good in battling terrorism? Explain.

2. Describe ways in which the U.S. government attempts to be efficient in how it spends money militarily. Give an example in which spending might be inefficient and explain why that might happen.

Visit www.prenhall.com/ayers for updates and web exercises on this Explore & Apply topic.

*T*HINKING
*C*RITICALLY

SUMMARY AND LEARNING OBJECTIVES

1. **Analyze tradeoffs facing both individuals and countries.**
   - Opportunity costs, which are the value of forgone alternatives, influence the choices people make.
   - The concept of opportunity cost makes clear that nothing is free. By considering the opportunity cost of an action, both people and countries can make better choices.

2. **Categorize the types of resources an economy possesses.**
   - Resources include land, labor, capital, and entrepreneurship. Land refers to natural resources in their natural states. Labor refers to the human ability to work. Capital is produced to increase future productivity. Physical capital includes buildings, machines, and equipment. Human capital represents acquired skills and abilities. An entrepreneur takes risks by combining the other resources in productive ways.
   - Human capital is different from physical capital because it is embodied within a person.

3. **Model a country's production possibilities, and how these possibilities respond to technological development.**
   - The production possibilities frontier represents all combinations of two goods that would be technologically efficient.
   - The production possibilities frontier typically has a bowed outward shape. Points outside the frontier are not now attainable. Points inside the frontier are inefficient. Inefficiency arises from unemployment and/or misallocated resources. Only points on the frontier are both attainable and efficient.
   - Opportunity costs are illustrated by the production possibilities frontier. Movement from one point to another on the frontier means that more of one good is produced, but less of the other. The amount by which the production of the other good decreases equals the opportunity cost of the increase in the first good.
   - Economic growth expands the frontier by shifting it outward. Such growth can occur if a country adds more capital or other resources, or experiences technological change that enhances its productivity. Specialized growth pivots the frontier outward in the direction of more output in the industry affected by technological change.

4. **Describe how economies can grow faster if they are willing to cut back on current consumption.**
   - Depreciation shifts the frontier inward because it decreases the amount of capital. The effect of depreciation on the frontier can be overcome by producing new capital, with the amount of that production being at least large enough to offset depreciation.
   - Capital production comes with an opportunity cost since it requires the sacrifice of current consumption.

5. **Visualize the flow of goods and services, resources, and money in the economy.**
   - The circular flow graph shows how economic activity depends upon markets. Flows of goods and services go toward the household sector as households make purchases. Goods and services are sold in the output market. Households earn the incomes needed to make those purchases by selling the resources they own to businesses. Resources are bought and sold in the input market. Money is used to make it easier for market exchanges to take place.

6. **Explain how people and countries gain from trade by specializing according to comparative advantage.**
   - Countries specialize according to their comparative advantage, as do people. A comparative advantage in the production of a good requires that a country have a lower opportunity cost of production than other countries. Trade according to comparative advantage allows countries to consume beyond their production possibilities frontiers, thus benefiting the countries that trade.
   - A country has an absolute advantage if it is able to produce something with fewer resources than other countries. It is not necessary to have an absolute advantage in the production of a good to benefit from specialization and trade.
   - A country's comparative advantage can be computed, which entails first computing opportunity costs of each good's production within a country and then comparing the results with the same computation for other countries. The country with the lowest opportunity cost of producing a good has the comparative advantage in that good. If there are just two countries and two goods, a comparative advantage by one country in one good implies a comparative advantage for the other country in the other good.

7. Convey how economic strength can lead to victory, sometimes without a fight.

- A stronger economy can produce more guns and more butter than a weaker economy. A stronger economy's production possibilities frontier will be outside that of a weaker economy. The difference in economic prosperity illustrated by the location of the production possibilities frontiers can lead to envy and resentment of wealthy countries by the citizens of relatively poor ones. Alternatively, poorer countries can aspire to peacefully become prosperous themselves.

KEY TERMS

opportunity costs, 30
land, 30
labor, 30
human capital, 30
capital, 31
entrepreneurship, 31
technology, 31

production possibilities frontier, 32
law of increasing cost, 34
economic growth, 36
money, 39
barter, 40
circular flow, 40
output market, 40

input market, 40
comparative advantage, 41
absolute advantage, 41
exports, 42
imports, 42

TEST YOURSELF

TRUE OR FALSE

1. If you decide to buy a Butterfinger candy bar, instead of an equally priced Almond Joy, the opportunity cost of your purchase is the value you would have received from that Almond Joy.
2. The axes of the production possibilities frontier are labeled price and quantity.
3. Economic growth is represented on a production possibilities frontier as a shift outward of that frontier.
4. The circular flow model of economic activity assumes that resources are owned by businesses.
5. With international trade, a country is able to produce outside its production possibilities frontier.

MULTIPLE CHOICE

6. The opportunity cost of a new city police contract is
   a. the amount of money it takes in order to provide the city with the most highly qualified personnel.
   b. the value of the other goods and services that the city and taxpayers will be forced to give up in order to pay for the contract.
   c. the cost to victims of crimes that the new contract would prevent.
   d. the value of the opportunities that city policemen acquire by accepting it.

7. Which of the following items is the best example of an economic resource?
   a. A stock certificate.
   b. A one-hundred dollar bill.
   c. A tractor.
   d. A plate of spaghetti and meatballs.
8. Which of the following is the best example of earning income from human capital?
   a. Melody takes a job as an interpreter for the hearing impaired.
   b. Josie invests her life savings into her own business, "Jeans by Josephine."
   c. Seth toils all day in the hot summer sun as a common laborer, just to earn enough money to keep food on the table.
   d. J.R. kicks up his heels and watches the royalty checks flow in from his oil fields.
9. A production possibilities frontier shows combinations of
   a. inputs that can produce a specific quantity of output.
   b. outputs that people consume.
   c. outputs that can be achieved as technology improves.
   d. outputs that can be achieved in a given time period with all available resources employed using current technology.

10. If a nation's production possibilities indicate that 1,000,000 battle tanks and 6,000,000 houses could be produced, or alternatively, 750,000 tanks and 8,000,000 houses could also be produced, the opportunity cost of each additional house would be
    a. 250,000 tanks.
    b. 8 tanks.
    c. 0.125 tanks.
    d. 2,000,000 houses.

11. As a nation develops economically, its production possibilities frontier
    a. remains stable.
    b. shifts toward the origin.
    c. shifts away from the origin.
    d. becomes steeper, but does not shift.

12. Suppose an economy produces only gizmos and widgets. If there is a technological advance in the production of widgets, the economy's production possibilities frontier will shift
    a. outward along the widget axis, but not along the gizmo axis.
    b. outward along the gizmo axis, but not along the widget axis.
    c. outward along both axes.
    d. inward along both axes.

13. Of the points listed in Self-Test Figure 2-1, the fastest rate of economic growth would occur at
    a. *A.*
    b. *B.*
    c. *C.*
    d. *D.*

14. All points along the production possibilities frontier are
    a. technologically efficient.
    b. allocatively efficient.
    c. economically efficient.
    d. equitable.

15. In a circular flow diagram, the output market is where
    a. goods and services are exchanged for money.
    b. resources are exchanged for money.
    c. consumer outlays of dollars are exchanged for wages, rent, interest, and profits.
    d. resources are exchanged for goods and services.

16. Money in the economy today
    a. is needed in order for barter to occur.
    b. is primarily commodity money.
    c. facilitates the circular flow of economic activity.
    d. is an economic resource along with land, labor, capital, and entrepreneurship.

17. In order to gain from trade, it is necessary to
    a. specialize according to comparative advantage.
    b. specialize according to absolute advantage.
    c. find a trading partner with an absolute advantage in something.
    d. find a trading partner without an absolute advantage in anything.

18. When a country can produce a good with fewer resources than any other country, the country has
    a. a comparative advantage.
    b. a resource advantage.
    c. an absolute advantage.
    d. an unfair advantage.

19. A country has a comparative advantage in the production of a good if it can produce that good _____ than can other countries.
    a. with fewer raw materials
    b. at a lower opportunity cost
    c. at a higher quality
    d. with fewer labor-hours

20. By having an efficient economy today, a country's future production possibilities frontier will allow the production of
    a. both more guns and more butter.
    b. more guns, but not more butter.
    c. more butter, but not more guns.
    d. neither more guns nor more butter.

SELF-TEST FIGURE 2-1
PRODUCTION POSSIBILITIES FRONTIER

QUESTIONS AND PROBLEMS

1. *[opportunity cost]* Provide plausible opportunity costs for each of the following choices.
   a. Valerie stays home from work to watch an especially interesting episode of the Ricki Lake program.
   b. Frank spends Saturday night watching videos with his friend Erica.
   c. Renee spends Saturday afternoon playing golf with her church singles group.

2. *[entrepreneurship]* Do management skills differ from entrepreneurial skills? Explain.

3. *[resources]* Explain the concept of capital, as it is used in economics. Part of your answer should distinguish between human capital and physical capital.

4. *[production possibilities frontier]* Suppose the country of Baseballia's production possibilities frontier between baseballs and bats is as shown in the table below.

BASEBALLIA'S PRODUCTION POSSIBILITIES FRONTIER

Number of Baseballs Produced per Hour	Number of Baseball Bats Produced per Hour
0	10
5	9
10	7
15	4
20	0

   a. What is the opportunity cost of producing 20 baseballs?
   b. What is the opportunity cost of producing 15 baseballs?

5. *[production possibilities frontier]* What would a straight-line production possibilities frontier between coconuts and fish on Castaway Island say about opportunity costs?

6. *[general growth]* Draw a production possibility graph that shows general growth. Briefly state how the numbers in the production possibilities frontier table in question #4 above would change if the economy of Baseballia experienced general growth.

7. *[production possibilities frontier]* Draw the original production possibilities frontier in Figure 2-7. How does the frontier change when technological change affects only the pumpkin industry?

8. *[money]* What is meant when money is described as a medium of exchange? Is money a part of the circular flow diagram?

9. *[circular flow]* In the circular flow diagram, how do households earn incomes?

10. *[trade]* California and France both produce wine.
    a. Without international trade, U.S. consumers would be unable to consume French wines, but they would still be able to consume California wines. Would this arrangement be better for the United States as a whole? For any particular groups within the United States?
    b. Do you think France imports U.S. wines? Explain.

11. *[trade]* Succinctly evaluate the validity of the following:
    a. "The United States is losing its competitive edge to other countries with more diligent and skilled workers. The problem is that we are becoming increasingly incapable of producing anything that other countries would want to buy. We are fast on our way to becoming a nation of burger flippers."
    b. "The U.S. standard of living has been the envy of the world. Unfortunately, because we have allowed imports from countries where working conditions are dismal and labor is cheap, our own standard of living is rapidly being pulled down to match the competition."

12. *[absolute advantage]* Briefly explain the difference between the concept of absolute advantage and the concept of comparative advantage. Which principle explains how countries specialize?

13. *[comparative advantage]* Since the principle of comparative advantage applies to people as well as economies, identify at least three areas in which you have a comparative advantage relative to your friends.

14. *[consumption possibilities]* Draw a graph of the production possibilities frontier. Then comment on the validity of the following statements, referring to the graph you have drawn:
    a. A country that trades with other countries will produce at a point outside its production possibilities frontier.
    b. A country that trades with other countries will consume at a point on its production possibilities frontier.

15. *[comparative advantage]* Explain the sport your favorite athlete has chosen to play in terms of that person's comparative advantage. How does an athlete's comparative advantage change with age?

16. *[computing comparative advantage]* Suppose that there are two countries, Tryhard and Trynot. In Tryhard, each hour of labor can produce either 8 units of good X or 8 units of good Y. In Trynot, each hour of labor can produce either 2 units of good X or 4 units of good Y. Compute the opportunity cost of: (a) one unit of X in Tryhard; (b) one unit of Y in Tryhard; (c) one unit of X in Trynot; and (d) one unit of Y in Trynot. If these countries trade only goods X and Y, which country will produce X? Which will produce Y? Explain.

 Visit www.prenhall.com/ayers for Exploring the Web exercises and additional self-test quizzes.

CHAPTER 3

DEMAND AND SUPPLY

A LOOK AHEAD

"Teach a parrot the terms 'supply and demand' and you have an economist!" That humor from Thomas Carlyle has been handed down for decades in introductory economics courses. While not literally true (we hope), it does point out how central the concepts of supply and demand are to economic analysis.

How are the prices of music CDs, apartment rents, and the prices of other goods and services determined? Why do people build so many homes where hurricanes are known to strike? What do cows eat? The answers? "Squawk, supply and demand!" This chapter fills in the details of these answers and shows how to answer a host of additional questions about the workings of supply and demand that underlie the market economy. The Explore & Apply section that concludes the chapter discusses how public policy might tap into the forces of supply and demand to improve our schools.

LEARNING OBJECTIVES

Understanding Chapter 3 will enable you to:
1. Distinguish between the general notions of demand and supply used in ordinary conversation and the precise notions employed in the study of economics.
2. Explain what it means to shift demand and supply and why shifts might occur.
3. Describe how the marketplace settles on the equilibrium price and quantity.
4. Specify how demand and supply shifts cause market equilibriums to change over time.
5. Identify the changes to equilibrium that result from simultaneous changes in demand and supply.
6. Discuss how vouchers use competition to improve the quality of schooling.

Competition provides consumers with alternatives. The competition by producers to satisfy consumer wants underlies markets, which are characterized by demand and supply. Market economies rely upon competition, and thus upon demand and supply, to answer the three basic economic questions: *What? How?* and *For whom?* The economic definitions of demand and supply are more precise than the fuzzy notion that demand is something a person wants or needs and supply is what is available. Rather, demand and supply are both defined as relationships between price and quantity. We start by looking at demand.

3.1 DEMAND

demand relates the quantity of a good that consumers would purchase at each of various possible prices, over some period of time, *ceteris paribus*.

quantity demanded the quantity that consumers would purchase at a given price.

Demand *relates the quantity of a good that consumers would purchase at each of various possible prices, over some period of time, ceteris paribus.*

Demand is a relationship, not a single quantity. For a given price, demand tells us a specific quantity that consumers would actually purchase if given the opportunity. This quantity is termed the **quantity demanded**. In other words, demand relates quantity demanded to price over the range of possible prices. To emphasize that demand is a relationship and not just a single point, demand is also sometimes called a *demand schedule*. A demand schedule is a table that shows possible prices and their quantities demanded. When the numbers in a demand schedule are plotted in a graph, the line that is plotted is called a *demand curve*. In other words, the terms demand, demand schedule, and demand curve all refer to the same thing.

Demand must be defined for a set period of time. For example, demand for coffee will be quite different if the period in question is one day, one week, or one year. Moreover, anything else that might influence the quantity demanded must be held constant. This is termed the *ceteris paribus* condition. It means that we only look at one relationship at a time, where *ceteris paribus* is the Latin for holding all else constant.

ceteris paribus holding all else constant.

Suppose we want to know how an increase in water rates will affect the amount of water people use on their lawns. To avoid mixing up the effects of price and rainfall, for example, we might estimate one demand curve for times of normal rainfall and another for times of drought. This approach allows us to focus exclusively on the relationship between price and quantity demanded.

BY WORD, BY TABLE, BY GRAPH

There are various ways to express relationships between variables. One is to provide a schedule, which is a table showing various values of the variables. Another is to show the data with a graph. For example, the data shown in Figure 3-1 make up a demand schedule. The data can be plotted on a graph to form the demand curve labeled Demand, also shown in the figure. The horizontal axis is labeled Quantity to denote the quantity demanded at each possible price. Since price is measured in dollars, the dollar sign provides the label for the vertical axis.

law of demand as price falls, the quantity demanded increases.

Note how the graph pictures an inverse relationship between price and quantity demanded. As price rises, quantity demanded falls. As price falls, quantity demanded rises. This relationship is termed the **law of demand**. It is an empirical law, meaning that no one enforces it, but buyers almost always adhere to it because it makes sense. When the price of an item falls, consumers not only can afford to buy more, but will also substitute the lower-priced good for higher-priced alternatives.

You've heard the saying "a picture is worth a thousand words." That saying usually applies to supply and demand analysis in general and to the law of demand in particular. While a table of data can be useful for applications calling for numerical calculations, a graph is ordinarily better suited for broader messages, such as the inverse relationship between price and quantity demanded. When the specific data are less important than the

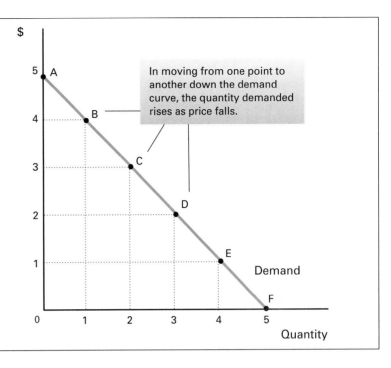

Demand		
Data point	Price ($)	Quantity demanded
A	5	0
B	4	1
C	3	2
D	2	3
E	1	4
F	0	5

In moving from one point to another down the demand curve, the quantity demanded rises as price falls.

FIGURE 3-1

DEMAND Demand slopes downward, showing that price and quantity demanded are inversely related. For example, as the price drops from $4 to $1, the quantity demanded rises from 1 unit to 4 units. This is seen as a movement from point *B* to point *E* along the demand curve.

QUICKCHECK

What is the minimum quantity demanded and the maximum quantity demanded in Figure 3-1?

Answer: At a price of $5, the quantity demanded is zero units, which is the minimum. At a price of $0, the quantity demanded is 5 units, the maximum. These quantities occur where demand intersects the axes.

general nature of the relationship, it is common to draw a graph without attaching any numbers to that graph, as is done in many of the graphs in this chapter and the rest of this book.

If you are uncomfortable with a graph without numbers, recall the simple solution mentioned in Chapter 2: Add some numbers. Even though the numbers would be artificial, the graphical relationship may then become easier to comprehend. For example, we could have labeled Figure 3-1 with different numbers or with no numbers at all. The graph would still impart the notion that price and quantity vary inversely.

SHIFTING DEMAND VERSUS MOVEMENTS ALONG A DEMAND CURVE

Price is not the only influence on how much people buy. Quantities purchased are also dictated by income, tastes, the prices of other goods, and various other factors. By holding all but price constant, the *ceteris paribus* assumption lets us focus on one thing at a time. This approach provides order to what otherwise might seem like a jumble of simultaneous changes.

QUICKCHECK

Would an increase in price decrease demand?

Answer: No, an increase in price would decrease the quantity demanded but not demand itself. A change in the price of a good represents a movement from one point to another along the same demand curve. In contrast, were demand to decrease, the entire demand curve would shift to the left.

What happens to demand when other influences on demand change? Changes in other aspects of the world have the potential to shift the entire demand curve, leading to a new relationship between price and quantity. This is shown by a change in the position of the demand curve—a shift. Anything that causes the curve to shift is termed a *shift factor.* **An** *increase in demand* **occurs when demand shifts to the right. A** *decrease in demand* **occurs when demand shifts to the left.** Figure 3-2 summarizes these shifts. Note that a change in the price of the good neither increases nor decreases demand—demand does not shift. Rather, **a price change would change the quantity demanded, which involves** *moving along the demand curve,* **but would not change the demand curve itself.** A lower price results in a movement down the demand curve, while a higher price causes a movement up the demand curve.

Consider an example of demand shifting that is associated with a fast-growing economy. An upward surge in the economy often causes family incomes to rise. With more income at their disposal, some families will decide to buy new homes. That decision increases the demand for new homes. To the extent that higher income causes consumers to

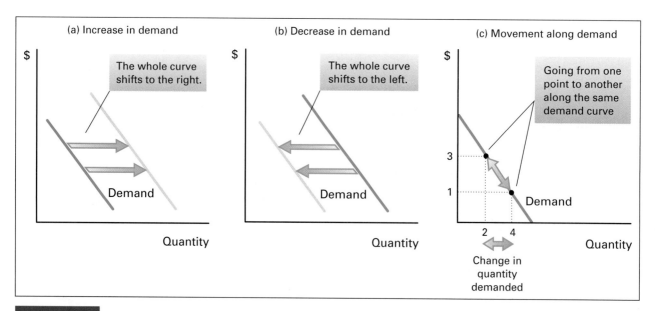

FIGURE 3-2

A SHIFT IN DEMAND VERSUS A MOVEMENT ALONG DEMAND Demand shifts when there is a change in any shift factor. An increase in demand moves the demand curve to the right, as shown in (a). A decrease in demand moves the demand curve to the left, as shown in (b). A change in price does not shift demand. Rather, a price change causes a movement along the demand curve to a new quantity demanded, as shown in (c).

buy more of any good at a particular price, the higher income increases demand, depicted by the rightward-pointing arrow in Figure 3-2(a).

Whether it be a hurricane's pounding surf that washes away expensive beachfront homes, a swollen river that engulfs entire communities along its course, or sliding mud that obliterates whatever stands in its way, the effects of wind and rain cost U.S. citizens billions of dollars annually. Much of this loss is a direct result of expensive structures being built in harm's way. For example, huge amounts of real estate development occur in some of the most at-risk areas, including California hillsides, property fronting the beaches of Florida, and in the flood plains of scenic West Virginia rivers.

Is the large amount of building in risky areas proof of people's shortsighted irrationality? More likely, it is evidence of the law of demand in response to government low-interest loans for rebuilding and other assistance that reduce the cost of disasters to their victims. Specifically, disaster assistance lowers the price of taking the risk to build in disaster-prone locations. The lower price leads people to do more building there. Thus, by the law of demand, the unintended consequence of compensating disaster victims for property losses is that there will be a larger amount of property lost when the next disaster strikes.

To reduce the amount of risk-taking, it is increasingly common for government aid to be contingent upon the recipients rebuilding in safer spots. Even so, disaster aid lowers the expected price of risk-taking for the rest of us. We respond to this lower price by daring to live closer to our country's scenic but dangerous places. ◄

CHANGES IN DEMAND

As listed in Table 3-1, various events are likely to shift demand. **For *normal goods*, an increase in income shifts demand to the right.** However, there are many goods that people buy less of as their incomes rise. These are termed **inferior goods**. **An increase in income shifts the demand for inferior goods to the left.** Is there anything you would buy less of as your income increases? Perhaps you would eat fewer hot dogs and cans of tuna, and more steak and fresh fish. If so, for you, hot dogs and tuna would be inferior goods, and steak and fresh fish would be normal goods.

Changes in the prices of substitutes and complements also shift demand. A **substitute** is something that takes the place of something else. Different brands of coffee are substitutes. So are coffee and tea. A **complement** is a good that goes with another good, such as ketchup on hot dogs or cream in coffee. The degree to which one good complements or substitutes for another will vary according to each person's tastes and preferences. For example, many coffee drinkers prefer to take their coffee black. For them, coffee and cream are not complements. Likewise, to the extent a consumer is loyal to a particular brand of a product, other brands might not be viewed as acceptable substitutes unless the price difference is dramatic.

What would happen to demand for a good if the price of a substitute changes? To answer questions like this one, it often helps to be specific. For example, consider how much Sparkle Beach laundry detergent shoppers purchase at various possible prices. Those quantities would go up or down depending upon the prices of Tide, Surf, All, and other possible substitutes. If the price of the substitutes rises, *ceteris paribus,* shoppers buy more Sparkle Beach. Their demand for Sparkle Beach shifts out. Likewise, should the substitutes be reduced in price, *ceteris paribus,* shoppers would buy less Sparkle Beach—demand shifts in. Thus, **demand varies directly with a change in the price of a substitute.**

Conversely, **demand varies inversely to a change in the price of a complement.** Since complements are the opposite of substitutes, a change in the price of a complement shifts

normal goods demand for these goods varies directly with income.

inferior goods demand for these goods varies inversely with income.

substitutes something that takes the place of something else, such as one brand of cola for another.

complements goods or services that go well with each other, such as cream with coffee.

TABLE 3-1   CHANGES IN DEMAND

SHIFT FACTORS	DEMAND SHIFTS TO THE LEFT WHEN	DEMAND SHIFTS TO THE RIGHT WHEN	EXAMPLES
Price of substitutes	The price of a substitute decreases.	The price of a substitute increases.	A decrease in the price of butter causes the demand for margarine to decrease. An increase in the price of butter causes the demand for margarine to increase.
Price of complements	The price of a complement increases.	The price of a complement decreases.	An increase in the price of computers decreases the demand for software. A decrease in the price of computers increases the demand for software.
Income, when the good is normal	The good is normal and income decreases.	The good is normal and income increases.	The demand for jewelry decreases when income decreases. The demand for jewelry increases when income increases.
Income, when the good is inferior	The good is inferior and income increases.	The good is inferior and income decreases.	The demand for thrift store clothing decreases when income increases. The demand for thrift store clothing increases when income decreases.
Population	Population decreases.	Population increases.	The demand for shoes decreases when population decreases. The demand for shoes increases when population increases.
Consumer expectations of future prices	Consumers expect the price to decrease in the future.	Consumers expect the price to increase in the future.	Demand for coffee decreases because consumers expect the price of coffee to decrease later. Demand for coffee increases because consumers expect the price of coffee to increase later.
Tastes and preferences	Tastes and preferences turn against the product.	Tastes and preferences turn in favor of the product.	The demand for action movies decreases because consumers prefer less-violent movies. The demand for action movies increases because consumers prefer more-violent movies.

demand in the opposite direction from what would occur if there were a change in the price of a substitute. For example, peanut butter is complementary to jelly. An increase in the price of jelly would decrease consumption of jelly and anything that goes with it. Demand for peanut butter would shift to the left. Likewise, a decrease in the price of jelly would shift demand for peanut butter to the right.

Changes in tastes and preferences will also shift demand. Over time, as some items become more popular, their demand curves shift out. Other items see their popularity fade and their demand curves shift in. Producers often use advertising in an attempt to influence tastes and preferences toward their particular brand of product.

Changes in population, in expectations about future prices, or in many other factors can cause demand to shift. **Demand will increase or decrease to the extent that population increases or decreases. A change in consumer expectations about future prices will shift demand in the present.** For example, if you expect prices to fall in the future, you might put off your purchases now, in effect shifting your current demand curve to the left. You would be treating future purchases as a substitute for current purchases. For some products, other

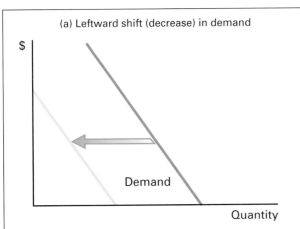

(a) Leftward shift (decrease) in demand

Demand

Demand shifts left when:
• Price of a substitute decreases.
• Price of a complement increases.
• Good is normal and income decreases.
• Good is inferior and income increases.
• Population decreases.
• Consumers expect price to fall in the future.
• Tastes and preferences turn against the product.

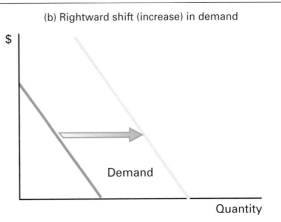

(b) Rightward shift (increase) in demand

Demand

Demand shifts right when:
• Price of a substitute increases.
• Price of a complement decreases.
• Good is normal and income increases.
• Good is inferior and income decreases.
• Population increases.
• Consumers expect the price to rise in the future.
• Tastes and preferences turn in favor of the product.

FIGURE 3-3

FACTORS THAT SHIFT DEMAND Factors that shift demand to the left are listed in (a), along with a graph showing the leftward shift. Factors that shift demand to the right are shown in (b), along with a graph showing the rightward shift.

factors could be significant, such as conjectures about future technologies that might make products with current technologies obsolete.

Summing up, when consumers buy less of a good at each price, demand shifts to the left. When consumers buy more of a good at each price, demand shifts to the right. Table 3-1 and Figure 3-3 summarize the causes of these shifts. A change in the price of the good causes a change in the quantity demanded, but does not shift demand. Rather, a change in price causes a movement along the demand curve.

NEW COKE? OR OLD COKE IN A NEW BOTTLE?   *S N A P S H O T*

It was either a stroke of marketing genius or just dumb luck. But what it did for demand is one for the record books. The year was 1985 when, losing market share to its arch-rival Pepsi, the Coca-Cola Company tossed aside its secret recipe and ceased making "the real thing." Instead, Coke drinkers were presented with a reformulated New Coke that tasted oh-so-syrupy sweet. It seems that taste tests found consumers favoring the sweeter taste of Pepsi over traditional Coke, but found New Coke beating all. Market research notwithstanding, New Coke was a huge flop.

"Bring back the real thing!" cried Coke customers, and back it came under the name Coca-Cola Classic. Curiously, even though the formula is the same as that of traditional Coke, Coke Classic has proven more popular. Was it the publicity? The near loss of something millions of Coke drinkers took for granted? Was it nostalgia? Whatever the reasons, the demand for Coke shifted to the right and has stayed shifted ever since. In the back of their minds, it's what Coke's owners were hoping to find. ◄

supply relates the quantity of a good that will be offered for sale at each of various possible prices, over some period of time, *ceteris paribus*.

3.2 SUPPLY

Supply *relates the quantity of a good that will be offered for sale at each of various possible prices, over some period of time, ceteris paribus.*

The first thing to note about supply is its symmetry with demand. Supply tells us the quantity that will be offered for sale at various prices. This quantity is termed the **quantity supplied**. Note that supply and quantity supplied are not synonyms. Supply refers to the entire set of data that relates price and quantity and is thus also called a *supply schedule* or *supply curve*. Quantity supplied is the quantity associated with a single point on that schedule. As price changes, quantity supplied changes, but supply does not.

Supply is often referred to as the supply schedule or supply curve in order to emphasize that it is not any single quantity. Like demand, supply must be specified for a set period of time, such as a day, month, or year. The *ceteris paribus* condition makes sure that other things are held constant, so that we can focus clearly on the relationship between price and quantity supplied.

quantity supplied the quantity that will be offered for sale at a given price.

BY WORD, BY TABLE, BY GRAPH

Just as with demand, supply can be presented as a table or as a graph. Figure 3-4 shows an example of supply. In contrast to the downward-sloping demand curve, the supply curve nearly always slopes upward to the right. This direct relationship between price and quantity supplied is known as the **law of supply**. As price rises, the quantity offered for sale by producers increases. The reason is that a higher price means higher revenue per unit sold, which will in turn cover the cost of producing some additional units.

law of supply as price rises, the quantity supplied increases.

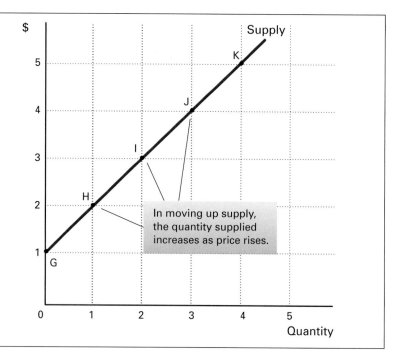

Supply		
Data point	Price ($)	Quantity supplied
G	1	0
H	2	1
I	3	2
J	4	3
K	5	4

In moving up supply, the quantity supplied increases as price rises.

FIGURE 3-4

SUPPLY Supply slopes upward. An increase in price leads to a greater quantity supplied. For example, an increase in price from $3 to $5 would cause the quantity supplied to increase from 2 to 4 units. This result is seen as a movement from point *I* to point *K* along the supply curve. The supply curve itself remains unchanged.

CHANGES IN SUPPLY

An *increase in supply* occurs when the entire supply curve shifts to the right, with more quantity supplied at each particular price. Likewise, a *decrease in supply* occurs when the entire supply curve shifts to the left, showing less quantity supplied at any particular price. A change in price does not shift supply, but rather causes a *movement along the supply curve.* Figure 3-5 illustrates these three possibilities.

Supply's most important shift factors differ from those for demand. Remember, for demand, the most important shift factors are income, prices of substitutes and complements, tastes and preferences, and consumer expectations about future prices. When it comes to supply, changes in expectations as to future prices are still important, but it is the expectations by producers, and not by consumers, that matter. The other important supply shift factors are different from the demand shift factors. In addition to producer expectations as to future prices, important shift factors include: (1) the number of firms; (2) prices of inputs; (3) technological change; (4) restrictions in production; (5) prices of substitutes in production; and (6) prices of jointly produced goods.

Why would expectations of future prices be important to a seller? To answer that question, suppose you own an oil field, and that it costs you $1 per barrel to pump your crude oil from the ground. How much oil would you offer for sale if the price were $15? $20? Why would you think twice about pumping your oil field dry if the selling price were $1.50?

For each possible current price, you would ask yourself how likely it would be for the price to go higher in the future. If you thought prices were on their way up, you would put off your pumping until later. If you expect prices to remain flat or to drop in the future, you would pump more now. If your expectations change, your entire supply schedule for pumping oil in the present would shift. For example, if you become convinced that the world is about to run out of oil, your supply curve in the present would shift far to the left, so that

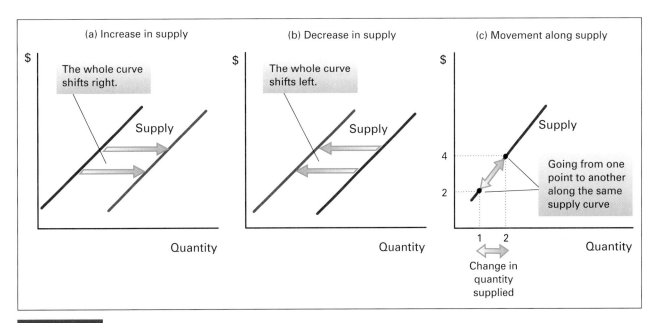

FIGURE 3-5

A SHIFT IN SUPPLY VERSUS A MOVEMENT ALONG SUPPLY Supply shifts when there is a change in any of its shift factors. An increase in supply moves the supply curve to the right, as shown in (a). A decrease in supply moves the supply curve to the left, as shown in (b). A change in price does not shift supply. Rather, a price change causes a movement along the supply curve to a new quantity supplied, as shown in (c).

you would retain plenty of oil to sell at high prices in the future. Thus, **today's supply curve shifts in the opposite direction from changes in expected future prices.**

If the price of labor or other input prices fall, firms see their expenses drop, and are willing to produce more at any given price. Hence, a decline in input prices increases supply, meaning that supply shifts to the right. Were input prices to increase, supply would decrease, meaning that it would shift to the left. In that case, fewer units are offered for sale at any given price. In general, **supply will shift in the opposite direction from changes in input prices.**

Firms adopt technological change in order to produce more output per unit of input. This has the same effect as a decrease in input prices. **Technological change in the production of any good shifts its supply to the right.**

Firms sometimes face restrictions in how they are allowed to do business. **Production restrictions decrease supply.** For example, a contract between a firm and its labor union might restrict the firm's ability to hire, fire, and make work assignments. Such restrictions have the potential to increase per-unit production costs. Likewise, automobile makers must meet exhaust-gas emission standards by installing catalytic converters, which adds to the cost of each car. For any given price, the automakers will offer fewer units for sale because of the increased expense of producing an automobile. This expense shifts the supply curve of automobiles to the left.

Additional shift factors could be important in some applications. For example, the 1990s saw thousands of acres in the South converted from cotton to corn because of the relatively high price of corn. As the price of corn rose, *ceteris paribus,* cotton plantings fell and the cotton supply curve shifted to the left. If the price of corn were to fall, conversely, the cotton supply curve would shift to the right. More generally, **supply varies inversely to the price of a substitute in production.** Be aware that substitutes in production are not the same as the substitutes in consumption that shift demand. After all, would you be willing to trade in your morning corn flakes for a hearty bowl of cotton flakes?

Turning to another agricultural example, some products are produced jointly, such as beef and leather. An increase in the popularity and price of beef would lead to a movement up the supply curve for beef. The greater quantity supplied of beef means that more cattle are raised for slaughter, which has the effect of shifting the supply of leather to the right. In brief, more leather would be offered for sale at each price of leather, in response to people consuming more steak and hamburger. Thus, **supply varies directly with the prices of products that are jointly produced.**

Summing up, when producers offer to sell less of a good at each price, supply decreases. When producers offer to sell more of a good at each price, supply increases. Table 3-2 and Figure 3-6 summarize these shifts. Remember that a change in the price of the good causes a change in the quantity supplied, but does not shift supply. Rather, a change in price causes a movement along the supply curve.

SNAPSHOT   ### THE LIVESTOCK GOURMET ON A HOT SUMMER DAY

While humans huddle by their air conditioners to escape the sweltering summer sun, life is good for some Iowa pigs and cattle—they enjoy a gourmet feast of tasty wet corn feed. On particularly hot days, farmers in the vicinity of the Cargill corn processing plant in Eddyville, Iowa, can buy this high-quality feed for a very low price. It's not that Cargill pities overheated animals. Rather, it is the availability of electricity that shifts out Cargill's supply of wet feed.

The many air conditioners that run on exceptionally hot days stress the ability of the local electric company to provide power. The ensuing power shortage leads to electricity cutbacks and leaves Cargill with huge piles of perishable wet feed, because there isn't enough electricity to dry and store it. The result is that, although power curtailment is not one of the more common things that shift supply, it's one that leaves some cows very contented. ◀

| TABLE 3-2 | CHANGES IN SUPPLY | | |

SHIFT FACTORS	SUPPLY SHIFTS TO THE LEFT WHEN	SUPPLY SHIFTS TO THE RIGHT WHEN	EXAMPLES
Number of sellers	The number of sellers decreases.	The number of sellers increases.	The supply of shoes decreases when the number of shoemakers decreases. The supply of shoes increases when the number of shoemakers increases.
The price of labor or other inputs	The price of labor or any other input rises.	The price of labor or any other input falls.	The wages of shoemakers rise, which decreases the supply of shoes. The wages of shoemakers fall, which increases the supply of shoes.
Production restrictions and technology	Government, labor union, or other restrictions on production practices increase cost.	Technological change lowers cost.	The garment workers' labor union negotiates extra holidays for its members, which increases the cost of making clothing, thus decreasing the supply of clothing. Technological improvements in sewing machines lower the cost of making clothing, thus increasing the supply of clothing.
Price of substitutes in production	The price of a substitute in production rises.	The price of a substitute in production falls.	The price of corn rises, causing the supply of wheat to decrease. The price of corn falls, causing the supply of wheat to increase.
Price of jointly produced products	The price of a jointly produced product falls.	The price of a jointly produced product rises.	The price of beef falls, causing the supply of leather to decrease. The price of beef rises, causing the supply of leather to increase.
Producer expectations of future prices	Producers expect prices to rise in the future.	Producers expect prices to decline in the future.	Wheat farmers expect the price of wheat to rise and so withhold wheat from the market, causing the supply of wheat to decrease. Wheat farmers expect the price of wheat to decline, and so rush wheat to the market, causing the supply of wheat to increase.

3.3 EQUILIBRIUM—DEMAND MEETS SUPPLY AND THE MARKET CLEARS

Now that we have taken a close look at demand and supply, let's put them together to see how prices are determined. We will first need to make clear the distinction between demand and supply at the individual level and at the market level.

MARKET DEMAND AND SUPPLY

Demand can be one individual's or the market's as a whole. Likewise, supply can be from one firm or all firms in the market. Most of the time when economists use demand and supply analysis, they have in mind demand and supply for the entire market. When necessary, the terms *market demand* and *market supply* can be used to clarify that demand and supply are for the entire market rather than for a single buyer or seller.

The market is the bringing together of buyers and sellers. While most people think of a market as a physical location, markets usually extend well beyond any single place. Markets can be local, regional, national, or multinational in scale. For example, gold, crude oil, and

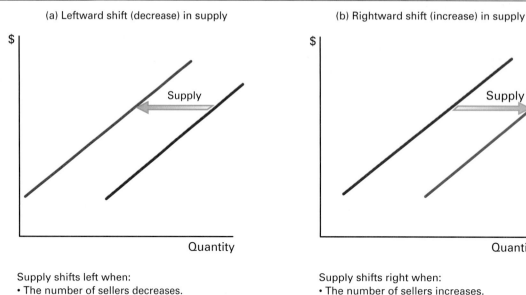

(a) Leftward shift (decrease) in supply

Supply

Quantity

Supply shifts left when:
• The number of sellers decreases.
• The price of labor or other input rises.
• Producers expect the price to rise in the future.
• Government, labor, or other restrictions on production practices increase cost.
• Price of a jointly produced product falls.
• The price of a substitute in production rises.

(b) Rightward shift (increase) in supply

Supply

Quantity

Supply shifts right when:
• The number of sellers increases.
• The price of labor or other input falls.
• Producers expect the price to fall in the future.
• Technological change lowers cost.
• Price of a jointly produced product rises.
• The price of a substitute in production falls.

FIGURE 3-6

FACTORS THAT SHIFT SUPPLY Factors that shift supply to the left are listed in (a), along with a graph showing the leftward shift. Factors that shift supply to the right are shown in (b), along with a graph showing the rightward shift.

many other commodities are sold in global markets, with only minor variations in price throughout the world.

Market demand is the sum of all the individuals' demands in that market. Summing individuals' demands is straightforward if you remember to add quantities, not prices. For each price, the quantity demanded in the marketplace is the sum of the quantities demanded by all consumers. On the graph of demand, as we will see in Figure 3-7, **market demand is the horizontal summation of individuals' demand curves.** An example will demonstrate this process.

For simplicity, we will consider a market with only two consumers, Jack and Jill. Jack and Jill are both interested in purchasing—what else?—pails of water. While climbing the hill for pails of water is great aerobic exercise, there is always some danger of tumbling down. So both Jill and Jack are willing to buy pails of water. The quantities they demand depend upon price, as shown by Jill's and Jack's demand curves in Figure 3-7. These demand curves combine into a market demand, as also shown in Figure 3-7. To obtain market demand, Jill's and Jack's quantities demanded are added at each possible price. As always, it is quantities that are added, not prices. Since quantity—the number of pails of water—is measured on the horizontal axis, we say that market demand is the horizontal sum of individual demand curves.

Market supply depicts the total quantity offered for sale in the market at each price. To obtain market supply, merely add the quantities offered for sale by all sellers at each price. Graphically, **market supply is the horizontal summation of each seller's supply curve.** Continuing with the example, Figure 3-8 shows the supplies of two sellers of pails of water— Wally and Wanda—and how their supplies sum to market supply.

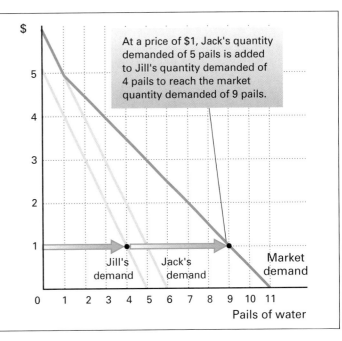

Market demand sums the quantities demanded by each buyer			
Price ($)	Jack's quantity demanded	Jill's quantity demanded	Market quantity demanded
5	1	0	1
4	2	1	3
3	3	2	5
2	4	3	7
1	5	4	9
0	6	5	11

At a price of $1, Jack's quantity demanded of 5 pails is added to Jill's quantity demanded of 4 pails to reach the market quantity demanded of 9 pails.

FIGURE 3-7

MARKET DEMAND Market demand is the horizontal summation of all buyers' demands. At a price of $1, Jill would be willing to purchase 4 pails of water and Jack 5 pails. Added together, the market quantity demanded would be 9 pails of water, as seen on the market demand curve. Likewise, at a price of $4, Jill's quantity demanded would be 1 pail of water and Jack's would be 2 pails. Taken together, the market quantity demanded would be 3 pails of water.

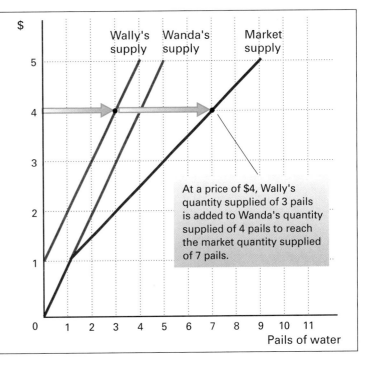

Market supply sums the quantities supplied by each seller			
Price ($)	Wally's quantity supplied	Wanda's quantity supplied	Market quantity supplied
5	4	5	9
4	3	4	7
3	2	3	5
2	1	2	3
1	0	1	1
0	0	0	0

At a price of $4, Wally's quantity supplied of 3 pails is added to Wanda's quantity supplied of 4 pails to reach the market quantity supplied of 7 pails.

FIGURE 3-8

MARKET SUPPLY Market supply is the horizontal summation of all sellers' supplies. At a price of $1, Wally would supply no pails of water and Wanda 1 pail. Adding these quantities, the market quantity supplied at $1 is 1 pail of water. If the price rises to $4, Wally supplies 3 pails and Wanda supplies 4 pails. The market quantity supplied is then 7 pails of water, as shown on the market supply curve.

ARRIVING AT AN EQUILIBRIUM

When supply and demand meet in the marketplace, a market price is created. While individual sellers are free to price their products however they wish, **there is only one price that *clears the market,* meaning that the quantity supplied equals the quantity demanded.** The market-clearing price and the resulting quantity traded comprise what is known as the **market equilibrium**, meaning that there is no tendency for either price or quantity to change, *ceteris paribus.*

market equilibrium a situation in which there is no tendency for either price or quantity to change.

Market equilibrium is determined by the intersection of supply and demand, as shown in Figure 3-9. A market equilibrium is associated with an *equilibrium price* and an *equilibrium quantity.* In our example, the market equilibrium occurs at a price of $3 and a quantity of 5 pails.

surplus the excess of quantity supplied over quantity demanded, which occurs when price is above equilibrium.

At any price above the equilibrium price, there would be a **surplus**, representing the excess of quantity supplied over quantity demanded. For example, a price of $4 would be too high, resulting in a surplus of 4 pails. In that case, Wally and Wanda would compete with each other for sales by lowering their prices. More generally, in any market in which a surplus occurs, some sellers would cut their prices slightly in order to be the ones that make the sales. Other suppliers would then be without customers, and would consequently lower their own prices enough to capture customers from their competitors. This leapfrogging process would continue until the quantity demanded and supplied are equal, which occurs at the equilibrium price.

shortage the excess of quantity demanded over quantity supplied, which occurs when price is below equilibrium.

A price that is below the equilibrium price results in a **shortage**, equal to the amount by which quantity demanded exceeds quantity supplied. For example, a price of $2 would be

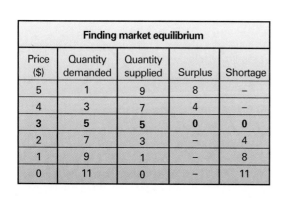

Finding market equilibrium				
Price ($)	Quantity demanded	Quantity supplied	Surplus	Shortage
5	1	9	8	–
4	3	7	4	–
3	5	5	0	0
2	7	3	–	4
1	9	1	–	8
0	11	0	–	11

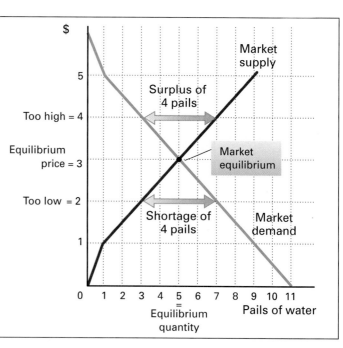

FIGURE 3-9

MARKET EQUILIBRIUM Market equilibrium occurs where demand and supply intersect. In this example, the equilibrium is at a price of $3 and a quantity of 5 pails. Any price above $3 would lead to a surplus, causing price to fall until the equilibrium is reached. Any price below $3 would lead to a shortage, causing price to rise until the equilibrium is reached.

too low and result in a shortage of 4 pails. Because there is not enough water to meet demand at that price, Jack and Jill would scramble to be the first to buy. More generally, whenever there is a shortage in any market, buyers compete against each other for the limited quantities of the goods that are offered for sale at that price. For sellers, shortages provide an opportunity both to raise prices and to increase sales, a doubly appealing prospect. Price would thus rise to its equilibrium value, the point at which the shortage disappears. Thus, without any guidance, the invisible hand of the market eliminates either surpluses or shortages and leads to the market-clearing equilibrium.

Suppose either supply or demand were to change. For example, suppose an increase in consumer income or a decrease in the price of a complement shifts demand to the right. One of the most common mistakes students make is to think this shift in demand would also shift supply. It would not, because demand is not a shift factor for supply. Rather, the rightward shift in demand leads to a movement up the supply curve and results in a new, higher equilibrium price and quantity. More generally, **a change in supply would cause a movement along demand. Similarly, a change in demand would cause a movement along supply.**

For practice, you might draw the basic supply and demand diagram, and then sketch a few shifts in either demand or supply. Note the effect on the equilibrium price and quantity. Note also that shifting demand does not cause a shift in supply or vice versa.

QUICKCHECK

In Figure 3-9, how much would be sold if the price is $4? If the price is $2?

Answer: Remember that each sale requires both a buyer and a seller. If the price is $4, then 3 pails of water would be sold, because 3 is the quantity demanded. If the price is $2, it would still be 3 pails of water sold, this time because 3 is the quantity supplied.

CHANGES IN THE MARKET EQUILIBRIUM

The market equilibrium will change whenever supply or demand shift. Taken one curve at a time, there are only four shifts possible:

1. An increase in supply, which shifts supply to the right.
2. A decrease in supply, which shifts supply to the left.
3. An increase in demand, which shifts demand to the right.
4. A decrease in demand, which shifts demand to the left.

These shifts and their effects on equilibrium price and quantity are shown and summarized in Figure 3-10. The four rows of the table, labeled case 1 through case 4, match the four graphs in the figure.

Whether it be in the market for meals, metals, or memory chips, we can expect both demand and supply to shift over time. To understand the effects on price and quantity when there are simultaneous shifts in supply and demand, look at each shift separately. In other words, we would combine two of the four cases listed in Figure 3-10. Table 3-3 summarizes the results from simultaneous shifts in supply and demand. Notice that in each of the cases in Table 3-3, the change in either equilibrium price or quantity is listed as uncertain to indicate that the direction in which the equilibrium price or quantity will move cannot be known without additional information. The direction in which either

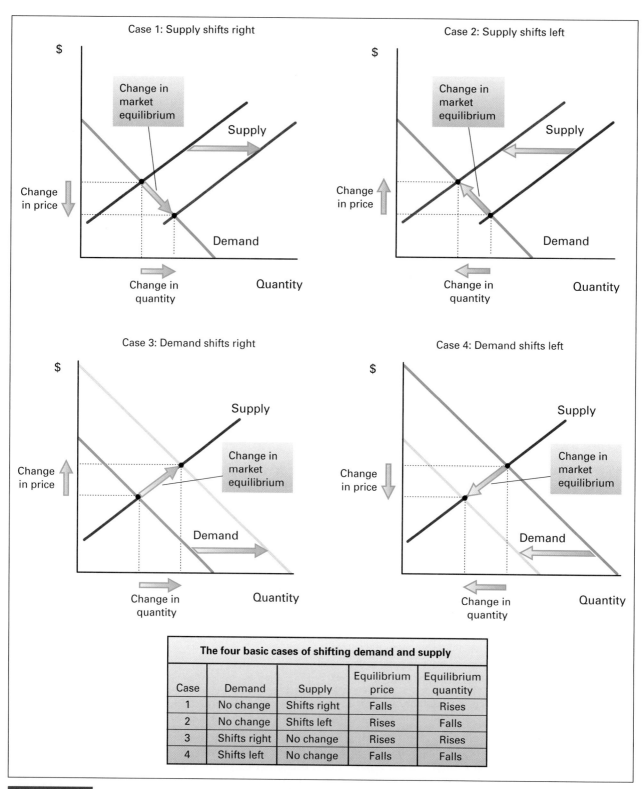

The four basic cases of shifting demand and supply

Case	Demand	Supply	Equilibrium price	Equilibrium quantity
1	No change	Shifts right	Falls	Rises
2	No change	Shifts left	Rises	Falls
3	Shifts right	No change	Rises	Rises
4	Shifts left	No change	Falls	Falls

FIGURE 3-10

EFFECTS OF SHIFTS IN DEMAND AND SUPPLY A shift in either supply or demand will affect the market equilibrium price and quantity, as seen in cases 1 through 4. When demand and supply shift simultaneously, the result can be found by first analyzing one shift and then the other. That process would involve combining two of the four cases.

TABLE 3-3	CASES 5 THROUGH 8 EACH COMBINE TWO OF THE FOUR CASES IN FIGURE 3-10			
CASE	**DEMAND**	**SUPPLY**	**EQUILIBRIUM PRICE**	**EQUILIBRIUM QUANTITY**
5 (cases 1 and 3)	Shifts right	Shifts right	Direction uncertain	Rises
6 (cases 2 and 4)	Shifts left	Shifts left	Direction uncertain	Falls
7 (cases 2 and 3)	Shifts right	Shifts left	Rises	Direction uncertain
8 (cases 1 and 4)	Shifts left	Shifts right	Falls	Direction uncertain

price or quantity changes will be uncertain when the shifts in demand and supply pull the equilibrium in opposite directions.

For example, if supply shifts to the right and demand shifts to the right also, we would look at the combination of cases 1 and 3 in Figure 3-10. This combination tells us that equilibrium quantity will definitely rise, but that equilibrium price might rise, fall, or remain unchanged. Specifically, when we look at them separately, both the demand and supply shifts result in a higher equilibrium quantity. However, case 1 pulls price lower while case 3 pulls price higher. Whether price rises, falls, or stays the same will depend on the relative strengths of those pulls. Figure 3-11 illustrates these possibilities by combining differently proportioned increases in supply and demand. Figure 3-11(a) shows identically proportioned increases in supply and demand, resulting in a constant price; Figure 3-11(b) shows a shift

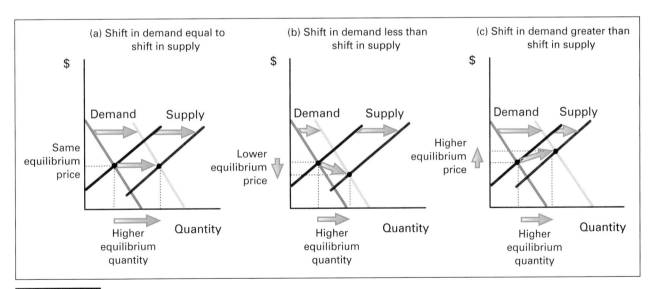

FIGURE 3-11

COMBINING AN INCREASE IN DEMAND WITH AN INCREASE IN SUPPLY When supply and demand both shift to the right, the equilibrium quantity increases. Equilibrium price might go up, down, or not change at all, depending upon the relative magnitudes of the shifts. Equal magnitude shifts are shown in (a), which leaves equilibrium price constant. As shown in (b), an increase in supply that exceeds the increase in demand causes a lower equilibrium price. By the same token, (c) shows that an increase in demand that exceeds the increase in supply causes equilibrium price to rise. These examples represent a combination of cases 1 and 3 from Figure 3-10.

FIGURE 3-12

A LARGE INCREASE IN SUPPLY COMBINED WITH A SMALL DECREASE IN DEMAND When demand shifts to the left by a smaller amount than supply shifts to the right, equilibrium price will fall and equilibrium quantity will rise. While both the shift in supply and in demand pull price downward, the two shifts pull quantity in opposite directions. The reason quantity rises in this example is that the shift in supply is larger than the shift in demand.

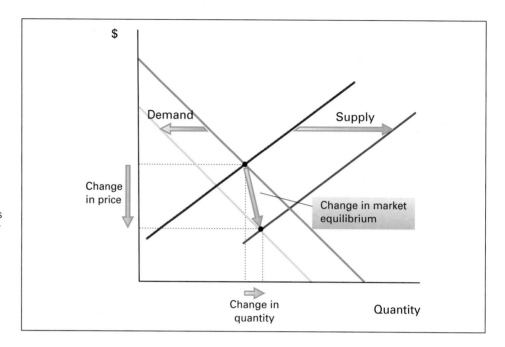

in demand that is weaker than the shift in supply, which causes the equilibrium price to fall; and Figure 3-11(c) shows a shift in demand that is larger than the shift in supply, resulting in a higher price.

Can you apply this analysis? For example, how would you interpret the observation that the price of digital camcorders has fallen in the last ten years, and people are now buying more? One possibility is case 1, in which demand stays constant while supply shifts to the right. Case 5 is more likely to represent reality, however, with both demand and supply shifting to the right. This result is shown in Figure 3-11(b). Demand shifted as population increased and camcorders became an increasingly popular addition to the gadgets of modern life. However, the increase in supply was even more pronounced, which explains why prices have fallen.

Continuing with the same example, suppose that video cell phones or other technologies take hold that cause demand for digital camcorders to fall in the future. If supply were to continue to increase, the result would be case 8. While the equilibrium price would definitely drop, the equilibrium quantity might rise, fall, or remain unchanged. Figure 3-12 illustrates the possibility that the equilibrium quantity would rise, which would occur if supply shifts to the right more than demand shifts to the left.

QUICKCHECK

List three cases in which shifts in demand and/or supply would result in a lower price and a greater quantity.

Answer: One case occurs when supply shifts to the right and demand does not change. A second case is when supply and demand both shift to the right, but the shift in supply is larger. A third case is when supply shifts right and demand shifts left, with the shift in supply being larger than the shift in demand. These cases are shown in Figures 3-10 (case 1), 3-11(b), and 3-12, respectively.

3.4 DEMANDING BETTER SCHOOLS, SUPPLYING BETTER SCHOOLS

Some people know the importance of education because they have it. I know the importance of education because I didn't.

—Frederick Douglass, ex-slave and abolitionist

"Our schools must be improved!" From kindergarten through the twelfth grade, the education of America's youth is a top concern of both the president and parents. There is less concern, however, about improving colleges; the reasons relate to demand and supply.

College students shoulder the high cost of college, with cost playing a major role in college choice. Consistent with the law of demand, the lower the price of a college education, *ceteris paribus,* the greater the number of students who will apply and the more education they will choose. To promote college education, government offers tax deductions, subsidies, and financial aid that in effect lowers its price.

High school seniors choose among a varied assortment of colleges. In lower grades, however, there is normally a powerful financial incentive to choose only the government-provided local public school. The reason is that taxpayer financing makes those schools free to the student.

Free public schooling was established in the nineteenth century to promote equal opportunity—an equal start in life. However, public schools are not all the same, and the gap between the best and the worst is not likely to close on its own. Schools in wealthy neighborhoods often spend more per pupil than schools in poor ones. Some schools are bureaucratic, inefficient, and ineffective, while others have strong academic reputations. Inefficient schools are insulated from competitive pressures to reform because even the best private schools find it hard to compete with "free" tuition. In addition, it would take moving to a new school district to enroll in a different public school.

If there were no free public schools, the invisible hand of the marketplace would cause schools to become efficient at responding to the demands of parents. While parents lack formal teaching credentials they could be guided by reputation or brand name in much the same way that they are guided in buying the family car and refrigerator. Schools that are most efficient at providing value would gain students, while others would lose them. However, because family incomes differ, the market outcome would not achieve equal educational opportunities for all children. The political outcome has been to sacrifice the efficiency of competition for the veneer of equity provided by equal access to free public schools. But is there a way to achieve our goal of equity in a manner that is less costly to the efficiency of free markets? Can we introduce competition to achieve more efficient schools?

Limited competition is provided by *charter schools,* a form of public school. Charter schools are started when a group of parents form or hire a nonprofit organization to set up a new school that meets state specifications. The new school receives a state contract called a charter to operate a school for a limited time, usually five years, after which the charter is renewed if the school meets educational standards. Because charter schools call for parental involvement, they are more accountable to parents than traditional schools. Recently, over 250,000 students were enrolled in about 800 charter schools in thirty-seven states.

INTRODUCTION TO VOUCHERS

Much more competition can be achieved through *vouchers,* which provide money that recipients can spend, although spending is restricted to a certain category of goods. The Food Stamp program provides low-income recipients with vouchers—food stamps—that can only be used on food purchases. Food Stamp recipients buy what they want rather than being forced to eat the offerings of a government-run food kitchen. A similar situation holds true when vouchers are applied to education. *School vouchers* provide parents with money that

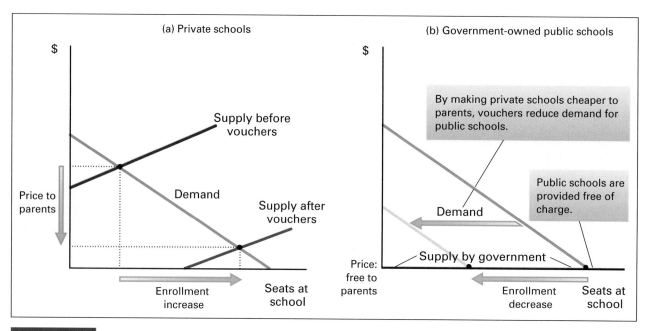

FIGURE 3-13

EFFECTS OF SCHOOL VOUCHERS Vouchers lower the price of private schooling, which increases the quantity demanded. The effect in the market for public schooling, a substitute, is to decrease demand and enrollments. Vouchers increase competition among schools, providing them with the incentive to provide the best value for money spent on education.

they must spend on schooling their children. With vouchers, the money is received by the school of each parent's choosing rather than being spent directly by the government-run public school.

School vouchers were first proposed in 1955 by Nobel-prize-winning economist Milton Friedman. Today, voucher programs of one sort or another are underway in Ohio, Florida, Texas, and elsewhere. Still, vouchers are poorly understood and controversial.

Figure 3-13 illustrates the effects of school vouchers, where public schools and private schools are substitutes. Vouchers lower the price of private schooling to parents, thus increasing their quantity demanded. Private schools are willing to increase the quantities they supply at each price because of the supplemental payment they receive from vouchers. Figure 3-13(a) shows this effect as a rightward shift in supply to parents who are provided vouchers. The result is a lower price and more children enrolled in private schools. Government-owned public schools, which are substitutes for private schools, offer unlimited enrollment at a price of "free" to parents. Vouchers result in a decrease in demand and enrollments in public schools, as shown in Figure 3-13(b).

With vouchers, the location, design, and operation of schools is driven by parental choice. Such radical change has proven difficult to enact into law. Most proposals for school vouchers retain support for public schools, either by restricting vouchers to apply to public schools only, or by providing vouchers just to students who attend "failing" public schools. A *pure voucher system* would permit children to attend any school, whether church sponsored or not. In the summer of 2002, the U.S. Supreme Court upheld a lower court ruling that allows vouchers so long as their purpose is to promote education, not religion. Similarly, financial aid is available to college students even if they attend a college operated by a religious denomination.

Opponents of vouchers fear that the competition for voucher money would cause schools to shortchange educational objectives and promote popular, but not very worthwhile, activities. For example, schools might de-emphasize academic achievement, while emphasizing football. Schools could also appeal to parents' religious preferences to gain enrollments and the dollars they bring.

Voucher opponents predict that competition would impede learning in other ways. For example, private schools might seek corporate sponsors who would pay for the right to put advertisements in school learning materials, thus possibly distracting students from learning. Voucher critics want to see schooling remain in the hands of educational professionals whose motives they feel would be more focused on learning and less on money.

Another criticism of vouchers relates to funding. Public schools are funded on the size of their enrollments. By reducing enrollments, vouchers would also drain public schools of money and jobs. Less money would cause the public schools to shrink in size. Just like inefficient companies in other sectors of the free market, inefficient public schools would whither and die. So, too, would inefficient private schools. The process might be hard on both the faculty and students.

Perhaps more time and experience with vouchers will clarify the issues. By promoting competition, vouchers offer the promise of improved schools. Would parents demand well for their children or should that choice be left to educational professionals? You be the judge.

1. Should educational quality be allowed to differ based on family income? Should vouchers be allowed to supplement a tuition payment at a private school, with the result that some children's quality of education would differ from other children's? Discuss.

2. *Myra:* I think voucher amounts should vary with household income. The more income, the less help—it's only fair.
   Fred: I think education should be free for everyone. Your income shouldn't have anything to do with how much voucher power you have.

   Evaluate Myra's and Fred's ideas. If a voucher plan is to be used, should the voucher amount depend upon a person's income?

THINKING CRITICALLY

Visit www.prenhall.com/ayers for updates and web exercises on this Explore & Apply topic.

SUMMARY AND LEARNING OBJECTIVES

1. **Distinguish between the general notions of demand and supply used in ordinary conversation and the precise notions employed in the study of economics.**
   - Supply and demand analysis captures the essential role of competition in the free marketplace. The what, how, and for whom questions you studied in Chapter 1 are answered by demand and supply in a market economy.
   - Demand is more than merely wanting a good or service. Demand is a relationship between price and quantity. By the law of demand, market demand curves slope downward, indicating an inverse relationship between price and quantity demanded. In other words, at each possible price there is a specific quantity demanded.
   - Like demand, supply is also a relationship between price and quantity. Supply shows the quantity supplied for each possible price. Unlike the demand

curve, market supply curves slope upward, reflecting the law of supply. Thus, price and quantity supplied are directly related.

2. **Explain what it means to shift demand and supply and why shifts might occur.**
   - Demand will shift with changes in the price of a substitute or complement, a change in income, a change in population, changes in expectations, and changes in tastes or preferences. An increase in demand shifts the demand curve to the right. A decrease in demand shifts the demand curve to the left.
   - Two goods are substitutes for each other when the goods are similar and serve the same purpose. An increase in the price of a substitute for a good will increase the demand for the good. Two goods are complements to each other when they are used

together. An increase in the price of a complement for a good will decrease the demand for the good.

- An increase in income will increase the demand for a normal good, but reduce the demand for an inferior good.

- There is a distinction between a change in demand and a change in quantity demanded. A change in demand means the demand curve shifts. A price change causes a movement from one point to another on a demand curve and results in a change in quantity demanded.

- Supply slopes upward, indicating a direct relationship between price and quantity supplied. A price change causes a change in quantity supplied and is seen as a movement along a supply curve. A change in supply means that the whole supply curve shifts. An increase in supply is seen as a shift to the right in the supply curve, while a decrease in supply occurs when the supply curve shifts to the left.

- Supply will shift with a change in the prices of substitutes in production, changes in the prices of jointly produced products, changes in union work rules or government regulations that change costs, changes in technology, changes in input prices, and changes in seller expectations.

- A shift in supply causes a movement along the demand curve, while a shift in demand causes a movement along the supply curve.

3. Describe how the marketplace settles on the equilibrium price and quantity.

- The interaction of supply and demand leads to a market equilibrium price and quantity, from which there is no tendency to change. Market equilibrium occurs at the intersection of demand and supply. At this point, quantity demanded equals quantity supplied.

- A market price that is less than the market equilibrium price will cause a shortage, in which case the price will adjust upward toward the equilibrium price. The shortage will be gone when the price reaches its equilibrium level. A price that is above the market equilibrium price will cause a surplus. The price will adjust downward toward the market equilibrium price until the surplus is eliminated.

4. Specify how demand and supply shifts cause market equilibriums to change over time.

- Demand and supply usually shift with the passage of time. When the demand or supply of a good shifts, then the good's price and quantity adjust to a new market equilibrium. There are four cases involving a shift in either demand or supply, but not both: an increase in demand, a decrease in demand, an increase in supply, and a decrease in supply.

- An increase in demand by itself causes an increase in the market equilibrium price and quantity. A decrease in demand by itself causes a decrease in the market equilibrium price and quantity. An increase in supply by itself causes a decrease in equilibrium price, but an increase in equilibrium quantity. A decrease in supply alone increases the equilibrium price and decreases the equilibrium quantity.

5. Identify the changes to equilibrium that result from simultaneous changes in demand and supply.

- More complicated cases involve simultaneous shifts in both demand and supply. Either the direction of change in equilibrium price or in equilibrium quantity will be uncertain in each of these cases.

- When demand increases and supply increases, the equilibrium quantity will increase, but the direction of change in the price will be uncertain. When demand increases and supply decreases, the equilibrium quantity will be uncertain, but the equilibrium price will increase.

- When demand decreases and supply increases, the equilibrium quantity will be uncertain, but the equilibrium price will decrease. When demand decreases and supply decreases, the equilibrium quantity will decrease, but the equilibrium price will be uncertain.

6. Discuss how vouchers use competition to improve the quality of schooling.

- School vouchers increase competition in the market for education. Vouchers are controversial because of the fear that the public schools would be harmed. However, the efficiency of public schools would likely be increased because of their need to compete with private schools for students and money.

KEY TERMS

demand, 54	inferior goods, 57	law of supply, 60
quantity demanded, 54	substitutes, 57	market equilibrium, 65
ceteris paribus, 54	complements, 57	surplus, 65
law of demand, 54	supply, 60	shortage, 67
normal goods, 57	quantity supplied, 60	

TEST YOURSELF

TRUE OR FALSE

1. If price rises, demand falls.
2. *Ceteris paribus*, if the price of Coca-Cola rises, the quantity sold of Pepsi will fall.
3. If something happens that leads producers to expect the price to rise in the future, supply will initially shift to the left.
4. If the market clears, there is likely to be a shortage.
5. If demand and supply both shift to the left, the equilibrium quantity will definitely fall but the equilibrium price might either rise, fall, or remain the same.

MULTIPLE CHOICE

6. The law of demand states that consumers
   a. must not buy more than they need.
   b. must not waste what they buy.
   c. must pay for what they buy.
   d. will buy more as the price falls.
7. Demand and supply curves are drawn assuming *ceteris paribus,* which means
   a. consumers and producers care only about money.
   b. that product is the only product in existence.
   c. to ignore all assumptions.
   d. that all other things are held constant.
8. Assume that used cars are an inferior good and that new cars are a normal good. If consumer incomes increase, the demand for
   a. used cars will decrease, and the demand for new cars will increase.
   b. used cars will increase, and the demand for new cars will decrease.
   c. both new and used cars will decrease.
   d. both new and used cars will increase.
9. An increase in the price of football tickets would cause the _____ basketball tickets, a substitute, to _____.
   a. demand for; increase.
   b. supply of; increase.
   c. demand for; decrease.
   d. supply of; decrease.
10. Which of the following would be most likely to shift the demand for widgets?
    a. A change in the price of widgets.
    b. Unionization of the widget industry.
    c. Discovery of a valuable use for by-products generated in the production of widgets.
    d. A news report that widget prices are expected to increase in the future.

11. An upward-sloping supply curve means that
    a. consumers will wish to purchase more at higher prices.
    b. consumers will wish to purchase more at lower prices.
    c. business firms will wish to sell more at higher prices.
    d. business firms that lower their prices will desire to sell more.
12. A decrease in supply is illustrated as
    a. a downward shift in the supply curve.
    b. a shift to the left in the supply curve.
    c. an upward movement along the supply curve.
    d. a downward movement along the supply curve.
13. Which event is most likely to result in an increase in the price of a Whopper hamburger at Burger King?
    a. French fries go up in price.
    b. New competing hamburger restaurants open.
    c. Beef prices increase.
    d. Scientists declare that hamburgers are a health hazard.
14. In Self-Test Figure 3-1, which of the following would cause a movement from point *A* to point *B*?
    a. An increase in the cost of inputs.
    b. A decrease in the cost of inputs.
    c. An increase in demand.
    d. A decrease in demand.

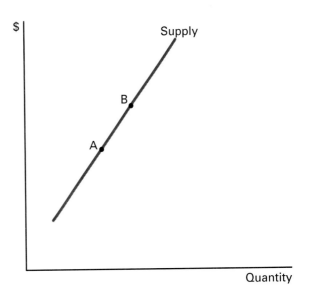

SELF-TEST FIGURE 3-1

15. Suppose a new technique is discovered that is expected to result in cars and houses of the future obtaining all of their energy requirements from roof-mounted solar panels. In the present-day market for oil, it is most likely that
    a. demand would shift to the right.
    b. demand would shift to the left.
    c. supply would shift to the right.
    d. supply would shift to the left.
16. If research reveals that carrot juice cures cancer, it is likely that
    a. the supply of carrot juice will increase, which will increase the quantity demanded.
    b. demand for carrot juice will increase, which will increase the quantity supplied.
    c. neither the demand for carrot juice nor the supply of carrot juice will increase.
    d. both the demand for carrot juice and the supply of carrot juice will increase.
17. Let Jack and Jill be the only two consumers in the market for pails of water. Jack's demand schedule is:

Price	Quantity Demanded
$1	10
$2	5
$3	0

Jill's demand schedule is:

Price	Quantity Demanded
$1	15
$2	10
$3	5
$4	0

Which of the following would be the market demand for pails of water?

a.

Price	Quantity Demanded
$1	12½
$2	7½
$3	2½
$4	0

b.

Price	Quantity Demanded
$1	15
$2	10
$3	5
$4	0

c.

Price	Quantity Demanded
$1	25
$2	15
$3	5
$4	0

d.

Price	Quantity Demanded
$1	15
$3	10
$5	5
$7	0

18. When there is an initial shortage, market prices eventually reach equilibrium because
    a. supply increases.
    b. price decreases.
    c. price increases.
    d. equilibrium output falls.
19. If the demand and supply of a product both decrease (shift to the left), then
    a. both price and quantity must fall.
    b. price rises, but quantity remains constant.
    c. quantity falls, but the change in price cannot be predicted without more information.
    d. price falls, but the change in quantity cannot be predicted without more information.
20. School voucher plans are likely to do all of the following EXCEPT
    a. increase the amount of control that parents have over schools.
    b. threaten the job security of teachers in the public schools.
    c. violate the constitutional separation between church and state.
    d. increase the amount of educational choices available.

QUESTIONS AND PROBLEMS

1. *[demand]* Do price and quantity demanded show an inverse or a direct relationship between each other? Draw a graph showing a plausible demand curve for milk. Be sure to correctly label the axes of your graph.

2. *[individual and market demand]* Draw a single graph indicating someone's demand curve for hot dogs. Be sure to label the axes of your graph appropriately. Label the demand curve with the words Individual's Demand.

On this graph, indicate what market demand would be if there were only two people willing to buy hot dogs, and if each had a demand curve identical to the one you just drew. Label this curve Market Demand.

3. *[demand]* Suppose Clare's demand for tomatoes is represented by the figures in the accompanying table. Draw and label the axes of a graph that shows Clare's demand for tomatoes. Scale the axes appropriate to the figures in the table. Plot the price–quantity pairs from the table in your graph, then connect the points plotted and label the resulting curve with the word Demand. Is the demand curve you plotted a straight line? Why are most of the demand curves in the text drawn as straight lines?

Price per Pound	Quantity Demanded per Week (in pounds)
$1.00	0
75 cents	1/2
50 cents	3/4
25 cents	1
Free	2

4. *[demand]* Why does insurance increase the number of homes that are built in areas prone to hurricane damage? Explain, using a graph of demand.

5. *[substitutes]* List at least five substitutes for your favorite soft drink, in order, starting with the best substitute, second best, and so on. Comment on whether the products on your list are good substitutes. How much would the price of your favorite soft drink have to increase before you would begin to purchase the best substitute?

6. *[complements]* Name at least one other good that would be a complement for each of the following goods: pencil, baseball, personal computer, postage stamp, sugar, and butter. What effect on the demand for each of these goods would there be if the price of a complement for the good were to increase (decrease)?

7. *[inferior goods]* Keeping in mind the economic definition of inferior goods, list several products that would be inferior goods for you personally. Do you think that these would also be inferior goods for most other people?

8. *[normal versus inferior goods]* When Mr. Johnson lost his job, thus cutting his income, his demands for various products changed. The accompanying table lists five normal goods and five inferior goods for Mr. Johnson. However, the goods may not be in the correct column. Bearing in mind the distinction between normal and inferior goods, use your best judgment to rearrange the goods by placing them in the correct column. Will the demand for the normal goods increase or decrease because of Mr. Johnson's income reduction? Will the demand for the inferior goods increase or decrease?

Normal Goods?	Inferior Goods?
Generic paper towels	Antique furniture
Restaurant food	Tickets to pro football games
Tommy Hilfiger clothing	Used cars
Fresh vegetables	Home-brewed coffee
Spam	Ramen noodles

9. *[demand]* As in the chapter, suppose Jack and Jill are the only two consumers in the market for pails of water. However, suppose that their demand curves change over time from the data in the chapter to the following:

Price	Jack's Quantity Demanded	Jill's Quantity Demanded
$1	10	15
2	5	10
3	0	5
4	0	0

a. Compute market demand.

b. Compute the quantities purchased in total and by Jack and Jill individually if the price per unit is $2.

c. Graph Jack's demand and Jill's demand on separate graphs. Note that, if you connect the data points you are given, you are actually inferring additional data. For example, connecting the data points on Jack's demand implies that Jack would be willing to purchase 2.5 pails of water at a price of $2.50 per pail.

10. *[demand versus quantity demanded]* Is there a difference between a *change in demand* and a *change in quantity demanded*? Explain.

11. *[direct or inverse supply curve]* Does a supply curve show a direct or an inverse relationship between price and quantity supplied? Draw a graph showing a plausible market supply curve for spinach. Be sure to correctly label the axes of your graph.

12. *[shift factors for supply]* In each of the situations that follow, state whether supply would increase or decrease. Sketch each shift by drawing a graph for each case.

a. The price of a substitute in production falls.

b. The price of a jointly produced product falls.

c. Sellers expect prices of their output will increase in the future.

d. The technology of production improves.

13. *[supply versus quantity supplied]* Explain why an increase in *quantity supplied* is NOT the same as an increase in *supply*. Which of these would be associated with a rightward shift in the supply curve? Which would be associated with a movement up the supply curve?

14. *[equilibrium]* Explain what is meant by saying that, at equilibrium, the market clears. Why do markets tend toward equilibrium?

15. *[surplus]* Will a surplus result from a price that is above the equilibrium price or a price below the equilibrium price? Why would a surplus be only temporary?

16. *[shortage]* Will a shortage result from a price that is above the equilibrium price or a price below the equilibrium price? What adjustment will take place so that the shortage eventually disappears?

17. *[surplus, shortage, equilibrium]* Fill in the surplus or shortage in the table below. In each case identify whether the number is a surplus, shortage, or neither. Identify the equilibrium price, and explain why a price above equilibrium would not last.

Price	Quantity Demanded	Quantity Supplied	Surplus or Shortage
$7	12	30	
$6	15	25	
$5	19	19	
$4	23	10	

18. *[adjustment to equilibrium]* Suppose that a market is initially in equilibrium. Now suppose that demand increases. At the initial equilibrium price, will the effect of the increase in demand be to create a surplus or a shortage? What must happen for the market to attain a new equilibrium?

19. *[shifts in demand and supply]* Fill in the missing information in the following table by stating whether equilibrium price and quantity will increase or decrease in each case.

Demand	Supply	Equilibrium Price	Equilibrium Quantity
Shifts to the right	Does not shift		
Shifts to the left	Does not shift		
Does not shift	Shifts to the right		
Does not shift	Shifts to the left		

20. *[shifts in demand and supply]* Using a graph of supply and demand, demonstrate how a leftward shift in demand, accompanied by a rightward shift in supply, can result in the equilibrium quantity rising. On a separate graph, demonstrate how the equilibrium quantity could alternatively have fallen.

 Visit **www.prenhall.com/ayers** for Exploring the Web exercises and additional self-test quizzes.

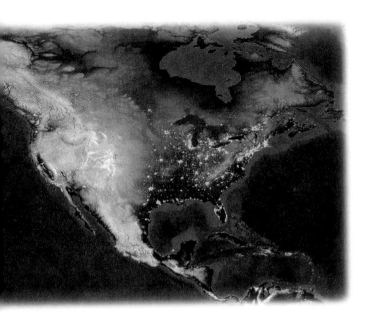

CHAPTER 4

THE POWER OF PRICES

A LOOK AHEAD

The United States shines like no other country, at least when looked at from outer space. Electric power and lighting are taken for granted as inalienable rights. Yet there was a time not long ago when the lights blinked out in California. The consequences were severe in terms of consumer annoyance and lost industry output. As we will see in the Explore & Apply section that concludes this chapter, the culprit was a policy that ignored some basic economic lessons concerning supply, demand, and market price.

Prices are powerful! They guide the marketplace to produce the right things in the right way and distribute them to those who place the most value upon them. Sometimes the results of the market price system seem unfair. But tampering with market prices can be perilous in terms of efficiency. As we will see, sometimes the effect is to harm the very people the policies intend to help.

LEARNING OBJECTIVES

Understanding Chapter 4 will enable you to:
1. **Interpret how demand represents marginal benefit and supply represents marginal cost.**
2. **Explain the concept of social surplus and how it is divided between consumers and producers.**
3. **Demonstrate how both exports and imports increase efficiency while simultaneously harming either consumers or producers.**
4. **Identify inefficiencies associated with price ceilings.**
5. **Show why price supports are unnecessary and potentially counterproductive.**
6. **Pinpoint the economic flaw in California's deregulation of electricity.**

Explore & Apply

79

price signals help consumers decide how much to buy and help producers decide how much to sell.

The marketplace depends upon **price signals,** meaning that the market price sends a message to consumers and producers. The price signals to consumers how much of a good they will wish to buy, and signals to producers how much of a good they will wish to sell. When the market equilibrium price rises, consumers respond by buying less of a good and producers respond by offering more for sale. Just the opposite is true when price falls. We start Chapter 4 by examining why these price signals are desirable. We then examine various public policies that are intended to either lower or raise prices from their market equilibrium values.

4.1 PRICE SIGNALS FOR EFFICIENT CHOICE

Consumers buy something because they expect that they will be better off by doing so. The same holds true when producers sell something. Therefore, when a consumer buys a good that a producer sells, both parties are better off. The mutual gains from such market exchanges lead the economy to greater efficiency. This section looks at how gains are measured, how much is gained by consumers and producers, and how market prices can maximize these gains, including when trade occurs internationally. Later chapters examine exceptions, such as possible reasons for restricting international trade.

MARGINAL BENEFIT AND CONSUMER SURPLUS

The demand curve depicts the quantity that would be purchased at each of various prices, *ceteris paribus.* Another way of looking at it is that the demand curve shows the maximum price the consumer would pay for each quantity that might be purchased. This maximum price is the consumer's **marginal benefit**—the incremental value of each additional item consumed. Figure 4-1 illustrates this way of looking at demand.

marginal benefit the incremental value of an additional unit of a good.

Consider Dwight, who is shopping for blue jeans. Dwight won't buy blue jeans if the price is over $20. He'll buy one pair if the price is $20, two pair if the price is $15, or three pair if the price is $10. In other words, the first pair is worth $20 to him, the second pair is worth an extra $15, and the third an extra $10. His marginal benefits from blue jeans, therefore, are $20 for the first pair, $15 for the second, and $10 for the third. Table 4-1 shows how demand translates into marginal benefit and total benefit. Dwight's *total benefit* from his blue

FIGURE 4-1

MARGINAL BENEFIT Demand is the marginal benefit to consumers. Marginal benefit declines as quantity demanded rises. The length of the arrows represents the marginal benefit of the quantities 1, 2, and 3, respectively.

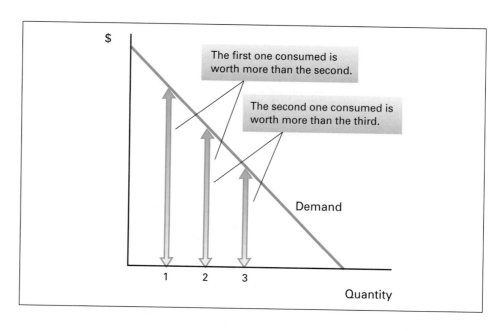

TABLE 4-1   DWIGHT'S DEMAND, MARGINAL BENEFIT, AND TOTAL BENEFIT

| (A) DWIGHT'S DEMAND FOR BLUE JEANS | | (B) DWIGHT'S BENEFITS FROM BUYING BLUE JEANS | | |
PRICE	QUANTITY	QUANTITY	MARGINAL BENEFIT	TOTAL BENEFIT
$20	1	1	$20	$20
$15	2	2	$15	$35
$10	3	3	$10	$45

jean purchases is the sum of his marginal benefit from each pair. So, if he buys three pair, the blue jeans would bring Dwight $45 worth of total benefit, where $45 = $20 + $15 + $10.

Since Dwight must pay for the blue jeans he buys, the remaining value to him of his blue jean purchases equals the total benefit from the blue jeans minus what he pays. This value is termed **consumer surplus,** which is the difference between the total benefit and total cost to the consumer. Graphically, it is the demand curve minus price, as shown in Figure 4-2(a). Therefore, if the price of blue jeans is $10, then Dwight would buy three pair at a cost of $30. Subtracting that $30 from his total benefit of $45 would leave him with a consumer surplus of $15, as shown in Figure 4-2(b).

consumer surplus consumers' total benefit minus cost; graphically, demand minus market price.

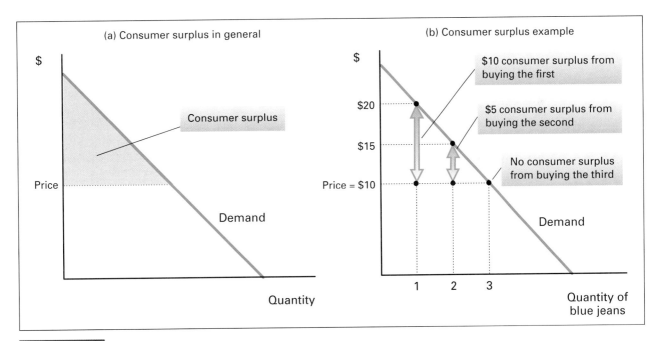

FIGURE 4-2

CONSUMER SURPLUS Consumer surplus is the area under the demand curve and above the market price. It is what consumers gain from their purchases after deducting the cost. The general idea is shown in graph (a).

Graph (b) applies this idea to the example of Dwight. At a price of $10 per pair of jeans, Dwight buys three pair and receives $15 worth of consumer surplus. His consumer surplus equals the sum of the consumer surplus from the first, second, and third pairs, which is $10 + $5 + $0 = $15. If the price were higher, Dwight's consumer surplus would be lower, as shown in Table 4-2.

TABLE 4-2   DWIGHT'S CONSUMER SURPLUS FROM BLUE JEANS

PRICE	QUANTITY BOUGHT	TOTAL BENEFIT	TOTAL PAID	CONSUMER SURPLUS
$20	1	$20	$20	$0
$15	2	$35	$30	$5
$10	3	$45	$30	$15

Table 4-2 computes Dwight's consumer surplus for three different prices of blue jeans. As you can see in that table, **consumer surplus varies inversely with price.** The greater the price, the less is consumer surplus, and the lower the price the greater is consumer surplus.

MARGINAL COST AND PRODUCER SURPLUS

Supply, like demand, can be viewed in two ways. A supply curve shows the quantity that would be offered for sale at each of various prices, *ceteris paribus*. The supply curve also depicts the minimum price that the producers of a good would be willing to accept for each quantity offered. That minimum price is the producer's *marginal cost,* which is the incremental cost of producing each additional item offered for sale. Figure 4-3 illustrates this way of looking at supply.

Consider Buddy, who sells blue jeans. Buddy won't offer any blue jeans for sale if the price is under $5. He is willing to sell one pair if the price is $5, two pair if the price is $7.50, or three pair at a price of $10. Those prices are also his marginal costs when he produces the first three pair of blue jeans. Table 4-3 shows how supply translates into marginal cost and total cost. Buddy's *total cost* of blue jeans sold is the sum of his marginal cost from selling each pair. So, if he sells three pair of blue jeans, he would incur total costs of $22.50, where $22.50 = $5 + $7.50 + $10.

The value Buddy receives from the sale of his product equals total revenue minus total cost. This value is termed **producer surplus,** which is the excess of revenue to producers over their costs of production. Graphically, it is the market price minus the supply curve, as shown in Figure 4-4(a) on page 84. If the price of blue jeans is $10 in our example, then

producer surplus producers' revenue minus production cost; graphically, market price minus supply.

QUICKCHECK

Suppose coffee costs $1 per cup at Handy Stop Shop and $1.05 per cup at Gas'n N Goin' next door. If you buy coffee at Handy Stop Shop, does this mean your consumer surplus from coffee is only five cents?

Answer: No, consumer surplus does not depend upon alternative prices for the same product. Rather, it asks you what is the most you would be willing to pay to avoid doing without the product altogether and then subtracts the price you actually pay. Thus, whatever your consumer surplus from a cup of coffee may be, it is five cents more if you buy your coffee at Handy Stop Shop than at Gas'n N Goin'.

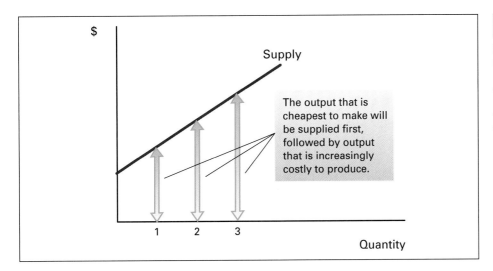

FIGURE 4-3

MARGINAL COST Supply is the marginal cost to producers. Marginal cost increases as quantity produced rises. The length of the arrows represents the marginal cost of the quantities 1, 2, and 3, respectively.

TABLE 4-3   BUDDY'S SUPPLY, MARGINAL COST, AND TOTAL COST

(A) BUDDY'S SUPPLY OF BLUE JEANS		(B) BUDDY'S COSTS OF PRODUCING BLUE JEANS		
PRICE	QUANTITY	QUANTITY	MARGINAL COST	TOTAL COST
$5	1	1	$5	$5
$7.50	2	2	$7.50	$12.50
$10	3	3	$10	$22.50

Buddy would sell three pair for a total revenue of $30, where total revenue is computed by multiplying price by quantity. Subtracting the total cost of $22.50 from the $30 would leave him with a producer surplus of $7.50, as shown in Figure 4-4(b).

Table 4-4 computes producer surplus for three different prices of blue jeans. As seen in that table, **producer surplus varies directly with price.**

TABLE 4-4   BUDDY'S PRODUCER SURPLUS FROM BLUE JEANS

PRICE	QUANTITY SOLD	TOTAL COST	TOTAL REVENUE	PRODUCER SURPLUS
$5	1	$5	$5	$0
$7.50	2	$12.50	$15	$2.50
$10	3	$22.50	$30	$7.50

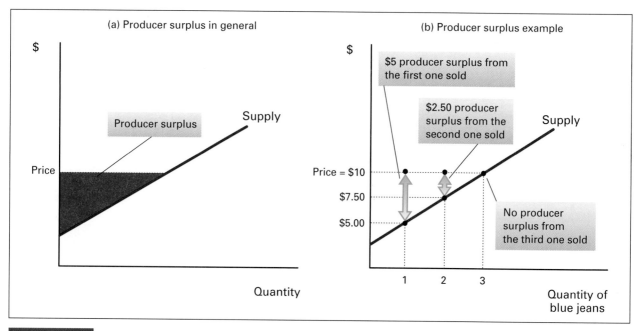

FIGURE 4-4

PRODUCER SURPLUS Producer surplus is the area above the supply curve and under the market price, as shown in (a). It is what producers gain from their sales after deducting their costs.

Graph (b) shows that, at a price of $10 per pair of jeans, Buddy sells three pair and receives $7.50 worth of producer surplus. His producer surplus equals the sum of his producer surplus from the first, second, and third pairs, which is $5 + $2.50 + $0 = $7.50.

QUICKCHECK

What is the difference in meaning between the terms surplus, consumer surplus, and producer surplus?

Answer: A surplus exists when the market price is above the equilibrium price, as discussed in Chapter 3. The surplus equals the quantity supplied minus the quantity demanded at that price. In contrast, consumer surplus refers to the value that a consumer receives in excess of what was paid for the purchase—it equals demand minus the market price. Producer surplus is the value a seller receives in excess of cost—it equals market price minus supply.

THE EFFICIENCY OF THE MARKETPLACE

social surplus the sum of consumer surplus and producer surplus.

Markets are efficient to the extent that they maximize social surplus, which is the sum of consumer and producer surplus. Social surplus is the difference between how much a good is worth and how much it costs to produce. It is the total value the economy gains by having the good produced and consumed. In the blue jeans example, the social surplus at a price of $10 would be $22.50, which equals $15 in consumer surplus for Dwight plus $7.50 in producer surplus for Buddy.

Any time marginal benefit exceeds marginal cost, social surplus would increase if more of the good were to be produced and sold. That is just what the marketplace does.

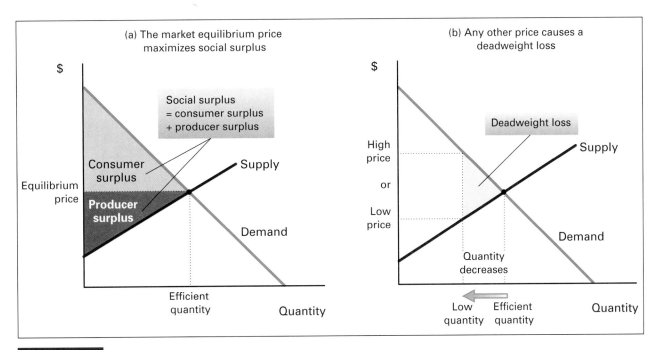

FIGURE 4-5

EFFICIENCY OF THE EQUILIBRIUM PRICE The market equilibrium price leads to the efficient quantity, as shown in (a). No other quantity would generate a larger total of consumer and producer surplus. Any other price, such as either of the prices shown in (b), would lead to a lower quantity sold. If the price is high, the quantity falls because consumers aren't willing to buy as much. If the price is low, quantity falls because producers aren't willing to sell as much. In either case, there is a triangular area of deadweight loss that shows how much social surplus is forgone relative to the amount at an efficient quantity.

Producers keep on selling until their marginal cost just equals the market price. Likewise, consumers keep on buying until their marginal benefit equals the market price. This means that marginal benefit equals marginal cost at the market equilibrium price and that social surplus is maximized. Any more output would add more cost than benefit. Thus, the *rule of efficiency* states that **the efficient output occurs when society's marginal benefit equals marginal cost.**

The marketplace achieves an efficient output through price adjustments. At the market equilibrium price, marginal benefit equals marginal cost and social surplus is maximized. Figure 4-5(a) illustrates how the market price—also the equilibrium price—signals an efficient quantity that maximizes social surplus. In this figure the intersection of demand and supply establishes the efficient quantity. Since demand represents marginal benefit and supply represents marginal cost, the rule of efficiency is satisfied. Any other price, such as the high price or low price shown in Figure 4-5(b), would lead to less output and a smaller social surplus.

The triangular area of forgone social surplus caused by inefficient pricing is called a **deadweight loss.** The size of the deadweight loss will decrease when the price is closer to the market price, but increase when the price moves farther away from its equilibrium value. Prices that differ from their equilibrium values will not persist because those prices will adjust toward equilibrium. The deadweight loss will in this way eventually disappear.

deadweight loss reduction in social surplus caused by inefficient price; shown graphically as a triangular area.

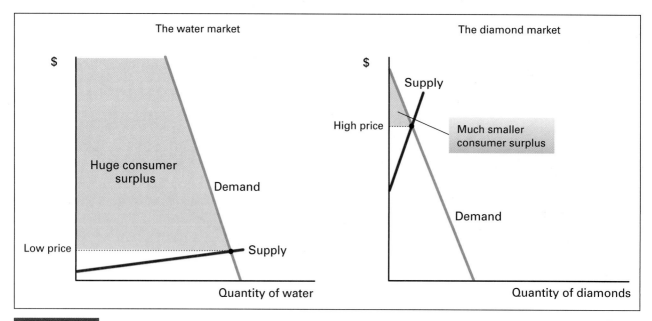

FIGURE 4-6

THE PARADOX OF DIAMONDS AND WATER Price measures the value of consuming one more unit of a good. Consumer surplus measures the total value to consumers from all of their consumption of the good. While the marginal benefit from a glass of water is far less than from a diamond, as revealed by the relatively low price of water, the total benefit from all water as measured by its consumer surplus is immensely larger than it would be for all diamonds.

SNAPSHOT   **THE PARADOX OF DIAMONDS AND WATER**

Some necessities that have a great deal of intrinsic worth are priced lower than luxuries we could easily do without. For example, people pay much more for a diamond than for a glass of water, which seems paradoxical. If we were stranded in Death Valley with neither water nor diamonds, which would seem the better bargain—a diamond for a nickel or a glass of water for a one-hundred-dollar bill?

The paradox disappears when we realize that price merely tells the value of a good at the margin. The last bit of water is not worth much when water is plentiful. It is the scarcity of diamonds that keeps that price high. To understand the total value of a good, though, we must look beyond price to consumer surplus. As shown in Figure 4-6, the consumer surplus from water purchases is vastly greater than the consumer surplus from diamond purchases. It is consumer surplus that truly measures the total value consumers receive from the things they buy. ◄

THE EFFICIENCY OF IMPORTS AND EXPORTS

Questions of efficiency often arise in the context of international trade. If a country chooses not to engage in international trade, the market prices of its goods and services would reflect only the supply and demand within that country. Those prices are called *domestic* prices. Opening an economy to international trade will change market prices in a country by bringing into its markets a world of new consumers and producers. *World prices* of goods and services are determined by the supply and demand from all countries.

Countries that trade buy goods and services from other countries—their *imports*. They also sell goods and services to other countries—their *exports*. Whether a country imports a good or exports a good will depend upon whether the good's world equilibrium market price is below or above what the country's price would otherwise have been—its domestic price.

In other words, **the result of trade is that the price in the domestic market will come to equal the world market price.** If the domestic price rises to meet a higher world price, then the country exports the good. If a lower world price causes the domestic price to drop, then the country imports the good, meaning that it is purchased from producers in other countries. In either case, there are some people within the country who gain and others who lose. However, as we will see, the gains can be expected to exceed the losses.

Figure 4-7 shows the case of a world price of a good that would lead a country to import that good. Domestic consumers will not be willing to pay any more than the world price. Producers will also refuse to sell for less than the world price. Because the domestic quantity supplied is less than the quantity demanded, consumers make up the difference with imports, as shown in Figure 4-7(a).

Adding together consumer surplus and producer surplus, it is apparent by looking at Figure 4-7(b) that the total increases. Specifically, allowing imports increases social surplus by the amount labeled. Although the lower price will cause producer surplus to shrink, the increase in consumer surplus is seen to more than compensate for that loss. Because the gains to consumers more than offset the losses to producers, efficiency calls for allowing imports.

Figure 4-8 is similar to Figure 4-7 except the world price is above the domestic price. In this case, the price difference causes the domestic quantity supplied to be greater than the domestic quantity demanded. This difference between quantity supplied and quantity

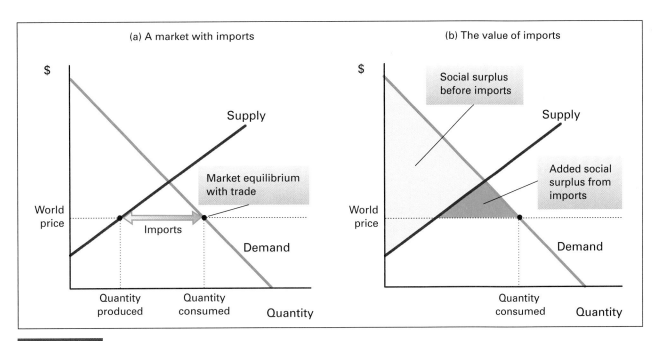

FIGURE 4-7

THE EFFICIENCY OF IMPORTS Imports result from a world price that is below what the country's equilibrium price would have been without trade. The lower world price causes the country's consumption to rise and production to fall, with the difference being the amount imported, as shown in (a).

Trade leads to an efficient quantity consumed because it increases the value of social surplus by the added triangular area shown in (b). However, the gains go disproportionately to consumers. Producer surplus is smaller because of the lower price.

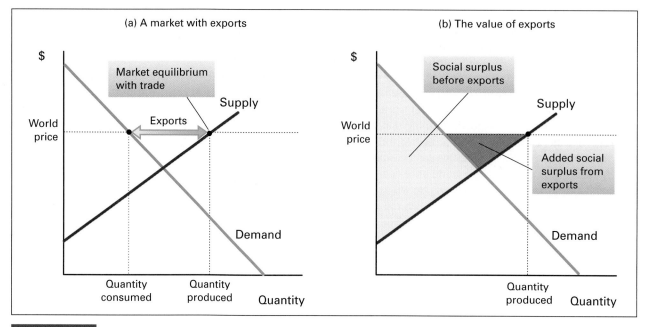

FIGURE 4-8

THE EFFICIENCY OF EXPORTS Exports result from a world price that exceeds what the country's equilibrium price would be without trade. The higher world price causes the country's consumption to fall and production to rise, with the difference being the amount exported, as shown in (a).

Trade leads to an efficient quantity produced because it increases the value of social surplus by the added triangular area shown in (b). However, the gains go disproportionately to producers. Consumer surplus is less because of the higher price.

QUICKCHECK

Since consumers gain from imports, but domestic producers lose, isn't a country just as well off to forgo imports altogether? Similarly, since consumers lose from exports, but domestic producers gain, isn't a country just as well off to do without exports? Explain.

Answer: No, consumers gain more from imports than producers lose. Likewise, producers gain more from exports than consumers lose. Thus, both imports and exports bring net gains to the country.

demanded results in an excess quantity of the product. This excess is exported, as shown in Figure 4-7(a).

Adding together consumer surplus and producer surplus in Figure 4-8(b) shows that the total increases. Specifically, allowing exports increases social surplus by the amount labeled. Although the higher price will cause consumer surplus to shrink, the increase in producer surplus is seen to more than compensate. Because the gains to producers more than offset the losses to consumers, efficiency calls for allowing exports.

In short, consumers come out winners from imports, but producers lose. Producers come out the winners from exports, but consumers lose. In each case, though, the gains exceed the losses. So, whether it be from imports or from exports, the country as a whole comes out the winner.

4.2 PRICE CEILINGS—HOLDING PRICES DOWN

In 1973, the Organization of Petroleum Exporting Countries (OPEC) succeeded in restricting oil supplies to Western countries and achieving a dramatic spike upward in energy prices. In response, Congress enacted temporary gasoline price controls, which capped price increases and cut into the social surplus. This action caused fuel shortages, with drivers losing much time and patience in long lines at the gas pumps. Yet the problem of gasoline shortages and wasteful gas lines has little to do with gasoline and much to do with the economics of a **price ceiling,** which is a law that establishes a maximum price that can be legally charged for a good. As discussed in the following sections, price ceilings arise in various contexts.

price ceiling a maximum price that can legally be charged for a good.

PROMOTING AFFORDABLE HOUSING—ARE RENT CONTROLS THE ANSWER?

With rising populations in competition for scarce land, major cities sometimes choose rent controls as a way to insulate tenants from higher housing costs. **Rent controls** hold the monthly price of rental housing to below its equilibrium level. Price tries to rise, but bumps up against the rent control ceiling. As we will see, the long-term consequences often differ from what proponents have in mind.

rent controls a price ceiling applied to the price of rental housing.

The market for rental housing is like other markets in which demand slopes down and supply slopes up. Demand slopes down because prospective tenants are unwilling to rent as many apartments when prices are high as when they are low. Some people continue living with their parents. Others choose to share rental homes and apartments with roommates. Still others live on their own, but rent smaller and less-desirable quarters than they would have preferred. The supply of rental housing slopes upward as higher rental prices motivate prospective landlords to partition off rental rooms, repair vacant apartments, and in other ways increase the quantity of housing supplied.

Figure 4-9 illustrates a housing market with rent controls in place. **For these rent controls to be meaningful, the ceiling price must be set below the market equilibrium price.** The result is a housing shortage, as shown in Figure 4-9(a), in which less housing is offered for lease, while more housing is demanded.

One effect of rent controls is to transfer wealth from current landlords to current tenants, as shown in Figure 4-9(b). Such **transfer payments,** in which one party's loss is another's gain, are not themselves inefficient since they merely redistribute social surplus. However, when transfer payments are caused by government price controls, there are multiple sources of inefficiency that shrinks social surplus. The first inefficiency is the deadweight loss triangle associated with a less-than-efficient overall quantity, such as labeled in Figure 4-9(b).

transfer payments the redistribution of social surplus from one party to another; rent controls create transfer payments from landlords to tenants.

A second source of inefficiency comes from misallocating apartments that are leased. For example, even though Tanisha in Figure 4-9 would get a larger benefit from the apartment than would Candice, the landlord would receive the same payment from either and so might well rent the apartment to Candice. Since any tenant would be constrained to pay the same rent and there are more potential tenants than available apartments, the landlord would find it easy to discriminate, whether on the basis of income, occupation, or anything else the landlord thinks is important. It might be difficult to prove if that discrimination was illegal, such as based on race, color, or creed.

A third inefficiency involves **search costs,** which are the costs of finding an apartment. Since landlords have plenty of prospective tenants for rent-controlled apartments, they do not need to advertise. As a result, some enterprising would-be tenants have taken up such tactics as reading the obituaries or, to get the jump, listening to police radios and checking out emergency rooms. In the absence of rent controls, there would be little or no need for such wasteful behavior.

search costs the costs of finding something; rent controls increase search costs for rental housing.

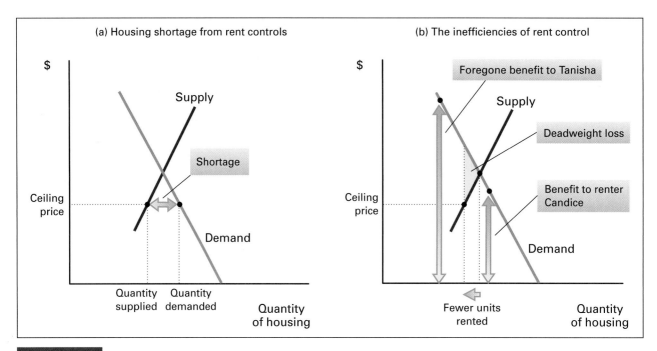

FIGURE 4-9

RENT CONTROLS A rent control law imposes a ceiling price that leads to a shortage of rental housing, as shown in (a). As shown in (b), the inefficiencies of rent controls include a deadweight loss from fewer units rented and an inefficient allocation of apartments among prospective tenants. For example, a landlord might rent an apartment to Candice, since she is willing to pay the ceiling price. However, that might leave Tanisha without an apartment, even though it is worth more to her.

The inefficiencies of rent controls are likely to get worse over time as demand grows with an increasing population while rent-controlled apartments are allowed to deteriorate. For example, New York City and Washington, D.C., have seen rent-controlled housing crumble for decades. A look at some of the aging cities of Europe also reveals deep scars from rent control. Paris has had some rent controls in place for over two hundred years. The rent-controlled apartment houses in Paris have seen little modernization in that time, with few apartment units containing their own plumbing facilities. In the rent-controlled period between 1914 and 1948, almost no new rental housing was constructed in all of France.

While rent controls have problems, there are also problems associated with removing them. The immediate effect of abolishing rent controls is that rents jump to their market equilibrium value. That value could be quite high if rent controls have been in place for a long time and the housing shortage has become severe. Higher rents would eventually shift supply to the right as old apartments are refurbished and new ones are built. However, this process would take time and the only immediate effect would be higher rents.

There are alternatives to rent controls. One alternative is to identify the needy and assign them housing vouchers. **Housing vouchers** are government grants that the recipient can spend only on housing. Thus, even though the price of rental housing may be high, housing vouchers can bring it within reach of impoverished tenants.

housing vouchers *government grants that recipients can spend only on housing.*

ANTI-GOUGING LAWS

price gouging *price increases in response to increased demand related to emergencies.*

Rent controls are far from the only time government seeks to keep prices down. For example, local governments have often attempted to protect consumers against **price gouging,**

QUICKCHECK

If rent controls are removed, is there likely to be as much illegal discrimination against apartment applicants?

Answer: No, uncontrolled rents will clear the market, meaning that the shortage of apartments will be eliminated. Landlords will no longer have the luxury of picking from a crowd of applicants all offering the same rent. In competing for tenants, landlords have a financial incentive to avoid discrimination. Those who insist on discriminating on the basis of irrelevant prejudices are by definition accepting less than the most valuable offer. Because the price of discrimination has risen, its quantity will fall.

which is the disparaging term for hiking up prices in response to temporary surges in demand. The idea is to promote equity. The cost is in terms of efficiency, though, because high prices in times of emergency prevent shortages and allocate sought-after goods to those who value them the most.

Profitably high prices also motivate rapid restocking, which means that prices do not stay high for long. For example, when hurricanes move toward the coast, oceanfront homeowners seek out plywood to board up their windows. If stores can raise prices, they have an incentive to send out extra trucks for new supplies. Otherwise, homeowners must scramble to snatch up and hoard supplies before the shelves go bare. If homeowners are lucky, stores might use the occasion to generate goodwill and restock promptly despite the extra costs.

Local governments also often have laws against *ticket scalping*—the practice of buying tickets at the price set by concert promoters and then reselling at whatever the market will bear. Scalping is a form of *arbitrage*, which means buying low and selling high. Arbitrage directs goods to their highest-valued uses, thus efficiently allocating seats at concerts, ball games, and other events. As for equity, however, opinions differ. Good seats get snared quickly by scalpers, many of whom hire stand-ins to buy up blocks of tickets. Those seats are made available to true fans, but the price might be much higher.

SCALPING THE STONES   *SNAPSHOT*

With four decades of touring under their belts, the Rolling Stones know all about how to please a crowd. And their fans know all about the crowd of scalpers that snatch up all the best tickets! Their techniques? One ticket reseller paid $20 each to the brothers of a college fraternity just for standing in the ticket line. That reseller hired over 150 stand-ins for a single Rolling Stones concert. Who could blame Stones' fans for crying that they "can't get no satisfaction"?

Some fans—those willing to spend extra money to avoid the time in line—were glad for the choice and convenience offered by the scalpers, who these days usually put their tickets up for auction at eBay, uBid, or other on-line auction sites. Others cried that it wasn't fair to fans or promoters, who want to generate excitement with below-market ticket prices. Which should it be? During their 2002–2003 World Tour, the Rolling Stones played in stadiums, arenas, and clubs in cities including Boston, Chicago, and Los Angeles. Concert tickets sold out quickly, leaving many fans with two choices: wait for another tour or pay an above-market price. The price of some tickets on eBay reached $3,000. The fans who didn't pay got to know all too well the words of Mick Jagger, "You can't always get what you want." If you have the money, though, "you can get what you need!" ◄

Although consumers are better off when prices are low, producers prefer them high. Both groups often turn to government for help. If politics dictates propping up prices, government can establish a **price floor,** also termed a **price support,** which sets a minimum price that producers are guaranteed to receive. One way to implement a price floor is for government to agree to buy at that floor price. This approach can cause surpluses to pile up at taxpayer expense. Such is the case of agricultural price supports. Note that the term *surplus* in this context refers to a quantity of output, specifically the excess of what is produced over what is consumed, not to the term social surplus that is also used in this chapter. We will also look at minimum wage laws, which have no budgetary cost to government but nevertheless do have significant costs to both job applicants and employers.

price floor (price support)
minimum price guaranteed to producers by the government.

AGRICULTURAL PRICE SUPPORTS

Although only 2 percent of the United States' labor force currently derives a living from agriculture, the political influence of agriculture has been strong enough to maintain agricultural price supports in the United States since the 1920s. These price supports have been justified on two counts. One is that they sustain the lifestyle of the family farm, an American tradition. However, the reality is that family farming has continued to decline, and a disproportionate amount of price support payments have gone to large farms and corporations. The second justification is that they ensure a plentiful supply of food for American consumers. This line of reasoning does not withstand the logic of economic analysis.

Figure 4-10 shows the effects of an agricultural price support, such as for corn or wheat. By holding price above the equilibrium, there is more farm output produced, but less consumed. The result is a surplus, as shown. Such agricultural surpluses have averaged many billion dollars' worth of foodstuffs annually in the United States. Agricultural price supports have increased in recent years, most notably with President Bush's 2002 signing of a farm bill estimated to cost taxpayers $190 billion over ten years. With the Census Bureau estimating the U.S. population to be about 287 million at the time of signing, the $190 billion cost

FIGURE 4-10

PRICE SUPPORTS Price supports cause a surplus because they prompt consumers to reduce consumption even as producers increase production. Applied to the grain market, the support price shown in this graph generates additional production at a cost that is greater than its value, causing a triangular area of deadweight loss. A second triangular area of deadweight loss results from the reduced consumption brought by the artificially higher price. Additional deadweight loss can be expected when government distributes the surplus grain it has purchased.

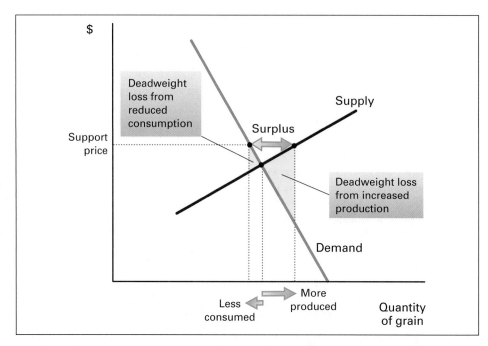

QUICKCHECK

What determines the amount of the surplus when there is a price support? Will there be a surplus if the support price is set below the equilibrium price?

Answer: Other things equal, the higher the support price, the larger will be the surplus. There will be no surplus when the support price is at or below the equilibrium price.

of the legislation translates to an average of $662 apiece from every man, woman, and child in the United States.

The effect of agricultural price supports is to transfer money from both taxpayers and consumers to those in the agriculture industry. Maintaining a high price redistributes social surplus from consumers to producers. There is a deadweight loss associated with both increased production and decreased consumption, as shown in Figure 4-10. Additional deadweight loss can be expected to occur because government must buy and dispose of the surplus quantity, which is nearly impossible to do in an efficient manner. Government cannot merely sell the surplus to the highest bidder, because it must prevent the surplus commodities it buys from being distributed to people who would otherwise purchase that product in the marketplace. To do otherwise would merely mean more of a surplus that government would be forced to buy, because those who received from government would buy less from farmers.

One option is to give the surplus quantity away in a relatively unpalatable form, such as by turning excess milk into powdered milk. Another option is to export the surplus in a manner that does not compete with other agricultural exports. For example, foreign aid to impoverished countries might work, to the extent that the aid does not supplant other food exported from the donor country. However, recipient countries often fear becoming too dependent upon food aid based on unpredictable agricultural surpluses. The dependency arises when farmers in those countries are driven out of business by the low food prices that years of plentiful food aid brings.

There are other options. To rid itself of surplus butter, for example, Denmark offers it for a reduced price if the buyer agrees to export that butter by baking it into Danish butter cookies. Still another common practice is to store surplus commodities until they are no longer edible and then discard them. It's like the fate of leftover food in a refrigerator!

THE MINIMUM WAGE

The **minimum wage,** which is a requirement that employers pay no less than a specified wage rate, has been a cherished American tradition since the Great Depression of the 1930s. We all remember our first jobs. We each remember how hard we worked to find a job and how we deserved no less than that minimum wage for the work we did. For many, the job served as a springboard toward great success in life. Backing for the minimum wage also arises out of American compassion for the downtrodden. Americans cherish the notion that no one should be exploited. On the face of it, the minimum wage seems like a good protection against such exploitation. On closer examination, however, the case is arguable.

People support the minimum wage with the idea of reducing poverty. The minimum wage has the potential to reduce poverty by increasing the wages paid to low-skilled labor. That is also its problem. The higher wage means that more people are willing to work. These extra workers include many college and college-bound students already on the road to success. The lure of a higher minimum wage would detour some short-sighted students away from that path—in other words, the opportunity cost of following it has become greater for them.

The higher wage for low-skilled labor also means that fewer jobs are offered. Fast-food restaurants, car washes, and other businesses "make do" with fewer people, but train and

minimum wage lowest wage legally allowed to be paid to workers.

TABLE 4-5   SELECTED STUDIES ON THE EFFECTS OF THE MINIMUM WAGE

AUTHOR(S)	YEAR PUBLISHED	FINDINGS IN BRIEF
Peterson	1957	The minimum wage reduces employment.
Mincer	1976	Unemployment caused by the minimum wage is concentrated among minority teens.
Hammermesh	1982	The minimum wage reduces teenage employment.
Behrman, Sickles, and Taubman	1983	The minimum wage helps whites and hurts blacks.
Bonilla	1992	Increase in the minimum wage leads to lower incomes for single parents.
Neumark	2002	Cities with local minimum wage laws experience less poverty, but a greater number of unemployed.

Source: The first four studies and many others are referenced in *50 Years of Research on the Minimum Wage,* Joint Economic Committee, 1995.

work them harder. They also may replace some labor with capital, such as automated dishwashers and car-washing equipment. The result is that along with higher wages comes a surplus of labor—or a shortage of jobs, depending upon how you look at it. The least employable—those with poor language, computational, or social skills—are out of luck. They cannot get that first job they need to start climbing the ladder of success. They cannot join the "jobs club"—it has become too exclusive.

Table 4-5 presents the findings from just a few of the many studies conducted over the last fifty years on the effects of the minimum wage. The overwhelming majority of them conclude that whatever help it provides to some recipients, the minimum wage also causes harm among those it is intended to help.

Figure 4-11 shows how minimum wage laws increase the number of people seeking low-skilled work while decreasing the number of jobs available. For example, Tony would not have worked for the equilibrium wage. With a minimum wage, however, Tony might wind up taking Dave's job, even though Dave would have been willing to work for less. Because higher wages are offset by fewer jobs, there is no guarantee that minimum wage laws actually increase the total amount firms spend to employ low-skilled workers.

As was the case with rent controls, minimum wage requirements make it easier to discriminate. With numerous applicants for each job opening, employers can pick and choose as they wish. It would be quite difficult to prove if they choose to discriminate on an illegal basis.

There are alternatives to the minimum wage. One alternative is for a so-called *living wage* that would increase the minimum wage so high that a person could live on it, or possibly even support a family on it. A living wage would be attractive to numerous prospective job seekers, but would accentuate the problems with the minimum wage, as previously discussed.

Another alternative is to subsidize the earnings of low-income workers. Such a subsidy is already embedded in the U.S. personal income tax—the earned income tax credit. The drawback is that earnings subsidies come at a high budgetary cost, because they reduce government tax collections or involve actual cash payments. Minimum wage laws also have high costs, but these costs are borne by businesses, consumers, and those unable to find a job.

Subsidies to education also serve as an alternative to the minimum wage. Such subsidies include free public schooling or government financial assistance to students attending private schools, subsidized student loans for college students, and subsidized tuition at

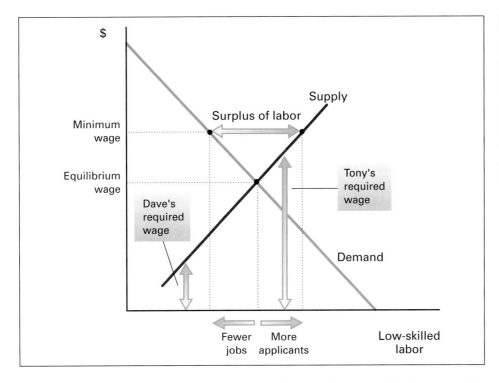

FIGURE 4-11

THE MINIMUM WAGE Minimum wage laws make it tough to find a job, especially for the least-experienced and least-skilled job seekers. The higher wage causes fewer jobs and more applicants. Some of the new applicants (such as Tony) take jobs from others who need the jobs more desperately (such as Dave).

public universities. The more widely available are educational opportunities, the more skills the workforce will acquire. The result is that the supply of low-skilled labor shifts to the left as the opportunity cost of accepting such jobs rises for workers with more human capital that can be applied elsewhere. As shown in Figure 4-12, the leftward shift in supply increases the equilibrium wage for low-skilled labor, which is the purpose of minimum wage laws. The advantage of education subsidies is that they help people develop their skills, leaving the low-skill jobs for those who need them most.

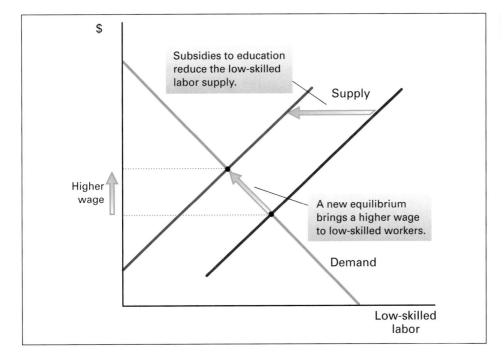

FIGURE 4-12

AN ALTERNATIVE TO THE MINIMUM WAGE Subsidies to education reduce the supply of low-skilled labor, which causes a higher equilibrium wage. Unlike the minimum wage, all workers willing to work at that higher wage will get jobs.

HOMELESS AND WITHOUT A JOB

The homeless often carry a disturbing sign—"Will Work for Food." Although the offers are often a sham, advocates for the homeless are quick to point out that many of the homeless are indeed eager to find steady work. More often than not, however, there are no steady jobs offered to them.

Lack of a home is itself an impediment to finding a job. For example, employers may worry about the employee's personal health and hygiene, and about whether or not the employee is a drifter. For these reasons, potential employers are usually unwilling to pay the minimum wage to the homeless. There are too many other applicants with fewer problems. While employers would be willing to offer jobs at lower wages, such job offers are prohibited.

The homeless are thus caught in the grips of a political vise. Minimum wages are one side of this vise while so-called flophouses that offer cheap nightly lodging are on the other side. Many flophouses have closed down, however, because the residents could not afford rent increases that would be needed to pay the expense of renovation. The law demands such renovation to provide accessibility for the physically challenged. It also requires security from hazards such as fires, lead in pipes and paint, and asbestos. Such government policies are intended to add fairness to what is sold in the marketplace. Together with minimum wages, however, those policies block access to those markets for the very people who need it most, the homeless. ◄

4.4 AROUND THE WORLD—BLACK MARKETS AS A SAFETY VALVE

Price controls are practiced throughout the world. In Taiwan, the Statute for Salt Administration applies price controls to salt. The price of oil is also regulated in order to provide Taiwanese companies with stable prices on what is an important input in manufacturing. Venezuela lifted its price controls in 1996 as a condition for receiving foreign aid. Belarus, a country that once was part of the Soviet Union, made a similar pledge. Price support programs have been common in agriculture. Belgium and other countries of Europe have found that attempts to cut price support programs have been met with vociferous protests from farmers.

black market market in which goods are bought and sold illegally; associated with price controls.

Any time government tries to hold prices above or below market equilibrium, it provides profit opportunities to those willing to take advantage of them. **Black market** activity is said to occur when goods are bought and sold illegally. Under rent controls, for example, it is not uncommon to hear of prospective tenants bribing landlords for an apartment. Sometimes this black market may seem somewhat gray, as when the bribes are merely offers of gifts, or agreements by tenants to "fix up the place." There are also many reports of people being hired "off the books" for less than the minimum wage, especially when the unemployment rate is high.

The black market is nothing more than the free market trying to assert itself when government has attempted to influence that market through taxes or regulation. Regulation could take the form of price controls or the outright ban of market activities. In either case, it is hard to keep willing buyers and sellers from negotiating mutually beneficial illegal deals.

Governments often owe a debt of gratitude to black markets that temper destructive policies. For example, Cubans rely heavily on the black market in their country. If they had to depend upon government rations, they could not obtain enough food to survive. Similarly, the shelves were often bare in the government stores when the countries of Eastern Europe were under communism. These countries relied in large measure on the industriousness of black marketers to keep their economies going.

Recognizing the critical role played by the black market in their economy, the centrally planned former Soviet Union legalized private for-profit agricultural production on approximately 3 percent of its arable land. Despite the small acreage involved, this market-driven component of agriculture produced nearly one-third of all Soviet agricultural output.

4.5 THE PRICE OF POWER

*ε*XPLORE
&
*ℐℰ*PPLY

It was the winter of 2001 when California flirted with disaster. This was no earthquake or tidal wave. Instead, California felt painful shortages of electricity, the lifeblood of modern commerce. Inadequate electric supplies prompted rolling blackouts that cut off electricity to 670,000 households and businesses for two hours at a time. In San Francisco and elsewhere across the state, traffic snarled and motorists screamed as traffic lights died, elevators ground to a halt, and computer screens abruptly turned black. The rolling blackouts were imposed without warning, so as not to alert burglars and robbers that security systems would fail. Even the technological elite of Silicon Valley were not immune, with Cisco Systems and other industry titans complaining of billions of dollars of lost commerce.

EFFECT OF ELECTRICITY DEREGULATION IN CALIFORNIA

Nature was not to blame for California's fiasco. State government was. In order to increase the efficiency with which electricity was generated and distributed at the wholesale level, California lawmakers deregulated the wholesale electricity market. Deregulation caused the state's wholesale electricity providers to compete for customers.

Competition reduces costs through weeding out inefficiencies. *Ceteris paribus,* greater efficiencies in wholesale electricity production and distribution cause the wholesale electricity supply to shift to the right and the price of electricity in the wholesale market to fall, as shown in Figure 4-13(a). Utilities pay less for the electricity they distribute and these savings are passed along to the utilities' residential and business customers. California lawmakers, therefore, felt comfortable promising California voters that their electricity rates

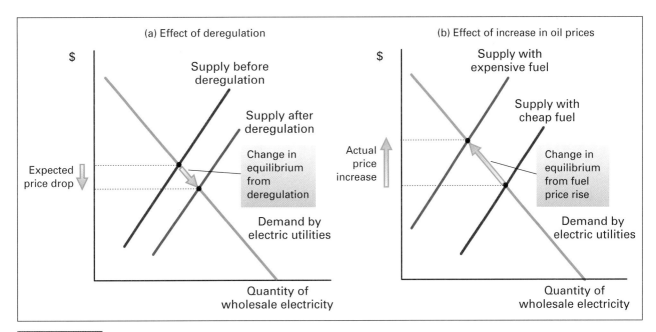

FIGURE 4-13

CALIFORNIA'S WHOLESALE ELECTRICITY MARKET Increased competition after deregulation was expected to shift supply to the right and lower electricity prices, as shown in (a). However, soaring prices of crude oil, coal, and natural gas—inputs into the production of electricity—more than offset the effects of deregulation. The result was that electricity supply in fact shifted to the left, causing the price to increase as shown in (b).

FIGURE 4-14

CALIFORNIA'S RETAIL ELECTRICITY MARKET Higher wholesale electricity prices caused the supply of retail electricity to shift to the left. Ordinarily, that would cause consumers to face a higher price of electricity. However, with retail electricity prices held down by California law, the result was a shortage as the market moved from point *A* to point *B*. The market would achieve the equilibrium shown at point *C* if controls were lifted and price allowed to rise.

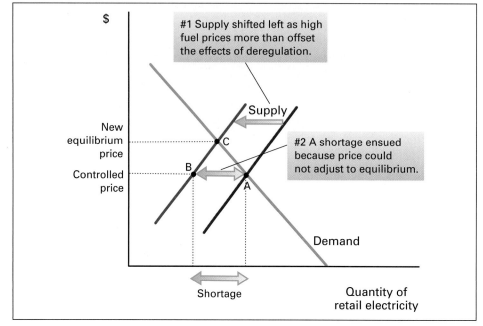

would not go up, at least not very much, and might even go down. Making this promise was a big mistake.

In the real world many things can change at once. In particular, world crude oil prices skyrocketed, more than doubling soon after California's deregulation of wholesale electricity took effect. The prices of natural gas, coal, and other substitutes for crude oil likewise increased. Since oil and other fuels are significant inputs into the production of electricity, rising fuel prices shifted the supply of electricity at the wholesale level significantly to the left. That leftward shift more than offset any rightward shift caused by deregulation. As shown in Figure 4-13(b), the decrease in the supply of wholesale electricity caused the wholesale price of electricity to rise sharply.

Left to itself, the marketplace will not allow a shortage for long. The price of electricity at the retail level will rise in response to a shortage. In turn, consumers will consume less electricity, and producers will provide more, until an equilibrium is reached. However, because of the lawmakers' promise that consumer electricity prices would be held in check, the market was not left to itself. Rather, rates were held down to less than the market equilibrium price. The result in the retail electricity market was a shortage, as shown in Figure 4-14.

There was no incentive for the utilities to provide additional electricity because the controlled price they were allowed to charge their customers was less than what they were paying for the electricity they bought on the wholesale market. Losses among the California utilities climbed to $13 billion (as reported by SoCal Edison and Pacific Gas & Electric) and they were teetering on the brink of bankruptcy before the state fashioned a plan to keep the power on. Under the terms of that plan, California borrowed $10 billion to tide the utilities through, with California taxpayers responsible for repaying this added debt. All in all, the decision by California lawmakers to hold electricity rates below the market equilibrium price turned out to be a very costly proposition for the very customers they sought to protect.

The restructuring of the electricity industry toward more competition is not just a California event. About half of the states are currently active in this effort, with electricity deregulation moving from the planning stage to reality in state after state. The experience of California, one of the first to deregulate, will be remembered and analyzed for what can be learned. The most vivid memory is sure to be of the electricity shortages. We must remember one more thing: price ceilings cause shortages.

Thinking Critically

1. Californians wound up paying a high "price" because the state held down the price of electricity. Explain.

2. California's tough environmental regulations were a factor in preventing the construction of new power plants in California in the 1990s. The result is that California wound up importing more of its power from elsewhere. Explain how that decision might or might not have been efficient. If the tough regulations were inefficient, why would California have imposed them?

Visit www.prenhall.com/ayers for updates and web exercises on this Explore & Apply topic.

SUMMARY AND LEARNING OBJECTIVES

1. **Interpret how demand represents marginal benefit and supply represents marginal cost.**
   - Marginal benefit equals the incremental value associated with the consumption of additional units of a good. The marginal benefit of any unit of a good is measured by how much consumers are willing to pay for it, as shown by their demand curves. The demand curve slopes downward, indicating the marginal benefit of additional consumption decreases.
   - Marginal cost equals the incremental cost associated with producing additional units of a good. The marginal cost is equivalent to the price required to induce a producer to supply a particular quantity. The supply curve slopes upward, depicting the increase in marginal cost that occurs as more units of output are produced.

2. **Explain the concept of social surplus and how it is divided between consumers and producers.**
   - Social surplus is the sum of consumer surplus and producer surplus.
   - Consumer surplus is the difference between the market price and the price that consumers are willing to pay. The total amount of consumer surplus is shown as a triangular area bounded by the market price and the demand curve.
   - Producer surplus is the difference between the market price and the price that producers would be willing to receive in order to sell their goods. Producer surplus is represented by the triangular area bounded by the market price and the supply curve.
   - Because social surplus is the sum of consumer and producer surplus, social surplus is also represented by a triangular area. This area is bounded by the demand curve and the supply curve.

   - A price that deviates from the equilibrium price will create a deadweight loss, which represents the loss of social surplus.
   - The paradox of diamonds and water is that the price of water, a necessity, is less than the price of diamonds. The paradox is resolved by recognizing that price reveals only marginal benefit. The consumer surplus from water is higher than from diamonds.

3. **Demonstrate how both exports and imports increase efficiency while simultaneously harming either consumers or producers.**
   - Exports occur when a country's domestic price of a good is below the world price of that good.
   - Imports occur when a country's domestic price of a good is above the world price of the good.
   - When a country opens its doors to trade, its domestic prices are replaced by world prices for traded goods.
   - Imports increase a country's social surplus. The bulk of the increase goes to consumers since consumer surplus increases with the consumption of imports, but producer surplus shrinks because of cuts in domestic production.
   - Exports also increase a country's social surplus. The bulk of the increase goes to producers since producer surplus increases with the production of more goods for export. Consumer surplus shrinks because production that is exported cannot be consumed by domestic consumers.

4. **Identify inefficiencies associated with price ceilings.**
   - For the sake of equity, government often seeks to change free-market prices. Unfortunately, because

price signals are basic to how markets operate, changing these signals sacrifices market efficiency.

- Anti-gouging laws are examples of price ceilings. Price ceilings hold price below the market equilibrium, resulting in shortages. Market quantity will be less than the equilibrium quantity, which is also the efficient quantity. The lower the price ceiling is set by government, the greater the shortage that results.

- Rent controls are an example of a price ceiling. A number of cities around the world have enacted rent control legislation, although a number of these laws have been repealed in the United States recently. When rent controls are present, the incentive to provide new rental housing is reduced.

- Housing vouchers are an alternative to rent controls. Housing vouchers avoid the shortages created by rent controls, but require that government set aside money for the vouchers.

5. Show why price supports are unnecessary and potentially counterproductive.

- When a price is kept higher than the market equilibrium price because of a government price floor, also called a price support, the result is a surplus in which production rises and consumption falls. The higher the price floor, the greater the surplus.

- Black markets are a response to price ceilings. Black markets are illegal, but arise anyway when price ceilings are present. Goods are sold in black markets at or above their market equilibrium prices.

- Minimum wage laws are another example of price floors. Minimum wages that are set above the market equilibrium wage decrease the quantity demanded of labor while increasing the quantity supplied of labor. The result is that minimum wage laws create unemployment.

- Educational subsidies provide many of the same benefits as the minimum wage. Educational opportunities reduce the ranks of low-skilled workers by shifting the supply of low-skilled labor to the left. The shift in supply increases the wages of the remaining low-skilled workers. In this way educational subsidies increase the wages of low-skilled workers without creating unemployment.

- When surpluses or shortages are present because of price ceilings and supports, markets are not efficient.

6. Pinpoint the economic flaw in California's deregulation of electricity.

- The flaw involved price ceilings. Rising fuel prices increased the wholesale price of electricity just as California was deregulating the market for wholesale electricity. Rather than being allowed to pass on their price increases, electric utilities serving consumers were forced to hold rates down because of government imposed price controls. The result was shortages of electricity and accompanying power outages.

KEY TERMS

price signals, 80	deadweight loss, 85	housing vouchers, 90
marginal benefit, 80	price ceiling, 89	price gouging, 90
consumer surplus, 81	rent controls, 89	price floor (price support), 92
producer surplus, 82	transfer payments, 89	minimum wage, 93
social surplus, 83	search costs, 89	black market, 96

TEST YOURSELF

TRUE OR FALSE

1. Consumer surplus is greater for diamonds than for water.
2. For an economy to be efficient, it must eliminate producer surplus.
3. A price ceiling set below the market equilibrium price results in a shortage.
4. Rent controls provide a good way to fight discrimination in housing.
5. Consumers in the United States have more food on their tables than they would without agricultural price supports.

MULTIPLE CHOICE

6. If Yvette would be willing to pay up to $10 for one gizmo, up to $8 for a second, and up to $6 for a third, and the price of gizmos is $6 apiece, then Yvette's consumer surplus totals
   a. $24.
   b. $18.
   c. $6.
   d. $4.

7. Efficiency requires that
   a. total consumer surplus equal zero.
   b. market prices be fair.
   c. marginal social benefit equal marginal social cost.
   d. people buy low and sell high.

8. The benefits of price ceilings are received by
   a. consumers able to buy the product.
   b. producers able to sell the product.
   c. all consumers.
   d. all producers.

9. If the government places a price ceiling of $1.20 on a good with an equilibrium price of $1.00, then
   a. there will be a shortage of the good.
   b. there will be a surplus of the good.
   c. neither a surplus nor a shortage will occur.
   d. if demand for the good decreases, the government will not let the price go below $1.00.

10. Over time, rent controls that remain in place lead to
    a. increased renovation of old apartments.
    b. a greater ability for tenants to move to the best apartment for their needs.
    c. increasingly severe housing shortages.
    d. rents that are higher than they would be if the controls were to be removed.

11. Housing vouchers offer an alternative to rent controls by
    a. ensuring that landlords keep their word to keep rents low.
    b. giving prospective tenants the ability to pay higher rents.
    c. setting up detailed standards landlords must adhere to in order to qualify for permits to offer rental units.
    d. constructing new, low-rent public housing on government-owned land.

12. Anti-gouging laws that keep prices of essentials low in times of emergency are likely to
    a. be efficient.
    b. lead to surpluses.
    c. lead to shortages.
    d. distribute the available goods fairly.

13. Ticket scalping is most likely to be
    a. neither efficient nor equitable.
    b. equitable, but not efficient unless on-line auctioning is banned.
    c. efficient, but of questionable equity.
    d. both efficient and equitable, but very unfair.

14. Of the following, the best example of a black market is
    a. the sale of secondhand furniture at a used-furniture shop.
    b. a mail-order purchase of a computer.
    c. renting an apartment for more than the rent-controlled price.
    d. discriminating against minority applicants for a job opening.

15. A price floor placed on a good is a _____ that will normally result in a _____.
    a. maximum price; shortage
    b. maximum price; surplus
    c. minimum price; shortage
    d. minimum price; surplus

16. Compared to a free-market equilibrium, agricultural price supports have the effect of
    a. increasing both the quantities supplied and demanded.
    b. decreasing both the quantities supplied and demanded.
    c. increasing the quantity supplied and decreasing the quantity demanded.
    d. decreasing the quantity supplied and increasing the quantity demanded.

17. Which of the following is NOT a way that governments dispose of agricultural surpluses?
    a. Let the surpluses rot in storage.
    b. Sell the surpluses to purchasers in the marketplace, without restrictions on the use or resale of the commodities involved.
    c. Give the surpluses away in an unappealing form to the poor.
    d. Give the surpluses to needy countries that are unable to afford enough food.

18. If the minimum wage is set below the equilibrium market wage, the effect will be
    a. a surplus of labor.
    b. neither a surplus nor a shortage of labor.
    c. unemployment of labor.
    d. higher wages.

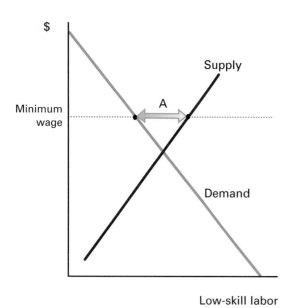

SELF-TEST FIGURE 4-1

19. In Self-Test Figure 4-1, the two-headed arrow labeled *A* represents the
    a. surplus of labor caused by the minimum wage.
    b. shortage of labor caused by the minimum wage.
    c. inefficiency of the minimum wage.
    d. efficiency of the minimum wage.
20. Minimum wage laws would most likely DECREASE
    a. the number of homeless people without jobs.
    b. opportunities for the least employable to gain job experience.
    c. discrimination in the job market.
    d. wages paid for low-skilled labor.
21. The reason California suffered from a shortage of electricity in 2001 is fundamentally because of
    a. insufficient regulation by the state.
    b. too many people.
    c. antiquated power lines.
    d. price controls on retail electricity.

QUESTIONS AND PROBLEMS

1. *[consumer surplus]* Compute consumer surplus in the market for pails of water, described in Figure 3-9.
2. *[consumer surplus]* Of all the purchases you have made in the last three months, which one has given you the largest amount of consumer surplus? State the amount of consumer surplus by subtracting what you paid for the item from the amount you would have been willing to pay.
3. *[social surplus]* Using a supply and demand graph, illustrate the area of social surplus. Explain how the area of social surplus can be broken down into two parts, the areas of consumer and producer surplus.
4. *[efficient output]* Is the efficient output equal to the equilibrium output? Explain.
5. *[diamonds and water]* Why is water so much cheaper than diamonds, when water is so much more important to human life?
6. *[imports and exports]* When the world price of a good is less than what a country's price would be without trade, will the country import or export the good? Will the country produce any of the good itself? Will it gain from trade? Explain, using a graph as part of your explanation.
7. *[imports and exports]* When the world price of a good is more than what a country's price would be without trade, will the country import or export the good? Will the country produce any of the good itself? Will it gain from trade? Explain, using a graph as part of your explanation.

8. *[price ceiling]* For a ceiling price to have any effect in a competitive market, must it be set above or below the equilibrium price? Explain by drawing two graphs. The first graph should show the ceiling price above the equilibrium price; the second graph should show the ceiling price below the equilibrium price. Each graph should be accompanied by an explanation noting the effects of the price ceiling in that graph.
9. *[efficient quantity; price ceiling]* Using the data provided in the accompanying table, fill in the last column and then provide answers to the following questions.

Price	Quantity Demanded	Quantity Supplied	Surplus (+) or Shortage (−)
$12	7	9	
11	8	8	
10	9	7	
9	10	6	
8	11	5	
7	12	4	

   a. What is the efficient quantity?
   b. What price results in the efficient quantity?
   c. Suppose a price ceiling of $8 is established. Does a surplus or shortage result? What is the amount of the surplus or shortage?
   d. Suppose a price ceiling of $7 is established. Describe its effect.

e. Suppose a price ceiling of $11 is established. What is its effect?

f. Suppose a price ceiling of $12 is established. Why does it have no effect?

10. *[efficiency versus equity]* Comment on the efficiency and equity aspects of ticket scalping.

11. *[price ceilings]* Do price ceilings increase or decrease social surplus? Explain.

12. *[rent controls]* Rent controls lower rents for those lucky enough to have apartments. However, there are several problems. List three inefficiencies of rent control.

13. *[price floors]* For a price floor to have any effect in a competitive market, must it be set above or below the equilibrium price? Explain by drawing two graphs. The first graph should show the price support above the equilibrium price; the second graph should show the price support below the equilibrium price. Each graph should be accompanied by an explanation noting the effects of the price support in that graph.

14. *[price floors]* Do price floors increase or decrease consumer surplus? Explain.

15. *[price floor]* Using the data in question #9, what would be the effect of a price floor set at a price of $8? What would be the effect of a price floor set at a price of $11? What would be the effect of a price floor set at a price of $12? Since the goal of a price floor is to increase the income of producers, which price(s) in the data table would logically be chosen as a floor price?

16. *[minimum wage]* Is the minimum wage law an example of a price ceiling or a price floor? Explain.

17. *[minimum wage]* Minimum wage laws are an American tradition. Although the laws seem caring and do raise wages for minimum wage labor, there are many problems. List five problems caused by minimum wage laws and briefly indicate why each occurs. Why are minimum wage laws so popular?

18. *[black markets]* What is a black market? Explain why black markets might arise as a consequence of price controls, but not as a consequence of price supports. What function do black markets perform? Are black markets legal?

 Visit www.prenhall.com/ayers for Exploring the Web exercises and additional self-test quizzes.

CHAPTER 5

MEASURING NATIONAL OUTPUT

A LOOK AHEAD

If we as a society are to achieve our macroeconomic goals, we'd best have ways of measuring our successes and failures. Government collects and makes available to anyone who is interested a vast amount of statistical information about our economy. This chapter starts with the measurement of the nation's aggregate output. Statistics on aggregate output provide a revealing glimpse of the health of the whole economy.

Accurate statistics can help paint a clear picture of the economy—where it's been, where it's at now, and where it's going. Statistics on the aggregate economy also guide decision makers in government as they allocate funds to education, defense, healthcare, and other government programs. It turns out that the data used by Congress are often wrong, and wrong in a way that is obvious to its members. The Explore & Apply section at the end of this chapter discusses how the use of the wrong numbers by Congress can make sense.

LEARNING OBJECTIVES

Understanding Chapter 5 will enable you to:
1. **Present three widely accepted goals for the economy.**
2. **Define gross domestic product (GDP) and discuss its components.**
3. **Distinguish real GDP from nominal GDP.**
4. **Track the stages of the business cycle.**
5. **Identify the advantages and disadvantages of static and dynamic scoring.**

EXPLORE & APPLY

Macroeconomics deals with the economy as a whole. The millions of individual microeconomic decisions of people, businesses, and government in their totality represent the nation's economy. Everyone thus influences the economy at least a little bit, and the performance of the economy likewise affects everyone.

5.1 MACROECONOMIC GOALS

Economic growth, full employment, and low inflation are the three primary goals of macro policy. Economic growth occurs when the economy's total output of goods and services increases. Higher living standards are a by-product of economic growth. In effect, growth enlarges the economic pie, allowing many people bigger slices. Table 5-1 shows a handful of the many ways in which the United States standard of living has improved. Economic growth in the United States has promoted changes in our living standards that range from greater computer ownership to greater life expectancy. Because the wealth of our nation increases as a consequence of economic growth, more of us are able to own our homes, go to college, and access the Internet.

An economy grows because of increases in available resources and improvements in technology. Economists usually believe that the economy can sustain a long-term growth rate of about 2.5 percent per year. Strong economic growth in the late 1990s offered hope that the U.S. economy is capable of growing faster than previously believed possible. Because of that strong growth, some optimists argue that a sustained growth rate of as much as 5 percent is possible. Over the long run, differences in the economy's growth rate can make a large difference in living standards. It would take about 29 years for aggregate output to double at a 2.5 percent growth rate, but only half that time in the more optimistic case of 5 percent annual growth.

Doubling times, such as that for aggregate output, can be estimated using the *rule of seventy-two*. Whatever the percentage growth rate of a variable is, dividing that number into 72 will reveal the approximate doubling time. For example, a 5 percent growth rate means that output doubles about every 14.4 years, because 72/5 equals 14.4.

In reality, economic growth does not occur smoothly. The economy surges and stumbles at periodic intervals. These ups and downs in the growth of output sometimes put the economy above, and other times below, its long-run sustainable growth rate.

High employment is a major goal of public policy. When economic growth falls short, unemployment is usually the result. Concerns over unemployment motivate economists to develop macro models designed to help us better understand its causes and identify policies to achieve full employment. In subsequent chapters you will study some of these models.

Inflation **is a sustained rise in the general price level.** Inflation is usually expressed in terms of the *inflation rate*, the annual percentage increase in the general level of prices. Policymakers in government seek to preserve the value of money by keeping the inflation rate low. In practice, the economy has experienced some inflation every year since 1955. Annual inflation reached a peak of 13.5 percent in 1980 before declining sharply after that. By 2001, the inflation rate had fallen to slightly less than 3 percent. When the inflation rate is low and stable, history shows that public concern over inflation subsides. However, even a seemingly low inflation rate, such as 3 percent, would cause the price level to double in about 24 years. If inflation were to reach 10 percent today, and stay at that rate permanently, it would take a little more than 7 years for the price level to double. Seven more years after that, the price level would have doubled again, and so forth. Such behavior of the price level explains why increases in the inflation rate merit concern, especially for people living on fixed incomes.

TABLE 5-1	EFFECTS OF GROWTH: SELECTED CHANGES IN THE U.S. STANDARD OF LIVING

INDICATOR, YEARS COMPARED, AND INDICATOR VALUES

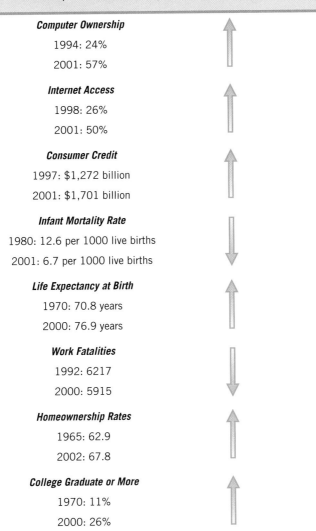

Computer Ownership

1994: 24%

2001: 57%

Internet Access

1998: 26%

2001: 50%

Consumer Credit

1997: $1,272 billion

2001: $1,701 billion

Infant Mortality Rate

1980: 12.6 per 1000 live births

2001: 6.7 per 1000 live births

Life Expectancy at Birth

1970: 70.8 years

2000: 76.9 years

Work Fatalities

1992: 6217

2000: 5915

Homeownership Rates

1965: 62.9

2002: 67.8

College Graduate or More

1970: 11%

2000: 26%

Sources: Various publications of U.S. government agencies, including the *Statistical Abstract of the United States.*

5.2 MEASURING NATIONAL OUTPUT

From the earliest days of American history, the government has kept statistical records. As the economy has grown larger and more complex, the importance of keeping track of the economy has increased. Policymakers rely on government data to design policies that will improve economic performance and help achieve the macro goals of economic growth, full employment, and low inflation.

The value of goods and services produced is the single most important measure of the nation's output. According to the circular flow of income, the value of national output must be identical to the value of national income. This equality occurs because every dollar that buyers spend on output represents income to the sellers of that output as depicted in the circular flow model shown in Chapter 2.

The economy's output of goods and services is diverse, running the gamut from A to Z, including the proverbial kitchen sink. One way to measure output is to classify the goods and services produced according to who is purchasing the output. To this end, purchases are classified by dividing the economy into four sectors, each identified with a different type of purchaser. These are the household, business, government, and foreign sectors. Each unit of output eventually finds its way to one of these sectors. The output is valued at *market value,* which is measured by market prices (the prices paid by the purchasers). Apples, oranges, the kitchen sink, and all other goods and services are valued by the common dollar-denominated yardstick of market prices.

gross domestic product (GDP) the market value of the final goods and services produced in the economy within some time period, usually one quarter or one year.

Output is measured by tallying the market value of *final goods and services*—those that are sold to their final owners. The most widely reported measure of the economy's output is **gross domestic product (GDP),** the market value of the final goods and services produced in the economy within some time period, usually one quarter or one year. Spending on *intermediate goods*—goods used to make other goods—is not included in GDP so as to avoid counting the same output twice. For instance, a new Ford Focus purchased by a consumer includes a new battery and tires as standard equipment. Since the total value of the Focus includes the value of these and other input components, the values of the new Focus and its inputs should not be counted separately. While the value of the Focus is included in GDP, the values of the battery, tires, and other intermediate goods are not included in GDP. On the other hand, replacement batteries and tires are counted because they are purchased by their final users. For this reason, GDP includes expenditures by car owners who replace their old tires and batteries with new ones from Sears, Wal-Mart, AutoZone, and other retailers.

In order to track spending in different parts of the economy, GDP is measured as the sum of spending on output by households, businesses, government, and the rest of the world. Thus, we turn our attention now to consumption spending, investment, government purchases, and the effect of foreign commerce on GDP. This way of looking at GDP is termed the *expenditures approach.* Another approach, the *incomes approach,* measures GDP as the sum of wages, rent, interest, and profit. The incomes approach is discussed in the Appendix to this chapter.

CONSUMPTION

consumption spending purchasing by households; makes up the majority of GDP spending.

Purchasing by households comprises **consumption spending**. Household spending makes up the majority of spending in the U.S. economy, generally close to 70 percent of total spending. This spending may be on services or on consumer durable or nondurable goods. Nondurable goods are consumed quickly, by definition in one year or less. Food is an example. Durable goods have an expected life span of more than one year, such as automobiles. Note that the purchases of new houses by consumers are included in investment spending, as explained below.

INVESTMENT

investment spending now in order to increase output or productivity later; includes spending on capital, new housing, and changes in business inventories.

Investment—spending now in order to increase output or productivity later—is the most variable component of GDP over time. Although there are many forms of investment, such as a college student's investment in the human capital provided by an education, GDP statistics record only three measurable types:

- Purchases by firms of **capital,** such as new factories and machines.
- Consumers' purchases of **new housing,** a form of consumer capital.
- The market value of the **change in business inventories** of unsold goods.

Purchases of capital allow firms the opportunity to increase their future outputs of goods and services. As such, a pickup truck purchased by a firm is counted as an investment. If that same truck had been purchased by you for your personal use, it would have been included in consumption. New homes are included under investment because they provide an ongoing stream of housing services over many years. In that sense the purchase of a new house is an investment.

To see why the change in business inventories is included as an investment, consider an increase in inventories. Inventories increase when firms deliberately produce more than they can immediately sell. Inventories also increase when demand falls short of firms' estimates, as when the economy slows down. Inventory investment is different from investment in capital in that an increase in inventories may be unintended. Nonetheless, accumulations of inventory represent investment because they allow for increased sales in the future. When goods in inventory are sold, inventory investment shows a decrease and other spending an equivalent increase.

Investment may be measured as either gross or net. **Gross investment** is the total amount of investment that takes place. Gross investment by private sector firms, *gross private domestic investment,* is the measure of investment used to compute GDP. It usually amounts to between 15 and 18 percent of GDP. **Net investment** is gross investment minus depreciation. Because plants and machines wear out or become technologically obsolete, net investment will be less than gross investment. A positive value for net investment measures the increase in the economy's productive capacity. A negative value for net investment means that depreciation exceeded the total amount of investment, which implies that the productive capacity of the economy declines. When the focus is on net investment, **net domestic product (NDP)** is a more appropriate measure than GDP. NDP equals GDP minus depreciation.

gross investment the total amount of investment.

net investment gross investment minus depreciation.

net domestic product (NDP) gross domestic product minus depreciation.

ARE DISASTERS GOOD FOR THE ECONOMY?

S N A P S H O T

Hurricanes, floods, and earthquakes are good for the economy, right? After all, they force people to spend more, which increases output. Isn't an increase in output a reason to rejoice?

Clearly, something is amiss with this reasoning. What is the key to understanding this faulty logic? Spending on additions to our stock of goods and services increases living standards. However, spending that follows natural disasters merely replaces goods in order to bring living standards back to some semblance of their former levels. ◄

GOVERNMENT PURCHASES

Governments at the federal, state, and local levels accounted for about 18 percent of the total purchasing of goods and services in the U.S. economy in 2001. Although estimates are

QUICKCHECK

What would a value of net investment equal to zero say about the economy's ability to produce goods and services?

Answer: Net investment equal to zero implies that the economy's productive capacity did not grow. The investment that occurred merely replaced depreciated capital. For example, if 100 machines wore out during the year, net investment equal to zero means that the 100 machines were replaced, and the total number of working machines remained constant.

imprecise, perhaps one-tenth of government purchasing could be classified as investment. Examples of government investment include new highways and other infrastructure, such as government-owned buildings, including schools, offices, and airports. Government also pays for social services provided by teachers, social workers, parole officers, and others. These are civilian goods and services. Defense goods, such as tanks, missiles, and the services of military personnel, are also purchased.

Government *transfer payments,* such as Social Security and unemployment benefits, are received by individuals who do not provide goods and services in return. **Government purchases and investment should be distinguished from government transfer payments. The latter are not included in the computation of GDP.** In Figure 5-1, transfer payments are contrasted to government expenditures that count toward GDP. The figure shows that transfer payments have become increasingly important over time. To the extent that transfer payments are used by the households that receive them to buy goods and services, they are counted as consumption spending. Through this backdoor route, the dollars received as transfers do ultimately contribute to GDP.

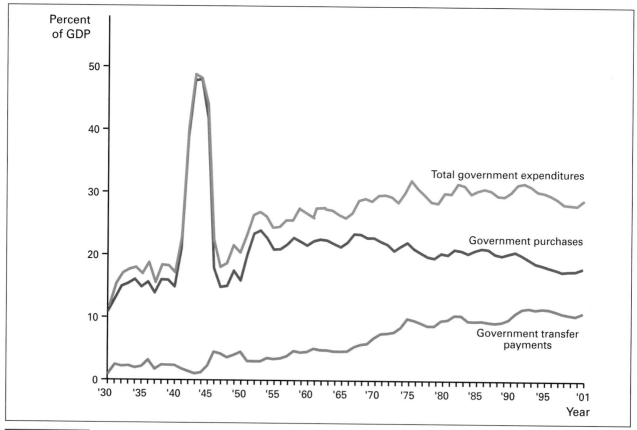

FIGURE 5-1

GOVERNMENT PURCHASES VERSUS GOVERNMENT TRANSFER PAYMENTS Government expenditures take two forms: purchases and transfer payments. When the government purchases goods and services GDP increases. However, transfer payments do not represent payments for production, and are not counted toward GDP. As a percentage of GDP, transfer payments have risen significantly over time, while government purchases are back to what they were at the start of the 1950s. The spike seen in the 1940s was caused by World War II.

Source: Computed from National Income and Products Account data.

Are each of the following included in computing U.S. GDP?
1. New Corvettes built in Bowling Green, Kentucky?
2. New Honda Accords produced in Marysville, Ohio?
3. New Accords produced in Japan, but purchased by U.S. residents?
4. New Ford cars produced in Ford plants in Great Britain and purchased by residents of Britain?

Answers: (1) Yes, although the value of any imported components would be subtracted. (2) Yes, since the nameplate or ownership of the company does not matter. As in (1), the value of imported engines, transmissions, or other components are not part of U.S. GDP. (3) No. Japanese-built Accords purchased by American consumers are an import. Recall that imports are subtracted from exports in the calculation of GDP. (4) No. U.S. GDP measures U.S. production, not production by U.S. firms in other countries.

NET EXPORTS

Some of the output produced by the economy is purchased by foreigners in the form of exports. Exports should be included when GDP is computed because they represent goods and services produced. However, consideration of the role of foreign commerce on GDP must not stop there. Because a portion of spending by U.S. consumers, businesses, and government is on imports, it is necessary to subtract imports from exports in order to compute GDP. In other words, a part of consumption spending, investment, and government purchases is on goods not produced in the United States. The value of these imports should not be counted in GDP.

Exports minus imports defines *net exports.* It is the value of net exports that goes into GDP. A negative value for net exports means that spending on imports is greater than spending on exports; a positive figure means that spending on imports is less than spending on exports. The value of net exports varies from year to year, but has been negative for many years. For example, in 2001, exports equaled $1.03 trillion, about 10.2 percent of GDP. Imports equaled $1.38 trillion, about 13.7 percent of GDP. Net exports were thus equal to −$0.35 trillion, about −3.5 percent of GDP.

net exports exports minus imports.

5.3 GROSS DOMESTIC PRODUCT—A CLOSER LOOK

We have just examined the four kinds of spending that, when added together, sum to GDP:

■ Consumption spending
■ Gross investment
■ Government purchases
■ Net exports

Let's show GDP as the sum of these in an equation, and then show their values in 2001, in trillions of dollars. The percentage each item contributes to GDP is shown in parentheses. The percentages shown are rounded, which is why they do not sum to 100 percent. Figure 5-2 illustrates the components of GDP graphically. Figure 5-3 shows their behavior over time.

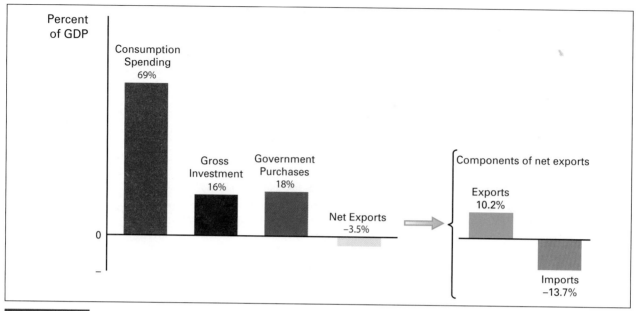

FIGURE 5-2

THE FOUR COMPONENTS OF GDP GDP equals the sum of the four categories of spending. Net exports equals the value of exports minus the value of imports. Net exports have a negative value because the value of imports outweighs the value of exports, as shown.

Source: Bureau of Economic Analysis, *National Income and Product Account Tables,* Table 1.1.

$$\underset{\substack{\$10.1}}{\text{GDP}} = \underset{\substack{+\ \$6.99 \\ (69\%)}}{\text{Consumption spending}} + \underset{\substack{+\ \$1.59 \\ (16\%)}}{\text{Gross investment}} + \underset{\substack{+\ \$1.86 \\ (18\%)}}{\text{Government purchases}} + \underset{\substack{-\ \$0.35 \\ (-3.5\%)}}{\text{Net exports}}$$

Note that net exports enters the equation with a minus sign because exports were less than imports.

There are other features of GDP that should be noted. One is that only private sector investment is counted in gross investment, since government investment is counted in government's contribution to GDP. Gross investment includes U.S. investment spending by foreign citizens as well as by U.S. citizens. Thus, if a citizen of France purchases a new condominium in New York City, the transaction enters GDP through investment. However, if this same person purchases U.S.-made business machines and ships them to France, the transaction enters GDP through net exports.

Per capita GDP is GDP per person. The total U.S. GDP in 2001 is seen to be $10.1 trillion ($10,082,200,000,000—a trillion is a million millions or a one followed by twelve zeros). This number is more easily placed into perspective when divided by the U.S. population that year of 284,796,887 people. Performing that division, we see that per capita GDP for 2001 was $35,401. This is the amount of output produced that each person would receive if output were divided equally among every person living in the United States, whether adult or child.

GDP AS VALUE ADDED

As an alternative to the expenditures approach, **GDP may also be viewed as the sum of values added in the economy.** Each firm takes inputs of materials and intermediate goods and

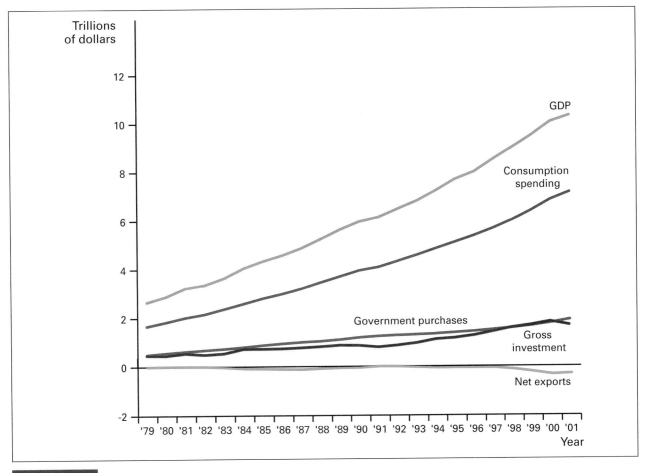

FIGURE 5-3

TRACKING GDP AND ITS COMPONENTS OVER TIME GDP is the sum of the four components shown in the figure: consumption spending, gross investment, government purchases, and net exports.

Source: 2002 Economic Report of the President, Table B-1; and Bureau of Labor Statistics, *National Income and Product Accounts Tables,* Table 1.1. Data are nominal values, meaning they have not been adjusted for price changes.

increases their value through the firm's production process. **Value added** equals the revenue from the sale of output minus the cost of purchased inputs.

value added the difference between revenue and the cost of purchased inputs.

Let's examine the computation of value added by looking at the steps in the production of a single jar of dill pickles. A seed company produces cucumber seeds that are sold to a farmer. Suppose it takes 30 cents worth of seeds to grow the cucumbers in a jar of dill pickles. Assuming the seed company buys no intermediate goods, this initial step generates 30 cents of value added by the seed company. The farmer who purchases the 30 cents worth of seeds subsequently sells the resulting cucumber crop to a pickle maker for $1.00. The farmer has added value equal to 70 cents. The pickle maker sells the pickles it produces to a supermarket for $1.50, and in so doing contributes another 50 cents in value added. When the supermarket sells the pickles to shoppers for $2.25 a jar, which is the market value of a jar of pickles, an additional 75 cents is contributed toward value added.

FIGURE 5-4

VALUE ADDED Value added is the firm's revenue minus the cost of the inputs it purchases from other firms. Jars of pickles sell for their market value, $2.25. Since pickles are a final good, GDP increases by $2.25 for each jar of pickles produced. Of the $2.25 in total value added, the seed company contributed 30 cents for supplying the seeds, the farmer 70 cents for growing the cucumbers, the pickle maker 50 cents for making the pickles, and the supermarket 75 cents for selling the pickles.

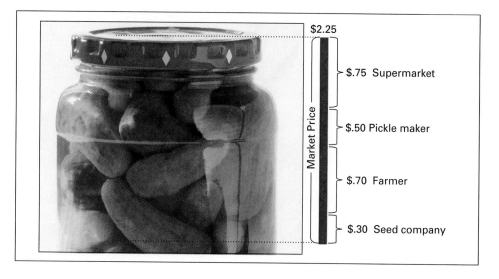

The $2.25 market value of the jar of pickles represents the value of the production of a final good, since that is the sum of money spent by consumers who will eat the dill pickles in question. The spending of the $2.25 on each jar of pickles is spending on a final good that increases GDP by that amount. This $2.25 worth of GDP can be computed by summing the values added at each step of production:

Increase in GDP from production of a jar of pickles = $0.30 + $0.70 + $0.50 + $0.75 = $2.25

Figure 5-4 illustrates the computation of value added for this example.

CONTRASTING GDP TO GNP

Until 1992, the chief measure of the economy's output was *gross national product (GNP)*. GNP differs from GDP in that the value added to production by resources located outside the United States, but owned by U.S. citizens, is counted in GNP. Unlike GDP, GNP excludes value added within the United States by foreign-owned resources. Typically, U.S. GDP and GNP differ by less than 1 percent, so that either can be used to evaluate the performance of the economy. Table 5-2 shows the relationship between GDP and GNP, using data from 2001. Other measures of an economy's output and the income created by the production of output are discussed in the Appendix to this chapter.

TABLE 5-2   ADJUSTMENTS TO GDP TO OBTAIN GNP

Gross domestic product in 2001 (billions of dollars)	$10,082.2
Plus: Income received from the rest of the world	316.9
Minus: Income payments to the rest of the world	295.0
Equals: Gross national product	10,104.1

Source: Bureau of Economic Analysis, *National Income and Product Account Tables,* Table 1.9.

Let's consider an example where the value of production would be included in U.S. GNP, but not U.S. GDP. Holden cars and light trucks are produced in Australia by Holden, Ltd., whose parent company is U.S. auto giant General Motors. Holden's income in the form of profit represents income earned by U.S.-owned resources. Thus, Holden is an example of a firm located in another country that contributes to U.S. GNP, as recorded in the second line in Table 5-2, *Income received from the rest of the world.*

Just as U.S. firms own factories in other countries, foreign companies also own factories in the United States. Consider American Honda Motor Company, owned by Honda of Japan. A company factory in Marysville, Ohio, produces Honda Accords sold in the United States. Earnings from the production of this factory and other Honda facilities located in the United States are examples of value added that is included in U.S. GDP. This value added must be subtracted from U.S. GDP when U.S. GNP is computed, as recorded in the third line in Table 5-2, *Income payments to the rest of the world.*

INTERPRETING GDP—THE UNDERGROUND ECONOMY, HOUSEHOLD PRODUCTION, AND INTANGIBLES

The value of many of the goods and services produced in our economy goes unreported in the GDP statistics. Market transactions that go unreported make up the **underground economy.** Some of these goods and services are illegal. For example, while a drugstore's sales of prescription medications are included in GDP, the crack cocaine sales of a drug dealer are not. The underground economy includes other goods and services that, while not illegal, are not reported to government so that their producers can avoid paying taxes. In sum, the existence of an underground economy means that GDP understates the economy's true output.

underground economy market transactions that go unreported to government.

The government's statisticians ignore some output deliberately, because they don't know how to place a value on it. For example, GDP does not include the value of *household production,* which is the production of goods and services for use within the household. So, if you cook your own dinner tonight, the value of that service does not appear in GDP. But if you eat out, the value does. That's because there is a market price for a restaurant meal but not for a home-cooked meal. As a result, if all married couples were to divorce and pay one another for their household services, GDP would skyrocket despite the economy not actually producing any more than it had before.

GDP is often used as a proxy for our well-being. This practice is convenient, but can also be misleading. For example, just looking at GDP, it might be hard to fathom how anyone could be nostalgic for the past. After all, GDP is up, and so is the variety of goods and services we can buy. Yet, there is more to life, including *intangibles* that cannot be measured easily. Unmeasured intangibles of value include simplicity, love, freedom, harmony, neighborliness, and many other qualities. On the downside, intangibles include pollution, loneliness, and traffic congestion.

Then there are the things that are measured, but that do not actually indicate that the people are better off. For example, increases in military spending increase GDP, but do nothing to increase a country's welfare above what it had been in the past if the spending is in response to heightened dangers in the world. Likewise, increased spending on cigarettes adds to GDP in the same way as increased spending on healthcare made necessary by previous smoking. It would be useful to have a single *measure of economic welfare* that could take into account the effects of intangibles on our overall standard of living. Although economists and social scientists have tried to develop such a measure, their efforts have failed to lead to a widely accepted alternative to GDP itself.

SHHH! WANT A ROLEX? HOW ABOUT A "HONEY DO"?

While it is obviously difficult to measure illegal activity, estimates place the underground economy at from 3 percent to 15 percent of total economic activity in the United States. Other countries see even higher percentages. As a general rule, the more burdensome a country's taxes and regulations, the larger its underground economy.

Most people think that the underground economy consists of prohibited goods and services, such as drugs and prostitution, along with stolen or counterfeit items. Yes, that Rolex watch being hawked on the street corner is probably fake or stolen. But there is much more. A significant portion of the underground economy consists of legal goods that are sold off the record in order to avoid taxes or regulatory requirements.

Examples of this type of underground activity include toxic wastes illegally dumped, workers illegally employed, goods sold without the collection of sales taxes, and services sold without required paperwork. Yes, the underground economy may even include that friendly handyman willing to take on the "honey-do-this, honey-do-that" odd jobs—no license inspected, no credit cards accepted, and no tax collected. ◀

DISTINGUISHING NOMINAL GDP FROM REAL GDP

Increases in the measured value of a nation's output, its GDP, may occur for two reasons:

■ Because of an increase in the output of goods and services. The more boats, books, beans, and other goods and services the economy produces, the greater will be the value of a country's gross domestic product.

■ As a consequence of price increases in the form of inflation. Inflation artificially "pumps up" the value of gross domestic product. An increase in GDP due solely to price increases does not increase economic welfare since there is no increase in output to make people better off.

In reality, when GDP rises there is usually a mix of both an increase in output and a price increase. Removing the effects of price changes from the value of GDP allows us to identify the changes in output.

nominal GDP GDP that is stated without adjusting for inflation.

real GDP the value of GDP after nominal GDP is adjusted for inflation.

Nominal GDP is the value of GDP expressed in current dollar terms. The nominal value may be thought of as "what you see is what you get." By contrast, **real GDP** adjusts the nominal value of GDP for inflation. Real GDP expresses GDP in terms of a constant value of money—dollars with the same purchasing power.

The *GDP price index*, also called the *GDP chained price index*, is an index of prices that measures price changes over time, linking each year with the next. An increase in the value of the GDP price index over time indicates that the general level of prices has increased. The GDP price index is used to compute real GDP, as follows:

$$\text{Real GDP} = \frac{\text{Nominal GDP}}{\text{GDP price index}} \times 100$$

Table 5-3 shows the values of U.S. nominal GDP and the GDP chained price index for selected years. These data are used to compute the values for real GDP shown in the last column. To see how the computation of real GDP works, let's pick a year, 2001 for example, and compute real GDP. Looking at the table we see that nominal GDP in that year equaled $10.082 trillion. The GDP chained index equaled 109.42. What then is the value of real GDP in 2001? Divide the nominal value by the value of the GDP price index and multiply by 100: ($10.082 ÷ 109.42) × 100. Performing this computation shows the real value of GDP in 2001 to be $9.215 trillion (rounded to the third place following the decimal). You should compute real GDP for additional years, using the values given in the

TABLE 5-3 U.S. NOMINAL AND REAL GROSS DOMESTIC PRODUCT, SELECTED YEARS

SELECTED YEARS	NOMINAL GDP (IN TRILLIONS)	GDP PRICE INDEX (IN CONSTANT 1996 DOLLARS)	REAL GDP (IN TRILLIONS OF 1996 DOLLARS) [NOMINAL GDP/GDP PRICE INDEX]
1961	$0.546	22.43	$2.434
1971	1.129	30.52	3.699
1981	3.131	62.37	5.020
1987	4.742	77.58	6.112
1988	5.108	80.22	6.368
1989	5.489	83.27	6.592
1990	5.803	86.53	6.706
1991	5.986	89.66	6.676
1992	6.319	91.85	6.880
1993	6.642	94.05	7.062
1994	7.054	96.01	7.347
1995	7.401	98.10	7.543
1996	7.813	100	7.813
1997	8.318	101.95	8.160
1998	8.782	103.20	8.510
1999	9.274	104.69	8.859
2000	9.825	106.89	9.192
2001	10.082	109.42	9.215

Source: Adapted from *2002 Economic Report of the President,* Tables B-1 and B-3, and Bureau of Economic Analysis, *National Income and Product Accounts.* Slight variations from the values in the sources may occur because of rounding.

table for nominal GDP and the GDP chained price index, to confirm your ability to perform this calculation. Your computations should be identical to those shown in the last column of Table 5-3.

Let's look more closely at Table 5-3. Observe that the GDP price index column states that the values for this price index are expressed relative to the purchasing power of the dollar in 1996. The arbitrary choice by government statisticians of the year 1996 as a reference point for the chained index has two implications. One is that the real GDP and the nominal GDP have the same value in 1996, as you can see by looking at the table. The second is that picking a particular year as a reference point for the GDP price index allows us to express real GDP in terms of a constant value of money, which in this case is the value of the dollar in 1996. Thus, the column heading for real GDP states that the figures given are expressed in 1996 dollars.

5.4 THE BUSINESS CYCLE—THE UPS AND DOWNS IN ECONOMIC ACTIVITY

Cycles in economic activity have been a feature of economies throughout history. In the twentieth century, the Great Depression of the 1930s stands out as an economic collapse of historic proportions in the United States and other countries around the world. Although most downturns in the economy are mild and short-lived, we still worry about the cyclical nature of our economy.

STAGES OF THE BUSINESS CYCLE

business cycle the uneven sequence of trough, expansion, peak, and recession that the economy follows over time.

recession a sustained decrease in real GDP.

The term **business cycle** refers to the expansions and contractions in economic activity that take place over time. Figure 5-5 shows the stages of a business cycle as a smooth curve. The low point in economic activity is called the *trough.* Following the trough is the *expansion* stage. When the expansion is ready to end, the economy reaches its *peak,* and then falls into **recession** in which real GDP decreases. An especially severe recession is termed a *depression.* Subsequently, another trough will mark the point where the process begins repeating itself.

The economic fluctuations represented by the business cycle are an example of *short-run* features in the economy. The business cycle occurs around an upward trend in real GDP. Economic trends describe persistent features in the economy. Thus, trends describe the *long-run* features of the economy.

FIGURE 5-5

STAGES OF THE BUSINESS CYCLE
The stages of the business cycle are not smooth in reality. The duration and intensity of stages can differ dramatically over time, although the long-run trend is upward.

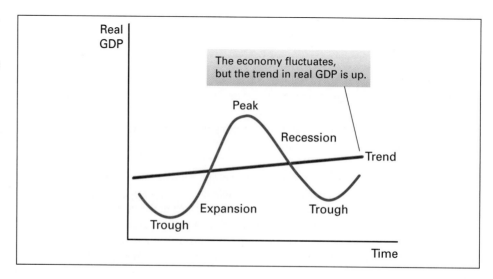

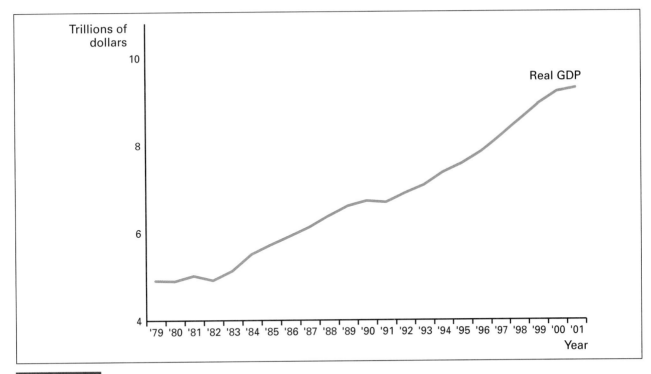

FIGURE 5-6

THE UPWARD TREND OF REAL GDP When real GDP is viewed over many years, the upward trend becomes apparent.

Source: 2002 Economic Report of the President, Table B-2, and Bureau of Economic Analysis, *National Accounts Data.*

In the real world, the ups and downs in the economy do not occur in such a smooth fashion. Expansions typically last much longer and are much stronger than recessions. Thus, the business cycle occurs within the context of a rising trend in real GDP. Figure 5-6 reveals the upward course of GDP over time. Figure 5-7 shows that, since the Great Depression of the 1930s, recessions in the United States have been infrequent, mild, and short lived. None of the post-war recessions has come close to matching the Great Depression in length or magnitude.

Who decides when the economy leaves one stage of the business cycle and enters the next stage? In the United States, that job is not left to government economists, whose judgment might be swayed by political considerations. Instead, an independent organization, the National Bureau of Economic Research (NBER), is entrusted with the dating of business cycle turning points. To accomplish this task, the NBER considers the depth and duration of the downturn, along with the dispersion of its effects throughout the economy.

Because important indicators of the economy, such as GDP, employment, and industrial production, sometimes move opposite to each other, the job of the NBER is a difficult one. In many instances, the NBER will not announce the onset of a recession until it has observed the indicators for months. There are also often delays in dating the beginning of expansions.

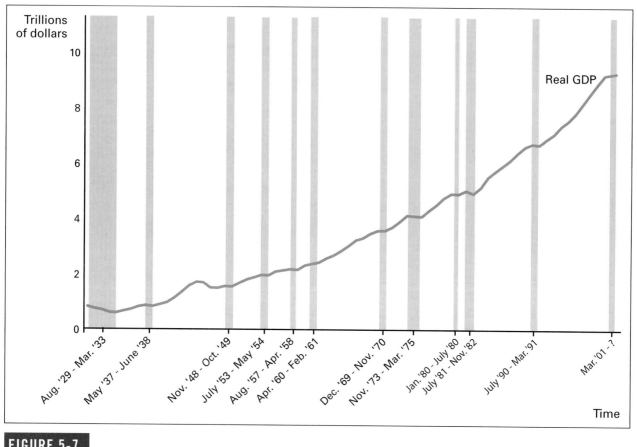

FIGURE 5-7

REAL GDP SINCE 1929 People living during the Great Depression of the 1930s would have found it difficult to agree with the idea that the trend in GDP was upward. In contrast, the ten recessions since the
end of World War II in 1945 have been relatively short and mild, thus reducing public fear that another
Great Depression might occur. Recessions are identified in the graph by the shaded vertical bars.

Source: Bureau of Economic Analysis, *National Accounts Data,* and National Bureau of Economic Research, *Business
Cycle Expansions and Contractions.*

SEASONAL ADJUSTMENTS—HELPING TO ISOLATE CYCLICAL EFFECTS

Many economic variables move either up or down at the same time each year. For example,
construction activity slows down during the winter because of bad weather and picks up
during the warmer months. Retail sales increase during the Christmas season. Agriculture
follows seasonal patterns. Thus, downswings in economic activity do not always indicate
recession, just as upswings do not always signal expansion.

These seasonal effects make it difficult to disentangle actual growth in economic variables from changes in them due to seasonal volatility. That is why most published economic
data are seasonally adjusted, using statistical models. Seasonal adjustments to data help
reveal the underlying trends. For example, when construction activity drops off in January,
the seasonally adjusted data can tell us whether the decline is merely the usual winter slowdown or whether construction is stronger or weaker than usual for that time of year.

Seasonal adjustments can reveal unusual strength or weakness in the economy. For
example, if the seasonal adjustment shows that the January decline in construction activity
is not as sharp as usual, and many other economic measures are also above their seasonal
norms, we have compelling evidence that the economy is expanding.

READING THE INDICATORS—LEADS AND LAGS

There are hundreds of economic indicators capable of illuminating various aspects of the economy. History has shown that some of these indicators, called **leading indicators**, will usually change direction before the economy does. Examples include the index of building permits, housing starts, and manufacturers' new orders for durable goods. These data series and several others are combined to form a composite index of leading indicators, which receives much attention from the media.

leading indicators statistics that are expected to change direction before the economy at large does, thereby indicating where the economy is headed.

Other indicators, the *lagging indicators,* usually change direction only after the economy has already done so. The unemployment rate and expenditures on new plants and equipment are examples. Many indicators change direction about the same time the economy changes direction. These are called *coincident indicators.* Examples include the index of industrial production and the prime interest rate charged by banks.

Investors and businesspeople need predictions about the future in order to plan effectively, which motivates their interest in the leading indicators. Unfortunately, the leading indicators do not always give an accurate prediction of the future direction of the economy, and thus must be used with care.

GLOBAL ECONOMY, YES—GLOBAL RECESSION, WHO COULD KNOW?   *SNAPSHOT*

In 1998, the economies of Asia and the Far East were in turmoil. Indonesia entered a depression. Bad bank loans in Japan caused the lengthy recession there to deepen. The Russian economy teetered on the brink of disaster. In the second half of the year, the U.S. stock market reacted so negatively that investors wondered if the long-feared "bear market" was upon them. President Clinton even called the situation the most dangerous for the world economy in fifty years. Yet, in the following two years, the U.S. economy boomed and the U.S. stock market soared to record heights.

April of 2000 ushered in a different phenomenon. This time it was U.S. stocks that came crashing down from their historic highs, with one major market indicator losing over a quarter of its value in a single week and continuing a generally downward course for over two years. As panic gripped Wall Street, finance ministers from around the world met in Washington to discuss the latest turn of events. Would the tightening financial situation crush developing countries in a financial vise? Would Wall Street's troubles become the world's?

Although investors and finance ministers alike sought definitive answers to those questions, seeking knowledge in the leading indicators and other evidence, there was really only one answer that could have been known for sure. And that was: "Time will tell." For the last sixty years, time has told that economic downturns have been mere blips against the upward trend in GDP. ◄

QUICKCHECK

Does the government declare when the economy enters a recession? Explain.

Answer: No, it is not a government agency that performs this task. Instead, the National Bureau of Economic Research, a private organization that is less likely to be influenced by politics than a government agency, is charged with the task of announcing that a recession has begun, and that a recession has ended.

XPLORE & PPLY

5.5 ASSESSING ECONOMIC PERFORMANCE— DARE WE PREDICT THE FUTURE?

The federal government must have answers, even if they are not the ultimate answers. It must know whether there are macroeconomic problems. If there are problems, it must know how serious those problems are. Otherwise, government cannot know which actions to take, or even whether to take action at all. Thus, it turns to economic statistics.

Some economists would say that government should ignore the aggregate economy, and just focus on prudent budgetary practices. If the government follows sensible rules, they say, the economy will take care of itself. However, whether or not the government's best macro policy strategy is active or passive, it is still necessary to track economic performance. The reason is that government policies affect the rest of the economy, which in turn affects government revenues and expenses. Without knowing revenues and expenses, government cannot budget effectively.

Of course, just knowing economic data does not mean that government will choose to budget sensibly. The federal budget deficit—a shortfall of federal revenues below expenses—is evidence. Until the surpluses of 1998–2001, the federal government incurred a budget deficit every year between 1960 and 1997. With an estimated $165 billion deficit in 2002, deficits are expected to continue. In response to citizen outrage over the earlier deficits, Congress revised its budgetary practices. As we will see, the result has been to give economic statistics a more central role than ever before.

In 1985, in an attempt to lead the federal budget into balance, Congress passed the Gramm–Rudman–Hollings Act. This legislation set specific deficit-reduction targets. Each time targets were not met, the act called for across-the-board budget cuts that would bring spending into line with those targets. According to the Gramm–Rudman–Hollings targets, the federal deficit was to be eliminated by 1991.

When 1991 rolled around, the federal budget deficit was $215 billion dollars, higher than it had ever been before. What happened? Well before 1991, Congress had modified and then abandoned the Gramm–Rudman–Hollings approach. The across-the-board budget axe was not used. It fell victim to special interests, especially the interests of Social Security recipients. Too much spending was exempted from cuts.

Congress instead instituted a different set of budgetary procedures to add integrity to the budget process. Specifically, in the Budget Enforcement Act of 1990 that expired in 2002, Congress legislated that policy changes should not increase the budget deficit. Thus, policy changes that would add to the budget deficit must be balanced by other changes that would offset that effect. Doing so sounds reasonable, but brings back that basic statistical problem—measuring the effects on government revenues and expenses of alternative public policies. As we will see, these statistics are not immune from politics.

DO LUXURY TAXES WORK?

Is government able to forecast the effects of policy changes? In 1990 Congress imposed a surcharge on luxuries including, among other things, new yachts and other luxury boats. Immediately after the so-called luxury tax took effect, orders for new yachts all but disappeared. Although the tax rate was higher, government revenue from boat sales was much lower. Overall the luxury tax did bring in more money, but the amount was about $13 million by 1993, rather than the $76 million over that period that was designated in the Congressional budget.

Although the revenue effect of the luxury tax could have been predicted with much greater accuracy, the Budget Enforcement Act did not allow Congress to do so in its budgetary calculations. Thus, the luxury tax surcharge was assumed to bring in $76 million dollars of extra revenue, which then allowed Congress to pass an additional $76 million of new spending programs.

This traditional manner of computing the effects of federal actions is known as *static scoring.* Static scoring assumes no general change in macroeconomic behavior as a result of government policy changes. Hence, the effect of the luxury tax on the demand for luxury goods was ignored. The alternative is called *dynamic scoring,* which does allow for consideration of all behavioral changes over time caused by changes in government policy.

Static scoring has led to other serious problems. Prior to the final passage of the internationally negotiated revisions to the General Agreement on Tariffs and Trade (GATT) in 1994, for example, Congress was nearly forced to abandon the agreement. Negotiations over the GATT had dragged on for over seven years, as countries around the world sought to retain their special trade protections. The final agreement dramatically lowered trade barriers, which had been America's objective all along. The problem was those static scoring rules.

Although the entire purpose of reducing trade barriers was to promote trade, static scoring rules assumed that the volume of trade would remain constant. Thus, any tariff cut was automatically scored as a revenue-loser by the same percentage that the tariffs were cut. Budget rules meant that tariffs could not be cut without other policy changes that would add revenues or cut expenditures in other areas to offset the purported revenue loss. It was only through an extraordinary act of juggling other elements of the budget that the congressional budgetary rules were finally satisfied.

Static scoring is stupid, you might say. Washington policymakers know that taxes can change our behavior. Static scoring has been a budgetary mainstay because it provides an obvious baseline estimate, the baseline being the status quo. Analysts may know that behavior will change, but are unlikely to agree on exactly what forms the changes will take or how significant will be their effects. Because of such disagreement, dynamic scoring must inevitably lead to controversy.

Everyone in the budget process knows that static scoring gives wrong answers. Still, as the saying goes, the devil you know is better than the devil you don't know. If the government were to follow a dynamic scoring standard, who could tell what controversies would lie buried beneath the surface?

Consider the possibilities. There was hot debate over President George Bush's recently enacted tax cuts when, on May 16, 2002, the Congressional Joint Committee on Taxation (JCT) issued a report urging Congress to modify its budget rules in order to allow dynamic scoring. The Committee pointed to economic studies suggesting that, while cutting tax rates would reduce the amount of tax revenue per dollar earned, a significant portion of that revenue loss would be offset by revenues gained from an increase in aggregate economic activity. Senate Majority Leader Tom Daschle objected. In a public letter to House Speaker Dennis Hastert on June 25, 2002, Daschle declared, "Having JCT include the macroeconomic effects into its cost estimates would subject the committee's work to huge potential errors and would only serve to undermine its credibility."

The problem of budgetary discipline also arises on the spending side. For example, advocates of social programs often find themselves attracted to the dynamic standard, arguing that cutting back spending on social programs could cause tax revenues to decline over time. The idea is that money spent on social programs helps to develop productive, taxpaying citizens who pay back many times more than they received. Thus, they sometimes argue, cutting social spending would threaten to increase rather than decrease budget deficits.

The issue of static versus dynamic scoring underscores the old adage that politics makes strange bedfellows. Conservatives seeking to cut taxes find themselves allied with liberals seeking to expand government spending on social programs. Both support dynamic scoring. On the other side are conservatives and liberals who fear political manipulation of the budget process. Whatever the immediate outcome of this tug-of-war, the issue will remain with us.

Is it better to continue with static scoring that we know gives wrong answers or to allow our elected officials the leeway to use their best judgments as to which forecasts to accept? Do we trust them to think well? Is it better to analyze and maybe get it wrong than not to analyze at all? Those are the questions.

Thinking Critically

1. Senate Majority Leader Tom Daschle was quoted in this Explore & Apply as declaring, "Having JCT include the macroeconomic effects into its cost estimates would subject the committee's work to huge potential errors and would only serve to undermine its credibility." Using your own words, explain what he meant and why others might disagree.

2. As a taxpayer, do you support static or dynamic scoring? Which do you think is more likely to lead to lower taxes? To higher taxes? Explain your answers.

 Visit **www.prenhall.com/ayers** for updates and web exercises on this Explore & Apply topic.

SUMMARY AND LEARNING OBJECTIVES

1. **Present three widely accepted goals for the economy.**
   - The three goals for the economy are economic growth, full employment, and low inflation.
   - An annual growth rate of 2.5 percent is usually considered sustainable. Evidence from the late 1990s suggests a possible sustainable growth rate of up to 5 percent.
   - The rule of seventy-two can be used to compute doubling times. For example, at a 2.5 percent rate of growth, the economy's output would double in approximately 29 years. A growth rate of 5 percent would cut this doubling time in half.
   - In order to know whether the nation is meeting its macro goals, government collects data that measure the aggregate economy.

2. **Define gross domestic product (GDP) and discuss its components.**
   - Gross domestic product (GDP) is the most widely reported measure of the aggregate economy. It measures the value of final goods and services produced by an economy within some time period. Intermediate goods are used to make other goods. To avoid double counting, GDP does not count the production of intermediate goods, since their value is included in the value of final goods.
   - GDP equals the sum of consumption, investment, government purchases, and net exports. Per capita GDP is GDP per person, computed by dividing GDP by the population. GDP is an imperfect measure of a nation's well-being, because it does not count the value of goods and services produced in the underground economy and at home.
   - The largest component of total spending in the United States is consumption spending, which includes most spending by consumers.
   - Total spending also includes investment, government purchases, and net exports. Investment is the sum of three items: spending on capital by businesses, spending on new housing by consumers, and the change in business inventories.
   - Government spending is the sum of spending on purchases of goods and services by governments at the local, state, and national levels. Government transfer payments are not directly included in the computation of GDP.
   - Net exports equal the value of exports minus the value of imports. Net exports have been negative in the recent past.
   - Gross national product (GNP) is computed by first adding income received from the rest of the world to GDP, and then subtracting income payments to the rest of the world. GNP and GDP typically differ by a relatively small amount.
   - The value of production that occurs at home is not counted in GDP. Neither is the value of goods and services produced for the underground economy. Thus, GDP is an imperfect measure of a nation's well-being.

3. **Distinguish real GDP from nominal GDP.**
   - A nominal value is expressed without regard to price changes. A real value has been adjusted for price changes. The GDP price index is used to compute real GDP from nominal GDP
   - Nominal GDP, when divided by the GDP price index and multiplied by 100, equals real GDP. Real GDP provides a more accurate measure of the economy's actual output over time than does nominal GDP. Nominal GDP will rise whenever production increases, but also because of inflation. Real GDP will only rise when production increases.

4. **Track the stages of the business cycle.**
   - The business cycle refers to the expansions and contractions in economic activity that take place over time. In the expansion phase, real GDP rises. Real GDP reaches its maximum at the peak of any business cycle. During the recession phase, economic activity declines. Real GDP reaches its lowest level at the trough of the business cycle.
   - The leading indicators are various data series that are supposed to predict turning points in the business cycle. Since they do not always predict accurately, anyone using them to make decisions must proceed with caution.

5. **Identify the advantages and disadvantages of static and dynamic scoring.**
   - Static scoring and its opposite, dynamic scoring, are alternative methods for gauging the effects of a policy action taken by government. In contrast to dynamic scoring, static scoring assumes that policy changes have no macroeconomic effects. Dynamic scoring is potentially more accurate than static scoring, but also allows for more opportunities to manipulate predicted outcomes to match political preferences.

KEY TERMS

gross domestic product (GDP), 108
consumption spending, 108
investment, 108
gross investment, 109
net investment, 109

net domestic product (NDP), 109
net exports, 111
value added, 113
underground economy, 115
nominal GDP, 116

real GDP, 116
business cycle, 118
recession, 118
leading indicators, 121

TEST YOURSELF

TRUE OR FALSE

1. Low unemployment is a widely accepted goal of macro policy.
2. The investment component of GDP includes spending on human capital.
3. Net exports equal about 5 percent of GDP.
4. When there is an increase in nominal GDP, there must also be an increase in real GDP.
5. When real GDP decreases during the business cycle, the lowest point is called the peak.

MULTIPLE CHOICE

6. Applying the rule of seventy-two, it would take _____ years for GDP to double at a steady growth rate of 3 percent in GDP.
   a. 216
   b. 72
   c. 24
   d. 3

7. A loaf of french bread is used by a bakery to cut into croutons that are sold to Bridgette. The value of the loaf of french bread is not counted in GDP because it is a(n) _____ good. The value of the croutons are counted in GDP because they are a(n) _____ good.
   a. final; intermediate
   b. intermediate; final
   c. consumption; investment
   d. investment; consumption

8. The consumption spending portion of GDP includes
   a. durable goods, nondurable goods, and services.
   b. goods, services, and new houses.
   c. intermediate goods, but not final goods.
   d. about 90 percent of all production that occurs in the economy.

9. Gross investment equals
   a. net investment plus depreciation.
   b. investment adjusted for the effects of inflation.
   c. a negative component of GDP.
   d. the change in business inventories.

10. The value of new houses is included in
    a. consumption.
    b. investment.
    c. government purchases.
    d. net exports.

11. Which of the following is an example of a transfer payment?
    a. A school district pays the salary of a teacher.
    b. A senior citizen is issued a Social Security check by the government.
    c. A farmer raises a field of corn from seed.
    d. A little boy and girl spend their allowances at Chuck E. Cheese's pizza restaurant.

12. How are transfer payments treated in the measurement of GDP?
    a. Transfer payments are included in the government component of GDP.
    b. Transfer payments are changes in business inventories and are thus included in the investment component of GDP.
    c. Transfer payments are subtracted in the computation of GDP.
    d. GDP does not count transfer payments directly.

13. Net exports are computed as
    a. exports minus depreciation.
    b. exports minus imports.
    c. exports minus GDP.
    d. imports minus exports.

14. U.S. gross national product (GNP)
    a. is another name for gross domestic product (GDP).
    b. excludes net exports, since its purpose is to compute national consumption and investment.
    c. includes production by U.S. firms in other countries and excludes production by foreign firms in the United States.
    d. is no longer computed, having been replaced by GDP.

15. Per capita GDP is
    a. GDP minus net exports.
    b. GDP adjusted for inflation.
    c. GDP per person.
    d. computed by taking the legal output and the illegal output of the economy and adding them together.

16. How is the output of goods in the underground economy treated in the computation of GDP?
    a. They are difficult to measure accurately, but the government estimates their value and adjusts GDP to reflect that value.
    b. They are included in GDP as one of the components of investment.
    c. Government produces goods for the underground economy and, thus, they are included in the government purchases component of GDP.
    d. They are not counted.

17. To compute real GDP when given nominal GDP, we must also know
    a. nothing else, since real and nominal GDP are generally equal.
    b. the value of consumption spending.
    c. the value of gross investment.
    d. the value of the GDP chain-type price index.

18. If the real value of GDP decreases from one year to the next, it is most likely that
    a. inflation is a problem in the economy.
    b. real GNP is up.
    c. consumption spending is down while government purchases are up.
    d. the economy is in a recession.

19. The leading indicators are
    a. a group of New York City investors who predict the stock market.
    b. government economists whose job it is to indicate solutions to problems with the economy.
    c. statistics that are used to predict the future direction of the economy.
    d. almost always wrong, but interesting anyway.

20. The primary difference between static and dynamic scoring is that
    a. static scoring is legal but dynamic scoring is illegal.
    b. static scoring considers real values of variables, but dynamic scoring considers nominal values.
    c. static scoring is favored by Congress, but dynamic scoring is favored by the president.
    d. static scoring assumes that behavior does not change when policies change, but dynamic scoring allows for the possibility of behavioral changes.

QUESTIONS AND PROBLEMS

1. *[macro goals]* List the three primary macroeconomic goals and briefly discuss why the achievement of these goals is desirable.

2. *[macro goals]* The U.S. Constitution refers to the rights of "life, liberty, and the pursuit of happiness." Explain how this constitutional right relates to the three primary macro goals. Does it appear from this phrase that the Constitution goes beyond promoting these goals? Explain.

3. *[macro goals]* After obtaining the most recent edition of the *Economic Report of the President* from your library or the Internet, compare the discussion of macroeconomic goals in this chapter with those discussed in the *Report.* Are all the goals mentioned in the chapter also in the *Report?*

4. *[final versus intermediate goods]* Explain why GDP excludes the value of intermediate goods, while including the value of final goods and services.

5. *[components of GDP]* Explain each of the four components of GDP. Include in your explanation answers to the following: (a) Is investment measured as gross or net? (b) Does the government component include transfer payments? (c) Which component has a negative value?

6. *[computing GDP]* Suppose you have the following information available to compute the GDP of the country of Traczania: Consumption spending = $150; Gross investment = $55; Net investment = $50; Government purchases = $75; Government transfer payments = $30; Imports = $25; Exports = $20. Compute Traczania's GDP.

7. *[GNP versus GDP]* Explain how gross national product (GNP) differs from gross domestic product (GDP). Is the difference between the values of GDP and GNP large or small in percentage terms?

8. *[GDP and household production]* Jane and John spent last Saturday morning cleaning their apartment. Is the value of those services counted in the measurement of GDP?

9. *[GDP and the underground economy]* What is meant by the underground economy? Is the output of the underground economy counted in measuring GDP?

10. *[value added]* Jay Jones runs a small business out of his home, making bird houses from scrap lumber that he finds in dumpsters. Last year Jay sold $8,000 worth of his birdhouses to happy birdwatchers. How much value added did Jim contribute to GDP last year? Is the value added equal to spending by consumers on his birdhouses? Explain.

11. *[per capita GDP]* What is *per capita* GDP? Under what circumstances would *per capita* GDP tell us more about the state of the economy than would GDP?

12. *[real versus nominal GDP]* What is the purpose of computing the real value of GDP?

13. *[GDP price index]* Explain how the GDP price index is used to compute real GDP.

14. *[business cycle]* Illustrate graphically the stages of the curve you draw. Be sure to include appropriate labels on the axes and on the business cycle.

15. *[business cycle]* Go to your library or the Internet and read at least three articles about the current condition of the economy in magazines such as *Business Week, The Economist,* or *Fortune,* or in a business newspaper such as the *Financial Times* or *The Wall Street Journal.* What stage of the business cycle is the economy currently in? Which single statistic is the most useful in answering this question? What economic problems are discussed in the articles you have read? Explain.

 Visit www.prenhall.com/ayers for Exploring the Web exercises and additional self-test quizzes.

APPENDIX 5

THE NATIONAL INCOME AND PRODUCT ACCOUNTS

The purpose of national income accounting is to summarize the millions of daily economic transactions in a form that economists, government planners, politicians, and others can easily use and understand. The development of the national income and product accounts began in the 1930s in response to the need to evaluate depressed economic conditions, and the growing realization that the government's existing collection of data meant that it already possessed the primary data that could be used to construct the accounts.

The Bureau of Economic Analysis (BEA), an arm of the U.S. Department of Commerce, is responsible for the preparation of the final reports detailing the national income and product statistics. These reports are prepared using data obtained from other government agencies. Individual tax returns, obtained from the Internal Revenue Service, are an important source of data. Survey data are also extensively employed.

Users of BEA data are familiar with the notion of preliminary and revised data. Preliminary data are estimates that are subject to change. Revised data incorporate changes in data made necessary as more complete information becomes available with the passage of time. Data may be revised several times before the BEA is satisfied with its accuracy. The process of revision can occasionally drag on for years.

Most data are available at quarterly or annual intervals, although some data are available monthly. The monthly Commerce Department publication, the *Survey of Current Business,* is the primary source of national income and product data. BEA-developed data can also be found in other government publications, including the annual *Economic Report of the President.*

In calculating GDP it is useful to recognize that every dollar of production creates an equivalent dollar of spending. **Since every dollar of spending generates a dollar of income for someone, the values of production and income are also equal.** Goods and services are produced and sold, with the dollars spent by purchasers being collected by businesses. These dollars go toward the payment of incomes—wages to workers, for example.

The equality of production and income means that GDP can be calculated in two ways, as seen in Table 5A-1. On the left side of the table, GDP is obtained by measuring the total value of production. The **expenditures approach** sums spending on consumption, investment, government purchases, and the value of net exports. On the right side of the table, the **incomes approach** sums various income items plus other charges against GDP. Proprietor's income is received by persons who own unincorporated businesses, such as farmers and physicians. Net interest is interest received by individuals minus individuals' interest payments.

TABLE 5-A1 TWO APPROACHES TO MEASURING GDP

EXPENDITURES APPROACH	INCOMES APPROACH
Personal Consumption Expenditures	**Compensation of Employees**
Durables	Wages and salaries
Nondurables	Supplements
Services	+
+	**Proprietor's Income**
Gross Private Domestic Investment	+
Business capital investment	**Rental Income of Persons**
New housing	+
Inventory change	**Corporate Profits**
+	+
Government purchases	**Net Interest**
Federal	+
State and local	**Other Charges Against GDP**
+	Capital consumption
Net Exports	Indirect business taxes
	Other items, net
=	Statistical discrepancy
	=
Gross Domestic Product	**Gross Domestic Product**

Source: Adapted from Federal Reserve Bank of Richmond, "The National Income and Product Accounts," *Macroeconomic Data: A User's Guide,* 3rd edition.

Because of imperfections in data collection, product and income are not exactly equal. This necessitates the inclusion of the statistical discrepancy as part of the "other charges" on the income side. Other complications associated with the income approach force the inclusion of several additional charges. Capital consumption measures depreciation in the nation's capital stock. Indirect business taxes are federal excise taxes as well as state and local sales taxes included in the value of purchases. These complications make the incomes approach less useful than the more straightforward expenditures approach for most macro analyses.

By making adjustments to GDP, other measures of aggregate economic activity can be calculated as follows:

■ *Gross national product (GNP):* GNP = GDP + income received by U.S. firms and workers outside the United States − income received by foreign firms and workers within the United States
■ *Net national product (NNP):* NNP = GNP − capital consumption
■ *National income (NI):* NI = NNP − indirect business taxes − business transfer payments − statistical discrepancy + subsidies less surplus of government firms

- *Personal income (PI):* PI = NI − corporate profits − net interest − Social Security taxes − wage accruals less disbursements + government transfer payments to persons + personal interest income + personal dividend income + business transfer payments to persons
- *Disposable personal income (DPI):* DPI = PI − personal tax and non-tax payments

As the adjustments show, national income accounting can be quite complex. Each of the measures defined above is used for a specific purpose, thus justifying the effort. For example, disposable personal income shows how much income people actually have available to spend. Economists use this data to forecast consumer spending.

EXERCISES

1. If you manage a major chain of retail stores, and are developing your plans as to how much inventory to stock for the Christmas season, which of the national income and output measures would you be most interested in? Why?
2. GNP rather than GDP was the primary focus of national income accounting until the early 1990s. Under what circumstances would GNP be of more interest to economists than GDP? Given the difference between GNP and GDP, why do you think that attention shifted to GDP?

CHAPTER 6

UNEMPLOYMENT

A LOOK AHEAD

Too many unfilled jobs and not enough qualified people—not a bad problem to have! The United States found
itself in just that situation as the twentieth century drew
to a close, with an unemployment rate that hovered at 4
percent, the lowest since 1969. Unfortunately, the recession that began in early 2001 caused unemployment to
reverse course. Adding to the stress, government mandates have lengthened the workweek for many full-time
workers and caused part-time jobs to become more com-
mon. Consequences of mandates affecting the workplace are examined in this chapter's
Explore & Apply section.

This chapter is about the labor force and unemployment. You will learn what it means
to be a labor force participant. You will also see how the unemployment rate is calculated.
We discuss the causes of unemployment within the framework of the four types of unemployment, as well as the economy's overall path toward full employment. While U.S. unemployment is the primary interest here, you will also see that unemployment is a problem
with global dimensions.

LEARNING OBJECTIVES

Understanding Chapter 6 will enable you to:
1. **Identify who is part of the labor force and who is not.**
2. **Explain how the unemployment rate is calculated.**
3. **Elaborate on unemployment in other countries.**
4. **Divide unemployment into different types and explain the implications of each.**
5. **Describe the natural rate of unemployment and its converse, full employment.**
6. **Discuss how the quality of employment can deteriorate when mandates increase
   labor costs.**

Explore & Apply

Employment and unemployment top the list of macroeconomic concerns. The reason is straightforward—most people's incomes come from their jobs. To understand unemployment, we must measure it in total and by types. Knowing what it is helps us to identify how much of it we can expect.

6.1 MEASURING UNEMPLOYMENT

An economy with unemployment is wasting resources and producing at a point inside its production possibilities frontier. The concept of unemployment applies to any resource that lies idle. In common usage, however, unemployment refers to idle labor.

THE LABOR FORCE AND UNEMPLOYMENT

labor force individuals age 16 and over, excluding those in the military, who are either employed or actively looking for work.

The U.S. *civilian labor force*—the **labor force**—is composed of individuals age 16 and over, excluding those in the military, who are either employed or actively looking for work. The labor force typically expands as the adult population increases. The labor force also expands as job opportunities improve, which causes some of the people not previously in the labor force to look for work.

The labor force can be divided into two parts, consisting of the employed and the unemployed. The employed are those who work for pay, and the unemployed are those who do not work, but are seeking jobs. The **unemployment rate** is the fraction of the labor force who are unemployed, expressed in percentage terms:

unemployment rate the ratio of the number of unemployed persons to the number of persons in the labor force.

$$\text{Unemployment rate} = \frac{\text{Number of unemployed}}{\text{Labor force}} \times 100$$

Table 6-1 shows the U.S. population, civilian labor force, and unemployment data from 1979 through 2001. When we take the ratio of the civilian labor force to the population age 16 and over, the result is the **labor force participation rate** (or just the *participation rate*):

labor force participation rate the ratio of the labor force to the population age 16 and over; expressed as a percentage.

$$\text{Participation rate} = \frac{\text{Labor force}}{\text{Population}} \times 100$$

Over this period there has been a consistent increase in the participation rate. This trend is primarily caused by the increase in the participation of women in the U.S. labor force.

Labor force participation and job creation depend on each other. When the economy is in the midst of a strong expansion, potential workers become aware that job opportunities are available that would be absent in a weaker economy. The result is that some persons who would choose not to join the labor force when job openings are relatively scarce are enticed to enter the labor force by the prospect of a good job. This job seeking is in addition to the normal expansion of the labor force that occurs when young graduates look for their first jobs and people who have temporarily left the labor force reenter it. The latter group includes women who return to the labor force after having left their jobs to raise families, and retirees who wish to supplement their incomes. When the expansion of the labor force brought on by a strong economy is added to the normal increase, the result is that the unemployment rate does not fall as much as it otherwise would. The reason is that the additional job seekers will be counted as unemployed until they find and accept work.

There are many influences on the labor force participation rate.

■ **Increased opportunities for women and minorities** have led to an increase in the participation rate over time.

TABLE 6-1	POPULATION, LABOR FORCE, AND UNEMPLOYMENT

YEAR	POPULATION AGE 16 AND OVER (MILLIONS)	LABOR FORCE (MILLIONS OF CIVILIANS)	LABOR FORCE PARTICIPATION RATE (IN PERCENT)	NUMBER OF UNEMPLOYED (IN MILLIONS)	UNEMPLOYMENT RATE (IN PERCENT)
1979	164.9	105.0	63.7	6.1	5.8
1980	167.7	106.9	63.8	7.6	7.1
1981	170.1	108.7	63.9	8.3	7.6
1982	172.3	110.2	64.0	10.7	9.7
1983	174.2	111.6	64.0	10.7	9.6
1984	176.4	113.5	64.4	8.5	7.5
1985	178.2	115.5	64.8	8.3	7.2
1986	180.6	117.8	65.3	8.2	7.0
1987	182.8	119.9	65.6	7.4	6.2
1988	184.6	121.7	65.9	6.7	5.5
1989	186.4	123.9	66.5	6.5	5.3
1990	188.0	124.8	66.4	6.9	5.5
1991	189.8	125.3	66.0	8.4	6.7
1992	191.6	127.0	66.3	9.4	7.4
1993	193.6	128.0	66.2	8.7	6.8
1994	196.8	131.1	66.6	8.0	6.1
1995	198.6	132.3	66.6	7.4	5.6
1996	200.6	133.9	66.8	7.2	5.4
1997	203.1	136.3	67.1	6.7	4.9
1998	205.2	137.7	67.1	6.2	4.5
1999	207.8	139.4	67.1	5.9	4.2
2000	209.7	140.9	67.2	5.6	4.0
2001	211.9	141.8	66.9	6.7	4.8

Source: *2002 Economic Report of the President,* Table B-35.

- **Opportunities for workers to take early retirement** have grown. Since retirees are not part of the labor force, the influence of improved retirement opportunities has been to limit the increase in the participation rate.
- **Better healthcare** has allowed workers who might have been too sick to stay in the labor force in earlier times to continue on.
- **Government aid,** such as generous welfare programs, can cause workers to stay out of the labor force.

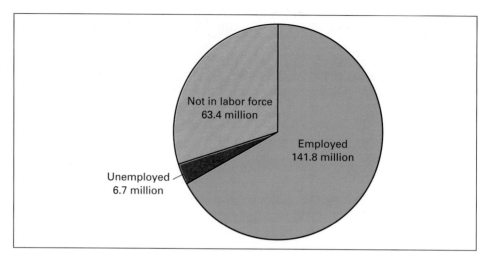

FIGURE 6-1

POPULATION AND LABOR FORCE
The U.S. adult population in 2001 of 211.9 million people is represented by the pie chart where each adult fits into one of the slices. Adults who have jobs are counted in the 141.8 million employed. Those who are unemployed are grouped in the slice that contains 6.7 million people. These two slices of the pie make up the labor force. The rest of the population, 63.4 million people, are grouped in the not-in-the-labor-force.

- **Individual attitudes** toward labor change. When people put great value on their involvement in the labor force, the participation rate will be higher than when work is not so highly valued for its own sake.

Figure 6-1 enlarges on Table 6-1 by showing labor force concepts in a pie chart, where the pie represents the adult population. There are three slices to the pie. Two of the slices represent people in the labor force, the employed and the unemployed. The third slice represents people not in the labor force. Figure 6-2 elaborates on Table 6-1 by breaking down the overall labor force participation rate in the table into the rates for men and women.

SNAPSHOT   ## DEMOGRAPHY—POPULATION STATISTICS TO LET US GLIMPSE THE FUTURE

Demography is the study of population statistics. Demographers offer us small glimpses of the future. Because birth rates and death rates change slowly, demographers can predict with little error how many people of various ages will comprise the labor force in ten, twenty, or even thirty years. Demographers tell us to expect an aging work force. The large numbers of baby boomers born from 1946 to 1964 were followed by the much smaller number of babies born in the 1970s and 1980s.

As the baby boomers grow older, and with fewer young workers to enter the labor force, the average age of the labor force must rise. An older labor force has important consequences, good and bad, for both the unemployment rate and our lifestyles. Middle-aged workers do not change jobs as often as young workers. As a consequence they are less likely to be unemployed. And while retirees look forward to taking it easy, their rising numbers will place increasing stresses on the nation's ability to provide for us all. With this glimpse of the future in hand, the nation can plan to deal with the problem of an aging labor force and growing population of retirees. ◄

UNEMPLOYMENT RATES IN THE UNITED STATES AND AROUND THE WORLD

As already mentioned, to be counted as unemployed a person must be at least 16 years of age and without work, but actively looking for a job. Separating the employed from the unemployed would seem easy, but there are many details to consider. For example:

- Are you employed if your job is not full time? Yes, people are counted as employed regardless of how many hours they work, just so long as it's one hour a week or more for pay.

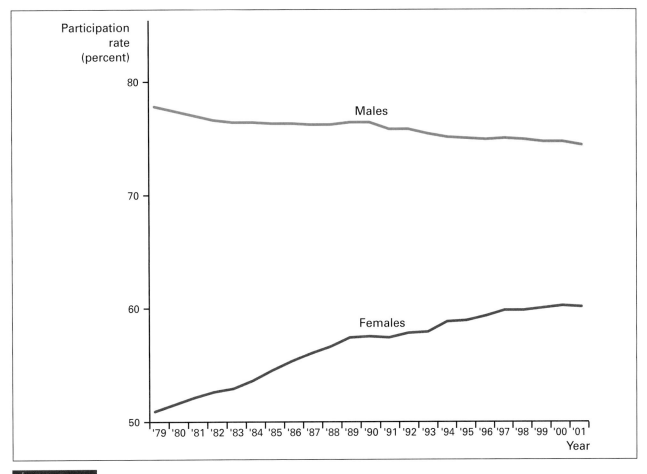

Source: 2002 Economic Report of the President, Table B-39.

FIGURE 6-2

LABOR FORCE PARTICIPATION RATES FOR MEN AND WOMEN The labor force participation rate of women has increased dramatically over time, from about 50 percent in 1979 to about 60 percent today. For men, the labor force participation rate has dropped slightly over time but has remained in the general vicinity of 75 percent. When men and women are taken together, the overall participation rate is about 67 percent, as seen in Table 6-1.

- Can someone who works without pay be counted as employed? Again, yes, just so long as that person is working in a family business for at least fifteen hours a week.
- Does going to school count as having a job? No. For students, school may seem to be a full-time job, but it's not considered that way by government statisticians. Neither are students counted among the unemployed, unless they are looking for jobs.

In the United States the Bureau of Labor Statistics (BLS) estimates the number of employed and unemployed, and hence the unemployment rate. The estimates are based on a monthly survey of households and employers, and a tally of unemployment insurance claims. The last column in Table 6-1 shows yearly average unemployment rates since 1979. Figure 6-3 offers a longer view of unemployment, showing yearly unemployment rates since 1947.

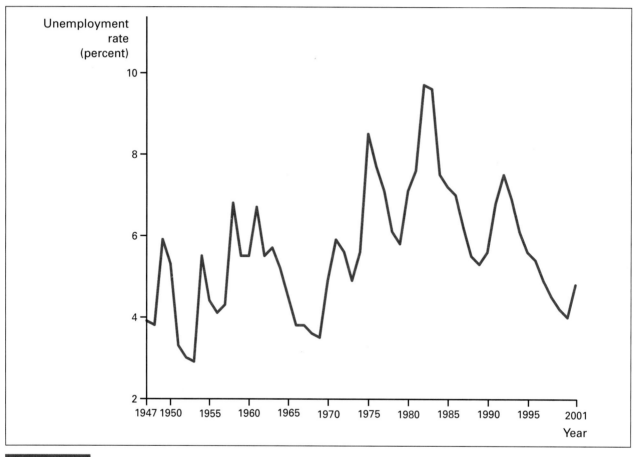

FIGURE 6-3

HISTORY OF THE U.S. UNEMPLOYMENT RATE The U.S. unemployment rate changes frequently. When the economy slows down, the unemployment rate rises. Faster economic growth promotes a lower unemployment rate. The unemployment rate fell significantly during the 1990s, but bounced upward in 2001 as the economy slowed.

Source: 2002 Economic Report of the President, Table B-35.

The unemployment rate, while useful, does not tell us all that we would like to know about the labor market. Some workers who have part-time jobs would like to have full-time jobs. Those workers are *underemployed.* Other workers would like to have a job, but have tried unsuccessfully to find one in the past and have given up looking. Because they have stopped looking, they are not counted in the unemployment statistics. Such would-be workers are called **discouraged workers.** Government estimates put the number of discouraged workers at 317,000 in mid-2002. **The presence of discouraged workers would cause the reported unemployment rate to understate true unemployment because discouraged workers are not in the labor force.** Concerns over the accuracy and meaning of the unemployment rate have led some economists to coin a saying about it: "The unemployment rate is like a hot dog. It's hard to tell what's in it."

People are unemployed for a variety of reasons, with some reasons of more concern than others. For example, some people are unemployed because they have voluntarily left their jobs. These unemployed persons are of less concern than the unemployed who have been involuntarily laid off. Some other people who are unemployed are actually earning

discouraged workers people who would like to have a job, but have given up looking; not counted as unemployed because they are not included in the labor force.

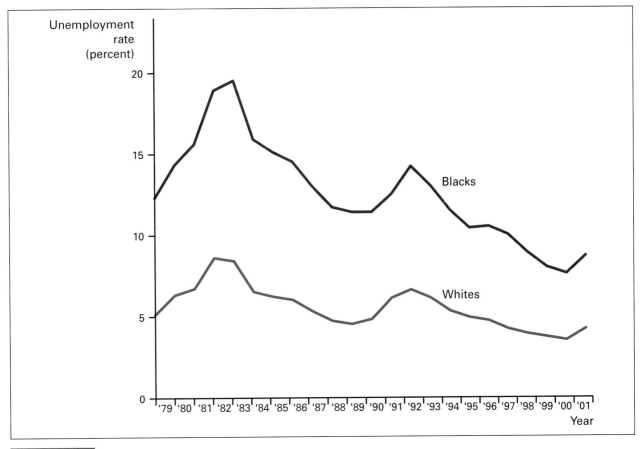

FIGURE 6-4

UNEMPLOYMENT RATES FOR BLACKS AND WHITES Despite recent signs of convergence, unemployment rates for blacks are consistently higher than unemployment rates for whites. However, when the unemployment rate among whites decreases (or increases), typically the black unemployment rate will also decrease (or increase).

Source: 2002 Economic Report of the President, Table B-42.

incomes in the underground economy. **The underground economy causes the reported unemployment rate to overstate true unemployment.**

Unemployment rates can vary among different segments of the population. For example, Figure 6-4 shows that the unemployment rate for blacks has been consistently higher than that for whites, although the gap has narrowed in recent years. Teenage unemployment is a significant contributing factor, with nearly 30 percent of black teenage males and 25 percent of black teenage females unemployed in 2001, compared to unemployment rates of 12.6 percent for white teenage males and 10.3 percent for white teenage females.

Historically, male unemployment rates have been close to female unemployment rates. However, when only heads of households are considered the unemployment rate for men is much less than for women. Figure 6-5 shows those unemployment rates over time. Unemployment among heads of households is particularly significant because it can affect the well-being of entire families.

The unemployment rate does not tell us the *duration of unemployment*—how long a person has been unemployed. Short spells of unemployment among workers are of less

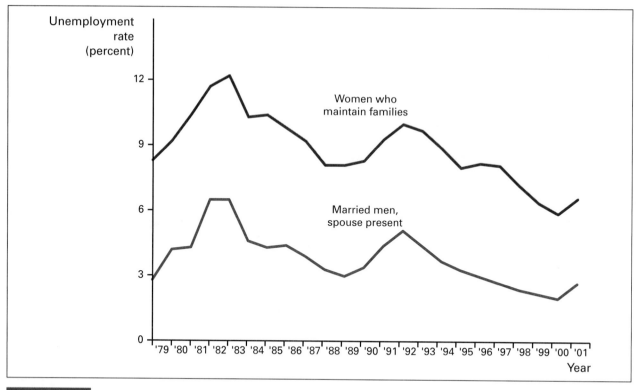

FIGURE 6-5

UNEMPLOYMENT RATES FOR MALE AND FEMALE HEADS OF HOUSEHOLDS The men and women in this graph provide the primary financial support for their families. The men have a significantly lower unemployment rate than the women.

Source: 2002 Economic Report of the President, Table B-42.

concern than long-term unemployment. The median duration of unemployment in 2001 was just under seven weeks. Figure 6-6 shows that unemployment tends to be of relatively short duration.

Having looked at unemployment in the United States, let's turn our attention to other countries. Recent unemployment rates for several major economies are presented in Figure 6-7 on page 142. By examining these data we can make a few generalizations about unemployment around the world. First, there is some tendency for unemployment rates to rise and fall together across countries. This tendency for unemployment rates to move together reflects the modern global economy that has led to increased economic interactions among countries. Note, however, that this tendency is not a hard and fast rule.

Four of the countries in Figure 6-7 experienced relatively high unemployment rates during the 1990s. While *changes* in the level of unemployment tend to move together, the *level* of unemployment itself is a different matter. Relative to their historical norms, Japan, France, Sweden, and Germany all exhibited high unemployment rates during the 1990s. The Japanese economy was bogged down in a stubborn recession during the period. France and Sweden suffered from high labor costs, along with traditions and government regulations that impeded their abilities to compete with other countries in the international marketplace. At the same time, Germany was dealing with the problem of integrating the economically backward East Germany into its economy.

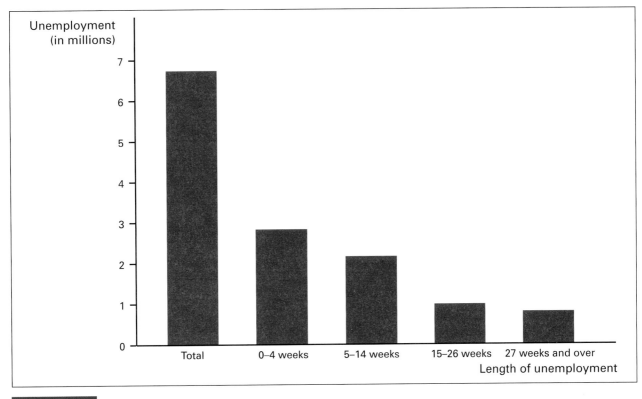

FIGURE 6-6

DURATION OF UNEMPLOYMENT Most unemployed people are unemployed for relatively short periods of time. The long-term unemployed, people who were unemployed for twenty-seven weeks or longer, make up only 11 percent of the total number of unemployed.

Source: 2002 Economic Report of the President, Table B-44. The data are for 2001.

QUICKCHECK

Suppose the labor force in the country of Ecommercia equals 150 million people. Six million of these have no job and are looking for work. Another one million people have no job but are not looking for work. What is the unemployment rate? What is the labor force participation rate?

Answer: The unemployment rate equals 4 percent (6 million/150 million) since the one million people not looking for work are not in the labor force. It is impossible to calculate the labor force participation rate without more information. Specifically, to compute the participation rate would require us to know the population age 16 and above as well as the size of the labor force.

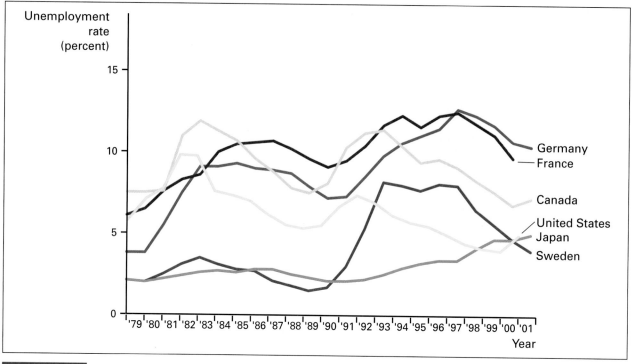

FIGURE 6-7

COUNTRY UNEMPLOYMENT RATES Unemployment rates around the world vary. Note that the United States, Sweden, and Japan succeeded in keeping their unemployment rates below 10 percent during the entire twenty-three years covered in the figure. The data are adjusted to U.S. methodologies.

Source: Comparative Civilian Labor Force Statistics, Ten Countries, 1959–2001, Table 2, U.S. Department of Labor.

6.2 IDENTIFYING TYPES OF UNEMPLOYMENT

Unemployment can be divided into the following four types:

- **Frictional Unemployment**—occurs when someone enters the labor market or switches jobs.
- **Seasonal Unemployment**—recurs periodically, according to the time of year.
- **Structural Unemployment**—caused by a mismatch between a person's human capital and that needed in the workplace. This mismatch can be caused by an evolving structure of the economy as some industries rise and others fall. It can also be caused by minimum wage laws or other structural *rigidities* that inhibit job creation or the movement of workers into new jobs.
- **Cyclical Unemployment**—results from a downturn in the business cycle and affects workers simultaneously in many different industries.

Structural and cyclical unemployment are usually of most concern, because they represent *involuntary unemployment,* meaning that employees have little choice in the matter. In contrast, frictional and seasonal unemployment frequently represent *voluntary unemployment,* which can be planned for and more easily overcome.

SEASONAL AND FRICTIONAL—WAITING FOR THE OLD OR SWITCHING TO THE NEW

Seasonal unemployment affects workers in agriculture, many tourism-related occupations, education, tax accounting, professional sports, and some other industries. There is usually

frictional unemployment
unemployment associated with entering the labor market or switching jobs.

seasonal unemployment
unemployment that can be predicted to recur periodically, according to the time of year.

structural unemployment
unemployment caused by a mismatch between a person's human capital and that needed in the workplace.

cyclical unemployment
unemployment from a downturn in the business cycle that affects workers simultaneously in many different industries.

little concern over this unemployment, because it can be planned for—it is part of the job. Workers are not even counted as unemployed if they have labor contracts that restart after the off-season, such as often occurs in teaching and professional sports.

Frictional unemployment occurs when people are between jobs, either because they were fired and have yet to line up new jobs or have quit voluntarily, such as in preparation for moving somewhere else or trying something new. Either way, their stay on the unemployment roles is likely to be brief. Frictional unemployment also includes many young people entering the labor market for the first time and older workers reentering the work force after an absence to raise children.

Changing jobs does not imply frictional unemployment. Most voluntary job switching is done without it; people line up new jobs before leaving their old ones. However, involuntary job changes, such as in response to layoffs and firings, commonly do result in frictional unemployment. In the case of involuntary frictional unemployment, publicly provided unemployment compensation acts as a safety net. It allows the job seeker to hold out longer in search of the best job opportunity.

STRUCTURAL—HUMAN CAPITAL MISMATCHES AND LABOR MARKET RIGIDITIES

Changes in the structure of the economy can give rise to structural unemployment, as demands for some types of goods and services give way to demands for others. This change in structure arises from such factors as technological change, international trade, and changing ways of doing business. For example, computers and telecommunications have opened doors to many types of jobs, but have cost many types of jobs, too.

Former telegraph operators exemplify structural unemployment. Once a valuable skill, the ability to speedily send coded messages over telegraph lines now has no market. Telegraph operators who were displaced by the technology of telephones could not easily find other employment at comparable wages. Their skills were not in demand. Until they retrained or found new jobs (usually at much lower wages), the ex–telegraph operators were structurally unemployed.

Rigidities that inhibit labor movement and the creation of new jobs can also cause structural unemployment. For example, the federal minimum wage law introduces a rigidity by making it difficult for workers with little human capital to find a job. Further rigidities arise from the regional nature of many jobs. For example, there may be pockets of unemployment in inner cities and some regions of the country, while there are plenty of job openings in suburbia or other states. If regional migration were without cost, such locational rigidities would vanish.

Human capital is often specific to a particular firm or kind of job—**specific human capital**—and does not apply readily to other firms or other jobs. As telegraph operators learned the hard way, workers with specific human capital are most prone to structural unemployment. It is a risk that people take voluntarily, since the best-paying jobs usually involve specific human capital. In contrast, **general human capital** involves such skills as language and math. General human capital is easily transferred from job to job. Those who possess it are less likely to be structurally unemployed. For most students, an undergraduate economics education represents general human capital. Economics majors are qualified to hold a variety of jobs in business and government. However, graduate training in economics is more specialized, and thus represents specific human capital. Students who earn a doctoral degree in economics usually build a career as a business or government economist, or as a college teacher of economics.

Structural unemployment is a necessary part of economic evolution. Without structural unemployment, there would be no progress—no industrial revolution, no railroad, no automobile, no computer. Those skilled workers who lose their jobs often find the transition to

specific human capital human capital that is specific to a particular firm or kind of job.

general human capital skills such as language and math that are easily transferred from job to job.

new jobs difficult, since economic change has depreciated the human capital that supported their incomes. They are usually forced to evaluate their alternatives, and either take a job with lower pay or drop out of the labor force to retire or learn new skills.

Examples of structural unemployment are frequently poignant, involving older workers who have advanced high up career ladders that collapse out from under them. Sometimes the reason involves imports. For example, the United States imports much of its steel from the countries of Europe and the Far East. Blast furnaces in America's "rust belt" that were built before World War II could not compete with the newer, more technologically advanced facilities in other countries. In response, America's primary steel producers laid off many highly skilled workers. Those skills and a powerful union had combined to increase steelworkers' earnings to levels far above what they could earn in other occupations. Does a 50-year-old ex-steelworker go back to school and start over, compete with teenagers for a minimum-wage job, or retire early and hope the money holds out? The choices are painful.

Structural unemployment is not only found in blue-collar jobs. Corporations have eliminated many white-collar managerial jobs in corporate downsizings in recent years. Like their blue-collar counterparts, former managers find that job openings are few and competition is fierce. Their choices are often little better than those of the 50-year-old steelworker just mentioned.

The government sometimes offers job-training programs to cushion the blows of structural unemployment. The question arises, though, as to the form of that training. For example, should the government train people to be hair stylists? That would take the jobs of other hair stylists or force them to work at lower wages. Such human capital is also so specific that it would not be pertinent for many of the structurally unemployed. The 50-year-old steelworker would probably not enroll.

SNAPSHOT   ## A WORLD WITHOUT CHANGE

Change is distressing. It disrupts our lives and makes us scramble to adapt to it. It causes stress in our lives, especially when it causes us to lose our jobs. Just ask the bank tellers who lost their jobs to automatic teller machines. Or the typewriter repair people who just never learned about computer keyboards. Or the many others whose skills became obsolete when technology or tastes changed against the industries or occupations in which they worked. They are the structurally unemployed.

When spending patterns change, so do the available jobs. The only way to avoid such disruption would be to freeze ourselves in time. For example, if change had been forbidden in the early 1960s, then we would still be watching the TV shows, listening to the music, and driving the cars of that era. Life would be pretty much like dwelling in a museum. ◀

CYCLICAL—A SYSTEMIC DISORDER

A troublesome form of unemployment is caused by downturns in the business cycle, *panics* as they were called in the nineteenth century. In these periodic downturns, which we refer to as recessions today, people in numerous sectors of the economy lose their jobs simultaneously. There just does not seem to be enough spending to go around, at least for awhile. Cyclical unemployment is thus a *systemic disorder*—a problem felt throughout the entire economy. The increase in U.S. unemployment in 1991 and 1992, and again in 2001 and 2002, exemplifies cyclical unemployment since those increases were associated with the mild recessions that occurred at those times.

Categorize each of the following cases according to the type of unemployment described: (1) long-term unemployment related to lack of marketable skills; (2) temporary unemployment related to finding a job or switching jobs; (3) unemployment related to a recession; (4) lack of a job because of the time of year.

Answer: (1) structural; (2) frictional; (3) cyclical, and (4) seasonal unemployment.

Cyclical unemployment is a temporary phenomena because recessions are temporary. As the economy pulls out of a recession, job creation leads the cyclically unemployed to return to their old jobs or find new ones. In this way cyclical unemployment diminishes and eventually disappears.

6.3 UNEMPLOYMENT INSURANCE AND THE NATURAL RATE OF UNEMPLOYMENT

Unemployed workers who qualify are able to collect state-provided *unemployment insurance* payments to help tide them over during a spell of unemployment. Benefits vary from state to state, paid for by taxes on employers. Workers who are laid off for economic reasons qualify for unemployment benefits, but workers who are fired do not. Otherwise, incentives would exist for workers to provoke their own firings in order to undeservedly collect benefits. Unemployment insurance programs were instituted on a widespread basis in the United States during the 1930s in order to alleviate some of the human suffering that accompanies unemployment. These programs partner the state governments with the federal government in providing cash benefits to the unemployed. Figure 6-8 shows how the average weekly unemployment check has grown over time.

By making it easier for the unemployed to stay unemployed, unemployment insurance contributes to a higher unemployment rate. If there were no unemployment insurance, the unemployed would be forced to take work or apply for welfare benefits as soon as their savings ran out, even if they were not happy with the jobs available to them. Unemployment insurance affords workers the time to find better jobs, thus increasing the *duration of unemployment*. Unemployment insurance programs build in some provisions that are designed to discourage idleness on the part of the unemployed. These provisions include a requirement that, to receive benefits, recipients must demonstrate evidence of applying for work each week. There are also limits on how long unemployment insurance can be received. Typically, unemployment insurance benefits are exhausted after one year or less.

In countries around the globe, unemployment rates average significantly closer to zero than to 100 percent. This is no coincidence. People look for ways to work because work puts food on the table. Even in the Great Depression of the 1930s, unemployment in the United States never exceeded 25 percent of the work force, and was as high as 20 percent for only four years, 1932–1935. Given that income is critical to living, however, it does not take many percentage points of unemployment to cause severe human trauma. The Great Depression was proof of the misery that high unemployment can bring.

Over time, the unemployment rate does not tend toward zero, exactly. Rather, the tendency is for unemployment to settle at a few percentage points above zero, due to the

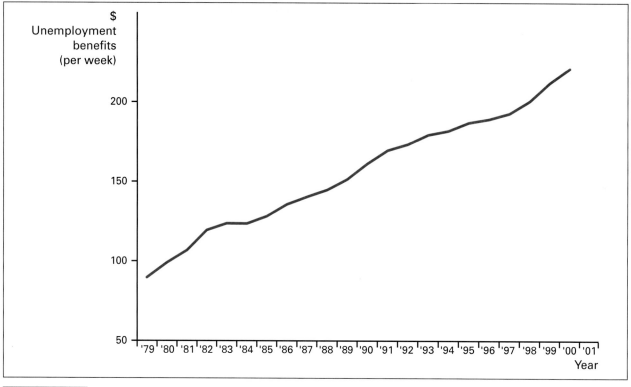

FIGURE 6-8

THE GROWTH IN THE AVERAGE WEEKLY UNEMPLOYMENT BENEFIT Average unemployment benefits have increased over time. The checks received by the unemployed are not intended to replace all of the income they earned when they had jobs.

Source: 2002 Economic Report of the President, Table B-45, and Employment and Training Administration.

natural rate of unemployment the minimum sustainable level of unemployment; associated with zero cyclical unemployment.

inevitable presence of seasonal, frictional, and structural unemployment. The minimum sustainable level of unemployment is termed the **natural rate of unemployment,** and is thought to be around 5 percent of the U.S. work force today.

The economy would tend toward a lower natural rate in the absence of unemployment insurance and other social *safety net* programs, such as Medicaid, food stamps, and additional programs designed to cushion the impact of unemployment or poverty. Without the safety net, the unemployed would be subject to greater misery, and a correspondingly greater incentive to grasp at any job offer, without regard to its long-term consequences for their future prospects. From an employer's perspective, minimum wage laws, liability laws, and many other policies discourage job formation because of the cost of complying with them. Other government policies, such as employment-related tax breaks for businesses, can have the opposite effect. Thus, government policies can and do affect the level of employment. Because of government actions, it is likely that the natural rate of unemployment has risen from a little over 2 percent a century ago to somewhere in the vicinity of 5 percent today.

full employment 100 percent minus the natural rate of unemployment.

The flip side of the natural rate of unemployment is **full employment,** which equals 100 percent minus the natural rate of unemployment. Because the natural rate of unemployment exceeds zero, full employment occurs when the employment rate is less than 100 percent. In short, economies will always have people who are looking for jobs.

QUICKCHECK

What are some reasons that the natural rate of unemployment is higher today than it was a century ago?

Answer: Unlike a century ago, the out-of-work today need not fear starvation or resort to private charity. Unemployment compensation, food stamps, and other programs provide a safety net that removes some of the urgency about finding a job right away. Another reason is structural unemployment caused by minimum wage laws, laws that did not exist a century ago.

FORECASTING JOBS LOST TO IMPORTS—NO MARKET FOR THE NATURAL RATE?

SNAPSHOT

We must have an income, and so we work. If we are out of work, we offer to work for less pay, which tends to drive wages down. As wages fall, prices fall. Our incomes then buy more goods, and more people can work to produce them. The process continues until all but about 5 percent of us have jobs. That is the logic of the natural rate of unemployment.

When it comes to international trade, though, the media has no patience for logic—it wants numbers to drum up interest! How many jobs do we gain from trade? How many do we lose? Reporters eagerly seek out so-called experts who provide numerical forecasts that international trade cuts down on aggregate employment. Other experts then reply with numbers showing just the opposite.

As usual, reality lies somewhere in the middle. Imports cost jobs in import-competing industries. However, the logic of a natural rate of unemployment leaves no room for international trade to have any lasting effect on unemployment in the aggregate. Workers who lose their jobs to imports would find other jobs. That is why, when faced with low-priced imported beef, many South Texas ranches switched from raising cattle to raising wild game for hunters. More generally, that is why, even as the United States imported a then-record $271.3 billion more goods than it exported in 1999, that year's unemployment rate was lower than it had been in thirty years! Unfortunately, logic usually lacks the eye-popping magic of charts with numbers, and therein seems to lie the market. ◄

*E*XPLORE
&
*A*PPLY

6.4 EMPLOYING LABOR—HIDDEN CONSEQUENCES OF THE LAW

Employers incur expenses associated with complying with employment laws and regulations. Hiring new employees is no longer as simple as advertising a job, interviewing the applicants, checking the references, and making the best choice. Firms must be careful to avoid lawsuits in this process. The lawsuits could come from the federal government, perhaps while it guards against discrimination. A lawsuit could also come from someone who was not hired. Such a lawsuit might allege an unfair hiring process. While many lawsuits involve an honest difference of opinion, frivolous lawsuits designed to harass defendants have resulted in the common use of the phrase "lawsuit abuse."

Jobs nowadays must be advertised using very careful wording. Prior to passage of the flurry of anti-discrimination laws in the mid-1960s, if a particularly appealing applicant came along, an employer could tailor the job to suit that applicant's unique abilities. Such actions today would wave the red flag of lawsuit over discriminatory treatment of those who were not hired. Hiring exactly according to a written advertisement avoids this problem, but also lowers the expected payoff to the firm from advertising a new opening. This caution

increases the cost of producing the firm's output. These costs are not measured in official statistics.

Information about prospective employees is increasingly hard to come by. The Equal Employment Opportunity Commission (EEOC) issues detailed guidelines about questions that are or are not appropriate to ask of job candidates. The same questions must be asked of each candidate. The employer cannot revise the list once interviewing has started, even if it becomes obvious that some pertinent questions have been overlooked. This very formal process makes it difficult for an employer to get a feel for whether an employee will fit into the organization.

Letters of recommendation are often nearly devoid of meaningful information. The threat of lawsuits bears much of the blame. After all, previous employers or others who know of reasons why someone should not be hired have no incentive to reveal it. Even if their information is true, they might still be sued for slander, defamation of character, or some other charge. There could even be dangers of lawsuits from future employers if letters of recommendation are misleadingly glowing.

Since the certain expense and uncertain outcome of a lawsuit is something few letter writers wish to face, letters of recommendation are often little more than reports on such dry, objective facts as a job applicant's previous position and duration of employment. The upshot is that hiring firms face an increasingly risky process, one less likely to match the best-qualified person to the job. This process increases per-unit production costs above what they might have been. It also affects the decision about whether to hire, since the hassles of hiring can be avoided by working current employees longer hours or more efficiently. The result is fewer employees per unit of output.

Government regulations and mandates have also increased employment costs. For example, the Americans with Disabilities Act mandates that firms accommodate a variety of employee disabilities. Usually, for example, a firm cannot simply fire a worker for showing up to work inebriated, since that might be a symptom of alcoholism. Alcoholism is a covered disability. Health and safety regulations, anti-discrimination laws, family leave requirements, and other government actions are intended to make the workplace better. They also increase per-unit production costs.

Such cost increases even arise from government-mandated protections for employees about to lose their jobs. For example, consider the requirement that firms notify their employees at least sixty days prior to closing a production facility and laying off employees that work there. In those sixty days, firms can expect to see both productivity and quality drop, perhaps precipitously. After all, employees are not usually motivated to do their best if they know that they will be out of work shortly. If they choose to produce at all, firms must be prepared for high absenteeism, low productivity, and even sabotage. In these ways, legislation designed to cushion the blow of unemployment has the unintended side effect of increasing firms' production costs.

DO GOVERNMENT POLICIES HELP EMPLOYEES?

Despite all the government presence in the employment process, life on the job isn't necessarily any easier. This is not surprising. The same incentives that reduce the number of employees firms wish to hire also motivate firms to obtain more productivity from the employees they already have. From the employees' perspective, finding new jobs is more difficult. Because all employers face similar incentives to increase productivity, employees have little recourse but to bear down and be more productive. Thus, we see the rise of workweeks that are much longer than the traditional forty hours. Table 6-2 shows the results of a survey of workers that identified those who work long hours, classified in the survey as 55 to 99 hours a week. The occupations shown are selected from those that exhibit the highest percentage of workers who fall into that classification. Men tend to work longer hours than women, an average of 44 hours for

TABLE 6-2	PERCENTAGE OF EMPLOYED WHO WORK 55 TO 99 HOURS A WEEK, BY OCCUPATION AND SEX

PERCENTAGES FOR MEN	
Physicians	44
Firefighters	41
Clergy	40
Restaurant and Hotel Managers	32
Vehicle Sales	26
Lawyers	25
Total:	10

PERCENTAGES FOR WOMEN	
Physicians:	32
Lawyers:	18
College Faculty:	16
Marketing Managers:	12
Restaurant and Hotel Managers:	12
Total:	3

Source: Daniel Hecker, How Hours of Work Affect Occupational Earnings, *Monthly Labor Review,* October 1998.

men and 41 hours for women. In addition to showing data for specific occupations, the table also shows that 10 percent of men and 3 percent of women work long hours.

Incongruously, we also see more temporary and part-time positions. The reasons for both trends are similar. Part-time and temporary workers are easier to hire and fire and require fewer federally mandated benefits. For example, firms will go to extraordinary lengths to stay below fifty full-time employees. By law, firms that exceed that threshold find themselves subject to an array of costly mandates and regulations. Part-time and temporary workers often provide the flexibility to avoid that threshold.

Taken as a whole, then, the increasing presence of well-intentioned laws pertaining to the workplace is threatening one of the mainstays of middle-class American existence, the forty-hour workweek. Part-time and overtime work is on the rise. Whether or not these changes are for the long-term good, is it any wonder that jobs seem stressful? Employment statistics measure the quantity of employment. We have no federal measure of its quality. The increasingly common reports of violence in the workplace give reason to wonder. According to the BLS, workplace violence accounted for 16 percent of the 5,915 workplace fatalities in 2000. Additionally, there were over 23,000 assaults and violent acts in the workplace that did not end in fatalities.

Few Americans would wish to repeal the laws or regulations that aim to eliminate discrimination and other workplace problems. However, a recognition of the costs of these mandates can help alleviate the unavoidable burdens. A little less stress on the job might contribute to a higher quality of life for all.

1. This Explore & Apply notes that laws and regulations are enacted in order to accomplish some worthy end. However, because these benefits are not elaborated upon, you might get the impression that legislation and litigation have imposed costs in excess of their benefits. Have they? Justify your answer with some specific examples.

2. What characteristics would a high-quality job have for you personally? If you worked at a job that failed to provide your desired characteristics, would you be willing to quit and join the ranks of the unemployed? Why or why not? What sorts of considerations would lie behind your decision?

 Visit www.prenhall.com/ayers for updates and web exercises on this Explore & Apply topic.

SUMMARY AND LEARNING OBJECTIVES

1. **Identify who is part of the labor force and who is not.**
   - The civilian labor force equals the number of persons age 16 and over who have a job or are looking for one. The labor force participation rate is found by dividing the labor force by the population age 16 and over. Currently, the U.S. labor force participation rate is about 67 percent.

2. **Explain how the unemployment rate is calculated.**
   - The unemployment rate equals the number of unemployed persons divided by the civilian labor force, multiplied by 100. The unemployment rate must be interpreted carefully, because of the existence of discouraged workers. Discouraged workers are not counted in the labor force because they have given up looking for work. If they were counted, the reported unemployment rate would rise.
   - The reported unemployment rate is higher than the true unemployment rate because of the underground economy. Note that the underground economy biases the reported unemployment rate in the opposite direction from discouraged workers.

3. **Elaborate on unemployment in other countries.**
   - There is a tendency for changes in unemployment rates across countries to move together. In contrast, the level of unemployment varies significantly across countries.

4. **Divide unemployment into different types and explain the implications of each.**
   - Unemployment of labor comes in four basic types: seasonal, frictional, structural, and cyclical.
   - Seasonal unemployment is related to the time of year. Examples include the department store Santa Claus without a job after Christmas, and the farm worker who becomes unemployed after the crop is harvested.
   - Frictional unemployment is associated with job switching and entry into the labor force. Frictional unemployment cannot be eliminated since, even though most job switches occur without unemployment time, there will always be some new jobs that cannot be lined up prior to departure from the old. Even when there is time between jobs, the frictionally unemployed typically do not stay unemployed for long.
   - Structural unemployment occurs when job skills become obsolete. Without skills that are in demand in the labor market, the structurally unemployed will remain unemployed for an extended time. Job training programs can reduce structural unemployment.
   - Cyclical unemployment is associated with the business cycle. During recessions, workers are laid off and the unemployment rate rises accordingly.

5. **Describe the natural rate of unemployment and its converse, full employment.**
   - The natural rate of unemployment is the minimum unemployment rate the economy can sustain in the long run. The natural rate changes over time. Currently, it is estimated to be around 5 percent.
   - A natural rate of unemployment implies the existence of full employment and the absense of cyclical unemployment.
   - Unemployment insurance programs offer financial support to the unemployed. However, they also offer an incentive to remain unemployed. Thus, the existence of unemployment insurance increases the unemployment rate.

6. **Discuss how the quality of employment can deteriorate when mandates increase labor costs.**
   - Because of various government actions, the expense of hiring and employing labor is higher than it otherwise would be. Employment-related government mandates are intended to create a more equitable workplace. However, the higher costs might cause some firms to cut back on their use of labor. Job stress and uncertainty can be a side effect.

KEY TERMS

labor force, 134
unemployment rate, 134
labor force participation rate, 134
discouraged workers, 138

frictional unemployment, 142
seasonal unemployment, 142
structural unemployment, 142
cyclical unemployment, 142

specific human capital, 143
general human capital, 143
natural rate of unemployment, 146
full employment, 146

TEST YOURSELF

TRUE OR FALSE

1. Persons over the age of 65 are excluded when the labor force is counted.
2. Recently, the U.S. labor force participation rate has been around 67 percent.
3. Persons who work but receive no pay, such as in a family business, are never counted as employed.
4. Frictional unemployment is associated with the business cycle.
5. The natural rate of unemployment is the unemployment rate associated with full employment.

MULTIPLE CHOICE

6. To be counted as employed, someone must work for pay
   a. at least 1 hour a week.
   b. at least 15 hours a week.
   c. at least 35 hours a week.
   d. for at least as many hours as that person wants to work.
7. The civilian labor force does not include
   a. workers under the age of 16.
   b. the unemployed.
   c. part-time workers.
   d. anyone working in a family business without pay.
8. The long-term trend in the labor force participation rate in the United States has been
   a. flat.
   b. up.
   c. down.
   d. cyclical.

9. To be counted as unemployed, an individual must
   a. not have a job.
   b. not have a job and be looking for work.
   c. not have a job, be looking for work, and be willing to accept the first job offer he or she receives.
   d. have held a job in the past, not have a job now, be looking for work, and be willing to accept the first job offer.
10. Discouraged workers
   a. are counted among the employed.
   b. are counted among the unemployed.
   c. would increase the unemployment rate if they were counted among the unemployed.
   d. have no effect on the labor force and unemployment statistics regardless of how or whether they are counted.
11. How does the underground economy affect the measurement of unemployment?
   a. It causes the reported unemployment rate to be higher than the true unemployment rate.
   b. It causes the reported unemployment rate to be lower than the true unemployment rate.
   c. It has no effect on the reported unemployment rate.
   d. It affects the reported unemployment rate in varying, but unpredictable, ways.
12. The duration of unemployment is an important aspect of unemployment because it tells us
   a. the probability that someone will become unemployed.
   b. the average age of the unemployed.
   c. how long people are unemployed.
   d. the lost income that is associated with unemployment.

13. Which type of unemployment is associated with a recession?
    a. Frictional.
    b. Seasonal.
    c. Structural.
    d. Cyclical.
14. Which type of unemployment is associated with technological change?
    a. Frictional.
    b. Seasonal.
    c. Structural.
    d. Cyclical.
15. Which type of unemployment is typically long term?
    a. Frictional.
    b. Seasonal.
    c. Structural.
    d. Cyclical.
16. The current best estimate of the natural rate of unemployment is around
    a. 0 percent.
    b. 1 percent.
    c. 5 percent.
    d. 7 percent.

17. The natural rate of unemployment
    a. remains constant over time.
    b. is higher today than a century ago.
    c. is lower today than a century ago.
    d. changes every day, so that it is sometimes higher than in the 1970s, but sometimes lower than then.
18. Full employment
    a. occurs only when 100 percent of the labor force is employed.
    b. equals 100 minus the natural rate of unemployment.
    c. is achieved when no one is frictionally unemployed.
    d. is a concept that is useful in the abstract, but never actually occurs in reality.
19. Unemployment insurance
    a. has no effect on the unemployment rate.
    b. increases the unemployment rate.
    c. decreases the unemployment rate.
    d. has unpredictable effects on the unemployment rate.
20. Mandates in the labor market arise from
    a. the market.
    b. government.
    c. firms.
    d. workers.

QUESTIONS AND PROBLEMS

1. *[civilian labor force]* How would the labor force be affected if those in the military were included? What effect would including the military in the labor force have on the unemployment rate?
2. *[labor force]* Can you think of a logical reason for excluding persons under the age of 16 from the labor force statistics, but not excluding persons over age 65 or even age 70 from the statistics? Explain.
3. *[labor force participation]* a) Provide several examples of individuals who would choose not to participate in the labor force. b) The labor force participation rate among men between 35 and 44 years of age is nearly 100 percent. What would explain such a high labor force participation rate?
4. *[labor force participation rate]* How is the labor force participation rate calculated? What is your best guess about the labor force participation rate among students in your economics class?
5. *[unemployment rate]* How is the unemployment rate calculated? Are discouraged workers included?
6. *[unemployment rates over time]* Use the data in Table 6-1 to answer the following questions.
    a. What is the highest unemployment rate in the table and what year did it occur?

    b. What is the lowest unemployment rate in the table and what year did it occur?
    c. Is there an easily discernable long-term trend in unemployment rates? Explain.
7. *[differences in unemployment rates]* Would you expect the average unemployment rate among high school graduates to be the same as the average unemployment rate among college graduates? Explain.
8. *[labor force and unemployment rate]* Suppose the country of Worklandia has a population of 100,000 persons age 16 and above. Of these persons 70,000 are working, 3,000 have no job, but are looking for a job, 7,000 of them are discouraged workers, and the rest are either students or retired. What is the labor force participation rate in Worklandia? What is the unemployment rate in that country?
9. *[types of unemployment]* List three instances when you or someone you know has been unemployed. For each, explain the type of unemployment, such as frictional, seasonal, structural, or cyclical.
10. *[structural unemployment]* Explain the role of human capital in the ability of an individual to find and keep a job.

11. *[seasonal unemployment]* Provide at least two examples of workers who are likely to become seasonally unemployed in each of the following cases.
    a. The day after Christmas.
    b. The day after the Super Bowl.
    c. The day after the last day of school.
12. *[influences on unemployment]* How does the "work ethic" of a country affect its labor force participation rate and its unemployment rate? Is it possible for a country to have too strong a work ethic? Explain.
13. *[natural rate of unemployment]* Why do economists reject the notion that the natural rate of unemployment equals zero? Why is the natural rate stated to be in the vicinity of 5 percent instead of an exact number?
14. *[full employment]* The employment rate in percent equals 100 minus the unemployment rate. What employment rate represents full employment in the United States? Explain.
15. *[imports and employment]* Explain why the logic of the natural rate of unemployment leaves no room for international trade to have any lasting effect on aggregate employment.

 Visit www.prenhall.com/ayers for Exploring the Web exercises and additional self-test quizzes.

CHAPTER 7

INFLATION

A LOOK AHEAD

Inflation—widespread, persistent price increases—can hurt people. It can change their behavior and keep them awake at night worrying about whether their incomes will keep up with prices. It can lower their standard of living when their incomes fall behind. In America, inflation has been a fact of life, but at least that inflation has been mild. In some other countries, inflation has been severe. In the Explore & Apply section in this chapter you will see how people make adjustments in their lifestyles in response to inflation.

Low inflation is a basic macroeconomic goal. As you read this chapter you will see why we prefer low inflation, the several ways that inflation is measured, and some ways that have been devised by people to defend themselves against the harmful effects of inflation.

LEARNING OBJECTIVES

Understanding Chapter 7 will enable you to:
1. **Describe inflation rates in the United States and other countries.**
2. **Discuss the effects of inflation that cause low inflation to be a macroeconomic goal.**
3. **Compute, interpret, and use a price index to compute a real value.**
4. **Identify problems with price indexes and efforts to improve them.**
5. **Explain how people respond to inflation, and how their responses affect its measurement.**

EXPLORE & APPLY

Do you notice price changes when you go shopping? Most people do, especially when prices are rising fast. This chapter will show you how changes in the cost of living are measured and why it is important to keep track of inflation.

7.1 THE GOAL OF LOW INFLATION

You have learned that there are three fundamental goals for our economy: economic growth, high employment, and low inflation. How well have we achieved the last goal? Let's take a look at the behavior of prices over time to answer that question.

MODERN HISTORY OF U.S. INFLATION

price level prices of goods and services in the aggregate.

The **price level** refers to the prices of goods and services, when considered in the aggregate. Even with no training in economics it is easy for you to recognize that the price level today is higher than it was when you were born. For example, by going to the library and taking a peek at twenty-year-old copies of your local newspaper, you would see that back then a basic economy car cost about $4,000, a man's dress shirt $10, a gallon of regular gas 80 cents, and a pound of bananas 20 cents. These items today might average about $13,000, $20, $1.40, and 40 cents, respectively. Many other items commonly purchased are also more expensive. A few items have gotten cheaper. Examples include television sets, cell phones, and other electronics. Overall, however, since most prices are higher, we say that the price level is also higher today than twenty years ago. Most of the time the price level increases from one year to the next.

inflation persistent, widespread increases in the price level.

Inflation is a persistent increase in the price level. Thus, inflation is not the same as a one-time increase in the prices of a few products. Rather, inflation involves widespread price increases, affecting the prices of many goods and services. Inflation can be mild, meaning that price increases are typically small for most goods, or severe, in which case price increases tend to be large. Any amount of inflation robs people of their purchasing power, *ceteris paribus*.

inflation rate the annual percentage increase in the price level.

The **inflation rate** is the annual percentage increase in the price level. We can compare the inflation rate in one year to the inflation rate in other years. In the United States, so long as the inflation rate stays at approximately 3 percent or less, most Americans are satisfied that the goal of low inflation has been accomplished. Once the inflation rate gets much over 3 percent, people tend to become worried.

As the inflation rate rises beyond the 3 percent threshold, people expect the federal government to "fight" inflation. In the United States, the last bout of relatively high inflation occurred in the 1970s. Every president in that decade fought for his political future by taking a stand against inflation. For example, in the mid-1970s President Ford tried to popularize a small lapel button that said WIN. WIN stood for Whip Inflation Now. Most people thought the WIN buttons were silly and ineffective. Partly because of inflation, candidate Jimmy Carter beat President Ford in the 1976 election. Ironically, the inflation rate had fallen every year of the Ford presidency, but promptly rebounded under Carter. When inflation rates reached new highs during the Carter years, Carter himself was turned out of office by Ronald Reagan's 1980 victory. As you can see, presidents may need to pay attention to inflation or pay the consequences. Because inflation was low during the last decade, it has become less of an election issue than it used to be.

Let's check the U.S. inflation rate over the years by looking at Figure 7-1. This figure shows the annual inflation rate in the United States since 1945, the last year of World War II. We can see that the inflation rate fluctuates. The somewhat high inflation in the late 1940s after World War II, and during the second year of the Korean War (1950–1953), subsided throughout the rest of the 1950s and early 1960s. Inflation began to increase as the Vietnam

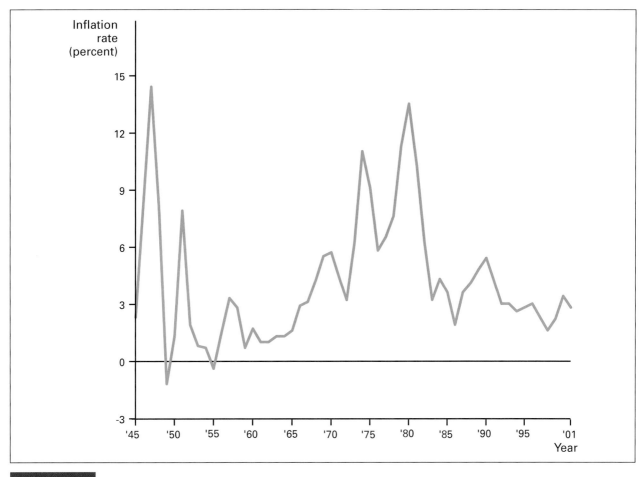

FIGURE 7-1

THE U.S. INFLATION RATE SINCE 1945 The annual inflation rate changes from year to year. The relatively high inflation rates in some years tell us that the goal of low inflation is sometimes elusive.

Source: 2002 Economic Report of the President, Table B-64. The inflation rates shown are based on the Consumer Price Index.

QUICKCHECK

What is the price level? How is the inflation rate related to the price level?

Answer: The price level refers to the prices of goods and services in the aggregate. An inflation rate is expressed as an annual percentage increase in the price level.

War heated up in the mid-to-late 1960s, continued to rise during the 1970s, and peaked in the early 1980s. Most of the 1980s were characterized by declining inflation rates. Inflation stayed relatively low in the 1990s. Although there are periodic fears that a new outbreak of high inflation is about to begin, such fears had not been realized by 2002, as the United States continued to experience the relatively low inflation that characterized the 1990s. As the figure shows, however, the inflation rate can rise significantly from one year to the next, so no one knows what the future holds.

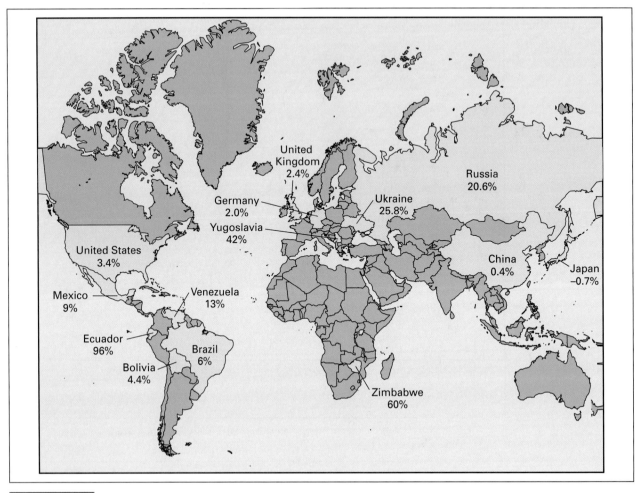

FIGURE 7-2

INFLATION RATES IN SELECTED COUNTRIES Inflation rates vary significantly from country to country. Developing countries tend to have higher inflation rates than do developed countries.

Source: Central Intelligence Agency, *The World Factbook, 2001.* All data are for 2000, except Yugoslavia, which is for 1999. Except for the United States, Brazil, and Venezuela, the data are estimated values. The inflation rates are for consumer prices.

INFLATION—A WORLDWIDE PHENOMENON

Inflation is not confined just to the United States. The Central Intelligence Agency (CIA) estimates that the average inflation rate in the world in 2000 was 25 percent. Throughout recent history, inflation has been most severe in developing nations, ones facing a variety of economic and social problems. The CIA estimates that developing countries had inflation rates between 5 percent and 60 percent in 2000, which is markedly higher than the typical 1 percent to 3 percent inflation rate in developed countries. A few countries, such as Japan, have had lower inflation rates than the United States. Figure 7-2 shows recent inflation rates for selected countries. The figure reveals that inflation is a near universal fact of life in the modern world.

Countries with very high inflation rates usually try to bring them down because high inflation is unpopular. Political instability can be the result of letting inflation get out of control. For example, Bolivia had an 11,000 percent (!) inflation rate in 1985, which brought about a change in its government the next year. Figure 7-2 shows that Bolivia has been able to successfully rein in the inflation of the 1980s. Other countries, including Brazil and Venezuela, have also suffered from very high inflation rates in the last decade or two. Similarly, they have brought their inflation rates down to no more than two digits, also documented in Figure 7-2. However, countries with a history of high inflation seem to swerve back and forth between extreme increases in the price level and relative price stability.

Seeking a solution to its high inflation, Ecuador, the country with the highest inflation rate in Figure 7-2, adopted a policy of *dollarization* in 2001. Dollarization replaces a country's currency with the U.S. dollar. By dollarizing its economy, Ecuador expects to be better off because its inflation rate should mirror the relatively low U.S. inflation rate. Dollarization should also provide for a more stable economy and government since the value of the dollar is relatively stable. Following dollarization, the inflation rate in Ecuador fell sharply from the value in the figure.

DEFLATION AND DISINFLATION

When the inflation rate is negative, *deflation* is said to occur. That would happen if the price level declined from one year to the next. Severe, persistent deflation has yet to occur in modern U.S. history, although the economy showed slight deflation in 1949 and 1955, which you can see in Figure 7-1. More recently, prices of raw materials and some other goods, such as personal computers, fell significantly in the late 1990s, but not enough that we could say there was deflation. As for other countries, Figure 7-2 shows that Japan experienced a small negative value for its inflation rate, indicating mild deflation in 2000.

Shoppers benefit from persistently falling prices by being able to buy more with their incomes, which means that their purchasing power is increased by deflation. For example, if deflation caused all prices to drop by 10 percent, then other things equal, everyone's income would buy 10 percent more. Borrowers, on the other hand, see declining values of the items they have purchased using debt, while the size of their debts remain constant. The family that borrowed $100,000 to finance the $100,000 purchase price of a new home would find that their home was worth only $90,000 after a 10 percent deflation, but their debt would stay at $100,000.

Deflation is not a macroeconomic goal because deflation tends to be associated with economies in trouble. In the 1930s, the U.S. economy experienced significant deflation during the Great Depression. Sixty years later, a decade characterized by recession and weak growth in Japan has also been associated with deflation in that country. The conclusion drawn by many economists is that deflation must be avoided in order for an economy to prosper.

Disinflation differs from either inflation or deflation. *Disinflation* means that the rate of inflation declines. For instance, if we observed inflation rates of 7 percent followed by 2 percent over two consecutive years, disinflation would have occurred. Disinflation is sometimes confused with deflation, but they are not the same. You can see in Figure 7-1 that disinflation occurs quite frequently. It is identified in the figure with dips in the line showing the inflation rate.

SNAPSHOT   **"WATCH FOR FALLING PRICES"—CAN WAL-MART HELP KEEP INFLATION IN CHECK?**

It's all about low prices at Wal-Mart. The slogan in the title is designed to keep customers coming back by convincing them that Wal-Mart strives to give them more for their money. You've probably seen the ads that show the old higher prices and the new lower prices of specific items.

How does Wal-Mart bring down those prices, and what effect does the retail giant have on inflation? Wal-Mart is able to cut prices when it finds ways to increase the efficiency with which it operates and thereby cut its operating costs. Efficiency increases help keep inflation in check. ◄

7.2 THE HARM FROM INFLATION

In spite of relatively little inflation in the United States in recent years, the fear of higher inflation persists. This fear causes people to pay attention to inflation data. Toward the middle of each month, the government makes public the inflation rate for the previous month in a news release that is reported by the media. Of course, even without access to inflation data, people can tell a lot about the inflation rate just by visiting their local supermarket or discount store. For many Americans, the ultimate inflation tale is the story told by a cash register tape.

Energy and food prices are subject to wide fluctuations caused by temporary shifts in their supplies. Excluding food and energy prices from the computation of the inflation rate reveals what is termed *core inflation.* The core rate of inflation is of special interest when food and energy inflation rates differ significantly from the overall inflation rate. Otherwise, core inflation and the overall inflation rate will not differ much. Table 7-1 shows the U.S. inflation rate and the core inflation rate. In 2000, for example, the core inflation rate of 2.4 percent is less than the inflation rate of 3.4 percent. That difference occurred because energy prices skyrocketed in percentage terms in 2000.

Even with relatively low inflation, as in recent years, select groups of people can be hurt. There will be some people whose incomes do not keep up with inflation and other people whose incomes keep up with or exceed inflation. The first group will be hurt; the latter group probably will not be.

Most workers expect and receive an annual raise in pay. To them a good pay raise is one that provides an increase in their purchasing power, meaning that it exceeds the inflation rate. In contrast, people who live on a fixed income see no increase in their income. Thus, inflation eats away at their purchasing power. Over time, through no fault of their own, their standard of living declines. **Inflation hurts those on fixed incomes.**

One group that can benefit from inflation is borrowers. Because inflation erodes the purchasing power of money, borrowers repay their debts with dollars that are worth less and less. Of course, on the other side are the lenders who receive those devalued dollars as the debts of the borrowers are paid off. Thus, when lenders and borrowers are compared, it is the lenders who are hurt by inflation.

Perhaps the greatest harm from inflation is the opportunity cost of the time and other resources spent trying to avoid the harm inflicted by inflation. One obvious response by consumers to inflation is to seek out substitute goods whose prices have not risen as much as the prices of similar goods. Shoppers must spend time, energy, gasoline, and other resources trying the dodge the inflation bullet.

Inflation motivates businesses to offer new products. The interest in cheaper substitutes motivated retailers to begin offering generic brands. Generic products, with plain labels like "Green Beans" and "Paper Towels," are cheaper than their brand name equivalents. Inflation might also cause businesses to trim the sizes of their products rather than raise their prices.

TABLE 7-1 THE CORE RATE OF INFLATION

The core rate of inflation excludes food and energy prices from the computation of the inflation rate. These items' prices are particularly volatile. By excluding them, we get a better idea of the price changes in a broad range of other goods and services. All data are percentages.

YEAR	INFLATION RATE (INCLUDES FOOD AND ENERGY PRICES)	CORE INFLATION RATE (EXCLUDES FOOD AND ENERGY PRICES)
1979	11.3	9.8
1980	13.5	12.4
1981	10.3	10.4
1982	6.2	7.4
1983	3.2	4.0
1984	4.3	5.0
1985	3.6	4.3
1986	1.9	4.0
1987	3.6	4.1
1988	4.1	4.4
1989	4.8	4.5
1990	5.4	5.0
1991	4.2	4.9
1992	3.0	3.7
1993	3.0	3.3
1994	2.6	2.8
1995	2.8	3.0
1996	3.0	2.7
1997	2.3	2.4
1998	1.6	2.3
1999	2.2	2.1
2000	3.4	2.4
2001	2.8	2.6

Source: 2002 Economic Report of the President, Table B-63. The inflation rates shown were computed using the Consumer Price Index.

ANTICIPATED AND UNANTICIPATED INFLATION

By making the distinction between anticipated inflation and unanticipated inflation, we can more easily discuss the gains and losses produced by inflation. *Anticipated inflation* is expected by the public. *Unanticipated inflation* is inflation that catches the public by surprise.

People can take anticipated inflation into account in wage negotiations, mortgage loans, the tax system, and a variety of other contractual agreements. In theory at least, everyone is thus able to defend against losses imposed by anticipated inflation. For example, if workers anticipate the inflation rate will be 3 percent next year, they can try to negotiate 3 percent wage increases to offset that inflation.

When inflation is unanticipated, the story changes. An increase in inflation that causes the inflation rate to be higher than expected provides borrowers with a windfall. Because borrowers win, lenders lose. To see this possibility, suppose I borrowed $1,000 from you to be repaid in one year. We both anticipate an inflation rate of 2 percent over the year, and agree that an additional 3 percent **interest** to compensate you for the use of your money is fair. Thus, we strike a deal that I will repay you $1,050: the original sum of $1,000 I borrowed, plus $20 (2 percent of $1,000) to make you whole for the loss of purchasing power you suffer because of inflation, plus another $30 (3 percent of $1,000) for giving up the use of your money for the year.

Now suppose inflation proves greater than we anticipated. For example, suppose inflation rises to 5 percent. The $1,050 I repay you provides you with no reward for giving up the use of your money. You lose. I win, because I was able to use your money without having to pay you for its use. In other words, I used your purchasing power, and later returned the same purchasing power to you. If inflation had risen to a rate greater than 5 percent, I would have returned less purchasing power to you than you had before. You would be an even bigger loser, and I would be a bigger winner.

interest payment made by a borrower to compensate a lender for the use of money.

INDEXING TO OFFSET INFLATION'S EFFECTS

A response to the winners and losers problem created by unanticipated inflation is called **indexing**—automatically adjusting the terms of an agreement to account for inflation. *Cost of living adjustment (COLA)* clauses in labor agreements are a form of wage indexing. COLAs call for periodic upward adjustments in the wages of workers to match increases in inflation. Social Security payments feature a COLA. People who receive monthly Social Security checks find those checks get larger each year because of the built-in COLA.

If we indexed our loan agreement in the previous section, we would agree to adjust the amount I repaid you according to the inflation rate. If the inflation rate were to be 5 percent over the year of our loan agreement, I would be required to repay you $1,080, equal to the $1,000 I borrowed, plus the additional 3 percent interest you wanted ($30), plus the 5 percent ($50) to make up for the reduction in purchasing power caused by inflation. In other words, an **interest rate**, the price of borrowed money, that is indexed to inflation rises when inflation rises and falls when inflation falls.

indexing automatically adjusting the terms of an agreement for inflation.

A number of high-inflation countries have resorted to indexation to deal with inflation. In the United States, variable-rate home mortgages are a form of indexing. When market interest rates rise because of inflation, home buyers find their monthly payments also rising because the interest rate built into their mortgage agreement rises accordingly. Traditional fixed-rate home mortgages are not indexed. Lenders who make fixed-rate loans take the risk of inflation-induced losses in exchange for a higher interest rate than is initially attached to an otherwise-similar variable-rate mortgage.

interest rate the price of borrowed money; expressed as a percentage.

Indexing can benefit savers. Millions of Americans have loaned money to the federal government by buying U.S. Savings Bonds, receiving fixed interest payments in return.

The fixed interest payments mean that these bonds are not indexed for inflation. Inflation thus reduces the purchasing power of the interest payments as the years go by. Because of people's fears of inflation, the U.S. Treasury began to offer indexed bonds called *Treasury Inflation-Protected Securities (TIPS)* in 1997. Savers who buy TIPS bonds will find their interest earnings rise as inflation rises and fall as inflation falls. This feature of these bonds makes them attractive to savers who worry about unanticipated inflation. Meanwhile, the old-fashioned savings bond is still available for other less-worried savers.

IS A LITTLE INFLATION GOOD FOR THE ECONOMY?

SNAPSHOT

Goal: low inflation. Why not just say, "Goal: zero inflation." Some say a little inflation is good for the economy. The argument goes like this: Rising prices create expectations of more inflation, and prompt consumers to buy now to beat the coming price increases. Those rising prices also provide businesses with more profits that they can use to expand their production of goods and services. Thus, GDP rises and unemployment is kept low.

Based on this view, inflation is like a mild stimulant to the economy, just as caffeine is to tired, overworked people. However, we should recognize that inflation causes consumer purchasing power to fall so that consumers cannot keep up the extra spending that inflation initially causes. Furthermore, experience from the 1970s showed that a little inflation can easily become a lot of inflation. That experience showed that inflation can become less like caffeine and more like a strong narcotic. Still, today we accept a little inflation and go about our business. ◄

7.3 MEASURING INFLATION

Which prices are going up the fastest? Is our income keeping up with price increases? Price indexes can help inform us about inflation.

A *price index* measures the average level of prices in the economy. There are several price indexes, each created for a specific purpose, with a different set of prices measured.

- The **consumer price index (CPI),** the best-known price index among the public, measures prices of typical purchases made by consumers living in urban areas.
- The **producer price index (PPI)** measures wholesale prices, which are prices paid by firms.
- The **GDP chained price index** and the **GDP implicit price deflator** are the most broadly based price indexes because they include prices across the spectrum of GDP.

Let's look at the CPI first since it is the most-used price index.

THE CONSUMER PRICE INDEX

To understand the CPI, let's start with the concept of the *base period*. **The base period is an arbitrarily selected initial time period against which other time periods are compared.** The CPI is assigned a value of 100 during the base period. For instance, the base period for the CPI is presently 1982 to 1984, and the CPI has been assigned an average value of 100 over that period of time.

Table 7-2 reproduces values of the CPI for selected years. The table shows, for example, that the CPI for 1951 equals 26. That value means that a dollar's worth of consumer purchases in the base period would have cost 26 cents in 1951. The table also shows that the CPI for 2001 equals 177.1. On average, a consumer would have needed $1.77 to pay for the

consumer price index (CPI) measures prices of a market basket of purchases made by consumers living in urban areas.

producer price index (PPI) measures wholesale prices, which are prices paid by firms.

GDP chained price index a price index used to compute real GDP by linking together successive years of data.

GDP implicit price deflator index of prices across the spectrum of GDP; ratio of nominal GDP to real GDP.

TABLE 7-2 | THE CONSUMER PRICE INDEX, SELECTED YEARS

The CPI typically rises year to year, as is seen here. The average value of the CPI for 1982, 1983, and 1984 equals 100 because the 1982–1984 period is the base period.

YEAR	CONSUMER PRICE INDEX
1951	26
1961	29.9
1971	40.6
1979	72.6
1980	82.4
1981	90.9
1982	96.5
1983	99.6
1984	103.9
1985	107.6
1986	109.6
1987	113.6
1988	118.3
1989	124.0
1990	130.7
1991	136.2
1992	140.3
1993	144.5
1994	148.2
1995	152.4
1996	156.9
1997	160.5
1998	163.0
1999	166.6
2000	172.2
2001	177.1

Averages to 100, the base-period value

Source: 2002 Economic Report of the President, Table B-60.

purchases that cost a dollar during the base period. Notice that the CPI for years before the base period exhibits values less than 100 because prices were lower than in the base period.

We can use the CPI data to compute the inflation rate. The inflation rate is calculated by taking the percentage change in the CPI as follows:

$$\text{Inflation rate} = \frac{\text{Change in price index}}{\text{Initial price index}} \times 100$$

For example, from Table 7-2, the CPI equaled 177.1 in 2001 and 172.2 in 2000. The change in the CPI between 2000 and 2001 was 4.9 units, equal to 177.1 minus 172.2. When 4.9 is divided by 172.2 and the result multiplied by 100, the annual rate of inflation is seen to be 2.8 percent:

$$\text{Inflation rate in 2001} = \frac{4.9}{172.2} \times 100 = .028 \times 100 = 2.8 \text{ percent}$$

The inflation rate you just computed is the same as shown in Table 7-1. All the inflation rates in that table are computed in the same way.

What prices are measured by the CPI? If it were possible to count all the consumer prices in the economy, the number of different prices would likely be in the millions. It is unrealistic to expect so many prices to be used in the computation of a price index. The calculation of the CPI is based upon the prices of selected goods and services that consumers typically purchase. **The collection of goods and services used in the calculation of the CPI is called the *market basket*.** The market basket represents a sampling of the items that consumers buy that make up a significant part of their budgets. The market basket is based on extensive surveys of consumer purchases. There are around 200 specific categories of goods and services in the market basket, ranging from apples to women's dresses. Each item in the market basket is assigned a *weight* that reflects its importance in consumers' budgets. For example, personal care items such as shampoo have a smaller weight than gasoline. The BLS computes the CPI for the market basket every month. This effort requires BLS employees in eighty-seven urban areas to collect a total of 80,000 different prices.

The 200 or so specific categories of goods in the CPI market basket are divided into eight broad expenditure categories, as shown in Figure 7-3. All goods and services in the market basket belong to one of these categories. The weight on each category, which reflects the relative importance of the categories to consumers, is also shown in the figure. The relative importance is stated as a percentage of total spending by the average consumer. For example, housing expenditures are the largest component of the expenditure categories, amounting to 40.9 percent of expenditures by average consumers. The weights are so important in contributing to the accuracy of the CPI that they are now updated every two years, rather than every ten years, as in the past. Current weights help to ensure that the CPI reflects how people are spending their money.

Weights can be used to identify the sources of inflation. For example, suppose that there is a price increase of 10 percent in housing, with no price changes for the other expenditure categories. The inflation rate as measured by the CPI would equal 4.09 percent, computed as 10 percent multiplied by 0.409 (the weight on housing, after it is converted from a percent to decimal form). The knowledge that the increase in the CPI is concentrated in the price of housing can be used to design policies that target inflation from that source.

Let's see how to compute a price index based on the CPI market basket of items. The formula for the consumer price index is:

$$\text{CPI} = \frac{\text{Cost of market basket at current prices}}{\text{Cost of market basket at base period prices}} \times 100$$

The consumer price index measures the increase in the price of the market basket between the current year and the base period. It uses base period quantities throughout.

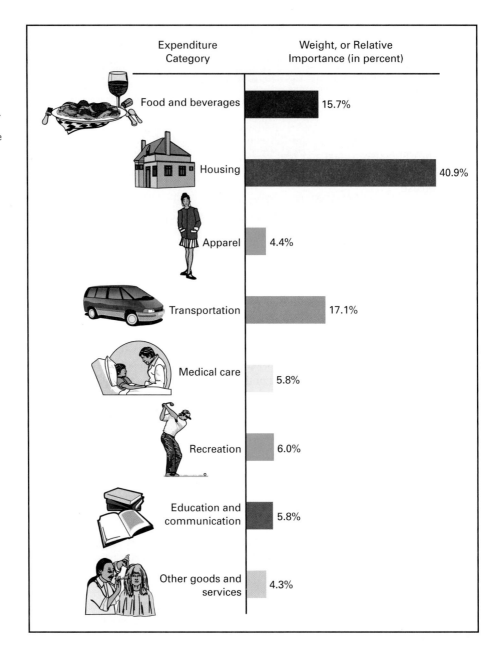

Expenditure Category	Weight, or Relative Importance (in percent)
Food and beverages	15.7%
Housing	40.9%
Apparel	4.4%
Transportation	17.1%
Medical care	5.8%
Recreation	6.0%
Education and communication	5.8%
Other goods and services	4.3%

An example in which this price index is calculated for a market basket of three goods can help clarify the procedure. Suppose we wish to calculate the price index for a market basket of apples, oranges, and bananas. In the base period 5 apples, 4 oranges, and 2 bananas are purchased. The prices in the base period were 30 cents each for apples, 20 cents each for oranges, and 10 cents each for bananas. Currently, apples are still 30 cents each, but oranges have also risen to 30 cents each, while bananas have risen to 20 cents each. These prices and quantities are presented in Table 7-3.

Perform the calculation as follows:

$$\text{Price Index example} = \frac{(.30 \times 5) + (.30 \times 4) + (.20 \times 2)}{(.30 \times 5) + (.20 \times 4) + (.10 \times 2)} \times 100 = \frac{3.10}{2.50} \times 100 = 1.24 \times 100 = 124$$

TABLE 7-3   DATA USED IN PRICE INDEX EXAMPLE

BASE PERIOD QUANTITIES	BASE PERIOD PRICES	CURRENT PRICES
Apples: 5	Apples: $.30 each	Apples: $.30 each
Oranges: 4	Oranges: $.20 each	Oranges: $.30 each
Bananas: 2	Bananas: $.10 each	Bananas: $.20 each

QUICKCHECK

What is the significance of the base period for the CPI? How is the base period selected?

Answer: The base period provides a point of reference to which the current price level can be compared. The CPI is set to a value of 100 during the base period. The selection of the base period is arbitrary.

In the base year the market basket cost $2.50. Now that same market basket costs $3.10. The index number of 124 indicates that the market basket costs 24 percent more than in the base year. The computation of this simplified price index gives you an idea of how the CPI is computed. The actual CPI calculation follows this procedure, but is more complicated because of some problems with price indexes that we will discuss a little later in the chapter.

CHANGING INCOMES, CHANGING LIFESTYLES, CHANGING WEIGHTS

SNAPSHOT

The twentieth century has run its course. Looking back we can see that the century was characterized by ever-increasing prosperity for Americans. Oh, there were interruptions on the way up—the Great Depression, then World War II, and a number of relatively mild recessions. However, the overall prosperity allowed for major lifestyle changes: a shorter workweek, a house in the suburbs, and a car in every garage.

Changes in people's lifestyles mean that the things that they spend their money on change. People can only spend so much on necessities like food and clothing before they have enough to meet their needs. The relative importance of necessities in their budgets thus falls. Their weights in the CPI market basket decrease. At the same time, new goods and services are introduced to the marketplace. When these are successful, the market basket weights will change to reflect that success. Thus, the expenditure category weights in Figure 7-3 are a snapshot of spending patterns at a point in time. The weights were different in the past and will be different in the future. ◀

USING THE CPI: NOMINAL VALUES VERSUS REAL VALUES

An increase in GDP due solely to price increases does not increase economic well-being. We can use a price index to adjust economic measures for the effects of inflation. The **nominal value** of a variable is not adjusted for inflation. The **real value** of a variable adjusts for inflation. The real

nominal value a value that is not adjusted for inflation.

real value a value that results from adjusting a nominal value for inflation.

value is expressed in terms of the value of the dollar during a selected base period. The time period chosen as the base period is not very important. What is important is that each year's measuring units be the same—dollars with the same purchasing power.

The distinction between real and nominal values is important not only to the study of macroeconomics, but also to individuals. Consider a worker whose weekly pay increases from $100 to $110. That worker has experienced a 10 percent increase in nominal income. If the price level remains constant, the worker's real income is also 10 percent greater. However, if the price level increases by 10 percent, the $110 of current income will purchase only as much as $100 purchased in the past. That means that the real income has not changed.

The following formula shows how to use a price index to compute a real value:

$$\text{Real value} = \frac{\text{Nominal value}}{\text{Price index}} \times 100$$

For example, suppose Jason earned nominal incomes of $39,000 a year in the base period and $40,500 in the current year, a 3.8 percent increase over the base period. Is Jason better off in the current year than in the base period? If the price index in the current year equals 105, then:

$$\text{Jason's real income} = \left(\frac{\$40,500}{105}\right) \times 100 = \$38,571.43$$

Jason's real income, which measures his purchasing power, has fallen since the base period. In terms of his real income he is not better off.

Figure 7-4 exemplifies the importance of real measures by showing the nominal and real values of the minimum wage since its enactment in 1938. As the figure shows, the purchasing power of the minimum wage has been in a long-term decline since the late 1960s, with periodic slight upticks when it is increased by Congress.

The distinction between a nominal and a real value is important in other instances. An *interest rate* is the price of borrowed money, expressed in percentage terms. If it is not adjusted for inflation, it is called a *nominal interest rate*. A *real interest rate* measures the percentage payment in terms of its purchasing power. To compute a real interest rate it is not necessary to know the value of a price index. Instead, all that is needed is the inflation rate and the nominal interest rate. To obtain the real interest rate, subtract the inflation rate from the nominal interest rate:

$$\text{Real interest rate} = \text{Nominal interest rate} - \text{Inflation rate}$$

Recall our earlier example where I borrow $1,000 from you. We agree that I am to repay you $1,050 in one year. The nominal interest rate is 5 percent (the interest payment of $50 divided by the amount borrowed). With an inflation rate of 2 percent, the real interest rate is only 3 percent. You, the lender in this example, will increase your purchasing power by 3 percent when the loan is repaid. The real interest rate in the United States is contrasted to the nominal interest rate in Figure 7-5 on page 170. The real interest rate and the nominal interest rate typically move in the same direction, but the nominal rate is higher than the real rate.

PRICE INDEXES FOR OTHER PURPOSES

Let's consider the three other price indexes mentioned earlier: the producer price index, the GDP implicit price deflator, and the GDP chained price index. The producer price index (PPI) focuses on the prices received by U.S. producers, as measured by the revenue they receive. The prices are those of the outputs sold by producers to other producers as intermediate goods, and sold by producers directly to consumers. The PPI often foretells increases in the CPI because price increases at the producer level will usually be passed on

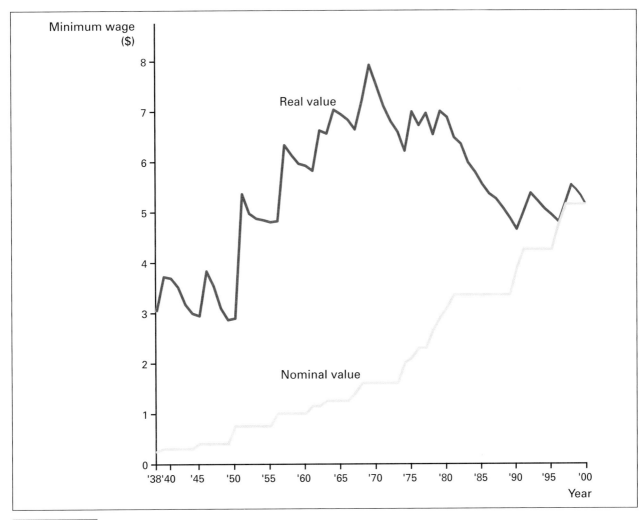

FIGURE 7-4

THE REAL AND NOMINAL VALUES OF THE MINIMUM WAGE, 1938–2000 The figure shows the nominal and real values of the minimum wage since its inception in 1938. The real value of the minimum wage is in terms of year 2000 dollars. Expressing the real value in terms of dollars in that year makes the real and nominal values identical in the year 2000, which you can see in the figure. You can also see that the minimum wage had the greatest purchasing power in 1968, when the nominal value of $1.60 would have bought the equivalent of a nominal wage of nearly $8.00 in 2000.

Source: Bureau of Labor Statistics.

later to consumer prices. Thus, the PPI is watched for hints about the future course of consumer prices.

Prior to 1978, the PPI was called the wholesale price index, a name that reflected the idea that many of the prices in the PPI are wholesale prices, rather than the retail prices used to compute the CPI. The name change occurred in order to emphasize that the prices in the PPI are those received by producers no matter who makes the purchase, whether it be another firm or a consumer.

The GDP chained price index and the GDP implicit price deflator, as you would guess from their names, are for gross domestic product. Both indexes, published by the Department of Commerce, use 1996 as the base period, meaning that the values of the indexes are equal to 100 in that year.

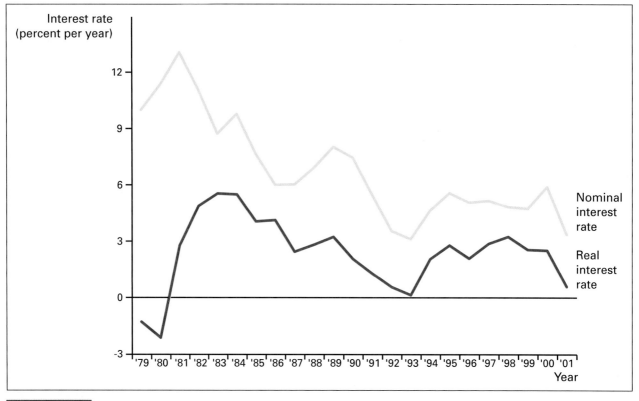

THE REAL AND NOMINAL INTEREST RATES The real interest rate was negative in 1979 and 1980 because the inflation rate was higher than the nominal interest rate. The rising real interest rates in 1981, 1982, and 1983 resulted from efforts to bring inflation under control.

Source: 2002 Economic Report of the President, Tables B-63 and B-73. The real interest rate was computed using the six-month T-bill rate as the nominal interest rate.

Let's look at the GDP implicit price deflator first. It is computed as:

$$\text{GDP implicit price deflator} = \frac{\text{Nominal GDP}}{\text{Real GDP}} \times 100$$

Let's apply the formula. In 2001 nominal GDP equaled \$10,082.2 billion and real GDP equaled \$9,214.5 billion. Substituting in the formula, we have:

$$\text{2001 GDP implicit price deflator} = \frac{10,082.2}{9,214.5} \times 100 = 109.42$$

This value says that the price level has risen over 9 percent since the 1996 base year. The GDP implicit price deflator is broad-based because it reflects price changes in the entire spectrum of goods and services that go into GDP.

In order to compute the GDP implicit price deflator, we must know the value of real GDP. Real GDP is computed from nominal GDP, using the GDP chained price index:

$$\text{Real GDP} = \frac{\text{Nominal GDP}}{\text{GDP chained price index}} \times 100$$

The computation of real GDP using this price index was shown in Chapter 5. Chain-type methods provide the best way to estimate a price index. We turn now to discussing why a chain-type index is superior, and how the computation of the CPI has been revised in response.

CHAIN METHODS TO IMPROVE PRICE INDEXES

The GDP chained price index is a type of *chain-weight* index, because it links quantities (weights) in two successive years, then moves forward a year and does that link again, and so forth. This continuous linking, two years at a time, forms a chain, and hence the name. For example, the calculation of 2002 GDP involves prices and quantities for 2001 and 2002. Similarly, the calculation of 2003 GDP involves prices and quantities for 2002 and 2003. A chain-type price index provides the most accurate data on changes in the cost of living, since it uses current weights in its computation. This consideration has led to changes in the CPI, including the decision to offer a new chained CPI alongside the traditional CPI.

Prior to 1999 the CPI was calculated using *fixed weights* throughout the market basket. Fixed weight price indexes provide consistently incorrect results because they assume that people do not change their consumption when prices rise. In fact, as prices change, people typically substitute relatively cheaper goods for goods that have become relatively more expensive. The inaccuracy introduced into the CPI by this behavior is termed the *substitution bias*. **The substitution bias causes inflation to be overstated.** This bias is inherent in a fixed-weight price index. Other biases creep into price indexes because it is difficult to account for quality changes that improve products. Similarly, unless a price index immediately takes into account the introduction of new products, it will be biased.

It was recognized long ago that the substitution bias caused the CPI to overstate inflation, and a solution to the problem was sought. Through the years since its inception in 1913, the method of computing the CPI has been improved repeatedly. In January 1999, the CPI was improved again to provide a partial solution to the substitution bias. That change better measures the cost of living when people respond to inflation by cutting their consumption of goods whose prices have risen the most, and increasing their consumption of items whose prices have not. The revision to the CPI has lowered the computed inflation rate slightly, providing a more accurate assessment of price changes.

In an effort to provide even more accurate inflation data, another type of CPI was introduced in August 2002. This CPI is called the C-CPI, with the first C standing for chained. A chained price index uses continuously updated expenditure weights. As discussed earlier in relation to Figure 7-3, the CPI weights are updated every two years. In contrast, the new C-CPI is chained monthly. In effect, the weights for the C-CPI are updated continuously.

The C-CPI supplements, but does not replace, the older CPI. Both price indexes are useful, but the method of computation is different. The current CPI assumes that the share of the consumer's budget spent on an item stays fixed for the two years between updates in the weights. Thus, it retains some of the disadvantage of a fixed weight index. The C-CPI makes no such assumption, and instead assumes that consumers substitute freely among items as prices change. Thus, the C-CPI may be viewed as an effort to overcome fully the problem of substitution bias.

QUICKCHECK

What is the substitution bias that causes the traditional CPI to overstate the impact of inflation on actual consumers?

Answer: Computing inflation using the traditional CPI will tell you the percentage by which the cost of goods in the market basket will have increased. However, consumers will substitute away from goods that have risen the most in price and toward those that have risen the least, thus mitigating the effect of that inflation.

7.4 LIVING WITH INFLATION

The consumer price index (CPI) is used in three ways:

- As an economic indicator. As such, it is used by the government and the public to determine whether the nation is meeting its goal of low inflation.
- To convert nominal economic values into real values. A worker's average real income is superior to nominal income as a measure of economic progress.
- To adjust selected monetary payments upward as prices increase. The annual cost-of-living adjustment in Social Security payments is an example.

Consider how people might react to a soaring CPI.

Hyperinflation is inflation out of control, with prices rising quickly. Take an annual inflation rate of 10,000 percent, for example. A look at the CPI would be unnecessary to conclude that inflation was out of control. A trip to any store would do that. What would a dollar be worth after just one year of such continuous hyperinflation? The answer: less than a penny. To put it another way, it would take over $100 at the end of a year of such hyperinflation to purchase what $1 would have purchased at the beginning of the year.

The most widely documented hyperinflation occurred in post–World War I Germany in the years 1922–1923. Germany had to pay war reparations to the Allies. Unable to raise enough money by taxing or borrowing, the German government turned to the printing press. Before the presses stopped and currency reform occurred, prices had increased by a factor of 1.5 trillion. In comparison, if the United States suffered an inflation of similar magnitude, a $50 sleeping bag would rise in price to $75 trillion.

Imagine a hyperinflated world. It would be difficult to carry enough cash to make a simple purchase since that purchase might cost you millions of dollars. You might want your wages paid daily, or even more often. That's because a dollar received now would have more purchasing power than a dollar received later—even a few hours later. You would also want to budget enough time to spend your money. You might take time off from work during the day to go spend your wages as soon as you receive them. Hyperinflation turns money into a hot potato: Get rid of it quickly before it loses more value.

Hyperinflation has also struck other countries. Imagine yourself peering from your apartment window in Buenos Aries, Argentina, in 1989. You spy an armored car pulling up to La Dora Restaurant down the street, and carting away sacks of money. It is midnight. You recall seeing the same event every night at midnight. Come to think of it, you'd seen bags of money carted away from that same restaurant every day at noon. Have you witnessed an illegal money laundering operation? Actually, these events were real, but represented the restaurant getting its money into an interest-earning bank account as quickly as possible. At a 1989 inflation rate of 100 percent per month, it did not take long for the Argentine currency to lose much of its value.

With prices changing quickly, everyone tries to adjust. One type of adjustment is the behavioral changes that individuals make in order to try to cope with inflation. Individual adjustments can be as simple as searching out cheaper places to shop and substituting chicken for steak. Some people barter—they enter into direct exchanges of goods and services with other people, with no need for money to change hands. Other people exchange their country's currency for foreign currencies that are stable in value. These adjustments can be stressful and costly in terms of a person's time.

Another type of adjustment revolves around the changes in business practices that increase the cost of doing business. For example, businesses must devote resources to constantly keep track of prices, making changes as often as necessary. Other businesses may be forced into costly redesigns of their products in response to higher labor and materials prices. These costs are likely to be passed on in the form of higher consumer prices. Higher prices, followed by higher costs, followed by even higher prices can result in an *inflationary spiral,* with inflation feeding on itself.

With all these examples of individual and business behavioral changes, you can see that hyperinflation would be a giant headache. The time needed to cope with it decreases individual productivity, which reduces the production of goods and services, in turn reducing the standard of living. Some of the adjustments that people make in response to hyperinflation are also made on a smaller scale in response to ordinary levels of inflation.

HOW INFLATION IS MEASURED USING THE CPI

The changes in behavior we've discussed make it more difficult to measure the inflation rate accurately. Since the CPI is widely used, it should reflect price changes as precisely as possible. Changes in product design present a particular challenge to the accurate measurement of inflation. To understand this point, recall the earlier example in which the prices of apples, bananas, and oranges were used to illustrate the computation of the CPI. Those computations implicitly assumed that the three products remained unchanged. Suppose, however, that improved varieties of all three goods have been introduced in the marketplace since the base period. The improvements offer consumers greater satisfaction, which they are willing to pay for. In this context, the value of the CPI does not accurately reflect inflation, but a willingness to pay for improvements in product quality. Thus, unless a price index adjusts for product quality improvements, the price index will overstate the inflation rate.

The CPI adjusts price changes for product improvements through a method called an *hedonic model.* Although hedonic models use statistical methods and are complicated in practice, in concept they are quite simple. In a hedonic model each product is viewed as a bundle of characteristics, where the model is used to estimate the value of each characteristic. Can you identify several characteristics of a college textbook that provide value? In the CPI, the number of pages, the type of cover (soft or hard), and the use of color are a few examples of the characteristics that affect the value of a textbook.

Let's see how the hedonic approach works. Suppose that the previous edition of your math textbook sold for $65, but that the new edition carries a price of $75. If both editions were identical, then the entire price increase would be viewed as inflation and would enter into the computation of the CPI. However, suppose the new edition has more pages and the book has gone from black and white to color. To a significant extent the two books are different products. A hedonic model estimates the value of the improvements in the book, concluding, let's say, that the increased pages have a value of $5, while color has a value of $4. Then $9 of the $10 price increase is accounted for by quality improvements. The remaining $1 of price increase not related to improvements increases the CPI. Although hedonic models help improve the accuracy of the CPI, they are not perfect.

Even if the CPI were perfectly accurate, your personal inflation experience would probably be different. The CPI measures changes in average prices. You may live in an area of the country that is experiencing price increases that outstrip the average. For a variety of reasons your purchasing may not mirror that of the average consumer. If you are chronically ill, you may spend a larger-than-average fraction of your income on medicines. If you are in college, increases in tuition will hit you harder than the average citizen. If you have a long commute between home and work, increases in the price of gasoline make your personal inflation experience different from the CPI.

Even relatively low inflation can add up over time. The rule of seventy-two allows an estimate of how many years it would take prices to double for any inflation rate. The calculation involved in the rule of seventy-two is simple: Take an inflation rate and divide it into seventy-two. The result is the time it takes prices to double. Figure 7-6 shows doubling times for selected annual inflation rates between 1 percent and 16 percent.

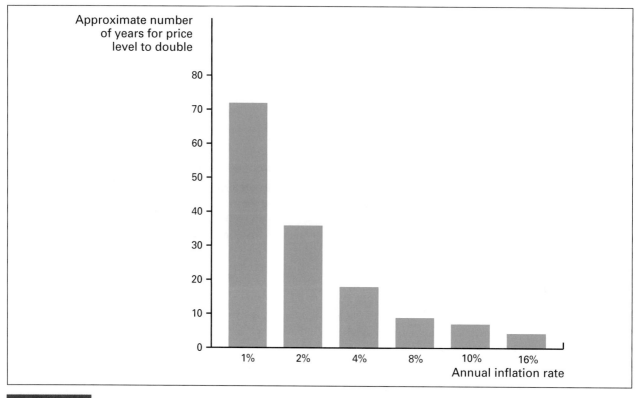

FIGURE 7-6

APPLYING THE RULE OF SEVENTY-TWO TO COMPUTE THE EFFECTS OF INFLATION The rule of seventy-two is used to compute the approximate doubling times. In this figure the rule of seventy-two is used to compute how long it would take the price level to double when the inflation rate takes on different values.

Figure 7-6 shows that an increase in the inflation rate can have dramatic long-term effects. For instance, a sustained 2 percent inflation rate would mean that it would take almost half of the average person's lifetime for prices to double. At a 4 percent inflation rate, not much higher than in recent U.S. experience, prices would double about four times over a lifetime. At a 10 percent inflation rate, prices would double a total of ten times for someone living into his or her seventies. No matter the inflation rate, living with inflation is what people must do.

*T*HINKING
*C*RITICALLY

1. Consumers often substitute cheaper goods for similar goods that have risen in price. From a student perspective, what are some substitutes for a new math textbook? Would these substitutes be acceptable substitutes from a professor's perspective? Explain.

2. How easy is it for consumers to identify improvements in personal computers? Since personal computers today are cheaper than they were five years ago, what effect does including them in the CPI market basket have on the inflation rate? Explain.

Visit **www.prenhall.com/ayers** for updates and web exercises on this Explore & Apply topic.

SUMMARY AND LEARNING OBJECTIVES

1. **Describe inflation rates in the United States and other countries.**
   - Inflation occurs when there is a sustained rise in the general price level, which includes the prices of many goods and services. The inflation rate is stated as an annual percentage increase in the price level. Over time, U.S. inflation rates have fluctuated up and down.
   - Inflation occurs in many countries. The inflation rate in some countries is quite high, but relatively low in other countries. Some countries that have experienced very high inflation rates have looked to a policy of dollarization to bring down inflation. Dollarization was enacted in Equador, which replaced its own currency with the U.S. dollar.
   - Deflation and disinflation sound similar, but are not the same. Deflation means a fall in the price level. Deflation would involve a decrease in the CPI. Disinflation is a fall in the inflation rate. Disinflation is illustrated by an inflation rate of 3 percent one year and 2 percent the next. This situation is not deflation because the CPI increases in both years. Deflation is not a macroeconomic goal since deflation is often associated with a weak economy.

2. **Discuss the effects of inflation that cause low inflation to be a macroeconomic goal.**
   - People on fixed incomes suffer from reduced purchasing power because of inflation. Compared to people who are able to earn larger incomes, those on fixed incomes lose because of inflation. Relative to lenders, borrowers gain from inflation. This effect of inflation occurs because borrowers repay their debts with money that will buy less because of the rise in the price level.
   - The core inflation rate excludes food and energy prices from the computation of the inflation rate. Under some circumstances it can provide a clearer picture of inflation and its harm.
   - Anticipated inflation is expected by people. Unanticipated inflation takes them by surprise. People are able to adjust their financial affairs to adjust for the effects of anticipated inflation.
   - Indexing allows people to take account of future inflation and protect their purchasing power. Social Security payments are an example of an indexed income since Social Security checks are adjusted upward in amount each year to reflect the prevailing inflation rate. Cost-of-living adjustments (COLAs) allow workers to receive automatic upward adjustments in their pay that are tied to the inflation rate.

3. **Compute, interpret, and use a price index to compute a real value.**
   - Several price indexes, including the consumer price index (CPI), the producer price index (PPI), the GDP chain-type index, and the GDP implicit price deflator, measure inflation. The CPI is the best known of these.
   - The base period for a price index is an initial time period, currently 1982 to 1984 for the CPI, to which prices in other time periods are compared. The base period is selected arbitrarily. By convention, the value of a price index equals 100 during the base period.
   - As the price level rises, the value of the CPI increases. The CPI for 2001 equals 177.1, which is interpreted to mean that the price level in 2001 is 77.1 percent higher than in the base period. Alternatively, it would take $1.77 to purchase what $1.00 purchased in the base period.
   - The CPI is calculated using items that urban consumers typically purchase, the so-called market basket of goods and services. There are about 200 categories of goods and services in the CPI, grouped into eight major expenditure categories. The relative importance of an expenditure category is used as a weight in the computation of the CPI. Currently, the CPI is computed using weights that are updated every two years.
   - The formula used to compute a price index is: Cost of market basket at current prices ÷ Cost of market basket at base period prices, multiplied by 100.
   - Price indexes are used to compute a real value from a nominal value. With knowledge of the nominal value of a variable and the value of a price index it is possible to compute the real value of the variable. Real values are useful to know. For example, the real value of the minimum wage over time shows us that the purchasing power of the minimum wage has varied significantly.
   - The producer price index (PPI) is used to measure inflation in the prices of goods and services sold by U.S. producers. The GDP implicit price deflator measures a broad spectrum of prices. It is computed as: GDP implicit price deflator = Nominal GDP ÷ Real GDP × 100. The GDP chained price index also measures prices across the spectrum of GDP.

4. **Identify problems with price indexes and efforts to improve them.**
   - The CPI is an imperfect measure of inflation. Using the CPI to measure inflation suggests that the effects of inflation are more severe than they really are. The reason has to do with biases in fixed-weight price indexes, including the substitution bias. A chain-weight index, such as the GDP chained price index, is intended to provide a better approximation to true inflation.

5. **Explain how people respond to inflation, and how their responses affect its measurement.**
   - The CPI is used for three purposes: an economic indicator, to find real values, and to adjust monetary payments. In the case of hyperinflation, behavior changes necessary to limit the harm caused by rapidly rising prices will be widespread. Behavioral changes create difficulties in computing and interpreting price indexes. Product design is a particular challenge. The CPI attempts to adjust for quality changes so as to avoid overstating price increases. The method used is called a hedonic model.

KEY TERMS

price level, 156
inflation, 156
inflation rate, 156
interest, 162

indexing, 162
interest rate, 162
consumer price index (CPI), 163
producer price index (PPI), 163

GDP chained price index, 163
GDP implicit price deflator, 163
nominal value, 167
real value, 167

TEST YOURSELF

TRUE OR FALSE

1. The goal of low inflation is explicitly stated to be an inflation rate of 0 percent.
2. Compared to other countries in recent history, the United States is among the group of four or five countries with the highest inflation rates.
3. Disinflation is associated with a fall in the price level.
4. Inflation hurts borrowers while benefiting lenders.
5. A chain-weight price index links quantities in one year to the next.

MULTIPLE CHOICE

6. Which of the following best fits the definition of inflation?
   a. A one-time increase in a few prices.
   b. A one-time increase in many prices.
   c. A sustained increase in a few prices.
   d. A sustained increase in many prices.
7. In which decade was U.S. inflation highest?
   a. 1960s.
   b. 1970s.
   c. 1980s.
   d. 1990s.
8. Deflation is associated with
   a. a rising price level.
   b. a falling price level.

   c. an inflation rate that is higher this year than last year.
   d. an inflation rate that is lower this year than last year.
9. The core inflation rate excludes
   a. energy prices.
   b. the price of medical care.
   c. food prices.
   d. both food and energy prices.
10. The distinction between anticipated and unanticipated inflation is important because
    a. unanticipated inflation is always greater than anticipated inflation.
    b. unanticipated inflation is harmful, but anticipated inflation is not.
    c. anticipated inflation is harmful, but unanticipated inflation is not.
    d. both types of inflation are potentially harmful, but people can make arrangements to minimize the damage from anticipated inflation.
11. Treasury Inflation-Protected Securities (TIPS) are an example of
    a. a policy to reduce the inflation rate.
    b. one of the goods in the CPI market basket.
    c. indexing to protect against unanticipated inflation.
    d. a deliberate effort to inflict harm on lenders when inflation rises.

12. When you see a value of the consumer price index (CPI) of less than 100, you know
   a. that there has been a misprint since the CPI cannot be under 100.
   b. nothing in particular since the CPI can be any value at any time.
   c. that there has been price inflation within the last year.
   d. that either you are looking at the CPI for a year prior to the base period, or there has been deflation since the base period.

13. The goods and services included in the computation of the consumer price index (CPI) are referred to as the _____
   a. base period.
   b. fixed weights.
   c. market basket.
   d. price level.

14. How is an inflation rate computed?
   a. The inflation rate equals the value of a price index.
   b. The inflation rate equals the change in the value of a price index.
   c. By the following computation: (change in price index/initial value of price index) multiplied by 100.
   d. By the following computation: change in price index multiplied by the initial value of the price index.

15. Using a price index, a real value is computed by
   a. multiplying a nominal value by the price index, and then dividing by 100.
   b. dividing a nominal value by the price index, and then multiplying by 100.
   c. averaging two nominal values.
   d. dividing the current nominal value by the base period nominal value.

16. The best way for workers to determine whether their earnings have kept up with inflation over the last ten years is to

   a. see if the nominal value of earnings is at least the same as ten years ago.
   b. see if the real value of earnings is at least the same as ten years ago.
   c. multiply the earnings figure from a decade ago by the current value of the consumer price index.
   d. multiply the current earnings figure by the value of the consumer price index from a decade ago.

17. When the real value of GDP is computed by the government
   a. the CPI is used.
   b. the PPI is used.
   c. the GDP chained price index is used.
   d. no price index is necessary because the real and nominal values of GDP are always identical.

18. A chained price index is
   a. the least accurate type of price index.
   b. superior to other types, because it links successive years of prices and quantities together.
   c. superior to other types, because it links the CPI and PPI together to cover more prices than either the CPI or PPI cover separately.
   d. superior to the CPI, but definitely inferior in accuracy to an implicit price deflator.

19. The substitution bias causes the CPI to
   a. overstate the effects of inflation.
   b. understate the effects of inflation.
   c. more accurately reflect the effects of inflation.
   d. be nearly useless as a measure of inflation.

20. When a country experiences hyperinflation it is likely that
   a. people will hold on to money.
   b. hyperinflation was a goal of that country's macro policy.
   c. cash will be spent very quickly.
   d. the country's standard of living will be improved.

QUESTIONS AND PROBLEMS

1. *[history of U.S. inflation]* Use the information conveyed by Figure 7-1 to characterize the decades of the 1950s, 1960s, 1970s, 1980s, and 1990s as to how well the goal of low inflation was met. Use your general knowledge of history and politics to speculate on why inflation remained under better control in some decades than others.

2. *[world inflation]* Are other countries' inflation rates similar to that of the United States? Explain, referring to the data in Figure 7-2.

3. *[deflation]* Refer to the example in the chapter that computes a price index for apples, bananas, and oranges. Provide price data for that example that illustrates deflation. Compute the price index using the prices you provided. Based upon your computation, state how a price index will behave when there is deflation.

4. *[core inflation]* Suppose that data shows the overall inflation rate equals 5 percent, but core inflation equals 3 percent. What is the cause of the difference in these

percentages? Which is more likely to provide the most accurate gauge of inflation? Explain.

5. *[harm from inflation]* The minimum wage is adjusted upward at unpredictable intervals. Congress must pass legislation increasing the minimum wage, legislation the president must sign before the increase takes effect. How is the group of minimum wage workers affected by inflation?

6. *[anticipated versus unanticipated inflation]* Why is unanticipated inflation usually considered more harmful than anticipated inflation?

7. *[indexing]* Is indexing practiced in the United States? Explain.

8. *[CPI base period]* Why does an understanding of the CPI require you to understand the base period concept?

9. *[CPI market basket]* Why does an understanding of the CPI require you to understand the concept of the market basket?

10. *[computing a price index]* Suppose that in the base period consumers purchase eight pounds of grapes, seven pounds of potatoes, and three pounds of bacon.

The prices per pound were $1, $.50, and $2, respectively. In the current year, these prices are $2, $1, and $3, respectively. Compute and interpret a price index using these data.

11. *[CPI]* Suppose that the CPI in year 5 equals 123 and in year 6 equals 130. What was the inflation rate in year 6?

12. *[real versus nominal values]* Three years ago Johnson earned $100 a week. Today he earns $125 a week. He would like to know whether his real income is higher today than it was three years ago. If the consumer price index increased from 150 to 175, has Johnson's real income risen, fallen, or remained the same? Explain.

13. *[chain weights]* What is the purpose of computing a chain-weighted price index? Is the CPI an example of a chain-weighted index?

14. *[real chained GDP]* Suppose that a country's nominal GDP equals $1,000. Also suppose its GDP chained price index has a value of 125. What is the value of this country's real GDP?

15. *[substitution bias]* Explain how the substitution bias in the CPI affects the reported inflation rate.

Visit www.prenhall.com/ayers for Exploring the Web exercises and additional self-test quizzes.

CHAPTER 8

A FRAMEWORK FOR MACROECONOMIC ANALYSIS

A LOOK AHEAD

The twentieth century ended with a string of prosperous years for the United States economy. Productivity surged and unemployment fell to record lows. Because of its success, the economy faded into the background of our collective consciousness. Then, as the twenty-first century unfolded, productivity sagged and unemployment reared its ugly head. Business profits were slim, bankruptcies were up, and stock prices were down. People with their jobs on the line or their savings decimated by stock-market declines demanded action from the federal government. In response they got tax rebates and interest-rate cuts, but nothing seemed to help.

Then came the terrorist attacks of September 11, 2001. A war on terrorism was declared. Immediately, the stock market plunged and 100,000 people were laid off in the airline industry alone. The monthly unemployment rate jumped by ½ percent, the largest one-month leap in twenty-one years. Some urged the government to take action to shore up the economy. Others said it would be best to wait and let the economy take care of itself. This chapter frames these choices and the tradeoffs involved. The Explore & Apply section that concludes this chapter pays particular attention to the macroeconomic consequences of the war against terrorism.

LEARNING OBJECTIVES

Understanding Chapter 8 will enable you to:
1. **Contrast the perspectives of classical economists to those of Keynesians.**
2. **Describe how full-employment output can change.**
3. **Explain why the price level does not matter in the long run.**
4. **Interpret and apply the aggregate demand–aggregate supply model.**
5. **Relate the difference between demand-side and supply-side inflation in the long run.**
6. **Interpret how the war against terrorism can cause both inflation and lower output, and ways in which these effects might be countered.**

*E*XPLORE
&
*A*PPLY

179

"Prior to 1929, kids had too much of everything. Then after the crash, they didn't have enough of anything. So they became too much concerned with economic problems. We began to think too much about sharing the wealth, instead of creating it. Youth should create something, and it should have something to create."

—*Perry Mason, by Earl Stanley Gardner, The Case of the Drowning Duck, 1942*

The above passage was written as America was preparing to enter World War II. Having endured a lingering depression for over a decade, the state of the U.S. economy was high on people's minds. Then World War II brought forth a massive civilian and military mobilization that brought with it a new resolve and new spending. After the war, the economic crisis was over and America prospered like never before. Unemployment fell from the 14.6 percent in 1940 (before the war) to 3.9 percent in 1946 (after the war had ended). The one and only Great Depression of the twentieth century was over.

In late summer of 2001, Americans were again troubled by a declining economy. Unemployment was under 5 percent, but up from its lows of under 4 percent. Stock prices had been in a jagged slide since March of the previous year. Business profits were squeezed and layoffs announced. Having lived comfortably for decades, U.S. citizens were not used to worrying about the overall economy, but that started to change.

Then came terrorist attacks that killed thousands of Americans. The Dow-Jones Industrial Average of stock prices reacted by falling nearly 15 percent in a single week, exceeded only by the 15.5 percent drop in 1933 during the depths of the Great Depression. Consumers held tight to their money and business investment was at a standstill. During October 2001, businesses cut their payrolls by 415,000 jobs, the largest one-month decline in over two decades. All at once, it seemed, everybody wanted to know what was to become of the economy. How did it work? What could be done?

8.1 KEYNESIAN SHORT-RUN AND CLASSICAL LONG-RUN PERSPECTIVES

long run involves underlying economic forces that make themselves felt over time.

short run a period of time during which the economy transitions to the long run.

Answering sweeping macroeconomic questions about employment, output, and inflation requires providing near-term events with a long-term perspective and context. This context is called the **long run,** which involves underlying economic forces that make themselves felt over time. For example, economic growth is a long-run consideration. In contrast, the **short run** represents more immediate and transitory economic developments, such as the increased unemployment in the months following the September 11 attacks. Much of the difference of opinion within the economics profession concerns how much weight to attach to short-run versus long-run outcomes. The issues are especially contentious when the policies that are best for long-run economic health come at the price of short-run problems.

KEYNESIAN AND CLASSICAL SCHOOLS OF THOUGHT

During the Great Depression of the 1930s, the biggest short-run problem was unemployment. It was against this backdrop that, in 1936, John Maynard Keynes authored *The General Theory of Employment, Interest, and Money.* In this path-breaking work, Keynes took issue with the mainstream of economic thinking at the time. Instead of accepting that government should sit back and wait for the economy to pull itself out of recession, he proposed ways in which government could actively manage the economy toward prosperity. Keynesian theory came to define the field of macroeconomics for nearly half a century. Before it, the field of macroeconomics did not even exist.

After the work of Keynes and the economic recovery seemingly brought about by the government spending of World War II, it appeared that government had a duty to shepherd the economy through times of economic distress. In the United States, that duty was embodied in the Employment Act of 1946. When the problem was too little spending and too few people employed, the government could go far toward solving the problem through spending more itself and giving its citizens incentives to do likewise. At the time, there seemed to be no macroeconomic tradeoffs in this course of action. As time progressed, however, efforts by the government to keep unemployment low started to cause the unwanted side effect of inflation in the 1960s and 1970s.

As a result, the emphasis in economics shifted away from short-run cures and toward looking for policies that would facilitate smooth long-run economic growth without significant inflation. From this perspective, government should not adjust its policies in order to promote spending when unemployment rises, but should rather provide the stability that allows the economy to adjust on its own.

Macroeconomic theory can be placed within either of two broad categories, depending on whether the emphasis is on short-run or long-run processes. These schools of thought are:

- **Keynesian,** which suggests that government action is an appropriate response to short-run macroeconomic problems.
- **Classical,** which suggests that a steady policy aimed at the long run best allows the economy to take care of itself.

Keynes himself was emphatic about the difference between these perspectives. He vigorously argued that the short run should be our focus because, as he put it, "In the long run we are all dead." Economists today commonly tap into both schools of thought, with their emphasis depending on the severity of short-run problems encountered. Later in this chapter, we will see how to use the models of aggregate demand and aggregate supply to provide the long-run framework of analysis. In the next two chapters, we will see how the framework can be developed to address short-run issues as well.

Keynesian a macroeconomic school of thought that emphasizes the short run and the importance of fiscal policy.

classical a macroeconomic school of thought that emphasizes the long run and reliance upon market forces to achieve full employment.

THE PHILLIPS CURVE—A MATTER OF INFLATIONARY EXPECTATIONS

Aggregate supply and aggregate demand analysis was motivated by the Phillips curve, named after British economist A.W. Phillips who first identified it. The **Phillips curve** is a graphical representation of data that, from the 1960s in the United States, depicted a distinct curvilinear tradeoff between low unemployment and low inflation, as seen in Figure 8-1. The evidence seemed so convincing that many economists at the time hailed the Phillips curve as a newly revealed fundamental truth.

By the end of the 1960s, the Phillips curve relationship was falling apart, as seen by the later data points in Figure 8-1. Data beyond the decade of the 1960s showed no systematic relationship between unemployment and inflation. The Phillips curve is now viewed as a

Phillips curve a graphical representation of data from the 1960s in the United States that shows a curvilinear tradeoff between low unemployment and low inflation.

QUICKCHECK

What is the essential difference between the Keynesian view and the classical view of the economy?

Answer: Keynesians emphasize the importance of the short run, while classical economists emphasize the importance of the long run.

FIGURE 8-1

THE PHILLIPS CURVE The Phillips curve showed a tight, inverse relationship between inflation and unemployment in U.S. data from the 1960s. In later decades, though, the relationship no longer held true.

Source: 2002 Economic Report of the President, Tables B-42 and B-43.

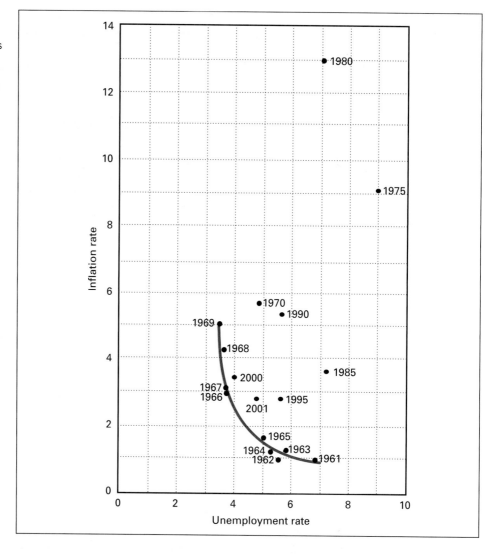

short-run phenomenon that did not hold up in the long run. The reason is thought to revolve around how people form their expectations.

inflationary expectations predictions about future inflation that people factor into their current behavior.

Whether we are particularly conscious of it or not, we each have **inflationary expectations,** meaning expectations about how much higher or lower prices will be in the future. For example, if we think that we are going to be paying less for everything later on, we might be willing to accept a wage cut. If we think we will be paying more for everything later on, however, we might demand a wage increase.

adaptive expectations when people form expectations as to future prices according to what their experiences have been in the past.

There are two ways for people to form their inflationary expectations. One way is through **adaptive expectations,** where we form our expectations about future prices according to our past experiences. So if the price level goes up at a rate of 2 percent per year, we would expect inflation of 2 percent to continue on into the future. If prices rise or fall in a manner inconsistent with the past, adaptive expectations could lead to our being fooled and slow to adjust our wage demands.

For example, a big new government spending program might add to both GDP and inflationary pressures in the short run before people catch on. In the 1960s, government spending in the United States did increase significantly in response to the Vietnam War and President Lyndon Johnson's Great Society social programs. The prolonged period of time in which the public was apparently tricked by unexpectedly high inflation suggests that the public was basing its expectations on what it had previously experienced rather than forming its opinions based on current policy actions. With a U.S. economy characterized by adaptive expectations in the 1960s, increased government spending would cause lower unemployment and higher inflation, exactly what was shown by the Phillips curve of the time.

By the 1970s, people and businesses had learned to factor the effects of inflation into their personal and business plans. Government could no longer inflate its way to lower unemployment. This limitation on government's ability to manage the economy was shown by the combination of high inflation and unemployment—**stagflation**—experienced in that decade. People had learned to predict more accurately the impacts of public policy.

stagflation the combination of high inflation and unemployment.

These days, public policy is unlikely to succeed if it depends on assuming that government knows more than participants in the marketplace. With the instant communications of the modern world, people are more likely to have **rational expectations** in which they correctly predict the implications of government policy action and thus cannot be systematically tricked. With rational expectations, we keep up with the news analyses and base our expectations on the best information available to us. Public policies that have been debated in Congress, commented on by the media, and passed into law are not likely to surprise us.

rational expectations when we base our expectations upon the best information available to us.

The rise of rational expectations explains the demise of the Phillips curve relationship of the 1960s. In those years, government actions that caused inflation also caused people to work more because they didn't recognize that inflation. People at the time were tricked by higher wages into working more. They later came to understand that the higher wages were only in nominal terms, not in real terms, because prices were rising to match. From then on, it became standard practice for workers to compare wage increases to their expected cost-of-living increases. The more experience they had with being surprised, the more attention they paid to inflation predictions in the media.

If people have rational expectations, government policy that is intended to stimulate the economy will have no predictable effect. In other words, the best guess is that policy actions will not change the economy much in either direction. The idea of rational expectations provides support to the classical argument that government should step back and let the macroeconomy take care of itself.

BUDDY, CAN YOU SPARE A THEORY?   *SNAPSHOT*

"Buddy, can you spare a dime?" The mood of the Great Depression was somehow captured in that poignant refrain. There just didn't seem to be enough spending to keep everyone working. So thought Keynes when, at the height of the Depression, he came out with what became known as the Keynesian theory. In short, if people weren't spending enough, the government should bridge the gap with spending of its own. So spend on the Civilian Conservation Corps, spend on the Works Progress Administration, spend on just about anything, and help beat the Depression!

Classical economists disagree, contending that it was time and not government spending that spelled the demise of the Great Depression in the 1940s. Some might say, "Something worked so why argue about it now?" The answer is not for the sake of the past, but is for the future. Hashing out how best to keep the economy humming and out of depression is what macroeconomic theory is all about. It's about not having to ask a stranger for a dime. ◄

8.2 MODELING THE LONG RUN WITH AGGREGATE SUPPLY AND AGGREGATE DEMAND

full-employment output (full-employment GDP) the real GDP the economy produces when it fully employs its resources.

A fundamental goal for the economy is to achieve **full-employment output,** also termed **full-employment GDP,** which is the real GDP the economy produces when it fully employs its resources. At any given point in time, actual output can be either above or below the amount associated with the full-employment amount. For example, in times of unemployment, actual output would fall short of full-employment output.

The economy can temporarily exceed full-employment output if workers accept overtime, work more than one job, or find new jobs exceptionally quickly. Whether actual GDP is above or below full-employment GDP, **the existence of a natural rate of unemployment implies that the long-run tendency is toward full-employment GDP.**

For most of its history, the U.S. economy has been successful at living up to its potential. In other words, actual GDP has been in the vicinity of *potential GDP,* which is the amount that we can expect the economy to achieve at full employment. This history is shown in Figure 8-2.

Periods of unemployment in which actual GDP falls short of potential GDP represent transition times in a market economy—the time markets take to adjust to their market-clearing equilibriums. During these times, there is a surplus of workers in the labor market. As they compete for jobs, workers drive down wages until the labor surplus is absorbed. In response to lower labor costs, competition forces output prices to fall, too. These wage and price adjustments reflect supply and demand in action in the many markets that make up the economy as a whole. These adjustments can take time, however, the significance of which forms the crux of the debate between classical and Keynesian economists.

LONG-RUN AGGREGATE SUPPLY

long-run aggregate supply the idea that, in the long run, the price level does not affect the amount of GDP the economy produces; graphically, long-run aggregate supply is vertical at full-employment GDP.

The economy supplies full-employment output in the long run, no matter the price level, as shown by the **long-run aggregate supply** in Figure 8-3(a) (see page 186). Because the price level is irrelevant to the potential for full-employment output, **long-run aggregate supply is always vertical.** The logic is the same as the logic behind the natural rate of unemployment discussed in Chapter 6. Specifically, **in the long run, the desire of people to receive income pushes unemployment down toward its natural rate and leads to full-employment output.**

The vertical long-run aggregate supply curve means that the same quantity of real GDP will be produced whether the price level is low, high, or in-between. In other words, the price level does not make a difference in determining the full-employment level of GDP. As evidence that the price level does not matter in the long run, consider that the price level today is quadruple that of the late 1960s. However, market wages have also adjusted upward. Other than requiring that we earn and spend about four times as much to obtain the same goods and services, the rise in wages and prices has had little long-run significance for the aggregate economy.

Over time, long-run aggregate supply shifts in response to changes in the amount of resources available to the economy and in the technology available to use these resources. For example, warfare or natural disasters could destroy resources, which would reduce full-employment output and shift aggregate supply to the left, as shown in Figure 8-3(a).

More commonly, economies add resources and improve technology over time. The result is economic growth that increases full-employment output and thus shifts long-run aggregate supply to the right, as shown in Figure 8-3(b).

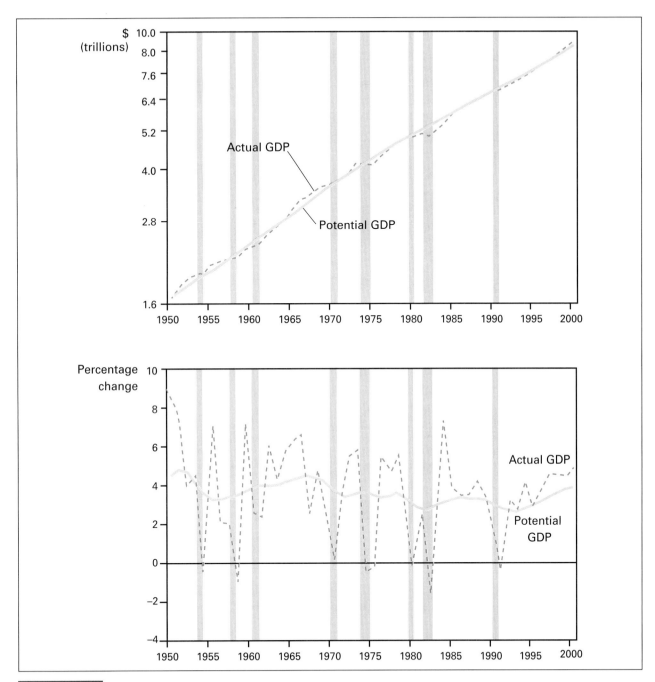

FIGURE 8-2

ACTUAL AND POTENTIAL GDP Over time and with some short-run zigs and zags, actual real GDP in the
United States has generally been close to the economy's full-employment potential. The upper graph
shows actual and potential GDP in trillions of dollars. The lower graph shows the percentage change
in both. Actual GDP is seen to be more volatile than potential GDP.

Source: Congressional Budget Office, 2001, using data from the Department of Commerce, Bureau of Economic
Analysis.

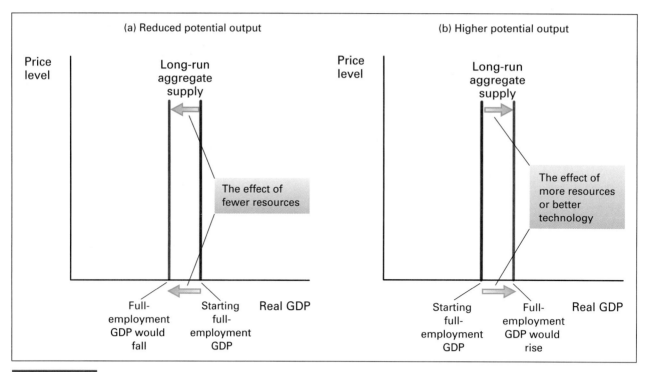

FIGURE 8-3

LONG-RUN AGGREGATE SUPPLY Long-run aggregate supply is graphed as a vertical line at full-employment GDP, which implies that the price level does not affect an economy's potential output in the long run. As shown in (a), a loss of resources reduces full-employment output and shifts aggregate demand to the left. Conversely, as shown in (b), long-run aggregate supply shifts to the right over time as the economy acquires greater resources and better technology that increase the amount of output produced at full employment.

QUICKCHECK

What would be the effect on long-run aggregate supply of an earthquake that destroys an economy's productive capacity? Why?

Answer: The long-run aggregate supply would shift to the left. This movement shows that, even if the country's work force is fully employed, there would be less output.

AGGREGATE DEMAND

Aggregate supply reveals how much real GDP the economy has to offer, whatever the price level. To understand what the price level will be requires that we look beyond the supply side of the economy. Therefore, we examine the demand side, using the concept of **aggregate demand,** which tells us how much real GDP consumers, businesses, and government would purchase at each price level.

In the microeconomy, a demand curve reveals the quantity of a good or service that would be purchased at each of various possible prices. For example, as the price of Pepsi rises, the quantity demanded falls because consumers substitute Coca-Cola and other beverages. In the event of a general inflation in the prices of all goods and services, though, consumers can no longer merely substitute away from products whose prices have risen. Yet, consumers can no longer buy as much as before, either, because the inflation has eroded their

aggregate demand relates how much real GDP consumers, businesses, and government will purchase at each price level; graphically, aggregate demand slopes downward.

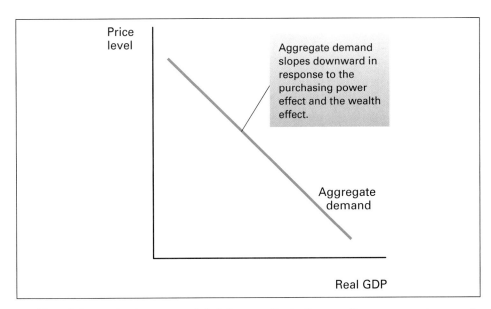

Price level

Aggregate demand slopes downward in response to the purchasing power effect and the wealth effect.

Aggregate demand

Real GDP

FIGURE 8-4

AGGREGATE DEMAND Aggregate demand slopes downward, which illustrates that a lower price level increases both the purchasing power of current income and the value of savings.

wealth and the purchasing power of their income. So, in the overall economy, an increase in the price level will also cut back the aggregate quantities that consumers purchase.

Likewise, a decrease in the price level will increase aggregate purchases. The reason is twofold. First, at a lower price level, money buys more goods and services. In other words, even if all of us continue to spend the same amount of money, a lower price level causes the real GDP we purchase to be greater. Second, a lower price level increases the inflation-adjusted value of money and personal savings. When people think that they have more wealth, they spend more of their current income.

The two effects of a price level change are summed up as follows:

■ **Purchasing power effect:** A lower price level allows consumers to receive more goods and services for any given number of dollars they spend. A higher price level means consumers receive fewer goods and services for any given number of dollars they spend.

■ **Wealth effect:** A lower price level causes consumers to spend more of their current incomes because the lower price level increases the value of their savings. Conversely, a higher price level would reduce the real value of savings and lead consumers to spend less out of current income.

purchasing power effect the effect of the price level on consumers' ability to buy goods and services.

wealth effect the change in the fraction of current income spent caused by a price-level change affecting the real value of savings.

Both the purchasing power effect and the wealth effect cause an inverse relationship between the price level and the quantity of GDP demanded. Thus, **aggregate demand slopes down** as shown in Figure 8-4.

QUICKCHECK

The lower the price of movies, the more movies you choose to see, according to the law of demand. Would this behavior be different if prices were to fall in the same proportion throughout the economy?

Answer: When the price of movies drops but other prices remain constant, consumers substitute movies for other forms of entertainment. That substitution effect of a price change would not occur if all prices dropped simultaneously. However, if the general price level falls, the purchasing power of your income increases and so you might watch more movies because of the purchasing power effect. You also feel wealthier and so might watch more movies on account of the wealth effect.

THE FULL-EMPLOYMENT EQUILIBRIUM

full-employment equilibrium the long-run macroeconomic equilibrium that occurs at a full-employment output.

Figure 8-5 shows a downward-sloping aggregate demand curve, along with a vertical long-run aggregate supply. The intersection of these two curves represents a long-run macroeconomic equilibrium, termed the **full-employment equilibrium** because it occurs at the full-employment output. The figure labels both the full-employment equilibrium and the price level that supports it.

At any price level above the full-employment price level, aggregate spending will be insufficient to support full-employment output. Unemployed workers will compete for jobs, which will drive down wages. Competition in the output market will force firms to lower prices in response to these lower wages. The lower price level that results means that spending will buy more output and thus lead to greater employment. The process continues until the economy reaches full employment and the corresponding full-employment GDP, as shown in Figure 8-5.

If the actual price level were below the equilibrium shown in Figure 8-5, the economy would "overheat," with aggregate purchasing power exceeding the economy's ability to produce. Firms would compete for workers, thus driving their wages up. Competitive firms would pass on these higher wages to consumers by raising their prices. The resulting increase in the price level would soak up the excess purchasing power, thus leading the economy back to its long-run equilibrium.

FIGURE 8-5

THE LONG-RUN MACRO EQUILIBRIUM The long-run macroeconomic equilibrium occurs where aggregate demand intersects long-run aggregate supply. Competition prevents the price level from remaining either too high or too low, resulting in a movement along the aggregate demand curve until full employment is reached.

For example, the high price level at point A on aggregate demand is associated with unemployment. As workers compete to get jobs, they drive down wages and production costs. Competition then forces down prices. In contrast, at point B, there are not enough workers to produce all the output people want to buy. Competition drives up wages and prices, a condition known as overheating.

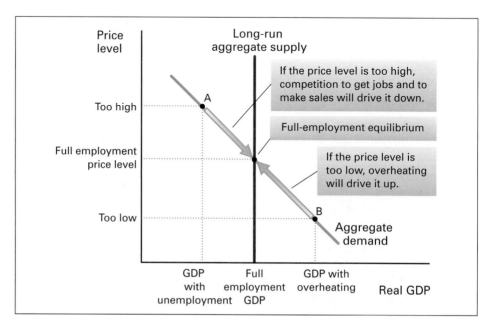

If products linger on the shopkeeper's shelf, the prices eventually get lowered to clear the inventory. If you can't find a job with the skills you have, you eventually acquire new ones. If no one will pay you what you ask, you eventually lower your salary expectations. However, if the headhunters are beating at your door with salary offers that you just can't pass up, then you demand a higher salary where you are or switch jobs.

These are stories told over and over for millions of people and products all across the land. Put together, it is nothing more than the economy heading toward full-employment output at an equilibrium price level. But the stories of how to get there are told in ways that are unique to the circumstances of the individuals and firms involved. Each and every story is significant—they are the micro behind the macro of economics. ◄

8.3 ROOT CAUSES OF INFLATION

To fight or prevent inflation, policymakers must identify the source. This section shows how the model of aggregate supply and aggregate demand can help by distinguishing between demand-side and supply-side causes of inflation. This distinction also has implications in regard to full-employment output.

DEMAND-SIDE INFLATION AND DEFLATION

Aggregate demand tends to increase—shift to the right—over time. This shift occurs in response to general growth in purchasing power as consumer spending increases, government spending increases, or, most generally, as more money circulates throughout the economy. The effect of an outward shift in aggregate demand is shown in Figure 8-6(a). *Ceteris paribus,* in the long run, the effect is to keep output the same and increase the price level. This effect is known as **demand-side inflation.**

Alternatively, if aggregate demand were to shift to the left, the effect would be **demand-side deflation** as shown in Figure 8-6(b). Demand-side deflation is not common, but can have significant disruptive effects when it happens. Many economists point to the difficulties of adjusting to a lower price level as being a root cause of the Great Depression.

SUPPLY-SIDE INFLATION AND DEFLATION

Changes on the supply side of the economy can also cause either inflation or deflation. If long-run aggregate supply were to shift to the left, we would see **supply-side inflation** in which the same amount of spending is able to buy fewer goods at higher prices. Supply-side inflation is shown in Figure 8-7(a) on page 191. Note that full-employment GDP decreases as long-run aggregate supply shifts to the left.

One possible source of supply-side inflation is a **supply shock,** which is an unexpected event that is major enough to affect the overall economy. Supply shocks, such as caused by wars or natural disasters, cause real changes in productive capacity. The terrorist attacks of September 11 caused a supply shock, the economic effects of which are discussed in this chapter's Explore & Apply section. Supply shocks are behind what is called the **real business cycle,** in which GDP rises or falls in response to major events that cannot be foreseen. Although we don't know what the shocks will be, we can be pretty sure that additional shocks will occur.

Aggregate supply might alternatively shift to the left in response to a change in the laws governing business practices within a country. Recent years have witnessed a number of

demand-side inflation occurs when aggregate demand shifts to the right. The result is a movement up the long-run aggregate supply curve to a higher price level, but no change in full-employment output.

demand-side deflation occurs when aggregate demand shifts to the left. The result is a movement down the long-run aggregate supply curve to a lower price level, but no change in full-employment output.

supply-side inflation occurs when long-run aggregate supply shifts to the left. The result is a movement up the aggregate demand curve to a higher price level and lower full-employment output.

supply shock an unexpected event that is major enough to affect the overall economy; shifts aggregate supply.

real business cycle when GDP rises or falls in response to major events that cannot be foreseen.

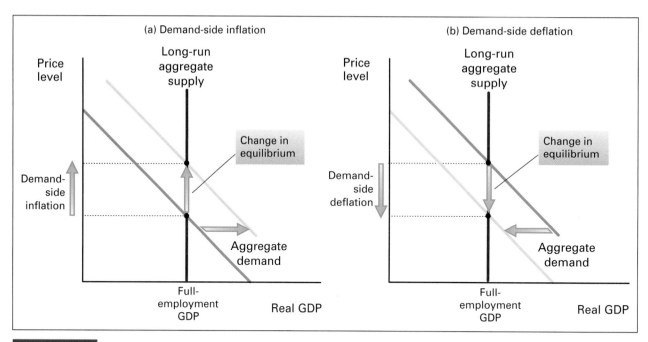

FIGURE 8-6

DEMAND-SIDE INFLATION AND DEFLATION Aggregate demand shifts to the right in response to increased government spending or increased spending by consumers, as shown in (a). The equilibrium price level increases, a result known as demand-side inflation. Spending might increase in response to an increase in the amount of money circulating in the economy.

Aggregate demand shifts to the left when there is less money circulating, such as when the government collects more tax revenue or when consumers are fearful and inclined to hoard cash. The leftward shift in aggregate demand pushes the price level down, resulting in demand-side deflation as shown in (b).

QUICKCHECK

Would the economy be better off if the government were to declare that all incomes shall henceforth be doubled? Use aggregate supply and aggregate demand analysis to support your answer.

Answer: If the economy is working up to its potential, then doubling everyone's income could not increase output, but would rather cause demand-side inflation that increases prices to offset the increased wages. With everyone having more money to spend, aggregate demand would shift to the right. The economy would move to a new long-run equilibrium at the same output and a higher price level.

---

laws and lawsuits that have changed the way firms can operate. Most notably, firms have seen their production costs increase in response to higher indirect employee costs, higher costs of complying with government regulations, and higher legal costs. Ongoing technological improvements that increase productivity can mask these effects.

On the bright side, technological change or an increase in resources increases the output associated with full employment. The result is a rightward shift in long-run aggregate supply. For example, the advent of e-commerce opened up possibilities for on-line shopping that have increased competition. It has also opened up possibilities for on-line payment

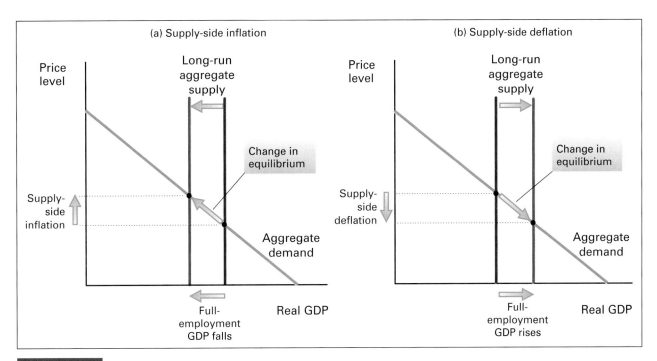

FIGURE 8-7

SUPPLY-SIDE INFLATION AND DEFLATION IN THE LONG RUN A leftward shift in long-run aggregate supply causes supply-side inflation, as shown in (a). Although unemployment remains unchanged, output falls and the price level rises. Explanations for this shift could include the destruction of resources in warfare or government restrictions on business practices.

In contrast, technological change or additional resources would shift aggregate supply to the right, resulting in supply-side deflation. In that case, without changing employment, output would rise and the price level would fall as shown in (b).

methods that have reduced the costs of making transactions. As aggregate supply shifts to the right, the economy moves down the aggregate demand curve to a lower equilibrium price level. This process is called **supply-side deflation,** and is associated with an increase in full-employment GDP, as shown in Figure 8-7(b).

supply-side deflation occurs when long-run aggregate supply shifts to the right. The result is a movement down the aggregate demand curve to a lower price level and higher full-employment output.

THE REAL BUSINESS CYCLE—SOME SHOCKING SURPRISES   *SNAPSHOT*

Cars, wars, oil cartels, computers, and earthquakes may not seem to have much in common, but they do. They have all shocked the economy in one way or another. How could ordinary citizens have foreseen the potential of the auto or the carnage of World War II? We did not know of the oil crisis of the 1970s before it happened, and we did not know that it would disappear in the 1980s. Nor can we know the extent to which technology will alter our lifestyles or when the next big earthquake will strike.

All of these things and more jolt the economy, either to make it more productive or to knock it back a notch. They represent real changes in aggregate supply to which businesses and individuals must adjust. Policymakers can predict these events no better than the rest of us, and so can do little to avert these disruptions to the smooth path of economic growth. When it comes to the real business cycle, then, it is best to expect the unexpected! ◀

8.4 CLASSICAL VERSUS KEYNESIAN—THE GREAT DEBATE

This chapter started with reference to the Great Depression, which was ended by World War II and the massive government spending associated with it. Keynesian analysis was thought to have been proven correct. As President Richard Nixon phrased it in 1972, "We are all Keynesians, now." However, just as Nixon was proclaiming that Keynes had won, the economics profession was focusing in a more classical direction. It began to emphasize its microeconomic foundations, such as incentives facing individuals and firms that can influence the performance of the overall economy.

Economic analysis influences people's politics and vice versa. For example, political liberals often adopt Keynesian policy prescriptions. The reason is presumably not because most liberals have studied the economy in detail and are convinced of the validity of the Keynesian economic model. More likely, political liberals tend to believe that an activist government can be a powerful force for good in the world. Keynesian economics calls for government to be just such a force. It provides justification for a large government, but leaves open specific categories of spending.

A similar analysis applies to political conservatives, who tend to adhere to a classical perspective on the role of government. Conservatives usually distrust big government, preferring instead a more laissez-faire approach. Classical analysis suggests that much government action does more harm than good to the macroeconomy, which is in keeping with the conservative perspective.

While some controversy in macroeconomics is positive, concerning factual issues of cause and effect, most disagreement among macroeconomists is normative. For example, modern Keynesian models incorporate classical analysis of the long run. What makes these economists and their models Keynesian is that they discount the significance of the long run, preferring instead to emphasize practical issues in the workplace that inhibit adjustments to full employment. Thus, the disagreement between modern Keynesians and classical economists often boils down to the degrees to which they are willing to trade off short- and long-run objectives.

EXPLORE & APPLY

8.5 FIGHTING TERRORISM—WHAT PRICE DOES THE ECONOMY PAY?

"The world is not ending."

—*New York Mayor Rudy Giuliani after the September 11 terrorist attack*

On September 11, 2001, hijackers turned four passenger airliners into terrorist bombs, demolishing the World Trade Center skyscrapers in New York City and destroying a portion of the Pentagon in Washington, D.C. One of the hijacked planes crashed in rural Pennsylvania. About three thousand people lost their lives from these attacks. Immediately, before any more hijackings could be committed, the U.S. Federal Aviation Authority grounded all planes until security could be tightened. It was only when expensive and time-consuming security measures were in place that planes resumed flying. The country prepared for war, the war against terrorism.

No one could know at the time just what would lie ahead. One thing was certain, however, and that was the addition of tighter security throughout the country. The added security measures meant that it became more expensive to do business. The security industry prospered, as demand and prices went up in that line of business. However, numerous other industries suffered as they faced higher costs of production and slower deliveries of their raw materials.

The added costs for security services cause an increase in the real costs of producing the final goods and services recorded in GDP. The economy's limited resources are thus not

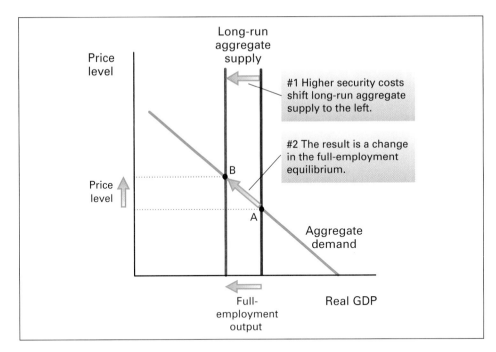

FIGURE 8-8

SUPPLY-SIDE EFFECTS OF TERRORISM The war on terrorism causes firms to spend more on security, which takes resources that could otherwise produce final goods and services. For this reason, the output associated with full employment decreases and shifts long-run aggregate supply to the left. The macroequilibrium adjusts from A to B, reflecting a higher price level and less output. Either an increase in full employment during wartime or the adoption of improved technologies holds the potential to offset these effects.

capable of producing as much final output, meaning that full-employment output falls. Note that full employment itself remains the same, but the output associated with it is less. The result is a shift to the left in the long-run aggregate supply curve, as shown in Figure 8-8, which leads to a new full-employment equilibrium at a higher price level and a lower level of output.

This shift can be moderated or even completely offset by advances in technology that increase productivity. For example, advances in monitoring and scanning cameras can reduce the need for security personnel, freeing them up to be productive in other ways. More generally, technology is applied to the workplace in order to increase productivity. To the extent it does so, the effect is to increase full-employment output and shift aggregate supply to the right, which is exactly opposite to the changes shown in Figure 8-8.

Other influences might also shift aggregate supply to the right. Looking back to World War II, we find that patriotism led to far more hours of work from the general population than was the norm either before or after the war. In effect, wartime full employment was higher than peacetime full employment. Taken by itself, the result was an increase in long-run aggregate supply.

HOW TERRORISM AFFECTS DEMAND

The 2001 terrorist attacks also had a significant effect on the demand side of the economy. The shock and uncertainty caused businesses to postpone new investment and consumers to postpone new purchases. For a while, it seemed everyone was hanging tight to their money and not allowing it to circulate as rapidly as it previously had. Airlines, hotels, amusement parks, and cruise ships all begged for customers. Some went bankrupt. Hundreds of thousands of Americans lost their jobs and millions more worried about their job security. The result was a leftward shift in aggregate demand. In other words, for any given price level, less output was demanded, as shown in Figure 8-9.

DEMAND-SIDE EFFECTS OF TERRORISM If the threat of terror makes people more cautious about spending, aggregate demand would shift to the left. The result would be:

#1 Firms throughout the economy would be unable to sell all of their output. Unemployment would rise and output would fall at first.

#2 To sell unsold output, firms would lower prices and the price level would fall.

#3 Output would return to the full-employment output once the price level adjusts to a new equilibrium.

The aggregate demand shift would be avoided if government's extra wartime spending exactly offsets the spending slowdown in the private sector, or as people return to their previous spending habits.

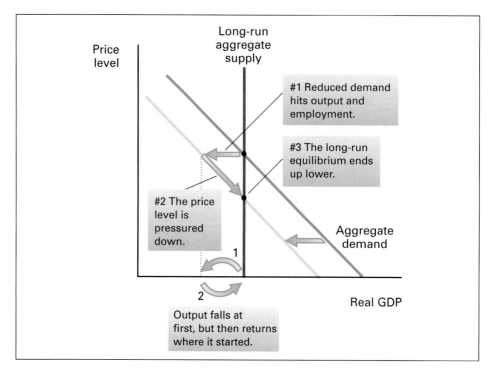

Taken by itself, this leftward shift in aggregate demand would have the effect of pushing prices lower, as shown. Before the price level would have a chance to adjust downward, output would fall and unemployment would rise. Were aggregate demand and aggregate supply both shifting left simultaneously, however, their influences would tend to offset each other in regard to price. Therefore, only output would fall.

There was considerable question following the September 2001 attacks as to how long it would take for consumers to resume their former patterns of spending. The answer was significant in terms of what the government should do. In particular, the government was not only spending additional money to combat the terrorists, but was also taking actions to lower borrowing costs and increase the amount of money circulating in the economy. The idea was to offset any drop in aggregate demand.

While intended to merely offset a drop in aggregate demand, such government actions ran the risk of going too far and actually increasing aggregate demand above what it had been before, particularly once the initial fears subsided and people returned to more normal spending patterns. If aggregate demand were to increase, demand-side inflation would be the result, as shown Figure 8-10(a). Figure 8-10(b) shows how the situation could easily get out of hand, with demand-side inflation adding to supply-side inflation, causing the economy to move from point A to point B, and on to point C in the figure. This situation is stagflation, in which output falls even as prices rise.

In response to the war against terrorism, there are also additional real and important macroeconomic consequences that lie hidden beneath the surface of the aggregate-demand/aggregate-supply model. For example, for the purposes of this model, it does not matter whether GDP is composed of military spending that we wish was unnecessary or spending on consumer goods and services that would be the alternative in peacetime. It matters to our standard of living, but we do not see these things in the aggregate economic analysis.

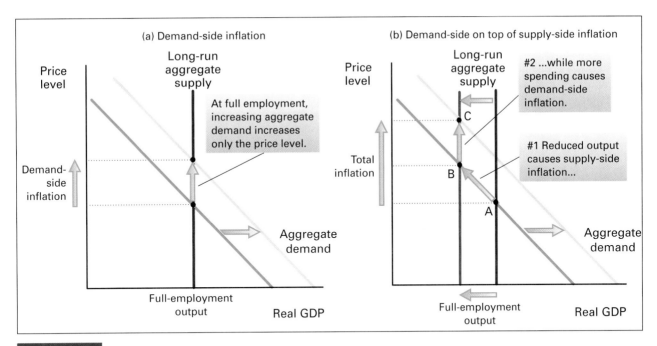

FIGURE 8-10

A DOUBLE DOSE OF INFLATION Graph (a) shows the demand-side inflation that could occur if government spending rises dramatically while the economy is already at full employment. The macro equilibrium would rise as shown. The higher government spending might reflect the costs of fighting a war, or merely the costs of tax and spending programs intended to offset an economic downturn.

The demand-side inflation might follow an initial supply-side inflation from higher costs of security and transportation. In graph (b), the leftward shift in long-run aggregate supply causes supply-side inflation. Because the economy is unable to produce as much output as previously, it moves up the aggregate demand curve from point A to point B. Then, if government steps in with additional purchases that increase aggregate demand, the economy experiences further inflation as it moves up the long-run aggregate supply curve from point B to point C. The combined effect is a double dose of inflation.

1. Identify some additional effects of the war on terrorism that would shift aggregate supply or aggregate demand.

2. What could cause wartime full employment to exceed peacetime full employment? Give some examples from the United States' actual wartime experience.

*T*HINKING
*C*RITICALLY

Visit www.prenhall.com/ayers for updates and web exercises on this Explore & Apply topic.

SUMMARY AND LEARNING OBJECTIVES

1. Contrast the perspectives of classical economists to those of Keynesians.
 ■ When the economy's resources are fully employed, the economy has attained full-employment output, also called full-employment GDP. Actual GDP could be at, above, or below the full-employment level of GDP.

 ■ The book *The General Theory of Employment, Interest, and Money* (1936) by John Maynard Keynes revolutionized economics and launched the new field of macroeconomics. Keynes distinguished between the short run and the long run, observing that "In the long run we are all dead." Keynesian economics takes a short-run perspective. Keynes's goal was to further the understanding of why the economies of the world remained mired in the Great Depression of the 1930s.

- Classical economics emphasizes the long run. It has achieved a resurgence of interest as the Great Depression recedes further into the past.

- The long-run tendency in the marketplace is toward the natural rate of unemployment and its associated output. That is the classical focus, but the process takes time. The reason for this tendency is rooted in the desire of people to receive income.

2. **Describe how full-employment output can change.**
   - Full-employment output changes each time the long-run aggregate supply curve shifts.

   - Long-run aggregate supply shifts in response to changes in the amount of resources and in the technology available to use these resources. Warfare or natural disasters could destroy resources, which would reduce full-employment output and shift aggregate supply to the left. More commonly, economies add resources and improve technology over time. The result is economic growth that increases full-employment output.

3. **Explain why the price level does not matter in the long run.**
   - As evidence that the price level does not matter in the long run, consider that the price level today is quadruple that of the late 1960s. However, market wages have also adjusted upward. Other than requiring that we earn and spend about four times as much to obtain the same goods and services, the rise in wages and prices has had little long-run significance for the aggregate economy.

4. **Interpret and apply the aggregate demand–aggregate supply model.**
   - The determination of real output, inflation, and employment is shown with the model of aggregate demand and aggregate supply.

   - The long-run aggregate supply curve is vertical at full employment. It will only shift as the economy's productive capacity changes. That shift will be outward as productive capacity increases.

   - The aggregate demand curve is downward sloping because a lower price level will increase the purchasing power of money and prompt people to spend more, the so-called purchasing power effect. The aggregate demand curve also slopes downward to the right because of the wealth effect. The wealth effect is the increase in the real value of savings that accompanies a lower price level.

- The long-run macroeconomic equilibrium is termed the full-employment equilibrium. It occurs at the point where the aggregate demand curve intersects the long-run aggregate supply curve. This equilibrium involves both full-employment output and a full-employment price level.

- When the price level is higher than the full-employment price level, the economy will experience unemployment and actual GDP will be less than full-employment GDP. The economy's tendency to adjust to full employment requires that the price level drop.

- When the price level is lower than the full-employment price level, the economy will overheat. Aggregate demand will be greater than long-run aggregate supply and actual GDP will exceed the full-employment level. Overheating causes the price level to adjust upward. Along with a higher price level will come a decrease in actual GDP back to its full-employment level.

5. **Relate the difference between demand-side and supply-side inflation in the long run.**
   - Increases in aggregate spending, such as those caused by additional consumer and government spending, shift aggregate demand outward and lead to demand-side inflation. Demand-side deflation would accompany a leftward shift in aggregate demand.

   - Inflation and deflation can also arise from shifts in the long-run aggregate supply curve. An outward shift in long-run aggregate supply leads to supply-side deflation. A leftward shift in long-run aggregate supply leads to supply-side inflation.

   - Structural changes in the economy influence inflation and deflation. An increase in the natural rate of unemployment will occur when legislation and other forces make it more difficult for employers to hire workers and for workers to switch jobs. Supply-side inflation is the outcome.

6. **Interpret how the war against terrorism can cause both inflation and lower output, and ways in which these effects might be countered.**
   - The war on terrorism will cause the macroeconomic equilibrium to change. Aggregate supply will shift to the left because of the need to devote resources to increase the country's security, causing the price level to rise. Aggregate demand will also shift to the left to the extent that uncertainty inhibits consumer spending, causing the price level to fall. Government spending can offset the drop in consumer spending. If aggregate demand rebounds strongly, the economy could see a combination of supply-side and demand-side inflation pushing the price level upward.

KEY TERMS

long run, 180
short run, 180
Keynesian 181
classical, 181
Phillips curve, 181
inflationary expectations, 182
adaptive expectations, 182
stagflation, 183

rational expectations, 183
full-employment output (full-employment GDP), 184
long-run aggregate supply, 184
aggregate demand, 186
purchasing power effect, 187
wealth effect, 187

full-employment equilibrium, 187
demand-side inflation, 189
demand-side deflation, 189
supply-side inflation, 189
supply shock, 189
real business cycle, 189
supply-side deflation, 191

TEST YOURSELF

TRUE OR FALSE

1. Both classical and Keynesian economists agree that the economy is most usefully characterized through a long-run perspective.

2. The long-run aggregate supply curve illustrates that full-employment GDP is independent of the price level.

3. One explanation for the downward slope of aggregate demand is the savings effect, which states that people save more as they earn more.

4. Supply-side inflation occurs when there is a decrease in aggregate supply.

5. The aggregate demand and aggregate supply model can explain inflation but not deflation.

MULTIPLE CHOICE

6. Full-employment GDP
   a. must be equal to actual GDP.
   b. must be less than actual GDP.
   c. must be greater than actual GDP.
   d. could be less than, equal to, or greater than actual GDP.

7. Because of the desire of people to have an income, the long-run tendency of the economy is to
   a. move up and down with the business cycle.
   b. produce the full-employment level of output.
   c. behave in unpredictable ways.
   d. exhibit stable prices.

8. "In the long run we are all dead" is a statement that best expresses
   a. Keynesian economics.
   b. classical economics.
   c. both Keynesian and classical economics.
   d. neither Keynesian nor classical economics.

9. The Phillips curve shows an inverse relationship between _____ and _____ .

a. inflation; unemployment
b. GDP; price level
c. supply-side inflation; demand-side inflation
d. aggregate demand; aggregate supply

10. A graph of long-run aggregate supply would show the curve to be
    a. upward sloping to the right.
    b. downward sloping to the right.
    c. vertical.
    d. horizontal.

11. In Self-Test Figure 8-1, point A represents
    a. total unemployment.
    b. an increase in unemployment.
    c. a decrease in aggregate demand.
    d. a smaller output associated with full employment.

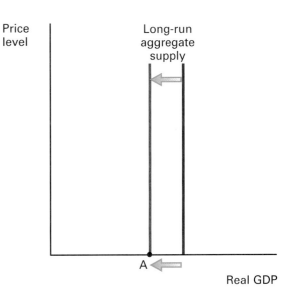

SELF-TEST FIGURE 8-1

12. Which of the following is most likely to cause the shift in aggregate supply shown in Self-Test Figure 8-1?
   a. An increase in aggregate demand.
   b. A decrease in aggregate demand.
   c. A decrease in consumer spending.
   d. The destruction of resources in warfare.

13. The aggregate demand curve is
   a. upward sloping to the right.
   b. downward sloping to the right.
   c. vertical.
   d. horizontal.

14. An aggregate demand curve
   a. shows the quantity of a good or service that will be purchased at each of various possible prices.
   b. reveals how much real GDP consumers, businesses, and government will purchase at each price level.
   c. portrays how much real GDP the economy will produce at various price levels.
   d. shows the relationship between interest rates and spending in the economy.

15. Graphically, a long-run macro equilibrium occurs
   a. anywhere along an aggregate demand curve.
   b. anywhere along the long-run aggregate supply curve.
   c. at the intersection of an aggregate demand curve and the long-run aggregate supply curve.
   d. at any value of real GDP so long as the long-run aggregate supply curve and an aggregate demand curve do not intersect.

16. If the economy starts at point *A* in Self-Test Figure 8-2, it is likely to see
   a. the price level increase over time.
   b. the price level decrease over time.
   c. unemployment rise over time.
   d. full-employment output fall over time.

17. Demand-side inflation occurs when
   a. the long-run aggregate supply curve shifts to the left.
   b. inflation causes the aggregate demand curve to shift to the left.
   c. the aggregate demand curve shifts to the right.
   d. inflation rises above 3 percent per year.

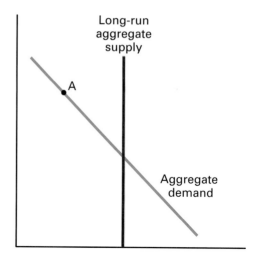

SELF-TEST FIGURE 8-2

18. Supply-side deflation is a phenomena associated with
   a. more government rules and regulations.
   b. decreased consumer spending.
   c. an aggregate demand curve that shifts to the right.
   d. improved technology.

19. The supply shock of a natural disaster is associated with a _____ shift in long-run aggregate supply and a _____ price level.
   a. leftward; lower
   b. leftward; higher
   c. rightward; lower
   d. rightward; higher

20. The war on terrorism could shift aggregate supply to the left and aggregate demand to the right as a consequence of increased government spending. The result would be
   a. demand-side inflation only.
   b. supply-side deflation only.
   c. a combination of demand-side inflation and supply-side inflation.
   d. a combination of demand-side deflation and supply-side deflation.

QUESTIONS AND PROBLEMS

1. *[classical versus Keynesian]* State the essential difference between the classical and Keynesian schools of thought. If you were a public policymaker and received conflicting advice from a classical and a Keynesian economist, how would you choose? Explain.

2. *[Phillips curve]* According to the Phillips curve, what characterizes the relationship between inflation and unemployment? Draw a Phillips curve, making sure to label the axes. Does evidence accumulated after the 1960s support those conclusions?

3. *[inflationary expectations]* What do you expect the inflation rate to be over the next year?

   a. Did you arrive at an answer to this question by adaptive expectations?

   b. What are rational expectations? Are rational expectations or adaptive expectations more likely to be accurate?

4. *[full-employment GDP]* Must actual GDP always be equal to full-employment GDP? Explain.

5. *[full-employment GDP]* Explain how it is possible for actual GDP to temporarily exceed full-employment GDP.

6. *[natural rate of unemployment]* Explain how the natural rate of unemployment discussed in Chapter 6 relates to long-run aggregate supply.

7. *[long-run aggregate supply]* Explain why the long-run aggregate supply curve is drawn as a vertical line. At what point on the horizontal axis is the long-run aggregate supply curve located? Why would the long-run aggregate supply curve shift outward?

8. *[long-run aggregate supply]* Why does the price level not make a difference to full-employment output in the long run? Illustrate your answer by drawing a long-run aggregate supply curve and explaining the implications of the vertical nature of the curve.

9. *[aggregate demand]* Define aggregate demand. Draw a graph of aggregate demand. What are the two effects that explain the slope of the aggregate demand curve?

10. *[long-run macro equilibrium]* Illustrate graphically and explain the long-run macro equilibrium.

11. *[aggregate demand/aggregate supply model]* Draw a graph that shows the long-run aggregate supply curve and an aggregate demand curve. Be sure to label the axes and the point on the horizontal axis that represents full-employment GDP. Illustrate on your graph an economy with unemployment. What is the cause of unemployment? Describe how the economy will adjust toward full employment.

12. *[aggregate demand/aggregate supply model]* Redraw the aggregate demand/aggregate supply graph you created in the preceding question. Illustrate on your graph an economy that is overheating. What is the cause of overheating? How will the economy adjust toward full employment?

13. *[inflation]* On separate graphs, show demand-side and supply-side inflation, labeling the axes, curves, and changes in output and the price level. Explain how the two might occur together.

14. *[deflation]* On separate graphs, show demand-side and supply-side deflation, labeling the axes, curves, and changes in output and the price level. Explain how the two might occur together.

15. *[Classical versus Keynesian]* Which group, political liberals or conservatives, is more likely to take Keynesian positions on the economy? Explain.

Visit www.prenhall.com/ayers for Exploring the Web exercises and additional self-test quizzes.

CHAPTER 9

SHORT-RUN INSTABILITY

A LOOK AHEAD

Debt is a four-letter word, one that has gotten many people in trouble. It can crimp one's lifestyle and even lead to personal bankruptcy. Many countries have felt the financial straitjacket of debt. In the United States, for example, the federal government has amassed debt of over $6 trillion and a deficit in the federal budget that increases that debt as the years go by. Irresponsible? Perhaps, perhaps not. As we will see in the Explore & Apply section that concludes this chapter, there is cause for both personal and national debt. There are also questions about the effect on the economy of policies that add more.

Deficit spending might be intended to offset economic downturns and reduce economic instability. As the economy transitions from one long-run equilibrium to another, it is buffeted by the short-run ups and downs of the business cycle. This chapter examines the issues of short-run instability by adding to the model of aggregate supply and aggregate demand introduced in Chapter 8. We will find possible ways for government tax and spending policies to help the economy out of recession. We will also uncover potential problems with these policy actions, including getting them to take effect at the proper time and creating inflation that can undermine the policy's intent.

LEARNING OBJECTIVES

Understanding Chapter 9 will enable you to:
1. **Explain why wages and prices might be slow to adjust downward, and what significance this can have.**
2. **Discuss how fiscal policy to stabilize the economy is subject to lags, and how the lags can be overcome automatically.**
3. **Explain how balancing the full-employment budget is consistent with a budget deficit.**
4. **Identify the characteristics and significance of short-run aggregate supply.**
5. **Describe demand-pull and cost-push inflation, and how they can be part of an inflationary spiral.**
6. **Analyze the rationale and limitations of deficit spending.**

$\mathscr{E}$XPLORE
&
$\mathscr{A}$PPLY

201

At any given point in time, the short-run instabilities of the business cycle often seem more compelling than the long-run tendencies discussed in the previous chapter. Whenever there is an economic downturn, the press and public call upon government to do something about it. People want action!

For example, the economic downturn that started in March of 2001, together with four years of surplus in the federal budget, led President Bush and Congress to authorize refunds of some tax payments in August of that year. Taxpayers received checks for up to $300 per person or $600 per couple. The idea was to energize the economy. In the time period between then and the shock of September 11 when terrorists struck the American homeland, however, there was no discernible increase in consumer spending.

To bring the economy out of what then appeared to be a deepening recession, President Bush requested, and Congress enacted, $100 billion worth of tax cuts and new spending. There was almost no opposition to following this policy action. Elected representatives of the people want to show their constituencies action, not inaction. However, from the perspective of macroeconomic theory, herein lies the great debate. While Keynesians argue for government action, recall that classical economists emphasize that markets are quite capable of doing their own adjusting.

9.1 SHORT-RUN STICKINESS ALONG AGGREGATE DEMAND

The debate over macro policy often comes down to the question of nothing more than whether to wait for a movement along aggregate demand or to take action to *manage aggregate demand*, meaning to shift the aggregate demand curve itself. We proceed by looking at the adjustment process along aggregate demand, and then by looking at some policy options for aggregate demand management.

If a market is not at equilibrium, forces of supply and demand will cause the price to change until the equilibrium comes about. That is the classical analysis: Wage and price adjustments will lead to a long-run macro equilibrium that is characterized by both full employment and its associated full-employment output. Keynesians do not dispute this point, but dispute its relevance when the economy faces immediate macroeconomic problems that call for prompt solutions. Of particular note is the existence of downwardly **sticky wages** and **sticky prices,** where downwardly sticky refers to an inflexibility that makes it difficult for wages and prices to fall. If wages are sticky, the downward movement in wages required to reach a long-run equilibrium could take too long. The downward stickiness could be due to labor contracts between a union and its employees. It could also be due to human psychology—when firms cut wages, their workers resent it.

One reason for wage and price stickiness is that some markets might not move to equilibrium easily. Changes in the demand for outputs make it appropriate for some wages and prices to rise or fall relative to other wages and prices. However, there is resistance to change—*rigidities*—within both labor and output markets. Stores have leases and contracts that are not easily adjusted. In some cases, the contracts are with unions that resist wage cuts.

In principle, wage and price stickiness might occur in either direction—whether for price increases or for price decreases. In practice, **wage and price stickiness is most pronounced in a downward direction,** meaning that there is more stickiness when markets resist lower wages and prices. For example, it is natural for workers to resent a wage cut, no matter what the macroeconomic circumstances might be. Firms that cut wages run the risk of lower productivity and lower quality output from their workers. The problem is often exacerbated by a lack of information and trust. When employers attempt to downsize or close operations, employees balk, which causes adjustments in employment and output to occur slowly.

sticky wages wages that are slow to adjust, usually in a downward direction.

sticky prices prices that are slow to adjust, usually in a downward direction.

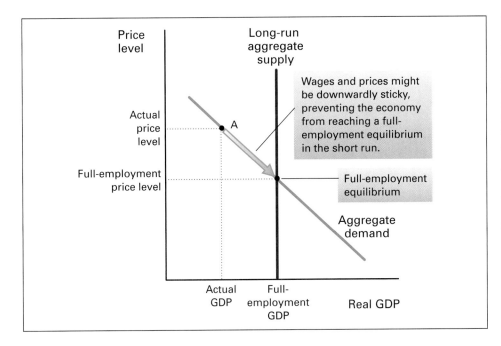

FIGURE 9-1

DOWNWARDLY STICKY WAGES AND PRICES Wages and prices that are downwardly sticky would prevent the economy from moving rapidly to a full-employment equilibrium. For example, the economy might start at point *A*, with a price level that is too high to reach full-employment output. In the long run, that price level will fall, but wage and price stickiness might prevent it from doing so in the short run.

Figure 9-1 sums up the significance of downwardly sticky wages and prices. While wages are not listed explicitly in this figure, wages paid by firms will be a big factor in determining their costs and the prices they charge. In other words, higher wages are associated with a higher price level. When the price level is too high to sustain a full-employment equilibrium, it must adjust downward to reach that equilibrium. Sticky wages and prices can get in the way of that adjustment.

For example, if the actual price level is above the full-employment price level, such as at point *A*, wage and price stickiness would prevent it from dropping fast enough that the full-employment equilibrium can be reached quickly. By delaying movement down the aggregate demand curve to a full-employment equilibrium, wage and price stickiness can mean a prolonged period in which both output and employment are below the economy's potential.

9.2 FISCAL POLICY TO STABILIZE THE BUSINESS CYCLE

Suppose the economy starts at an **unemployment equilibrium,** characterized by a price level that is too high to achieve full-employment GDP, but that refuses to fall because of sticky prices. If the price level cannot fall to correct the unemployment equilibrium, the only solution is to shift aggregate demand rightward by increasing spending power. The shift can be accomplished by **fiscal policy,** which is government policy toward taxation and spending. It can also be accomplished through *monetary policy,* which has to do with varying the quantity of money that is available to spend. We will examine specific fiscal policy tools in Chapter 11 and the tools and goals of monetary policy in Chapter 14. Here we focus on **stabilization policy,** which refers to the general strategies of fiscal policy government can use to manage aggregate demand in order to reduce economic fluctuations.

unemployment equilibrium a short-run equilibrium GDP that is less than full-employment GDP.

fiscal policy government tax and spending policy.

stabilization policy general strategies of fiscal policy government can use to manage aggregate demand in order to reduce economic fluctuations.

expansionary fiscal policy (fiscal stimulus) occurs when government adds to aggregate expenditures by lowering the amount of tax revenue it collects or increasing the amount of its spending.

FISCAL STIMULI AND FISCAL DRAGS

When the economy finds itself stuck at an unemployment equilibrium, Keynesians advocate using **expansionary fiscal policy,** also called a **fiscal stimulus,** which is increased government spending or reduced taxation intended to *stimulate* aggregate demand and return the

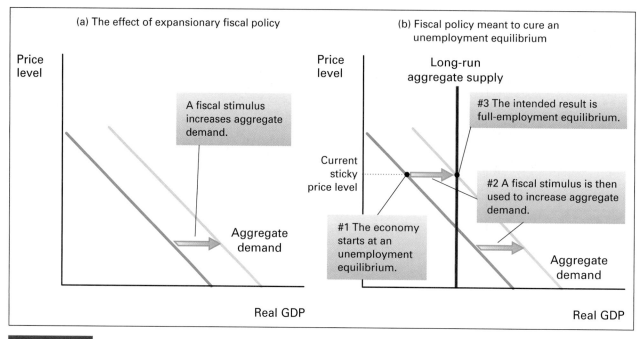

FIGURE 9-2

EXPANSIONARY FISCAL POLICY Expansionary fiscal policies shift aggregate demand to the right by adding to government and/or consumer spending, as shown in (a). When the economy starts at an unemployment equilibrium, Keynesians would suggest using expansionary fiscal policy to shift aggregate demand to the right. As shown in (b), the idea is to shift aggregate demand just far enough to reach long-run aggregate supply at full-employment output and achieve a full-employment equilibrium.

economy to full employment. The Works Progress Administration and other New Deal public works programs of President Franklin Roosevelt are examples of stimulative fiscal policies. Indeed, World War II seemed to prove the validity of Keynesian economics, since the massive amount of government spending it involved paved the way from the Great Depression of the 1930s to the prosperity of the 1950s. With more government spending, aggregate demand shifts to the right, as shown in Figure 9-2(a). The Keynesian idea is to shift it just enough to reach full-employment output, as shown in Figure 9-2(b), thus solving unemployment problems without causing inflation.

Alternatively, when the economy *overheats*—or grows so fast that inflation threatens—government can use a **contractionary fiscal policy,** also called a **fiscal drag,** to slow it down. Contractionary fiscal policy might involve higher taxes or less government spending. Figure 9-3(a) and (b) illustrate how contractionary fiscal policy can shift aggregate demand to the left to avoid overheating.

contractionary fiscal policy (fiscal drag) occurs when the government reduces aggregate expenditures by increasing the amount of tax revenue it collects or reducing the amount of its spending.

FISCAL POLICY CHOICE: DISCRETIONARY OR AUTOMATIC?

Both expansionary and contractionary fiscal policy are examples of **discretionary policy**—public policy adjusted at the discretion of lawmakers. Unfortunately, even the best intentioned discretionary public policy is unlikely to follow the Keynesian policy prescription of managing aggregate demand in order to counter short-run instability. The reason has to do with the three *fiscal policy lags:*

discretionary policy public policy adjusted through explicit changes made by lawmakers.

recognition lag time before policymakers recognize that a problem exists.

■ The **recognition lag**—It takes time to know that the economy is in a recession. For example, although not an official standard, it usually takes approximately two consecutive

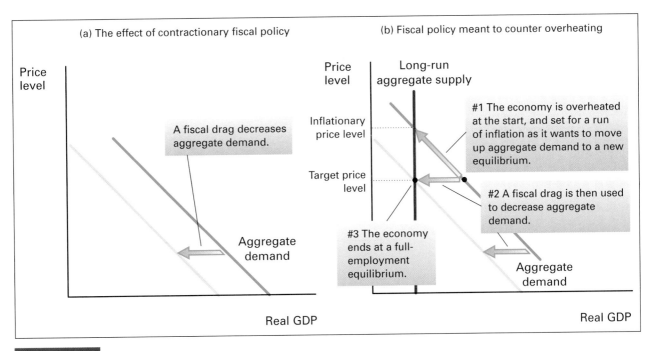

FIGURE 9-3

CONTRACTIONARY FISCAL POLICY Contractionary fiscal policies shift aggregate demand to the left by reducing government and/or consumer spending, as shown in (a). When the economy starts overheating, such that it is likely to cause inflation as it moves up aggregate demand to a long-run equilibrium, contractionary fiscal policy can be used to shift aggregate demand. As shown in (b), the idea is to shift aggregate demand just far enough to the left to reach long-run aggregate supply at the current price level so as to achieve a full-employment equilibrium.

quarters of declining GDP before the authoritative National Bureau of Economic Research (NBER) declares a recession. In late November of 2001, the NBER declared that the economy was in a recession that started in March of that year.

- The **action lag**—Tax and spending bills are not passed overnight. The fiscal stimulus aimed at the 2001 recession was not passed until 2002.

- The **implementation lag**—It's great to build a highway, but most people expect to have it planned out before crews are sent to lay asphalt! Once spending is authorized, the details must be planned and the money spent, which takes time. It also takes time before tax changes can take effect.

action lag time between when the problem is recognized and when policies are enacted.

implementation lag time between when policies are enacted and when they take effect.

Because of fiscal policy lags, the business cycle may have turned by the time the money starts flowing from an expansionary fiscal policy. The spending may be more likely to cause inflation than to reduce unemployment. Policy lags make it very difficult, if not impossible, to *fine-tune* the economy to even out the ups and downs of the business cycle. Fine-tuning would require that contractionary fiscal policy start when the economy pushes above full-employment GDP. Likewise, when the economy sinks to less than full-employment GDP, then finely tuned fiscal policy should be expansionary. Figure 9-4 shows both possibilities.

Instead of discretionary policy, lawmakers can rely on **automatic stabilizers.** Automatic stabilizers are components of existing fiscal policies that stimulate the economy when it is sluggish and act as a drag when it overheats. The U.S. economy has automatic stabilizers embedded within its system of taxation and spending.

automatic stabilizers features embedded within existing fiscal policies that act as a stimulant when the economy is sluggish and act as a drag when it is in danger of inflation.

Consider automatic stabilizers on the tax side. As personal and corporate incomes fall during recession, so too does the amount collected by the federal government in personal

FISCAL POLICY TIMING The best time for contractionary fiscal policy is when the economy starts to overheat, meaning that it is exceeding full-employment GDP. The best time for expansionary fiscal policy is when the economy has fallen into a recession below the full-employment GDP. Lags make it hard to fine-tune discretionary fiscal policy such that it follows these prescriptions. Automatic stabilizers, in contrast, tend to push down the economy's peaks and push up its troughs without any change in the policies themselves.

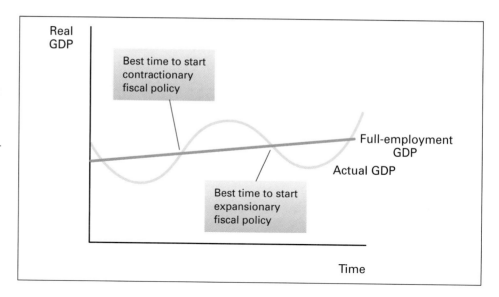

and corporate income taxes. The reduced tax burden on individuals and companies helps reduce the severity of that recession. Alternatively, if the economy is booming, income taxes bring in revenue, which is contractionary because it removes some of the excess purchasing power. No policy action is necessary.

On the spending side, payments for welfare, unemployment compensation, and other social programs rise as the economy slows and more people seek these safety-net services. Conversely, this spending falls when the economy heats up, just as Keynesian policy prescribes. Again, the action to stabilize the economy is automatic; no policy adjustments are needed. Taken as a whole, the automatic stabilizers are intended to be expansionary if the economy is below full employment and contractionary when the economy is overheating. **If the economy is at full employment, fiscal policy should be neutral, since there is no need to either stimulate or slow down economic activity.**

BALANCING THE BUDGET

balanced budget occurs when government revenue equals government spending.

Fiscal policy might lead to a **balanced budget,** which occurs when tax revenue inflows just equal government expenditure outflows. Government spending and revenues are recorded in the *federal budget.* Interpreting this budget is often difficult, since the budget is separated into so-called on-budget and off-budget items. Together these items represent the *unified budget,* which is most commonly used.

Whether fiscal policy is discretionary or is accomplished by automatic stabilizers, economists often suggest that it should be set so that the budget roughly balances over the course of the business cycle. The idea is that, when the economy is overheated and contractionary policy is in order, the government would run a **budget surplus** in which tax revenue exceeds government spending. When economic health is poor and expansionary policy is needed, the government would then choose a **budget deficit** in which government spending exceeds tax revenue. The surpluses could help pay for the deficits.

budget surplus occurs when government collects more revenue than it spends.

budget deficit occurs when government collects less revenue than it spends.

full-employment budget estimate of government revenue and spending were the economy to be at full employment.

In practice, however, there is a significant tilt toward the expansionary side, even when the economy is doing well. To assess this tilt, we can look at the **full-employment budget,** which is an estimate of what government revenue and spending would be were there full employment. The full-employment budget has usually been in deficit in recent years. For example, despite being in the vicinity of full employment for much of the past two decades,

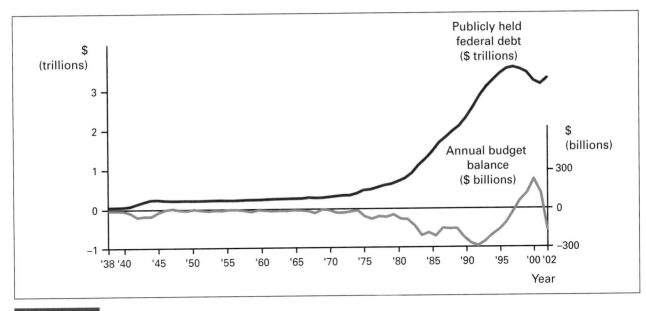

FIGURE 9-5

THE U.S. BUDGET Budget deficits have been the norm in modern U.S. history. These deficits have added to the national debt over time. This figure shows the portion of the debt held by the public. Including debt from one government agency to another, the national debt totaled over $6 trillion in 2002.

Source: 2002 Economic Report of the President, Table B-78.

the U.S. government has run substantial budget deficits in the large majority of those years, as seen in Figure 9-5. The result of the accumulation of past budget deficits and surpluses is, on balance, a U.S. **national debt** of over $6 trillion by the end of 2002. Roughly half of this debt is owed within government (mostly to Social Security), with the other half owed to the public. The latter portion of debt is shown in Figure 9-5. The national debt increases when there are budget deficits and decreases when there are budget surpluses. This is money owed by the U.S. government, mostly to American citizens. Budget deficits and the national debt will be further discussed in this chapter's Explore & Apply section.

national debt how much money the government owes.

SQUANDERING THE SURPLUS?   *SNAPSHOT*

For four glorious years—from 1998 through 2001—the United States government experienced the luxury of a budget surplus. The national debt got a chance to decline for the first time in three decades. It was more than nice. The declining national debt instilled hope that the country could actually afford its commitments, such as to Social Security for the looming wave of retiring baby boomers. Then reality struck.

First came the stock market slide and later a mild recession, which caused the government to pay out more in unemployment insurance and other assistance. The September 11 terrorist attacks added the need for massive amounts of government spending on national security. All of this combined to create a mentality in Washington, D.C., of spend and spend some more. By the middle of 2002, the economy was expanding, but so too was government spending. With massive new commitments to agriculture, the military, and for homeland security, a return to the days of budget surpluses was no longer in sight. ◄

QUICKCHECK

(a) Once federal spending is approved, why is there an implementation lag? Use a new highway as an example. (b) Must all fiscal policies have a long implementation lag? Explain.

Answer: (a) Projects must first be planned. A new highway requires a considerable amount of surveying before the specifics of its route and features are established. Land must then be acquired. There continues to be a sequence of employing different types of labor and other inputs for different phases of the construction. The final product may not be completed for several years. (b) Projects that require little planning will have a shorter implementation lag.

9.3 THE SHORT-RUN ADJUSTMENT PROCESS

In principle, as seen earlier in Figure 9-2, expansionary fiscal policy can shift aggregate demand rightward until it achieves full-employment output at the current price level. In practice, however, the economy does not behave quite this simply. The most notable complexity is a tendency toward inflation when policymakers try to stimulate aggregate demand. In order to understand this response, we will distinguish between aggregate supply in the short run and aggregate supply in the long run.

SHORT-RUN AGGREGATE SUPPLY

Recall that aggregate supply tells how much output the economy has to offer at each possible price level, based on the potential productivity of its resources. In the long run, the price level does not matter to this potential. In the long run, higher wages that are only the result of inflation will have no influence on behavior as workers recognize that the higher wages are merely necessary to pay for higher costs of living. Therefore, in the long run, aggregate supply is unaffected by the price level, causing it to be vertical. However, **short-run aggregate supply**—the amount of output the economy has to offer in the short run—will slope upward.

> **short-run aggregate supply** tells how much output the economy will offer in the short run at each possible price level.

Figure 9-6 shows the upward-sloping short-run aggregate supply as it relates to long-run aggregate supply, which is always vertical at full-employment GDP. In the short run, the amount of output produced can even exceed full-employment GDP, as workers offer to work overtime or seek out extra jobs. Conversely, if workers expect more inflation than actually occurs, the output they would produce at the actual price level would be less than full-employment GDP.

Two reasons for the upward slope of aggregate supply are as follows:

> **structural rigidities** impediments within the economy that slow adjustment to a long-run equilibrium.

- **Structural rigidities**—As new spending power is added to the economy, it tends to raise wages and prices where it first hits, before eventually diffusing throughout the economy. Wages and prices in the sectors of the economy most directly affected by the spending will rise before the extra spending can circulate more generally throughout the economy. The result is a higher output in those sectors, but also a higher overall price level.

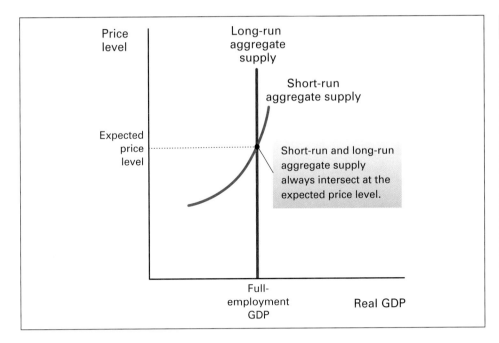

FIGURE 9-6

SHORT-RUN AGGREGATE SUPPLY
Short-run aggregate supply slopes upward, intersecting long-run aggregate supply at the expected price level. Structural rigidities and the production effect explain the upward slope of short-run aggregate supply. According to the production effect, a drop in the price level can lead workers to cut back on hours of work, causing GDP to fall. An increase in the price level would have the opposite effect, possibly leading to output that exceeds full-employment GDP.

■ **The production effect**—When the price level rises and labor supply curves remain unchanged, firms can profit by increasing output and employment. If the economy is already at full employment, firms will employ workers overtime, thus allowing the economy to exceed full-employment output temporarily.

the production effect when a higher price level causes firms to increase output, employing workers who are willing to work extra hours to the extent that they do not correctly anticipate inflation.

The production effect relies upon workers being fooled by inflation or deflation. After all, if the price level changes, workers should adjust their own labor supply curves accordingly. In the event of inflation, for example, individual wage requirements should rise, thus shifting each worker's labor supply curve upward. However, while it is easy for workers to know past rates of inflation, it is much more difficult to recognize price-level changes in the present. People seeing wages going up are likely to first respond by offering to work more and then adjust their inflationary expectations later. Since an increased price level is associated with higher wages, a higher price level brings forth more work effort as workers are fooled by inflation, but only in the short run. For the economy to be in long-run equilibrium, workers must have accurate wage and price expectations. For this reason, **short-run aggregate supply always intersects long-run aggregate supply at the expected price level.**

The intersection of aggregate demand and short-run aggregate supply constitutes a **short-run macroeconomic equilibrium,** as shown in Figure 9-7. In this case, the macro equilibrium is also an unemployment equilibrium, because it occurs at less than full-employment GDP. The short-run macro equilibrium consists of an equilibrium price level and an equilibrium GDP. These are labeled in the figure as actual price level and actual GDP, since the short run is where the economy actually is at any given point in time. As before, short-run aggregate supply intersects long-run aggregate supply at the expected price level.

short-run macroeconomic equilibrium where the economy tends in the short run, given by the intersection of aggregate demand and short-run aggregate supply.

The long-run aggregate supply is a reference toward which the economy tends over time. Therefore, whereas the long-run equilibrium occurs where aggregate demand intersects long-run aggregate supply, the short-run equilibrium is where aggregate demand intersects short-run aggregate supply.

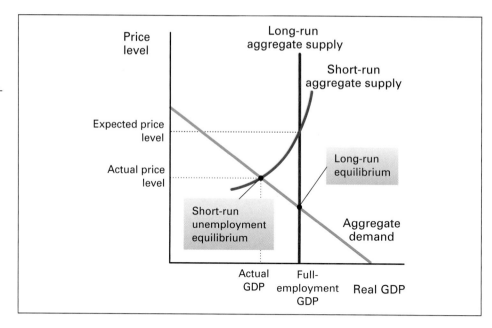

SNAPSHOT   **"TOMORROW IS ANOTHER DAY!"**

"I will never go hungry again!" avowed Scarlett O'Hara in the movie *Gone With the Wind*. She was determined to make a better future. In the meantime, though, she was forced to work with what she had. For Scarlett, it was the red earth of her one-time plantation *Tara*. For the economy, it is the output and price level that actually do occur. Collectively, we must first take stock of where we are before we can make progress toward where we want to be. In other words, it takes a short run to make it through to the long run! ◄

demand–pull inflation occurs when a rightward shift in aggregate demand moves the economy up short-run aggregate supply; associated with greater employment and output.

DEMAND–PULL INFLATION

Chapter 8 discussed demand-side and supply-side inflation in the context of changes in either aggregate demand or long-run aggregate supply. That discussion involved the long run. Here we discuss the short-run counterparts. Consider first **demand-pull inflation**, which is caused by an increase in aggregate demand that pulls the economy up the short-run aggregate supply curve, such as shown in Figure 9-8. **Demand–pull inflation occurs when a rightward shift in aggregate demand moves the economy to both a higher output and a higher price level.**

Demand–pull inflation might be caused by expansionary fiscal policy that is meant to move the economy toward full employment. For example, suppose the economy starts at the unemployment equilibrium given by the intersection of aggregate demand and short-run aggregate supply, labeled point 1 in Figure 9-9. To reach full employment, the government might select the fiscal policy stimulus of spending an extra $20 billion on new ballistic-technology military equipment. The idea would be to shift aggregate demand far enough to the right to reach full-employment GDP at the current price level, as shown by point 2 in the figure.

Instead of full employment at the current price level, though, the result of the extra spending is likely to be inflation plus a less-than-intended increase in output, given by point 3 in Figure 9-9. The reason is that the added demand for jobs would be concentrated in the defense industry. Workers with the human capital used in the defense industry would be in great demand and would see their salaries increase, a situation that would contribute to

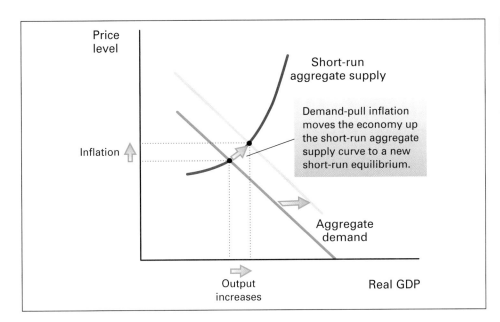

FIGURE 9-8

DEMAND-PULL INFLATION
Stimulative fiscal policy shifts aggregate demand, moving the economy up the short-run aggregate supply curve. The result is an increase in output along with demand–pull inflation.

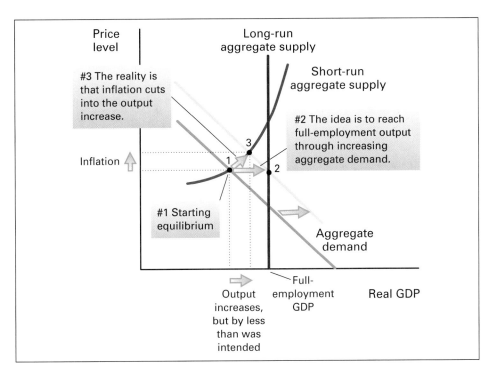

FIGURE 9-9

INFLATION FROM FISCAL STIMULUS Expansionary fiscal policy shifts aggregate demand. While the intention might be to move the economy to full-employment output at a constant price level, the reality is a movement up the short-run aggregate supply curve. Some of the added spending that is intended to increase output is instead eaten up by inflation.

inflation. Meanwhile, job seekers without the required skills would remain unemployed. The result is shown as a movement up the short-run aggregate supply curve in the general direction of full-employment output, but also in the direction of a higher price level.

COST–PUSH INFLATION

Inflation could also arise from an upward shift in the short-run aggregate supply curve. Because the short-run aggregate supply curve intersects long-run aggregate supply at the

FIGURE 9-10

SHORT-RUN AGGREGATE SUPPLY SHIFTS Short-run aggregate supply shifts in response to a change in the expected price level. Whatever the expected price level may be, that is where short-run aggregate supply and long-run aggregate supply intersect and the long-run equilibrium occurs.

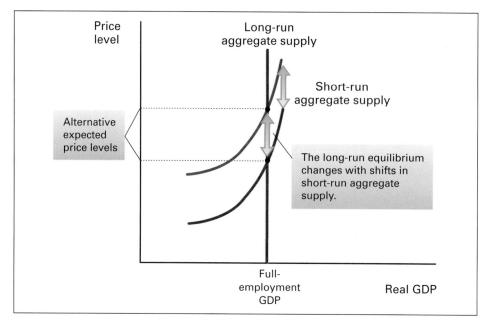

expected price level, a change in the expected price level will shift short-run aggregate supply vertically, as shown in Figure 9-10. For example, if the expected price level increases, short-run aggregate supply shifts vertically upward until its intersection with long-run aggregate supply occurs at the new expected price level. Likewise, if the expected price level decreases, short-run aggregate supply shifts downward, intersecting long-run aggregate supply at the new expected price level.

Such shifts are likely because workers revise their expectations over time. For example, as inflation rose significantly from 2 percent in 1960 to 6 percent in the early 1970s, most people commenced to factor inflation into their labor supply decisions—they developed inflationary expectations, and could be fooled only by actual inflation that turned out differently from what they came to expect. Thus, stimulative fiscal policies that shifted aggregate demand to the right were offset by upward shifts in the short-run aggregate supply curve.

cost–push inflation occurs when an upward shift in short-run aggregate supply causes the economy to move up the aggregate demand curve to a higher price level and less output.

When aggregate supply shifts up, the economy moves up the aggregate demand curve to a point of higher prices and lower output, as shown in Figure 9-11. Inflation that is caused in this way is called **cost–push inflation. Cost–push inflation reduces output and increases the price level.** Recall from Chapter 8, that this combination is known as *stagflation*—the simultaneous occurrence of inflation and economic stagnation.

SNAPSHOT   ## A SQUEEZE ON CHARMIN

In 1971, in an attempt to combat inflation, President Nixon signed a price freeze into law. Shortly afterward, Canadian paper companies increased the price of wood fiber, which eroded the profits of tissue manufacturers. Johnny Carson, true to his form as host of *The Tonight Show,* could not pass up making light of this touchy subject.

In his opening monologue, Johnny joked about toilet paper shortages in New Jersey. Guess what? Even though it had not really been very difficult to find toilet paper in New Jersey, a shortage quickly developed. People rushed to the stores to snatch up all brands of toilet tissue. Manufacturers had no special incentive to restock, so the shelves stayed bare. Thus was the start of the Great Toilet Paper Squeeze of 1971! That was also the last we saw of price freezes in the United States. ◀

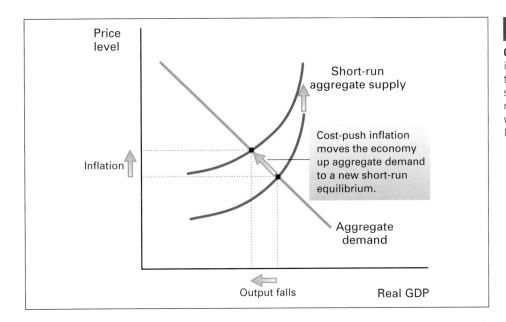

FIGURE 9-11

COST–PUSH INFLATION When an increase in inflationary expectations causes an upward shift in short-run aggregate supply, the result is cost–push inflation, in which output falls and the price level rises.

QUICKCHECK

What is the difference between cost–push inflation and demand–pull inflation?

Answer: Cost–push inflation involves a movement up the aggregate demand curve as prices rise. It is caused by the inflationary expectations of workers and firms that drive up production and output costs. Demand–pull inflation occurs when the aggregate demand curve shifts outward, which causes a movement up the short-run aggregate supply curve.

9.4 SHORT-RUN PATHS TO LONG-RUN STABILITY

Over the course of time, an economy is constantly in the short run. However, the short runs differ from one year to another. If they differ very much, there is likely to be trouble, as we will see below.

THE INFLATIONARY SPIRAL

The shifting short-run aggregate supply becomes a moving target for government policy-makers. If government chases an upwardly shifting aggregate supply with ever more stimulative policies that shift out aggregate demand, the result would be the reinforcement of inflationary expectations. As inflationary expectations rise, short-run aggregate supply shifts up and output falls, which prompts more fiscal stimuli in an ever-repeating cycle. The result is an ongoing **inflationary spiral** of rising and falling output along with a continually rising price level, as shown in Figure 9-12.

In the inflationary spiral, demand–pull and cost–push inflation feed upon each other. Cost–push inflation is caused by past experiences with inflation, which were most likely caused by policies that had allowed aggregate demand to increase. To counter cost–push inflation and keep the economy near full employment, policymakers might choose to expand aggregate demand again. That would reinforce inflationary expectations in future periods, causing another round of cost–push inflation. Thus, if government responds to cost–push inflation by stimulating aggregate demand, the result is likely to be an inflationary spiral of demand–pull inflation followed by more cost–push inflation, continuing in a cycle that goes on and on.

inflationary spiral fluctuating output along with continually accelerating inflation.

FIGURE 9-12

SPIRALING INFLATION When stimulative policy increases aggregate demand, the result can be an inflationary spiral, which is an ongoing sequence of demand–pull inflation (arrows 1 and 3 pointing upward to the right), followed by cost–push inflation (arrows 2 and 4 pointing upward to the left) as short-run aggregate supply shifts to reflect higher expectations of inflation. Output is seen to fluctuate near the full-employment level.

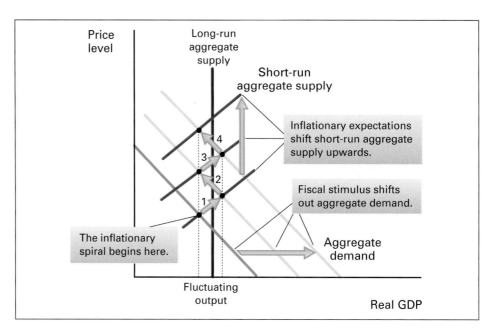

QUICKCHECK

How can government policy to stimulate the economy cause spiraling inflation? Explain with reference to demand–pull and cost–push inflation.

Answer: Government stimulative policy can shift aggregate demand to the right, leading to demand–pull inflation by moving the economy up the short-run aggregate supply curve to higher output. As workers get hit by this inflation, they demand higher wages, which shifts short-run aggregate supply upward, causing in turn cost–push inflation and its associated reduction in output. Government might respond to the falling output and associated higher unemployment with additional fiscal stimulation, thus taking the economy into a second round of demand–pull inflation. The pattern continues, with output rising from the demand–pull inflation and falling from the cost–push inflation, while the price level rises all the time. That sequence forms the inflationary spiral.

CLASSICAL OR KEYNESIAN—BOTH SEEK THE SAME STABILITY

Figure 9-13 depicts a sustainable long-run macro equilibrium, in which the expected and actual price levels are equal. The expected price level is given by the intersection of short- and long-run aggregate supply. The actual price level is given by the intersection of short-run aggregate supply and aggregate demand. Because these intersections both occur at the same point (a point on long-run aggregate supply), the economy is at full employment. Whether achieved through government policy intended to manage aggregate demand, or through a hands-off policy of giving short-run aggregate supply time to

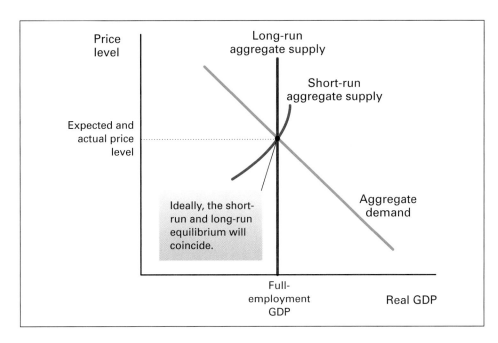

FIGURE 9-13

THE MACRO POLICY IDEAL Macro policy aims to achieve the full-employment output and a stable price level, which occurs when the actual price level equals that which is expected. The actual price level is given by the intersection of short-run aggregate supply and aggregate demand. The expected price level is given by the intersection of short-run aggregate supply and long-run aggregate supply.

adjust on its own, this long-run macro equilibrium is usually considered to be the ideal outcome of macro policy.

To achieve long-run stability and avoid the inflationary spiral, classical economists advocate maintaining the policy goal of low inflation, no matter the short-run consequences. The United States followed that policy in the early 1980s, after a decade when inflation had risen to the double-digit range. The result was a couple of years of jarring recession during which people adjusted their inflationary expectations downward. Afterward, the economy returned to full employment, but at a much lower rate of inflation.

Table 9-1 summarizes the differences between the classical and Keynesian approaches. Bear in mind that both schools of thought have the same goal for the economy, which is to

TABLE 9-1   SUMMARY OF CLASSICAL AND KEYNESIAN VIEWS

	CLASSICAL	KEYNESIAN
Focus	Long-run issues, especially economic growth.	Short-run issues, especially unemployment.
Prices and Wages	Prices and wages will adjust upward or downward as needed to reach a full-employment equilibrium.	Prices and wages adjust upward without difficulty, but are downwardly sticky and thus unable to lead the economy from an unemployment equilibrium to full employment.
Fiscal Policy	Government should not attempt to manage aggregate demand.	Government should actively adjust taxes and spending in order to manage aggregate demand.
Shortcoming	Remedying unemployment requires patience.	Remedying unemployment can lead to demand–pull inflation and possibly an inflationary spiral.

reach full-employment output without inflation. The essential difference is that the Keynesians will set aside long-run goals to combat the short-run hardships of unemployment, while classical economists "keep their eyes on the horizon" to obtain a sustainable long-run equilibrium of stable prices and full employment.

9.5 DEFICITS AND DEBT—DO WE SPEND TOO MUCH?

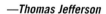

I place economy among the first and most important virtues, and public debt as the greatest of dangers.

—Thomas Jefferson

Why do babies cry? You'd cry, too, if you were born over $21,000 in debt. On average, that is how much debt Uncle Sam has already rung up for each U.S. citizen, babies included. The federal government continues to add to that national debt each year in which it operates with a budget deficit. In 2002, the budget deficit was $106.2 billion and the gross national debt stood at $6.24 trillion. About half of this debt was owed from one government agency to another, with the other half owed to the public.

The national debt can be thought of as the *stock* or inventory of accumulated past budgetary imbalances, and the deficit as a *flow* that adds to that debt. That debt represents almost 60 percent of the $10.4 trillion value of U.S. GDP. Interest payments alone account for about 14 percent of total federal government spending.

Is it fair? Is our government doing the right thing by spending our next generation's money, without them having any voice in the matter? After all, in the 1773 Boston Tea Party, the colonists of Massachusetts rebelled against unjust English taxes. Their rallying cry of "Taxation without representation is tyranny!" provided one more spark to the fire that formed the United States of America. Is our government engaging in tyranny against future American citizens?

To answer these questions, ask yourself when debt is justified. You may run up debt to pay for a college education. If you expect a payback in the form of a better income down the road, some debt while in college seems justifiable. What if you "own" a home? Few people own their homes outright. Yet most homeowners, even those with hefty mortgages to pay off, do not consider themselves debtors. Government statisticians count them as debtors, though.

Most people are willing to take on debt when that debt allows the purchase of assets of greater value. The homeowner who takes on a mortgage and the lender who offers that mortgage figure that the value of the house is more than enough to cover the balance due on the mortgage. Indeed, most homeowners with mortgages view the difference between the value of their homes and what they still owe as a primary source of their savings.

Government statisticians take a different view. When the government measures how much Americans have saved, it subtracts from that savings figure the amount that is owed on mortgages. The value of the homes is left out because it is difficult to measure. Since there are so many homeowners with mortgages in the United States, America's savings rate then appears artificially low when compared with that of other countries.

Likewise, when the government reports its own debt, it does not offset this debt with the value of the assets it owns. After all, how do you value assets of the government? Those assets include such things as parks, highways, military bases, military equipment, a judicial system, and much more. Taken as a whole, we know the value is quite high. We also know that new babies born as U.S. citizens will obtain benefits from these assets for years to come. From this perspective, expecting future citizens to bear some of the costs does not seem so bad.

Would the next generation accept this deal, to be born with both the privileges and obligations of being a U.S. citizen? While we cannot ask them, we can observe their parents answering that question with their actions. It would be most unusual to find an expectant mother seeking to leave the United States so that her baby would be born elsewhere. In contrast, immigrant couples frequently seek entry into the United States so their babies can be born as U.S. citizens.

Just because most people believe that, on balance, there is a positive value to living in the United States does not tell us that the United States has the right amount of debt. If the accumulation of debt exceeds the accumulation of assets, the value of our country diminishes over time. Conversely, if the United States holds down debt by cutting back on public investments, the country runs the risk of missing out on investment opportunities that would look good in hindsight. U.S. opportunities for economic growth would diminish, meaning that long-run aggregate supply would not shift rightward as rapidly as it could.

THE RELATIONSHIP BETWEEN THE BUDGET DEFICIT AND THE TRADE DEFICIT

As a country, we often accuse ourselves of being on a spending binge, one we will have to pay for later. As evidence, we point to both the federal budget deficit and the U.S. *trade deficit*. The trade deficit is the amount by which the value of goods we import exceeds the value of goods we export. Because we spend more of our dollars on foreign goods than foreigners return in exchange for American goods, foreigners have extra dollars left over to invest in the United States. Those investments represent future obligations of this country to other countries. Yet, while it is the collection of our individual actions that leads us to a trade deficit, we don't usually consider ourselves to be personally engaging in irresponsible spending.

The $106 billion budget deficit differs from the amount of the trade deficit, which has been running well over $400 billion in recent years. Still, the two are related, so much so that they have been dubbed the *twin deficits*. By running a budget deficit, the U.S. government leaves more money in the pockets of consumers, some of which they spend on imports. Those U.S. dollars that consumers spend on imports come back to the United States, such as when foreigners buy U.S. exports or invest in the United States.

When the government borrows money to finance the budget deficit, that borrowing tends to draw more investment dollars into the United States in response to the expanded investment opportunities. To obtain dollars to invest in the United States, foreign investors must bid them away from other uses, such as foreign purchases of U.S. products. For this reason, holding all else constant, the higher the federal budget deficit, the higher the trade deficit.

The existence of the twin deficits runs counter to the idea that government fiscal policy can spend the economy out of an unemployment equilibrium. The problem is illustrated in Figure 9-14. If the government attempts to shift aggregate demand to the right through deficit spending, it generates offsetting effects that shift aggregate demand back to the left. Specifically, the higher U.S. trade deficit reflects a reduction in spending on U.S. goods as foreigners substitute purchases of U.S. debt for purchases of U.S. products.

By the same token, the same higher interest rates that cause foreigners to invest in the United States rather than buy U.S. goods will likewise *crowd out* private sector investment, because the more money investors put into secure government debt, the less there is left over for private sector investments. Together, these effects might offset the government's expansionary fiscal policy and leave the economy back where it started, as seen in Figure 9-14.

FIGURE 9-14

CAN FISCAL STIMULI WORK? The effectiveness of deficit spending that is intended to shift aggregate demand to the right may in practice be offset by an enlarged trade deficit, together with less consumption and investment spending at home by U.S. residents.

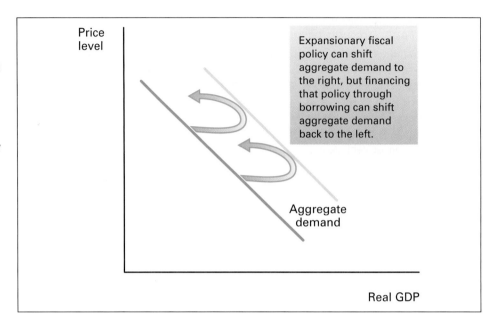

About 80 percent of government debt is owed to itself or to private U.S. investors. Nevertheless, as the federal government adds to its debt, so too do U.S. citizens. Attracting additional foreign investment accumulates obligations to repay that debt in the future. Is that dangerous? After all, Bolivia, Argentina, and many other struggling countries have endured economic crises brought about by foreign debt obligations that they were unable to repay.

When it comes to the United States, the dangers of foreign debt are few. Latin American and other debtor countries ran into problems repaying their debts in large part because their debts were denominated in U.S. dollars, which meant they had to acquire those dollars. To the extent that the United States owes financial debt to citizens of other countries, that debt is also denominated in dollars. The critical difference is that those are our dollars; we control the presses that print the money.

Some people worry over a sudden exodus of foreign investment, possibly as a means to exert political pressure. Such worries are unfounded. If foreigners for some reason wish to stampede out of the United States, they would have to leave behind all but a small fraction of their assets. By investing in the United States, foreigners allow us political and economic control over things of great value to them. In that way, foreigners acquire a strong interest in having our economy perform well and in maintaining good political relations.

We have seen that a budget deficit and consequent increase in the federal debt can be justifiable. We have also seen that this expansionary fiscal policy tends to increase the trade deficit and international debt, but that the consequences of those increases are not as worrisome as many people think. Just how much debt is the right amount, however, remains an open question.

1. Keynesian fiscal policy suggests that deficit spending can be justified to pull the economy out of an unemployment equilibrium. Yet federal budget deficits have characterized most years in recent decades, even when the economy has been at or near full employment. What are some likely explanations for this expansionary fiscal policy?

2. "Our federal government exploits babies by giving them a huge debt upon birth—a debt they did not ask for, but will be forced to repay. Let's care for our children and grandchildren. It's time for the government to stop running budget deficits and to start repaying our massive public debt!" Evaluate this view, including in your discussion an assessment of the proper role of government debt.

Visit www.prenhall.com/ayers for updates and web exercises on this Explore & Apply topic.

SUMMARY AND LEARNING OBJECTIVES

1. **Explain why wages and prices might be slow to adjust downward, and what significance this can have.**
   - A short-run unemployment equilibrium occurs when the price level is above the full-employment price level. The economy would operate at a point on the aggregate demand curve that is above the full-employment equilibrium point.
   - Keynes suggested that sticky wages and prices might hinder the economy's adjustment to full-employment output, if the economy starts at a short-run unemployment equilibrium.

2. **Discuss how fiscal policy to stabilize the economy is subject to lags, and how the lags can be overcome automatically.**
   - An expansionary fiscal policy is associated with more government spending and/or tax cuts. Either of these fiscal policy actions would shift the aggregate demand curve to the right.
   - A contractionary fiscal policy, which involves either less government spending or tax increases, would shift aggregate demand to the left.
   - Discretionary fiscal policy is the term applied to deliberate changes in fiscal policy that are designed to affect the macroeconomy.
   - Discretionary fiscal policy is subject to errors because of the three fiscal policy lags. These lags include the recognition lag, the action lag, and the implementation lag. The recognition lag refers to the length of time before a problem is recognized. The action lag refers to the amount of time it takes to decide on an appropriate policy response and pass the legislation that reflects policy. The implementation lag occurs because policy changes take time to begin to affect the economy.
   - Working to counter the problems of an unemployment equilibrium and overheating are the automatic stabilizers that are built into the economy. When the economy slows down, the automatic stabilizers increase government spending. When the economy overheats, government spending tends to decrease. An example of the automatic stabilizers is unemployment benefits.

3. **Explain how balancing the full-employment budget is consistent with a budget deficit.**
   - The federal budget records the revenue and spending of the federal government. A balanced budget occurs when the two are equal. A budget surplus is when revenue exceeds spending, and a budget deficit is when spending exceeds revenue. Because the federal budget has mostly been in deficit, the United States has compiled a national debt of over $6 trillion.
   - The full-employment budget estimates what federal revenue and spending would be if the economy were at full employment. It's sometimes argued that the government should balance its budget over the course of the business cycle, running surpluses during booms and deficits during recessions. Doing so would help stabilize the economy. It also means that the government could have a budget deficit or a surplus even though the full-employment budget is balanced.

4. **Identify the characteristics and significance of short-run aggregate supply.**
   - Unlike long-run aggregate supply, which is vertical, short-run aggregate supply slopes upward to the right. This means that in the short run an increase in the price level will result in an increase in real GDP.
   - The upward slope to the short-run aggregate supply curve occurs for two reasons. The first is structural rigidities. As new spending takes place, it tends to raise wages and prices in selected sectors of the economy. That spending also increases production and employment.

■ The second reason for the upward slope to short-run aggregate supply is the production effect. A rise in the price level can prompt firms to profitably employ labor for more hours. Overtime work can result in an economy that temporarily produces more than the full-employment level of output. The production effect relies upon workers' labor supply curves remaining constant, which will only occur if workers are unaware of the true level of inflation.

■ Short-run aggregate supply always intersects long-run aggregate supply at the expected price level. The reason is that a long-run macro equilibrium requires that workers and firms have accurate price expectations.

5. **Describe demand–pull and cost–push inflation, and how they can be part of an inflationary spiral.**

■ Demand–pull inflation describes an increase in the price level that results from an increase in aggregate demand.

■ Cost–push inflation occurs in response to an upward shift in the short-run aggregate supply curve. The short-run aggregate supply curve will shift upward whenever there is an increase in inflationary expectations on the part of workers or firms. The effect of cost–push inflation is to reduce real GDP.

■ Demand–pull inflation can lead to cost–push inflation and an inflationary spiral, which refers to a sequence of demand–pull and cost–push inflation that creates an ongoing rise in the price level. Demand–pull infla-tion increases output and the price level. This increase in the price level sets off an increase in infla-tionary expectations that leads to cost–push inflation and an accompanying reduction in real GDP. To counter the cut in production, policymakers would see to it that aggregate demand increased, thus caus-ing another round of demand–pull inflation. This process could continue indefinitely.

6. **Analyze the rationale and limitations of deficit spending.**

■ An enduring feature of the modern American econ-omy is the presence of a budget deficit, trade deficit, and huge national debt. These features are related, with ongoing budget deficits adding to the national debt and also attracting foreign investment dollars. Because those foreign investment dollars might other-wise have gone to purchase American goods and ser-vices, the budget deficit and trade deficit are often called the twin deficits.

■ Although people worry a great deal about the large deficits and national debt, at least some of this bor-rowing is offset by assets. For example, while future taxpayers inherit debt, they also inherit roads, a sys-tem of government, and other assets of value.

■ If the government attempts to shift aggregate demand to the right through deficit spending, the trade deficit and other offsetting effects might shift aggregate demand back to the left.

KEY TERMS

sticky wages, 202
sticky prices, 202
unemployment equilibrium, 203
fiscal policy, 203
stabilization policy, 203
expansionary fiscal policy (fiscal stimulus), 203
contractionary fiscal policy (fiscal drag), 204

discretionary policy, 204
recognition lag, 204
action lag, 205
implementation lag, 205
automatic stabilizers, 205
balanced budget, 206
budget surplus, 206
budget deficit, 206
full-employment budget, 206

national debt, 207
short-run aggregate supply, 208
structural rigidities, 208
the production effect, 209
short-run macroeconomic equilibrium, 209
demand–pull inflation, 210
cost–push inflation, 212
inflationary spiral, 213

TEST YOURSELF

TRUE OR FALSE

1. An unemployment equilibrium will be corrected if wages and prices are able to adjust downward.

2. The implementation lag occurs because it takes time to recognize that a problem exists with the macroeconomy.

3. Aggregate demand will increase in response to a fiscal stimulus.

4. Balancing the budget over the course of the business cycle results in surpluses in some years and deficits in others.

5. When workers expect a higher price level, short-run aggregate supply will shift upward.

MULTIPLE CHOICE

6. In Self-Test Figure 9-1, which of the arrows is most likely to be affected by downwardly sticky wages and prices?
   a. *A.*
   b. *B.*
   c. *C.*
   d. *D.*

Price level   Long-run aggregate supply

A

D

C   B

Aggregate demand

Real GDP

SELF-TEST FIGURE 9-1

7. When wages and prices are described as possibly being sticky, it is meant that they
   a. adjust quickly.
   b. adjust slowly.
   c. never adjust.
   d. do not need to be adjusted.

8. An example of an automatic stabilizer is
   a. the U.S. income tax system.
   b. the Internet.
   c. sticky wages.
   d. the full-employment equilibrium.

9. The federal budget deficit
   a. has not existed since 1997.
   b. is the accumulation of all federal debts.
   c. equals the national debt minus the budget surplus.
   d. is the amount by which government spending exceeds its revenue over the course of a year.

10. Short-run aggregate supply always intersects long-run aggregate supply at
    a. the expected price level.
    b. the actual price level.
    c. the long-run equilibrium price level.
    d. an unemployment equilibrium.

11. If the economy starts at the point indicated in Self-Test Figure 9-2 and aggregate demand does not shift, the long-run equilibrium would occur at point
    a. *A.*
    b. *B.*
    c. *C.*
    d. *D.*

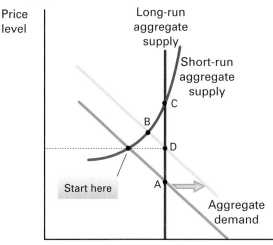

Price level   Long-run aggregate supply

Short-run aggregate supply

C

B

D

Start here

A

Aggregate demand

Real GDP

SELF-TEST FIGURE 9-2

12. If the economy starts at the point indicated in Self-Test Figure 9-2 and aggregate demand shifts to the right as shown, the new short-run equilibrium will occur at point
    a. *A.*
    b. *B.*
    c. *C.*
    d. *D.*

13. In Self-Test Figure 9-2, the expected price level is associated with point
    a. *A.*
    b. *B.*
    c. *C.*
    d. *D.*

14. The short-run aggregate supply curve holds
    a. the price level constant.
    b. real GDP constant.
    c. workers' labor supply curves constant.
    d. nothing constant.

15. Suppose the economy is in an unemployment equilibrium. An increase in aggregate demand caused by a fiscal stimulus
    a. must cause a fall in the price level.
    b. will most likely cause a rise in the price level.
    c. cannot affect the price level.
    d. will affect the price level, but in an unpredictable way.

16. Cost–push inflation occurs when
    a. the long-run aggregate supply curve shifts to the right.
    b. the short-run aggregate supply curve shifts upward.
    c. the short-run aggregate supply curve shifts downward.
    d. a shift in aggregate demand moves the economy up the short-run aggregate supply curve.

17. In an inflationary spiral, output
    a. always rises.
    b. always falls.
    c. alternately rises and falls.
    d. remains constant.

18. In an inflationary spiral, the price level
    a. always rises.
    b. always falls.
    c. alternately rises and falls.
    d. remains constant.

19. When the expected and actual price level are equal, the macroeconomy is
    a. overheated.
    b. in an unemployment equilibrium.
    c. experiencing inflationary expectations.
    d. at the long-run macro equilibrium.

20. The difference between the federal budget deficit and the national debt is that the budget deficit represents the
    a. accumulation of past debts, while the national debt is the amount by which spending exceeds revenues each year.
    b. amount by which spending exceeds revenues each year, while the national debt represents the accumulation of past deficits and surpluses.
    c. amount of money the country owes that it cannot pay back.
    d. amount of money the United States owes foreign countries, while the budget deficit represents the amount of money the United States owes in total.

QUESTIONS AND PROBLEMS

1. *[sticky wages and prices]* Illustrate graphically an unemployment equilibrium and explain how downwardly sticky wages and prices can prevent the economy from reaching the long-run macro equilibrium.

2. *[expansionary fiscal policy]* Show an unemployment equilibrium on a graph and explain how an expansionary fiscal policy can achieve full employment.

3. *[overheated economy]* Explain the appropriate fiscal policy response when the economy overheats.

4. *[fiscal policy lags]* What are the three fiscal policy lags that complicate the task for policymakers of using fiscal policy to manage the economy? Explain each of the lags.

5. *[automatic stabilizers]* Write a brief essay on the contribution that the automatic stabilizers play in creating a stable economy. Provide examples of the automatic stabilizers and use them to illustrate their significance. Why is there an interest in using fiscal policy to stabilize the economy when the automatic stabilizers are available?

6. *[federal budget]* When the economy is at full employment, should the federal government run a budget deficit, surplus, or neither? Explain.

7. *[full-employment budget]* Is the full-employment budget usually balanced? Explain.

8. *[national debt]* How was the U.S. national debt of over $6 trillion created? Who is owed this debt?

9. *[short-run aggregate supply]* Illustrate graphically the short-run aggregate supply curve. Also include on your graph the long-run aggregate supply curve. At what point must the short-run aggregate supply curve and long-run aggregate supply curve intersect? Label the correct axis accordingly.

10. *[structural rigidities]* In regard to the short-run aggregate supply curve, what is the significance of structural rigidities? Your explanation should be stated within the context of an example of structural rigidities.

11. *[production effect]* In regard to the short-run aggregate supply curve, what is the significance of the production effect? Your answer should be stated within the context of workers' labor supply curves.

12. *[short-run unemployment equilibrium]* When the actual price level is below the expected price level, explain why there will be a short-run unemployment equilibrium. If fiscal policy shifts aggregate demand to the right, explain what will happen to the actual price level.

13. *[demand–pull and cost–push inflation]* On separate graphs, show demand–pull and cost–push inflation, labeling the axes, curves, and changes in output and the price level.

14. *[inflationary spiral]* Explain how cost–push inflation might prompt policymakers to take actions that subse-

quently cause demand–pull inflation. Then explain how this demand–pull inflation could lead to another round of cost–push inflation. What is the sequence of demand–pull inflation followed by cost–push inflation called? Illustrate this process graphically using the aggregate demand–aggregate supply model.

15. *[macro thought]* Summarize the Keynesian and classical views on fiscal policy.

 Visit www.prenhall.com/ayers for Exploring the Web exercises and additional self-test quizzes.

CHAPTER 10

AGGREGATE EXPENDITURES

A LOOK AHEAD

Spend your money and give people work. It sounds like such a patriotic thing to do: Buy, buy, and buy some more. In doing this, you will help out others, but you might also find yourself on the verge of personal bankruptcy. Is this really the way the economy works? Should you consume for the sake of giving others jobs? Is spending the key to keeping economic depression at bay? This chapter's Explore & Apply examines the Great Depression, noting what we thought we knew then and what we think we know now.

Interpreting the Great Depression is not the only place where economists disagree. As the joke goes, "If you line up all the economists in the world end to end, you still won't reach a conclusion!" The joke is itself quite a stretch, because economists share a great deal of common ground. The model of aggregate supply and aggregate demand represents that meeting of the minds. This chapter highlights the demand side of the economy, using Keynesian analysis that at one time defined the whole field of macroeconomics. The Keynesian model of the economy is implicit within the aggregate demand curve we have already studied.

LEARNING OBJECTIVES

Understanding Chapter 10 will enable you to:
1. **Summarize the perspective of Keynes and Keynesian economics.**
2. **Illustrate the income–expenditure model.**
3. **Explain the adjustment process to an expenditure equilibrium.**
4. **Describe how new spending can have a ripple effect throughout the economy.**
5. **Distinguish the tax multiplier from the balanced-budget multiplier.**
6. **Graph the relationship of the income–expenditure model to aggregate demand.**
7. **Compare economic analyses of the Great Depression.**

ℰXPLORE
&
𝒜PPLY

Whether about workers displaced by the Industrial Revolution of the nineteenth century or workers displaced by decreases in air travel in the last few years, there have always been concerns about insufficient demand to keep everyone employed. For example, if we have what we need and new technology can produce it with fewer people, what are the remaining people to do? Or what if people start making do with fewer goods and services? How can the economy keep everyone employed?

As discussed in Chapter 8, economists are relatively unconcerned with these questions in the long run, as markets have time to adjust—the evidence across time and across countries suggests that there is always something to do, if only a person has the time to find it. As people discover those jobs, they move the economy toward its full-employment output. In this process price levels adjust, which is why the model of aggregate supply and aggregate demand includes the price level explicitly on the vertical axis. In contrast, in the model presented in the current chapter, the price level is not a variable. Here we dig deeper into the demand side of the economy, using a Keynesian model that focuses on the short run, before prices have time to adjust. We will see how the aggregate demand curve is derived from the Keynesian model.

10.1 "IN THE LONG RUN, WE ARE ALL DEAD"

With the famous line above, John Maynard Keynes (1883–1946) spotlighted the need to address immediate problems facing the unemployed. In response to the pressing problems of the Great Depression, Keynes offered a new, short-run perspective that came to be called *Keynesian economics.* Prior to that time, economists emphasized long-run economic tendencies, viewing short-run fluctuations around the long-run trends as transitory problems that would correct themselves. That long-run way of looking at the macroeconomy became known as *classical economics.* Both classical and Keynesian perspectives are still used today.

In keeping with a short-run perspective, Keynes chose to ignore long-run tendencies toward full employment. In a nutshell, he took the view that problems of unemployment could be solved if only people and their government would buy more goods and services. Recall that consumption directly accounts for almost 70 percent of GDP. It also motivates business investment spending. The Keynesian model is based around understanding how much spending is likely to occur at different levels of GDP and how the government can influence that spending to make sure that the economy lands at full employment.

The Great Depression was a long time ago, beginning in 1929 and ending with the United States' entry into World War II in late 1941. Since Keynesian analysis seemed to explain how the economy went from depression to prosperity in that period, it should come as no surprise that the Keynesian model was popular in the 1950s and 1960s. However, the model did not seem to apply in the 1970s, during which time the U.S. economy faced serious problems of both inflation and unemployment.

The 2001 recession and the eagerness of politicians to embrace demand-side remedies in the months that followed propelled the Keynesian model into the spotlight once more. President George W. Bush implemented a Keynesian-style policy of tax rebate checks, which were mailed out in the summer of 2001. Then, following the attacks of September 11, both the president and Congress were eager to spend, with the justification that extra spending was needed to spur the economy. For example, the farm aid legislation passed in 2002 was by far the largest such bill ever, with a projected ten-year cost of $190 billion. The focus upon increased government or private spending is very much in keeping with the Keynesian model, as we will see.

10.2 THE INCOME—EXPENDITURE MODEL

One person's spending is another person's income—the two go hand in hand. Likewise, the circular flow model from Chapter 2 tells us that aggregate income and output must be equal.

Aggregate national income = Aggregate national output

Money spent on a cheeseburger, for example, is split into income to the employees and owners of the restaurant, as well as to the suppliers of the cheese, meat, and other inputs that go into the burger. For this reason, gross domestic product can be viewed as a measure of both output and income, as noted on the horizontal axis of Figure 10-1. That figure depicts the **income–expenditure model,** which shows planned and actual expenditures at each possible real GDP.

The 45-degree line in Figure 10-1 maps the GDP from the horizontal axis to the vertical axis. The vertical axis is labeled expenditure, because GDP measures output by adding up the value of all final goods and services that are purchased. Those purchases are expenditures that sum to the economy's **aggregate expenditures.** So, if the economy has produced $5 trillion worth of GDP, we collectively have made $5 trillion worth of aggregate expenditure to buy it.

Unfortunately, what we plan to spend and what we earn are not always the same. We might plan to spend $7 trillion when our aggregate income is only $5 trillion. In that case, $5 trillion is not an equilibrium GDP, because our spending plans cannot be sustained. The **aggregate expenditure function** tells what the economy's planned spending will be at each level of real GDP. There will be only one GDP that matches up planned spending and actual output. That GDP occurs at the **expenditure equilibrium,** which is given by the intersection

income–expenditure model shows planned and actual expenditures at each possible real GDP.

aggregate expenditures consumption + investment + government + net exports.

aggregate expenditure function shows the economy's planned aggregate expenditures for each possible level of real GDP.

expenditure equilibrium the level of GDP that the economy tends toward in the short run, at a given price level.

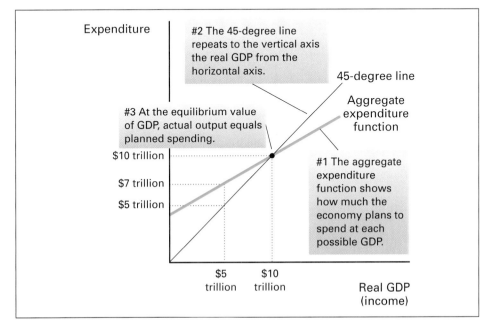

FIGURE 10-1

THE INCOME–EXPENDITURE MODEL The income–expenditure model shows planned and actual expenditures at each possible real GDP, where GDP measures both aggregate output and income. The model contains three components:

#1 The aggregate expenditure function shows how the economy's spending plans are based on its GDP. For example, at a GDP of $5 trillion, we would plan to spend $7 trillion.

#2 The 45-degree line notes the amount that the economy actually produces. So at a GDP of $5 trillion, we in fact have only $5 trillion of new output.

#3 The expenditure equilibrium is the one point at which planned expenditures and actual GDP are the same. In this case, the expenditure equilibrium occurs at $10 trillion.

of the aggregate expenditure function and the 45-degree line in the income–expenditure model shown in Figure 10-1. We'll now examine this model more closely.

COMPONENTS OF AGGREGATE EXPENDITURES

The aggregate expenditure function shows that the economy's planned spending depends upon its income, the latter measured by actual GDP. Aggregate expenditures can be divided into the following two types:

autonomous spending spending that would occur even if people had no incomes.

induced spending spending that depends upon income.

- **Autonomous spending** would occur even if people had no incomes.
- **Induced spending** depends upon income.

Autonomous spending includes both investments and goods and services that will be purchased no matter what the national income might be. For example, if it became necessary, people would draw upon their accumulated wealth to buy such necessities of life as food and shelter. Even college students without any earnings have been known to draw down their parents' bank accounts in order to pay for room and board at school!

Figure 10-2 shows how aggregate expenditures equal the sum of autonomous and induced spending. Autonomous spending by itself shows up as a horizontal line, since it does not vary with income. In contrast, induced spending is entirely dependent upon income. Therefore, the line showing induced spending starts at zero GDP and rises from there. When autonomous spending and induced spending are added together, the result is an aggregate expenditure function that has both a positive vertical intercept and a positive slope. In other words, the aggregate expenditure function starts at autonomous spending and rises from there.

The components of aggregate expenditures are merely the components of GDP, which are:

GDP = Consumption + Investment + Government purchases + (Exports − Imports)

or, for short,

$$GDP = C + I + G + (X - M)$$

Exports minus imports is alternatively termed *net exports,* as presented in Chapter 5.

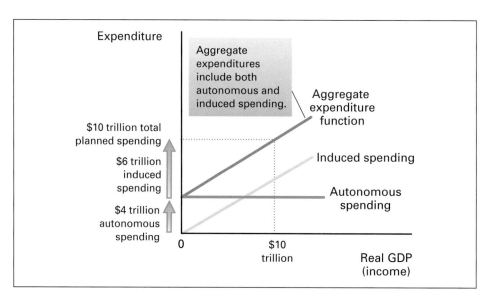

FIGURE 10-2

AUTONOMOUS AND INDUCED SPENDING Aggregate expenditures have an autonomous component that does not vary with actual GDP and an induced component that does. The higher the GDP, the more consumers will want to spend. For this reason, induced spending and aggregate expenditures in total both rise as GDP increases. There is only one point at which planned aggregate expenditures equals actual GDP. That equality occurs only at the expenditure equilibrium, which is $10 trillion in this example.

Expenditure

Aggregate expenditures include both autonomous and induced spending.

Aggregate expenditure function

$10 trillion total planned spending

$6 trillion induced spending

$4 trillion autonomous spending

Induced spending

Autonomous spending

0          $10 trillion   Real GDP (income)

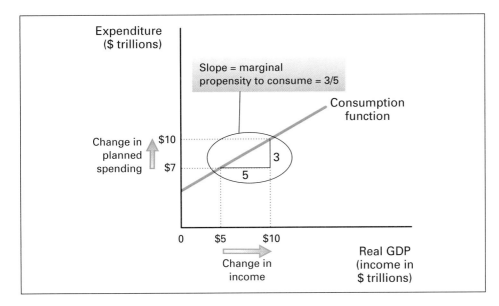

FIGURE 10-3

THE CONSUMPTION FUNCTION
The consumption function shows how much consumers intend to spend at various possible values of GDP, which is the economy's actual income. The slope of the consumption function is the marginal propensity to consume, given by the change in planned spending divided by the change in income.

Far and away the largest component of GDP is consumption. Plotting consumption spending against GDP gives the **consumption function,** as shown in Figure 10-3. Because of autonomous spending, the consumption function has a positive vertical intercept. From there, it slopes upward because of the **marginal propensity to consume (mpc),** which is the fraction of incremental income that people spend. It is computed as the slope of the consumption function, equaling 3/5 in the example shown in Figure 10-3. A worker with an mpc of 3/5 and who is given a $1/hour raise would spend sixty cents out of that dollar and save the rest.

The fraction of additional income that people save is termed the **marginal propensity to save (mps).** Adding together the marginal propensity to save and the marginal propensity to consume must yield a total of one, since there is nowhere else for income to go:

$$mpc + mps = 1$$

Investment and government purchases are of roughly comparable size. Figure 10-4 shows these components, where for simplicity planned government purchases and planned investment spending are assumed to be completely autonomous and thus to be constant as GDP changes. For this reason, the slope of the aggregate expenditure function and consumption function are the same, both equaling the marginal propensity to consume.

MODELING THE EXPENDITURE EQUILIBRIUM

Recall that the expenditure equilibrium occurs where the aggregate expenditure function intersects the 45-degree line, as shown in Figure 10-1. At the expenditure equilibrium, the economy's actual GDP equals its planned spending. **When the economy is not at equilibrium, actual GDP and planned spending differ. The difference shows up in business inventories.** In particular, businesses plan to maintain some amount of inventories, but cannot predict exactly how much of their products consumers will buy. For example, toy sellers cannot predict exactly how many Xbox video games and other items consumers will buy at Christmas. The result is that business plans go awry and they find themselves with either

consumption function shows planned consumption spending for each possible level of real GDP.

marginal propensity to consume (mpc) the fraction of additional income that people spend.

marginal propensity to save (mps) the fraction of additional income that people save.

FIGURE 10-4

THE AGGREGATE EXPENDITURE FUNCTION The aggregate expenditure function shows planned spending at each possible quantity of real GDP. It equals the sum of consumption, investment, and government. (Net exports would also be included.) In the example, autonomous expenditures are 2 + 1 + 1 = $4 trillion. If GDP is $5 trillion, planned expenditures would be $7 trillion, including $3 trillion in induced consumption. The slopes of the aggregate expenditure function and consumption functions are equal, both being the marginal propensity to consume.

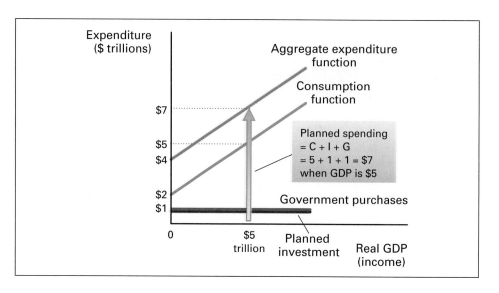

QUICKCHECK

Does the aggregate expenditure function include actual investment or planned investment? What are the other types of spending that make up aggregate expenditures?

Answer: The aggregate expenditure function shows planned spending, including planned investment spending. The aggregate expenditure function sums planned spending on consumption, investment, government spending, and net exports.

---

too little inventory or too much inventory. Unintended inventory changes show up as the difference between planned and actual investment, as follows:

Expenditure equilibrium: Aggregate expenditures = Actual GDP

where

Aggregate expenditures = Consumption + Planned investment + Government + Net exports

and

Actual GDP = Consumption + Actual investment + Government + Net exports

which implies that the expenditure equilibrium occurs where planned investment = actual investment.

Another way to understand the expenditure equilibrium is to consider what would happen if real GDP were either above or below it. If the economy produced less than the equilibrium, planned spending would exceed output. With buyers clamoring for more than the economy in fact produces, businesses would see their inventories decline.

The next step after a decline in inventories is a surge in orders to suppliers, as businesses would want to replace those inventories. In response, manufacturers and other suppliers would increase output. The result is an increase in GDP produced.

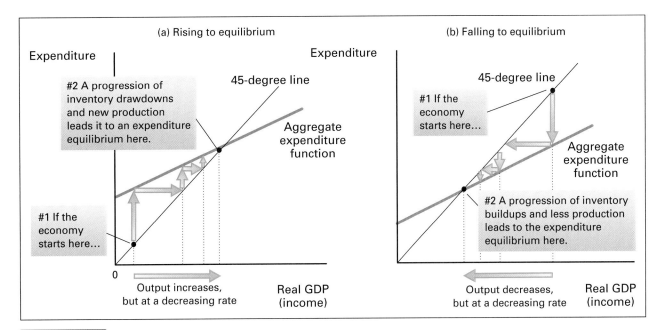

FIGURE 10-5

THE EXPENDITURE EQUILIBRIUM When GDP is below the expenditure equilibrium, there is an unintended drop in business inventories. Output is increased to replace these inventories, as shown in (a). Producing more output adds to income, leading to more consumption. Therefore, inventories drop again, production rises again, and on and on, as depicted by the sequence of arrows in the graph. The process continues until an expenditure equilibrium is reached. At that equilibrium, actual GDP and planned spending are equal and there are no unplanned inventory changes.

Graph (b) shows the process in reverse. In this case, the economy starts by producing more than can be sold, leading to inventory buildups. Then come order cutbacks, layoffs, lower incomes, and lower consumption. That causes more inventory buildup, which leads to more layoffs, and so forth as shown by the sequence of arrows. The process continues until an expenditure equilibrium is reached.

The process does not stop there. The workers in the factories would take home more pay, and spend some of it. That extra spending is induced consumption (induced by the extra income). Inventories are then drawn down again, which means that firms will again increase output. This process continues, but not forever. At each round, the increases in output and income get smaller until, eventually, an equilibrium is reached.

Figure 10-5 illustrates the process of moving to the expenditure equilibrium. The economy starts at a GDP that is below equilibrium. The initial inventory drawdown and resulting increase in output is the vertical arrow at point 1. As the amount of GDP produced rises to replace these lost inventories, real GDP increases and adds induced spending that leads to a second inventory drawdown, which is not as large as the first. Additional rounds of inventory drawdowns and output increases lead to the expenditure equilibrium shown as point 2.

Conversely, if production were to exceed the equilibrium, planned spending would not keep pace with production and inventories would build up. In response to the buildup in inventories, firms would cut back output and jobs as Boeing did in 2002 following the drop in air travel after September 11. The output cuts cause income to drop. In turn, induced spending falls and inventory levels would continue to be high. Firms would continue to postpone ordering and GDP would continue to fall until an expenditure equilibrium is reached. At the expenditure equilibrium, there are no further unplanned changes in inventories.

QUICKCHECK

What sorts of situations would occur if the economy is not at an expenditure equilibrium?

Answer: The situations would depend on whether the economy is producing more or less than the expenditure equilibrium GDP. If the economy is producing more, there'll be an inventory buildup and consequent reduction in production. If the economy is producing less than the equilibrium GDP, inventories will be drawn down and firms will order increased output.

SNAPSHOT   **CHRISTMAS STOCKINGS AND JANUARY RESTOCKINGS**

Jingle jingle jingle! These are not the bells retailers listen for in those merry days before Christmas. They are the chimes of coins landing in the cash register drawer. How many coins? That can only be known at the end of the year. And what a Christmas present it would be to see those shelves bare!

Empty shelves following Christmas would provide a present for the economy, too. The new year would start with new orders to the warehouses and additional orders to the factories. More orders mean more jobs and more income and spending. The effect of retailers underestimating Christmas demand on the macroeconomy would be an increase in GDP toward its true equilibrium value. The only hint of a Grinch would be if the economy is already at full employment. In that case, inflation would surely dampen the exuberance of the new year.

There is a flip side to this happy story. The retailers might have overestimated Christmas shopping enthusiasm. In that case, the shelves would overflow and the after-Christmas orders would not go. The days of January would be grim as employment drops along the path to a lower expenditure equilibrium. ◀

10.3 CHANGING THE EXPENDITURE EQUILIBRIUM

An expenditure equilibrium implies that there are no unplanned inventory buildups or drawdowns that would prompt a change in business plans. Thus, all businesses must correctly forecast the demand for their products. The world is not that precise. Because there will always be some forecasting errors, the economy can only approximately achieve an equilibrium. In addition, that equilibrium will change when the aggregate expenditure function changes, such as in response to people changing their consumption preferences or businesses changing their investment preferences. The reasons could be as simple as attitudes toward world events, with planned expenditures increasing when we are optimistic and decreasing when we are pessimistic. Then there is government, which can change the aggregate expenditure function directly by altering its spending policies, or change it indirectly by altering tax policies that affect consumer spending or business investment.

THE MULTIPLIER EFFECT

multiplier effect sequence of spending that takes the economy from one equilibrium to another.

When there are changes in autonomous spending, the changes are magnified by the **multiplier effect,** which is a sequence of cause and effect, much like the ones shown in Figure 10-5. However, instead of taking us from a disequilibrium to an equilibrium as in that figure, the multiplier effect takes the economy from one equilibrium to another.

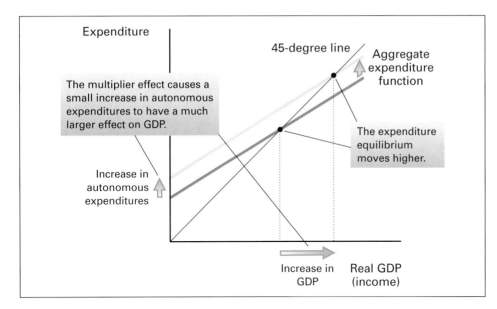

FIGURE 10-6

THE MULTIPLIER EFFECT The multiplier effect is the induced spending caused by a change in autonomous spending. The higher the marginal propensity to consume, the steeper the aggregate expenditure function and the greater the multiplier effect. Through the multiplier effect, a change in autonomous spending results in a much larger change in equilibrium GDP. The example shows this result for an autonomous spending increase.

The multiplier effect works as follows: Adding autonomous spending causes a higher GDP, which causes more induced spending. That's because money that one person spends autonomously adds to the income of others, which in turn induces them to buy more output. This process generates an ongoing cycle of greater income and greater output. At each stage in this cycle, however, some income is likely to be saved, thus eventually bringing the cycle to a halt.

For example, suppose that Dawn spends her wages to buy boots at Betty's Bargain Basement. Dawn's spending in turn provides Betty with income that she spends at J-Mart, which in turn, well, you get the story! Through this multiplier effect, as shown in Figure 10-6, any given change in autonomous spending adds up to a considerably larger change in equilibrium GDP.

The strength of the multiplier effect depends upon the proportion of income that is devoted to consumption. To the extent that people save their incomes, for example, those savings represent a *leakage* out of the multiplier process. Table 10-1 illustrates how the value of the marginal propensity to consume determines the increase in spending as income rises from zero to $5,000. The table assumes that autonomous spending is $1,000. Although actual values of mpc and mps depend upon consumer confidence, the table will (for simplicity) assume that the mpc is a constant 0.6, meaning people spend sixty cents out of each additional dollar of income. Savings are also shown in the table, because income not spent is saved. Thus, the mpc of 0.6 implies an mps of 0.4. A negative value for savings, which occurs at lower income values in the table, means that there is *dissaving*—spending out of existing savings.

The multiplier effect works through the following formula:

Change in autonomous spending × Expenditure multiplier = Change in equilibrium GDP

In this equation, the **expenditure multiplier** is the multiple by which equilibrium real GDP grows as a result of an increase (an *injection*) of new autonomous spending. The expenditure multiplier is sometimes called the *autonomous expenditure multiplier* for clarity or merely just the *multiplier* for short. If autonomous spending rises, **the expenditure equilibrium will rise by the increase in autonomous spending multiplied by the expenditure multiplier.** The price level is assumed to remain unchanged.

expenditure multiplier 1/(1 − mpc) or 1/mps; when multiplied by a change in autonomous spending, gives the change in equilibrium GDP.

| TABLE 10-1 | SPENDING DEPENDS UPON THE MARGINAL PROPENSITY TO CONSUME (MPC) |

(Assume autonomous spending = $1,000, mpc = 0.6, mps = 0.4)

INCOME	SPENDING	SAVINGS
$0	$1,000	−$1,000
$1,000	$1,600	−$600
$2,000	$2,200	−$200
$3,000	$2,800	$200
$4,000	$3,400	$600
$5,000	$4,000	$1,000

For example, if investors gain confidence in the economy and so increase their autonomous investment spending, equilibrium GDP would rise by more than that amount. Specifically, the equilibrium GDP would equal the increase in autonomous investment multiplied by the multiplier. Conversely, if autonomous spending were to decrease, the expenditure multiplier would reveal how much real GDP would fall.

If people always spend every penny of income they receive, the expenditure multiplier would be infinite and the multiplier formula would lead to an infinite GDP. For example, if Ann were to receive $1,000 in income, she would spend $1,000. That would provide others with $1,000 in income, which they would spend, thus providing others with $1,000 in income, and so forth. In practice, however, leakages and possible price increases eventually bring the multiplier process to a halt. For example, if the mps were to equal 0.2, Ann would only spend $800, and 20 percent of that $800 would be saved by those receiving it, so that the next round of spending would amount to only $640.

The multiplier is computed as the reciprocal of the percentage of new income that isn't spent on consumption. If the only options for using additional income are to spend it or save it, the multiplier formula becomes the reciprocal of the marginal propensity to save:

$$\text{Expenditure multiplier} = \frac{1}{(1 - \text{mpc})}$$

or, equivalently,

$$\text{Expenditure multiplier} = \frac{1}{\text{mps}}$$

Again, **the multiplier is multiplied by a change in autonomous spending to reveal the change in equilibrium GDP.** The change in autonomous spending could be undertaken by the government, businesses, or consumers. For example, if government spending rises by $10 billion, and the marginal propensity to save is 0.2, the expenditure equilibrium will rise by (1/0.2) multiplied by $10 billion, which equals 5 multiplied by $10 billion, or $50 billion.

Note that nothing in the foregoing analysis indicates whether the expenditure equilibrium occurs at full employment. However, **there must be some idle resources for the multiplier effect to occur.** If an injection of new spending occurs when the economy is already at full employment, consumers and others bid up prices by seeking to buy more output than

QUICKCHECK

Suppose the marginal propensity to consume is .75. Using the expenditure multiplier, what is the effect on equilibrium GDP of an extra $10 billion federal spending program?

Answer: If the economy is below full employment, and the price level remains constant, the effect equals $40 billion. This result is obtained by multiplying $10 billion by the expenditure multiplier. Because the mpc equals .75, and because the sum of mpc and mps must equal 1, the mps must equal .25. The multiplier thus equals $1/.25 = 4$.

the economy is capable of sustaining. The result is inflation, implying a rising price level that offsets the multiplier effect by making money not go as far in real terms. Thus, rising prices thwart the multiplier effect, even to the extent that extra spending might cause no increase at all in real GDP.

If the expenditure equilibrium occurs below full-employment GDP, there will be unemployment, and thus downward pressure on prices until full-employment GDP is achieved. However, this point is where Keynes draws the line from his classical predecessors. Regarding the expenditure equilibrium, Keynes wrote, "There is no reason for expecting it to be *equal* to full employment." Keynes went so far as to dismiss any possibility for prices to fall, because that process would only occur in the long run. Remember, "In the long run, we are all dead." Accordingly, **Keynesian multiplier analysis assumes a constant price level.**

RECESSION AND INFLATION WITHIN THE INCOME–EXPENDITURE MODEL

If the expenditure equilibrium lies below full-employment GDP, it is called an **unemployment equilibrium.** Along with the unemployment equilibrium comes an **output gap,** in which actual GDP falls below full-employment GDP, as shown in Figure 10-7. At an unemployment equilibrium, there is too little planned spending for the economy to achieve full-employment GDP. The shortfall in spending is called a **recessionary gap,** which is a shortfall in the aggregate expenditure function below that necessary to achieve a full-employment equilibrium.

The recessionary gap is shown in Figure 10-7. Keynes suggested that the government could increase spending by just this amount and the multiplier effect would do the rest. More generally, an increase in autonomous spending in an amount equal to the recessionary gap would shift up the aggregate expenditure function by just enough to lead to a full-employment equilibrium. This result assumes a constant price level. As we saw in Chapter 9, expansionary fiscal policy might raise the price level and have a diminished effect on output, particularly as the economy approaches full-employment GDP.

If the expenditure equilibrium occurs past full-employment GDP, multiplier analysis does not apply because inflation will not allow it to stay there. This possibility is referred to as an **inflationary gap,** which is the excess of the aggregate expenditure function above that consistent with a full-employment equilibrium. The inflationary gap is shown in Figure 10-8. Because the productive capacity of the economy could not keep up with the economy's appetite to buy, the result would be inflation. Inflation would continue until it eroded the real value of planned aggregate expenditures and shifted the aggregate expenditure function down to intersect the 45-degree line at a full-employment equilibrium.

unemployment equilibrium a short-run equilibrium GDP that is less than full-employment GDP.

output gap the amount by which full-employment GDP exceeds actual GDP.

recessionary gap shortfall in the aggregate expenditure function below that necessary to achieve a full-employment equilibrium; this gap might persist in the short run unless the government takes action.

inflationary gap excess in the aggregate expenditure function above that necessary to achieve a full-employment equilibrium; this gap will be corrected by inflation.

FIGURE 10-7

THE RECESSIONARY GAP The recessionary gap is the shortfall in the aggregate expenditure function below that needed for full employment. Note that the recessionary gap is much smaller than the output gap, which is the shortfall in actual GDP below full-employment GDP. The recessionary gap could be closed by shifting the aggregate expenditure function up with additional autonomous spending. The gap is how much extra autonomous spending is needed.

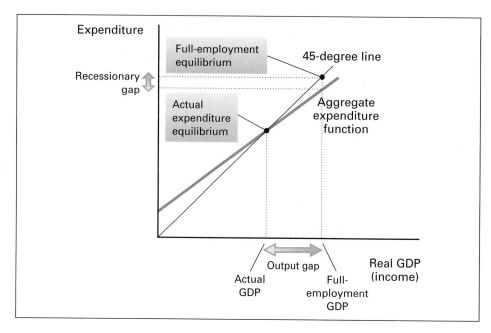

FIGURE 10-8

THE INFLATIONARY GAP The inflationary gap is the excess in the aggregate expenditure function above that needed for full employment. In trying to produce more than is possible, the economy overheats and produces inflation. In turn, the inflation shifts down the aggregate expenditure function and closes the gap.

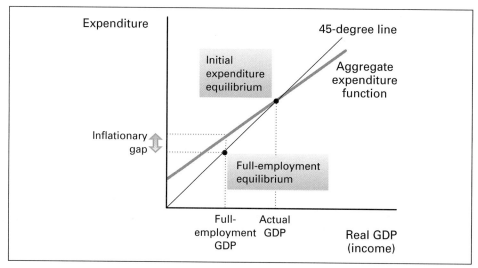

SNAPSHOT **CONSUMED WITH CONFIDENCE**

Are you a confident consumer? Do you plan to purchase a new house or car in the next year? Various surveys attempt to measure consumer confidence each month, with an eye to predicting how consumers are going to behave in the near future. These surveys underscore an important point: Spenders will become savers when they fear the economy is on the verge of turning down. That's because they fear that hard times might require them to dip into their savings and so they feel more comfortable building up those savings.

When consumers spend less, businesses have to throttle back production. Workers, in turn, might lose their jobs. In this cyclical pattern, a lack of consumer confidence becomes a self-fulfilling prophecy for the economy. That's probably why there always seems to be a government official or economist reassuring us that all is well with the economy. If we believe the economy is sound, we keep spending and our spending helps keep the economy sound. ◄

MAKING POLICY WITH MULTIPLIERS

To prevent an unemployment equilibrium, in which the economy is stuck in recession, Keynesians argue that either autonomous spending or the multiplier itself must be increased. The multiplier will increase to the extent that people decrease their marginal propensity to save. Because savings represent a leakage out of the multiplier process, Keynesians emphasize the value of consumption. If people consume a greater fraction of their income, the multiplier increases and equilibrium occurs at a higher GDP.

For example, if the marginal propensity to save were to equal 1, that would mean that people save every dollar they receive. In that case, the expenditure multiplier would equal 1/1 = 1, meaning that the effect of an extra dollar of spending is that dollar and no more. If the mps equals 0.2, in contrast, people save only twenty cents per dollar of additional income. In that case, an extra dollar of spending would generate $1 multiplied by (1/0.2), giving a result of $1 multiplied by 5, which equals a $5 increase in equilibrium spending and output. Thus, a decrease in the marginal propensity to save means that equilibrium income will be a greater multiple of autonomous spending.

How can the multiplier be increased or autonomous spending be stimulated? According to Keynes, when business conditions are bad, the private sector is unlikely to make it better! Because he doubted increases in private sector spending, Keynes was a strong advocate of increasing government spending during recessions.

Keynesian analysis also suggests that the government can use tax cuts to stimulate the economy. However, Keynesians note that people might save some of their higher after-tax income rather than spend it all. In other words, the **tax multiplier**—the expansionary effect of a tax cut or contractionary effect of a tax increase—would be less than the expenditure multiplier by the amount of the initial round of spending.

> **tax multiplier** — mpc/(1 − mpc); when multiplied by a change in taxation, gives the change in equilibrium GDP.

For example, if the government spends a dollar, taxpayers with an mpc of seventy percent will get that dollar and proceed to spend seventy cents. If the government merely cuts taxes by a dollar, the first effect to be felt on the economy is that taxpayers will spend their mpc of, in this case, seventy cents. So the tax multiplier starts at the marginal propensity to consume and proceeds from there. The result is that, instead of a multiplier of $1/(1-\text{mpc})$, the tax multiplier formula is:

$$\text{Tax multiplier} = \frac{-\text{mpc}}{(1 - \text{mpc})}$$

and

Change in taxes owed to government × Tax multiplier = Change in equilibrium GDP

The tax multiplier is preceded with a negative sign because an increase in taxation reduces after-tax income and thus reduces aggregate expenditures. Because the tax multiplier is smaller than the expenditure multiplier, **Keynesians view extra government spending as the most effective policy to cure a recession.**

In this model, financing extra government spending with an identical increase in taxation would have an expansionary effect because the expenditure multiplier exceeds the tax multiplier. The **balanced-budget multiplier** combines the expenditure multiplier for an increase in government spending and the tax multiplier because taxes would increase to finance that spending. Adding these multipliers together gives a balanced budget multiplier of one, as follows:

> **balanced-budget multiplier** the effect on equilibrium GDP per dollar of additional government spending when that spending is paid for by additional taxation; this multiplier equals one.

$$\text{Balanced budget multiplier} = \frac{1}{(1 - \text{mpc})} - \frac{\text{mpc}}{(1 - \text{mpc})} = \frac{(1 - \text{mpc})}{(1 - \text{mpc})} = 1$$

and

Change in balanced-budget government spending × 1 = Change in equilibrium GDP.

In other words, when financed by a tax increase, an increase in government spending increases equilibrium GDP by exactly the amount of that extra spending, without a further multiplier effect.

Critics of Keynesian analysis contend that Keynesian multiplier analysis is flawed because it ignores the impact of how government spending is financed. Specifically, the tax multiplier and balanced-budget multiplier analysis assumes that tax rates have no effect on incentives to work or invest. For example, to the extent that higher taxes reduce expected after-tax returns on investments, tax increases might be expected to reduce investment. Alternatively, if government spending is financed by borrowing, the borrowing is likely to drive up interest rates and cause a *crowding-out effect,* which means that less money will go to private sector investments because it is going to finance the government instead. Such reductions in investment spending are not included in the Keynesian multipliers, but will be considered in Chapter 12.

SNAPSHOT   **THE PARADOX OF THRIFT—DOES SAVING MORE SAVE LESS?**

The baby boomers are aging. Their retirement looms and their lifestyles are threatened. Maybe they should save their money. "A penny saved is a penny earned," Benjamin Franklin told us. However, Keynesians might not agree.

According to Keynesian analysis, when consumers plan to save a higher fraction of their incomes, the result is a flatter aggregate expenditure function and a smaller multiplier. All else equal, the result is a lower equilibrium GDP. The economy winds up saving a higher fraction of a smaller income. Our incomes might drop so much that our total savings might even be lower than before—that's the *paradox of thrift.* In this Keynesian model, the baby boomers should keep on spending.

Economists today are not so quick to discard Ben Franklin's advice, at least not for the long run. In the long run, the paradox of thrift does not exist. Instead, price levels adjust to take the economy to a full-employment GDP no matter what fraction of income we save. But if you worry about escaping a short-run unemployment equilibrium, frugality might be something for the economy to avoid. ◀

10.4 AGGREGATE DEMAND—AN EXPENDITURE EQUILIBRIUM FOR EACH PRICE LEVEL

When the price level changes, the aggregate expenditure function shifts and generates a different expenditure equilibrium. The reason is that a change in the price level changes the real value of consumer wealth. For example, a higher price level represents inflation that erodes wealth and purchasing power. In response, there is less planned spending at each level of GDP, meaning that the aggregate expenditure function shifts down. Autonomous and induced

QUICKCHECK

If the price level rises, what happens to the aggregate expenditure function and the aggregate demand curve?

Answer: The aggregate expenditure function shifts down as the real value of wealth falls in response to the higher prices it takes to buy goods and services throughout the economy. However, the aggregate demand curve does not change. Rather, there is a movement up the curve to a point that reflects the new higher price level and lower expenditure–equilibrium GDP.

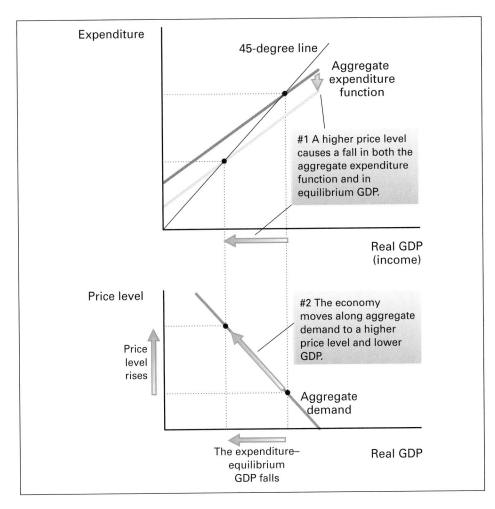

FIGURE 10-9

FROM THE INCOME–EXPENDITURE MODEL TO AGGREGATE DEMAND
As the price level rises, planned real spending falls, as shown by the downward shift in the aggregate expenditure function in the top graph. The result is that the expenditure equilibrium falls. Aggregate demand, shown in the bottom graph, is nothing more than a plot of the expenditure equilibrium that would occur at each of the various possible price levels. When the price level rises, therefore, the demand-side GDP falls and the aggregate demand curve slopes down.

spending are both less, because inflation has diminished the real value of savings. The expenditure equilibrium drops to a lower GDP, as shown in the upper portion of Figure 10-9.

If we were to plot the expenditure equilibrium for each price level, the result would be the aggregate demand curve that we've used in the previous two chapters. To see how, consider again Figure 10-9. The lower portion of this figure illustrates that a higher price level is associated with the lower expenditure equilibrium, the same information as above but now plotted explicitly. This relationship between the price level and the expenditure equilibrium is nothing more nor less than aggregate demand.

If the price level remains constant and the aggregate expenditure function shifts for any other reason, aggregate demand shifts as well. The reason is that the price level, while not itself changed, would now be associated with a different expenditure equilibrium. This result is shown in Figure 10-10.

Holding the price level unchanged, the top graph in Figure 10-10 shows the aggregate expenditure function shifting down in response to a decrease in autonomous spending. Perhaps the decrease is the result of lower government spending or higher taxation. The decrease in the autonomous expenditure function causes the expenditure equilibrium to occur at a lower real GDP. Since the price level has not changed, the result is that aggregate demand shifts to the left, as shown in the bottom portion of Figure 10-10. There is now a lower expenditure–equilibrium GDP at the current price level. The equilibrium GDP would be lower at any other price level, as well.

FIGURE 10-10

SHIFTING BOTH THE AGGREGATE EXPENDITURE FUNCTION AND AGGREGATE DEMAND If the autonomous expenditure function shifts for a reason other than a change in the price level, the aggregate demand curve would also shift. In the example shown in the top graph, the aggregate expenditure function shifts down in response to a decrease in autonomous spending. As a consequence, the expenditure–equilibrium GDP is lower. Also as a consequence, as shown in the lower graph, aggregate demand shifts to the left. The shift in aggregate demand shows the lower expenditure–equilibrium GDP at the existing price level and at various other possible price levels.

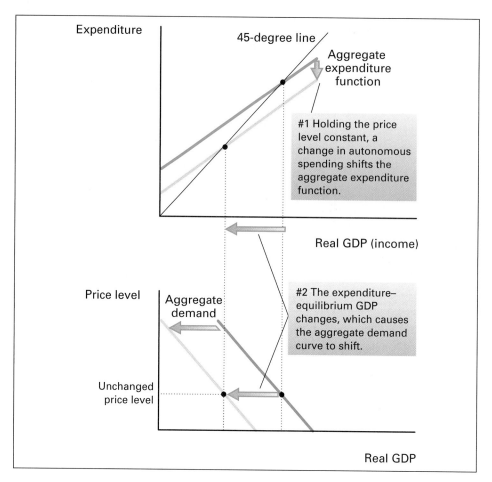

#1 Holding the price level constant, a change in autonomous spending shifts the aggregate expenditure function.

#2 The expenditure–equilibrium GDP changes, which causes the aggregate demand curve to shift.

$\mathscr{E}$XPLORE
&
$\mathscr{A}$PPLY

10.5 THE GREAT DEPRESSION—AT THE TIME AND WITH THE BENEFIT OF TIME

Nearly every American has been haunted by the images—grainy flickering newsreel pictures and black-and-white stills of bread lines, bank runs, hunger, and desperation from which we cannot turn away. These images of the Great Depression have become part of our subconscious. Many fear that it may happen again. We even capitalize the words to emphasize its place in our heritage. Otherwise, future generations might dismiss it as just a long recession. The United States' survival through the Great Depression gives us hope that Americans can overcome whatever adversity might strike.

Some years are indelibly stamped on our collective memory. One such year is 1929. In August of 1929 the U.S. economic expansion reached its peak. Was the subsequent drop just another bump on the road to permanent prosperity? Most people, if they even noticed the economic downturn at all, thought so.

After all, the "Roaring 20s" witnessed unprecedented prosperity as the average American family seized the opportunity to buy its first automobile, as well as a radio that would tune in the soap operas, dramas, and comedies offered by the expanding web of network-affiliated stations. Many also dabbled in stocks, shares of ownership in the booming businesses around them. It was a new age of permanent prosperity in which the consumer and investor both shared in the wealth.

There were a few missed beats as the economy marched forward in time to the music of this new age of jazz, flappers, and speakeasies. A couple of brief, mild economic downturns did occur along with a more severe recession at the beginning of the decade. Farmers in particular did not share in the general prosperity. However, the wealthy made out quite well. The Revenue Act of 1926 legislated huge tax cuts, fueling the demand for stocks issued by companies like General Motors (GM), General Electric (GE), and the Radio Corporation of America (RCA).

There were also more intellectual pursuits if one so desired. For example, 1922 saw the publication of Ludwig von Mises's *Socialism: An Economic and Sociological Analysis*, followed the next year by John Maynard Keynes's *Tract on Monetary Reform*. But why bother to read the difficult works of these and other intellectuals when there was so much easy money to be made in the new national pastime—stock picking? This was one gamble where everyone could win, or so it seemed until October 29, 1929, "Black Tuesday." The stock market crashed and did not recover. The party was over and the country would not fully recover for over a decade.

The 1929 crash of the stock market was followed by deepening economic troubles, which most people blamed on the market crash. The economy did not begin to recover until 1933. The recovery, never strong enough to convince the country that its troubles were behind it, was interrupted by a second severe downturn in 1937. Thus, in the course of more than a decade a nation struggled to overcome its economic troubles.

DID KEYNES UNDERSTAND HOW TO FIX THE ECONOMY?

The tools of Keynesian economic analysis can help us understand the problems of recession and its meaner relative, depression. In Figure 10-11, we see a situation in which GDP starts far short of that needed for full employment. In order for the economy to produce full-employment GDP, the aggregate expenditure function must be shifted upward to intersect the 45-degree line at the higher level of GDP. Keynes called for the government to make this shift happen by filling the recessionary gap with extra autonomous spending. If the government would just spend this extra amount, the multiplier effect would take over and bring the economy to full employment.

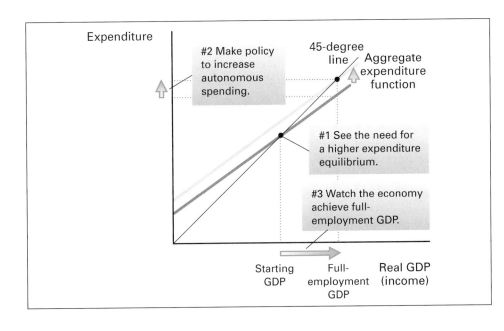

FIGURE 10-11

KEYNES'S CURE FOR DEPRESSION
When the economy is in depression, Keynes suggests the government should take action. First, observe the extent of the problem. Second, solve it by increasing aggregate demand enough to fill the recessionary gap, shown by the arrows pointing upward. Third, await the multiplier effect that will lift the economy to full-employment GDP.

Unfortunately, this analysis does not answer several important questions. If we grant that the crash of the stock market destroyed enough wealth to push the aggregate expenditure function down from the full-employment level, why did the aggregate expenditure function continue to shift downward until 1933? Once the economy did begin to recover in 1933, why was the recovery so weak? What could have been done to strengthen the recovery? The Keynesian analysis neither tells us why the Great Depression occurred, nor why the economy remained trapped so long.

Even today, economists differ over the cause or causes of the Great Depression. The simplest explanation is that the stock market crash caused the aggregate expenditure function to shift downward as previously described. However, economists are well aware of the dangers of the *fallacy of causation* in which an event is attributed to another event that preceded it. Just because one event occurs before a second one does not mean that the first event caused the second one. Many economists would label the stock market explanation as an example of the fallacy of causation. After all, the economic downturn began in August of 1929, while the market did not crash until October.

What else could have caused the Great Depression? In the 1992 presidential debate that CNN broadcast on *Larry King Live,* candidate Al Gore presented candidate Ross Perot with a framed picture of Senators Smoot and Hawley, authors of the *Smoot–Hawley Tariff Act,* passed in 1930. Gore criticized Perot for favoring raising tariffs on imports into the United States. Many analysts believe that the Smoot–Hawley tariffs turned what might have been an ordinary recession into an economic disaster. By smothering international trade with high tariffs and precipitating retaliation by other countries, the Smoot–Hawley Act disrupted commerce. Soon the depression had spread to become a worldwide phenomenon.

We know that other suspects lurk in the pages of history. Economist Milton Friedman points his finger at the Federal Reserve, America's central bank. The Federal Reserve failed to rescue the banking system and allowed bank failures to multiply. By the time President Roosevelt declared a so-called bank holiday on his Inauguration Day, March 4, 1933, about a third of the country's money had been swallowed by bank failures. As one survivor of the era, Vince Olsen, put it, "A nickel would go a long way in those days. The problem was that nobody had a nickel." If the Fed had acted decisively to save the nation's banks and its money supply, the Great Depression would not have occurred.

Others point to the nation's unequal distribution of wealth as the culprit, decrying such actions as the Revenue Act of 1926 that cut the federal income tax on a million-dollar income from $600,000 to $200,000. As the rich took a larger fraction of national income and wealth, some argue that the nation began to save too much, resulting in too little aggregate demand. In addition to advocating government spending, for example, Keynes also urged consumers to increase the marginal propensity to consume and in that way get more money circulating in the economy.

With the passing of the Hoover presidency into history on March 4, 1933, President Franklin D. Roosevelt took the oath of office while promising the American people a New Deal. The nation witnessed an energetic, if not always successful, effort to banish the Great Depression through legislation. The first theme of action was to reform the nation's financial and banking system to make banks stronger and safer. However, the government did not repay the money lost when banks failed. A program of deposit insurance was not enacted until June of 1933, and that program was not retroactive.

A second theme of the New Deal, the one for which it is most widely known, is embodied in various pieces of legislation to provide "relief" in the form of money and services for those in distress. The government attempted to set up a social safety net so that business downturns would no longer bring such personal devastation.

A third theme is government influence over market prices. Prime examples are minimum wage laws and agricultural price floors. The purpose of these actions was to put purchasing power into the hands of workers and farmers, a very large group in those days.

Support for workers was also embodied in legislation that supported the efforts of labor unions to organize workers.

There was a widespread belief early on that a balanced federal budget would be the soundest fiscal policy. Thus, the Revenue Act of 1932 raised tax rates from a 25 percent maximum rate to 63 percent. Keynes abhorred that policy.

Even years prior to its publication date in 1936, drafts of Keynes's *General Theory of Employment, Interest, and Money* were the talk of the town in Washington. The ideas of this already well-known English economist offered the best hope that the country could find a way out of the Great Depression. Keynes suggested that an economy ought to use government deficit spending to stimulate the economy and close any recessionary gap. A tax cut might achieve the same result, but with less certainty because taxpayers might save the money received from a tax cut rather than spend it. Thus, the Keynesian remedies for unemployment can be summarized as "spend, spend, spend." Only the government has deep enough pockets for that.

Keynes recommended that the deficit spending that governments use to fight off recessions should be balanced by a budget surplus during good economic times. The problem is that the Keynesian medicine of deficit spending has proved to be an addictive drug for governments around the world. Severe, protracted unemployment such as in the Great Depression has not been seen since.

Economists today pay homage to Keynes for his powerful logic and insights into the role of aggregate demand in the macroeconomy. But economists also recognize the importance of money, taxes, aggregate supply, property rights, international trade, and other factors in promoting a healthy economy.

THINKING CRITICALLY

1. Why would deficit spending prove to be addictive to governments? Would a deficit created by tax cuts be more or less desirable than a deficit created by more government spending? Explain

2. What practical difficulties would a government face in closing a recessionary gap with government spending? Can you identify any alternatives besides a tax cut to close such a gap?

Visit www.prenhall.com/ayers for updates and web exercises on this Explore & Apply topic.

SUMMARY AND LEARNING OBJECTIVES

1. **Summarize the perspective of Keynes and Keynesian economics.**
   - Keynesian economics takes a short-run perspective, whereas classical economics emphasizes long-run tendencies and views unemployment as a temporary phenomenon that will be corrected by market forces. In response to the classical contention that unemployment will be corrected by the market, Keynes wrote, "In the long run, we are all dead."

2. **Illustrate the income–expenditure model.**
   - Keynesian economics is portrayed with an income–expenditure model. There are two curves in the income–expenditure graph. The first is a 45-degree line. Since at every point along any 45-degree line the value on one axis equals the value on the other axis, the 45-degree line in the expenditure–equilibrium graph illustrates all points where spending and real GDP are equal. The second curve is the aggregate expenditure function, which shows how much spending is planned at each level of real GDP.
   - An expenditure equilibrium occurs when aggregate planned spending equals real GDP, shown graphically by the intersection of the aggregate expenditure function and the 45-degree line. When real GDP and aggregate planned spending are equal, the economy's output of goods and services are all purchased.

- Planned spending can be autonomous or induced. Autonomous spending is the amount of spending that would occur if people had no incomes. Even if people had no incomes, autonomous spending would be some positive amount because people would spend out of accumulated savings.
- Induced spending is the spending that occurs because people earn incomes. Induced spending is in addition to autonomous spending. The larger one's income, the greater his or her induced spending.
- The aggregate expenditure function sums the four components of aggregate spending: consumption, planned investment, government spending, and net exports (net spending by foreigners).

3. **Explain the adjustment process to an expenditure equilibrium.**
   - An expenditure equilibrium is associated with inventories of goods and services that are neither being drawn down nor built up.
   - Aggregate spending that is less than real GDP causes a recessionary gap. A recessionary gap is associated with unemployment because planned spending is less than production, which results in a buildup of inventories of unsold goods. Producers would cut back production to eliminate an additional buildup of inventories. Production cutbacks typically involve layoffs of workers. Thus, a recessionary gap leads to higher unemployment.
   - An inflationary gap is the opposite of a recessionary gap. An inflationary gap leads to a decrease in inventories. Businesses will increase production in an effort to restore inventories to their desired level.
   - In addition to recognizing the implications of differences between planned and actual investment, Keynesian analysis also points out the significance of various aspects of consumer behavior. The marginal propensity to consume (mpc), which is the fraction of an additional dollar that is spent, plays a key role in the aggregate expenditure function. The maximum value of the mpc is one, indicating that 100 percent of an additional dollar is spent. The minimum value of the mpc is zero, indicating that none is spent. Typically, the value of the mpc for the economy will be somewhere between zero and one.

4. **Describe how new spending can have a ripple effect throughout the economy.**
   - Keynesian economics emphasizes the distinction between saving and spending. Every additional dollar of income must either be spent, or by definition, saved. The fraction of an additional dollar of income that is saved is the marginal propensity to save (mps).
   - The sum of the marginal propensity to consume and the marginal propensity to save must equal 1 [mpc + mps = 1]. The reason is that the fraction of an additional dollar not spent must be saved. For example, if consumers spend ninety cents of each additional dollar of income they receive, they save ten cents by definition. Thus, the mpc = 0.9 and the mps = 0.1.
   - Multiplier effects of spending are an important element of Keynesian economics. Induced spending and autonomous spending both contribute to reaching an expenditure equilibrium. When saving or consuming are consumers' only options, the expenditure multiplier equals 1/mps.
   - The expenditure multiplier assumes there are unemployed resources in the economy. It also assumes a constant price level.
   - Rather than rely upon downward price adjustments, Keynes recommended increased government spending to move the economy to full employment. This spending will spread and, through the multiplier effect, lead to even more spending.

5. **Distinguish the tax multiplier from the balanced-budget multiplier.**
   - The tax multiplier shows the expansionary effect of a tax cut or the contractionary effect of a tax increase on the economy. The tax multiplier will have a value of $-\text{mpc}/(1 - \text{mpc})$, which is less than the expenditure multiplier.
   - Combining the expenditure multiplier with the tax multiplier gives a balanced-budget multiplier that equals one. This means that an increase in government spending financed by higher taxes increases equilibrium income by the amount of extra government spending.
   - One objection to Keynesian multiplier analysis is that the tax multiplier ignores how changing taxes changes work and investment incentives. Keynesian multiplier analysis also ignores the crowding-out effect, which occurs when government borrowing reduces funds available for private sector investment.

6. **Graph the relationship of the income–expenditure model to aggregate demand.**
   - The income–expenditure model can be used to derive an aggregate demand curve. A higher price level shifts the aggregate expenditure function downward; a lower price level shifts it upward. The relationship

between the price level and the expenditure–equilibrium GDP is plotted in aggregate demand.

■ If the aggregate expenditure function shifts for any reason other than a change in the price level, aggregate demand will shift. The new aggregate demand curve shows the new expenditure equilibrium for the existing price level and for each other possible price level.

7. Compare economic analyses on the Great Depression.

■ There is disagreement over the cause or causes of the Great Depression. There is also disagreement over the success of Keynesian policy in pulling the country out of that depression. Keynesian analysis models the Great depression as a severe recessionary gap.

KEY TERMS

income–expenditure model, 227
aggregate expenditures, 227
aggregate expenditure function, 227
expenditure equilibrium, 227
autonomous spending, 228
induced spending, 228

consumption function, 229
marginal propensity to consume (mpc), 229
marginal propensity to save (mps), 229
multiplier effect, 232
expenditure multiplier, 233

unemployment equilibrium, 235
output gap, 235
recessionary gap, 235
inflationary gap, 235
tax multiplier, 237
balanced-budget multiplier, 237

TEST YOURSELF

TRUE OR FALSE

1. John Maynard Keynes offered a long-run perspective on the macroeconomy in the *General Theory.*
2. If you had no income, you would still engage in autonomous spending.
3. The marginal propensity to consume is normally less than one.
4. An expenditure equilibrium occurs where the aggregate expenditure function intersects the vertical axis.
5. An injection of new autonomous spending will leave equilibrium real GDP unchanged when the marginal propensity to save equals 0.5.

MULTIPLE CHOICE

6. An expenditure equilibrium is
   a. achieved when aggregate demand involves no induced spending.
   b. the level of real GDP the economy tends toward in the short run, at a given price level.
   c. when tax revenue is exactly equal to government spending.
   d. the point where the economy is always at.
7. Suppose actual spending equals planned spending. Then we can say that
   a. the economy is at an expenditure equilibrium.
   b. real GDP is the most it can possibly be.

   c. autonomous spending equals zero.
   d. aggregate demand has shifted to the left.
8. Referring to Self-Test Figure 10-1, point *A* represents
   a. autonomous spending.
   b. induced spending.
   c. an unemployment equilibrium.
   d. the multiplier effect.

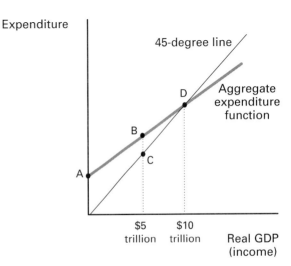

SELF-TEST FIGURE 10-1

9. Referring to Self-Test Figure 10-1, an economy that produces real GDP equal to $5 trillion would have
   a. a recessionary gap equal to $B - C$.
   b. an output gap equal to $B - C$.
   c. an inflationary gap equal to $B - C$.
   d. a drawdown of inventories equal to $B - C$.

10. Referring to Self-Test Figure 10-1, point D represents
    a. full-employment GDP.
    b. an expenditure equilibrium.
    c. induced spending.
    d. the inflationary gap.

11. In the income–expenditure model, the 45-degree line shows
    a. the amount of autonomous spending.
    b. the amount of induced spending.
    c. the expenditure multiplier.
    d. that the economy's income is actually the same as its output.

12. The aggregate expenditure function includes all of the following EXCEPT
    a. consumption.
    b. planned investment.
    c. net exports.
    d. unintended changes in business inventories.

13. The marginal propensity to consume equals
    a. the fraction of total income that people consume.
    b. the fraction of additional income that people consume.
    c. the fraction of savings that people plan to spend within the next year.
    d. one in most cases.

14. The sum of the marginal propensity to consume and the marginal propensity to save equals
    a. the amount of a person's income.
    b. zero.
    c. one.
    d. a value greater than zero, but less than one.

15. The expenditure equilibrium will rise by the increase in _____ _____ multiplied by the expenditure multiplier.
    a. autonomous spending
    b. aggregate demand
    c. induced spending
    d. idle resources

16. To cure a recession, Keynes suggested that the most effective action the government could take would be to
    a. reduce government regulations.
    b. raise wages.
    c. reduce prices.
    d. increase government spending.

17. According to the balanced-budget multiplier, a simultaneous increase of $50 billion in both government spending and taxation would
    a. have no effect.
    b. increase equilibrium output by $50 billion.
    c. decrease equilibrium output by $50 billion.
    d. decrease output by $50 billion multiplied by the crowding-out effect.

18. Crowding out
    a. is what Keynesian economic policies aim to achieve.
    b. occurs if government borrowing increases interest rates.
    c. refers to the effort to move large numbers of people out of poverty with Keynesian policies.
    d. happens every time there is an increase in aggregate demand.

19. The paradox of thrift, if true, suggests that people should
    a. save more.
    b. spend more.
    c. vote more often.
    d. spend the same amount of money, but spend it more wisely.

20. In Self-Test Figure 10-2, the arrow labeled A represents the
    a. marginal propensity to consume.
    b. amount of inflation that can be expected to close an output gap.
    c. increase in autonomous spending needed to close a recessionary gap.
    d. amount of inflation that can be expected to close an inflationary gap.

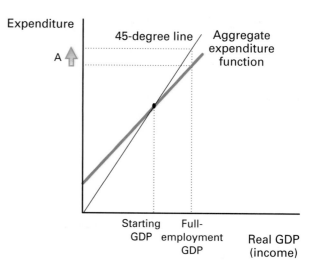

SELF-TEST FIGURE 10-2

QUESTIONS AND PROBLEMS

1. *[Keynesian versus classical perspectives]* "In the long run, we are all dead." Evaluate this quote from a macroeconomic perspective, taking first a classical position and then a Keynesian position.

2. *[income equals output identity]* The circular flow model implies that aggregate national income equals aggregate national output. Review the circular flow model in Chapter 2 and then explain why this implication is present in the model.

3. *[45-degree line]* What role does the 45-degree line play in the model of expenditure equilibrium?

4. *[autonomous and induced spending]* Provide an estimate of your family's autonomous spending. What is your family's approximate actual spending? What is the difference between the actual spending figure and your estimate of autonomous spending called? Why is actual spending different from autonomous spending?

5. *[expenditure equilibrium]* Illustrate graphically an expenditure equilibrium. Be sure to label the axes. Show the amount of autonomous spending, the amount of induced spending, and the point that represents the expenditure equilibrium.

6. *[recessionary gap]* Using the graph you created in the previous question, illustrate and explain the effects of a recessionary gap.

7. *[inflationary gap]* Apply the income–expenditure model to illustrate a situation in which business inventories are being unintentionally depleted. Explain the effects of this inventory depletion within the context of that model.

8. *[mpc and mps]* Explain why the sum of the marginal propensity to consume (mpc) and the marginal propensity to save (mps) must equal one. What value do you estimate your personal mpc to have?

9. *[expenditure multiplier]* What is the formula for the expenditure multiplier? What role does the expenditure multiplier play in the expenditure equilibrium? What assumption does the expenditure multiplier make about the price level?

10. *[expenditure equilibrium]* Suppose the marginal propensity to save is 0.4 and autonomous spending is $1 trillion.
    a. Identify the value of the expenditure equilibrium.
    b. To increase the expenditure equilibrium by $1 trillion, what change in autonomous spending would be needed? Why is this amount less than $1 trillion?

11. *[Keynesian policy]* Why does Keynesian economics view an increase in government spending as a better cure for a recession than a tax cut?

12. *[mps and equilibrium income]* Suppose there is a decrease in the mps. Does Keynesian analysis predict an increase, decrease, or no change in equilibrium income? Explain.

13. *[balanced-budget multiplier]* The balanced-budget multiplier can be shown to equal one. What is the significance of this for the expenditure equilibrium?

14. *[paradox of thrift]* What is the paradox of thrift? Is it relevant to the economy today?

15. *[deriving aggregate demand]* Using two possible price levels, show how aggregate demand can be derived from the income–expenditure diagram. Label the axes and all curves and equilibrium points on both the income–expenditure graph and the aggregate demand graph.

 Visit www.prenhall.com/ayers for Exploring the Web exercises and additional self-test quizzes.

CHAPTER 11

FISCAL POLICY IN ACTION

A LOOK AHEAD

To take from the rich and to give to the poor was the model of Robin Hood of storybook fame. Some considered him a hero, others thought he was nothing more than a thief. So it is with our system of taxation and income redistribution: We hate to pay but we like to receive. As Winston Churchill put it, "Taxation is the price we pay for living in a free society." However, we do demand a say in what sort of taxes we are expected to pay, as well as the choices our government makes in spending those taxes. Those choices are the subject of this chapter.

One such choice involves how to pay for homeland security. Both government and industry have found themselves facing higher costs to maintain security. The airline industry was particularly hard-hit. Paying for added security in air travel and elsewhere in the economy is the subject of this chapter's Explore & Apply section. We will see that there are repercussions elsewhere in the economy when government picks up the tab for security in air travel or security in any other industry.

LEARNING OBJECTIVES

Understanding Chapter 11 will enable you to:
1. **List the major sources of revenue for government in the United States.**
2. **Explain the principles of tax equity and how they apply.**
3. **Interpret why the U.S. income tax is structured as it is, and why critics suggest changing it.**
4. **Show why workers pay more Social Security tax than they see withdrawn on their pay stubs.**
5. **Justify the use of consumption taxes, including the value added taxes of Canada and Europe.**
6. **Discuss issues of market efficiency and tax equity as they relate to security costs.**

Chapters 9 and 10 have discussed fiscal policy, both in terms of budgetary balance and with respect to possible effects on equilibrium GDP. This chapter examines issues of implementing fiscal policy, for not all tax and spending programs have an equal effect on the economy. Effects on efficiency and equity can differ significantly among policy options, even if the tax and spending totals are the same.

11.1 POLICY IN PRACTICE

In this world nothing can be said to be certain, except death and taxes.

—*Benjamin Franklin*

Few things are less popular than taxes, since taxes represent money that is taken from us involuntarily by the government. However, we all like to be the recipients of government spending. If we live in the U.S. economy, with its large variety of both taxes and government activities, we are likely to see both.

SPENDING AND TAXATION

transfer payments the redistribution of income from one group to another.

Government spending in the United States encompasses a vast array of programs. Some of these programs go toward the purchase of goods and services, such as highways or national defense. Others are regulatory programs, such as those conducted by the Occupational Safety and Health Administration or the Environmental Protection Agency. In addition, a large fraction of government spending goes toward **transfer payments** that redistribute income to the needy. Transfer payments include unemployment compensation, welfare, and other *safety-net programs* that provide economic security. Transfer payments account for approximately 44 percent of total federal spending. Figure 11-1 shows the growth in transfer payments and other components of federal spending over time.

Because taxes take roughly 30 percent of gross domestic product (GDP), taxpayers are acutely concerned that they not be taken advantage of—in other words, that all pay their fair share. This is the goal of equity. Because taxes can discourage work effort and investment, a second goal in taxation is efficiency. **To achieve efficiency, taxes that are intended to raise revenues should do so in a manner that affects our behavior the least.** Efficiency in taxation gives citizens the greatest possible incentive to be productive.

marginal tax rate tax rate on additional income.

Figure 11-2 illustrates the relative importance of revenue sources for the U.S. federal government. The personal income tax is the single largest source, providing 50 percent of all revenues. As U.S. citizens accumulate income over the course of the year, the federal personal income tax claims those earnings at incremental rates that increase from 10 percent to 15 percent, to 27 percent, to 30 percent, to 35 percent, and to 38.6 percent. This incremental tax rate on incremental income is known as the **marginal tax rate,** which equals 27 percent for most American taxpayers.

Marginal tax rate = Additional taxes owed as a percentage of additional income

In other words, the average citizen pays twenty-seven cents to the IRS on each additional dollar he or she earns. Marginal tax rates are shown in Table 11-1. Note that the marginal tax rate differs from the *average tax rate,* which equals a person's total tax liability divided by total income at the end of the year.

Average tax rate = Total taxes owed as a percentage of total income

The amount of income withheld from your paycheck is based on your projected average tax liability.

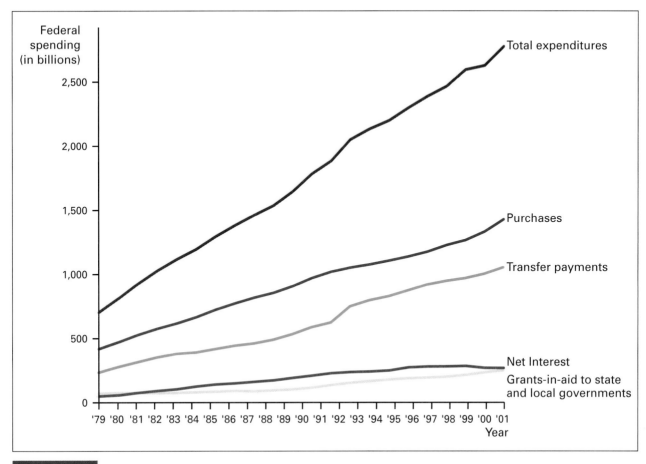

FIGURE 11-1

FEDERAL SPENDING Spending by the federal government has grown rapidly over the last century, especially spending on transfer payments, interest on the national debt, and grants-in-aid from the federal to state and local governments. Slightly more than half of federal purchases are related to national defense.

Source: 2002 Economic Report of the President, Table B-83.

TABLE 11-1 MARGINAL PERSONAL INCOME TAX RATES FOR SINGLES, 2002

TAX RATE	TAXABLE INCOME
10%	up to $6,000
15%	$6,001–$27,950
27%	$27,951–$67,700
30%	$67,701–$141,250
35%	$141,251–$307,050
38.6%	$307,051 or more

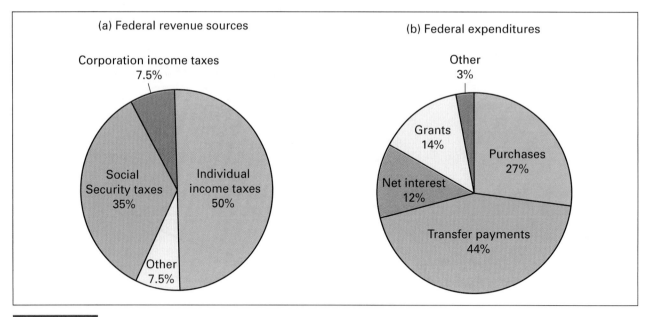

FIGURE 11-2

FEDERAL REVENUE SOURCES AND EXPENDITURES

Source: 2002 Economic Report of the President, Table B–80. The data are for 2001.

Source: National Income and Product Accounts Tables. The data are for 2001.

As seen in Figure 11-2(a), Social Security taxes, inclusive of the hospitalization portion of *Medicare*—health insurance for the elderly—account for 35 percent of federal revenues, second only to the share of the personal income tax. The Social Security tax is a *payroll tax,* in which the government deducts a flat 7.65 percent from the amount of money the employer pays, plus another 7.65 percent from the amount of money the employee receives. Taken together, the Social Security tax collects 15.3 percent of a worker's payroll income, up to a maximum individual income of $84,900 in 2002, after which only the 2.9 percent Medicare hospitalization tax continues to be collected.

Figure 11-2(b) shows how the taxes collected are spent. The largest category of spending is on transfer payments, especially Social Security. Other federal spending goes to purchase goods and services, pay the interest on the national debt, provide grant monies to state and local governments, and a variety of other government subsidy programs.

The corporation income tax takes in approximately 30 percent of corporate profits, and brought in revenues of $151.1 billion in 2001, equaling about 7.5 percent of total federal revenues. The corporation income tax has proven to be quite controversial over time because,

tax incidence identifies those who eventually wind up paying a tax.

while it may seem fair to tax corporations as though they are people, the **tax incidence** of the corporation income tax—meaning who ultimately winds up paying the tax—is on real people who directly or indirectly own the corporations and who also pay personal income taxes or other taxes relating to that ownership.

Figure 11-3(a) shows state and local revenue sources. Most states rely heavily on a combination of individual income taxes, sales taxes, revenue from the federal government, and other charges. Major sources of revenue at the local level include property taxes and sales taxes. Figure 11-3(b) shows how state and local governments spend their revenue. The "Other" category is very large because it includes many types of expenditures. Examples include libraries, hospitals, police protection, fire protection, and much more.

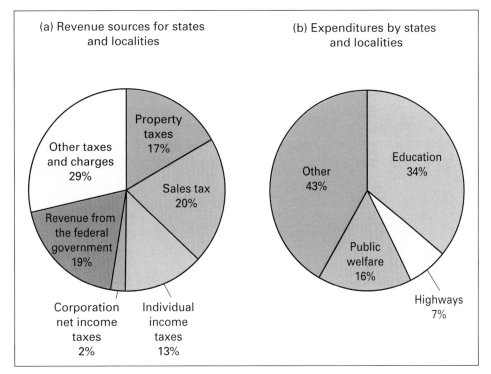

(a) Revenue sources for states and localities

- Property taxes 17%
- Sales tax 20%
- Individual income taxes 13%
- Corporation net income taxes 2%
- Revenue from the federal government 19%
- Other taxes and charges 29%

(b) Expenditures by states and localities

- Education 34%
- Highways 7%
- Public welfare 16%
- Other 43%

FIGURE 11-3

STATE AND LOCAL GOVERNMENT REVENUE SOURCES AND EXPENDITURES

Source: 2002 Economic Report of the President, Table B–86. The data are for 1998–1999.

Source: 2002 Economic Report of the President, Table B–86. The data are for 1998–1999.

States have to be careful not to tax any one source of revenue much more heavily than do other states, or that revenue source will migrate to the less-taxing state. This problem plagued New York in the 1960s and 1970s, as the poor moved in to receive generous welfare benefits, while many of the wealthy moved away to avoid paying the high income taxes that financed those benefits.

When all the revenues received by all units of government are added together, the result is that **government revenues in the United States are over 30 percent of the value of production.** Another way of looking at this is that the average American must work until "Tax Freedom Day" each year—declared by the Tax Foundation to be April 27 as of 2002—in order to have enough money to pay the government.

"DON'T TAX YOU, DON'T TAX ME—TAX THAT FELLOW BEHIND THE TREE."

SNAPSHOT

That was how former U.S. Senator Russell Long of Louisiana put it. In the abstract, taxes sound great. Higher taxes can eliminate the need for government borrowing and can pay for more of the public services we value. There is only one problem. We want to keep our own money and for that reason want those taxes to be paid by people other than ourselves.

Some localities have found a way to do just that through *tax exporting*, which is getting nonresidents to finance government. For example, speed zones on roads through small towns allow those towns to collect revenue from unsuspecting motorists. The payments on their speeding tickets keep property taxes down, while the out-of-towner is never heard from again.

Bigger cities resort to surcharges on rental cars and lodging, since few people will change their travel plans because of such a tax. Although convention planners do pay attention, most tourists and business travelers have probably left town before they know what's hit them. Travelers might grind their teeth and mutter. The locals merely smile as their government pockets the cash. ◄

EVALUATING EQUITY

Taxes are used to redistribute income from the haves to the have-nots, and in the process remedy some of the inequities that arise in a free-market economy. People's views on equity vary widely, however, which means that issues of equity in taxation—*tax equity*—become a matter of hot debate. Some basic principles can help frame this debate. The two most fundamental principles of tax equity are as follows:

- The **benefit principle** states that a fair tax is one that taxes people in proportion to the benefits they receive when government spends the tax revenues.
- The **ability-to-pay principle** states that those who can afford to pay more taxes than others should be required to do so.

benefit principle states that a fair tax is one that taxes people in proportion to the benefits they receive when government spends those tax revenues.

ability-to-pay principle states that those who can afford to pay more taxes than others should be required to do so.

The gasoline tax would appear to satisfy the benefit principle of tax equity, because gasoline tax revenues are *earmarked* for—restricted to—highway construction and repair. The more someone drives, the more government-funded highways the person drives on, and the more gasoline tax the person pays. In general, *user fees* are designed to meet the benefit principle of tax equity.

The benefit principle cannot be applied to programs whose purpose is to redistribute income. To see why not, consider food stamps (like money but only spendable on food). According to the benefit principle, food stamp recipients should pay for the cost of those food stamps. However, this would have the effect of defeating the fundamental purpose of the food stamp program, which is to help those in need. Food stamps are of no help if you have to pay for them! Thus, to justify redistributional programs, a different principle of tax equity is invoked—the ability-to-pay principle. The idea of the ability-to-pay principle is that the more a person is able to pay, the more that person should pay.

progressive tax a tax that collects a higher percentage of high incomes than of low incomes.

regressive tax a tax that collects a higher percentage of low incomes than of high incomes.

proportional tax a tax that collects the same percentage of high incomes as of low incomes.

Many people interpret the ability-to-pay principle to mean that taxes designed for redistributing income should be progressive. A **progressive tax** collects a higher percentage of high incomes than of low incomes. In contrast, a **regressive tax** collects a higher percentage of low incomes than of high incomes. A **proportional tax** collects the same percentage of income, no matter what the income is. A *flat tax* that taxes all income at the same tax rate would be proportional. In practice, proposals for a so-called flat tax almost always provide for some exemptions that make the tax progressive overall.

The key here is percentage. A tax that collects $1,000 from a poor person earning $10,000 and $10,000 from a rich person earning $1 million is regressive, because the poor person pays 10 percent of his or her income, whereas the rich person pays only 1 percent.

Sometimes it is hard to determine whether or not a tax is progressive. For instance, consider the Social Security tax, which is defined broadly to include the Medicare tax. The Social Security tax may be considered either proportional, regressive, or progressive, depending on which aspects of the system are under scrutiny. Up to the 2002 limit of $84,900 of payroll income received, the tax is proportional at 15.3 percent. Because the marginal payroll tax rate beyond that point drops to only 2.9 percent (the Medicare component),

QUICKCHECK

If your tax bill rises as your income rises, does that mean the tax is progressive?

Answer: Not necessarily. For the tax to be progressive, it must not only collect more revenue from you as your income rises, but it must also take a higher fraction of your total income.

the average tax rate declines with income and the overall tax is regressive. However, if Social Security benefits are included along with the taxes, the Social Security system as a whole is highly progressive, as will be discussed in more detail later in this chapter.

PROGRESSIVE—WHAT'S IN A WORD?

The terms *progressive* and *regressive* are loaded—they make an implicit normative judgment about what is good and bad. After all, who could argue against progress? Would you prefer to regress? That would be moving backward, not forward. Bear in mind, though, that there is nothing magical about the terms.

The ability-to-pay principle of equity says that, to finance government, the rich should pay more than the poor. It does not specify whether the higher taxes should be less than, more than, or exactly in proportion to the higher income. For instance, it would make life simpler if we had one flat-rate income tax, with no exemptions, deductions, exclusions, and so on. Such a tax would be proportional, but would it be fair? That judgment is entirely up to you. ◄

TRADING OFF EFFICIENCY AND EQUITY

Economic efficiency involves getting the most valuable output from the inputs available. It bakes the biggest economic pie. In general, taxes are efficient to the extent that they do not change our behavior, with the most efficient tax being the one we cannot influence or escape.

To see how taxes cause inefficiency, consider an increase in the income tax. Some workers, especially those who are not heads of households, would cut back their work efforts. Even those who do not cut back would find that getting ahead in the workplace would bring less reward. For this reason, people are less likely to invest their time and money to acquire more human capital. Corporate income taxes mean that businesses also don't invest as much, either, because the corporation income tax cuts down on the return to that investment.

For an efficient tax, we can turn to the *head tax*. In short, if you have a head, you pay the tax! Since head taxes are efficient and require virtually no paperwork, should all of our other taxes be replaced by head taxes? You probably see the problem. While the economic pie would be large, most of us would consider it to be sliced very unfairly. In other words, head taxes would not be equitable.

Not only are tax laws written with an eye toward equity, but government spending is often targeted toward promoting equity directly through provision of a social safety net. This safety net targets the needy with both cash transfers and **in-kind benefits,** which are any benefits other than money. Social Security is far and away the largest cash transfer program, redirecting a significant amount of current earnings to current retirees. The largest in-kind program is Medicaid, which provides health insurance for the impoverished.

in-kind benefits a government-provided good or service, as opposed to cash.

A tradeoff between efficiency and equity pervades our system of tax and spending programs. Ideally, to provide a broad and generous safety net, the government might guarantee good housing, good food, and good health insurance for everyone. The better the guarantees, however, the more the programs will cost and the less the incentives will be to work and invest. There are three reasons for this inefficient reduction in work incentives, as follows:

- There is less need to better yourself to the extent that the government guarantees you a comfortable lifestyle. As the saying goes, necessity is the mother of invention.
- If you choose to forge ahead anyway, your greater ability to take care of yourself causes you to lose eligibility for many welfare-type programs. Over some ranges of income, the

loss of benefits from Medicaid, subsidized housing, food stamps, and other welfare programs more than offsets the value of extra income earned.

■ Obtaining the money for safety-net programs requires the government to either tax or borrow, which would need to be repaid from future tax revenue. With taxes comes less incentive to work and invest.

We could eliminate the second problem if we offer eligibility to everyone, regardless of income. However, that policy would accentuate the third problem.

There is no ready answer to the dilemma of choosing between a generous safety net and incentives for economic productivity. This is an area of seemingly endless political debate and compromise. We don't want the income tax burden to be so high that our economy stagnates because we have little to gain personally by being productive. However, our economy can afford to provide some degree of economic security for those in need. Choices of this sort are why policymakers face what has been called *the big tradeoff* between efficiency and equity in the design of government tax and spending programs.

11.2 SOCIAL SECURITY

Social Security is far and away the government's largest program, with the Social Security tax alone accounting for more than a third of Federal revenue, as was shown in Figure 11-2. For this reason, we use Social Security as our focus to examine the issues that arise in fiscal policy.

Social Security collects taxes on all payroll income, and allots the proceeds for *OASDI* and *HI,* which stand for old age, survivors, and disability insurance, and hospitalization insurance, respectively. The hospitalization portion is more commonly known as Medicare. The combined employer and employee Social Security tax rate is 15.3 percent of the first $84,900 of that income as of 2002, where the threshold has been adjusted upward over time in response to wage inflation. For income over that threshold, the Social Security tax is eliminated except for the 2.9 percent Medicare component. The rates have risen over time, as shown in Figure 11-4.

Turning to Social Security's impact on wages, consider Figure 11-5, which illustrates the economy's supply and demand for labor. The sellers are the people who offer labor; the buyers are firms. The supply of labor is shown as a vertical line because the quantity of labor supplied depends primarily on the natural rate of unemployment rather than on the specifics of tax policy. The portion of the Social Security tax paid by employers reduces their after-tax demand for labor by the same percentage as the tax, since the value of labor to the firm is reduced by the amount of tax that must be paid for that labor. This reduction is shown in the figure by a downward shift in labor demand, a shift that is just sufficient to cover Social Security taxes.

As seen in Figure 11-5, requiring the firm to pay Social Security taxes causes the equilibrium wage to be lower by exactly the amount of the tax. In effect, the tax burden has been *shifted* from employers to employees. The result is that workers effectively pay the full 15.3 percent Social Security tax. Many employees are unaware of the true magnitude of the Social Security tax, because only half of the combined 15.3 percent rate appears on their pay stubs.

INCOME REDISTRIBUTION—NOT JUST FOR EQUITY

pay-as-you-go referring to Social Security, meaning that current workers pay for current retirees.

Social Security is primarily **pay-as-you-go,** meaning that current workers pay for people who are currently retired. In this way, **Social Security redistributes income from one generation to another.** This redistribution started off in a small way. When Social Security was first established in 1934–1935, the first pension was not planned to begin until 1942. The tax rate was initially set to reach only 5 percent in total, with 2½ percent levied on the pay of

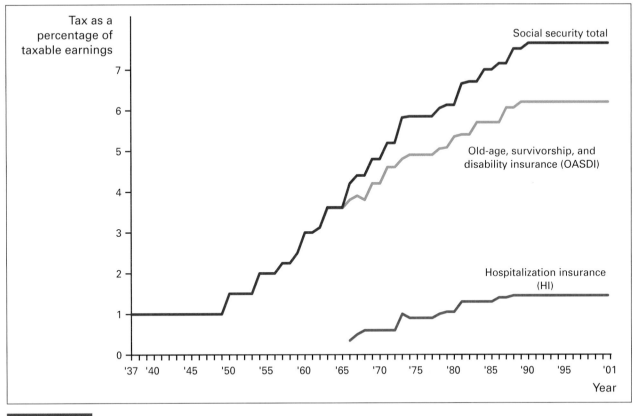

FIGURE 11-4

SOCIAL SECURITY TAX RATES OVER TIME Social Security rates are shown as a percentage of taxable earnings. Rates apply to both employees and employers, so that the total tax rates are double those shown. Hospitalization insurance is more commonly known as Medicare.

Source: U.S. Social Security Administration, data updated March 22, 2001.

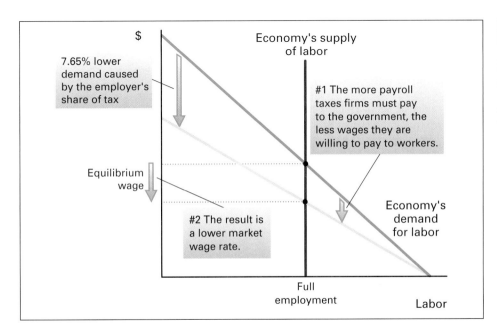

FIGURE 11-5

EFFECT OF SOCIAL SECURITY TAX ON WAGES The employer share of the Social Security tax is passed on to workers in the form of lower wages. The market-equilibrium wage rate falls by 7.65% as firms' willingness to pay for workers falls by 7.65% in response to the employers' 7.65% share of the Social Security tax.

workers and another 2½ percent on the employers doing the paying. In contrast, the current combined tax rate is 15.3 percent.

In 1945, the ratio of workers to retirees was about 50 to 1. It is currently about 3 to 1, and predicted to drop to only about 2 to 1 by 2030. Therefore, the burden on workers rises. To keep benefits constant, the Social Security Administration estimates that, by 2034, the tax rate would need to rise to almost 21 percent (18 percent, excluding Medicare). Without a tax increase, benefits would need to fall to three-fourths of their current amount.

Social Security also redistributes income within generations. The ratio of payments to retirees relative to the amount they contributed in their working years is much higher for the low income than for the high income. Payments are also adjusted on the basis of need, which is determined in part by the number of dependents a person has. Thus, even though the Social Security tax took out the same portion of each person's income when he or she was working, the percentage that Social Security gives back is much higher for the poor.

On an after-tax basis, Social Security may even pay the retired low-income worker more than he or she earned when working. A worker at the maximum income subject to Social Security tax, in contrast, is likely to receive only about 30 percent as much as when employed. The upshot is that, when Social Security taxes and payments are combined, the Social Security system is highly progressive. Low-income workers have money redistributed their way from the tax dollars paid by higher-income workers.

The redistribution from higher-income workers to lower-income workers is one reason participation in Social Security is required by law. If it were optional, workers with above-average incomes would quit, leaving no money to redistribute. Workers would also be deterred from joining voluntarily by intergenerational redistribution, which gives current retirees a much better deal than can be expected by current workers.

If the present structure of Social Security were to be offered by any private business, the owners of that business would be prosecuted for fraud for running an illegal *ponzi scheme,* in which the money from current investors is used to finance paybacks to longer-term investors. Ponzi schemes are very risky; if new investors ever stop coming, the most recent investors lose their money.

Social Security has a significant advantage over the typical ponzi scheme, however. New investors are forced into the system by the government and its power to tax. However, if the government changes its mind down the road, investors who have yet to receive a pay-back could lose out. Even if Social Security were fully financed, though, the low returns it offers would dissuade potential investors. Figure 11-6 illustrates these returns. Note that the return to those born in early years greatly exceeds the return to those born in later years.

A TRUST FUND OF IOUS

Social Security trust fund the buildup of Social Security tax revenues above what is paid out in benefits; kept in the form of government bonds.

There is a **Social Security trust fund,** which is the depository for Social Security tax revenues. The trust fund is currently building up because tax revenues exceed Social Security payouts. However, the size of that trust fund pales in comparison to the expected future demands against it. Moreover, all savings held in the Social Security trust fund take the form of special government bonds. Since a bond is merely a promise to pay in the future, savings within the Social Security trust fund are nothing more than government IOUs.

To pay those IOUs, the government must either create extra money or collect extra tax dollars in the future. Either way, future taxpayers pay. If the government creates new money, taxpayers pay the tax of inflation that eats away the value of their earnings. Otherwise, the trust fund bonds would be redeemed out of general tax revenues, which would require higher personal income taxes or other general taxes. Even if the Social Security trust fund were to stack a warehouse full of its special government bonds, it would still be up to future taxpayers to pay them off. Thus, for the economy as a whole, balances in the Social Security trust fund are not in themselves real savings.

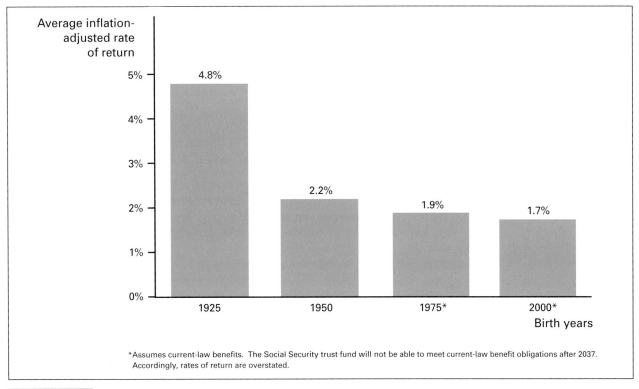

FIGURE 11-6

RETURNS FROM SOCIAL SECURITY The rate of return from Social Security has fallen from generation to generation.

Source: June 2002, http://www.whitehouse.gov/infocus/social-security/.

Social Security also reduces private savings to the extent that people expect to receive Social Security checks in the future. Workers substitute the government's promises for their own savings. Moreover, because the Social Security tax reduces take-home pay, current workers have less money that could be saved. The reduction in the national saving rate because of Social Security means there is less money for investment, and thus less economic growth, as will be discussed in the next chapter. The result is that, when current workers retire, the economic capacity of the country to support them will be smaller than if Social Security never existed in the first place.

For the Social Security trust fund to represent real savings, it must generate real capital that will increase the country's production possibilities in years to come. This could come about either directly through investment in capital or indirectly through a pay-down in other government debt. If tax inflows into Social Security are greater than the payment outflows, the surplus that is used to buy federal bonds could in turn be used by the Treasury to buy back its other bonds and thereby reduce the national debt. A lower national debt would reduce the crowding-out effect and make room for greater private investment that increases the economy's productive capacity. When Social Security reaches a point where it must cash in its government bonds and draw down its trust fund, the federal government could then increase federal debt once more. In the interim, though, the economy would have grown to be better able to support that debt. That is the ideal situation, but one that is politically difficult to implement. Instead, we are faced with a continuing Social Security budget surplus that is more than used up by other government spending. As a result we see an overall federal deficit that is projected to continue.

Rather than use the trust fund to pay down other government debt, the federal government might directly invest the Social Security trust fund in the production of real capital. It could take one of two routes:

- The **government could produce the necessary capital itself.** Government production may be justified to the extent that the needed investment applies to the provision of public goods, such as highway infrastructure needed for smoothly flowing traffic. Beyond this, however, direct government investment would lead the economy in the direction of command and control.
- The **government could invest the money in the marketplace, perhaps establishing or designating mutual funds to buy stock in private companies.**

In either case, the danger is that the investments would move the economy toward inefficient central planning and be allocated to firms based on politics rather than economic merit.

The amounts in question are not inconsequential. For the Social Security trust fund to be **fully funded**—able to pay off all its future obligations without recourse to future taxation—it would need to own well over a year's worth of GDP. In other words, the buildup of savings in the Social Security trust fund would need to greatly expand the country's current productive capacity for that savings to be real in a macroeconomic sense. Having the government take over such a large part of the economy's ownership of capital would not be capitalism as we know it in the United States.

fully funded the idea of having enough revenue in the Social Security trust fund to be able to pay off all obligations to current workers without recourse to taxing future workers.

SUPPLEMENTING SOCIAL SECURITY

individual retirement accounts (IRAs) tax-free savings accounts earmarked for retirement income.

Individuals do save for their own retirement. **Individual retirement accounts (IRAs)** promote that saving by allowing a limited amount of tax-free or tax-prepaid contributions, the latter termed *Roth IRA*. The contribution limit in 2002 is $3,000, which is scheduled to rise to $4,000 in 2005. The government has been reluctant to increase that limit very much, because any increase in tax-free savings would deplete current tax revenues. The government has also been content to accumulate bonds in the Social Security trust fund, because the special Social Security bonds that the Social Security Trustees buy from the Federal Treasury mean that any extra money collected by Social Security taxes are transferred into general government revenues that can be spent wherever the government chooses.

If the government wants to promote private saving, its options include:

- Increasing or eliminating the contribution cap on IRAs.
- Eliminating the taxation of income that is saved.
- Requiring that individuals save some fraction of their earnings for their own retirement.

QUICKCHECK

Most people consider investing in government bonds to be very secure. Yet, the Social Security trust fund's investment in government bonds is a source of insecurity. Explain.

Answer: At a personal, microeconomic level, government bonds are very secure because they are backed by the full faith and credit of the government. They will be repaid. When it comes to the macroeconomy, however, the bonds do not represent real savings because they are just IOUs that must be repaid by future taxpayers. They do not add to the productive capacity of the economy directly.

The third option has led to proposals for **Personal Security Accounts,** which would be financed by a payroll tax but be under the individual's own control and ownership. **Personal Security Accounts could only supplement, not replace, Social Security as it now stands,** for three reasons:

Personal Security Accounts
savings accounts individuals own, but that they are forced to contribute to by the government.

- **Social Security depends on current workers to support current retirees.** With Personal Security Accounts, workers are saving to support themselves.
- **Social Security redistributes income from wealthier workers to poorer ones.** With Personal Security Accounts, workers keep their own savings.
- **Personal Security Accounts are riskier, with workers making their own investment choices.** They would still need a Social Security fallback in case their personal investment choices lose their value.

While politically contentious, proposals for Personal Security Accounts have been looked on favorably by American presidents of both political parties. President Bill Clinton even included the idea in his 1999 State of the Union address. Workers who get to keep control of their own savings might be more inclined to accept the double tax of paying for current retirees and also building up savings for their own retirement. Such an approach has the economic advantage of maintaining a free-market allocation of investment. Companies that offer mutual funds and other forms of investment would compete for savings, and the winners would be those companies that offer the best services and investments.

11.3 TAX REFORM

The debate over Social Security taxes is a microcosm of the debate over taxes in general. It seems like nearly every year there is a move afoot to reform our taxes. Perhaps this is because taxes are always a compromise. Those who pay want to pay less. Those on the receiving end want to receive more. Within the give and take of the political process, though, the economic goals of efficiency and equity are treated with considerable respect by legislators interested in the country's prosperity.

A tax is efficient only if it does not *distort* relative prices within the economy, since price signals are what allocate resources to their highest-valued uses. By taxing all income equally, distortions are minimized. Efficiency thus calls for a *broadly based tax,* meaning one that it is difficult to escape, where the **tax base** refers to that which is taxed. **It is less disruptive to the workings of the economy to tax as wide a spectrum of income or consumption as possible at a low rate, rather than to single out a few things for especially high rates of taxation.** By spreading taxes broadly, people have few ways to escape them and not as much incentive to try; inefficient changes in behavior are kept to a minimum. Much of the complexity of the current income tax code stems from innumerable provisions that remove income from taxation, thus narrowing the tax base.

tax base that which is taxed.

IMPROVING THE INCOME TAX

The ability-to-pay principle of equity suggests that some income should be taxed more than other income, depending on how needy the person is. Exempting low incomes concentrates the tax base and leads to inefficiencies. Thus, the personal income tax is a compromise between efficiency and equity. Unfortunately, the compromise accomplishes neither goal fully and is also complicated.

Even the concept of income is not altogether easy to pin down, since income is more than money. For example, if you drill a water well in your backyard and inadvertently strike oil, your wealth spikes upward. That change in wealth is income, even if you do not sell any of that newly discovered oil until next year or beyond. A **comprehensive measure of income** would subtract a person's wealth at the beginning of the year from wealth at the end of the year, and then add back in the person's consumption during the course of that year. Consumption is added because it represents income that is spent.

The government does not use this comprehensive measure of income in computing the amount of personal income taxes to collect. It would be too complicated and intrusive for the government to attempt an assessment of how valuable each person's assets are at the end of each year. After all, assets include homes, cars, stocks, stamp collections, and much more. Moreover, even if the government could estimate these values, there is the problem of *liquidity*—of converting assets into cash. Liquidity is necessary to pay taxes. The federal government does not want to be responsible for kicking Grandma out of her house, just because property values around her have increased and she does not have the liquidity to pay the taxes on her rising comprehensive income.

The result is that the tax code looks at only a subset of comprehensive income: that which is liquid. If people sell their illiquid assets, they obtain liquidity and are subject to taxation on their *realized capital gains,* the increase in the value of assets between when they were bought and when they were sold. Even here, however, there are exceptions. For example, Grandma would fall under an exemption for the elderly, if she were to sell her house. Throughout the tax code, there is special treatment for special-interest groups. As you can see, even Grandma has a special-interest loophole.

So-called *loopholes* include the various exemptions, deductions, exclusions, and credits that complicate the tax code. Despite their notoriety, there are often economic principles behind these **tax expenditures,** so termed because they sacrifice tax dollars. The basis of tax expenditures frequently revolves around equity. For example, the concepts of vertical equity and horizontal equity are two ways to judge whether a tax meets the ability-to-pay principle.

Vertical equity concerns the proper tax burden for people of differing abilities to pay. It involves determining how *much* more someone with more ability to pay should in fact pay. That determination is not easy. For example, it seems vertically equitable for the top 10 percent of taxpayers ranked by income to pay more in federal taxes than any other percentile. However, is it vertically equitable to ask them to pay approximately twice as much as all other percentiles combined? That is in fact the situation in the United States when it comes to federal taxes. While the richest 10 percent might think it an undue burden for them to finance two-thirds of federal spending, the majority of voters do not appear to mind.

Horizontal equity, which suggests that people with equal means should pay equal taxes, is more straightforward. Yet, even ignoring differences in wealth, equal monetary incomes do not imply an equal ability to pay. Differences in the abilities to pay of households with identical incomes explain why there are tax exemptions for children, deductions for major medical expenses, and other features of the tax code that attempt to compensate for facets of life that hit some people harder than others.

There are many alternatives to the particular set of taxes chosen in the United States. For example, some have suggested that the United States should adjust its income tax to become a **consumed-income tax,** in which dollars that are saved would not be counted as income when the tax is applied. The consumed-income tax would remove the bias against saving that is present in a more general income tax, which taxes money when it is earned and also taxes interest on that money when it is saved. The flip side is that, although a consumed-income tax would promote savings, some people view it as a tax deduction for the rich and not for the poor, because the ability to save rises sharply with income.

QUICKCHECK

What is the difference between the ability-to-pay principle of taxation and vertical equity?

Answer: The ability-to-pay principle of taxation is that those who have a greater ability to pay should pay more taxes, but the principle does not say how much more. The idea of vertical equity requires an interpretation of the ability-to-pay principle, specifying how much more tax those with higher incomes should pay. There is no widespread agreement on what constitutes vertical equity, although there is widespread agreement that those with a greater ability to pay should in fact pay more taxes.

CONSUMPTION TAXES—FIRST CHOICE AROUND THE WORLD

Most of us are familiar with state or local *sales taxes* that collect a percentage of the prices consumers pay. Sales taxes are one form of **consumption tax,** which takes money as you spend it rather than as you earn it. This tax gives people a greater incentive to save, and may be partly responsible for the higher saving rates in other countries relative to the United States. Most countries of the world, including Canada and the countries of Europe and the Far East, rely much more heavily on consumption taxes as a source of public revenues than does the United States.

consumption tax a tax on spending rather than on income.

The most common form of consumption tax in other countries is the **value added tax (VAT).** A VAT collects the difference between what companies earn in revenues and previously taxed costs, which would mostly be the cost of material inputs. For example, the wheat farmer would pay a tax on the difference between revenues from the sale of the crop and the costs of fertilizer and other materials used to grow it. Taxing value added yields the same tax revenues as a retail sales tax set at the same rate, since the price of a final product is nothing more than the sum of the values added. Some advocate that the United States adopt the VAT as a means of promoting increased national saving. Others point out that it could help resolve trade disputes with Europe, which has complained that its industries must compete with tax-free U.S. exports. Two recent rulings from the World Trade Organization support that claim.

value added tax (VAT) a form of consumption tax that collects the difference between what companies earn in revenues and their previously taxed costs.

Just as with the income tax, value added taxes and sales taxes should be broadly based in order to achieve efficiency. Singling out some goods to tax while leaving others untaxed would distort choices away from the more highly taxed goods, since taxing sales in an industry shifts its supply curve, as shown in Figure 11-7. The tax will add an additional marginal cost of sales, which will shift the supply curve up by the percentage at which the tax rate is set. Tax revenues will equal the quantity of output multiplied by the amount of tax per unit, determined by the market equilibrium with the tax in place. The area of these tax revenues is labeled in the figure.

In Figure 11-7(a), the tax is assessed only on one good and not on substitutes for that good. In Figure 11-7(b), the tax is assessed on the same good and also on substitutes for the good. The difference is that demand will be steeper in (b), because consumers are unable to avoid the tax by buying untaxed substitutes for the good. The result is that the broadly based tax shown in (b) will be less distorting to consumer choice and therefore more efficient. It will also bring in more revenue because there is a greater quantity of output sold.

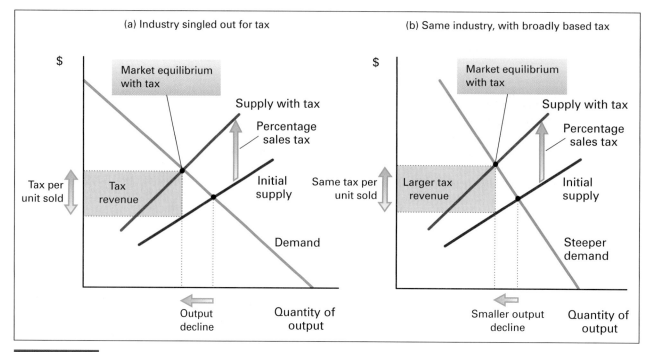

FIGURE 11-7

THE TAX BASE AND TAX REVENUE Taxes should usually be broadly based in order to be efficient. Graph (a) depicts an industry that is singled out for a sales tax. Supply in that industry is reduced, as the new supply curve appears higher by the amount of the sales tax percentage. The resulting equilibrium occurs at a new lower quantity and a higher price, inclusive of the tax. Tax revenue equals the tax per unit sold at the new market equilibrium multiplied by the new equilibrium quantity, as labeled by the shaded rectangle.

Graph (b) shows the exact same thing, with one difference: substitutes for the product are also taxed, which means that demand is steeper because consumers are less able to shift away from the taxed good. Therefore, the quantity purchased does not fall as much and tax revenue is consequently somewhat more. Because the broadly based tax causes less change in behavior, it is more efficient.

SNAPSHOT   **E-COMMERCE—A TAXING QUESTION**

Go to the store and pay sales tax; go on-line and skip it! Such has been the practice throughout the forty-seven states that impose sales taxes. To some it seems fair and reasonable. They say, "Let the Internet stay tax free!" To others, requiring shippers to pay sales tax for items shipped out of state is just too complex.

New taxes are never popular. Consumers enjoy buying tax-free items over the Internet, and do not take kindly to a tax that causes these items to cost more. Nonetheless, tax revenue must come from somewhere. Broadening the tax base by taxing e-commerce would allow lower sales tax rates overall without changing the amount that government collects in total. Maybe consumers just don't think that those tax cuts would happen!

As for complexity, modern database software should be able to handle it with ease. If a significant number of companies were required to charge taxes that varied from locality to locality and from state to state, you can bet that profit-seeking software makers would be eager to help out. So don't be too surprised to see a tax on e-commerce, even though nobody likes a tax. ◀

11.4 PAYING FOR HOMELAND SECURITY

Airplanes, buildings, oil pipelines, water supplies, nuclear power plants, letters in the mail—the list of potential terrorist targets is seemingly endless. Defending these points of vulnerability can potentially be accomplished in many different ways. Who is to pay for all these security measures?

Three possibilities suggest themselves:

1. **Use general tax revenues,** such as the $28 billion of financing budgeted in 2002 for the Office of the Homeland Security.
2. **Levy taxes on specific industries** for which the federal government provides security. For example, air travelers are assessed a surcharge to help defray the expenses of federally provided airport security. That approach is in keeping with the benefit principle of taxation, in which the beneficiaries of government spending are the ones who pay the taxes.
3. **Mandate that industries facing terrorist threats be responsible** for security, with any costs merely absorbed by the companies or passed along to their customers.

To gain perspective on which is the best alternative, consider the example of safeguarding air travel. To guard against the threat of bombs and hijackings, airline passengers are screened by means of federal marshals, surveillance equipment, X-ray machines, wands, and so forth. This screening is expensive and is a genuine cost of providing air transportation. If each airline company has to pay those costs on its own, the costs would be reflected in supply, just as would any other cost of doing business. To the extent that heightened concerns over security cause companies to increase spending on security, supply shifts to the left and the quantity of air travel decreases. This result is shown in Figure 11-8 as the movement from point 1 to point 2.

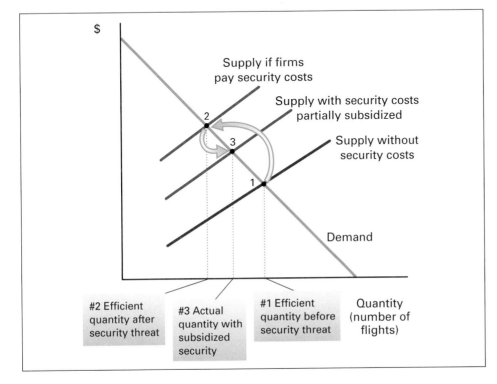

FIGURE 11-8

PAYING FOR SECURITY IN THE AIRLINE INDUSTRY The cost of protecting against security threats shifts the supply curve for the threatened industry to the left. The result is that the price of air travel increases and the number of flights decreases as the market equilibrium changes from point 1 to point 2. For example, the need to provide airport security increases the cost of air travel and shifts supply to the left as aging planes are not replaced and some airlines go out of business. The new equilibrium is associated with fewer flights and higher fares.

Government subsidies can offset some of these effects, such as shown by the equilibrium point 3. In the case of airlines, government has provided direct financial assistance to airlines and also provides a great deal of airport security. Only some of those subsidies are financed by a surcharge on passenger tickets.

USE OF SUBSIDIES AS AN OPTION

Alternatively, the federal government could give airlines *subsidies,* in which government picks up some of the cost of providing security. Figure 11-8 shows that when the government partially subsidizes increased security spending, it achieves the output given by point 3, which is greater than if firms are forced to pay all of the costs themselves, but less than if there was no security threat. The reason is that the leftward shift in supply as a result of increased security needs is partially offset by a rightward shift in supply as firms are able to obtain government money to pay for some of that added security. If government were to provide the security itself, or if subsidies to firms in the industry were to cover the entire cost of security, there would be no shift in supply. In that case, price and output would remain unchanged.

Comparing the alternative approaches requires us to specify our goals. The two most fundamental goals in economics are efficiency and equity, both of which might come into play in considering the best policy. Meeting the goal of efficiency requires that each good be produced only up to the point for which its marginal benefit equals its marginal cost. As discussed in Chapter 4, the market accomplishes this mission to the extent that the intersection of demand and supply is also the intersection of marginal benefit and marginal cost. However, **if the costs of necessary security measures are paid for by government subsidies, the market supply will no longer represent the complete marginal cost**. Instead, the output will be greater than the efficient quantity and the price will be lower than the price that achieves efficiency.

When the government gets directly involved in providing security, such as with screening mail for anthrax or checking airline passengers for weapons, the same principles of market pricing apply. With the mail, screening costs are reflected in the postage we pay. With airline security, the government adds a security charge of $2.50 to each passenger's ticket. Both of these practices are consistent with market efficiency.

Government action and taxation cannot replace the marketplace in one element of efficiency, however. In particular, the government lacks competition to ensure that its actions are technologically efficient. For this reason, for example, we have little way of knowing if the anthrax screening procedures used by the United States Postal Service are the most cost-effective. Likewise, there might be alternative combinations of equipment, personnel, and passenger waiting times that could achieve an equal amount of airport security, combinations that the government has little incentive to optimize. These possible inefficiencies represent a cost of government actions, not a definitive reason against taking those actions.

The upshot of this discussion is that when government does take action, efficiency suggests that it should tailor its practices as closely as possible to those of the marketplace. Rather than just using general tax revenues to provide government services, the implementation of user fees tailors price adjustments from industry to industry to match the costs of increased security in the various industries.

Politics does not always ensure that user charges are assessed in the right amount or even assessed at all, in which case, distortions can occur in the pattern of economic activity away from what is efficient. In particular, if the costs to government of providing security are not reimbursed by user fees, the result is a subsidy to the industries government is protecting. This subsidy comes from general tax revenue, which reduces the amount of income taxpayers have to spend throughout the rest of the economy. When incomes are reduced by the taxes that pay for security, the demand for many goods and services will decrease, such as shown in Figure 11-9. For those industries, output is reduced.

The myriad of new security measures to safeguard against terrorism have costs that cannot be avoided. Whether it be taxpayers or customers, someone will pay. Economic

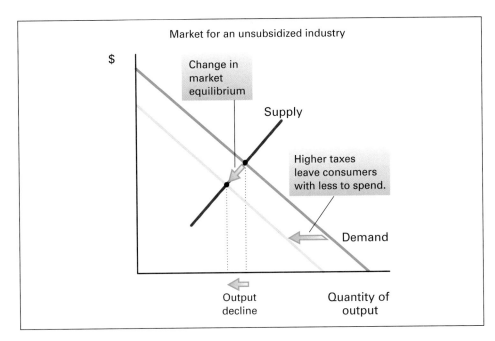

Market for an unsubsidized industry

Change in market equilibrium

Supply

Higher taxes leave consumers with less to spend.

Demand

Output decline

Quantity of output

$

FIGURE 11-9

THE HIDDEN COST OF SUBSIDIES
When the economy is at full employment, subsidizing some industries hurts other industries. When government uses tax dollars to pay the subsidies, it reduces demand for the various unsubsidized goods and services by reducing the after-tax income consumers have available to spend. The result is that output shrinks in the unsubsidized portion of the economy.

analysis can provide guidance to policymakers on how to design taxes in an efficient manner. Whether policymakers follow this advice is of course up to them.

*𝒯*HINKING
*𝒞*RITICALLY

1. How much security would the airline industry have to provide to ensure that you would travel as much as before the terrorist attacks? What is the maximum user fee for security you would be willing to pay to secure your safety when you travel by airplane?

2. How much individual liberty would you be willing to give up to increase the odds against other terrorist attacks such as those that occurred on September 11, 2001? For example, do you favor racial profiling that targets individuals with a particular appearance? Explain how the loss of individual liberty represents a cost to society of terrorism.

Visit www.prenhall.com/ayers for updates and web exercises on this Explore & Apply topic.

SUMMARY AND LEARNING OBJECTIVES

1. **List the major sources of revenue for government in the United States.**
   - Taxes are used by government to pay the costs of providing public goods. Taxes also finance income redistribution through the provision of transfer payments. Safety-net programs that provide economic security transfer tax dollars to those in need. Welfare and unemployment compensation are examples.
   - Two goals for taxes are equity and efficiency. Tax equity is about fairness. The goal of efficiency in taxation is to

maintain incentives for people to be productive. To raise revenue efficiently, a tax should be designed to change people's behavior the least.
   - A marginal tax rate is different from an average tax rate. A marginal tax rate states the percent of additional income that is collected in taxes. An average tax rate states the percent of total income that is taken in taxes.
   - Taxes take about 30 percent of GDP. The personal income tax raises the largest share of the federal government's revenue. Federal personal income tax rates

start at 10 percent for people with very low taxable incomes and increase to 15 percent, 27 percent, 30 percent, 35 percent, and 38.6 percent as incomes rise. This series of tax rates provides an example of marginal tax rates, since each of these rates applies to increments of income.

■ The federal government also collects Social Security taxes, including a Medicare hospitalization tax. There is also a corporate income tax that takes about 30 percent of corporate profits.

■ Tax incidence refers to who ultimately pays a tax. In the case of the corporate income tax, the tax ultimately reduces the income of shareholders.

■ State and local governments also collect taxes. States' individual income taxes, sales taxes, and revenues from the federal government make up most of the revenues states receive. Local governments tend to rely on property taxes and sales taxes for their revenues.

2. Explain the principles of tax equity and how they apply.

■ The two fundamental principles of tax equity are the benefit principle and the ability-to-pay principle. The benefit principle provides the justification for earmarked taxes, such as the gasoline tax. It suggests that those who pay a tax should be the same as those who receive benefits from how that tax revenue is spent. The benefit principle cannot apply to redistributional programs, since the point of those programs is to provide assistance from taxpayers to the needy.

■ The ability-to-pay principle states that those with more ability to pay taxes should actually pay more taxes. The federal income tax is modeled according to this principle, applying it with the further concepts of horizontal and vertical equity.

■ Horizontal equity adjusts income to reflect a person's special circumstances, such as if the person has high medical bills or a family to support. The idea is that people who are equally well off before paying taxes should be equally well off after paying taxes. Vertical equity attempts to pin down how much more people with a greater ability to pay should indeed pay.

3. Interpret why the U.S. income tax is structured as it is, and why critics suggest changing it.

■ A tax may be progressive, regressive, or proportional. A progressive tax collects a larger fraction of income as income increases. The federal income tax is progressive since the marginal tax rate rises as a person's income reaches a threshold level. For example, the income tax starts at 10 percent for low-income indi-

viduals and rises to 38.6 percent for those with relatively high incomes.

■ A regressive tax collects a smaller fraction of income as income increases. For example, a tax that collects $1,000 from a person earning $10,000 and $10,000 from a person earning $1,000,000 is regressive since the first person pays 10 percent of his or her income toward the tax, while the second person pays only 1 percent of income toward the tax.

■ A proportional tax collects the same fraction of income as income changes. If the person earning $1,000,000 in the previous example paid $100,000 in taxes, the same 10 percent as the low-income person, then the tax would be proportional.

■ A flat tax applies a single tax rate to all income. Thus, a flat tax is an example of a proportional tax. While the tax rate is the same for all taxpayers, recognize that people with higher incomes still pay higher taxes. A flat tax, if enacted, would be transparent (meaning easily monitored). In reality, any flat tax likely to be enacted would involve exempting low incomes.

■ It can be difficult to tell whether a tax is progressive, regressive, or proportional. Depending on whether Social Security benefits are included with the tax, Social Security can be viewed as representing a progressive, regressive, or proportional tax.

■ In pursuing the twin goals of equity and efficiency in the tax system, there are tradeoffs. More equity can mean less efficiency, and vice versa. In the pursuit of equity, government programs provide cash and in-kind benefits.

■ An efficient tax does not distort relative prices within a country. Efficiency calls for a broadly based tax that virtually everyone must pay.

4. Show why workers pay more Social Security tax than they see withdrawn on their pay stubs.

■ The Social Security tax is the second-largest source of federal revenue. Both employees and employers contribute toward Social Security taxes, each paying 7.65 of a worker's gross pay to the federal government, for a total of 15.3 percent. The burden of employers' contributions is shifted to workers in the form of lower worker pay. Thus, the ultimate incidence of the Social Security tax is on workers because the market wage rate declines by the amount of the employer's share of the tax.

■ The Social Security system is a pay-as-you-go system, with current workers paying for the benefits received by current retirees. It is predicted that the system will run out of money in the relatively near future.

Individual retirement accounts promote saving for retirement. Personal Security Accounts, although politically contentious, might supplement Social Security if enacted into law.

5. **Justify the use of consumption taxes, including the value added taxes of Canada and Europe.**
   - A consumption tax takes revenue for the government as people spend their money rather than as they receive income. Sales taxes are one form of a consumption tax. Many countries impose a consumption tax called a value added tax (VAT). As its name suggests, the VAT taxes value added, which is the difference between a firm's previously taxed costs and its

revenues. A VAT will yield the same tax revenue as a sales tax set at the same percentage.
   - Whatever taxes are imposed, a broader tax base, associated with eliminating tax "loopholes," combined with lower tax rates can reduce possibilities for inefficient behavior brought about by efforts to avoid taxes.

6. **Discuss issues of market efficiency and tax equity as they relate to security costs.**
   - The terrorist threat imposes additional costs on firms in specific industries, such as the airline and pipeline industries. These costs could be paid for by government subsidies to firms. Subsidies often run counter to market efficiency.

KEY TERMS

transfer payments, 250
marginal tax rate, 250
tax incidence, 251
benefit principle, 254
ability-to-pay principle, 254
progressive tax, 254
regressive tax, 254
proportional tax, 254

in-kind benefits, 255
pay-as-you-go, 256
Social Security trust fund, 258
fully funded, 260
individual retirement accounts
   (IRAs), 260
Personal Security Accounts, 261
tax base, 261

comprehensive measure of
   income, 262
tax expenditures, 262
vertical equity, 262
horizontal equity, 262
consumed-income tax, 262
consumption tax, 263
value added tax (VAT), 263

TEST YOURSELF

TRUE OR FALSE

1. The tax rate on incremental income is called the marginal tax rate.
2. Broadening the tax base is a very inefficient way to raise revenues.
3. Tax shifting refers to people being able to delay paying taxes until after April 15.
4. A progressive tax is any tax that takes more money from the rich than from the poor.
5. A flat tax collects the same number of dollars from everybody.

MULTIPLE CHOICE

6. An average tax rate is
   a. additional taxes owed as a percentage of additional income.
   b. total taxes owed.
   c. total taxes owed as a percentage of total income.
   d. the percentage of income not collected in taxes.

7. The corporate income tax takes about _____ percent of corporate profits.
   a. 10
   b. 20
   c. 30
   d. 50
8. The two most important sources of revenue for local governments are sales taxes and
   a. personal income taxes.
   b. corporate income taxes.
   c. Social Security taxes.
   d. property taxes.
9. A value added tax is an example of a
   a. property tax.
   b. Social Security tax.
   c. income tax.
   d. consumption tax.

10. The benefit principle and the ability-to-pay principle refer to
    a. whether a tax is progressive or regressive.
    b. principles of tax efficiency.
    c. principles of tax equity.
    d. legal principles that question the constitutionality of Social Security.

11. The gasoline tax
    a. is used to fund various government programs.
    b. is the best example of a progressive tax.
    c. seems to satisfy the ability-to-pay principle.
    d. reflects the benefit principle, since those who pay the tax tend to receive the benefits.

12. If a tax collects 5 percent of the income of those making less than $100,000 and 10 percent of the income of those making $100,000 or more, then the tax is
    a. progressive.
    b. regressive.
    c. proportional.
    d. flat.

13. If a tax collects $1,000 per person, no matter what a person's income might be, then the tax is
    a. a head tax, which is regressive.
    b. progressive.
    c. a user fee.
    d. proportional.

14. Efficiency in taxation
    a. is less important than equity in taxation.
    b. is best exemplified by the progressivity of the income tax.
    c. is increased when a tax is also more equitable.
    d. often involves a tradeoff with equity.

15. An efficient tax
    a. distorts relative prices.
    b. changes peoples' behaviors.
    c. is paid entirely by employers.
    d. may not be equitable.

16. When added together, the employer share and the employee share of the Social Security tax total just over _____ percent of an individual's wages.
    a. 5
    b. 10
    c. 15
    d. 24

17. Personal security accounts would be financed by
    a. employers.
    b. government.
    c. individuals.
    d. small- to medium-sized firms, but not large corporations.

18. Savings in the Social Security system consist of
    a. IOUs.
    b. shares of stock.
    c. mostly hundred-dollar bills.
    d. gold.

19. Which statement best exemplifies horizontal equity?
    a. Poor people should pay less in taxes than rich people.
    b. Taxes should be based on a person's age instead of income.
    c. The income tax should be replaced by a sales tax.
    d. People with equal incomes after deducting for special circumstances should pay the same amount in taxes.

20. Self-Test Figure 11-1 is most likely to represent which of the following?
    a. A subsidized industry.
    b. An unsubsidized industry, when other industries receive significant subsidies.
    c. An unsubsidized industry, when other industries likewise receive no subsidies.
    d. An industry that subsidizes its customers.

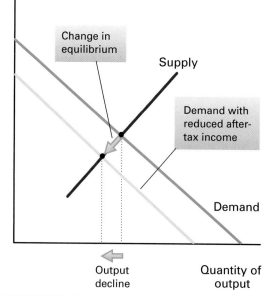

SELF-TEST FIGURE 11-1

QUESTIONS AND PROBLEMS

1. *[tax revenues]* Without looking at the pie charts in the text, draw a pie chart showing sources of federal revenue. Slice the pie you draw in order to show the relative importance of each source of revenue. After you finish your drawing, compare it to the pie chart in the text and make any corrections needed to your drawing.

2. *[tax revenues]* Repeat the first exercise, but this time show sources of state and local revenue.

3. *[marginal tax rate]* If Sam earns $100,000 a year and pays $10,000 in income taxes, can you determine his marginal tax rate? Explain.

4. *[average tax rate]* If Sue earns $100,000 a year and pays $10,000 in income taxes, can you determine her average tax rate? Explain.

5. *[tax base]* What is the tax base? Why is it efficient to lower tax rates while broadening the tax base? Explain.

6. *[tax equity]* Most people want taxes to be fair. Yet there are strong disagreements over what constitutes tax equity. Using an example and the concepts of equity discussed in this chapter, explain why such disagreement can reasonably persist.

7. *[tax equity]* Which principle of tax equity, the benefit principle or the ability-to-pay principle, is in closest agreement with your own personal idea of what is fair? Explain.

8. *[progressive versus regressive]* Suppose that you have been chosen by the president of your college or university to design a tax system that would tax students at your school in order to provide funding for student athletics. You will be allowed to impose a tax on one of the following: tickets to school football games, soft drinks from vending machines on campus, or textbooks sold from your campus book store. Evaluate each alternative within the context of equity, efficiency, and whether the tax you choose would be regressive or progressive.

9. *[flat tax]* On balance, do you think it is a good idea to adopt a flat tax? If such a tax is adopted, how much income should be exempted? Explain your reasoning.

10. *[payroll tax]* Is the term payroll tax another way of referring to the income tax? Explain.

11. *[Social Security tax]* Using a graph and labeling the axes, curves, and all relevant information, demonstrate how employees wind up paying the employer portion of Social Security taxes.

12. *[taxes and incentives]* Why is it difficult to design aid to the poor that provides work incentives? Explain with reference to cost and the level of the safety net.

13. *[tax reform]* Income taxes provide the government with information about your earnings. Information from tax returns has been used to convict bootleggers, narcotics smugglers, and others with large unreported incomes of tax law violations, even when the government could not prove that their income was obtained illegally. Some supporters of tax reform would prefer to abandon the income tax altogether and replace it with a value added tax or other tax that leaves no paperwork trail and keeps individuals' affairs out of the eyes of government. Do you think the information contained in income tax returns should be used by the government in prosecuting crime? Should we fear that the government will go overboard and misuse tax information to infringe on civil liberties? Explain.

14. *[tax reform]* Distinguish between horizontal and vertical equity. How do these concepts relate to the issue of tax reform?

15. *[consumption tax]* Do governments in the United States impose a consumption tax? If so, what is the most common type? Do governments in other countries impose a consumption tax? If so, what is the most common type?

 Visit www.prenhall.com/ayers for Exploring the Web exercises and additional self-test quizzes.

CHAPTER

ECONOMIC GROWTH

A LOOK AHEAD

Packets of electronic data surge from your keystrokes or from your voice. Instantly, you and your co-worker can see the results on your computer screen, hear the results with your headset, or both. It does not matter if your colleague is in New Jersey or New Guinea—the computers and networks of today are found all around the globe. It seems that the possibilities for collaborating on business projects have been expanding at light speed. In reality, today's fiber-optic transmission lines really *do* transfer data packets at the speed of light. Along with new possibilities for interacting and sharing comes new productivity and a *new economy*, the topic of this chapter's Explore & Apply section.

The technology and capital for economic growth do not appear by magic, however. Economies produce them, and produce more and better types if the right incentives are in place. Growth like this offers the only means to maintain or improve living standards in the face of an expanding population. In this chapter, we focus on the incentives for economic growth, and ways to adjust public policies to make those incentives stronger.

LEARNING OBJECTIVES

Understanding Chapter 12 will enable you to:
1. **Identify the sources of economic growth.**
2. **Describe the role of saving and investment in the process of capital formation.**
3. **Analyze how taxation affects both saving and investment activity.**
4. **Provide justification for subsidized higher education.**
5. **Summarize new growth theory and supply-side economics.**
6. **Discuss the key role of labor productivity in economic growth.**

Explore & Apply

economic growth the change in real GDP over time.

In Chapter 11, we saw that government tax and spending policies could change incentives, such as the incentives to work, to save, and to acquire human capital. In turn, these changes affect **economic growth,** which is usually measured by the change in real GDP over time. (Sometimes a real GNP measure is used, instead.)

Economies turn resources into outputs of greater value. The possibilities for doing so expand over time as the economy develops new technologies and acquires new resources. In other words, the economy's possibilities for production increase, which is why Chapter 2 showed economic growth to be an outward shift in the production possibilities frontier. This chapter examines the process more closely to see how the rate of economic growth might be improved. If the growth is in per-capita real GDP, a country can look forward to a better standard of living for its people.

12.1 THE SEEDS OF GROWTH

Economic growth does not just happen. It takes a combination of resources and technology, along with a policy environment to nurture that combination. These are the matters to which we now turn.

SOURCES OF GROWTH—LABOR, TECHNOLOGY, CAPITAL FORMATION, AND ENTREPRENEURSHIP

The U.S. economy has probably been studied more extensively than the economy of any other country. Evidence from the United States reveals quite a bit about what factors are important to growth, as the United States has a history of increasing real GDP. Table 12-1 summarizes U.S. economic growth according to the terms of office of recent presidents.

From 1947 to 1973, the average real GDP growth rate averaged around 4 percent. Real GDP growth diminished in the 1970s to under 3 percent during the Carter administration. GDP growth picked up steam a couple of years into the Reagan administration to give an annual growth rate average over Reagan's eight years of 3.5 percent. It then stumbled again to less than 2 percent in the following four years under George Bush. Growth was picking up in the final months of the first Bush administration to average a bit under 4 percent in the

TABLE 12-1   ANNUALIZED GROWTH RATES BY PRESIDENCY

PRESIDENCY	YEARS	GROWTH RATE
Kennedy–Johnson	1961–1968	4.9
Nixon–Ford	1969–1976	3.0
Carter	1977–1980	2.7
Reagan	1981–1988	3.5
Bush I	1989–1992	1.7
Clinton	1993–1999	3.7
Bush II	2001–2002(I)	2.5

Source: BEA's NIPA Revision, Released 3–30–2000. Clinton and Bush II growth rates were computed by the authors from NIPA annual growth rates. Bush's rate is current through the first quarter of 2002.

eight years of the Clinton administration. Shortly before Clinton left office, growth slowed and recession took hold in President George W. Bush's first year in office.

While growth is stated above in terms of presidential administrations, growth is not directed from the top down. It is also sometimes hard to know what the economy's growth rate is at any given point in time, because it takes time to compile the data used to report GDP. This lag can have political repercussions. For example, following the election of President Bill Clinton in 1992, it was widely speculated that President Bush would have instead been re-elected if only voters had recognized the then-occurring economic recovery just a little sooner.

Most U.S. economic growth is attributable to increases in labor and capital, as well as technological change. Both technological change and additional capital increase **labor productivity,** which is output per hour worked. Although there is still some question as to why U.S. economic growth began turning upward in the mid-1990s, many analysts believe that technological change, embodied in the personal computer and the Internet, played a significant role. In turn, technological change increased labor productivity. Increases in labor productivity mean that more GDP is produced for each hour worked by the labor force. Figure 12-1 shows the change in labor productivity in the United States since 1959.

labor productivity output per hour worked.

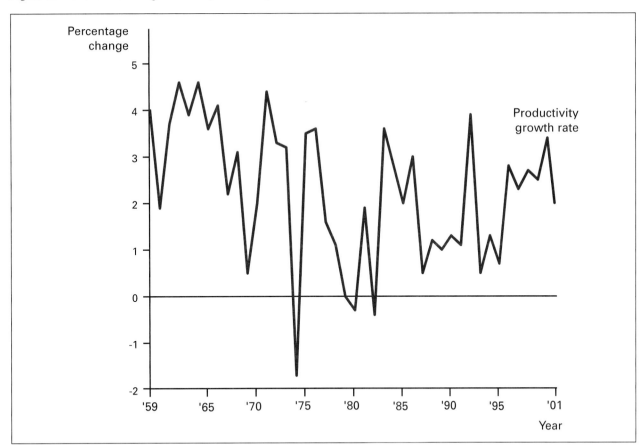

FIGURE 12-1

THE ANNUAL CHANGE IN LABOR PRODUCTIVITY Labor productivity rises and falls as additional capital is made available to workers. Technological change can also contribute to a rise in labor productivity as better equipment on the job makes labor more productive. The business cycle also affects labor productivity, with productivity typically falling in the early part of a recession, and rising as the economy later pulls out of the recession. Government regulations also affect labor productivity.

Source: 2002 Economic Report of the President, Table B-50, and Bureau of Labor Statistics. The data represent output per hour of all persons in the business sector.

The figure makes clear that labor productivity does not necessarily increase each year. Why does the growth rate in productivity decrease in some years, and even fall in others? One important factor is economic slowdowns. When the economy slows down, or enters a recession, labor productivity tends to fall at first because businesses decrease the production of goods and services in response to reduced aggregate demand. However, they also try to retain their workers in order to avoid the costs of recruiting and training new workers when aggregate demand picks back up. Thus, less production, combined with the same amount of labor, must decrease labor productivity. Later, when a recession nears its end, production is at first increased without a corresponding increase in labor employed. Labor productivity rises at that point in the business cycle.

capital formation the creation of new capital.

Labor productivity is associated with how much capital—both physical capital and human capital—labor has at its disposal. The labor productivity statistics suggest correctly that the United States has been quite successful at accumulating capital. The creation of new capital is termed **capital formation.** Capital formation requires initiative, since producing capital requires that people identify what additional outputs need to be produced or technologies should be employed. In market economies, entrepreneurs make these choices based on their best judgments of what is most profitable, meaning of most value to both consumers and producers. The struggle for profit weeds out entrepreneurs who do not make these choices well. Thus, one of the keys to capital formation is allowing this competitive search for profit. Where central planning is practiced, that key is lost. Thus, in Cuba, North Korea, and other economies in which government exercises too heavy a hand, the quantity and quality of capital formation is impaired. Figure 12-2 shows capital formation in the United States over time.

S N A P S H O T

THE ENTREPRENEURIAL ROAD TO RICHES—TAKING THE RISK AND SHARING THE REWARD

The odds of striking it rich as an entrepreneur may not be great—one in two hundred, they say—but the potential payoff does motivate people to try. If successful, the economy wins the products and the entrepreneurs gain a tidy profit.

Entrepreneurial success stories lie behind the companies we take for granted. Former economics major Sam Walton used the concept of one-stop shopping at everyday low prices to smash Wal-Mart's way to success, and in the process propel the Walton family to first place among America's wealthy. Bill Gates amassed his fortune by positioning Microsoft to provide the industry-standard interface for the personal computer. Talk on the phone? Craig McCaw said "take it with you," and took home $11.5 billion from his sale of McCaw Cellular Communications Corporation. Chat over coffee? Howard Shultze earned his fortune by opening Starbucks Coffee Company as a place to hang out over a steaming brew. FedEx your important papers? That was Fred Smith's idea. It was Domino's that delivered for Tom Monaghan, and Motown that recorded Berry Gordy's profit.

The common theme to the success stories of America's modern entrepreneurs is insight into what the public likes to do and how they could do it better or more conveniently. But it takes more. Without the risks inherent in trying to build companies from the ground up, there would be neither entrepreneurial success nor the economic growth that it engenders. ◄

QUICKCHECK

How can entrepreneurship increase labor productivity?

Answer: Entrepreneurship can add to productivity by organizing resources in better ways.

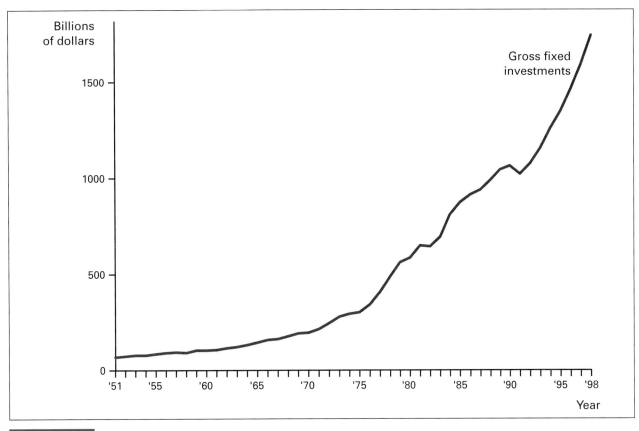

FIGURE 12-2

CAPITAL FORMATION Economic growth is associated with the creation of new capital, termed capital formation. Capital formation usually rises, but has dipped during recessions.

Source: National Income and Product Accounts, Table 5.16. The data are for gross fixed investment, and include both private and government investment.

NURTURING GROWTH—SAVING AND INVESTMENT

Capital formation requires investment, which can be coordinated centrally through government. For example, government ordinarily finances the construction of highways, because it would be very difficult for private investors to acquire rights of way or to charge for highway usage. Indeed, rebuilding highways, especially bridges on the U.S. interstate highway system, is thought to be one of the major investment needs in the United States today.

More typically, investment is a decentralized process that responds to supply and demand in the marketplace. Investors finance the capital formation that is necessary to take advantage of market opportunities. For example, investors who expect to profit from the sale of gum balls, livestock feeders, big-screen televisions, or any other product must first finance the capital necessary to produce that product. Firms invest when they wish to do any of the following:

- Expand their scale of operations
- Implement better production techniques
- Produce new goods that their old factories are ill-suited to manufacture

To acquire human capital, individuals invest in themselves. This investment includes the time and money it takes to attend college or otherwise acquire new skills.

Private investors have a strong personal incentive to invest wisely. Because their own resources are on the line, private investors can be relied on to investigate closely which products are likely to succeed and which are not. While no one can foresee the future with certainty, investors who judge the best are rewarded in the marketplace with additional funds for further investment.

saving putting aside income for later use.

Saving is when income is put aside for later use. Central to understanding the process of capital formation is the observation that **saving provides the funding for investment.** In general, the more saving, the more investment. Sometimes people invest their savings themselves, such as when they buy houses or stocks. Other times, savers deposit their money into financial intermediaries, such as banks and mutual funds, which then invest that money.

Savers look to investments for good returns without excessive risk. Without aiming to do so, **government reduces private saving and investment.** This reduction happens in two ways. First, **government taxes away income that might be saved.** Second, **government taxes the returns on investments,** thus making them less attractive. In contrast, **government also adds to investment** to the extent that it directly invests the tax revenues it receives. The government investment in highways is an example. So, too, are government investments in schools, the criminal justice system, and elsewhere in the economy. In turn, these investments are used in the private sector. For example, the production of gum balls, restaurant meals, family vacations, and innumerable other goods and services benefit from an efficient transportation system, educated workers, and the system of laws.

Without government, aggregate saving and investment would be equal. This equality would be true because money saved would either be directly invested or would find its way into investment through banks and other financial institutions. With government, the situation is more complicated because tax dollars can be directed toward government investment or government consumption purchases. Thus, the total amount saved plus the total amount taken in taxes must equal the sum of private investment, government investment, and government spending on consumption items. Lumping together private and government investment, and simply calling the sum investment, we have the following equality:

$$\text{Investment} + \text{Government consumption} = \text{Saving} + \text{Taxation}$$

or, equivalently,

$$\text{Investment} = \text{Saving} + \text{Taxation} - \text{Government consumption}$$

Some investment funds also come from abroad and, likewise, some saving becomes investment in other countries.

Investment is a current expense that is made in the expectation of receiving income in the future. When firms borrow to finance new investment, the expected future income must be sufficient to pay off the amount borrowed, plus interest. The amount of interest depends upon the interest rate. **Higher real interest rates raise the cost of investing.** Some investments that would be undertaken at low real interest rates will not be undertaken when those rates are high. This result causes the investment demand curve to slope downward, as shown in Figure 12-3.

The money for investment comes from saving. While people will save some money whether they are paid interest or not, in general the higher the interest rate, the greater the supply of saving. For this reason, the supply of saving curve is shown as upwardly sloping in Figure 12-3. There is only one point of equilibrium, which determines the actual interest rate. The market equilibrium equates the quantity of saving supplied to the quantity of investment demanded, as shown in the figure.

Investment is also affected by other factors, such as business confidence (which encompasses expectations about the future), current economic growth, and opportunities pre-

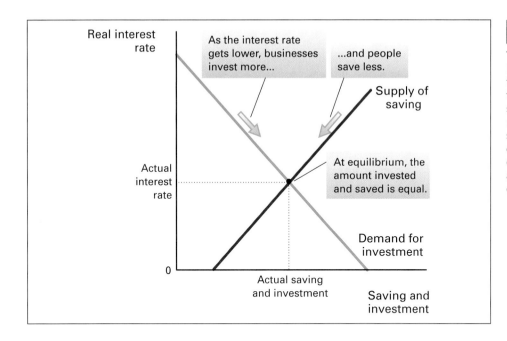

FIGURE 12-3

THE EQUILIBRIUM INTEREST RATE
Interest rates are determined in the marketplace by the intersection of investment demand and saving supply. This rate determines the quantity of actual saving and investment. The equilibrium will change if either demand or supply shifts, such as in response to changes in confidence about the future.

sented by technological change. Increases in any of these variables would shift the investment demand curve to the right. Decreases would shift it to the left.

Government fiscal policy can also shift investment demand. An expansionary fiscal policy can stymie the capital formation needed for economic growth. Specifically, when the government increases spending or cuts taxes in order to stimulate the economy, it often finances the difference with borrowing by selling government bonds to investors. However, **government borrowing is in competition with private sector borrowing, and thus can cause higher interest rates.** The resulting reduction in private investment spending is called the **crowding-out effect** of expansionary fiscal policy. In other words, the crowding-out effect represents money that would have gone to private sector investment, but instead goes to finance government borrowing. However, because so much goes on at once in the macroeconomy, it is difficult to interpret from investment data whether, and to what extent, the crowding-out effect actually occurs.

crowding-out effect when government borrowing attracts money that would otherwise have gone to private sector investment.

12.2 INFLUENCING GROWTH THROUGH PUBLIC POLICY

The world's economies represent a mix of markets and government, with government actions holding the potential to either help or hinder economic growth. Understanding the likely effects of public policies requires an understanding of the incentives facing prospective investors. The key elements are risk and return.

THE INVESTMENT DECISION—RISK AND RETURN

Success represents the 1 percent of your work that results from the 99 percent that is called failure.

                                                   —*Soichiro Honda, founder, Honda Motor Company*

Private investors do not know with certainty which products will sell and which will not. They accept some risk of failure, in the hopes of getting a return that compensates for that risk. There is always risk ex ante, meaning before the outcome is known. Investors assess

expected return the value of an investment if successful, multiplied by the probability of success; expressed as a percentage.

actual return the value an investment actually had, judged after the fact; expressed as a percentage.

the **expected return**—the value of the investment if successful, multiplied by the probability of success. The **actual return** can be viewed ex post, meaning after the fact. Ex post, an investment might have turned out fabulously, or it might have failed miserably.

As an example of the difference between expected return and actual return, consider movies. Some movies reap unexpected success at the box office and prove extremely profitable for their investors. In contrast, other movies, some with huge budgets and high expectations, are flops at the box office and lose enormous amounts of money for their investors.

The uncertain return on investment has important implications for public policy toward industry. Consider pharmaceuticals. The production cost of many cutting-edge drugs is very low, although their prices are often quite high. The high prices help pay for the many years of research and testing required to bring a successful drug to market. They also help pay for the many more drugs that failed to make it through the research and testing phase. In November 2002, Vice President Ferdinand Massari of Drugmaker Pharmacia put it this way, "For every new drug you see in the store, there are probably 10,000 that were tested and didn't make it!"

If prices for pharmaceutical drugs are held down by government regulation that aims to make drugs more affordable, less investment would occur in the pharmaceutical industry because there would be less expectation of profit. Investors would be less willing to accept the considerable risk of failure in the hope of only a modest profit from success. The result would be a slower pace of growth in that industry, leading to fewer new drugs. **Thus, the tradeoff is whether to make current drugs more affordable or to allow the quest for profit to lead to new and improved pharmaceuticals down the road.**

THE INCENTIVE EFFECTS OF TAXATION

In addition to regulation, taxes can also affect growth. For example, the United States personal income tax discourages saving behavior by taxing interest income earned on savings, but not taxing the alternative of current consumption. Figure 12-4 shows how a tax on saving increases the market interest rate and discourages investment. Savers face a lower return because of the tax, which makes them unwilling to save as much at each real interest rate. For this reason, taxing the return to saving shifts the supply of saving curve to the left,

FIGURE 12-4

EFFECT OF THE INCOME TAX The personal income tax requires savers to pay a tax on their interest incomes, which reduces people's willingness to save and shifts the supply of saving curve to the left. The result is a higher equilibrium interest rate and less actual saving and investment.

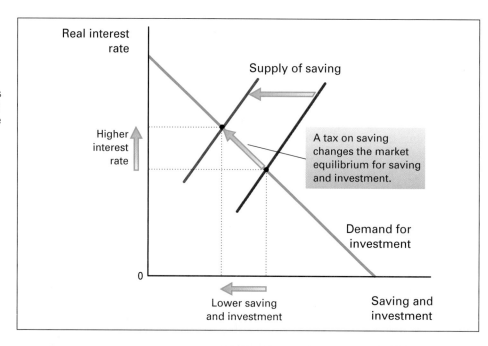

resulting in a higher equilibrium interest rate and less saving and investment. In this way, taxation of the return on saving discourages both saving and investment.

Because saving is so important to economic growth, there is concern over the low *personal saving rate* in the United States in recent years. Figure 12-5 illustrates the fluctuations in the percentage saved out of disposable personal income since 1929. In 2000 and 2001, the personal saving rate plunged to lows not seen since the Great Depression.

Investment is also discouraged by other taxes, such as the tax on capital gains. **Capital gains** represent the difference between the current market value of an investment and its purchase price. The **capital gains tax** takes a percentage of this difference when the investment is sold. Because investors know about the capital gains tax when making investment decisions, it too diminishes capital formation. The reduction in investment demand means that banks pay lower interest rates on savings. Likewise, individuals who invest directly in stocks or anything else subject to capital gains taxation also see their expected returns reduced. The upshot is that the capital gains tax leads to less saving and investment.

capital gains the difference between the current market value of an investment and its purchase price.

capital gains tax a tax on the capital gains from investments that are sold.

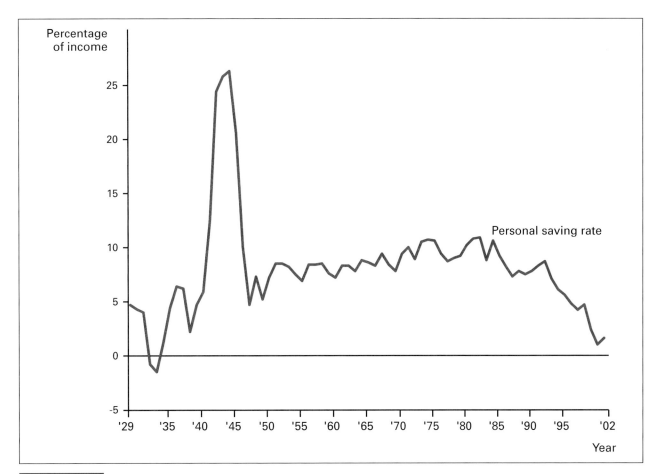

FIGURE 12-5

U.S. PERSONAL SAVING RATE The personal saving rate was low during the Great Depression because incomes were low. The personal saving rate soared during World War II because goods were rationed and people could not spend as much as they wished. In the 1990s, the personal saving rate fell as Americans consumed more and saved less.

Source: National Income and Product Account Tables. The personal saving rate equals personal saving as a percentage of disposable personal income.

> ## QUICKCHECK
>
> **Explain why the capital gains tax discourages investment.**
>
> **Answer:** Investors place their money at risk in the hope of seeing their investments grow. By taking a cut out of that expected return, the capital gains tax reduces the expected payoff and thus makes the investment less attractive.

SUBSIDIZING RESEARCH AND DEVELOPMENT

external benefit when some benefits are received by third parties who are not directly involved in the decision.

Even without the inhibiting effects of taxes and regulations, the private sector may not devote an efficient amount of financial capital toward increasing future productivity. This shortfall occurs when there are external benefits from investment in research and development (R&D). An **external benefit** occurs when some benefits are received by third parties who are not directly involved in a decision, such as the decision to research or invest. In effect, these third parties siphon off benefits that would otherwise have gone to the firms undertaking the R&D. The result is a lower expected benefit to investors, which is likely to reduce the amount of resources they devote to R&D.

research aimed at creating new products or otherwise expanding the frontiers of knowledge and technology.

development when technology is embodied into capital.

While often lumped together, there is a significant distinction between research and development. **Research** is aimed at creating new products or otherwise expanding the frontiers of knowledge and technology. **Development** occurs when that technology is embodied into capital or output. For example, research may be aimed at uncovering a superconducting material that allows electricity to flow unimpeded at ordinary temperatures. If the research is successful, many companies could then incorporate the advance in knowledge (research) to design their own products (development), such as transmission lines, electromagnets, or computers.

property rights rights of ownership.

External benefits are most prominent at the research stage, especially when the research involves the creation of knowledge that can be applied to the production of many different products, as in the example just given. It is difficult for any one investor or group of investors to assert ownership—**property rights**—over the range of applications that can arise from basic advances in knowledge. For this reason, given that the odds of achieving a significant knowledge breakthrough are quite small, private investors usually avoid investments in basic research.

To correct this market failure, and perhaps as a counterweight to the Federal tax code's general distortion against investment, the government subsidizes research. Sometimes the government funds research directly, such as cancer research at the National Institutes of Health. Sometimes subsidies are indirect, such as public support of universities that require faculty to conduct research along with their teaching. There is controversy over how generous these subsidies should be, however, since the diffusion of knowledge throughout the economy makes measuring the value of basic research practically impossible.

Much more controversy exists when government subsidizes development. For example, the U.S. Department of Energy funded a variety of alternative energy demonstration projects after the dramatic rise in world oil prices in 1973. However, most of the investments in windmills, solar energy, shale oil, and other forms of alternative energy were never commercially viable. Even gasoline blended with ethanol (alcohol made from corn) survives in the marketplace only because of ongoing government subsidies.

Such investments are examples of development rather than basic research. Development by one firm does give other firms ideas about what will be successful and what will not, and thus involves external benefits. However, this situation holds true for airline services, fast-food locations, new toys, and a host of other goods and services offered in the marketplace. Competitors learn from each others' successes and mistakes. Such minor external benefits pervade any market economy. It would be inefficient to single out some and not others.

QUICKCHECK

Explain why government subsidies are more likely to be justified in the case of research than for development.

Answer: In the research stage, there is less certainty of having a commercially viable product. Moreover, research can often be applied to many products. The result is external benefits that the researchers themselves might not capture. Thus, without government subsidies, there is likely to be too little research done. In the case of development, in contrast, profit is a much stronger motivation and government subsidies are less needed.

UNIVERSITIES—ADVANCING THE FRONTIERS OF KNOWLEDGE

SNAPSHOT

New ideas and information can confer significant external benefits, particularly if businesses can apply the knowledge to develop more valuable goods and services. The trouble is that the value of new ideas and information is often not known until they are produced, and then the applications could be in a variety of industries. Firms that engage in basic research might be unable to claim property rights to this growth in the knowledge base, since patent laws more effectively protect development than research. Firms that advance the knowledge base might even see competitors use that knowledge as well as, or better than, they do themselves.

So, where are advances in knowledge to come from? Often it is universities that are the sources. Government and academia both recognize the role of universities in engaging in valuable research that companies fear to undertake on their own. Government subsidies or grants often provide the funds that make it possible. ◄

12.3 PROPERTY RIGHTS AND NEW GROWTH THEORY

The prospect for business profits in the future can lead to research and development in the present. While not new in itself, this idea is a cornerstone of what is called **new growth theory.** New growth theory stresses the association between productivity growth over time and technological advances that are embodied in new capital. Since no one can know beforehand which lines of research will prove fruitful and which will fail, economies that handsomely reward productive ideas will grow the fastest. Productive ideas can include all sorts of things, including how to make wireless local computer networks, how to genetically engineer a disease-preventing potato, how to organize a firm, and any number of other thoughts.

new growth theory emphasizes the importance of new ideas in generating economic growth, and of intellectual property rights in providing the profit incentive to generate those ideas.

According to new growth theory, the ideas behind new technologies are promoted most effectively by allowing individuals to claim property rights, and the associated monopoly power, over ideas they have. *Monopoly power* is the idea that others can only imitate, but not duplicate your product. Profits associated with monopoly power provide the incentive to create even better ways of doing things. The idea that private property is the key to growth, however, is far from new.

New growth theory contrasts with mainstream prescriptions for growth in the decades following the Great Depression of the 1930s and World War II. The viewpoint at that time was that government was the centerpiece of economic development. This view of growth was consistent with the high degree of confidence in government that characterized that period in history. For example, the American public works projects and World War II itself were seen as instrumental in moving the economy from the ravages of depression to decades of peace and prosperity. Aid to Europe under the Marshall plan was also credited with getting that continent back on its feet. Confidence in the ability of government to direct the economy along a pathway of growth rose in the 1930s with the New Deal, and peaked during the period from the 1950s through the early 1970s.

Although new in contrast to the prevailing economic wisdom of that period, new growth theory actually taps into themes that have been central to economic analysis for centuries. For example, private property is central to Adam Smith's idea of the invisible hand of the marketplace, discussed in Chapter 1, which gives entrepreneurs an incentive to invest and grow the economy in their search for profit. Likewise, private property and the unfettered freedom to use it form a central theme of the *Austrian school* of economic thought, which got its start with the writings of Ludwig von Mises (1881–1973) in the early twentieth century. **Austrians emphasize that government rules and regulations that restrict the use of private property impede progress, which in von Mise's words, "is precisely that which the rules and regulations did not foresee."**

12.4 SUPPLY-SIDE POLICY

supply-side economists (supply siders) economists who emphasize incentives for productivity and economic growth, such as lower marginal tax rates and less regulation.

Those economists who particularly emphasize policies aimed at growth are called **supply-side economists,** or **supply siders** for short. Supply siders focus on increasing the value of what the economy can produce in the long run (the supply side), rather than on any desire to change consumers' spending behavior (the demand side). Supply siders figure that the short-run business cycle will sort itself out over time, and will lead to a larger economic pie in the long run if government does not intrude. This long-run, free-market orientation places supply siders squarely within the classical school of economic thought.

The objective of supply-side policy is to ensure that the output associated with full employment is as high as possible. Supply-side policies are designed to increase productivity, such as through increasing capital formation. The intended effect of such policies is to shift long-run aggregate supply to the right, as depicted in Figure 12-6.

FIGURE 12-6

GOAL OF SUPPLY SIDERS Supply-side economists seek to increase productivity, which would cause long-run aggregate supply to shift to the right. This increase would increase long-run per-capita GDP.

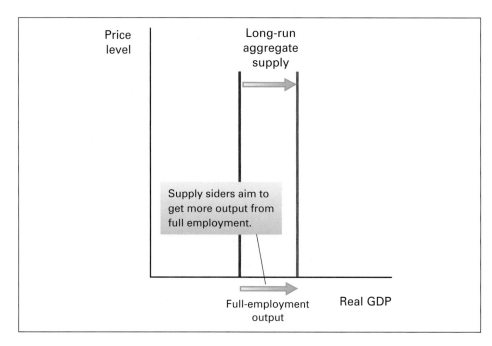

Full-employment output will change in response to changes in *structural features of the economy*, including resources and technology. Structural features also include government policies that change how workers and firms behave. Examples include unemployment compensation, minimum-wage laws, and other public policies that affect the natural rate of unemployment.

Supply siders are concerned with any government policies that might cut productivity or lead to structural unemployment. They look with suspicion at the work disincentives embedded in many safety-net programs, and at regulations that make it more costly for firms to hire and fire employees. They emphasize that regulations should be designed with an eye toward minimizing their impact on productivity.

Supply siders are most known for their focus on tax policies. They recommend keeping marginal tax rates low in order to leave a higher fraction of incremental earnings in the hands of individuals and investors. In this way, there is more incentive to invest and be productive. The result is a higher full-employment output. The reason is partly that there will be more work effort provided at the full-employment equilibrium in response to greater marginal rewards for that effort. Mostly, however, output will be greater because investors will have greater incentives to build up the economy's stock of physical and human capital, and thereby increase the productivity of its labor.

Because the concern of the supply siders is with the long run, they have little use for activist fiscal policies designed for short-run goals. **Supply siders often see an expansionary fiscal policy as an excuse for a greater government presence in the economy, and worry about the increased regulatory and tax burdens that presence may bring.**

Following the election of President Ronald Reagan, the U.S. Congress passed sweeping changes in the tax code. The 1982 tax changes adopted the supply-side agenda of cutting marginal tax rates in order to promote growth. Such growth was intended to provide greater prosperity in the future, as well as a greater tax base over time. Beginning in 1983, after the tax cuts took effect, and lasting through the end of that decade, the economy witnessed real economic growth every year along with an inflation rate that was much lower than in the preceding decade. The average growth rate from 1983 through the end of the Reagan presidency in 1988 was a very respectable 4.1 percent.

Because Congress did not curtail spending in line with its tax cuts, the federal government ran a large budget deficit in the 1980s. The budget deficit exceeded 6 percent of GDP in 1983, although it fell to just under 3 percent by 1989. The Reagan-era budget deficits look like Keynesian fiscal policy run amok, with the fiscal stimulus of a tax cut applied to marginal tax rates at the high end of the income spectrum, rather than to rates paid by those struggling to make a good life for themselves. **Critics thus refer to supply-side policies as *trickle-down economics*.** The term suggests that the policies intend to make the rich richer, so that they might spend a bit more and help the rest of us. **In fact, that is not the process that the supply siders have in mind.** Supply siders aim at productivity, not spending.

The U.S. economy grew in the 1980s after the tax cuts. The rich did indeed get disproportionately richer, at least in terms of the income they reported to the IRS. They also became more productive and paid more taxes. While the tax cuts of the 1980s reduced real federal tax revenues from most groups in the economy, the tax cuts greatly increased tax revenues from the highest income groups. The top 5 percent of income earners increased their share of total income tax payments from 36 percent in 1980 to 43 percent in 1990. Upward mobility also became more commonplace as a result of the lower tax rates. Looking at the lowest fifth of the income distribution in 1980, for example, 86 percent had advanced beyond that by 1988, with 16 percent even making it all the way to the top fifth of the income distribution.

FIGURE 12-7

THE LAFFER CURVE Increasing tax rates will increase tax revenues, but only up to a point. After that point, higher tax rates are self-defeating and actually reduce tax revenues. At a tax rate of 100 percent, there would be no personal incentive to earn any income at all.

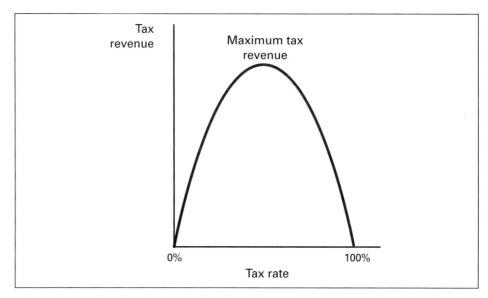

SNAPSHOT

ON THE BACK OF A NAPKIN

At a tax rate of zero percent, the government collects no revenue. It can increase revenues by increasing tax rates, but there are limits. After all, a tax rate of 100 percent would also generate no tax revenue—no one would bother to earn money if Uncle Sam took it all. Arthur Laffer, a young UCLA economist, discussed this at lunch one day in the 1970s. He sketched the hump-shaped relationship between tax rates and tax revenues on the back of his napkin. Ever since, as shown in Figure 12-7, that sketch has been called the *Laffer curve.*

Promoted by some of the supply siders, the Laffer curve proved to be a potent idea in the early 1980s. It surely would be nice if government could cut its tax rates and see both the economy and its tax revenues grow. Congress went on to cut tax rates in 1982, and—lo and behold—the economy grew and the rich wound up paying more taxes. They paid more taxes because economic growth meant there were more of them and they had more income.

Unfortunately, although overall federal tax revenues increased by $1.1 trillion in the 1980s, that was not enough to overtake government spending. The Laffer curve became a laughingstock among the I-told-you-so crowd. Yet, no one can dispute its logic. Perhaps, if the right tax is found to cut, the Laffer curve will rise to prominence once more. ◀

EXPLORE & APPLY

12.5 THE NEW ECONOMY—IS IT REAL?

We have entered a new era in which brains count for more than brawn.

—Royal Bank of Canada Newsletter

American prosperity seemed strong and enduring in the 1990s. The vitality of the economic boom indicated that the economy had changed in some fundamental way. The media needed a catch phrase that would describe what was happening and help define the decade for posterity. In this way, America's economy became the "new economy." That expression was soon on just about everyone's lips, symbolized by the wealth created in California's Silicon Valley. The fast-growing, entrepreneurial firms that dot Silicon Valley were a hallmark of the new economy. Today, the question is whether the new economy is still alive, or ever really was.

You may remember the old economy, with its emphasis on boring old industries, its recurring recessions and high unemployment, its inability to eliminate poverty, and its association with government budget deficits and a host of other ills. Contrast that mental picture to the new economy, which emphasizes the application of technology to raise living standards. The new economy is about high technology and its promise to revolutionize everyday life. From the spectacular special effects in the movie *Twister*, improved treatments for AIDS, and on-line auctions at e-Bay, the range of impacts associated with the new economy is wide.

How much about the new economy is ballyhoo? Consider that new economy centerpiece, the Internet. Over half of U.S. households are currently connected, and that number continues to grow. The Internet provides access to information and entertainment, and allows people to communicate instantly with each other. For buyers and sellers, the Internet provides opportunities to meet in cyberspace to transact business. The problems and failures associated with the Internet are often glossed over, however, when these benefits are raised in conversation. Try as we might to prevent them, problems like crippling new yet-to-be-named viruses threaten millions of computers. Hackers are another problem, able to penetrate allegedly secure web connections and steal millions of dollars. In addition, Internet failures include the liquidation of many Internet businesses that never came close to making a profit. For example, buying groceries on-line from home through Webvan was once touted as a threat to traditional supermarkets. No more!

The Internet bubble, exemplified by Webvan and a host of other failed on-line firms, began to deflate near the end of the longest economic expansion in U.S. history. That upswing in the economy began in the early 1990s and ended with the recession that started in March 2001. Some economists began to question whether the new economy was dead, or even whether it ever existed at all. Let's try to answer such questions, using the framework of macroeconomics.

The three macro goals of high growth, high employment, and low inflation all fell into place for the United States during the presidency of Bill Clinton. Economists will study this era for years to come, seeking to establish with certainty all the factors that accounted for the nation's superior economic performance. Alan Greenspan, chairman of the Federal Reserve at the time, has commented that the economy was revitalized by fundamental changes in the 1990s. Behold technology.

HOW TECHNOLOGY IMPACTS GROWTH

The new economy is characterized by the application of technology to increase business productivity. The growth of computers in the workplace increases the productivity of labor. More productive labor means incomes rise in the long run. Furthermore, increased productivity is the closest thing to a "magic bullet" for the economy. Increased productivity can translate into meeting the three macro goals. Strong productivity growth can keep the economy growing, keep workers employed, and act as a brake on inflation.

Before we discuss how productivity growth can strengthen the economy, let's examine the U.S. productivity data in Table 12-2. This table shows that, when cheaper and easier-to-use technology was provided to workers throughout the economy in the 1990s, workers became more efficient. Output per worker increased. Businesses increased production in response.

Table 12-2 tracks economic performance for three separate time periods: 1979 to 1990, 1990 to 1995, and 1995 to 2000. Row (1) shows the acceleration in the growth rate of labor productivity between 1995 and 2000 relative to the earlier years in the table. In the 1995 to 2000 time period, each year American workers produced 2.7 percent more output per hour worked than in the previous year. Compared to the earlier periods, labor productivity roared ahead in the mid-to-late 1990s.

Rows (2) through (4) explain the sources of growth in labor productivity: increases in capital, labor, and technological change. Note that information technology capital, such as

TABLE 12-2   SOURCES OF CHANGE IN UNITED STATES LABOR PRODUCTIVITY, 1979–2000

ITEM	1979 TO 1990	1990 TO 1995	1995 TO 2000
(1) Output per hour (Labor productivity)	1.6	1.5	2.7
(2) Contribution of capital	0.8	0.5	1.1
• Contribution of information technology capital	0.5	0.4	0.9
• Contribution of other capital	0.3	0.1	0.2
(3) Contribution of labor	0.3	0.4	0.3
(4) Contribution of technological change and other factors	0.5	0.6	1.4

Source: Adapted from *Multifactor Productivity Trends,* Bureau of Labor Statistics, USDL 02–128, March 12, 2002. Row (4) shows multifactor productivity, which measures the joint influences of technological change, efficiency improvements, and other influences on economic growth.

computers, fax machines, and so forth, contributed significantly to soaring labor productivity in the 1995 to 2000 period. The same is true of technological change, as shown in row (4). The data in this table allow us to separate the hoopla about the new economy from the substance. What we see is that something fundamental did indeed change in the mid-1990s. Technological change, especially as it related to increases in information technology capital like computers, contributed mightily to the burst in labor productivity, which in turn contributed mightily to the nation's increased prosperity.

The current new economy is not the first time in American economic history that everyone sensed a permanent change for the better because of technology. The Industrial Revolution in the late 1700s was the first. In the United States, that revolution was sparked when Samuel Slater illegally smuggled from England the plans for the textile mill he built in Rhode Island. Throughout history, the economy has been revitalized again and again. The railroad, the automobile, radio, television, and now the computer and the Internet have created new economies in turn.

As in the current new economy, those episodes from history were also filled with hype, speculation, and excess. Life was made better, too, because in spite of the hype, what was new was real. So, the next time you place an order for a music CD at Amazon.com, remember that the new economy is much more. Most fundamentally, it is the building block for economic growth.

*T*HINKING
*C*RITICALLY

1. Until the widespread adoption of personal computers and word processing software in the mid-to-late 1980s, office paperwork was usually typed on an electric typewriter. Describe how the productivity of typists was increased when they shifted to the new technology. Also describe how the human capital that typists needed was changed by the new technology.

2. Should government subsidize Internet access for the poor? Explain, making reference to the benefits and to the problems that could be expected.

Visit **www.prenhall.com/ayers** for updates and web exercises on this Explore & Apply topic.

SUMMARY AND LEARNING OBJECTIVES

1. Identify the sources of economic growth.

■ Labor, capital, technological change, and entrepreneurship are important determinants of growth.

■ In the United States, economic growth averaged about 4 percent from 1947 to 1973, but growth fell off after that. From 1992 until the recession that started in 2001, the growth rate in the United States was again in the vicinity of average during the earlier era.

■ Economies grow through accumulating resources. They have the most control over capital, which in turn improves labor productivity. New capital requires capital formation. Entrepreneurs must identify new products or new technologies and produce new capital according to these opportunities.

2. Describe the role of saving and investment in the process of capital formation.

■ Funds for investment come from savings. Together, investment demand and the supply of saving determine the amount of investment.

■ Government both increases and decreases investment. Taxes reduce saving that could be used for investment. However, the government invests some of the taxes it collects, making investments in highways, schools, airports, and elsewhere.

■ The following equation describes the fundamental relationship between investment, saving, and government: Investment = saving + taxation − government consumption. The right-hand side of the equation shows that investment is financed by dollars that are saved and paid in taxes. However, some tax dollars pay for government consumption, and this item must be subtracted.

■ Government fiscal policy can result in a crowding-out effect in which government spending replaces private investment.

■ The interaction of investment demand with the supply of saving creates an interest rate equilibrium. The equilibrium real interest rate makes the actual amount of investment equal to the amount of saving. Graphically, this model of investment shows the investment demand curve to be downward sloping and the supply of saving curve to be upward sloping.

The market equilibrium occurs at the intersection of these two curves.

3. Analyze how taxation affects both saving and investment activity.

■ Taxing interest income reduces the supply curve of saving, which leads to a higher equilibrium real interest rate and less investment. A second example is the capital gains tax, which imposes a tax on the rise in value of an investment. Some current regulations also discourage investment.

4. Provide justification for subsidized higher education.

■ Government promotes technological advancement through subsidies for basic research, such as is conducted at colleges and universities. Otherwise, the existence of external benefits would lead to too little of such research.

5. Summarize new growth theory and supply-side economics.

■ New growth theory recognizes the key role played by research and development in economic growth. This school of thought promotes the idea that property rights to ideas must be protected in order for businesses to have the incentive to engage in research and development.

■ Supply siders seek to minimize structural features of the economy that discourage work effort and capital formation. Reducing regulations and marginal tax rates have been two of their emphases. Supply siders believe that their policies will shift the long-run aggregate supply curve to the right.

6. Discuss the key role of labor productivity in economic growth.

■ The new economy is seen as more than just a catch phrase. Information technology capital and technological change both contributed to the rise in productivity that occurred after 1995. This rise in labor productivity has been a key ingredient of economic growth.

KEY TERMS

economic growth, 274
labor productivity, 275
capital formation, 276
saving, 278
crowding-out effect, 279
expected return, 280

actual return, 280
capital gains, 281
capital gains tax, 281
external benefit, 282
research, 282

development, 282
property rights, 282
new growth theory, 283
supply-side economists (supply
  siders), 284

TEST YOURSELF

TRUE OR FALSE

1. An economy will grow faster when it chooses to produce more consumer goods and fewer capital goods.
2. Saving is used to finance investment.
3. Higher real interest rates shift the investment demand
   curve to the left.
4. A tax on saving shifts the supply curve of saving to the
   left, thus increasing the real interest rate.
5. Supply-side economics favors more government regulation relating to the health and safety of workers.

MULTIPLE CHOICE

6. Technological change and additional capital
   a. increase labor productivity.
   b. decrease labor productivity.
   c. have no effect on labor productivity.
   d. affect labor productivity in unpredictable ways.
7. U.S. economic growth
   a. has generally been characterized by a 5 percent or
      more growth rate since the 1960s.
   b. varied with each president.
   c. was on a downward trend in the 1990s, but has
      recently reversed its course.
   d. is no longer considered an important economic goal.
8. Capital formation is also referred to as
   a. property rights.
   b. technology.
   c. the real interest rate.
   d. investment.
9. Investment equals
   a. saving − taxation.
   b. saving + taxation.
   c. saving + taxation + government consumption.
   d. saving + taxation − government consumption.
10. In Self-Test Figure 12-1, the movement from point A to
    point B is most likely to be caused by
    a. external benefits from research.
    b. external benefits from development.
    c. supply-side policies.
    d. the personal income tax.

11. In Self-Test Figure 12-1, the movement from point A to
    point B is most likely to cause
    a. less capital formation.
    b. more capital formation.
    c. higher capital gains.
    d. more saving.
12. In Self-Test Figure 12-1, axis C should be labeled as
    a. planned investment.
    b. actual investment.
    c. actual saving.
    d. the real interest rate.
13. Higher real interest rates
    a. increase the amount of investment.
    b. decrease the amount of investment.
    c. have no effect on the amount of investment.
    d. have varying and unpredictable effects on invest-
       ment.

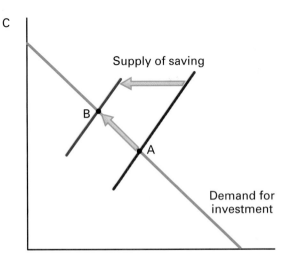

SELF-TEST FIGURE 12-1

14. The crowding-out effect refers to
    a. the crowds of people who attend sports events and rock concerts.
    b. the crowd mentality of investors who rush to buy the latest "hot" stocks.
    c. private sector borrowing that makes it difficult to finance the government.
    d. the reduction in private investment spending when the government borrows.

15. The capital gains tax takes a percentage of
    a. the purchase price of an investment.
    b. the selling price of an investment.
    c. the difference between the purchase price and the selling price of an investment.
    d. the expected return on an investment minus its actual return.

16. External benefits
    a. are most likely during the research phase.
    b. are most likely during the development phase.
    c. are equally likely during the research and development phases.
    d. explain why firms undertake research and development.

17. Research and development are the cornerstones of
    a. supply-side economics.
    b. the Laffer curve.
    c. old growth theory.
    d. new growth theory.

18. Supply siders emphasize
    a. increases in aggregate demand.
    b. higher real interest rates.
    c. a balanced federal budget.
    d. policies that shift the long-run aggregate supply curve to the right.

19. The Laffer curve shows that the effect of increasing taxes too much is
    a. less economic growth.
    b. less tax revenue.
    c. more unemployment.
    d. that only the rich get richer.

20. The new economy is characterized by
    a. the application of technology to increase business productivity.
    b. the need to rebuild bridges and highways to account for today's heavier traffic loads.
    c. widespread goofing off as workers are less accountable for their actions.
    d. the extra pollution it causes.

QUESTIONS AND PROBLEMS

1. *[labor productivity]* What is meant by the term labor productivity? What factors most strongly affect your personal labor productivity (or, if you have no job, the labor productivity of your closest family member with a job)? What actions can a person take to increase his or her labor productivity?

2. *[labor productivity]* Explain why the growth rate in labor productivity usually falls during the early part of a recession, but rebounds when the economic begins to improve.

3. *[capital formation]* Does capital formation affect labor productivity? Explain.

4. *[capital formation]* Provide examples of the kinds of capital formation that might have occurred when each of the following entrepreneurs launched his or her business:
    a. Bill Gates (Microsoft)
    b. Sam Walton (Wal-Mart)
    c. Howard Schultz (Starbucks Coffee)
    d. Berry Gordy (Motown Records)

5. *[government effect on investment]* Explain how government both reduces and increases investment at the

same time. In light of your answer, interpret the following equation from the chapter: Investment = saving + taxation − government consumption.

6. *[saving and investment]* Why does the supply of saving slope upward? Why does investment demand slope downward? Identify the equilibrium in this market.

7. *[saving and investment]* Illustrate graphically and explain the significance of the market equilibrium real interest rate.

8. *[saving and investment]* Illustrate graphically the effect of an increase in the demand for investment on the real interest rate. Could an increase in the supply of saving offset the interest rate effect your graph illustrates? Explain.

9. *[government investment]* List three examples of government spending that might be considered investment. Would the private sector have undertaken these projects if government did not? Explain.

10. *[effect of taxation]* Using a supply and demand graph, explain how taxation of interest earnings reduces the amount of saving and investment.

11. *[crowding-out effect]* An expansionary fiscal policy can reduce private investment spending through the crowding-out effect. Explain how the crowding-out effect could occur.

12. *[personal saving rate]* Figure 12-5 shows that the personal saving rate was very high in the United States during World War II (1942–1945), but is extremely low today. Speculate as to why the war brought about high annual savings rates. Would you expect that the war on terrorism would lead to an upward spurt in the personal saving rate?

13. *[research and development]* What is the difference between research and development? Why is the argument for the government subsidizing research stronger than the argument for subsidies to development?

14. *[theories of growth]* Explain the similarities and dissimilarities between new growth theory and supply-side economics.

15. *[supply-side economics]* Explain why critics of supply-side economics refer to it as "trickle-down economics." Explain why supply siders object to this characterization. Which president is known for promoting a supply side agenda?

16. *[Laffer curve]* How could the Laffer curve be used by government policymakers. Illustrate your explanation with a graph showing the Laffer curve.

 Visit **www.prenhall.com/ayers** for Exploring the Web exercises and additional self-test quizzes.

CHAPTER 13

MONEY, BANKING, AND THE FEDERAL RESERVE

A LOOK AHEAD

"Closed by Order of the Federal Deposit Insurance Corporation." Such signs were posted on hundreds of banks in the 1980s. For the individual depositor, bank failure is an unsettling event, but usually just a minor inconvenience. Depositors soon regain access to their money, along with receiving word of the name of the bank that has taken over their accounts.

Most depositors need not worry about permanently losing their savings because of bank failures. The government's deposit insurance, currently in the amount of $100,000 per bank account, has offered peace of mind to depositors since the 1930s. In this chapter's Explore & Apply section, you will learn why bank failures, although rare today, can occur and why they are worrisome to people. While repeated bank failures usually have little impact on individuals, they can ultimately reduce public confidence in the banking system and make bank loans less available.

Commercial banks are the banks we find on Main Street. The Federal Reserve (the Fed) is the U.S. *central bank,* a special kind of bank charged with regulating money and commercial banks. Together, the commercial banks and the Federal Reserve make up the U.S. banking system, which plays an instrumental role in shaping the quantity of money. Money, in turn, is itself at the heart of the macroeconomy. This chapter begins by examining money, its functions, and how it is measured. A discussion of banking and the Fed completes the chapter.

LEARNING OBJECTIVES

Understanding Chapter 13 will enable you to:
1. Identify the types, functions, and liquidity of various money measures.
2. Describe key elements of the banking industry.
3. Discuss how banks create money.
4. Describe the structure, functions, and policy tools of the Federal Reserve.
5. Work through the process of monetary expansion using the deposit multiplier.
6. Explain why the banking crisis of the 1980s occurred and whether another banking crisis could happen.

Explore & Apply

293

Meeting the macro goals of high employment, low inflation, and economic growth is made easier by the existence of money and banks, including a central bank. In previous chapters money has stayed in the background, but here it comes front and center, along with banks and the Federal Reserve.

13.1 MONEY

money what is used to buy and sell things.

barter exchange of one good for another.

Money is whatever is commonly used in an economy to buy and sell things. To put money into perspective, imagine a world in which it did not exist. To fulfill our wants, we would have to either swap one good for another—**barter**—or produce on our own all the goods and services we consume. Both alternatives are inefficient. Money provides us with higher living standards; that's why money is no fad and never goes out of style. In one form or another, money has been in continuous use from the earliest days of civilization. Among the important qualities of money are *portability* and *divisibility*. Money should be easy to carry around, and divisible to make it convenient to spend and receive change.

THE CHARACTERISTICS OF MONEY

Everyone knows what money is. It's the rectangular pieces of paper with pictures of presidents and the shiny metallic coins that we carry with us when we go shopping, right? Not quite. If it has value, is portable, and doesn't turn to mush, it has probably served as money somewhere. Among Native Americans, wampum (seashells) was used as money. Livestock, produce, tobacco, colonial currency, foreign currency, and furs were money at various times in the early days of America.

Gold was money for thousands of years. Given the long history of monetary gold, it may surprise you that gold is not used as money in the United States today. What, then, performs the role of money? Government-issued currency and coins are money, but they are most assuredly *not* the largest part of the money that we own. The electronic notations of bankers representing checking account money hold that distinction, as we'll see in the next section.

Money performs the following functions:

medium of exchange the purchasing function of money.

store of value the function of money related to holding wealth.

unit of account a use of money that occurs when the value of one item is compared with the value of another in terms of monetary units.

fiat money money not backed by a commodity; money by decree of law.

- **Medium of exchange.** Money is used to make purchases. Money must be acceptable to sellers, who will find it so only if they believe that others will, too.
- **Store of value.** Money is a means of holding wealth, but by no means the only one. Real estate, jewelry crafted of precious stones and metals, and stocks and bonds also serve as stores of value, because they are not perishable. Conversely, food and clothing are not used as money.
- **Unit of account.** The market values of goods and services are expressed as prices, which are stated in terms of money. The monetary unit varies from one nation to another. These monetary values are used for a variety of purposes, including measuring GDP and comparing goods.

Fiat money is money because the law says it is. Paper currency and current U.S. coins are examples. Because the government accepts fiat money, individuals and businesses do as well. Look at your paper money and see this reminder that our money is fiat money: "This note is legal tender for all debts, public and private." Gold and silver coins, once a commonplace form of money in the United States, are examples of *commodity money.* Commodity money is made from precious metals. In contrast, coins today are made from cheaper metals. The silver dimes that once filled change drawers in store cash registers have been replaced by dimes made of cheaper metals. Paper currency in the United States is not backed by gold, silver, or any other precious metal. As fiat money it does not need to be.

Unfortunately, commodity money is subject to **Gresham's law**—bad money drives out good. In other words, people have the incentive to nick, shave, or otherwise reduce the metallic content of coins. A little bit of gold shaved from the edges of enough coins can add up to a nice little nest egg. When the shaved coins are spent, they will be accepted by sellers who do not examine them closely. If they notice later, anyone possessing such an altered coin tries to spend it first and hoard the better, unaltered ones that contain more precious metal. This practice forces recipients of commodity money to examine it carefully, weigh it, and even bite it. People do not wish to examine their money this closely, and thus turn to fiat money instead. Of course, fiat money must be designed so that it is not easily counterfeited.

The governments of virtually all nations today hold a monopoly on the production of fiat money. The profit from the difference between the value of money and the cost of producing it is called *seigniorage.* For example, the U.S. Mint has reported that the cost of making 1,000 pennies, with a face value of $10, was $8.21 in 2000. The difference between the face value and the cost, equal to $1.79, is an example of seigniorage. Seigniorage is much greater for higher denomination coins and paper money.

> **Gresham's law** bad money drives good money out of circulation.

DEBIT OR CREDIT?

SNAPSHOT

That plastic card that you swipe through the reader at your local Home Depot could be a traditional credit card, like those used for more than fifty years, but it is increasingly likely to be a more recent invention, the debit card. What is the difference? The debit card immediately transfers the amount of your purchase out of your checking account and into the store's deposit account. In effect, it saves you the trouble of writing a check, and eliminates the possibility of bouncing a check. You can't use a debit card to make a purchase unless you have the amount of your purchase in your account.

In contrast, a credit card provides you with a loan in the amount of the purchase. When you receive your monthly statement you must repay at least part of the loan. The debit card came much later than the credit card because debit cards would not be practical without high-speed computer networks. Debit cards make it easier for consumers to spend their checking account money. Like credit cards, debit cards are not money. Even if every bank depositor were issued a debit card tomorrow, the amount of money that exists would not change. It would just be easier to spend. ◀

LIQUIDITY: M1, M2, AND M3

When paper money and coins are deposited in banks, money changes form. Deposits into checking accounts create **demand deposits,** also termed *checkable deposits.* More money is held in the form of checkable deposits than in any other form. These deposits are money

> **demand deposits** checking account deposits at commercial banks.

because checks—orders to a bank to make payment—are generally accepted by sellers. Traveler's checks are also generally accepted by sellers of goods and services. In addition, currency may be transformed into any of several "near monies," such as balances in savings accounts.

liquidity how easily and quickly an item can be turned into a spendable form.

Liquidity refers to how easily and quickly something of value can be converted into spendable form. An item is highly liquid if it is spendable without delay. Money is highly liquid, but some types of money are more liquid than others. Three definitions of money, termed the *monetary aggregates,* categorize various types of money according to how liquid they are. The monetary aggregates include M1, M2, and M3. M1 is the most liquid of these and totaled $1.2 trillion in 2001. M2 is slightly less liquid and totaled $5.5 trillion that year, while M3, which is much less liquid, totaled $8.0 trillion. The specific components of each category are as follows:

M1 most liquid measure of money; currency plus demand deposits, traveler's checks, and other checkable deposits.

■ **M1:** The sum of currency and coins in the hands of the public, demand deposits, other checkable deposits, and traveler's checks. These forms of money are the most easily and

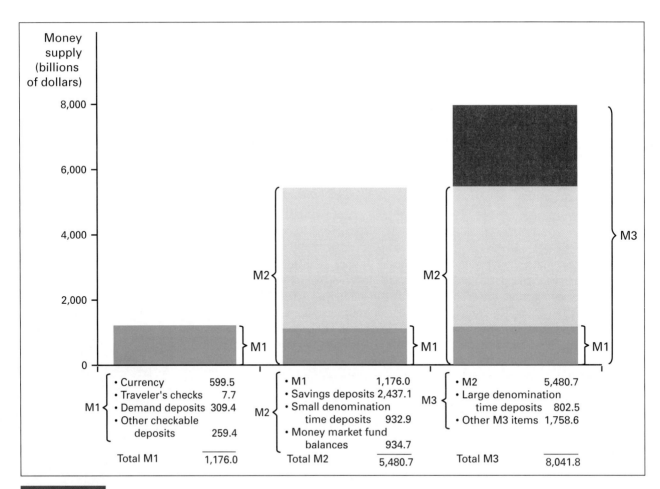

FIGURE 13-1

THE COMPONENTS OF M1, M2, AND M3 The M1 measure of the money supply includes only the most liquid items. Less-liquid items are added to arrive at M2 and M3. The bars rise in height when the additional components of the M2 and M3 money supply are added. Values are in billions of dollars.

Source: Money Stock Measures, June 13, 2002. The data shown are for April 2002. The values in the figure vary slightly from those in the source because of rounding.

immediately spendable. **Currency stored in bank vaults is not counted in the money supply because it is not available to make purchases.**

■ **M2:** M1 plus the balances in savings deposits, "small" time deposits, and balances in money market mutual funds. *Time deposits* are certificates of deposit (CDs), which can be withdrawn without penalty only after some period of time, such as one or five years. The Fed considers CDs small if they are less than $100,000!

M2 obtained by adding savings deposits, small time deposits, and money market fund balances to M1.

■ **M3:** M2 plus large time deposits (at least $100,000), and several other near monies. These additional components of M3 are even less likely to be spent than the items in M2.

M3 expands M2 by adding large time deposits and several other near monies.

Figure 13-1 illustrates how the M2 and M3 measures of the quantity of money build on the M1 measure. Figure 13-2 shows that the money supply, whether measured by M1, M2, or M3, grows each year.

Because currency and coins are immediately spendable, they are completely liquid. Demand deposits are only slightly less liquid, because businesses often require check writers to present some form of identification before the check is accepted. Savings account deposits are slightly less liquid than demand deposits, but can be converted into demand deposits or currency with a trip to the bank.

Financial assets, such as stocks and bonds, are not counted in the money supply figures. They are nonetheless relatively liquid because they can be readily sold in the financial marketplace at fair market value, although brokerage fees reduce their liquidity. In contrast, most nonfinancial assets are not very liquid. For example, automobiles, furniture, and personal belongings are difficult to sell quickly at their market value. Similarly, the sale of real estate usually involves large broker's fees.

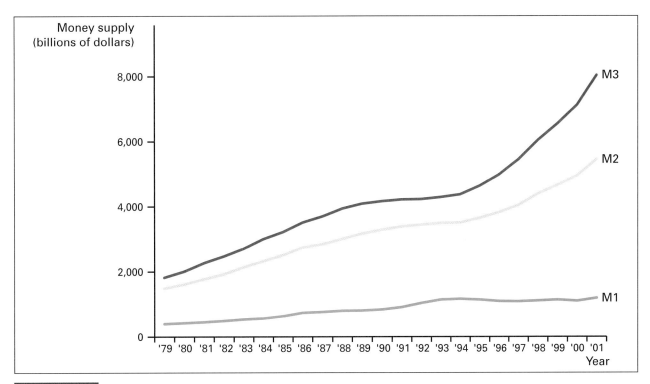

FIGURE 13-2

THE GROWTH OF THE M1, M2, AND M3 MONEY SUPPLY Over many years the money supply grows larger, no matter whether measured as M1, M2, or M3.

Source: 2002 Economic Report of the President, Table B-69. The 2001 data are preliminary.

> ### QUICKCHECK
>
> State the effect on the money supply in each of the following instances:
> a. Check printing companies print more blank checks.
> b. An individual deposits $9,000 in currency into a checking account in the bank.
> c. An individual moves $500 from a savings account to a checking account.
>
> **Answer:** (a) The printing of more blank checks does not change the money supply since it is the balances in demand deposit accounts that are measured by M1. (b) Depositing currency into a checking account leaves the money supply the same. (c) Moving balances from a savings account to a checking account leaves the M2 money supply the same. The M1 money supply increases because this move increases demand deposits.

S N A P S H O T   **THE EURO—OUT WITH THE OLD AND IN WITH THE NEW**

U.S. residents take it for granted that the same dollar bills are just as spendable in New York as New Orleans. Europeans, on the other hand, have historically had to contend with changes in currency and coins even for short trips that cross borders between countries. That has recently changed.

January 1, 1999 marked an historic moment in monetary history. The three-year transition to a new monetary unit began in eleven of the countries making up the European Monetary Union. The German mark, the French franc, the Italian lire, and the other familiar currencies issued by many European countries began to disappear in 2002, replaced by the euro. More countries may also make the jump to the euro as time passes. The Monetary Union also requires a new European Central Bank to conduct monetary policy, which was once the job of central banks in individual countries.

Why would countries risk confusion by dropping their familiar currencies, not to mention the loss of control over their own money? These changes are all part of a long-term effort to integrate the economies of Europe to make them more competitive with the United States and Japan in the global marketplace. A common currency will also ease the burdens on harried travelers who would rather worry about the price of lodging in the night's ski chalet than about having the right currency to pay that price! ◀

13.2 MONEY AND BANKING IN THE UNITED STATES

As Americans moved westward during the first 100 years of the country's existence, new banks were needed to facilitate commerce whenever towns grew up. For the most part, banking regulation was weak, and so banks were easy to start. The legacy of that frontier history lives on, as the United States today has more banks than any other country. Currently, about 8,500 U.S. commercial banks accept deposits and make loans.

THE BANKING SYSTEM

Since the mid-1980s the number of banks in the United States has plummeted because of bank failures and bank mergers. More specifically, the number of banks fell an astonishing 41 percent between 1986 and 2000. During this period the United States has seen the rise of megabanks—large banks that do business in many locations. Megabanks thrive in today's climate of *interstate banking* as legal barriers against branching across state lines have fallen. On-line banking from home or work using the Internet has become common, allowing people to check their account balances, pay bills, or transfer funds among accounts. The fact is that banks are becoming ever more national, and even international, institutions in terms of their reach.

Banks are regulated by both state and federal governments. Bank regulation is designed to protect against unsound banking practices that could bankrupt both depositors and government insurance funds. Bank regulation is controversial. Since regulations inhibit banks from responding to the demands of their customers, regulations can lead to inefficiencies in the financial system. For example, under the Glass–Steagall Act of 1933, banks were barred from offering insurance and brokerage services. The act was intended to keep banks away from risky investment activities that could endanger the banking system. Over time, the inefficiencies created by Glass–Steagall were recognized and a number of its provisions were relaxed because of changes in the law, regulatory interpretations, and court decisions. Yet the act stayed on the books.

Congress finally killed off the Glass–Steagall Act in 1999 after twelve attempts to do so in the prior twenty-five years. Why was it so difficult to abolish a law that many, including Federal Reserve Chairman Alan Greenspan, felt inhibited the competitiveness and efficiency of the U.S. financial system? For one reason, insurance and brokerage firms were happy that banks could not enter their markets to compete with them. For another, smaller banks were content to stay out of these businesses and were pleased that their larger competitors were forced out, too. The lesson? Good economics and good politics do not always go hand in hand.

To understand how our banking system operates, it is useful to consider a simplified *balance sheet* showing the assets and liabilities of a bank, as seen in Table 13-1. The assets are things that a bank owns, and reveal how banks use funds. In a balance sheet, assets are always listed on the left side. The liabilities are what the bank owes, and reveal how a bank raises funds. Liabilities are listed on the right side.

Take a look at bank assets first. The two most liquid assets, vault cash and deposits held by the Federal Reserve, are normally lumped together to form what are called cash assets. Bank deposits at the Fed are cash assets for banks because banks can cash in their deposits at the Fed in the same way that you can go to your bank and withdraw cash from your checking or savings accounts. The sum of vault cash plus deposits with the Fed is called **bank reserves.** Bank reserves are highly liquid and so are available immediately to meet

bank reserves vault cash plus deposits held by the Fed.

TABLE 13-1 A BALANCE SHEET—MAJOR ASSETS AND LIABILITIES OF BANKS

ASSETS	LIABILITIES
Vault cash (part 1 of bank reserves)	Customer deposits
Deposits held by the Federal Reserve (part 2 of bank reserves)	Federal funds
Loans	Discount loans
Securities	
Other	

depositor withdrawals. This liquidity provides banks with a margin of safety should depositor withdrawals unexpectedly increase.

Banks hold some fraction of their deposits on reserve to meet the cash needs of their customers. Individual banks are also required by law to meet the *reserve requirements* imposed by the Fed. The current reserve requirement of approximately 10 percent for demand deposits means that banks must hold at least $10 in reserves for every $100 of customer deposits. Reserves in excess of **required reserves** are called **excess reserves.** Hence, total reserves equal required reserves plus excess reserves.

required reserves bank reserves held to meet the Fed's reserve requirement; expressed as a percentage of deposits.

excess reserves the amount of bank reserves that exceed the amount needed to meet the reserve requirement.

Bank reserves are a non-income-producing asset. This characteristic motivates banks to minimize the amount of bank reserves held so long as the banks are meeting the reserve requirement and are satisfied with the margin of safety provided by the quantity of reserves held. If bank reserves provide banks with no income, how then do they earn revenues? Loans and securities provide the answer.

The next asset in Table 13-1 is loans, which represent promises by borrowers to repay borrowed funds. Bank loans go to both the household and business sectors. Banks lend to borrowers in order to earn income in the form of interest. Bank loans are extended to borrowers for many purposes, such as to finance a business, a car, home improvements, and college tuition. Interest rates that borrowers pay on a bank loan vary, mainly depending on the purpose of the loan, and the risk to the bank that the loan will not be repaid in full. One interest rate on bank loans that is widely known to the public is the *bank prime lending rate.* This interest rate applies to short-term business loans. When there are changes in interest rates, the prime rate is usually singled out by the news media to represent interest rates in general.

bonds interest-paying investments; also called securities.

Interest payments on investments purchased by banks also provide banks with income. *Securities,* in the form of **bonds,** are interest-paying investments. The government issues bonds when it borrows money from investors in order to pay the expenses of government that are not covered by tax collections. Large business firms also issue bonds in order to borrow money. Investors that purchase bonds include individuals, banks, and other financial institutions. Many people are familiar with U.S. Savings Bonds, which provide a safe investment vehicle for small savers. Banks do not invest in these bonds. Neither do they invest in bonds issued by business firms. Instead, they mostly purchase federally issued short-term bonds called *T-bills,* which is short for *Treasury bills.* T-bills are an attractive investment because their owners can easily convert them to cash. T-bills come in large denominations of $10,000 each. To the federal government, T-bills and other Treasury bonds are debt because they represent money the government borrows.

Although banks are prohibited by law from investing in risky securities, loans to borrowers do carry a risk of non-repayment. Sometimes loans go sour when borrowers are unable to repay them. It is normal for a small fraction of loans to be uncollectible. The expenses generated by bad loans raises the cost of borrowing and reduces the profits earned by banks. If the amount of bad loans goes beyond norms, banks might not be able to pay off their depositors. That possibility is why the *Federal Deposit Insurance Corporation (FDIC)* insures deposit accounts up to $100,000. This insurance reduces the likelihood of bank runs, in which numerous depositors simultaneously seek to withdraw funds because of fears about the financial soundness of a bank. The tradeoff is that FDIC insurance allows banks to make riskier loans without scaring away their depositors. These depositors know that their funds are secure no matter how many unsound loans a bank may make.

Banks also own other assets, such as their buildings, equipment, and fixtures. These assets are needed in order to do business with the public.

federal funds rate interest rate on loans that banks make to other banks.

Now take a look at the liabilities in Table 13-1. Bank deposits are liabilities because they are funds owed to depositors. Banks also raise funds by borrowing, both from each other and from the Federal Reserve. Funds borrowed from other banks are called *federal funds.* The interest rate that banks charge on loans to other banks is called the **federal funds rate.** The federal funds rate is determined by the supply and demand in the marketplace for fed-

> ## QUICKCHECK
>
> A bank has $1,000 in deposits and holds $250 in reserves. If the reserve requirement is 20 percent, what is the quantity of excess reserves?
>
> **Answer:** Required reserves equal 0.2 multiplied by $1,000, or $200. Since total reserves equal $250, excess reserves must be $50.

eral funds. Most of the funds borrowed in the federal funds market are repaid the next day. Although the federal funds rate is not widely known among the general public, as you will soon see, it is probably the most significant interest rate in terms of the Federal Reserve's monetary policy influence on banks.

Borrowings by banks from the Federal Reserve are called *discount loans* because the Federal Reserve is said to "discount" its loans. To discount a loan means that banks are required to pay the interest on loans from the Fed when the loans are made rather than as they are repaid. The rate of interest charged is termed the **discount rate,** which is set by the Fed. Funds borrowed by banks at the so-called "discount window" at the Fed are typically repaid quite rapidly because banks need these funds to meet a temporary shortfall in the reserve requirement.

discount rate interest rate set by the Fed on loans it makes to banks.

For simplicity, the balance sheet in Table 13-1vignores *net worth,* which is assets minus liabilities. By definition, the value of the sum of the assets must equal the value of the sum of the liabilities plus net worth for any balance sheet.

KEY BANK INTEREST RATES

Table 13-2 shows yearly data for the prime rate, federal funds rate, and the discount rate since 1979. Observe that the prime rate is greater than the federal funds rate and the discount rate every year. This difference illustrates the idea that banks can borrow funds at interest rates lower than the interest rates they charge borrowers. In this way, banks profit from their loans. Observe also that in general the three interest rates move in the same direction over time. Thus, year to year increases or decreases in the cost of borrowing for banks is translated into increases or decreases in the cost of borrowing for their customers.

In addition to banks, there are other *financial intermediaries,* bank-like institutions that accept funds from savers in order to make loans or investments. With minor exceptions, the discussion of banks in this text also applies to credit unions and savings and loans. Insurance companies, mutual funds, pension funds, and finance companies are examples of nonbank financial intermediaries, because, although they are not banks, they invest the funds they raise.

DO BANKS DISCRIMINATE IN MAKING LOANS?

SNAPSHOT

"Redlining!" Some banks have been accused of this illegal practice, which makes it tough to get a loan if you're in a low- and moderate-income neighborhood. Redlining violates the 1977 Community Reinvestment Act (CRA), which requires banks to service their entire community. The law does not require them to abandon sound banking principles, and banks defend themselves by noting that the profit motive prompts them to reject risky loans no matter the neighborhood.

The Federal Reserve assesses bank compliance with the CRA. It's found that of over 5,800 banks examined since 1990, just 38 have been in "substantial noncompliance" with the law, with another 208 rated as "needs to improve." Bank examinations, such as those called for by the CRA, provide a transparency to bank decision making that can help us know the extent of redlining and other potential problems in the banking system. ◄

TABLE 13-2   KEY INTEREST RATES: THE PRIME RATE, FEDERAL FUNDS RATE, AND DISCOUNT RATE

YEAR	PRIME RATE	FEDERAL FUNDS RATE	DISCOUNT RATE
1979	12.67	11.20	10.29
1980	15.26	13.35	11.77
1981	18.87	16.39	13.42
1982	14.85	12.24	11.01
1983	10.79	9.09	8.50
1984	12.04	10.23	8.80
1985	9.93	8.10	7.69
1986	8.33	6.80	6.32
1987	8.21	6.66	5.66
1988	9.32	7.57	6.20
1989	10.87	9.21	6.93
1990	10.01	8.10	6.98
1991	8.46	5.69	5.45
1992	6.25	3.52	3.25
1993	6.00	3.02	3.00
1994	7.15	4.21	3.60
1995	8.83	5.83	5.21
1996	8.27	5.30	5.02
1997	8.44	5.46	5.00
1998	8.35	5.35	4.92
1999	8.00	4.97	4.62
2000	9.23	6.24	5.73
2001	6.91	3.88	3.40
2002	4.75	1.79	1.25

Source: Federal Reserve. Interest rates for 2002 are those effective June 2002. All others are yearly averages.

HOW BANKS CREATE MONEY

When a bank makes a loan, the quantity of money in the economy increases. To see how, suppose you hope to borrow the cost of a new PT Cruiser, $18,000, from your bank, Homestate University National Bank. After discussing your loan request with loan officer Softheart, the loan is approved. Soon you'll be behind the wheel of your first new car.

If you receive the loan as currency, the amount of currency in the hands of the public, which includes you, is greater than before the loan. Recall that this currency, while inside the bank's vault, was not included in the money supply. Once you receive the $18,000, the M1, M2, and M3 money supplies increase by that amount.

You might not feel safe with $18,000 cash on your person. For this reason, you probably received the loan in the form of a $18,000 check deposited in your checking account. Again, the M1, M2, and M3 money supplies increase by $18,000. We can illustrate the effect of a loan on a bank's balance sheet by referring to the changes in Homestate University National Bank's balance sheet, seen below. The bank acquires an asset, your IOU promising to repay the loan. Customer deposits increase on the other side of the balance sheet because the bank increases your account by $18,000 when the loan is made.

HOMESTATE UNIVERSITY NATIONAL BANK: BALANCE SHEET CHANGES WHEN A LOAN IS MADE

ASSETS		LIABILITIES	
Loans	+ $18,000	Customer deposits	+ $18,000

When you pay for your new car, the bank's balance sheet will change again. Customer deposits decrease by $18,000 since you no longer have that money in your account. Bank reserves will also fall by $18,000 since the bank will either lose $18,000 in vault cash, or see its deposits at the Fed reduced by that amount. The balance sheet effects are shown below.

HOMESTATE UNIVERSITY NATIONAL BANK: BALANCE SHEET CHANGES WHEN A LOAN IS SPENT

ASSETS		LIABILITIES	
Reserves	− $18,000	Customer deposits	− $18,000

When borrowers repay bank loans, the quantity of money falls. If a loan is repaid with currency, the money supply decreases because there is less currency in the hands of the public. If a loan is repaid by writing a check, the money supply falls due to fewer demand deposits. Say that you repay your $18,000 loan all at once. That wipes out your IOU and increases the bank's reserves, as shown.

HOMESTATE UNIVERSITY NATIONAL BANK: BALANCE SHEET CHANGES WHEN A LOAN IS REPAID

ASSETS		LIABILITIES
Reserves	+ $18,000	
Loans	− $18,000	

13.3 MEET THE FED

In the United States, it is the Federal Reserve that performs the central banking functions at the heart of the monetary system. So, in addition to looking at money and banks, we are now ready to look at the Federal Reserve. The Fed is known to the public for engineering changes in short-term interest rates. However, the Fed does much more. Let's take a look at the Fed and its responsibilities.

STRUCTURE AND FUNCTIONS OF THE FEDERAL RESERVE

In England, it is affectionately known as the "Old Lady of Threadneedle Street," but it is officially called the Bank of England. In Germany, it is the Bundesbank; in Canada, the Bank of Canada; and in Hong Kong, the Hong Kong Monetary Authority. What is it? A central bank, a bank that is an arm of the government charged with seeing to it that the monetary system functions efficiently. In Europe as a whole it is called the European Central Bank. The U.S. central bank is called the Fed, short for **Federal Reserve System.** It was created by the *Federal Reserve Act of 1913* in response to recurring problems of bank failure and the belief that a central bank could contribute to U.S. economic stability. With its creation, Congress sought to provide the banking system with the stabilizing influence of a central bank. To this end, the Fed does the following:

Federal Reserve System U.S. central bank; conducts monetary policy, holds bank deposits, and performs several other functions.

- **Functions as a banker's bank.** The Fed holds reserves for commercial banks.
- **Functions as a lender of last resort.** The Fed lends reserves to sound banks that are temporarily short of reserves. Withdrawals by depositors deplete reserves. If depositors become concerned about a bank's ability to pay, the rush to withdraw funds can create a bank run.
- **Supervises banks.** Banks are held accountable for complying with the federal laws and regulations that apply to banks. The Fed is one of several government agencies that is responsible for overseeing compliance.
- **Conducts monetary policy.** The Fed was established for the purpose of providing an elastic money supply—a quantity of money that responds to the demands of the economy. Monetary policy involves the Fed in changing short-term interest rates and the quantity of money.
- **Issues currency.** Paper money in the United States is mostly made up of Federal Reserve Notes, which you can verify by looking at the front of the currency in your wallet or purse. Currency is printed by the U.S. Treasury, but put into circulation by the Fed.
- **Clears checks.** When you write a check, the check must clear, meaning that your bank must reduce your account by the amount of the check. The Fed operates facilities that process and transport checks to the banks upon which they are written so that the banks can clear them.

Congress also sought to keep the Fed *independent,* meaning free from political pressures that might lead it to take actions that would harm the economy in the long run. Because the Fed does not depend upon Congress for its income, but instead earns income from its investments and from providing banking services, the Fed is one of the more independent central banks around the world. This fact is important because evidence shows that countries with independent central banks suffer less inflation. To further insulate the Fed from the political process, the Fed is divided into three components:

- The *Board of Governors,* which is responsible for the overall direction of the Federal Reserve and its policies.
- The *Federal Open Market Committee (FOMC),* which conducts monetary policy.
- The *Federal Reserve Banks,* which regulate and provide a variety of services for banks.

There are seven members of the Board of Governors. They are appointed to fourteen-year nonrenewable terms by the president, with the advice and consent of the Senate. Terms are staggered so that one term expires every two years, which minimizes political influence over the Fed. One of the seven is named by the president to chair the Board. The chairperson, who serves a four-year renewable term, is the most powerful individual in the Fed and one of the most powerful people in the country. As of 2002, Alan Greenspan held the position.

The FOMC consists of twelve members, the seven members of the Board plus four rotating district bank presidents, as well as the president of the New York District Bank. The president of the New York Fed is always a member of the Committee because New York City is the hub of the United States' financial markets. The FOMC usually meets at intervals of approximately four to six weeks, making adjustments in the conduct of monetary policy in accordance with its assessment of economic conditions.

There are twelve regional Federal Reserve Banks, as shown in Figure 13-3. Together with their branches, these Banks perform the routine functions of the Fed. Chances are that you have benefited from their services today. Federal Reserve Banks issue currency, which bears the location of the issuing bank. Commercial banks within a district make deposits of reserves into their district's Federal Reserve Bank. Federal Reserve Banks also operate the Fed's check-clearing operations, which allow funds to be expeditiously transferred from check writers' accounts to the accounts of the banks that cash the checks. These banks also participate in the supervision of commercial banks in their districts.

INFLUENCING THE MONEY SUPPLY: OPEN MARKET OPERATIONS

The principal method the Fed uses to influence the money supply is called open market operations. **Open market operations** occur when the Fed enters the financial marketplace to buy or sell government securities, such as Treasury bonds or Treasury bills. The Fed does not itself issue government securities; the U.S. Department of the Treasury issues Treasury bonds and bills. The Fed can only obtain them in the open market, hence the name. Open market operations allow currency, in the form of Federal Reserve Notes, to make its way into circulation.

open market operations buying and selling of Treasury bonds and Treasury bills by the Fed; tool of monetary policy.

For example, suppose your Aunt Elvira sells a bond to the Fed for $10,000. The Fed issues a check written on itself, payable to Aunt Elvira. When she deposits the check in her checking account at Investors' National Bank, demand deposits in the banking system increase by the amount of the check. Thus, the money supply increases. If she had cashed the check instead, currency in the hands of the public would have increased. Either way, the money supply rises.

When an individual buys a bond sold by the Fed, the money supply decreases. Suppose the buyer pays for the bond by writing a check. When the buyer's bank pays the Fed, the buyer's checking account is reduced by the amount of the check. Thus, demand deposits decrease, as does the money supply.

The bulk of the Fed's open market operations involve banks directly. An open market sale to a bank by the Fed decreases bank reserves. Fewer reserves mean that the bank is able to do less lending. Thus, open market sales tend to reduce the money supply. A greater volume of open market sales is consistent with a tighter policy.

An open market purchase by the Fed from a bank increases bank reserves, which in turn tends to increase the money supply because banks have more money to loan. However, whether loans are actually made and the money supply actually increased depends on the willingness of banks to make loans and on the desire of the public to borrow. **Thus, the Fed influences, but does not control, the money supply.**

However, by conducting open market operations, **the Fed controls the monetary base.** The **monetary base** is the sum of currency held by the public plus bank reserves. **An open market purchase by the Fed always increases the monetary base by the amount of the purchase; an open market sale always decreases the monetary base by the amount of the sale.**

monetary base sum of currency in circulation plus bank reserves.

Let's look at four kinds of open market operations, and examine their balance sheet effects.

- Fed buys a $10,000 bond from a member of the public, and the seller deposits the funds received in a commercial bank.

Board of Governors of the Federal Reserve System, Washington, D.C.

● Federal Reserve Bank city

● Federal Reserve Branch city (by district):

2. Buffalo
4. Cincinnati, Pittsburgh
5. Baltimore, Charlotte
6. Birmingham, Jacksonville, Miami, Nashville, New Orleans
7. Detroit
8. Little Rock, Louisville, Memphis
9. Helena
10. Denver, Oklahoma City, Omaha
11. El Paso, Houston, San Antonio
12. Los Angeles, Portland, Salt Lake City, Seattle

FIGURE 13-3

THE FEDERAL RESERVE SYSTEM The Federal Reserve System is divided into twelve district national banks—those chartered by the federal government—are automatically members of the Federal Reserve. Banks with state charters may join at their option. Whether or not they are members of the Federal Reserve System, however, all banks have nearly equal access to the Fed's services and are subject to its regulations. Thus, although only about 4,000 banks are formal members, in practical terms all banks fall under Federal Reserve regulation.

Source: http://www.federalreserve.gov/otherfrb.htm.

BANK BALANCE SHEET CHANGES: PUBLIC SELLS BOND

ASSETS		LIABILITIES	
Reserves	+ $10,000	Customer deposits	+ $10,000

■ Fed buys a $10,000 bond from a commercial bank.

BANK BALANCE SHEET CHANGES: BANK SELLS BOND

ASSETS		LIABILITIES
Bonds	− $10,000	
Reserves	+ $10,000	

■ Fed sells a $10,000 bond to a member of the public. The buyer writes a check to pay for the bond.

BANK BALANCE SHEET CHANGES: PUBLIC PURCHASES BOND

ASSETS		LIABILITIES	
Reserves	− $10,000	Customer deposits	− $10,000

■ Fed sells a $10,000 bond to a commercial bank. The bank pays for the bond by having its account at the Fed reduced by $10,000.

BANK BALANCE SHEET CHANGES: BANK PURCHASES BOND

ASSETS		LIABILITIES
Reserves	− $10,000	
Bonds	+ $10,000	

In which of the four types of open market operations did the money supply immediately change at the completion of the transaction? To answer that question look for a change in customer deposits. When the Fed buys or sells a bond to the public, the money supply changes immediately. When the transaction involved a bank, there was no immediate change in the money supply. However, when bank reserves increase, banks are able to make more loans. When bank reserves decrease, the opposite is true. This means that **any open market operation has the potential to change the money supply, if not now, then later.**

In which cases did the monetary base increase? Since all four cases saw a change in bank reserves, the monetary base changed in all cases. As previously stated, any open market operation changes the monetary base immediately.

QUICKCHECK

If Aunt Elvira, who sold a $10,000 bond to the Fed, deposited the Fed's check into her savings account, would the money supply increase?

Answer: The M1 money supply would remain unchanged. However, M2 and M3 would rise, because these measures include savings accounts.

THE MONEY MULTIPLIER AND THE MONETARY BASE

The effects of open market operations do not stop with the initial purchase or sale. Secondary effects magnify changes in the money supply or monetary base. For example, an open market purchase from an individual increases the money supply once when the seller receives the proceeds of the sale. If those funds are deposited in a bank, and then loaned to someone, the money supply increases again. This process can continue over and over.

money multiplier the amount by which a new deposit is multiplied to arrive at the actual increase in the money supply; maximum value is given by the deposit multiplier.

The *money multiplier* shows the total effect on the money supply of each dollar of open market operations. To see how the money multiplier works, return to Aunt Elvira's sale of a bond to the Fed. When her checking account increased with the deposit of the Fed's check, we saw that demand deposits in the banking system increased.

If we assume for simplicity that Investors' National Bank was just meeting a 10-percent reserve requirement prior to the $10,000 deposit, then the bank will find itself holding excess reserves of $9,000. Actual reserves have increased by $10,000, but the bank is only required to hold 10 percent of that amount, equal to $1,000, as required reserves. The bank is thus able to make loans up to the amount of excess reserves and still meet the reserve requirement.

As it happens, your best friend wishes to borrow $9,000 to finance the purchase of a used Saturn automobile. After your friend speaks with loan officer Pushover at Investors' National Bank, the loan is approved. That loan increases the money supply by $9,000. The auto dealer deposits your friend's check into the dealer's bank. That bank will then have excess reserves to lend. The amount of required reserves equals $900, so excess reserves equal $8,100, the amount that can be loaned.

This lending–depositing–lending sequence could continue. Someone can borrow $8,100. When the loan is spent and someone else deposits the $8,100 in his or her bank, that bank will have excess reserves, which it is able to lend. At each succeeding step in the process, the sum of money loaned, which is new money, grows smaller because each succeeding bank in the sequence must hold a portion as required reserves. Thus the process is eventually exhausted when the last bank in the sequence has essentially nothing left to lend.

What is the total of new money created when the expansion of the money supply is complete? The answer depends on the money multiplier.

$$\text{Money supply} = \text{Money multiplier} \times \text{Monetary base}$$

The money multiplier can vary according to loan prospects and people's behavior, and is thus hard to calculate with precision. However, an upper bound can be found by calculating the *deposit multiplier*—**the maximum possible value of the money multiplier.** The deposit multiplier is calculated by assuming that all money is held as demand deposits and that banks do not hold excess reserves. In practice, the true value of the money multiplier will be less than the deposit multiplier.

deposit multiplier upper bound on the value of the money multiplier; computed as 1 divided by the reserve requirement.

The deposit multiplier is the reciprocal of the percentage reserve requirement, meaning

$$\text{Deposit multiplier} = \frac{1}{\text{Reserve requirement}}$$

For example, if the reserve requirement equals 10 percent, then 1 divided by 10 percent equals 1/0.1, which gives a deposit multiplier of 10. To use this multiplier, multiply the Fed's original open market purchase of $10,000 by the multiplier, 10. The total of new money in that case is $100,000.

You can follow the process of money creation that follows an open market operation by referring to Figure 13-4. The process starts when Aunt Elvira deposits the $10,000 she received from the Fed in Investors' National Bank. Let's refer to Investors' National Bank as

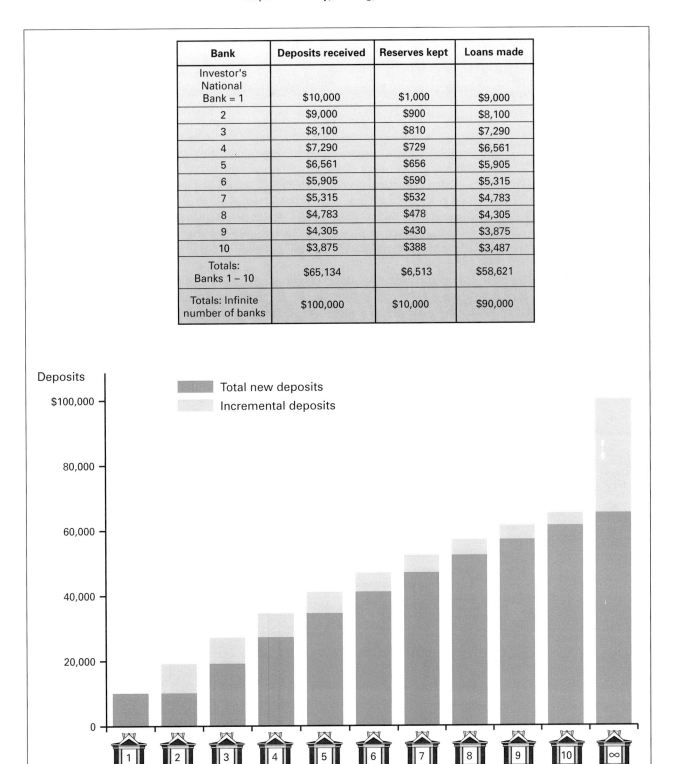

Bank	Deposits received	Reserves kept	Loans made
Investor's National Bank = 1	$10,000	$1,000	$9,000
2	$9,000	$900	$8,100
3	$8,100	$810	$7,290
4	$7,290	$729	$6,561
5	$6,561	$656	$5,905
6	$5,905	$590	$5,315
7	$5,315	$532	$4,783
8	$4,783	$478	$4,305
9	$4,305	$430	$3,875
10	$3,875	$388	$3,487
Totals: Banks 1 – 10	$65,134	$6,513	$58,621
Totals: Infinite number of banks	$100,000	$10,000	$90,000

FIGURE 13-4

CREATION OF DEPOSIT MONEY, 10 PERCENT RESERVE REQUIREMENT You can track the expansion in the money supply by following the actions of the banks in the table. The graph presents the same informa-tion visually.

Bank 1, and follow the actions of the other banks in the process. Note that each loan expands the money supply.

- **Bank 1.** The bank keeps required reserves of 10 percent of the $10,000 deposit, equal to $1,000. It makes loans totaling $9,000 ($10,000 deposit − $1,000 reserve requirement = $9,000) with the rest.
- **Bank 2.** The $9,000 loan from Bank 1 is spent by the borrower, and is then deposited in Bank 2 by the person receiving the money. Bank 2 keeps $900 in reserves. It loans the $8,100 difference between the $9,000 deposit and the $900 it keeps in reserves.
- **Bank 3.** The borrower of the $8,100 spends the amount of the loan, and the individual receiving that money deposits it in Bank 3. Bank 3 keeps 10 percent in reserves, equal to $810. It loans the balance, $7,290, to a customer.
- **Banks 4 to 10.** Each of these banks keeps 10 percent of the deposit it receives as reserves, and makes loans with the other 90 percent. By the time that Bank 10 has completed its role in the process, $65,134 has been received as deposits by Banks 1 through 10, and $58,621 in loans have been made.
- **All other banks.** The process described continues through an infinite number of banks. Because the amount of deposits received shrinks with the involvement of each additional bank, there will be a limit on the amount of deposit money that is created. The deposit multiplier formula allows you to compute that amount of money, which is $100,000 in this case.

The following three factors affect the money multiplier, and thus the actual expansion of the money supply:

- **The reserve requirement:** Changes in the reserve requirement would change the deposit multiplier, and thus the maximum value of the money multiplier. A lower reserve requirement means that banks are able to lend a greater fraction of deposits; a higher reserve requirement has the opposite effect.
- **The public's desire to hold currency instead of deposits:** If people hold more of their money as currency and less as deposits, banks will have fewer dollars to lend. If Aunt Elvira had taken the original $10,000 from the sale of her bond as currency and buried it in her backyard, the multiple expansion of the money supply would not have taken place, thus reducing the multiplier effect.
- **The bank's desire to hold excess reserves:** Excess reserves may be held in order to meet unexpected depositor withdrawals, or because lending opportunities seem poor. Reserves that are not loaned out do not add to the money supply. **Excess reserves reduce the multiplier effect.**

OTHER TOOLS OF THE FED

In response to unexpected customer withdrawals, banks may wish to borrow from the Fed in order to maintain their required reserves. Recall that loans from the Fed to banks are called discount loans, and the rate of interest charged is called the discount rate. An increase in the discount rate makes it more costly for banks to borrow; a decrease makes it less costly.

Increases in the discount rate tend to decrease the quantity of money by prompting banks to borrow less from the Fed. Conversely, a decrease in the discount rate leads banks to borrow more from the Fed, which tends to increase the amount of money in circulation. Thus, **a change in the discount rate tends to cause the money supply to change in the opposite direction.**

Changes in the discount rate are typically front-page news because they are an easily understood signal of the Fed's policy intentions. The Fed may wish to see the money supply

| TABLE 13-3 | THE FED'S MONETARY POLICY OPTIONS |

TIGHTER MONETARY POLICY	LOOSER MONETARY POLICY
Open market sale of securities	Open market purchase of securities
Increase in discount rate	Decrease in discount rate
Increase in reserve requirement	Decrease in reserve requirement

QUICKCHECK

When the Fed lowers the discount rate, why does it become more likely that the money supply will increase?

Answer: A lower discount rate lowers the cost to banks of borrowing reserves from the Fed. Banks that are short of reserves are more likely to borrow reserves from the Fed and less likely to borrow from other banks. Thus, more funds are available in the banking system to lend to the public.

grow faster to stimulate growth and employment. An increase in the discount rate signals a tighter policy. Perhaps the Fed would like to slow down monetary growth to fight inflation.

The Fed could change the money supply dramatically by altering the reserve requirement. A decrease in required reserves would increase the money multiplier and spur monetary growth. An increase in the reserve requirement would reduce the money multiplier and thus decrease the money supply. Excess reserves, which banks are able to lend to borrowers, would become required reserves, which cannot be used to make loans.

The Fed is reluctant to increase reserve requirements because banks without sufficient excess reserves would be forced to sell securities or call in loans—actions that could prove disruptive to the bank and its customers. Thus, while potent, changes in reserve requirements are rarely used as an instrument of monetary policy. Table 13-3 summarizes the Fed's options in setting monetary policy. A *tight monetary policy* is intended to slow the economy down in order to keep inflation in check. A *loose monetary policy* is intended to have an expansionary effect on the economy. Monetary policy is discussed in detail in the next chapter.

EXPLORE & APPLY

13.4 THE BANKING CRISIS OF THE 1980s—COULD IT HAPPEN AGAIN?

Fifty years is a long time. Yet two rounds of legislation, fifty years apart, set the stage for the banking crisis of the 1980s. The first round of the U.S. banking system's structuring that led to today's banking system occurred in the 1930s. Following upon the heels of bank runs after the stock market crash in late 1929, the 1930s witnessed the closure of many banks. The consequent loss of depositors' money led to New Deal legislation that created the Federal Deposit Insurance Corporation (FDIC) to insure funds deposited in banks, as well as to the passage of the Glass–Steagall law to restrict the investment-related activities of banks. The purpose of the FDIC insurance was to restore public confidence in the banking system; the purpose of Glass–Steagall was to prevent bank failures by keeping banks away from risky investments.

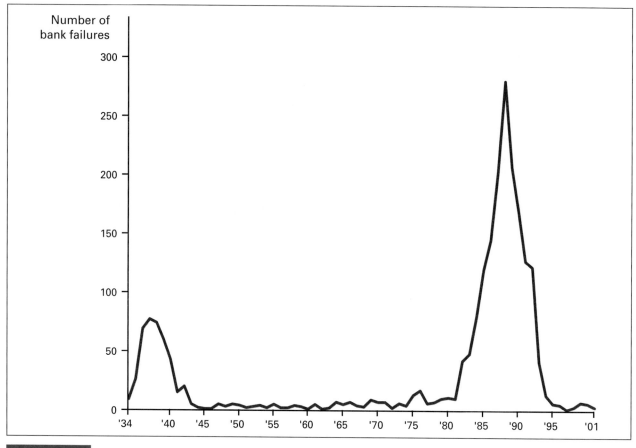

FIGURE 13-5

ANNUAL NUMBER OF U.S. BANK FAILURES Bank failures in the United States soared in the 1980s and did not return to normal until the mid-1990s. The number of bank failures in this period far exceeded those during the Great Depression of the 1930s.

Source: Federal Deposit Insurance Corporation.

For many years afterward, bankers lived on Easy Street. Bank failures were rare, as shown in Figure 13-5. Bankers could pay depositors low interest rates because of the FDIC insurance and because depositors had few alternatives. The financial climate was also favorable, with low inflation and stable interest rates as the norm. In the 1960s, though, the climate started to change. Inflation was no longer quite so low and the public intuitively understood that a 3 percent interest rate on deposits meant that savings accounts were not a very attractive use of money. Bankers had to start competing for deposits with more than a free toaster for every new account.

The second round of legislation that shaped today's banking system occurred with the passage of the *Depository Institutions Deregulation and Monetary Control Act of 1980 (DIDMCA)*. This legislation loosened the regulatory knot that was holding back the banks. Regulation Q, which limited the interest rates banks could pay on deposits, was also rolled back. Now banks were freer to compete for depositors' money. But how could they pay the higher interest rates that they needed in order to compete, and yet still maintain their profitability? The answer is that in the competition for deposits that came to characterize the latter 1970s and the 1980s, banks had to take on a large volume of what proved to be high-risk loans and investments. The alternative was to keep their rates on deposits low and see depositors flee to other banks, savings and loans, money market mutual funds, or even the bond market, all of which offered higher returns. After all, with the FDIC insurance, the only thing depositors cared about was high interest rates.

If it hadn't been for the FDIC insurance, depositors would likely have shopped for banks that invested wisely. They would have had to pay attention to the ratings in *Consumer Reports* magazine, or other publications that would have found it informative to their readership to profile the safety ratings of banks. Such actions by depositors would have been the only way to ensure that their money was safe.

MORAL HAZARD

The problem of *moral hazard* occurs when people change their behavior because of insurance. When the price of risk goes down, people will do riskier things. It is clear that the moral hazard problem led both depositors and bankers to take on more risk than they otherwise would have accepted. For the bankers' part, they could seek out lending opportunities with higher returns but greater risk without experiencing howls of protest from depositors worried about the safety of their deposits. Depositors could sleep soundly as long as their deposits did not exceed the $100,000 FDIC limit.

In practice if not in law, the government even guaranteed deposits above the $100,000 level by adopting a policy of "too big to fail," and by encouraging the merger of insolvent banks—those whose asset values fell below the value of their liabilities—with sound banks. Both of these government policies were equivalent to insurance. A large bank that was deemed too big to fail because its failure might diminish public confidence in the banking system was allowed by bank regulators to continue to operate. Some other troubled banks were forced to merge with sound banks. In these cases the sound banks acquired only the good loans of the merged bank. The government took over ownership of the bad loans.

The market also found a way to extend deposit insurance to those with deposits of more than $100,000 through deposit brokering. Deposit brokers could guarantee that any amount of deposits was insured by breaking up large deposits into blocks of amounts less than $100,000 and then placing these blocks with different banks. For example, a $1,000,000 deposit could be placed into ten different banks in $100,000 blocks. With this innovation, the FDIC limits became meaningless.

Could another massive wave of bank failures occur? The healthier economy of the 1990s did much to restore bank profitability and cut bank failures. Although the economy turned down in the 2001 recession, the number of bank failures remained steady. There is always some increase in bad loans when the economy turns down, however. To the extent that bank loans are for the most part sound, banks will be able to survive an uptick in the number of loans that are not repaid. Thus, the answer to the question is equivalent to asking about the soundness of bank loans. So long as deposit insurance creates moral hazard issues, that answer will remain unclear.

1. Based upon what you have learned about the U.S. banking system, reply to the following questions:
   a. To prevent bank failures should there be more or less regulation of banks?
   b. Make a case for the position you take. For example, if you believe that more regulation is called for, explain what regulations you would want to see enacted. If you believe in less regulation, explain why.
   c. Critique the position you took in part a. For example, if you favored more regulation, for what reasons might that be a bad idea? If you favored less regulation, what are the dangers?

2. Should another wave of bank failures occur in the future, what response should the government take? Specifically, should the government try to keep banks going or should it let them fail? What would be the consequences of each policy for the economy?

 Visit www.prenhall.com/ayers for updates and web exercises on this Explore & Apply topic.

SUMMARY AND LEARNING OBJECTIVES

1. **Identify the types, functions, and liquidity of various money measures.**
   - Money increases economic efficiency by eliminating the need to barter.
   - Money performs three functions. Money must be a medium of exchange, meaning that it is usable to make purchases. Money also functions as a store of value and a unit of account.
   - Paper currency in the United States is an example of fiat money, which is money because the government says it is money. Commodity money in the form of U.S. silver or gold coins is no longer minted. One shortcoming of commodity money is that it is subject to Gresham's law—bad money drives good money out of circulation.
   - An item has the characteristic of being liquid when it is easily and quickly spendable. Currency is highly liquid.
   - Various parts of the money supply exhibit varying degrees of liquidity, although in general any component of the money supply can be considered liquid in relative terms. The M1, M2, and M3 money supplies are defined according to decreasing liquidity, respectively.
   - M1 is the most liquid measure of the money supply because it contains only currency and coins in circulation; checking account balances, also known as demand deposits; and the value of traveler's checks.
   - M2 adds to M1 savings account balances plus small time deposits and money market mutual funds. M2 is considered a less-liquid measure of the money supply because savings account balances are not spendable without first converting them to currency or demand deposits.
   - M3 adds to M2 several additional items that are typically less liquid than the items making up M2. Thus, M3 is considered the least liquid measure of the money supply.

2. **Describe key elements of the banking industry.**
   - The U.S. banking system includes 8,500 or so commercial banks that accept deposits and make loans.

   - Bank regulation is designed to provide for a stable banking system.
   - A bank's balance sheet shows its assets and liabilities. The assets include vault cash, deposits held by the Federal Reserve, loans, and securities. Vault cash plus deposits held by the Federal Reserve equals bank reserves. Banks must meet the reserve requirement set by the Federal Reserve. Assets show what a bank does with funds that are deposited with it.
   - Loans and securities, which are government bonds, provide banks with income.
   - The liabilities include customer deposits, federal funds, and discount loans. Federal funds are the amount of reserves that a bank has borrowed from other banks. Discount loans are funds borrowed from the Federal Reserve.
   - The Federal Deposit Insurance Corporation (FDIC) insures deposit accounts up to a maximum of $100,000.
   - Key interest rates include the prime rate, the federal funds rate, and the discount rate. The prime rate is also called the bank prime lending rate. This interest rate applies to short-term business loans. The Federal funds rate is the interest rate on funds that banks borrow from other banks. The discount rate is set by the Fed and applies to loans that the Fed makes to banks.

3. **Discuss how banks create money.**
   - Banks create money when they make loans. When loans are repaid, the money supply decreases.
   - A borrower is provided with deposit money through the stroke of the banker's pen when the loan is granted.

4. **Describe the structure, functions, and policy tools of the Federal Reserve.**
   - The Federal Reserve controls the monetary base and thereby influences the quantity of money.
   - The Federal Reserve is composed of three primary parts: the Board of Governors, the Federal Open Mar-

ket Committee, and twelve regional Federal Reserve District Banks.

- The tools of monetary policy are open market operations, changes in the discount rate, and changes in the reserve requirement. Most monetary policy is conducted through open market operations.

- Open market operations occur when the Fed buys or sells securities. Fed purchases of securities tend to increase the money supply. Fed sales of securities tend to cause the money supply to decrease.

- The Fed also influences interest rates, which in turn affect other aspects of the economy.

5. **Work through the process of monetary expansion using the deposit multiplier.**

- The monetary base is the sum of currency in circulation plus bank reserves. The money supply equals the money multiplier multiplied by the monetary base.

- An initial deposit of new money into a bank results in an expansion of money through the money multiplier effect. The maximum value of the money multiplier is called the deposit multiplier. The value of the deposit multiplier is computed by taking the reciprocal of the reserve requirement. Thus, when the reserve requirement equals 10 percent, the deposit multiplier equals 1/.10, which is 10.

- With a deposit multiplier of 10, a $10,000 open market purchase by the Fed could conceivably result in an expansion of the money supply by $100,000. This expansion of the money supply would occur as the result of a lending–depositing–lending sequence.

6. **Explain why the banking crisis of the 1980s occurred and whether another banking crisis could happen.**

- The number of bank failures in the United States soared during the 1980s and early 1990s. Banks failed because of bad loans. The role of moral hazard created by the FDIC deposit insurance helps to explain the incentive to make risky loans.

- The strong economic growth of the 1990s helped bring down the number of bank failures as the decade unfolded. However, bank loans that appear to be sound can sour when the economy is in a recession. Moral hazard arising from deposit insurance remains a feature of the banking system, which could lead to additional bank failures.

KEY TERMS

money, 294
barter, 294
medium of exchange, 294
store of value, 294
unit of account, 294
fiat money, 294
Gresham's law, 295
demand deposits, 295

liquidity, 296
M1, 296
M2, 297
M3, 297
bank reserves, 299
required reserves, 300
excess reserves, 300
bonds, 300

federal funds rate, 300
discount rate, 301
Federal Reserve System, 304
open market operations, 305
monetary base, 305
money multiplier, 308
deposit multiplier, 308

TEST YOURSELF

TRUE OR FALSE

1. In fulfilling its medium of exchange function, money is set aside in savings accounts.

2. M3 includes only currency and checking account balances.

3. Federal funds represent bank reserves that have been borrowed by commercial banks at the discount window at the Fed.

4. The importance of the Federal Open Market Committee (FOMC) is that it conducts monetary policy.

5. An open market purchase of securities by the Fed would tend to increase the money supply.

MULTIPLE CHOICE

6. Barter is most likely to occur when
   a. money takes the form of commodity money.
   b. M1 is the dominant form of money.
   c. Gresham's law requires people to barter.
   d. there is no money.

7. The U.S. one dollar coin is an example of
   a. commodity money.
   b. fiat money.
   c. money that is neither commodity money nor fiat money.
   d. something that looks like money, but is not since it is coined from nearly worthless metals.

8. Which is NOT a function of money?
   a. Standard of measurement.
   b. Unit of account.
   c. Store of value.
   d. Medium of exchange.

9. The liquidity of money refers to its
   a. country of origin.
   b. denomination.
   c. store of value function.
   d. medium of exchange function.

10. Currency held in bank vaults is
    a. part of the M1 money supply.
    b. part of the M2 money supply.
    c. part of the M3 money supply.
    d. not part of the M1, M2, or M3 money supply.

11. The value of stocks is
    a. part of the M1 money supply.
    b. part of the M2 money supply.
    c. part of the M3 money supply.
    d. not part of the M1, M2, or M3 money supply.

12. Which statement about the Glass–Steagall Act is correct?
    a. The act was passed in the 1980s in response to the increase in bank failures of that decade.
    b. The act was repealed in 1999.
    c. Banks deposits were insured by the act, which also created federal deposit insurance.
    d. Bank reserves are required to be held as vault cash or as deposits at the Fed under the terms of the act.

13. A bank's total reserves equal
    a. required reserves.
    b. excess reserves.
    c. required reserves + excess reserves.
    d. required reserves − excess reserves.

14. Suppose a bank makes a loan in the amount of $1,000. Which of the following statements is correct about the immediate effect of the loan?
    a. The loan increases the money supply by $1,000.
    b. The loan leaves the money supply the same as it was before the loan.

    c. The loan changes the money supply by some amount that is impossible to determine from the information given.
    d. The loan decreases the money supply by $1,000.

15. Which of the following is NOT a function or activity of the Federal Reserve System?
    a. Lender of last resort.
    b. Accepts deposits from the public.
    c. Supervises banks.
    d. Clears checks.

16. If the money supply equals $100 and the money multiplier equals 10, then the monetary base must equal
    a. $1,000.
    b. $100.
    c. $10.
    d. an amount that cannot be determined from the information given.

17. If the reserve requirement were 20 percent and the Fed purchased $100 of securities in an open market purchase, then the money supply could potentially expand by a maximum of
    a. $5.
    b. $20.
    c. $100.
    d. $500.

18. Discount rate changes by the Fed
    a. change the interest rate on discount loans by the Fed to commercial banks.
    b. are a tool of monetary policy that is clearly superior to open market operations.
    c. tend to have no effect on the money supply.
    d. cause the reserve requirement to increase.

19. Which of the following is consistent with a looser monetary policy?
    a. Open market sale of securities.
    b. Closer supervision of banks by the Fed.
    c. Decrease in discount rate.
    d. Increase in reserve requirement.

20. The most likely explanation of the bank and savings and loan failures in the late 1980s is the combination of a downturn in the economy and
    a. deposit insurance.
    b. fraud.
    c. too much government oversight of investments by banks.
    d. collusion among a few giant banks aimed at reducing consumer choice.

QUESTIONS AND PROBLEMS

1. *[money]* Suppose it became lawful for anyone to issue money without any government restrictions of any kind. What factors would influence an individual to either accept or reject privately issued money? What institutions might arise in the free market to help a person decide whether to accept or reject a particular private monetary note?

2. *[money]* Although the castaways on *Gilligan's Island* were marooned for several years on an "uncharted desert isle" they apparently had no money and saw fit not to adopt any item to use as money. Speculate on the circumstances under which a group of people stranded without money on an island might see fit to invent money. In your discussion be sure to include answers to the following questions: What form might their money take? Would a smaller or larger group of people be more conducive to the invention of money? Would the length of time they expected to remain on the island be a factor in how useful money would be to them? Would barter be a good alternative to money?

3. *[monetary aggregates]* List the components of M1, M2, and M3. Explain why the additional items in M3 make it a less-liquid measure of the money supply than M1.

4. *[balance sheet]* Create a personal balance sheet for yourself. The value of your assets equals the value of the things you own. Your liabilities equal what you owe to others. Their value equals the amount of your loans outstanding, including the interest owed on the loans. On your personal balance sheet, what is the ratio of assets that are not liquid to assets that are liquid? Since liquid assets generally offer lower rates of return, why bother to hold them? Explain.

5. *[balance sheet]* Are loans an asset or a liability to a commercial bank? Explain.

6. *[bank reserves]* What are the two places that banks can use to keep their reserves? Speculate on the decision process by which a bank decides how much of its reserves to keep in each place.

7. *[bank liabilities]* List and explain three major liabilities of commercial banks. Are a bank's liabilities best described as its sources of funds or its uses of funds? Explain.

8. *[Fed's functions]* Suppose that you are the president of a commercial bank. List the functions of the Federal Reserve System. Then describe how your bank would interact with the Fed in relation to each function.

9. *[Fed's components]* List and briefly describe the three components of the Federal Reserve System.

10. *[monetary policy]* Explain the following sentence from the text: "The Fed influences, but does not control, the money supply."

11. *[open market operations]* What are open market operations? What form would open market operations take if the Fed wished to see an increase in the money supply?

12. *[money multiplier versus deposit multiplier]* Distinguish between the money multiplier and the deposit multiplier. Why is the value of the money multiplier likely to be less than the value of the deposit multiplier?

13. *[deposit multiplier]* What is the formula for the deposit multiplier? Compute the value of the deposit multiplier when the reserve requirement equals 25 percent.

14. *[federal funds rate versus discount rate]* What is the federal funds rate? What is the discount rate? Are the two rates necessarily equal?

15. *[monetary policy]* What Fed actions are consistent with a looser monetary policy? Which are in accord with a tighter policy?

 Visit www.prenhall.com/ayers for Exploring the Web exercises and additional self-test quizzes.

CHAPTER 14

MONETARY POLICY AND PRICE STABILITY

A LOOK AHEAD

The 1977 amendment to the Federal Reserve Act of 1913 spells out the objective of monetary policy: to "promote effectively the goals of maximum employment, stable prices, and moderate long-term interest rates." The Fed was created to be independent and free to act without interference from the president, Congress, big business, or big labor. The Fed would not be beholden to any branch of government, nor to any special-interest group. The Explore & Apply section in this chapter looks at the issue of Federal Reserve independence, and how it promotes a healthy, stable economy.

This chapter revolves around monetary policy and its goals. Monetary policy is established by the Fed, the U.S. central bank that we introduced in the previous chapter. In this chapter we describe the Fed's monetary policy along with the economic theory that guides such policy. Monetary policy affects interest rates, inflation, unemployment, and economic growth, which directly affect the lives of us all. Because of its broad effects, there is often contention over what monetary policy should be. Thus, this chapter also offers a view of the factors that motivate that disagreement.

LEARNING OBJECTIVES

Understanding Chapter 14 will enable you to:
1. **Distinguish between an expansionary and contractionary monetary policy.**
2. **Describe the significance of the money market and the motives for holding money.**
3. **Explain the equation of exchange and its role in the conduct of monetary policy.**
4. **Discuss the monetarist school of thought and its implications for monetary policy.**
5. **Interpret the relationship between monetary policy and interest rates.**
6. **Address the importance of central banks staying independent of political pressures.**

$\mathscr{E}$XPLORE
&
$\mathscr{A}$PPLY

The Fed's role in the economy has expanded greatly since its creation in 1913. At that time, the Fed was mainly seen as a "lender of last resort," for troubled banks. As we see in this chapter, the Fed's role today is much more.

14.1 THE AIMS OF MONETARY POLICY

There have been three great inventions since the beginning of time: fire, the wheel, and central banking.

—Will Rogers

Federal Reserve monetary policy encompasses the three macro goals discussed in Chapter 5: high employment, low inflation, and economic growth. *Low inflation* is referred to as *price stability*. In its efforts to keep employment high the Fed must take care not to set off higher inflation. **Many economists argue that price stability should be the Fed's primary goal.** That argument is based on the premise that the economy tends toward full employment, and that monetary policy's greatest impact is on the price level. Nonetheless, the Fed itself makes monetary policy decisions within the context of both employment and inflation because that is what it is legally required to do.

Two realities can help you better understand the conduct of monetary policy:

- **There are conflicts and tradeoffs involved in pursuing a particular monetary policy.** For instance, in bringing down the high inflation of the 1970s the Fed's monetary policy shift toward higher interest rates in the fall of 1979 was widely blamed for creating the two recessions that occurred in the early 1980s. In that particular circumstance, lower inflation came at the cost of a higher unemployment rate.
- **The Fed develops monetary policy surrounded by a whirl of political considerations.** The debates in Congress over appropriate Fed policy can be intense. Unemployment and inflation exact a toll in human suffering.

If you've been unemployed, you know the problem—you don't have enough money to spend! If unemployment in the economy is excessive, as in a recession, the problem is the same: Cyclical unemployment stems from spending that is insufficient to purchase the full-employment level of output at current prices. Thus, to cure the recession, either prices must fall or the quantity of money available to be spent must rise. In general, to maintain full employment, the quantity of money must rise to keep pace with the economy's productive potential. The Fed strongly influences the money supply by conducting open market operations, changing the discount rate, and changing the reserve requirement, as discussed in the previous chapter. The Fed is thus able to utilize these tools of monetary policy to achieve the goals of monetary policy.

If the quantity of money rises too much, then the problem is not one of too little spending power to sustain full-employment output. Rather, the problem is that too much money will be chasing the goods and services that the economy is capable of producing, thus driving up their prices and causing a general inflation. **An overwhelming amount of evidence shows excessive growth in money to be the root cause of inflation.** This evidence is from the United States and from many other countries, and covers episodes of inflation throughout history.

The quantity of money affects aggregate demand, as shown in Figure 14-1. An increase in the money supply is associated with an **expansionary monetary policy,** also called a *looser monetary policy* because the Fed is in effect loosening the purse strings to stimulate the economy with more money. **An increase in the money supply shifts aggregate demand to the right, and thus allows more aggregate output to be purchased at each**

expansionary monetary policy monetary policy designed to stimulate the economy; also called a looser monetary policy.

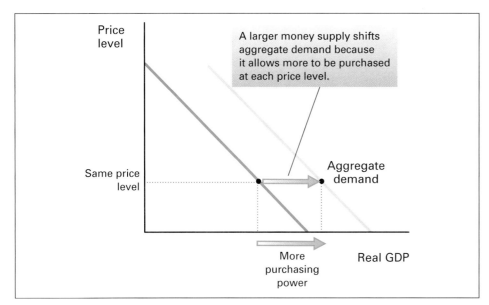

Price level

A larger money supply shifts aggregate demand because it allows more to be purchased at each price level.

Same price level

Aggregate demand

More purchasing power

Real GDP

FIGURE 14-1

EXPANSIONARY MONETARY POLICY An expansionary monetary policy shifts aggregate demand to the right, which means that more output can be purchased at any given price level. A looser monetary policy is designed to stimulate the economy.

possible price level. However, to the extent that the increased money supply causes the price level to rise, its effect in terms of increasing real GDP will be reduced or eliminated. That possibility is discussed later in the chapter when we consider the quantity theory of money.

Conversely, a **contractionary monetary policy** would have the effect of drying up liquidity and tightening the economy's purse strings, and is thus alternatively called a *tighter monetary policy*. The effect of a tighter monetary policy would be just the opposite of the expansionary policy shown in Figure 14-1.

There are two monetary policy targets that the Fed can influence as part of monetary policy:

■ *The money supply.* By increasing or decreasing the growth rate of the money supply, the Fed can attempt to stimulate or slow down the economy. Prior to July 2000, the Fed set target ranges for the growth of the M2 money supply. M2 targets are no longer set because the relationship between the size of the M2 money supply and economic performance is not as clear as it was in prior years.

■ *Short-term interest rates.* The Fed can also manipulate short-term interest rates, such as the interest rate on short-term government securities, up or down. Lower short-term interest rates stimulate the economy, while higher rates are aimed at slowing it down.

The Fed selects a monetary policy based on whether its focus is on adjustments in the money supply or manipulation of interest rates.

Short-term interest rates provide the current monetary policy focus. To understand this focus, we start by examining the motives for holding money.

contractionary monetary policy monetary policy intended to slow down the economy; also called a tighter monetary policy.

14.2 THE MONEY MARKET

Why do people hold on to some of their money rather than invest it? The answer to that question can help us understand the role of money in the economy and how changes in the quantity of money affect the economy. We begin by examining the demand for money.

THE DEMAND FOR MONEY

Why do people typically keep at least some of their wealth as money and not something else? Many other forms of wealth seemingly offer greater returns, or perhaps greater satisfaction. For instance, if you are fascinated by stocks, bonds, and other financial investments, why not invest all your money in those forms of wealth? If your tastes run to hot sports cars, wouldn't you want to hold your wealth in cars in the form of a Ferrari? Whatever your wants, why not just indulge yourself? There are good reasons, as we shall see.

demand for money quantities of money that people would like to hold at various nominal interest rates, *ceteris paribus;* the demand curve for money shows an inverse relationship between the quantity of money demanded and the interest rate, and thus slopes downward.

The fact is that people hold some of their wealth as money. The **demand for money** is the quantities of money that people would prefer to hold at various nominal interest rates, *ceteris paribus.* The demand curve for money is illustrated in Figure 14-2. The quantity of money is on the horizontal axis. The nominal market interest rate, on the vertical axis, represents the opportunity cost of holding money. In effect, it is the "price" of holding money because it represents the interest foregone when money is held rather than used to purchase some interest-earning asset, such as a savings bond. Money demand slopes downward because people will hold less money when the market interest rate (the price of money) is high. Likewise, people will hold more money when the market interest rate is low.

For example, if you hold currency, which pays no interest, instead of a U.S. Savings Bond that pays a market interest rate equal to 7 percent, then the 7 percent interest that you forego is the opportunity cost of holding currency. What would the opportunity cost be if you were holding your money as a demand deposit at a bank that paid you 2 percent interest? In this case the opportunity cost would be the difference between the 7 percent market rate of interest and the 2 percent interest you earned at the bank. Thus, the opportunity cost would be 5 percent.

Let's return to the question of what motivates people to hold money. Why hold money and suffer the loss of the interest income that you could earn by investing in a bond? Three motives make people willing to pay the price of holding money:

transactions motive holding money to make purchases.

- **Transactions motive:** money is held because of the everyday need to buy goods and services. Thus, there is a *transactions demand for money* because we know we're going to need to fill the car with gas, buy lunch at the cafeteria, grab a soft drink from the vend-

THE DEMAND FOR MONEY The demand for money shows an inverse relationship between the market interest rate and peoples' holdings of money.

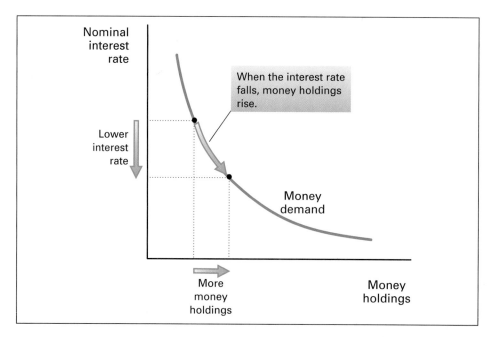

ing machine between classes, and write a check to make a payment on our credit card when we get home.

- **Precautionary motive:** unforeseen circumstances motivate people to hold more money than called for by their transaction demands. Thus, the *precautionary demand for money* arises from the possibility that people will need extra cash or money in their bank accounts to pay the dentist to fix a broken crown, the auto mechanic for a new radiator, or to buy that new computer at a low sale price that won't last long.

- **Speculative motive:** people may speculate with some of their money in the sense that they prefer to hold money rather than invest it when stocks, bonds, and other financial investments appear unattractive at their current returns. The *speculative demand for money* increases when people believe that future returns on investments will rise. For example, if people believe that interest rates on bonds will be going up in the near future, the smart thing to do is to wait before investing in bonds.

precautionary motive holding money to cover unforeseen needs or wants.

speculative motive money held because current investment opportunities are unattractive.

CASH—AN ENDANGERED SPECIES?   *S N A P S H O T*

With checking accounts and an abundance of credit and debit cards, why carry cash? In certain backwaters of the marketplace, cash still reigns as king. From illegal drug deals, to neighborhood garage sales and campus vending machines, cash is in the catbird seat. For lawbreakers, the opportunity cost of holding cash seems a small price to pay to avoid the paper trail left by checks and bank deposit slips. For the general public, cash is sometimes the most convenient way to buy things. The bottom line? Demand for cash is reduced by financial innovations such as 24-hour ATM machines and sweep accounts that automatically transfer funds from a person's savings account to his or her checking account. Even so, cash is not yet an endangered species. ◄

THE MONEY MARKET EQUILIBRIUM

Like markets for goods and services, the **money market** is characterized by demand and supply. You have just seen that the demand for money is illustrated by a downward-sloping curve. In Figure 14-3 the money market is illustrated by adding a money supply curve to the demand curve for money. The money supply curve is drawn as a vertical line because we are assuming that it is this quantity of money that is supplied to the economy by the Fed. A vertical money supply curve such as this one implies that the money supply is independent of the interest rate. In other words, any interest rate is consistent with the quantity of money shown. The question then is what will the actual market interest rate be?

money market the market where the determination of the interest rate is by the demand and supply of money.

The intersection of demand and supply establishes the money market *equilibrium* in Figure 14-3. The equilibrium interest rate is indicated on the interest rate axis in the graph. This interest rate equates the quantity of money demanded to the money supply. Figure 14-3 is an alternative to viewing the interest rate as determined by saving and investment, which you studied in Chapter 12.

THE SUBSTITUTABILITY OF MONEY AND BONDS

The market interest rate will adjust to the equilibrium interest rate. A market interest rate that is above the equilibrium interest rate will fall until the equilibrium interest rate is reached. Similarly, a market interest rate that is below the equilibrium interest rate will rise. **The key to understanding interest rate changes is to realize that money, bonds, and other investments are substitutes for each other.** When people see relatively high market

FIGURE 14-3

MONEY MARKET EQUILIBRIUM In the money market, the nominal interest rate is the price at which money can be bought (borrowed) or sold (loaned). The equilibrium interest rate occurs at the intersection of the money supply curve and the money demand curve. Market forces will adjust the interest rate until the equilibrium is reached. If the interest rate starts too high, there will be an excess supply of money that causes the rate to fall. If the interest rate starts too low, there will be an excess demand for money that causes the rate to rise.

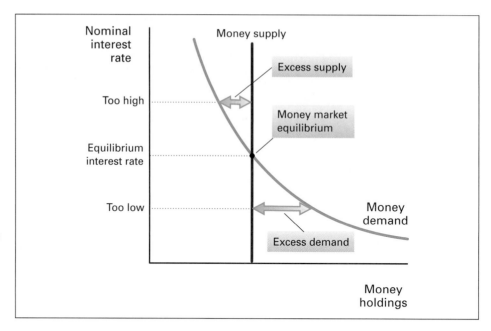

interest rates they will economize on their cash holdings in order to own bonds and other assets that pay those high interest rates. However, when interest rates are relatively low the opportunity cost of holding cash is also low. Therefore, people will hold more cash and fewer bonds.

At any market interest rate other than the equilibrium interest rate in Figure 14-3, the quantity of money demanded will not equal the money supply and the market interest rate will have to adjust to the equilibrium interest rate. To see how this would occur, consider a market interest rate greater than the equilibrium interest rate. This graph shows that the quantity of money demanded is less than the quantity of money supplied when the market interest rate is above its equilibrium value, called an *excess supply of money*. People will react to an excess supply of money by purchasing bonds. In this way people rid themselves of their excess money holdings. When people increase their demand for bonds the interest rate responds by decreasing, since it does not need to be so high to attract buyers to bonds. The decrease in the interest rate will continue until it equals the equilibrium level.

Now consider an interest rate that is below the market equilibrium rate. In this case the quantity of money demanded is greater than the money supply, called an *excess demand for money*. In their efforts to increase their holdings of money, people will sell their bonds. This increase in the supply of bonds must increase the interest rate on bonds because a higher interest rate is needed to make the additional bonds attractive to investors. The market interest rate will increase until it equals the equilibrium interest rate.

Table 14-1 summarizes the adjustment to equilibrium in the money market. The rows of the table are labeled (1) through (3) and show the three possible states of the money market. The columns offer a description of each aspect of the money market for each of the possible states.

The preceding analysis of the money market can help us to understand how monetary policy works. We will return to the money market and how it relates to monetary policy once we look at a theory from economic history that establishes the link between money and prices.

TABLE 14-1	INTEREST RATE ADJUSTMENT AND THE SUBSTITUTION BETWEEN MONEY AND BONDS			
IF THE INTEREST RATE IS	**QUANTITY OF MONEY DEMANDED IS**	**QUANTITY OF INTEREST-PAYING ASSETS DEMANDED IS**	**PUBLIC'S ATTEMPTED RESPONSE**	**INTEREST RATE RESPONSE TO PUBLIC'S ACTION**
(1) at equilibrium	equal to the quantity of money supplied	equal to the quantity supplied of interest-paying assets	No change in the holdings of money or bonds	No change in interest rate
(2) above equilibrium	less than the quantity of money supplied	greater than the quantity supplied of interest-paying assets	Increase holdings of bonds and decrease holdings of money	Interest rate decreases
(3) below equilibrium	greater than the quantity of money supplied	less than the quantity supplied of interest-paying assets	Decrease holdings of bonds and increase holdings of money	Interest rate increases

14.3 GUIDING MONETARY POLICY

The Fed maintains confidentiality when it comes to what economic variables determine monetary policy. For example, transcripts of the Federal Open Market Committee (FOMC) meetings are not released to the public until five years after those meetings take place. Thus, the public remains somewhat in the dark about the details of monetary policy decisions, relying upon the twice-a-year testimony of the chair of the Fed before Congress for clues.

Observers speculate that, in recent years, the Fed has usually followed a **price rule,** by which it conducts monetary policy with the aim of keeping price increases among certain basic commodities, perhaps including gold, within a low target range. The following of a price rule indicates that the Fed's prime concern will often be relative price stability, which means low inflation. We next turn to the equation of exchange, which provides a model to help us understand the cause of inflation and the rationale for monetary policy based on a price rule.

price rule conducting monetary policy in order to keep price increases in basic commodities within a low range.

THE EQUATION OF EXCHANGE—MONEY AND PRICES

The **equation of exchange** was originally proposed in the nineteenth century as a means of explaining the link between money, prices, and output. The equation of exchange reveals that the amount of money people spend must equal the market value of what they purchase, as follows:

$$M \times V = P \times Q$$

equation of exchange $M \times V = P \times Q$; M represents the quantity of money, V is velocity, P is the price level, and Q is aggregate output.

The equation of exchange applies to the aggregate economy. Let's look over the equation one variable at a time.

- *M:* The quantity of money is indicated by M in the equation. Money is used to purchase goods and services.
- *V:* The average number of times money changes hands in a year is called the **velocity of money** (*V*). The dollar you spend today was spent by someone else earlier, and will be spent again later. The typical dollar will change hands more than once as consumers buy the economy's output of goods and services.

velocity of money the number of times a dollar changes hands in a year.

Total spending is calculated by multiplying the money supply by velocity, as shown above in the left side of the equation of exchange. On the right side we have:

- *P:* P is a price index, such as the GDP price index, that shows the level of prices in the economy.
- *Q:* The aggregate output of goods and services is represented by Q.

When P and Q are multiplied, the result is the dollar value of aggregate purchases. The total amount of purchasing in an economy is equivalent to the economy's nominal GDP. Thus, **the equation of exchange says that aggregate spending, the left side of the equation, equals nominal GDP, the right side. Because the value of what is bought must equal the value of what is sold, the equation of exchange is always true.** Thus, we may expand the equation of exchange to include the interpretation of each side:

$$M \times V \text{ [total spending]} = P \times Q \text{ [nominal GDP]}$$

quantity theory of money a theory based upon the equation of exchange; shows that the effect of a change in the money supply is a proportional change in the price level; assumes velocity and aggregate output remain constant.

The equation of exchange forms the basis for the **quantity theory of money.** The quantity theory assumes:

- The velocity of money (V in the equation of exchange) is independent of the quantity of money in the long run. In other words, V is assumed not to change when the money supply changes, so that we can treat V as a constant value.
- Aggregate output, Q, is also independent of the quantity of money in the long run. Aggregate output depends upon the productive capacity of the economy and is assumed to be at its maximum level. This means that Q can also be treated as a constant.

These two assumptions leave only M and P, money and the price level, to vary. Thus, the effect of a change in the quantity of money must be a proportional change in the price level. An increase in the money supply brings a proportionally higher price level. Conversely, a decrease in the money supply lowers the price level proportionally to the decrease in the money supply. Except for determining the price level, the quantity theory suggests that money does not matter, because the economy will always operate at the full-employment level of real GDP. For this reason, the quantity theory cannot explain recessions.

A numerical example can help you grasp the quantity theory. Suppose that an economy's money supply equals $100 and that the velocity of money is constant and equals 2. Each dollar thus changes hands twice each time period, indicating that total spending in the economy is $200 during that time period. This $200 of total spending is also equal to nominal GDP. Suppose now that the money supply rises to $130, and that in accordance with the quantity theory, velocity remains constant at a value of 2. Total spending must then rise to $260. Because the quantity theory assumes that aggregate output (Q) is always at its maximum level, aggregate output cannot rise. There is only one way for the right side of the equation of exchange to rise to a value of $260—through an increase in the price level (P)!

The link between money and prices can also be clarified by imagining what would happen if, by government decree, we all woke up tomorrow with twice as much money as we have today. One dollar bills would be worth $2 each, five's would be worth $10 each, $100 in a savings account would be transformed into $200, and so forth. Nothing real would have changed, though. Dunkin Doughnuts would still have the same amount of doughnuts for sale as before, the number of new cars for sale at the dealerships would still be the same, and so on down the line for every good and service. Furthermore, if the economy were at full employment, the ability of the economy to produce more goods and services would be no more than before the increase in the quantity of money. What would you expect to happen next? With everyone having twice as much money to spend as the day before, prices would start to rise immediately in response. In fact, if everyone knew that there was exactly twice as much money, prices would immediately double. Even if people did not know that the total money supply had doubled, prices would still double quickly because of the doubling

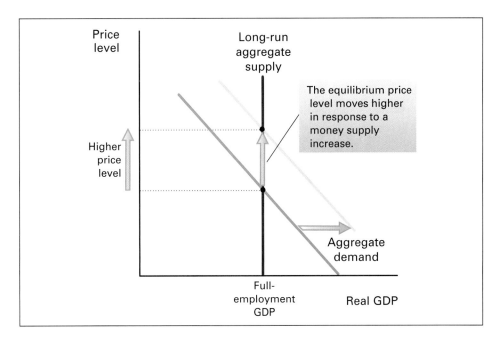

FIGURE 14-4

THE QUANTITY THEORY The quantity theory of money is that, in the long run, an increase in the money supply has no effect except to cause inflation. Aggregate demand shifts out and the economy moves up the long-run aggregate supply curve to a new equilibrium at a higher price level.

of demand for goods and services brought about by the doubling of the quantity of money. This exercise in imagination predicts exactly what the quantity theory of money predicts.

The quantity theory can be illustrated with the model of aggregate supply and aggregate demand, as shown in Figure 14-4. An increase in the money supply shifts aggregate demand to the right, because additional money provides greater purchasing power at any given price level. The long-run effect is to move the economy to a new equilibrium at a higher price level. Output remains the same at its full-employment level, as shown in the figure.

TAXATION THROUGH INFLATION—WHAT A MONEY MAKER!   *S N A P S H O T*

The Fed must keep in mind the equation of exchange when conducting its monetary policy. Otherwise, the temptation might be for the Fed to merely buy back as much government debt as possible. The open market purchases of Treasury bonds and Treasury bills that this would require might seem like a painless way to reduce or even eliminate government debt. But painless it is not, as newly printed money used to buy those Treasury securities would cause inflation that eats away at the value of all of our savings. The effect is much like a tax, and indeed is often referred to as the tax of inflation. ◄

QUICKCHECK

If the money supply quadruples, other things being equal, what does the quantity theory predict?

Answer: The quantity theory predicts the price level would quadruple. Prices increase proportionally to the increase in the money supply.

THE MONETARIST PRESCRIPTION

monetarism school of thought that emphasizes the importance of the quantity of money in the economy and a rule for monetary policy; associated with economist Milton Friedman.

Monetarism is a school of economic thought, associated with Nobel prize-winning economist Milton Friedman (1912–), that offers a modern version of the quantity theory. Monetarists readily agree with one contention of the original quantity theory: Velocity and aggregate output are independent of the quantity of money in the long run. However, unlike the quantity theory, monetarism acknowledges the existence of a short run.

According to the monetarist view, the quantity of money may indeed affect velocity and aggregate output in the short run. Thus, neither V nor Q in the equation of exchange is viewed as constant by monetarists.

■ *Changes in Q.* A reduction in the growth rate of the money supply may cause a reduction in aggregate output, Q. This effect could occur if people cut their purchases of goods and services because there is less money to spend. If that happens, the economy slows down. Hence, monetarism offers an explanation of how too little money can lead to a recession. Table 14-2 summarizes the monetarist view of how changes in the quantity of money affect the economy. The effects of both a looser and a tighter policy are described. A looser policy promotes an increase in nominal GDP through the means of increased spending. A tighter policy slows down the economy, reducing nominal GDP, by making money harder to come by, and thus reducing spending.

■ *Changes in V.* The velocity of money can change because of changes in people's need to hold money. For example, the widespread use of debit cards, ATM machines, and other technologies cause people to economize on their money holdings, and thus cause velocity to increase. Figure 14–5 shows the value of velocity over time, confirming that V increased from the mid 1980s to the mid 1990s. If V were constant, the effects of monetary policy would be more predictable. As seen in the figure, velocity is relatively stable from one year to the next, so that the effects of monetary policy are relatively predictable.

To avoid the recession that could result from too little money, or the inflation that could result from too much money, **the monetarist policy recommendation is for the Fed to increase the money supply at a steady rate, equal to or slightly greater than the long-run growth in aggregate output.** If the long-run growth of output tends to be about 2.5 to 3 percent, a steady annual monetary increase of about 3 percent or slightly higher is called for. The idea is to provide sufficient money so that the economy's additional output could be purchased without setting off significant inflation. Figure 14-6 shows the annual growth rates for the M2 money supply over time. The figure shows that money growth has varied significantly from year to year, which runs counter to the monetarist recommendation.

TABLE 14-2   **MONEY AS AN INSTRUMENT OF MONETARY POLICY— THE MONETARIST VIEW**

EXPANSIONARY (LOOSER) MONETARY POLICY

Increase in the quantity of money → Increased aggregate spending → Increased nominal GDP

CONTRACTIONARY (TIGHTER) MONETARY POLICY

Decrease in the quantity of money → Decreased aggregate spending → Decreased nominal GDP

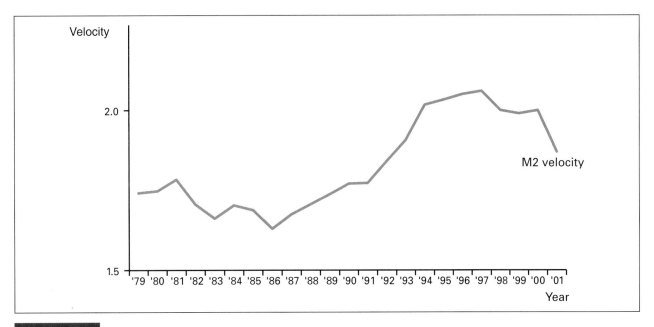

FIGURE 14-5

M2 VELOCITY Changes in velocity complicate monetary policy by making it more difficult for the Fed to achieve its targets. Velocity took an upward turn in the 1980s, as people became more comfortable with financial innovations that allowed them to reduce their money holdings.

Source: Computed by the authors using data from the *2002 Economic Report of the President.* M2 velocity equals nominal GDP divided by M2.

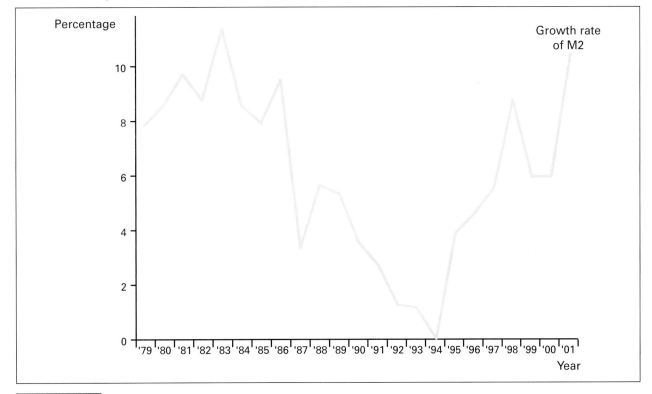

FIGURE 14-6

THE ANNUAL GROWTH RATE OF M2 OVER TIME The M2 money supply has not grown at a steady rate, but has exhibited significant variation over time.

Source: 2002 Economic Report of the President, Table B-69.

Figure 14-7 illustrates a monetarist version of monetary policy. A macro equilibrium is illustrated by the intersection of the long-run aggregate supply curve and the aggregate demand curve. Economic growth is shown by a rightward shift in long-run aggregate supply. If aggregate demand were to remain unchanged after the increase in long-run aggregate supply, the price level would have to fall in order for consumers to be able to purchase the increased production. In contrast, **monetarists recommend growth in the money supply that just matches the growth in long-run aggregate supply,** thereby avoiding the need for price level adjustments. Thus, the new aggregate demand curve in Figure 14-7 intersects the new long-run aggregate supply at the original price level.

The Fed is sometimes accused by monetarists of being too quick to increase or decrease the growth rate of the money supply. Monetarists claim that an activist policy by the Federal Reserve accentuates economic instability. Monetarists have compared the Fed to a driver who jerks a car's steering wheel first one way, and then the other, before accidentally steering the car off the road and over a cliff. The Fed, of course, denies that monetary policy can accurately be characterized this way. To monitor the Fed, monetarists have established a *Shadow Open Market Committee,* a group of economists that examine monetary policy with a critical eye.

Could the Fed ever adopt monetarism as the guiding principle of monetary policy? That is unlikely for there are some practical problems in implementing monetarism. The basic problem is that the Fed does not control the money supply—it only influences the quantity of money. The Fed controls only the monetary base, as explained in the previous chapter. Growing the monetary base at a slow and steady rate does not mean that the money supply will do likewise. Consumer pessimism or optimism about the economy can greatly affect the money multiplier, which relates the monetary base to the money supply.

FIGURE 14-7

MONETARIST POLICY Monetarists seek to match money-supply growth to growth in the country's productive potential. By doing so, aggregate demand shifts to the right just enough to keep the price level constant.

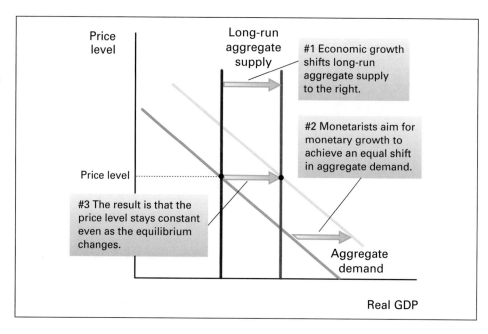

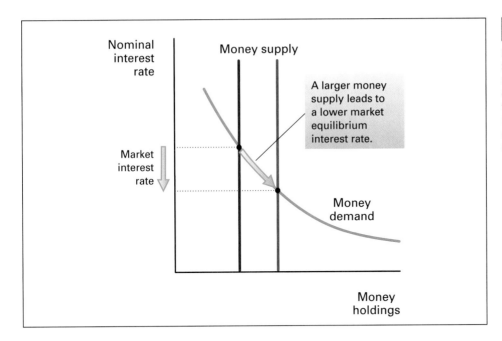

FIGURE 14-8

INTEREST RATES AND THE MONEY SUPPLY An increase in the money supply lowers the interest rate. After the increase in the money supply, the initial interest rate would no longer equate quantity supplied with quantity demanded, so the interest rate falls.

CHANGING THE MONEY SUPPLY

When the Fed conducts open market operations or employs one of the other monetary policy tools to change the money supply, we can trace the outcome in the money market. Refer to Figure 14-8 where an increase in the money supply is shown as a rightward shift in the money supply curve. The result is a lower interest rate.

In Table 14-1, row (2) explained why the increase in the money supply pushes the interest rate down. Once the money supply has been increased, the interest rate associated with the initial equilibrium is too high and the quantity of money demanded is less than the quantity of money supplied. People will buy more bonds in an effort to reduce their money holdings.

QUICKCHECK

Outline the effects of a decrease in the money supply. Why would the Fed pursue a policy that decreases the money supply?

Answer: A decrease in the money supply shifts the supply curve of money to the left and, *ceteris paribus,* causes the interest rate to increase. The interest rate must rise because, at the initial interest rate, the quantity of money demanded is greater than the quantity supplied. In an effort to increase their money holdings, the public sells bonds. In order for those bonds to be sold, the market interest rate will have to increase. A decrease in the money supply describes a contractionary (tighter) monetary policy. The Fed would pursue such a policy to slow down the economy, perhaps to head off an increase in inflation. The decrease in the money supply would shift aggregate demand to the left.

COMPLICATIONS IN CONDUCTING MONETARY POLICY

There are a number of possible difficulties that the Fed could face in designing an effective monetary policy. Five significant possibilities are:

- *Large unpredictable shifts in the demand for money.* Our analysis of monetary policy using the money market showed shifts in the supply of money combined with a stable, unchanging demand curve for money. If there are large unpredictable shifts in the demand for money, then interest rates will fluctuate unpredictably. While it is true that the demand curve for money can shift, we would expect such shifts to mostly occur slowly in response to technological change in financial markets.

- *Interest rate insensitivity among consumers and businesses.* If consumers and businesses ignore interest rate changes in making their spending decisions, then monetary policy would be ineffective. For example, if *expectations* about the future of the economy are pessimistic, it could be that lower interest rates would not increase aggregate demand because spending would not pick up.

- *An unresponsive interest rate caused by a liquidity trap.* A *liquidity trap* occurs when a demand curve for money becomes horizontal at some very low interest rate, as shown in Figure 14-9. Increases in the money supply won't push the interest rate down as when the demand curve for money is downward sloping. A liquidity trap occurs when consumers hold all increases in the money supply rather than buying bonds. The public might hold off from buying bonds if they expect interest rates to increase significantly in the future.

- *Lags in the effects of monetary policy.* Changes in the money supply affect the economy with, as Milton Friedman put it, a "long and variable lag." Today's change in monetary policy may not take effect for months or even years, at which time economic conditions may be quite different from what they were at the moment when the policy was implemented. Therefore, the effects of monetary policy are hard to predict. The long and variable lag in the effects of monetary policy is why monetarists call for a steady increase in the supply of money. Consider the lags in the context of the money market. When new money is put into circulation, it takes time for the public to adjust their holdings of money and bonds. Thus, the interest rate changes that accompany changes in the money

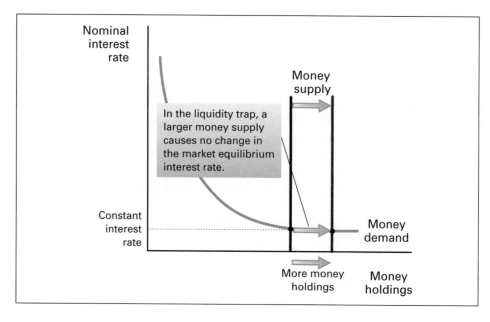

FIGURE 14-9

THE LIQUIDITY TRAP Interest rates might become so low that people ignore them. In that case, increasing the money supply merely increases the amount of cash that people hold.

supply may not take place immediately. Then, even after the interest rate changes take hold, there can be a lag before the public decides to change its spending. The problem of lags complicates the execution of monetary policy since the Fed's monetary policy actions may not move the economy in the desired direction for many months or even years.

- *Differential effects of monetary policy.* Certain sectors of the economy, such as housing and the automotive sector, are more interest-rate sensitive than other sectors because purchases of these goods are typically financed with borrowed money. Thus, monetary policy affects these sectors of the economy more than other sectors. For example, a tighter monetary policy that raises interest rates throws more auto and construction workers out of their jobs than workers in other industries. This seems unfair to many people.

In spite of these potential difficulties, the Fed typically conducts monetary policy with a great deal of confidence that monetary policy will be able to achieve its ends.

14.4 THE FEDERAL FUNDS RATE AND MARKET INTEREST RATES

Monetary policy is more than just adjusting the money supply, since monetary policy can also operate through short-term market interest rates. The means by which monetary policy works through interest rates is presented in Table 14-3. This view of the way money affects the economy is Keynesian in its origins. You should compare this table to Table 14-2, which showed how interest rates are not relevant when the quantity of money is the instrument of monetary policy.

Monetary policy goals can be achieved through changes in interest rates. **A key interest rate is the federal funds rate, the interest rate on reserves banks lend to each other.** The federal funds rate, introduced in the last chapter, is the price paid by banks that borrow reserves from other banks. For example, suppose Homestate University National Bank borrows reserves from Coastal Plains National Bank in order to satisfy the reserve requirement that was discussed in the previous chapter. If the federal funds rate is 5 percent, when Homestate repays the reserves it borrowed, it will have to include an interest payment to Coastal Plains that reflects the 5 percent federal funds rate.

The Fed does not directly set the federal funds rate, but can meet its federal funds rate target by changing the quantity of bank reserves through the conduct of open market operations. Open market sales of bonds by the Fed reduce the quantity of bank reserves because banks that buy bonds from the Fed pay for them by transferring the ownership of reserves to the Fed. When banks have less reserves to lend to each other, the result is an increase in the

TABLE 14-3 INTEREST RATES AS AN INSTRUMENT OF MONETARY POLICY— THE KEYNESIAN VIEW

EXPANSIONARY (LOOSER) MONETARY POLICY

Increase in the quantity of money → Lower interest rates → Increased borrowing → Increased aggregate spending → Increased nominal GDP

CONTRACTIONARY (TIGHTER) MONETARY POLICY

Decrease in the quantity of money → Higher interest rates → Decreased borrowing → Decreased aggregate spending → Decreased nominal GDP

TABLE 14-4   THE INTEREST RATE EFFECTS OF OPEN MARKET OPERATIONS

FEDERAL RESERVE ACTION	BANK RESERVES	FEDERAL FUNDS RATE	SHORT-TERM MARKET INTEREST RATES
Open market sale of securities to banks	Decrease (reserves go to the Fed to pay for securities)	Increases, as reserves leave the banking system	Increase
Open market purchase of securities from banks	Increase (reserves are received from the Fed in payment for securities)	Decreases, as reserves are pumped into the banking system	Decrease

federal funds rate. The higher price of reserves is likely to be passed along to borrowers in the form of higher interest rates on bank loans. Conversely, open market purchases of bonds by the Fed tend to reduce the federal funds rate, and can thus lead to lower interest rates on consumer and business loans.

The path by which open market operations affect short-term market interest rates is illustrated in Table 14-4. When the federal funds rate changes because of Fed actions that manipulate the quantity of bank reserves, short-term market interest rates tend to adjust in the same direction. Thus, when the federal funds rate increases, short-term market interest rates tend to go up. When the federal funds rate decreases, short-term market interest rates tend to go down. Consumers shopping for loans find their monthly payments increased or decreased accordingly. The higher monthly payments that go along with higher market interest rates tend to discourage consumer borrowing. The lower monthly payments that accompany lower market interest rates tend to encourage such borrowing.

Monetary policy that targets short-term interest rates can be tight (contractionary) or loose (expansionary), just as with monetary policy that works through the money supply. A tight policy causes real interest rates in the economy to rise, with the goal of keeping inflation in check. If successful, then a tight monetary policy would lead to nominal interest rates that are not much higher than the real rates. For example, if tight monetary policy kept the inflation rate down to zero, real interest rates would equal nominal interest rates. You can see this point clearly by substituting zero for the inflation rate in the equation for the nominal interest rate:

$$\text{Nominal interest rate} = \text{Real interest rate} + \text{Inflation rate}$$

A loose monetary policy causes real short-term interest rates to fall, which leads to more lending by banks to consumers. Such a policy is usually advocated when the economy is weak and inflation is not a problem. Figure 14-10 shows the average yearly federal funds rate since 1979. The nominal federal funds rate is the rate as stated. The real federal funds rate is computed using the equation for a real interest rate.

$$\text{Real interest rate} = \text{Nominal interest rate} - \text{Inflation rate}$$

Because interest rates are an expense to businesses and many households, some politicians and businesspeople argue that the Fed should aim to keep them low. Although the Fed could try to keep real rates low by expanding the money supply, the long-run result would likely be inflation that might cause nominal interest rates to soar as time passes. The reason is that the Fed's open market purchases that are intended to drive down interest rates will, in the long run, increase the money supply and thus inflation. **Monetary policy cannot lower interest rates in the long run, except through lower inflation.** A Fed policy that ignored this principle is often held responsible for the upsurge of U.S. inflation in the 1970s.

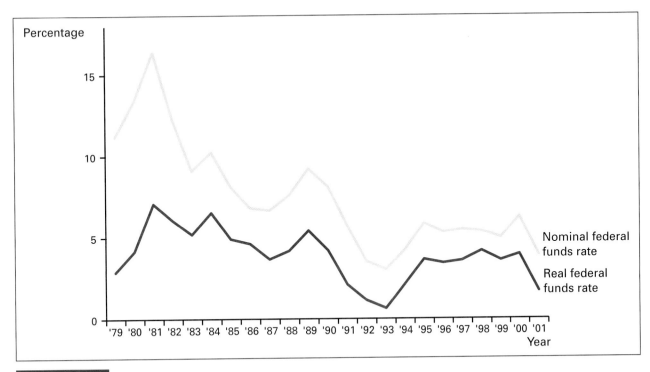

FIGURE 14-10

THE NOMINAL AND REAL FEDERAL FUNDS RATE The real federal funds rate is calculated as the nominal rate minus the change in the GDP implicit price deflator. The real federal funds rate provides a better indicator of the stance of monetary policy than does the nominal rate.

Source: 2002 Economic Report of the President, Tables B-3 and B-73, and National Income and Product Accounts, Table 8.1.

The role of the federal funds rate in monetary policy can be appreciated by referring to Figure 14-11. Part of this figure reproduces an actual Federal Reserve press release intended to inform the public about monetary policy. The wording of this press release suggests that monetary policy was unchanged since the Fed's goal was to keep the federal funds rate unchanged. Press releases like this one are provided to the public on a recurring basis by the Fed. The graph showing the drastic drop in the intended federal funds rate throughout 2001. The goal of a lower federal funds rate was motivated by the Fed's effort to shake off the recession that started in 2001.

FED WATCHING—FROM WALL STREET TO MAIN STREET   *SNAPSHOT*

Because the Fed is so powerful, its actions directly affect people's lives. The stock market, mortgage interest rates, returns on investments in bonds—all these and more are subject to the Fed's influence. The consequence is that Fed watching is something of a national sport. Economists, stock market analysts, and policymakers follow the money supply figures closely. The general public is more likely to have a greater interest in how Fed actions affect interest rates. The monthly payment on that new house or car depends not only on how good a deal the consumer is able to find, but also on monetary policy! Hints as to the future direction of monetary policy can be found when the chair of the Fed testifies before Congress each February and July. In between, the Fed issues press releases that explain monetary policy goals. ◄

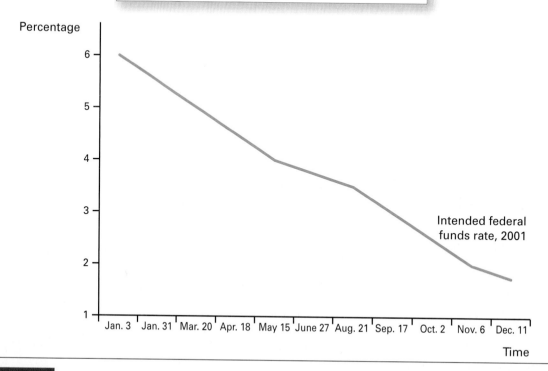

Federal Reserve Press Release

Press Release

Release Date: May 7, 2002

For immediate release

The Federal Open Market Committee decided today to keep its target for the federal funds rate unchanged at 1 3/4 percent.

The information that has become available since the last meeting of the Committee confirms that economic activity has been receiving considerable upward impetus from a marked swing in inventory investment. Nonetheless, the degree of the strengthening in final demand over coming quarters, an essential element in sustained economic expansion, is still uncertain.

In these circumstances, although the stance of monetary policy is currently accommodative, the Committee believes that, for the foreseeable future, against the background of its long run goals of price stability and sustainable economic growth and of the information currently available, the risks are balanced with the respect to the prospects for both goals.

Intended federal funds rate, 2001

FIGURE 14-11

MONETARY POLICY THROUGH THE FEDERAL FUNDS RATE The Federal Reserve press release shows the significance of the federal funds rate. The rate was set at 1.75% in December 2001 and not changed again until it was adjusted downward to 1.25% in November 2002. As seen in the graph, the intended federal funds rate was lowered numerous times in 2001.

Source: Federal Reserve web site. The press release is dated May 7, 2002.

14.5 HOW INDEPENDENT SHOULD A CENTRAL BANK BE?

The Federal Reserve is unique among government agencies in being subject to relatively few explicit government directives. The Fed has a great deal of independence to conduct monetary policy as it pleases, without interference from Congress, the president, or special-interest groups.

The fear that originally motivated Congress to insulate the Fed from politics is that political pressures could influence the Fed to pursue an expansionary monetary policy at the wrong moment—a policy that would ultimately lead to excessive inflation. Evidence suggests that the inflationary effects of monetary policy do not set in immediately, but appear only after a time lag. Thus, if the Fed were subject to political pressure, decision making could favor short-term popularity at the possible expense of long-term economic goals.

One source of the Fed's independence from political pressure is the structure of the Board of Governors. The president of the United States appoints governors to fourteen-year nonrenewable terms. Governors thus are given the freedom to make policy decisions without the worry of reappointment. Once on the Board, a governor is free to follow the dictates of conscience rather than the decrees of the president or Congress.

Typically, government agencies are funded by Congress. In contrast, the Fed funds itself. By retaining independent control of its own purse strings, the Fed retains independence of action. The Fed's secret of financial independence? The Fed is a banker's bank, and as such earns interest from the discount loans it makes to commercial banks. However, the major source of the Fed's earnings is interest from its holdings of Treasury securities—securities it may have purchased with newly printed Federal Reserve Notes! In recent years the Fed's income has totaled more than a whopping $30 billion each year, much of which it is required to turn over to the U.S. Treasury.

Another source of Federal Reserve independence is found in the financial markets. The Fed's policy actions have the potential to disturb the stock and bond markets, providing substantial gains or inflicting massive losses on the owners of stocks, bonds, and other financial instruments. Financial market participants, called "bond market vigilantes" in the press, stand ready to bail out of investments when they perceive the Fed's actions will threaten the value of those investments. That threat of a sell-off of stocks or bonds influences the Fed to act responsibly in the best long-term interests of the economy.

Even homeowners help keep the Fed independent. Higher expected inflation causes increases in interest rates. The interest rates on adjustable rate home mortgages go up when other interest rates rise. Homeowners with that type of mortgage will see their monthly house payments pushed up by the upward surge in interest rates that accompanies expected inflation. Hence, this segment of the public has a vested interest in seeing that the Fed acts to keep inflation in check.

For the reasons discussed, people have an interest in a stable monetary policy. Thus, the president's appointments to the Board do not go unnoticed. In 1983, for instance, the desire to keep financial markets from losing value influenced Republican President Reagan to reappoint then Board Chairman Paul Volcker even though Volcker had first been appointed to the Board by President Carter, a Democrat. Volcker was perceived by the markets as an experienced policymaker, independent and above politics, and thus a stabilizing influence on the economy. Similarly, President Clinton, a Democrat, was influenced to reappoint Chairman Greenspan, a Republican.

POSSIBLE DRAWBACKS OF THE FED'S ROLE

Critics argue the Fed has too much power, and charge it with decision making that favors its own self-interests and those of special interests, such as bankers. In this view, the Fed is akin to an aristocracy exercising power at the expense of the greater economic welfare.

Ostensibly, however, the Fed operates in the public interest. But what is the public interest? Possible goals include stable prices, stable interest rates, a stable foreign exchange value of the dollar, and stable overall economic activity, at a level sufficient to ensure high employment. Unfortunately, these economic variables fluctuate over time, sometimes severely.

Monetarists view the Fed with suspicion. Many monetarists believe that market economies are inherently stable, and that fluctuations in economic activity occur because of unstable monetary policies. If the monetarist view is true, then the Fed must be reined in, since its exercise of monetary policy is harmful. Thus, monetarists seek to limit Federal Reserve power. Others, especially those on Wall Street with a stake in financial stability, look to the Fed to keep the economy humming. While varying views of the Fed are unlikely to be reconciled, it remains true that Fed watching is a national pastime.

Thinking Critically

1. Since members of the Federal Reserve Board have so much power, should they be elected directly by the public? Explain.

2. How could the Federal Reserve hurt the economy? Provide some examples of Fed actions that could be harmful and of the damage that could be done. How can the Fed help the economy? Provide examples.

 Visit **www.prenhall.com/ayers** for updates and web exercises on this Explore & Apply topic.

SUMMARY AND LEARNING OBJECTIVES

1. Distinguish between an expansionary and contractionary monetary policy.

- Monetary policy has three goals: high employment, low inflation, and economic growth, which are the three macro goals introduced in Chapter 5. Many economists argue that price stability, meaning low inflation, should be the Fed's primary goal.

- There are sometimes tradeoffs and conflicts in monetary policy. For example, efforts to reduce inflation can slow the economy.

- Evidence shows that excessive growth in the money supply is the cause of inflation.

- Monetary policy works through aggregate demand. An expansionary monetary policy shifts aggregate demand to the right, while a contractionary monetary policy shifts aggregate demand to the left.

- The Fed can influence the two instruments of monetary policy. These instruments are the money supply and short-term interest rates. Prior to July 2000 the Fed set target ranges for the growth of the M2 money supply. M2 targets were abandoned in response to the murkiness of the relationship between M2 and economic performance.

2. Describe the significance of the money market and the motives for holding money.

- The demand for money is made up of the quantities of money that people wish to hold at various interest rates. The interest rate is the price paid for holding money because, when money is held, people forego the receipt of a certain amount of interest earnings. The demand curve for money is downward sloping, flattening out at a low interest rate.

- People demand money for three reasons. The first is the transactions motive, which occurs because people must hold a certain amount of money to make purchases. The second is the precautionary motive, which causes people to hold money for a "rainy day." The speculative motive for holding money comes into play when investments offer relatively unattractive returns and people would rather hold cash than stocks, bonds, and other investments.

- The money market is characterized by the demand for, and supply of, money. A money market equilibrium occurs at the intersection between the demand curve and the supply curve of money. At equilibrium the quantity supplied of money will equal the quantity demanded. A key feature of money market equilibrium is the equilibrium interest rate. The market rate of interest will adjust to equal the equilibrium interest rate.

- Money, bonds, and other interest-earning investments are substitutes. At relatively high interest rates the public will economize on cash holdings, which pay zero interest, and purchase bonds for the interest they pay. At relatively low interest rates the public is more willing to hold cash since the opportunity cost of holding cash, the lost interest that could be earned if bonds were held instead, will be low.

3. **Explain the equation of exchange and its role in the conduct of monetary policy.**

   ■ The equation of exchange is $M \times V = P \times Q$. This equation is an identity, meaning that each side of the equation must always equal the other side. The equation says that total spending ($M \times V$) equals the value of production ($P \times Q$). The equation of exchange forms the basis for the quantity theory of money.

   ■ The quantity theory of money makes two assumptions about the variables in the equation of exchange. For one, velocity, V, is assumed to be constant. For the other, aggregate output, Q, is assumed to be at its maximum value, which is achieved when there is full employment in the economy. Thus, the quantity theory states that an increase in the money supply, M, on the left side of the equation of exchange will be accompanied by a proportional increase in the price level, P, on the right side of the equation of exchange.

   ■ The quantity theory of money is illustrated graphically by the model of aggregate demand and aggregate supply. The long-run aggregate supply curve is vertical at full-employment GDP. An increase in aggregate demand occurs when there is an increase in the money supply. The increase in aggregate demand has no effect on output, but increases the price level.

4. **Discuss the monetarist school of thought and its implications for monetary policy.**

   ■ Monetarists argue that the Fed should target a slow and steady growth path for the money supply, so as to provide enough money for economic growth, but not so much as to cause an unacceptable level of inflation. The monetarist prescription for monetary policy is illustrated by Figure 14-7, which shows that an increase in long-run aggregate supply that is accom-

panied by a proportional rise in aggregate demand will leave the price level unchanged. According to monetarist doctrine, the way to achieve the desired proportional increase in aggregate demand is to increase the money supply proportionally.

   ■ Monetary policy actions can increase or decrease the money supply. An increase in the money supply will lower the interest rate, stimulate spending, and thus shift aggregate demand to the right. A decrease in the money supply will increase the interest rate, slow down spending, and thus shift aggregate demand to the left.

5. **Interpret the relationship between monetary policy and interest rates.**

   ■ Nominal interest rates are expressed without regard to inflation. A real interest rate is computed by subtracting the inflation rate from the nominal interest rate.

   ■ The federal funds rate is the interest rate on reserves that banks with excess reserves lend to other banks that are in need of reserves. By conducting open market operations, the Fed is able to achieve its target for the federal funds rate.

   ■ The Fed also influences other interest rates, which in turn affect other aspects of the economy. If the Fed is successful at controlling inflation, real and nominal interest rates will be close together.

6. **Address the importance of central banks staying independent of political pressures.**

   ■ Central bank independence is thought to insulate central banks from political influences and thus make it more likely that price stability is achieved.

   ■ Independence arises from a number of sources, including the twelve regional Federal Reserve district banks, the Board of Governors' non-renewability of terms of appointment, financial market considerations, and the Fed's interest earnings on Treasury securities.

KEY TERMS

expansionary monetary policy, 320
contractionary monetary policy, 321
demand for money, 322
transactions motive, 322

precautionary motive, 323
speculative motive, 323
money market, 323
price rule, 325

equation of exchange, 325
velocity of money, 325
quantity theory of money, 326
monetarism, 328

TEST YOURSELF

TRUE OR FALSE

1. Federal Reserve policymaking has as its chief aim the reduction of interest rates to 3 percent or less.
2. The precautionary motive for holding money is illustrated by consumers who have cash that they plan to spend soon.
3. The equation of exchange is written as $M \times Q = P \times V$.
4. The quantity theory of money assumes that the quantity of money is a constant.
5. The Fed conducts monetary policy ignoring the federal funds rate.

MULTIPLE CHOICE

6. Conflicts in meeting the goals of Fed policymaking
   a. never occur.
   b. occur, but are ignored by the Fed.
   c. occur, and are considered by the Fed in choosing monetary policy actions.
   d. occur only when the president and Congress disagree about the proper course of monetary policy.
7. The demand for money represents the quantities of money that people want to hold
   a. for transactions purposes only.
   b. at different income levels.
   c. at various interest rates.
   d. at banks.
8. The demand curve for money
   a. does not exist.
   b. is upward sloping.
   c. is vertical.
   d. is downward sloping.
9. The speculative demand for money occurs because
   a. people want to make purchases.
   b. of the need to save for a rainy day.
   c. money that is stolen must be replaced.
   d. sometimes investments are not attractive to people and so they hold money instead.
10. A money market equilibrium occurs
    a. when aggregate demand equals long-run aggregate supply.
    b. the transactions demand for money equals zero.
    c. when the interest rate has adjusted to the level that makes the quantity of money supplied equal to the quantity of money demanded.
    d. when real interest rates and nominal interest rates are equal.
11. The equation of exchange dates to the _____ century.
    a. seventeenth
    b. eighteenth
    c. nineteenth
    d. twentieth

12. The equation of exchange says that the quantity of money multiplied by _____ equals total spending.
    a. the price level
    b. velocity
    c. GDP
    d. the equilibrium interest rate
13. The quantity theory of money assumes that aggregate output is
    a. never at the full-employment level.
    b. always at the full-employment level.
    c. equal to one minus velocity.
    d. unpredictable and unexplainable.
14. The quantity theory of money is best at explaining
    a. how aggregate output is determined.
    b. how the price level is determined.
    c. the significance of interest rates to the economy.
    d. how much money people will save every year.
15. Monetarism recommends that monetary policy
    a. focus on low interest rates.
    b. focus on the stock market, aiming to increase stock prices.
    c. expand the money supply at a steady rate.
    d. be turned over to Congress.
16. Which of the following is most likely to cause the movement indicated by the arrow in Self-Test Figure 14-1?
    a. An increase in aggregate supply.
    b. A decrease in aggregate supply.
    c. An increase in the money supply.
    d. A decrease in the money supply.

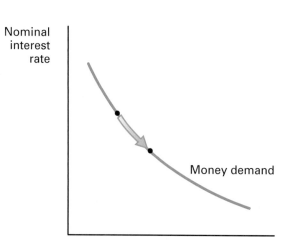

SELF-TEST FIGURE 14-1

17. An increase in the money supply will shift
   a. aggregate supply to the right.
   b. aggregate supply to the left.
   c. aggregate demand to the right.
   d. aggregate demand to the left.
18. A tight monetary policy is associated with
   a. low short-term interest rates.
   b. high short-term interest rates.
   c. alternating increases and decreases in interest rates.
   d. the money supply only, and not interest rates.
19. A monetary policy that aims to keep real interest rates low in the long run by expanding the money supply
   a. is considered the best monetary policy by economists.

   b. could lead to higher interest rates because of higher inflation created by the expansion of the money supply.
   c. would most likely cause deflation.
   d. would violate congressional regulation of the Fed.
20. Operating funds to support the Federal Reserve come mostly from
   a. the budget of the president of the United States.
   b. the Congress.
   c. garage sales, bake sales, and the other charitable fundraisers.
   d. interest earnings.

QUESTIONS AND PROBLEMS

1. *[goals of monetary policy]* List three goals for monetary policy. Explain why there could be conflicts between these goals.
2. *[tradeoffs in monetary policy]* Explain the possible tradeoff if monetary policy is designed to bring down a high inflation rate. In general, why are there tradeoffs in monetary policy?
3. *[monetary policy]* Distinguish between expansionary and contractionary monetary policy. Show graphically their effects on aggregate demand.
4. *[instruments of monetary policy]* What are the two targets of monetary policy? Why would the Fed pick one over the other?
5. *[demand for money]* What are the three motives for holding money? Explain these motives by writing three brief scenarios involving college students acting in ways that illustrate each motive.
6. *[demand for money]* Explain why the "price" of holding money is the interest rate. Will the public wish to hold more or less money as the interest rate decreases?
7. *[demand for money]* Draw a demand curve for money. Be sure to label the axes. Refer to the answer you wrote in question #5 above to explain what could make your personal demand curve for money shift to the right.
8. *[money market equilibrium]* What is meant by an equilibrium in the money market? Illustrate graphically and discuss.
9. *[adjustment to equilibrium]* What causes an excess demand for money? Explain. Is there such a thing as an excess supply of money?

10. *[money and bonds]* Why are money and bonds substitutes? Under what circumstances would someone prefer to be holding bonds rather than money?
11. *[quantity theory of money]* Write the equation of exchange. Define each variable in the equation and then explain why the left side of the equation must equal the right.
12. *[quantity theory of money]* Suppose M = the money supply = \$200, V = velocity = 2, and Q = quantity of output = 100 units. What is the price level? According to the quantity theory of money, what happens to the price level if the money supply triples to \$600?
13. *[quantity theory of money]* Using the model of aggregate demand and long-run aggregate supply, illustrate the effect of an increase in the money supply predicted by the quantity theory of money.
14. *[monetarism]* What is monetarism? How does it relate to the quantity theory of money? What monetary policy would a monetarist recommend?
15. *[monetarism]* Monetarists refer to a "long and variable lag" in the effects of monetary policy. What does this phrase mean? Why does the long and variable lag lead monetarists to call for the Fed to expand the money supply at a steady rate?
16. *[interest rate instrument]* What is the Keynesian view of how an increase in the quantity of money affects nominal GDP? Explain.
17. *[interest rates]* What is your bank's current nominal interest rate on savings deposits? What is the real interest rate on savings deposits? If the real rate is negative,

would people continue to hold dollars in savings accounts? Why?

18. *[federal funds rate]* What is the federal funds rate? Explain its significance to monetary policy.

19. *[interest rates and monetary policy]* Some people urge the Fed to aim at keeping interest rates in the economy

very low, both in the short run and the long run. Yet the policies that keep interest low in the long run might sometimes require high interest rates in the short run. Explain, making reference to the distinction between real and nominal interest rates.

   Visit www.prenhall.com/ayers for Exploring the Web exercises and additional self-test quizzes.

CHAPTER **15**

INTO THE INTERNATIONAL MARKETPLACE

A LOOK AHEAD

Technology and trade are bringing together people from different countries. Sometimes they come as immigrants to a new land. They bring with them the resources of labor and human capital. In the process they change what a country can do and wants to do. As to the immigrants themselves, sometimes they stay and sometimes they don't, as discussed in the Explore & Apply section at the end of this chapter.

Countries currently trade with each other more than ever before in history. Specialization and comparative advantage cause countries to benefit from trade. Yet, no field of economics is more controversial and less understood by the public than international trade. This fact comes as no surprise, since international trade involves all of the elements of the economy within a country's borders—its *domestic* economy. In addition, international trade must also take into account foreign currencies and conflicting interests among countries. Some background information and supply and demand analysis can shed light on this area that at first seems so murky.

LEARNING OBJECTIVES

Understanding Chapter 15 will enable you to:
1. **Identify the balance of payments accounts and their significance.**
2. **Analyze how international trade costs jobs in some industries and creates jobs in others.**
3. **Interpret exchange rates and explain how forces of supply and demand determine their values.**
4. **Describe why an appreciating dollar helps U.S. consumers, but hurts U.S. producers.**
5. **Discuss why immigration policies are controversial.**

*E*XPLORE
&
*A*PPLY

The European Community is breaking down the economic barriers among its member countries. The Chinese have embraced international trade as a key to their economic growth. The United States, Canada, and Mexico are ever more closely intertwined economically because of the North American Free Trade Agreement (NAFTA). The Brazilians have granted foreign investors huge stakes in that country's railroad and telecommunications infrastructure. Chrysler Corporation, once the third largest of the big three U.S. automakers, has combined operations with Daimler-Benz, the huge German automaker, to become DaimlerChrysler. The message is clear. Countries around the world are going global. To see how global, we need only check the balance of payments accounts.

15.1 MEASURING INTERNATIONAL TRANSACTIONS

balance of payments accounts measure of a country's economic interactions with other countries.

Countries trade with one another in order to increase their standards of living. Each country records the details of trade in its **balance of payments accounts.** The balance of payments accounts of the United States measure the economic interactions of the United States with other countries. These interactions include the sale of American-made goods and services to other countries, and the purchase of foreign-made goods and services by Americans.

The balance of payments accounts contain subaccounts that categorize the major types of international economic interactions. The two primary subaccounts are:

- the current account
- the capital and financial account

THE CURRENT ACCOUNT

exports goods and services a country sells to other countries.

imports goods and services a country buys from other countries.

current account account that records the monetary value of imports and exports of goods and services, adjusted for international incomes and transfers.

A country **exports** goods and services when it sells them to another country. A country **imports** goods and services when it purchases them from another country. The **current account** measures the values of

1. **exports of goods and services,** along with income received from abroad.
2. **imports of goods and services,** along with income payments made abroad.
3. **net transfers,** including gifts and foreign aid.

The balance on the current account is the dollar value of exports minus the dollar value of imports, adjusted for international incomes and net transfers. Figure 15-1 shows some leading imports and exports of the United States. Figure 15-2 on page 346 shows the percentage of total U.S. output accounted for by exports and imports.

balance of trade the monetary value of exported goods minus the monetary value of imported goods.

trade deficit a negative balance on the merchandise trade account, given when the dollar value of imported goods exceeds the dollar value of exported goods.

The current account divides trade into categories of merchandise and services. The **balance of trade** refers to the merchandise portion only, meaning that it is the value of exported merchandise—tangible goods—minus the value of imported merchandise. The balance of trade is currently in deficit—the **trade deficit**—which means that the value of imported merchandise exceeds the value of exported merchandise. In 2001, U.S. merchandise exports equaled $718.8 billion, while merchandise imports equaled $1,145.9 billion. Thus, when the value of those imports is subtracted from the value of those exports, the trade deficit stood at $427.1 billion that year. This amount represented 4.2 percent of the country's gross domestic product (GDP).

When it comes to services—intangible items—the United States exports more than it imports. The result is that the services component of the current account is in *surplus*. Services encompass a diverse array of activities, including the U.S. schooling of foreign citizens, the leasing of rights to broadcast U.S. television shows and movies, and even haircuts for foreign tourists. A wide range of financial and consulting services is also included. Thus,

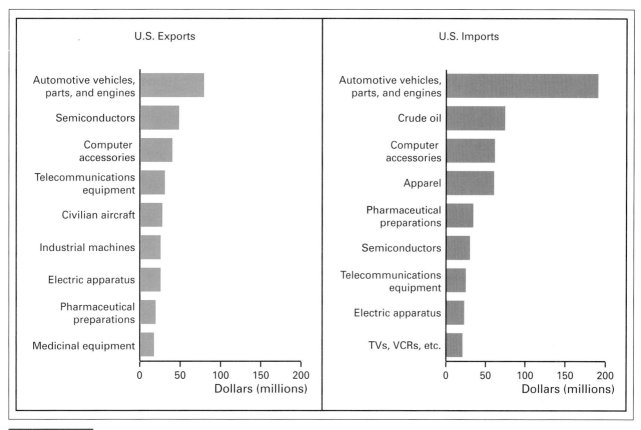

LEADING U.S. MERCHANDISE EXPORTS AND IMPORTS [BILLIONS OF DOLLARS] Many products, when broadly defined, are both imported and exported. An example is automotive vehicles, parts, and engines. However, the exported goods that fall into this category may exhibit different characteristics than those that are imported. Also, note that some goods, crude oil and apparel for example, are among the leading imports, but are not exported in quantities large enough to be included among the leading exports.

Source: U.S. Department of Commerce, *U. S. International Trade in Goods and Services,* June 20, 2002. Data values are totals for 2001.

if only services were included, the United States would show a surplus in its current account. **Largely because the trade deficit exceeds the services surplus, the current account as a whole is in deficit.**

THE CAPITAL AND FINANCIAL ACCOUNT

The *capital and financial account,* usually referred to as just the **capital account,** looks at flows of investment into and out of the country. Investments counted in the capital account are primarily of two types:

- **Direct investments:** Examples include foreign investments involving the purchase of tangible income-producing property in the United States such as office buildings, golf courses, and manufacturing plants. Likewise, U.S. investments in similar foreign properties are included in the capital account.

capital account records the monetary value of capital inflows from other countries (foreign investment in the United States), and outflows to other countries (U.S. investment abroad).

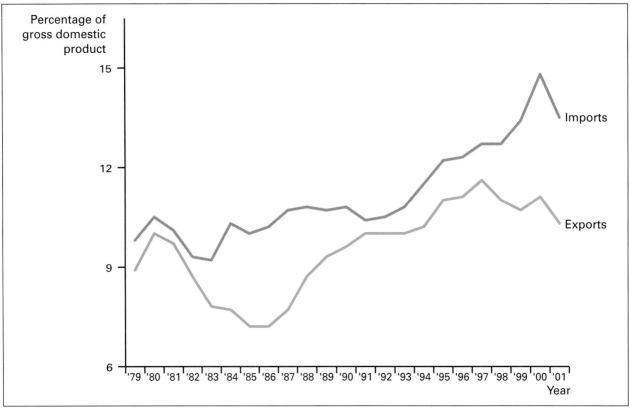

FIGURE 15-2

U.S. EXPORTS AND IMPORTS AS A PERCENTAGE OF GROSS DOMESTIC PRODUCT Whether for imports or exports, the data show an increasingly prominant role for international trade in the U.S. economy.

Source: Calculated from data in the *National Income and Product Accounts Tables,* Table 1.1.

■ **Financial investments:** Financial investments are primarily purchases of stocks and bonds. Examples include foreign purchases of stocks issued by American firms and of U.S. government Treasury bonds. The capital account also includes purchases of foreign stocks and bonds by Americans.

The balance on the U.S. capital account is the dollar value of capital inflows minus the dollar value of capital outflows, with adjustments for government transactions. *Capital inflows* represent dollars that foreigners spend on investments in the United States. *Capital outflows* represent dollars that United States citizens and firms spend on investments abroad. Thus, when looking at the direction of cross-border dollar movements, capital inflows are similar to exports, and capital outflows are similar to imports.

BALANCING PAYMENTS

The balance of payments accounts taken as a whole must have a balance that equals zero. The reason is that, when goods and investments are exchanged among willing buyers and sellers, each buyer and seller must always receive something of equal market value in exchange. For example, consider an export. The recorded worth of both the product sold and dollars received is exactly the same. However, under principles of double-entry bookkeeping, these entries go into different accounts. The result is that, while individual subaccounts

QUICKCHECK

Suppose a country records merchandise exports of $150 billion, merchandise imports of $200 billion, exports of services in the amount of $100 billion, and imports of services of $60 billion. Does this country have a trade deficit? Considering only these transactions, does the current account show a deficit or surplus?

Answer: The trade deficit is $50 billion (computed as: $150 billion minus $200 billion). The services component shows a surplus, in the amount of $40 billion (computed as $100 billion minus $60 billion). The current account deficit would be $10 billion, which is smaller than the trade deficit of $50 billion because of the surplus in services.

can have surpluses and deficits, the overall market value of what is lost and what is gained must be in balance.

Even though the market value of what enters and leaves a country is said to be equal when transactions are voluntary, countries still gain from trade. How can this be? The answer lies in the nature of any kind of trade. Sellers value the goods or investments they sell at less than market value, or they would not care to sell them. Likewise, buyers value the goods and investments they buy at more than market value, or they would not care to buy them. Thus, whenever international transactions occur, both parties gain. These gains are not measured in the balance of payments accounts, because they would be impossible for government statisticians to know.

Even with what is supposed to be measured, the statistical data are imprecise. To force the accounts into balance, it is necessary to include an entry termed *statistical discrepancy.* The statistical discrepancy is often quite large, because data collection is subject to large errors, such as caused by poor recordkeeping, tax evasion, and illegal imports and exports.

Figure 15-3 shows the size of the current account and capital account items in 2001. There is a $393 billion deficit in the current account. When it comes to the capital account, in recent years capital inflows of foreign investments in the United States have exceeded outflows of U.S. investment in other countries, putting the capital account in surplus. The surplus equaled $382 billion in 2001, meaning that $382 billion more investment dollars flowed into the United States than went in the other direction. When the statistical discrepancy is brought in to the balance of payments at the bottom of the table, you can see that the result equals the balance on the current account with the sign reversed. This outcome confirms that the balance of payments accounts as a whole must have a balance of zero, a balance that is forced by the statistical discrepancy. Figure 15-3 also shows in a graph the balance on the current account and capital account since 1982. Figure 15-4 summarizes the balance of payments accounts by presenting them in the form of a flowchart.

15.2 THE IMPACT OF INTERNATIONAL COMMERCE

Although international trade increases the aggregate value of a country's consumption, that does not mean that all share in those gains. The reason a country opens its doors to international trade, like the purpose of market trade within countries, is to get more value from the country's resources. However, while the economic pie grows because of trade, some of the slices get smaller. In other words, while there is more to go around, some people will wind up with less.

Current Account	
Exports of goods	$719
Imports of goods	−$1,146
(Balance of trade = −$427)	
Exports of services	$279
Imports of services	−$210
(Balance of services = $69)	
Net income adjustment	$14
Adjustment for net transfers	−$49
Balance on current account	**−$393**
Capital and financial account	
Net capital account transactions	$1
Foreign investment in the U.S.	$752
U.S. investment in other countries	−$371
Balance on capital and financial account	***$382***
Statistical discrepancy	$11

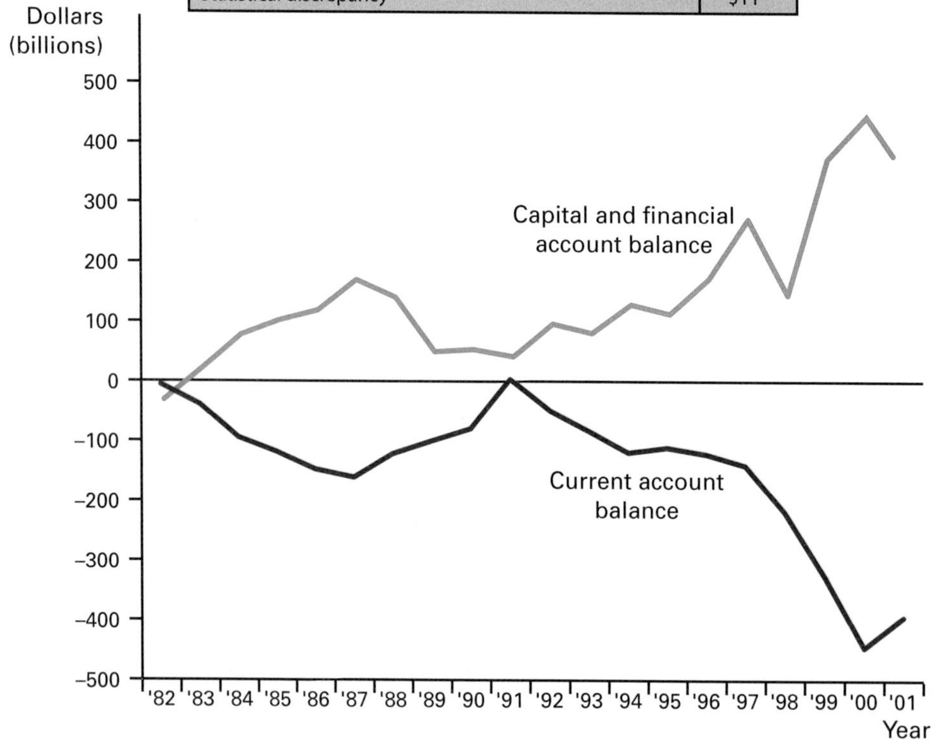

FIGURE 15-3

THE U.S. BALANCE OF PAYMENTS The table in this figure shows the balance of payments items and their 2001 values in billions of dollars. The graph shows the balance on the current account and capital account over time.

Source: Survey of Current Business, August 2002, Table F.2.

BEHIND THE NUMBERS—JOB OPPORTUNITIES LOST AND GAINED

Opportunities in specific industries and types of occupations can change markedly because of international trade. While the manufacturing of goods is still an important part

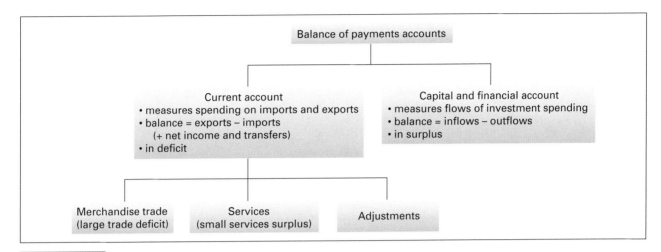

FIGURE 15-4

THE BALANCE OF PAYMENTS ACCOUNTS The U.S. balance of payments accounts record the dollar values of economic interactions between the United States and other countries. The two main subaccounts are the *current account,* which measures goods and services, and the *capital and financial account* (usually just called the *capital account*), which measures investment. The current account is in deficit while the capital account is in surplus. Although not pictured, the poor quality of data used to compute the current account and capital account causes there to be another account called *statistical discrepency* to reconcile the two.

The *balance of trade* refers to the value of exported merchandise minus the value of imported merchandise, which is a portion of the current account. This value is currently quite negative and is called the trade deficit. The services portion of the current account shows a surplus, which reduces the current account deficit to less than the trade deficit.

of the U.S. economy, many U.S. manufacturing industries have shrunk in relative importance as imported goods have replaced those made in the United States. For example, a generation ago, consumer electronic goods such as the TVs and radios that were purchased by U.S. consumers were made by American manufacturers in American factories. Today, that is not the case. Even RCA, which stood for Radio Corporation of America, is now owned by the French. While jobs making televisions are hard to find in the United States because of imports, the global economy has created a bounty of jobs in travel services, entertainment industries, and many other industries that produce goods and services popular with foreigners.

The United States has an abundance of both physical and human capital relative to most, but not all, other countries. This means that the United States is likely to specialize in goods that are *capital intensive.* In other words, for the United States to gain from international trade, it exports goods that use a high proportion of capital in their production, such as airplanes, financial services, and movies. Even U.S. farm exports are capital intensive relative to farm products in other countries because U.S. farmers use so much farm equipment relative to labor in growing and harvesting their crops. In return, the United States imports goods that use a high proportion of labor and land, such as textiles and crude oil.

However, there are exceptions. For example, Japan is in some respects more capital intensive than the United States, which explains why Japan exports so many electronic goods to this country. Over all, though, international trade causes the United States to specialize somewhat in capital-intensive goods. Exports thus increase the demand for different kinds of capital in the United States and increase the prices paid for capital. The prices paid for capital represent income to the owners of capital, including human capital.

By increasing the return to human capital in the United States, international trade opens up attractive employment opportunities for those who have acquired skills and abilities. The return to a college education, a significant source of human capital, is higher than

TABLE 15-1	EXAMPLES OF U.S. JOBS GAINED FROM EXPORTS AND LOST TO IMPORTS

EXAMPLES OF U.S. JOBS GAINED	EXAMPLES OF U.S. JOBS LOST
Aircraft workers	Textile workers
Software designers	Shoemakers
Stockbrokers	Electronics assembly line workers
TV and movie castmembers	Steelworkers
Travel agents	Autoworkers

it would be without international trade. Conversely, job opportunities for low-skilled labor in the United States are harmed by international trade, as imports of labor-intensive goods lead to lower wages and fewer job openings in those industries. Table 15-1 shows examples of jobs lost and gained by U.S. workers as a result of trade. The United States can gain jobs when it can export more of a particular good because of trade, or in response to technological changes that are promoted by trade. Workers who lose jobs because of trade are eligible for help from the Federal Trade Adjustment Assistance Program and other government programs.

SNAPSHOT   ## YOU CAN'T COMPETE WITH SUNSHINE

The trade deficit is huge, at over 4 percent of U.S. GDP. In 1992, presidential candidate Ross Perot even claimed to hear "a giant sucking sound" of jobs being pulled to low-wage countries. For centuries, people have needlessly worried about the jobs that are lost, as though there are only a limited number to go around. Some still do worry, but both long-standing economic theory and the last two decades worth of hard factual evidence from the United States tell us to leave those worries behind.

In recent decades, the United States has run a string of trade deficits, several setting new records. At the same time, it has seen some of the lowest unemployment in its history. The reason is simply that people produce in order to earn the income that allows them to consume. They find their comparative advantages. It does not matter if some things are imported cheaply. As French economist Frédéric Bastiat observed a century and a half ago, French candlemakers lost jobs in competition with sunlight, an import that is completely free. But that did not mean France would have been better off boarding up all its windows. Likewise today: We don't make sunlight and few of us even make candles; we make other things. ◄

EFFECTS OF CAPITAL FLOWS AND IMMIGRATION

International investment can substitute for trade. For evidence, look no further than the highways you travel each day. America's best-selling Japanese cars, the Honda Accord and Toyota Camry, are both made in the United States. The parent Japanese companies built manufacturing plants in Ohio and Kentucky instead of relying on importing cars from Japan.

Immigration can also substitute for trade by affecting trade patterns and the distribution of income within a country. Both capital investment and labor can move among countries, although there are usually some barriers to this migration. In the case of labor, governments commonly limit the number of immigrants overall and from particular countries. Those who want to immigrate must have sufficient money to at least pay for transportation

> ## _QUICKCHECK_
>
> **How can the international movement of capital substitute for international trade? Use autos as an example.**
>
> _Answer:_ Capital flows can lead to production of a good within a country instead of its import from abroad. For example, the Camrys and Accords driven in the United States would be imports were it not for Toyota's and Honda's investment in manufacturing facilities in the United States.

to their new home. Immigrants commonly face difficulties of language and culture, and perhaps discrimination.

The barriers to capital movements arise from diverse sources. Investors often lack information about the risks involved in setting up shop in another country. Many of these risks are referred to as _political risks_ because they involve instabilities associated with governments. For example, investors in a foreign land might worry that its government would confiscate their property without paying them for it.

These kinds of political risks are in addition to general business risks associated with investing, and help slow down the flow of capital from one country to another. A further barrier to capital movements occurs when a government limits or refuses to allow foreign investment in the country.

If a country has abundant capital relative to labor, it tends to have lower prices than other countries on capital-intensive goods. That country then tends to export goods that are produced with a relatively high proportion of capital and import goods that are relatively labor intensive. Likewise, labor-abundant countries tend to export goods that require a lot of labor to produce and import goods that require a lot of capital. Immigration provides countries that have relatively less labor an opportunity to increase their amounts of labor. The increase in labor would allow the country the chance to produce within its borders some products that it would previously have imported.

15.3 EXCHANGE RATES

A world traveler quickly discovers that there are dollars, pesos, yen, the baht, and many more currencies. Even countries that use the same name for their currencies usually do not actually share a common currency. For example, although Canada and the United States both use dollars, Canadian dollars are not the same money as American dollars. However, Ecuador is an exception to the rule. Its currency is the dollar—the same U.S. dollar that Americans use. Other countries may share a currency, as is the case with the euro, the common currency for Germany, France, and many other European nations.

Our world traveler probably will need another country's currency when crossing an international border. How can that new currency be acquired? Different monies can be exchanged for one another in _currency markets,_ also known as **foreign exchange markets.** Travelers are familiar with the obvious manifestations of currency markets. Hotels, banks, and airports frequently offer a currency exchange for the convenience of foreign tourists and businesspeople. Even taxi drivers are sometimes willing to offer these services.

foreign exchange markets markets in which currencies are bought and sold.

The amount of one country's currency that trades for a unit of another country's currency is called an **exchange rate.** In short, an exchange rate is the price of one currency in terms of another. With exchange rate information, cross-border travelers are equipped to compute how much foreign currency they will be able to obtain for their money. Travelers crossing the border between the United States and Canada in mid-2002 who looked up the exchange rate for these currencies found that one U.S. dollar exchanged for about

exchange rate price of one currency in terms of another.

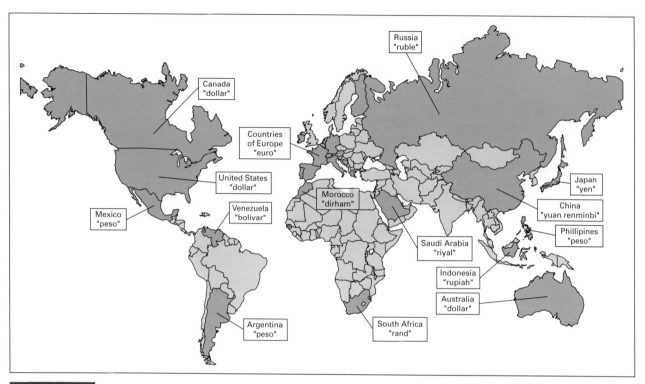

FIGURE 15-5

CURRENCIES OF THE WORLD There is a diversity of currencies in use in the world's many countries. Some countries share a common currency, such as the euro or U.S. dollar, but most countries have their own separate currencies. Thus, the U.S. dollar differs from the Canadian dollar and the Mexican peso differs from the Phillipines peso.

1.5 Canadian dollars. An American with $10 U.S. in hand would be able to acquire $15 Canadian. While exchange rates are of direct interest to travelers, they affect all of us, as we will see in the following sections. Figure 15-5 shows the currency of various countries.

MARKET EQUILIBRIUM EXCHANGE RATES— HOW MANY YEN CAN A DOLLAR BUY?

Figure 15-6 illustrates how a currency market operates. The specific example in the figure is for Japanese yen in exchange for U.S. dollars. In this market Americans seek to buy yen (demand) and the Japanese are sellers of yen (supply).

The horseshoe-shaped arrow indicates that, with minor exceptions, U.S. dollars spent on yen never physically make it to Japan. Likewise, virtually none of the yen purchased by Americans ever makes it to the United States. Rather, currencies are exchanged electronically through banks in major financial centers, such as New York, Tokyo, and London.

Although global in nature, the basic operation of this market is easily understood using supply and demand analysis, as depicted in the center of Figure 15-6. Those on the demand side for yen include U.S. buyers of imported goods and services from Japan. They also include U.S. investors interested in such things as Japanese property, stocks, and bonds. Those supplying yen have the same sort of interests, except now the roles are reversed. They may be wanting U.S. goods or services, or U.S. investments. The exchange of currencies thus represents the exchange of goods, services, and investments—both buyers and sellers have a use for each other's currencies.

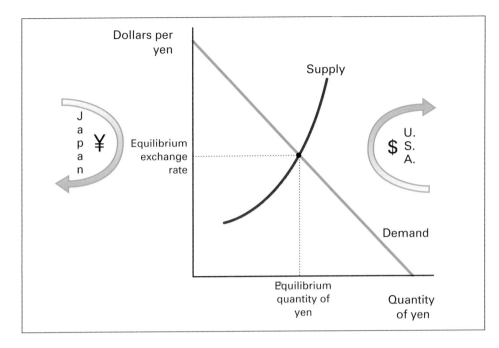

FIGURE 15-6

THE FOREIGN EXCHANGE MARKET—BUYING YEN WITH DOLLARS The equilibrium exchange rate makes sure that all dollars spent on yen are bought by others spending yen for dollars. In essence, the dollars bounce back to be spent in the United States, and the yen bounce back to be spent in Japan.

As usual with supply and demand analysis, the horizontal axis represents the quantity of a good, and the vertical axis represents its price. Quantity here is the total amount of one currency, and price is its value per unit in terms of the other currency. That price is the exchange rate. In our example, we look at the quantity of yen and see its price in terms of dollars per yen. The market equilibrium exchange rate is associated with the intersection of demand and supply, as shown in Figure 15-6. In mid-2002, that exchange rate was roughly $.0085 per yen, meaning that each Japanese yen cost a little less than one U.S. penny.

At the market equilibrium exchange rate, the total quantity of yen offered for sale is just equal to the total quantity of yen purchased. Moreover, the total number of dollars being spent to obtain yen is just equal to the total number of dollars being received by those selling yen. In other words, all dollars that U.S. residents spend on Japanese imports are received by Japanese sellers of yen. The sellers of yen enter the currency market because they want dollars for some reason.

Exchange rates can greatly affect the prices we see at our local stores. For example, imported products will seem cheaper if the dollar *strengthens,* meaning that it appreciates against many currencies. A stronger dollar buys more of other currencies, although just how much purchasing power is needed to make the dollar strong or how little to make it weak is a normative issue—a matter of subjective opinion. U.S. consumers and U.S. tourists abroad both like a strong dollar. Consider a ceramic vase that costs thirty pesos in Mexico. If the exchange rate is three pesos per dollar, the vase costs the U.S. tourist $10. However, if the exchange rate is six pesos per dollar, the vase costs only $5.

Moreover, not only does a stronger dollar mean that the price of imports is lower to U.S. consumers, it also means that U.S. firms must keep their own prices lower to the extent that their products and imports are good substitutes among consumers. For example, U.S. airlines that fly to Europe must keep their fares competitive with those of Virgin Atlantic, KLM, and other airlines based in Europe even when those airlines' fares decrease in response to a stronger dollar.

Although U.S. consumers benefit from a stronger dollar, U.S. producers of products that compete with imports and foreign tourists in the United States prefer to see the dollar weaken. A weak dollar means that U.S. goods and services seem cheap to foreigners, and foreign goods and services seem expensive to U.S. citizens. For example, the exchange rate between the dollar and the yen in June of 2002 was about 120 yen per dollar. However, it was over twice that (250 yen per dollar) in 1982, two decades earlier. The Japanese tourist in 2002 thus had more than double the spending power in the United States of that same tourist in 1982. Conversely, it seemed to the U.S. tourist visiting Japan in 2002 that everything was twice as expensive as it had been on a previous trip twenty years earlier.

purchasing power parity theory that prices would be the same around the world for easily tradeable items.

Some have argued that exchange rates will adjust until there is **purchasing power parity,** meaning that prices would be the same around the world for easily tradeable items. If there were purchasing power parity, a dollar should buy you the same amount of rice in New York as it does in New Delhi. In reality, there are often too many costly details of trade for purchasing power parity to be a good guide. The most significant of these details are transportation and storage costs that increase the price of traded goods. Other details involve public policies and even the cost of real estate where the item is sold. For example, the high price of real estate in New York City raises the price of rice in New York City relative to its price not only in New Delhi, but also relative to its price in New Paltz, which is just upstate.

SNAPSHOT

BUYING THE BIG MAC

Cashiers ring up Big Mac sales all around the world in all sorts of different currencies. When the Big Mac price is converted to a common denominator of dollars, as seen in Table 15-2, its price varies wildly from place to place. For example, it is less than a dollar in South Africa to more than four dollars in Switzerland. How can this be? There are world prices of oil, grain, ball bearings, and all sorts of other things. Is there no world price of a Big Mac?

The answer is that there is no world price for many items, including perishables such as Big Macs. No one flies from Australia to sell you a burger. If they did cart one along in their luggage, we suggest you not eat it . . . no matter the price! ◄

CURRENCY APPRECIATION AND DEPRECIATION

As we have just seen, exchange rates do not remain constant. Currency **appreciation** occurs when a currency gets stronger. **Depreciation** occurs when the currency becomes weaker. Figure 15-7 illustrates currency appreciation and depreciation.

appreciation when a currency buys more of other currencies; makes imports cheaper and exports more expensive.

depreciation when a currency buys less of other currencies; makes imports more expensive and exports cheaper.

TABLE 15-2 — THE PRICE OF A BIG MAC

COUNTRY	IN LOCAL CURRENCY	IN U.S. DOLLARS
Australia	$3.00 (Australian dollars)	$1.69
Canada	$2.99 (Canadian dollars)	$2.19
China	9.90 Yuan	$1.19
Japan	294 Yen	$2.50
Mexico	21.9 Pesos	$2.22
Russia	35 Rouble	$1.10
South Africa	9.7 Rand	$0.96
Switzerland	6.3 Swiss francs	$4.23

Source: The Economist, 2001.

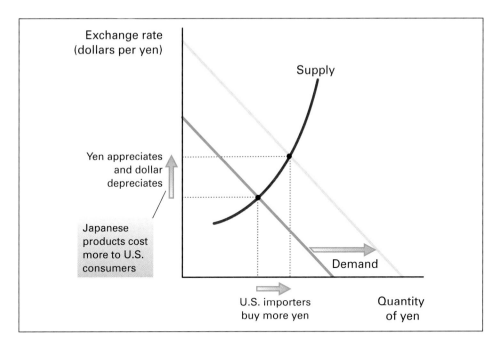

Exchange rate (dollars per yen)

Supply

Yen appreciates and dollar depreciates

Japanese products cost more to U.S. consumers

U.S. importers buy more yen

Demand

Quantity of yen

FIGURE 15-7

DEPRECIATION OF THE DOLLAR AGAINST THE YEN The dollar depreciated and the yen appreciated as U.S. consumers desired more Japanese products in the 1990s than in the 1980s. An increased demand for Japanese products shifts the demand curve for yen to the right. The figure assumes the supply curve of yen does not shift. The combination of an increased demand for yen along with an unchanging supply curve yields a higher price for yen.

In Figure 15-7 the demand curve for yen shifts to the right, such as occurred in the 1990s relative to the position of the demand curve in the 1980s. The supply curve of yen is assumed to remain constant. The price of yen in terms of dollars thus rises as shown by the upward pointing arrow on the vertical axis. Since Americans must pay more for yen, we conclude that the dollar has weakened. Since the Japanese receive more per yen, we conclude that the yen has gotten stronger. This scenario illustrates appreciation of the yen and depreciation of the dollar. The dollar depreciation between 1982 and 2002 saw its value drop from 250 yen per dollar to 120 yen per dollar. Instead of getting over 2 yen for a penny, as in 1982, by 2002 a penny would buy closer to one yen.

The depreciation of the dollar against the yen from the early 1980s through the mid-1990s can be traced to an increase in U.S. demand for yen, which drove the dollar price of those yen higher. A dominant force behind the strong yen during this period was the demand by American importers for yen to buy the Japanese electronics and automobiles that they sold to U.S. consumers.

Depreciation of the U.S. dollar could alternatively be caused by changes in the supply of foreign currency, such as in response to changes in foreign attitudes toward traveling to the United States, investing in the United States, or buying U.S. products. For example, a private lawsuit filed in U.S. courts in August 2002 sought to seize over $1 trillion worth of Saudi Arabian and other Middle Eastern assets in the United States as compensation for terrorist attacks. If foreign investors fear that U.S. courts might seize their assets because of their countries' alleged misdeeds, those investors would have a powerful incentive to invest elsewhere.

Governments sometimes try to influence the market exchange rates. The huge volume of global currency transactions overwhelms the efforts of any individual country. Countries have been slightly more effective when they work in synchrony. The most important of these joint efforts is conducted through a group of eight countries, called *the G8,* whose members include the United States, Great Britain, France, Germany, Japan, Italy, Canada, and Russia. While these countries slightly affect exchange rates through their buying and selling of currencies in the marketplace, their most effective tools involve monetary and fiscal macroeconomic policies that can change the demand for products and investments that underlie supply and demand in the foreign exchange markets. Even so, the currency markets are so huge that governments can hope for little more than to tweak them slightly in one direction or another. For example, **the value of currencies exchanged worldwide in a single week exceeds the value of an entire year's worth of U.S. output.**

This was not always the case. In the period after World War II, governments from around the world adhered to the *Bretton Woods agreement.* The Bretton Woods agreement was a treaty signed in 1944 at Bretton Woods, New Hampshire, by most of the world's major trading countries. This agreement *pegged* the dollar to gold ($35/ounce) and all other currencies to the dollar, thereby implying *fixed exchange rates.* Governments agreed to take whatever actions would be necessary to maintain these rates.

As world commerce grew over the next thirty years, however, the size of currency transactions overwhelmed the ability of governments to follow through on that agreement. The system of fixed exchange rates was modified in stages and was ultimately abandoned as unworkable during a run on the dollar in 1972. This run consisted of dollar selling that overwhelmed the governments' abilities to maintain the agreement, thereby precipitating a financial crisis. American tourists abroad felt this crisis personally, as many tourists were stranded, unable to find anyone willing to risk accepting their rapidly depreciating currency. Since that time, the system has been one of **floating exchange rates,** meaning that exchange rates have been allowed to adjust to whatever level the market dictates. However, **because governments still take actions intended to affect market exchange rates, the system is referred to as a** *managed float* **or** *dirty float.*

floating exchange rates exchange rates that adjust according to the forces of supply and demand; called managed float or dirty float if the government attempts to influence these forces.

Government inability to control exchange rates was highlighted by the precipitous depreciation of Asia's currencies as their values tumbled during the Asian currency crisis of 1998. By late July 1998, for example, the Indonesian rupiah had dropped to 14,000 per dollar from 2,600 per dollar one year earlier. This plunge of the rupiah occurred in spite of efforts by the Indonesian government to prevent it. The depreciation of the rupiah's value in the currency market meant that the 2,600 rupiah that would have exchanged for one dollar in July 1997 would exchange for only about eighteen cents one year later. To put matters another way, U.S. goods imported into Indonesia and paid for with rupiah cost over five times as much in the summer of 1998 than in the summer of 1997.

This abrupt depreciation of the rupiah dramatically increased the purchasing power of dollars in Indonesia and decreased the purchasing power of rupiah in the United States. When the rupiah fell, U.S. investors saw the value of their investments in Indonesia drop. However, many U.S. investors viewed the drop as a buying opportunity, since Indonesian investments seemed available at what looked like bargain-basement prices. However, the precipitous drop also sparked rioting and political unrest, which scared potential foreign investors worried about the security of their investments. These concerns also kept down foreign tourism, even though prices in Indonesia would seem very cheap to those who made the trip.

SNAPSHOT   **DOUBLING THE WRONG MONEY WON'T MAKE YOU RICH**

Interest rates among countries often vary quite dramatically. Yet, it's not a good idea to merely invest your money in countries with the highest interest rates. The value of those high interest rates can be eaten up by the cost of a depreciating currency. Indeed, the highest interest rates are in countries with the highest inflation rates, meaning that the country's currency loses its purchasing power over time. That loss of purchasing power is not just for goods and services, either. It applies equally strongly in the foreign exchange markets.

When you go to convert that foreign currency back to your own, reality hits! You'd find that the lavish interest gains you'd made are eaten away by the higher price you must pay for your own currency. That reality is called *interest rate parity,* meaning that expected returns on investments will be equal across countries, after accounting for expected inflation, risk, and exchange rate adjustments. The foreign exchange markets make it so. ◀

Suppose you are planning a trip from your home in the United States to France.
  a. Would your meals and hotel cost you more if the U.S. dollar depreciated or appreciated against the French franc just as you embarked on your trip?
  b. If the reason for your trip was to find customers in France for a product you make in the United States, which event, depreciation or appreciation of the dollar, would benefit your business?

Answer:
  a. Recall that when a currency depreciates it loses value. If the dollar depreciated against the franc, then it would take more dollars to buy the same number of francs. For this reason, as a tourist you would be better off financially if the dollar appreciated. It would take fewer dollars to buy the same number of francs. Thus, U.S. travelers going abroad prefer an appreciating dollar.
  b. As a producer of a product, the reasoning is different. An appreciating dollar means that the franc depreciates. As the franc loses value, it means that a citizen of France must spend more francs to get the same number of dollars. As a consequence, U.S. products sold in France carry higher price tags. U.S. producers prefer a depreciating dollar because it makes U.S. goods cheaper when they are sold in other countries.

COMPARATIVE ADVANTAGE AND EXCHANGE RATES— THE MARKET RESPONSE TO CURRENCY PRICE SIGNALS

Companies that import or export products do so in response to market prices, prices that depend centrally upon exchange rates. **Relatively higher prices at home than abroad lead to imports, while relatively lower prices at home than abroad cause exports. The result of the prices in the free market is that countries export goods in which they have comparative advantages, opportunity costs that are lower than for other goods they could produce. They import goods for which other countries have a comparative advantage.** To see the effects of market prices on what will be imported and exported, we consider a hypothetical market for flash memory chips and crude oil, as shown in Table 15-3.

We make the simplifying assumption that there are only two countries, Japan and England. Prices in Japan are given in its currency, the yen (¥), and prices in England in its currency, pounds (£). The relative prices of memory chips and oil in Japan imply that a barrel of oil costs the equivalent of 2.5 memory chips. That is, in Japan 5,000 yen could buy

TABLE 15-3   **RELATIVE PRICES WITHIN COUNTRIES IN THE ABSENCE OF TRADE**

COUNTRY	PRICE OF A MEMORY CHIP	PRICE OF A BARREL OF OIL	OPPORTUNITY COST OF A BARREL OF OIL	OPPORTUNITY COST OF A MEMORY CHIP
Japan	¥2,000	¥5,000	2.5 memory chips (= ¥5,000/¥2,000)	2/5 of a barrel of oil (= ¥2,000/¥5,000)
England	£3	£5	1.67 memory chips (= £5/£3)	3/5 of a barrel of oil (= £3/£5)

TABLE 15-4   OPPORTUNITY COSTS OF MEMORY CHIPS AND OIL BEFORE AND AFTER TRADE

COUNTRY	OPPORTUNITY COST OF A BARREL OF OIL BEFORE TRADE	OPPORTUNITY COST OF A BARREL OF OIL AFTER TRADE	OPPORTUNITY COST OF A MEMORY CHIP BEFORE TRADE	OPPORTUNITY COST OF A MEMORY CHIP AFTER TRADE
Japan	2.5 memory chips	2 memory chips	2/5 of a barrel of oil	½ of a barrel of oil
England	1.67 memory chips	2 memory chips	3/5 of a barrel of oil	½ of a barrel of oil

either one barrel of oil or 2.5 memory chips. By purchasing a barrel of oil, the buyer gives up 2.5 memory chips. In England, a barrel of oil effectively costs 1.67 memory chips because £5 could buy either one barrel of oil or 1.67 memory chips. By similar reasoning, a memory chip costs 2/5 of a barrel of oil in Japan and 3/5 of a barrel of oil in England. The opportunity costs of memory chips and barrels of oil in each country are shown in the last two columns of Table 15-3.

The data in Table 15-3 show that Japan has a comparative advantage in the production of memory chips because the opportunity cost of memory chips is lower in Japan than in England. Recall that comparative advantage occurs whenever the country can produce a good at a lower opportunity cost than could other countries. Looking at England, we see its comparative advantage is in the production of oil because the opportunity cost of oil is lower in England than in Japan. This means that Japan will export to England some of the memory chips it produces, while importing some of its oil from England.

Were the two countries to trade, the terms at which the countries could exchange oil for memory chips would settle somewhere between the two countries' opportunity costs of oil measured in terms of memory chips. For example, the exchange rate between the two goods might be two memory chips per barrel of oil. Equivalently, then, a memory chip would trade for one-half a barrel of oil. Currency exchange rates would adjust to make it happen.

The equilibrium exchange rate causes each country to export the good for which it has a comparative advantage and import the other good. In this way, both countries are better off by specializing and trading, meaning that their consumption possibilities would grow beyond their production possibilities. By trading, Japan obtains a barrel of oil in trade for 2 memory chips, which is less than the 2.5 memory chips a barrel of oil would cost in Japan. Trade allows England to obtain memory chips at the cost of one-half a barrel of oil rather than the cost of three-fifths of a barrel of oil that would prevail without trade.

Table 15-4 summarizes this example. Note that trade causes each country's opportunity costs to converge. A comparison of the before-trade and after-trade opportunity costs in Japan shows that Japan imports oil and exports memory chips. Likewise, a comparison of the before-trade and after-trade opportunity costs in England shows that England exports oil and imports memory chips.

15.4 IMMIGRATION AND THE MELTING-POT WORLD

We came over on different ships, but we're all in the same boat now.

-Dr. Martin Luther King, Jr.

Traditionally, the United States has been called the melting pot of the world. U.S. citizens are proud of their diverse ancestries and the symbolism of the welcoming arms of the Statue of Liberty. Today immigrants account for about 8 percent of the U.S. population.

While the number of immigrants varies from year to year, between 1820 and 2001 over 67 million immigrants found a new home in the United States. Figure 15-8 shows the annual number of immigrants during that period. The spike in immigration from 1989 to 1991 was caused by an amnesty for undocumented immigrants.

The United States is not alone in its role as melting pot. People of different races, religions, languages, and customs have come to live together in more and more nations. Jamaicans, Indian's, and others from countries within the old British Empire fill the sidewalks of London, Algerians fill those of Paris, and Turks fill those of Berlin. Immigration touches many nations, either because many of their citizens would like to emigrate to another country, or because their country is a favorite destination for immigrants.

IMMIGRATION POLICY DEBATE

Increasingly, many countries, including the United States, are ambivalent about the ideal of the national melting pot. This was not the case when John F. Kennedy, the great-grandson of an Irish immigrant, published *A Nation of Immigrants* in 1958. The future president of the United States struck a reverent stance toward immigration in his book, respectfully praising the economic and cultural contributions to the nation from immigrants. Subsequently, the Immigration Act of 1965 opened the door to a new wave of mass immigration into the

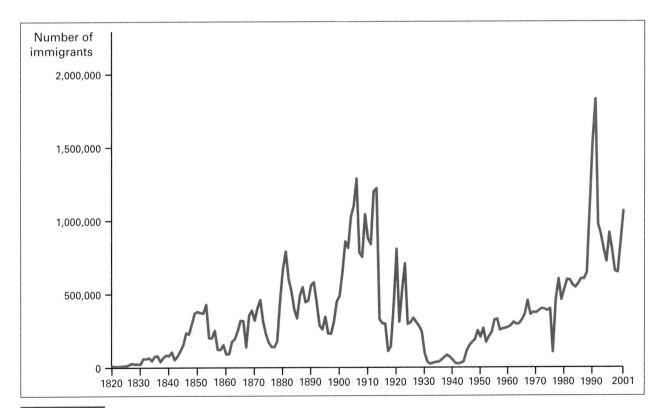

FIGURE 15-8

ANNUAL U.S. IMMIGRATION SINCE 1820 The number of immigrants varies each year, but since 1989 immigration has reached highs that match or exceed the immigration that took place in the first two decades of the twentieth century.

Source: Immigration and Naturalization Service, *Fiscal Year 2000 Statistical Yearbook,* Table 1, and *Legal Immigration, Fiscal Year 2001.*

United States, averaging about 800,000 persons per year in recent years. Today, in many other countries as well as the United States, citizens are questioning their government's open-door immigration policies. There are numerous reasons for this opposition to further immigration, but not because of the effects of immigration on trade patterns. Instead, opposition arises from the following root causes:

- Ethnic tensions arising from competition over jobs, which occurs prior to the assimilation of the newcomers into the existing culture.
- A backlash stemming from concerns that immigration has high economic costs, such as in terms of subsidized education and social programs.
- Concerns that immigration exposes the country to terrorism.

The U.S. Census Bureau estimates that by the year 2050, the immigration rates established by the 1965 act will result in a U.S. population of up to 500 million people, which is about twice the population counted in the 1990 census. The nation wonders how the economy can absorb that much population growth without social and environmental stress and reduced standards of living.

If the melting pot is not to boil over into ethnic warfare on our streets, can a host country develop a role model for immigrants of the future? It could be Albert Einstein, whose development of the theory of relativity made him a household name, or Werner von Braun, whose knowledge of rocketry played a key role in enabling the U.S. space program to reach the moon.

But superstar immigrants are few and far between. Perhaps the country seeks immigrants of the sort profiled in a series of *Saturday Evening Post* and *Country Gentlemen* articles in the 1940s: the Chinese-American Wongs of San Francisco; the Mexican-American Gonzalezes of San Antonio; the Norwegian-American Offerdahls of Wisconsin; and the half-dozen otherwise anonymous families able to succeed with their individual visions of the American Dream.

Immigration affects the economy in a variety of ways. Most controversially, immigration can change relative wages. Immigration of low-skilled workers can increase competition for low-skilled jobs and drive wages for those jobs down. Conversely, immigration of skilled workers can drive down wages that are available to other workers with similar skills. In effect, immigration has the potential to either widen or reduce the wage gap between the skilled and unskilled.

Immigrants also buy products and influence the buying habits of consumers in their new home country. Foreign products have often become popular after being introduced by immigrants. For example, without Chinese immigrants and their descendants, would Chinese food have become the lunch and dinner staple that it is in the United States today?

Another way that immigration can affect trade patterns is through the skills that immigrants bring to their new country. Suppose a group of immigrants with rug-weaving skills arrive in a country that has traditionally imported rugs. These immigrants might well be able to start a rug-weaving industry in their new country. At the least, that country would import fewer rugs. It might even be possible for that country to begin exporting rugs at some point. Also, opportunities for success in a country encourage particularly inventive and entrepreneurial immigrants. The entrepreneurship and development of technology arising from the efforts of these immigrants expands the country's production possibilities and in the process changes its patterns of trade.

Whether or not a country allows easy immigration has a lot to do with the ownership of resources and the distribution of income within that country. For example, immigration can decrease the incomes and job opportunities for workers who find themselves in competition with the immigrants. Also, if immigrants can obtain subsidies from longer-term citizens, the well-being of those citizens could easily fall, even as the country's output goes up. Thus, whether a country wants to allow easy immigration depends on its objective. If the country seeks to maximize the well-being of its longer-term citizens, it has to consider immigration's effects on those citizens' incomes and tax burdens, and might choose a relatively tight immigration policy.

As a middle ground, many countries make special provisions for guest workers. *Guest workers* are temporary immigrants who are granted limited rights to work and live in a country. For example, Switzerland depends on its Italian guest workers. Saudi Arabia depends on guests from the Philippines and numerous other countries. For years the United States depended on guest farm workers from Mexico under the *Bracero* (translated into English, Bracero means "arm") program that ended in 1964. As the U.S. unemployment rate dropped to 4.5 percent in 1998, shortages of cheap labor revived interest in the program. Subsequently, various proposals for new Bracero programs were put forth. For example, Mexico's President Vicente Fox proposed a modern version of the Bracero program in March of 2002.

Sometimes, guests become permanent, as with many of the Turkish workers invited into Germany. The same is true of the many temporary immigrants into the United States who make their way into the ranks of those with full citizenship. It is well to remember that, without the entrepreneurial drive of yesteryear's immigrants, the United States would not have produced the economy that beckons to so many more immigrants today.

1. Develop an immigration policy for the United States that considers the following factors:
   a. The effect of immigration on wages and skill differentials in wages.
   b. The country of origin of the immigrants, including whether you think a quota is desirable for each country.
   c. The effect of immigration on the national culture.
   d. Any other factors you consider to be significant.

2. To help with the burden of Social Security, some people suggest that we "import the young to care for the old." The idea is that the United States would offer foreigners a stake in America in exchange for their tax contributions. Is this a good idea?

*T*HINKING
*C*RITICALLY

Visit www.prenhall.com/ayers for updates and web exercises on this Explore & Apply topic.

SUMMARY AND LEARNING OBJECTIVES

1. **Identify the balance of payments accounts and their significance.**
   - The current account records the value of imports and exports of goods and services, with adjustments for international incomes and transfers. Since U.S. imports exceed U.S. exports, the current account is in deficit.
   - The current account includes trade in services and merchandise. The balance on merchandise trade is currently quite negative, and is called the trade deficit. Trade in services shows a surplus, but that surplus is smaller than the trade deficit.

   - The capital account measures international investment flows, which currently are characterized by more foreign investment in the United States than U.S. investment abroad, indicating a surplus. Capital inflows involve investment in the United States by foreigners. Capital outflows occur when there is investment in other countries by U.S. firms and citizens. Investments are of two types: direct investments and financial investments.
   - The balance of payments' balance must equal zero by definition. Because of errors in measurement in the

current account and capital account, the balance is forced to zero by including an item called the statistical discrepancy. When the statistical discrepancy is included with the capital account, the result equals the balance on the current account with the sign reversed.

2. **Analyze how international trade costs jobs in some industries and creates jobs in others.**
   - While trade may eliminate specific jobs, in the aggregate a country's total employment will be unaffected.
   - Countries that have abundant capital tend to specialize in the production of capital-intensive goods and export capital-intensive goods to other countries. Likewise, countries that have abundant labor tend to specialize in and export labor-intensive goods.
   - The United States is relatively capital abundant, both in terms of physical and human capital. International trade increases the demand for capital, thus increasing its price. The returns to the human capital possessed by U.S. workers are increased by trade, along with the job opportunities in industries that make use of that human capital. Jobs for low-skilled labor decrease because of trade.

3. **Interpret exchange rates and explain how forces of supply and demand determine their values.**
   - The price of a country's currency in terms of another country's currency is an exchange rate. Exchange rates are determined by the demand and supply of currencies.
   - Exchange rates vary over time. A currency appreciates (gets stronger) when its value in the foreign exchange market rises. A currency depreciates (weakens) when its value falls in the foreign exchange market.

4. **Describe why an appreciating dollar helps U.S. consumers, but hurts U.S. producers.**
   - As a country's currency appreciates, it is able to buy more of other countries' currencies. Currency appreciation results in lower prices for the country's imports, but higher prices for its exports. As a country's currency depreciates, its exports become cheaper, but the price of its imports rises. This effect occurs because currency depreciation increases the price of other currencies.

5. **Discuss why immigration policies are controversial.**
   - Immigration is a controversial issue in the United States and many other countries. Immigrants offer their skills and their culture. Some immigrants come to stay in their new country, but others arrive as guest workers, who will probably return to the countries of their births.

KEY TERMS

balance of payments accounts, 344
exports, 344
imports, 344
current account, 344
balance of trade, 344

trade deficit, 344
capital account, 345
foreign exchange markets, 351
exchange rate, 351
purchasing power parity, 354

appreciation, 354
depreciation, 354
floating exchange rates, 356

TEST YOURSELF

TRUE OR FALSE

1. The United States has a deficit in its balance of payments accounts.
2. The balance on the current account equals the dollar value of exported goods minus the dollar value of imported goods.
3. By increasing the return to human capital in the United States, international trade opens up attractive employ-

ment opportunities for those who have acquired skills and abilities.

4. If foreign investors decide that investment opportunities in the United States are better than they used to be and so increase their investments in the United States, the dollar is likely to appreciate.
5. An appreciation in the dollar means that consumers pay less for imports.

MULTIPLE CHOICE

6. The balance of payments accounts refer to
   a. the value of exports minus the value of imports.
   b. the values of all international transactions between a particular country and other countries.
   c. a statement of all international transactions among all nations.
   d. a record of spending and taxes collected by the federal government.

7. In the balance of payments accounts, the current account includes
   a. capital flows and merchandise trade.
   b. trade in goods and services.
   c. immigration and trade.
   d. capital flows and services.

8. Which statement best describes a trade deficit?
   a. The dollar value of exported goods is less than the dollar value of imported goods.
   b. Both the dollar value of imports and the dollar value of exports decrease.
   c. The foreign exchange value of a country's currency has increased.
   d. A country invests too much overseas.

9. Which of the following represents a direct investment?
   a. U.S.-grown timber is shipped to Japan.
   b. A shipload of new Korean automobiles is exported to the United States.
   c. A U.S. firm builds a factory in Ireland.
   d. A U.S. citizen gets a haircut abroad.

10. New international investments are measured by the
    a. current account.
    b. capital account.
    c. statistical discrepancy.
    d. trade deficit.

11. The dollars paid by U.S. importers to buy foreign products
    a. circulate abroad until foreigners buy U.S. products.
    b. circulate abroad and do not return.
    c. circulate abroad until Americans buy foreign investments.
    d. usually do not physically leave the country.

12. If the United States were to eliminate international trade, it would be likely to have
    a. an unpredictable impact on the return to human capital.
    b. no change in the return to human capital.
    c. a lower return to human capital.
    d. a greater return to human capital.

13. The euro will strengthen against the dollar when
    a. the demand for euros increases.
    b. the supply of euros increases.
    c. the demand for dollars increases.
    d. the dollar also strengthens against the euro.

14. Suppose that an American import firm purchases some English ironstone dinnerware from an exporter in London. The dinnerware costs £5,000. At the exchange rate of $3 = £1, the dollar price of the dinnerware is
    a. $15,000.
    b. $10,000.
    c. $2,500.
    d. $1,666.67.

15. Currently, currency exchange rates are determined primarily
    a. in the marketplace by demand and supply.
    b. by a computer model developed by the United Nations.
    c. by international gold flows.
    d. in accordance with international agreements negotiated by countries.

16. In Self-Test Figure 15-1, the vertical arrow shows that the dollar
    a. has appreciated.
    b. exhibits purchasing power parity.
    c. exhibits interest-rate parity.
    d. has depreciated.

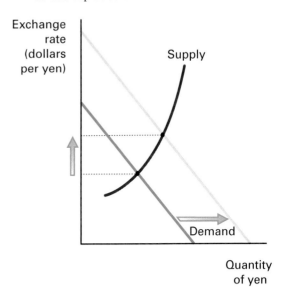

SELF-TEST FIGURE 15-1

17. If German-made goods have the same price in Germany this year as last year, but the euro depreciated against the dollar during the year, then the dollar price of German goods sold in the United States would _____ and Americans would buy _____ from Germany.
    a. increase; less
    b. increase; more
    c. decrease; less
    d. decrease; more

18. Depreciation in a country's currency will cause
    a. the country's exports to drop.
    b. an increase in the number of tourists visiting that country.
    c. windfall gains to speculators holding large quantities of that country's currency.
    d. widespread fear of contracting the disease, and hence a reluctance to accept payment in that currency.

19. Suppose two countries, France and Portugal, produce wine and cloth. If Portugal has a comparative advantage in the production of cloth, then

    a. Portugal must depreciate its currency.
    b. the opportunity cost of cloth is higher in France than in Portugal.
    c. wine will be exported from Portugal to France.
    d. these countries will choose not to trade with each other.

20. Approximately _____ immigrants legally enter the United States in an average year.
    a. 100,000
    b. 800,000
    c. 2,000,000
    d. 4,500,000

QUESTIONS AND PROBLEMS

1. *[balance of payments accounts]* Discuss the role of the current account in balance of payments accounting. In recent years, has the balance on the current account been positive or negative? Explain.

2. *[balance of payments accounts]* Discuss the role of the capital account in balance of payments accounting. Is the balance on the capital account positive or negative? Explain.

3. *[balance of payments accounts]* Critique the following statement: "There is usually a deficit in the U.S. balance of payments."

4. *[balance of payments accounts]* "The United States runs a trade deficit." Specifically, what does this statement mean? Briefly distinguish the trade deficit from the current account deficit.

5. *[trade and jobs]* Suppose the United States decides to prohibit all imports and exports. Would this approach reduce unemployment in the United States? Explain.

6. *[exchange rates]* Suppose Middle-Eastern investors decide to sell their U.S. investments. What would be the effect on the exchange rate between the dollar and Middle-Eastern currencies? In what way would that harm Middle-Eastern investors who do not sell their U.S. investments?

7. *[exchange rates]* Paperback novels sold in North America typically have two prices marked on their covers, one in U.S. dollars and another in Canadian dollars. Fifty years ago, there would probably only have been one price. Why?

8. *[currency depreciation]* In terms of demand and supply, what causes a currency to depreciate? How does the depreciation of a currency affect its imports and exports?

9. *[exchange rates]* Suppose the U.S. federal government adopts the policy of "What's good for General Motors is good for the country." To this end, the government decides to prohibit the import of all motor vehicles from other counties. Assuming other countries do not change their own trade policies, what would be the impact on the value of the dollar relative to other currencies? What would be the effect on the quantity of other items imported? What would be the effect on jobs in U.S. industries that did not participate in the making of autos?

10. *[exchange rates]* In 1998 the new Volkswagen Beetle and Mercedes-Benz M-class sport utility vehicles were unveiled. Explain, using the concepts in this chapter, why Mercedes-Benz chose to produce its new sport utility vehicle in Alabama rather than in Germany. Why would Volkswagen have decided at about the same time to make the new Beetle in Mexico rather than the United States?

11. *[exchange rates]* Find a recent issue of The *Wall Street Journal* newspaper or other financial publication or web site and check on the exchange rates between several currencies of your choice and the U.S. dollar. Has the dollar strengthened or weakened within the last year relative to these currencies?

12. *[comparative advantage]* Suppose there are only two countries, A and B. Country A is endowed with abundant resources of all types and a highly intelligent and motivated labor force. Country B has few natural resources and its workers cannot seem to do anything well. Both countries are self-sufficient, each subsisting on goods X and Y. The price of both X and Y in country A is $1. In country B, the price of X is £1 and the price

of Y is £2. Neither country trades with the other, but both are about to start.

a. If trade were to occur, what would be its pattern; that is, which country would specialize in which product(s)? Why?

b. As Trade Minister for country A, would you recommend trading with country B? Why, or why not? What if you were trade minister for country B?

13. *[comparative advantage]* Using the example of memory chips and oil production in Japan and England discussed in the chapter, provide a few examples of the characteristics that might explain the comparative advantages held by each country. In other words, what characteristics of Japan would explain why Japan would export memory chips, and what characteristics of England would explain why England would export oil?

14. *[comparative advantage]* Suppose that, without international trade, one Alphanian alpha (the currency of Alphania) would buy either one bottle of wine or one yard of cloth. In the country of Betalia, one Betalian beta would buy either one bottle of wine or two yards of cloth. Which country has a comparative advantage in wine production and which in the production of cloth? Why?

15. *[exchange rates]* In the previous question, what exchange rate between the alpha and the beta would allow both Alphania and Betalia to gain from trade? With trade, what would happen to the price of:

a. cloth in Alphania?

b. cloth in Betalia?

c. wine in Alphania?

d. wine in Betalia?

 Visit www.prenhall.com/ayers for Exploring the Web exercises and additional self-test quizzes.

CHAPTER 16

POLICY TOWARD TRADE

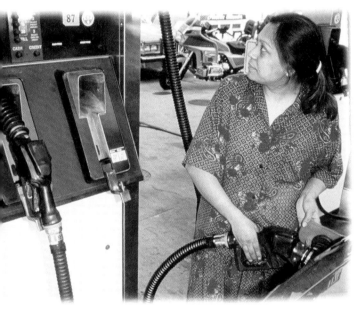

A LOOK AHEAD

We walk in them. We talk on them. We drive them. We wave them in the air and shoot them in the sky on Independence Day. What are they? Imports! It's not that we couldn't make all of our own shoes, phones, cars, flags, and fireworks. It is just not in our comparative advantage to do so. Instead, the price signals of the marketplace lead us to specialize and trade. But what about oil? Do we import so much of it that we are held hostage to oil politics? Are the costs of those imports merely the prices the importers pay, or do those imports add security costs, too? As we will see in this chapter's Explore & Apply section, economic analysis can shed light on such questions.

We begin with a discussion of the gains from trade and the policy instruments available in the trade-warfare arsenal. We will see that countries can "beggar thy neighbor" with protectionist policies, but risk losing their own prosperity in the process. To keep protectionist policies at bay and to promote freer trade, countries have joined together in regional trade agreements, reached a major multilateral trade accord termed the GATT, and established the World Trade Organization to enforce the GATT. We'll discover that there is still plenty of controversy over cases in which trade restrictions might be justified.

LEARNING OBJECTIVES

Understanding Chapter 16 will enable you to:
1. **Use the concept of a world price to explain imports, exports, and the gains from trade.**
2. **Discuss the GATT and other trade agreements among countries.**
3. **Distinguish among the various barriers to trade that countries might impose.**
4. **Assess the arguments for and against protectionist policies.**
5. **Examine whether an oil import fee can promote energy security.**

Explore & Apply

In Chapter 2, we discussed the efficiency of trade. It does not matter if that trade is among individuals, states, or countries—trade can increase our consumption to more than what we can produce ourselves. Yet, over the years, trade has frequently been restricted, and only sometimes for good reason. We start by examining who wins and loses from trade. We then turn to trade agreements . . . and to trade disagreements.

16.1 ASSESSING GAINS FROM TRADE

International trade occurs in response to differences between the price of a good in the country's own market—its domestic market—and the price that the good sells for in the rest of the world—the *world price*. When a country opens its doors to international trade, the price in the domestic market will come to equal that in the world market. If this adjustment means that the domestic price rises to meet the higher world price, then the country exports the good. If the world price causes the domestic price to drop, then the country imports the good, meaning that it is purchased from producers in other countries. In either case, there are some people within the country who gain and others who lose. However, as we will see in this section, the gains can be expected to exceed the losses.

GAINS FROM IMPORTS

We have previously seen how people and countries gain by specializing according to comparative advantage and then trading with others. Here, we look at that general concept as it applies to markets for imports and exports. We proceed by imagining a country that embraces **free trade**—with no policies designed to influence imports or exports—after previously allowing no foreign commerce at all.

free trade international commerce unhindered by policy obstacles.

Before free trade, the country's prices would have been based solely on its own domestic supply and demand curves. However, goods and services that are widely traded among countries have a *world price,* which is the price that the good trades for in the global marketplace. The world price of a good is determined by supply and demand for the good from all trading countries. **Free trade implies that a country's producers must accept world market prices, which would entail a higher price for some goods and a lower price for others.**

Figure 16-1 shows the case of a good's world price that would lead a country to import that good. The supply and demand for the good within the country, labeled "Domestic supply" and "Domestic demand" in the figure, intersect at the price that prevails when the country chooses not to trade, labeled "Price if no trade." However, the world price is less than this domestic price. Domestic consumers will not be willing to pay any more than the world price once free trade is allowed. Producers will also refuse to sell for less than the world price. Thus, it is the intersection of the world price with supply and demand that determines the domestic quantity supplied and demanded, respectively. Because the domestic quantity supplied is less than the quantity demanded, consumers make up the difference with imports, as shown in Figure 16-1.

Imports allow domestic consumers to pay a lower price for goods. They benefit from a lower price per unit for goods that they buy. **They also gain by consuming more of the good,** supplementing the lower quantity supplied by domestic producers with imports from other countries. The gains to consumers are measured by the increase in consumer surplus, defined as the difference between demand and price as discussed in Chapter 4.

Figure 16-2 repeats Figure 16-1, but with the areas of consumer and producer surplus labeled. Without imports, consumers would have received as consumer surplus the area labeled *A* in Figure 16-2, since that is the difference between demand and the price if there was no international trade. With the lower world price, however, consumer surplus

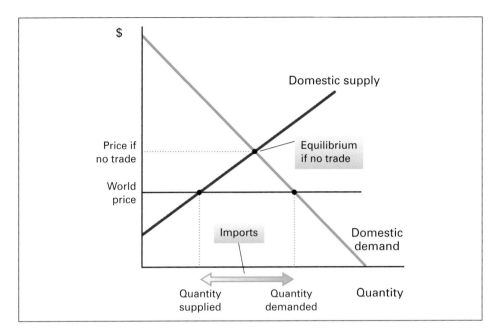

FIGURE 16-1

IMPORTS—EFFECTS ON PRICE AND QUANTITY Imports result from a world price that is below the country's price prior to trade. The lower price causes the country's consumption to rise and production to fall, with the difference being the amount imported.

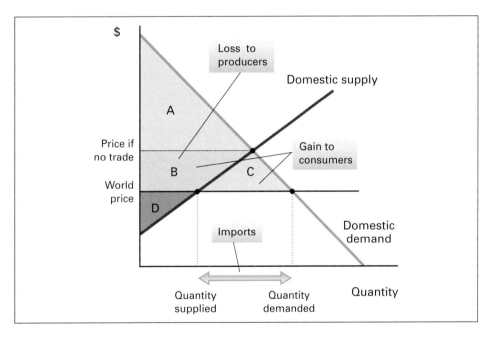

FIGURE 16-2

GAINS AND LOSSES FROM IMPORTS Imports benefit consumers more than they harm producers. Consumer surplus rises from area *A* to areas *A + B + C*, while producer surplus drops from areas *B + D* down to area *D*. Since the gains to consumers exceed the loss to producers, the country on balance is better off.

increases to the areas *A + B + C*, since that is the difference between demand and the new, lower price.

The price drop from imports causes producers to lose, however. In general, producer surplus is defined as the difference between price and supply. In Figure 16-2, producer surplus had been areas *B + D*, which is the difference between the market price without international trade and supply. After the lower price that results from international trade, however, producer surplus drops to only area *D*. Note that consumers gained areas *B + C* while producers lost only area *B*. The implication is that **the gains to consumers from imports more than offset the losses to producers, which reveals that the country as a whole is better off allowing imports.** This result is seen in Table 16-1.

TABLE 16-1	EFFECTS OF REMOVING TRADE BARRIERS IN CERTAIN U.S. INDUSTRIES, (MILLIONS OF DOLLARS)

INDUSTRY	TARIFF OR EQUIVALENT	CONSUMER GAIN	PRODUCER LOSS
Ball bearings	11.0%	64	13
Benzenoid chemicals	9.0	309	127
Canned tuna	12.5	73	31
Ceramic articles	11.0	102	18
Ceramic tiles	19.0	139	45
Costume jewelry	9.0	103	46
Frozen orange juice concentrate	30.0	281	101
Glassware	11.0	266	162
Luggage	16.5	211	16
Polyethylene resins	12.0	176	95
Rubber footwear	20.0	208	55
Softwood lumber	6.5	459	264
Women's footwear, except athletic	10.0	376	70
Women's handbags	13.5	148	16
Dairy products	50.0	1,184	835
Peanuts	50.0	54	32
Sugar	66.0	1,357	776
Maritime transport	85.0	1,832	1,275
Apparel	48.0	21,158	9,901
Textiles	23.4	3,274	1,749
Machine tools	46.6	542	157

Source: Cletus C. Coughlin, "The Controversy Over Free Trade: The Gap Between Economists and the General Public," *Federal Reserve Bank of St. Louis Review* Jan/Feb 2002, Table 1. Estimates are for 1990.

GAINS FROM EXPORTS

Figure 16-3 is similar to Figure 16-1 except the world price is above the domestic price. In this case, the price difference causes the domestic quantity supplied to be greater than the domestic quantity demanded. This difference between quantity supplied and the quantity demanded results in an excess quantity of the product. This excess is exported, as shown in the figure.

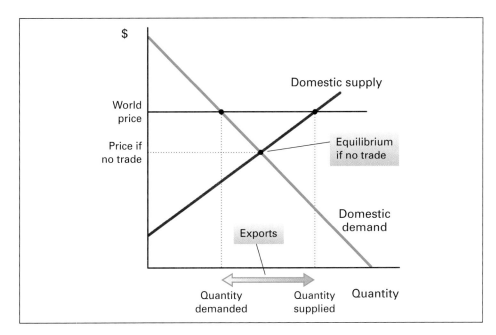

FIGURE 16-3

EXPORTS—EFFECTS ON PRICE AND QUANTITY Exports result from a world price that is above the country's price prior to trade. The higher price causes the country's consumption to fall and production to rise, with the difference being the amount exported.

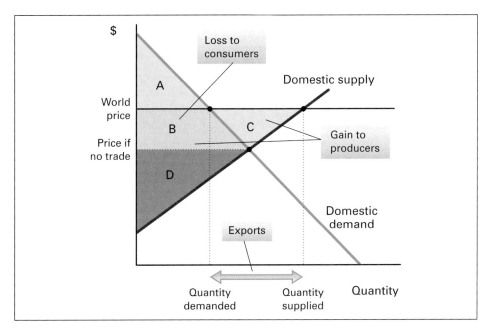

FIGURE 16-4

GAINS AND LOSSES FROM EXPORTS Producers gain more from exports than consumers lose. The country's consumers see their consumer surplus drop from areas $A + B$ to only area A. However, producer surplus rises from area D to areas $B + C + D$. Since the gain to producers exceeds the loss to consumers, the country is better off.

In the case of exports, producers win and consumers lose. Producers win because they sell more at a higher price. Their gain is measured by the increase in producer surplus. Figure 16-4 repeats Figure 16-3, but with consumer and producer surplus labeled. Producer surplus increases from area D, which is what producer surplus would be without international trade, to areas $B + C + D$, which is producer surplus with the higher price that prevails in the world market.

Consumers lose because they must pay the higher world price, and thus consume less. Their consumer surplus drops from areas $A + B$ to only area A in Figure 16-4. Because producer surplus increases by areas $B + C$ while consumer surplus only shrinks by area B,

> ## QUICKCHECK
>
> **Since consumers gain from imports, but domestic producers lose, isn't a country just as well off to forgo imports altogether? Similarly, since consumers lose from exports, but domestic producers gain, isn't a country just as well off to do without exports? Explain.**
>
> **Answer:** No, consumers gain more from imports than producers lose. Likewise, producers gain more from exports than consumers lose. Thus, both imports and exports bring net gains to the country.

producers gain more than consumers lose. So, on balance, **the country as a whole gains by allowing exports.** In short, both imports and exports lead to more gains than losses.

16.2 TRADE AGREEMENTS

open economy an economy with no restrictions on economic interactions with other countries.

Countries must choose how wide to open their doors to international trade. An **open economy** is one that erects no barriers to international trade and investment. In contrast, a *closed economy* shuts itself off from foreign investment and trade.

MULTINATIONAL EFFORTS TOWARD FREE TRADE— THE GATT AND THE WORLD TRADE ORGANIZATION

Controversy has been the hallmark of efforts toward free trade. Australians witnessed intense anti-trade sentiments firsthand during the 2000 Olympic Games. Australia, like the United States and some other countries, was the site of violent demonstrations in which protesters rebuked the industrialized nations for purported economic exploitation of less-developed countries. Those protesters neglected to point out the reasons that less-developed countries chose open economies, namely that there are benefits from trade in which both countries gain. Trade policies can reduce or enhance an economy's openness.

Countries design their trade policies with an eye toward their own self-interests. Since governments are by nature political, trade strategies usually contain a mix of political and economic objectives. However, most countries recognize that their interests are usually best served by freeing up trade with other countries. This lesson was learned the hard way during the Great Depression of the 1930s. In a misguided fight against the high unemployment of those days, the United States and other countries engaged in *trade wars,* situations in which countries punish each other and themselves through retaliatory trade restrictions.

General Agreement on Tariffs and Trade (GATT) an agreement signed by most of the major trading countries of the world, which limits the use of protectionist policies; enforced by the World Trade Organization.

Most countries have signed the **General Agreement on Tariffs and Trade (GATT)** that aims to avoid trade wars and promote free trade. The GATT was initially signed in 1947 by the twenty-three major trading countries of the world at that time. Over the intervening years, the agreement has been updated and membership has grown to 110 countries. Since 1995, the GATT has been administered by the **World Trade Organization (WTO),** an arm of the GATT created to settle trade disputes among GATT members and monitor compliance with provisions of the GATT.

World Trade Organization (WTO) international organization formed to administer the General Agreement on Tariffs and Trade.

The initial impetus for the GATT agreement was the prohibitively high **tariffs**—taxes on imports—imposed by the United States and some other countries in the decade prior to World War II. Most significantly, the **Smoot-Hawley Act** was passed by the U.S. Congress in 1930 as a means to fight the unemployment of the Great Depression. The Act raised import tariffs to an average rate of 52 percent on more than 20,000 products, a level that was so prohibitively high that imports nearly ceased.

tariff tax on imports.

Smoot-Hawley Act legislation passed by the U.S. Congress in 1930, the Act raised tariffs so high that imports nearly ceased.

Supporters of the Smoot-Hawley Act were surprised by the ultimate outcome. They had expected that high tariffs would protect jobs. But with imports cut back, U.S. exports and foreign investment flows into the country slowed to a trickle because foreigners could not finance their purchase without selling their goods and services to Americans. Rather than lower U.S. unemployment, the Smoot-Hawley Act was followed by even higher unemployment! Such *beggar-thy-neighbor* protectionist policies didn't work for the United States or anybody else. The high tariffs promoted political animosity and isolationism among countries and led to economic tensions that contributed to World War II.

The GATT required significant tariff reductions. It has been strengthened over the years through rounds of trade negotiations that have achieved further reductions in tariffs. The negotiations have also placed restrictions on **quotas,** which limit the quantity of imported products a country allows, and on other **nontariff barriers,** which is a catch-all category for the variety of other actions a country can take to restrict trade. Most recently, the *Uruguay round* of negotiations took eight years of often contentious bargaining before being ratified by the United States and other countries in late 1994. It established the World Trade Organization and dealt with various thorny issues, such as:

quota quantity limit on imports.

nontariff barriers any of a variety of actions other than tariffs that make importing more expensive or difficult.

- **Tariffs:** Tariffs have been cut by an average of about 40 percent worldwide on thousands of products and eliminated altogether on others, such as beer, toys, and paper. After a phase-in period, the percentage of products that can be imported *duty-free* into industrialized countries will more than double to 44 percent of all imported goods.
- **Agricultural subsidies:** *Subsidies* represent financial assistance to domestic producers. This assistance can lead to inefficient patterns of trade. After particularly heated debate, countries agreed to reduce trade-distorting subsidies to agriculture. Agricultural subsidies have been estimated to cost consumers $160 billion per year.
- **Services:** For the first time, global trade rules will be interpreted to cover services. To reach agreement, many of the details were left vague, especially in regard to banking and other financial services.
- **Intellectual property rights:** New rules were enacted to better protect patents and copyrights, including rights to copy computer software. For example, Malaysia announced in August 2002 that it would begin to crack down on pirated software.

The good intentions of these agreements are not always carried out in reality. For example, the United States and other countries have found it difficult in terms of their own internal politics to make a serious dent in agricultural subsidies. When members violate the GATT agreement, affected countries can turn to the World Trade Organization for recourse. For example, in the late summer of 2002, the World Trade Organization ruled that the United States corporate income tax unfairly subsidized exports. The WTO authorized countries of the European Union to impose up to $4 billion worth of retaliatory tariffs on goods imported from the United States. In response, the United States is considering revising some of its corporate income tax provisions, and might in this way be able to avert many of these penalties.

REGIONAL TRADING BLOCS

The European Union is an example of a regional **trading bloc,** which is an agreement that lowers trade barriers among member countries. The European Union is considered a trading bloc because it has lower trade barriers among its member countries than to the rest of the world. By signing the **North American Free Trade Agreement,** commonly known as **NAFTA,** the United States, Canada, and Mexico also formed a trading bloc. This bloc is envisioned to someday expand southward to include countries of Central and South America, some of which are currently in their own trading bloc called the *Mercosur.*

trading bloc agreement among a group of countries that provides for lower trade barriers among its members than with the rest of the world.

North American Free Trade Agreement (NAFTA) trading bloc that includes the United States, Canada, and Mexico.

Have you bought a pickup truck imported into the United States from Europe recently? It's not likely, in part because of a decades-old 25-percent tariff that the United States imposed in response to a threatened trade war long since forgotten. The pickup tariff was merely a shot across the bow, so to speak, because Europeans had never had a pickup-truck presence in the United States. The tariff was enacted by the United States as part of strategic maneuvering—a trade game—in which both the United States and Europe were each seeking to both restrict and free up trade in ways that would be of most benefit to their own political constituencies. ◄

To the extent that regional trading blocs reduce tariffs and other trade restrictions, the trading blocs promote trade among their members. This trade can come from two sources. First is the **trade creation effect,** which involves an increase in world trade. The trade creation effect is efficient, since it allows countries to specialize according to comparative advantage.

The second is the **trade diversion effect,** which represents trade that would have occurred with countries outside the trading bloc, but that is diverted to countries within a trading bloc solely in response to lower tariff rates within the bloc. An example of trade diversion would be if NAFTA is what induced IBM to assemble its laptop computers in Mexico instead of Taiwan. **Trade diversion is inefficient, since it causes trade to respond to price signals from the government—relative tariff rates—rather than to comparative advantage.**

Economists generally support regional trading blocs as a step toward free trade. However, even supporters of regional agreements have reservations about trade-diversion effects. There are also concerns that regional trading blocs may turn inward and erect higher barriers to the rest of the world. Not only would contentious trading blocs jeopardize gains from trade, they could also be a threat to world peace.

trade creation effect trade that would otherwise not take place; adds to efficiency; caused by lower trade barriers among members of a trading bloc.

trade diversion effect trade among members of a trading bloc that would more efficiently be conducted with other countries outside of the bloc.

Q U I C K C H E C K

Distinguish the trade diversion effect from the trade creation effect of a regional trading bloc. Why is the trade diversion effect inefficient?

Answer: Both the trade diversion effect and the trade creation effect are associated with the formation of regional trading blocs. Member countries of a trading bloc have lowered barriers to trade among themselves, but have not lowered barriers for trade with countries outside the bloc. Lower trade barriers lead to increased trade, which is efficient and is termed the trade creation effect. Unfortunately, there is also the trade diversion effect, which distorts the pattern of existing trade from what it would otherwise have been. Specifically, the trade diversion effect increases trade within the bloc at the expense of trade that would otherwise have occurred between member countries and other countries outside the bloc.

16.3 TRADE POLICY OPTIONS

Counter to the spirit of the GATT and regional trading blocs, all major countries have some restrictions on trade. For better or worse, countries often seek to protect individual industries or sectors of their economies from foreign competition. Policies that accomplish this goal are termed *protectionist,* even though these policies usually harm rather than protect the economy as a whole. Protectionist policies come in two basic forms: tariffs and nontariff barriers. Nontariff barriers can be either quotas—quantity restrictions on imports—or any of a variety of other actions that make importing more difficult. Consider the tariff.

TARIFFS

A tariff is a tax on an imported product. Demand for an imported product tells the quantities of the product consumers would purchase from foreign sources at each possible price. This demand is sometimes called *residual demand,* since it represents demand that is left over after consumers have bought from domestic suppliers. Because buyers have the ability to substitute domestically made products for foreign-made products, the quantity demanded of imports is typically quite responsive to price, leading to a flatter demand curve than for the market as a whole. Likewise, because suppliers of foreign-made goods can sell their products in many countries, the supply of imports is also relatively flat.

Tariffs increase the cost of selling imported products. This increase in turn increases the prices of those products in the domestic market and, by the law of demand discussed in Chapter 3, reduces the quantity that will be sold. That is how a tariff restricts imports. Figure 16-5 illustrates how a tariff raises the price and decreases the quantity of imports, relative to what would have occurred in the free market. Note that the increase in price is less than the amount of the tariff, indicating that importers are often not able to merely pass along the entire tariff to consumers.

By raising barriers to the entry of foreign products, **tariffs can be viewed as a form of price support for domestic producers.** The higher price of imports causes the demand curve to shift to the right for domestic products that are close substitutes. For example, an import tariff on Toshiba laptop computers increases demand for Dell, Compaq, and IBM laptop computers, which in turn causes a new, higher equilibrium price and quantity for those products. The higher price and quantity sold by domestic producers are why an import tariff is said to protect those producers from foreign competition.

Tariffs are said to be *transparent,* meaning that their effects on prices are clear for all to see. The United States has an extensive array of tariffs, most of which are currently below 6 percent and falling. Most other major trading countries also have similar tariffs. With some

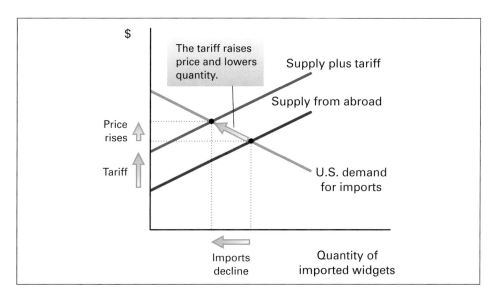

FIGURE 16-5

EFFECTS OF A TARIFF Import tariffs raise prices paid by consumers and thus cause them to buy fewer imports. A tariff on a good imported into the United States helps American producers who can sell at the higher price, but that help comes at the expense of consumers who must pay the higher price.

TABLE 16-2 EFFECTIVE U.S. TARIFF RATES BY SECTOR, 1992–2000 (IN PERCENT)

SECTOR	1992	1993	1994	1995	1996	1997	1998	1999	2000
Food and live animals	1.99	2.07	1.81	1.42	1.41	1.19	1.34	1.36	1.18
Beverages and tobacco	3.33	3.66	2.71	1.76	1.90	2.04	1.10	1.21	0.95
Crude materials, inedible, except fuels	0.36	0.36	0.32	0.24	0.21	0.20	0.20	0.16	0.16
Mineral fuels, lubricants and related materials	0.47	0.48	0.50	0.42	0.35	0.32	0.42	0.35	0.20
Animal and vegetable oils, fats and waxes	1.05	1.19	0.91	0.64	0.53	0.70	0.84	0.76	1.05
Chemicals and related products, n.e.s.	3.64	3.95	3.81	2.23	1.93	1.73	1.56	1.24	1.03
Manufactured goods classified chiefly by material	3.47	3.31	3.16	2.71	2.56	2.42	2.14	1.91	1.76
Machinery and transport equipment	2.00	2.02	1.86	1.53	1.35	1.14	0.94	0.85	0.73
Miscellaneous manufactured articles	8.41	7.81	7.70	6.86	6.45	6.18	5.88	5.54	5.49
Commodities and transactions not classified elsewhere in the SITC	0.02	0.03	0.03	0.05	0.07	0.06	0.10	0.09	0.03
All sectors	3.15	3.07	2.91	2.43	2.20	2.07	1.95	1.76	1.59

Source: United States International Trade Commission, *The Economic Effects of Significant U.S. Import Restraints,* June 2002, page 146.

exceptions, tariff rates are kept low by the GATT. The decrease in U.S. tariff rates in recent years is seen in Table 16-2.

QUOTAS

Import quotas are an alternative to import tariffs and can accomplish the same goals as a tariff. Unlike an import tariff, an import quota restricts the quantity of imports directly and thus cuts off supply from abroad at the quota quantity, as shown by the vertical segment of supply in Figure 16-6. The figure illustrates how the truncated supply from abroad under a quota leads to an increase in prices at home.

GATT limits the extent to which countries can impose import quotas, but does allow quotas for agricultural products and to avoid disruption to countries' domestic economies. While not as widespread as tariffs, most countries have some import quotas.

For example, the United States used to restrict the import of sugar through a set of country-by-country quotas, but have converted them to tariffs with an equivalent effect—*tariff-rate quotas.* These tariff-rate quotas increase the cost of sugar in the United States relative to what it is in the rest of the world. Consumers feel the effects when they buy sugar and sweetened products. Indeed, a primary reason for the use of corn sweetener in U.S. soft drinks has been the high price of sugar in the United States.

As an alternative to tariffs and import quotas, the United States and some other countries have chosen to negotiate **voluntary export restraints,** in which individual exporting countries agree to limit the quantities they export. For example, the *multi-fiber agreement,* currently scheduled for elimination by 2004, sets country-by-country quotas on clothing

voluntary export restraints an alternative to import quotas in which exporting countries agree to voluntarily limit their exports to the target country; leads to higher price received by exporting countries.

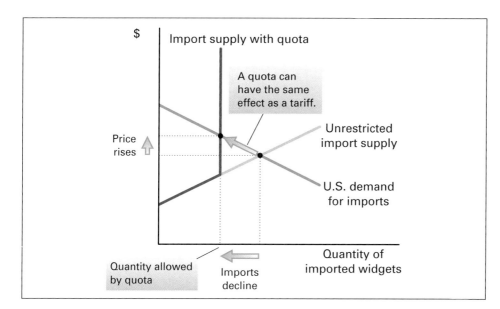

FIGURE 16-6

EFFECTS OF A QUOTA Like an import tariff, a quota also reduces the quantity of imports and increases price in the domestic market. The quota truncates supply from abroad at the maximum allowable import quantity, thus causing import supply to become vertical at that point.

QUICKCHECK

Why are exporting countries better off to agree to a voluntary export restraint than to have the importing country restrict imports with an import quota?

Answer: If the importing country imposes an import quota, exporting countries compete to fill that quota, which drives the prices they receive lower. In contrast, by accepting a voluntary export restraint, the countries are not in competition with one another and can thus receive higher prices for their exports.

exports to the United States and some other countries. The alternative would be for the United States or other importing countries to impose import quotas.

The United States offers to forgo quotas in favor of voluntary export restraints in order to maintain good relations with the governments of the other countries involved. Exporting countries know that if they do not agree to the voluntary export restraints, they may face either quotas or some other retaliatory action. Exporting countries can also charge higher prices per unit under a voluntary export restraint than they could if they face import quotas. Exporting countries charge more because they are not competing against one another—they each have their preassigned export restraints and are not allowed to fill those of other exporting countries.

AN ASSORTMENT OF NONTARIFF BARRIERS TO TRADE

Quotas and voluntary export restraints are examples of nontariff barriers to trade, which include all ways other than tariffs that countries make importing difficult. Most nontariff barriers do not restrict imports explicitly; their effects are less obvious than quotas. For example, paperwork and red tape delays can inhibit trade. Under the administration of President Salinas in the early 1990s, for example, Mexico established a clever system to fight corruption and in the process reduce hidden nontariff barriers. The policy required that any application for a license to import a product into Mexico be automatically approved, if not acted on within ninety days. Prior to that time, unless illegal bribes were paid, applications were often delayed until after the market opportunity to sell the product was gone.

Sometimes, nontariff barriers are incidental to accomplishing other objectives. For example, the United States inspects the manufacturing processes of some products made domestically. It cannot do that for most imports, and so resorts to sampling. For this reason, entire shipments of such products as canned foods from China have been discarded because sampling revealed some to be contaminated, labeled improperly, or otherwise not up to U.S. standards. While sampling does increase the cost of importing and is thus a nontariff barrier, its primary purpose is presumably to protect public safety.

At other times, the effects of nontariff barriers on trade seem intentional, but are hard to prove. For example, Japan made it difficult to sell Louisville Slugger baseball bats in its country for many years, because the bats did not meet Japan's guidelines for use in baseball games. Since the Louisville Slugger was the best-selling bat in the world market, U.S. trade negotiators asserted that the Japanese regulators had set their standards for bats in order to restrict competition from U.S. imports.

Still other times, motives conflict. Europe does not allow the import or sale of beef from cattle fed the bovine growth hormones. While illegal in Europe, use of bovine growth hormones was allowed in the United States. Since the U.S. government would not certify its beef exports as hormone-free, the United States was for a time barred from exporting beef to Europe. That ban was lifted after the U.S. restricted imports of some minor European products and threatened to go much further if the Europeans did not back down. Since buyers in either the United States or Europe could always contract with cattle ranchers for whatever sort of animals they desire, U.S. negotiators argued that no government certification would be necessary.

SNAPSHOT   ## MADE IN MEXICO, BRICK BY BRICK

Americans need not be told which state is responsible for producing the goods they buy. By law, however, they do have a right to know the country of origin for imports. This information must be labeled on each imported item. The law applies to all products, including bricks from Mexico. No big deal, perhaps, except when you realize that brick kilns in Mexico are rarely high-tech. The cost of imprinting *Mexico* into each brick bound for El Norté is a significant fraction of the entire cost of producing that brick. If that labeling requirement forms a nontariff barrier that reduces Mexican brick exports, U.S. brickmakers don't complain! ◀

16.4 THE FREE TRADE DEBATE

If the arguments for and against free trade were to be counted, the free trade side would come up very short. However, the number of objections is not important. It is their validity that matters. **The objections to free trade commonly have limited applicability or are based on questionable logic.** For example, the previous chapter took issue with worries over cheap foreign labor threatening domestic jobs. This section takes a brief look at some additional significant arguments and counterarguments.

NATIONAL DEFENSE—VALID BUT OVERUSED

If imports or exports seriously threaten national defense, it makes sense to restrict them. There is no argument there. However, translating national defense interests into policy requires judgments and debate. For example, the United States restricts the export of certain computers and technology. However, if the United States is an unreliable supplier to other countries, will new technologies evolve elsewhere in places where the government allows producers to reap the profits from exports? Also, how much consideration should be given civilian uses for products that could also be used in war?

The judgments are often difficult and the source of debate. In 1998, for example, President Clinton's decision to allow China to launch U.S. companies' satellites sparked a heated debate in Congress about the role of satellite and satellite launch technology in the production of intercontinental missiles, which the United States naturally does not want the Chinese aiming its way.

TRADE SANCTIONS—DO THEY WORK?

The United States sometimes uses *trade sanctions,* which restrict trade with countries such as Cuba and Iraq that have policies it opposes. Note that Cuba's Fidel Castro and Iraq's Saddam Hussein have had remarkable staying power, even as the trade sanctions contributed to the poverty of their economies. Trade sanctions allowed them to rally their citizens and point the blame outside their borders. **Despite their lack of effectiveness, trade sanctions are often popular with the public.** For example, when a Chinese fighter jet slammed into a U.S. spy plane in April 2001, and the Chinese government refused to let the crew return home, Americans overwhelmingly backed imposing sanctions. Perhaps in response, diplomacy prevailed and the Americans were allowed to return home.

Another question is whether economic sanctions punish the wrong people, including those in the country that imposes them. For example, the United States would be an unreliable source of goods and services if buyers must fear that their governments might do something that would irritate the United States and cause it to impose trade sanctions. Given the multinational nature of business today, buyers may decide to locate new businesses in countries that are more reliable. Thus, U.S. threats of trade sanctions can backfire and cause U.S. companies to be at a competitive disadvantage relative to similar companies located elsewhere in the world.

ENVIRONMENTAL, HEALTH, AND SAFETY STANDARDS— A LEVEL PLAYING FIELD WITHOUT A GAME

Some U.S. industries cannot produce products as cheaply as similar products from abroad, perhaps because foreign producers face weak government regulation of production. For example, they might not need to do as much to protect the environment and the health and safety of their workers. Should the United States attempt to estimate the extra costs of complying with U.S. standards and then add that cost to imports by imposing an appropriate set of tariffs? Some critics of current trade policy suggest that this approach is the only way to achieve a *level playing field.*

For the United States to impose its own standards on other countries, when effects are localized, would benefit neither the United States nor those countries. Such action could easily be interpreted by those countries' citizens as an act of U.S. arrogance or imperialism. For example, environmental costs of production in poor countries are often less than in the United States because of weaker laws or law enforcement. Higher levels of pollution are likely to be efficient for these countries, because environmental quality is a *normal good*—as incomes rise, people demand more. Poor countries value spending extra income on food and shelter more highly than on extra environmental quality. Thus, poor countries have a higher opportunity cost of environmental quality and might efficiently specialize in industries with a higher pollution content. In contrast, by valuing environmental quality highly, U.S. citizens might prefer that heavy polluters go elsewhere.

DUMPING—RARELY STRATEGIC

dumping selling a good to another country for less than its cost of production.

Dumping is defined as the selling of a good for less than its cost of production. Dumping occurs for many reasons. For example, a company might have overestimated demand for its product and find itself stuck with too much—a clearance sale, so to speak. Alternatively, a company may be selling output at a price that covers wages, materials, and other operating expenses of production, but does not cover the cost of its capital and other costs that it must pay whether it produces or not. Even though the company loses money, it would lose more by not selling. Perhaps it is even able to offset these losses by selling at a higher price in another market where it faces less competition.

Dumping for the above reasons occurs within a country, as well as in international trade. However, dumping is illegal across countries according to the GATT. The United States presumes dumping whenever a foreign company charges less in the United States than it does at home, irrespective of its costs. **The GATT and U.S. law permit anti-dumping tariffs when dumping harms a domestic industry.** However, the world cried foul when, in 2002, the United States slapped anti-dumping tariffs of up to 30 percent on imported steel. Japan immediately retaliated by placing a 100-percent tariff on the token $5 million worth of steel it imports from the United States. Both Europe and Japan took their cases to the World Trade Organization, and have both promised hundreds of millions of dollars worth of additional retaliation if the WTO rules that the United States applied its tariffs inappropriately. A final ruling by the WTO is expected in March 2003.

strategic dumping dumping with the intention of driving the competition out of business.

Consumers gain from the low prices that result from dumping. The only strong economic argument in favor of restricting dumping occurs in the special case of strategic dumping. **Strategic dumping** is dumping that aims to drive the competition out of business so that the firms doing the dumping can monopolize output and drive prices up in the future. However, the prospects for successful strategic dumping are highly questionable in most industries. After all, in a world marketplace, there are numerous potential competitors. Even companies that have been driven out of a particular line of business can often reenter it in the future, should an increase in price make it profitable to do so.

INFANT INDUSTRIES—WHERE ARE INVESTORS?

infant industries startup industries that might be unable to survive the rigors of competition in their formative years.

Developing countries often try to nurture new industries they hope will one day become a source of export earnings. These **infant industries** are thought to need protection in the rough world marketplace. The infant industry argument claims that the government must first identify promising industries and then erect import barriers to protect them. When the infants grow strong enough to fend for themselves, the government should remove the barriers.

The infant industry argument is unconvincing if markets function efficiently. In the free marketplace, *venture capitalists* and other private investors will often support firms through many years of losses. They will do so if they expect that the firms will eventually become profitable and reward their patience. If private investors do not foresee profits down the road, they will withhold their funds, and the businesses will fail.

Unfortunately, there is much less assurance that the government will pick industries that are likely to survive on their own. **Governments often use political considerations to select so-called infant industries.** Even if governments do attempt careful economic analysis, such analyses are unlikely to match those of investors with their own money at risk. The result is that governments around the world have protected industries that never grew strong enough to withstand foreign competition. By requiring government subsidies to stay afloat, and by charging prices above those in the rest of the world, such industries have proven to be expensive for governments and consumers alike.

QUICKCHECK

There are more arguments against free trade than there are in favor of it. Even so, economists are for the most part staunchly pro free trade. Why?

Answer: The arguments against free trade constitute exceptions to the rule that free trade promotes prosperity through increased efficiency. Oftentimes, even the purported exceptions to that rule turn out to be invalid.

FREE TRADE—A WIN-WIN SOLUTION   *SNAPSHOT*

Is limiting free trade just another protectionist barrier, or are the Europeans more aware of the dangers than are Americans? Perhaps the topic would be the sale of beef from livestock fed growth hormones, a practice allowed in the United States but banned in Europe as previously discussed. Perhaps the topic is antitrust. The U.S. Justice Department gave the green light to a merger between General Electric Corporation and Honeywell Corporation, two titans of industrial might. The Europeans put the kibosh on the merger, though, by ruling that the combination was too mighty and could not be allowed to do business in Europe. Maybe good arguments. The result was trade that was less free.

In this international marketplace with so many countries with so many ideas as to what is okay to do and what is not, it is a wonder that free trade can survive at all. Yet it does, to the tune of over $1 trillion in imports and exports done every month by the countries of the world. The protectionists might win a battle here and there, as well they should. But the gains in living standards brought about by free trade are what give us all victory. ◄

16.5 ENERGY SECURITY—A QUESTION OF OIL IMPORTS

A business scenario can be put together that could have us back on the moon within 10 to 15 years.

—Dr. "Jack" Schmitt, Apollo 17 astronaut and last man on the moon

EXPLORE & APPLY

The business strategy Dr. Schmitt had in mind revolved around that most precious of possessions, energy. As he described it in a speech he gave to the Australian Institute of Physics Biennial Congress, in the summer of 2002, his particular plan involved gathering helium-3 from the moon to use in energy-creating fusion reactions here on earth. The cost? Dr. Schmitt estimated it at 200 billion Australian dollars (110 billion U.S. dollars).

While traveling to the moon to gather fuel might seem an outlandish idea, it is but one of many possibilities for developing *alternative fuels,* so-called because they provide an alternative to the traditional fossil fuels of coal, natural gas and crude oil. These alternative fuels have one thing in common—they all cost more than the oil and other fossil fuels that they would replace. For that reason, without government assistance, the marketplace has not financed the development and production of such alternative fuels as ethanol, wind power, and solar power. Those fuels could not compete with cheaper oil. But is oil really cheaper?

The price of oil in the world market has fluctuated from under $20 per barrel to over $30 per barrel in the last few years. However, the cost of importing that oil into the United States might be significantly higher. There are costs that the importers do not currently pay that perhaps the country as a whole does pay. These are the costs having to do with energy freedom.

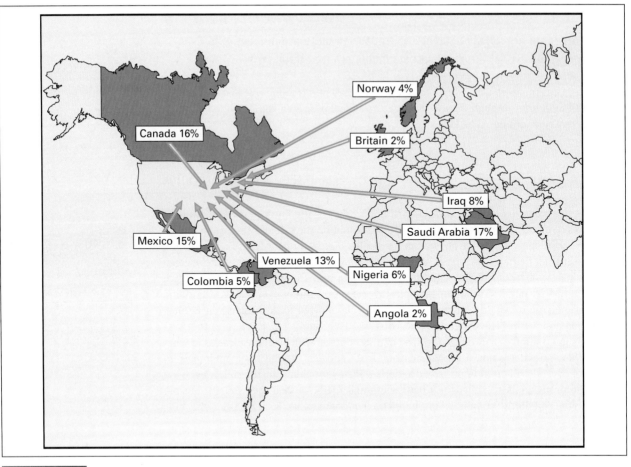

FIGURE 16-7

THE SOURCES OF OIL IMPORTED TO THE UNITED STATES The United States imports oil from many places, with about half coming from the Americas.

Source: Gibson Consulting.

HOW AN OIL IMPORT FEE AFFECTS OIL PRODUCTION

The U.S. economy consumes tremendous amounts of petroleum, about 777 million gallons per day as of January, 2002. If placed in one-gallon gas cans, they could encircle the globe six times over. That is 18.5 million barrels of oil per year, with a total price tag of over $50 billion. The U.S. imports 55 to 60 percent of the oil it uses, with imports exceeding 50 percent of the total for the first time in 1994. Much of that oil comes from countries of this hemisphere, as seen in Figure 16-7. However, because the oil market is global, a disruption in oil exports from the Middle East would bring Europeans and other countries into competition for oil that would otherwise go to the United States. By the same token, the U.S. presence in the world oil market increases petroleum prices and the wealth of oil exporters. This situation means that:

■ **The United States is vulnerable to political instability in the Middle East and in other oil-exporting countries.** The United States has spent a large amount of money and put many lives at risk in its efforts to bring peace to the Middle East. It's impossible to know how much of this effort has been motivated by the U.S. interest in secure energy sources.

■ **The United States is a source of income for Middle Eastern countries with interests hostile to those of the United States.** For example, the "axis of evil" identified by President Bush in 2001 includes the governments of Iraq and Iran, two countries with a large amount of oil-related income. Likewise, oil money from the Middle East has been pointed to in Congress as providing funds for terrorist organizations.

These *external costs* of oil imports are not reflected in the price paid by importers. To "internalize" them, the United States could levy an *oil import fee*, a common name for an import tariff when applied to oil.

An oil import fee would raise the price of imported oil and encourage the development of alternative fuels. U.S. producers would produce more, and consumers consume less, as shown in Figure 16-8. For ease of analysis, the United States is shown in the figure as a price taker in the world oil market.

If the United States raises the price of imported oil, U.S. oil companies will produce more domestic oil, which increases the price of domestic oil relative to oil available on the world market. The higher price would attract resources from elsewhere in the economy to increase production from existing U.S. oilfields, as well as to increase the search for new supplies. Likewise, some existing industries that consume large amounts of oil would shrink or leave the country. For example, a higher oil price in the United States relative to other countries would probably cause petrochemical production to be moved abroad.

Since oil is a nonrenewable resource, opponents of oil import fees argue that such a fee would "drain America first." Down the road, as U.S. wells are pumped dry more quickly, the United States might be forced to rely even more heavily on foreign supplies. In that view, oil import fees might help in the present, but would make matters worse over time. The economy would grow faster and stronger with cheaper energy and be better positioned to weather energy disruptions if they ever do materialize.

Also, higher oil prices could prompt the substitution of coal and nuclear power, both of which can harm the environment. Oil production itself can cause significant environmental damage. For example, the General Accounting Office estimated in July 2002 that oil companies pumping oil from Alaska's North Slope oil fields will face about $6 billion worth of

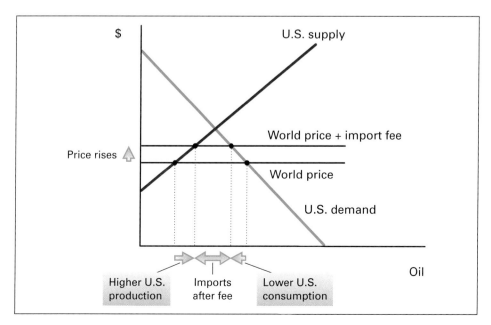

FIGURE 16-8

AN OIL IMPORT FEE An oil import fee would reduce oil imports and increase the U.S. price of oil. Part of the reduction in oil imports would be offset by less oil consumption due to the higher price. The rest would be offset by U.S. oil producers increasing output, also in response to the higher price. The increased U.S. production would deplete U.S. oil reserves more quickly, although the higher price might also prompt additional oil discoveries or development of alternative fuels.

environmental cleanup costs when their wells run dry. Since the opening of the Trans-Alaska pipeline in 1977, oil companies have pumped more than 13 billion barrels of oil and provided about 20 percent of the oil produced in the United States. The prospect of additional environmental damages to the Alaska National Wildlife Refuge caused the U.S. Congress to reject President Bush's proposal to allow oil exploration in that area.

The subject of oil import fees is obviously contentious, with the topic discussed off and on for decades. While the United States does not have an oil import fee, it does have another policy that gives it a measure of protection from the uncertainties of oil politics. Specifically, the United States maintains a *Strategic Petroleum Reserve* in the form of a huge quantity of oil that the U.S. government has been stashing away each year, and that President Bush ordered to be filled to capacity in 2002. That reserve was tapped only once when, in the face of oil prices that had doubled to more than $30 per barrel in 2000, President Clinton ordered a limited sale of oil from the reserve. Whether for this reason or other reasons, the price did drop back after President Clinton's action.

*T*HINKING *C*RITICALLY

1. Would the U.S. military have less to do in the Middle East if the United States did not import so much oil? Should this cost differential be covered by an oil import fee? Explain.

2. Does the Strategic Petroleum Reserve accomplish the objectives of an oil import fee? Explain.

 Visit www.prenhall.com/ayers for updates and web exercises on this Explore & Apply topic.

SUMMARY AND LEARNING OBJECTIVES

1. **Use the concept of a world price to explain imports, exports, and the gains from trade.**
   - Goods and services that are broadly traded in the world marketplace have a world price, which is determined by the world supply and demand. Free trade means a country will accept the world price, whether it is higher or lower than the country's price before trade.
   - When the world price is below a country's price prior to trade, the country will import the good.
   - Imports increase consumer surplus, but reduce producer surplus. The overall effect is to make the country better off than before trade.
   - A country will export a good whose world price is above the country's price prior to trade.
   - Exports reduce consumer surplus, but increase producer surplus. The increase in producer surplus is more than the loss of consumer surplus, so the country is better off than before trade.

2. **Discuss the GATT and other trade agreements among countries.**
   - The General Agreement on Tariffs and Trade (GATT) is a multilateral agreement, meaning that many nations have signed it. The 110 GATT signatories include the United States, Canada, Mexico, and countries of Europe. The GATT agreement is administered by the World Trade Organization, which was created to settle trade disputes among countries.
   - Many issues are addressed in the GATT agreement and its updates, such as those made in the Uruguay round of negotiations in 1994. The GATT seeks to cut tariffs, encourage duty-free imports, reduce agricultural subsidies, apply trade rules to services such as banking as well as goods, and protect property rights through the enforcement of rules relating to copyrights and patents.
   - Regional trading blocs are an increasingly common feature of the global economy. An example is the North American Free Trade Agreement that includes the United States, Canada, and Mexico.
   - Regional trading blocs promote trade among their own members. The trade creation effect is efficient, occurring because member countries can more easily specialize according to the principle of comparative advantage. The trade diversion effect occurs when trade that would have occurred with countries outside the trading bloc if the trading bloc did not exist is

instead diverted to countries within the trading bloc. Trade diversion is inefficient because it is a response to differences in tariffs rather than to comparative advantage.

3. **Distinguish among the various barriers to trade that countries might impose.**
   - Tariffs are taxes on imported products. A tariff shifts the supply curve of a product upward by the amount of the tariff. However, the price of the product will usually rise by less than the amount of the tariff because importers are not able to pass on the entire amount of the tariff. Nonetheless, a tariff will decrease the quantity imported of the product it is placed on.
   - Tariffs are a type of price support for domestic producers. Since tariffs increase the price of imported goods, domestic producers experience an increase in the demand for substitutes for the imports, which leads to higher prices in the domestic market.
   - To be transparent means the effects are readily clear to all. Tariffs are an example of a transparent protectionist policy.
   - The United States and most countries have lengthy lists of products that are subject to tariffs. For the most part these tariffs are kept low by the GATT. In the United States, most tariffs are below 6 percent.
   - Quotas impose a numerical limit on imports. A quota cuts off the supply of an imported product once a predetermined number of units of the product have been brought into the country.
   - A country's desire to reduce imports can be achieved by imposing either a tariff or a quota since both tariffs and quotas decrease imports. However, tariffs are more transparent than quotas since consumers usually know little about the existence of quotas or their effect on the price of an import. Quotas on agricultural products are allowed by the GATT, but in general quotas are not as widespread as tariffs.
   - A voluntary export restraint is a quota agreement negotiated between countries. A country would prefer that its exports be subject to a voluntary export restraint rather than a quota. The reason is that a quota induces exporting countries to lower their prices as they compete with each other to fill the quota. In contrast, with a voluntary export restraint in place each exporting country is allowed to sell only so much and no more to the other country. This means that each exporting country need not lower its price below that of other exporting countries to sell its product.
   - Various other nontariff barriers to trade can be imposed by a country to reduce imports. For example, complicated import rules and regulations in a particular country make it difficult for other countries to sell their goods in that country.

4. **Assess the arguments for and against protectionist policies.**
   - Protectionist trade policies seek to protect a country's industry from foreign competition. Because most countries recognize the benefits that come from more international trade, they have jointly agreed to limit their use of protectionist policies by becoming signatories to the General Agreement on Tariffs and Trade (GATT).
   - There are a number of possible exceptions to the principle of free trade, although application of these exceptions is often subject to debate. These exceptions include the national defense argument. It may be wise for a country to restrict exports of goods that could be used by another country for hostile purposes. Another arguable justification for not trading arises when a trading partner acts in ways that a country disapproves of, and trade sanctions are imposed. A third questionable justification is that a level playing field should be achieved before trade is allowed. For example, a level playing field would require other countries to adopt U.S. environmental policies.
   - Sometimes exporting countries are accused of dumping, which is selling a good for less than the cost of production. The GATT makes dumping illegal and allows a country to impose anti-dumping tariffs in response.
   - The infant industry argument for protectionism argues that a country's new industries need to be protected from foreign competition until they are able to compete effectively against the same industries already existing in other countries. This argument is weak if markets function efficiently, since investors will fund new industries that they expect will eventually be profitable.

5. **Examine whether an oil import fee can promote energy security.**
   - An oil import fee might be used to adjust the price of imported oil upward so as to include costs associated with maintaining energy security. The effect would be to encourage use of alternative energy sources, some of which are likely to be environmentally harmful. The Strategic Petroleum Reserve is intended to accomplish some of the same objectives as would an oil import fee.

KEY TERMS

free trade, 368
open economy, 372
General Agreement on Tariffs and
     Trade (GATT), 372
World Trade Organization (WTO), 372
tariff, 372

Smoot-Hawley Act, 372
quota, 373
nontariff barriers, 373
trading bloc, 373
North American Free Trade
     Agreement (NAFTA), 373

trade creation effect, 374
trade diversion effect, 374
voluntary export restraints, 376
dumping, 380
strategic dumping, 380
infant industries, 380

TEST YOURSELF

TRUE OR FALSE

1. The GATT was created in 1995 in order to lower tariffs.
2. A tariff raises the price of an import but leaves the quantity imported the same.
3. Quotas are transparent, but tariffs are not.
4. A country with protectionist policies seeks to encourage imports.
5. Dumping is legal but controversial, with the GATT refusing to take a stand on whether dumping should be outlawed.

MULTIPLE CHOICE

6. The arrow shown in Self-Test Figure 16-1 represents
   a. imports.
   b. exports.
   c. consumer surplus.
   d. producer surplus.

7. When a country imports a good, it will
   a. gain more in consumer surplus than it loses in producer surplus.
   b. gain more in producer surplus than it loses in consumer surplus.
   c. find that its gain of consumer surplus is exactly offset by its loss of producer surplus.
   d. find that its gain of producer surplus is exactly offset by its loss of consumer surplus.

8. When the world price of a good is greater than a country's price before trade, free trade will result in that country
   a. importing the good and experiencing an increase in consumer surplus.
   b. importing the good and experiencing a decrease in consumer surplus.
   c. exporting the good and experiencing an increase in consumer surplus.
   d. exporting the good and experiencing a decrease in consumer surplus.

9. The GATT was created in response to
   a. the Great Depression of the 1930s.
   b. the Cold War of the 1950s and 1960s.
   c. Reaganomics, the economic policies of President Reagan in the 1980s.
   d. President Clinton's desire to forge closer relationships with China in the 1990s.

10. The World Trade Organization
   a. is a trading bloc that consists of the United States and the countries of Japan and China.
   b. has many member countries, but not the United States.
   c. competes with the GATT for members, with about half the world's countries belonging to the GATT and the other half belonging to the World Trade Organization.
   d. is a component of the GATT that administers the GATT agreement.

SELF TEST FIGURE 16-1

11. An import tariff shifts the _____ curve of imports upward and _____ the price of the good paid by the consumer.
    a. supply; increases
    b. supply; decreases
    c. demand; decreases
    d. demand; increases

12. The effects of a quota will be to _____ the quantity of imports and _____ the price consumers pay for them.
    a. increase; increase
    b. increase; decrease
    c. decrease; increase
    d. decrease; decrease

13. Which is an example of a voluntary export restraint?
    a. A tariff.
    b. A quota.
    c. The multi-fiber agreement.
    d. The GATT.

14. Nontariff barriers to trade
    a. are illegal under GATT.
    b. are allowed by GATT, but are not currently used by any country.
    c. have the effect of reducing a country's imports.
    d. are a good way to increase a country's exports.

15. Trade sanctions
    a. are generally acknowledged to be one of a countries most effective policy weapons.
    b. have been effective in accomplishing America's goals in regard to Cuba.
    c. were strongly supported by the American public as a means of getting China to release some downed U.S. flyers.
    d. have caused Saddam Hussein of Iraq to lose his grip on power there.

16. Which of the following is NOT offered as a reason to restrict trade?
    a. Infant industries.
    b. Dumping.
    c. Level playing field.
    d. Comparative advantage.

17. Strategic dumping is intended to
    a. result in a cleaner environment.
    b. pollute the environment.
    c. lead countries to seek a mutually beneficial agreement relating to the environment.
    d. drive competitors out of business.

18. The trade diversion effect is
    a. efficient.
    b. inefficient.
    c. equitable, with no effect on efficiency.
    d. inequitable, with no effect on efficiency.

19. The trade creation effect is
    a. efficient.
    b. inefficient.
    c. equitable, with no effect on efficiency.
    d. inequitable, with no effect on efficiency.

20. In Self-Test Figure 16-2, the effect of the oil import fee shown would be to
    a. decrease price by *A*.
    b. decrease the quantity produced in the United States by *B*.
    c. decrease the quantity produced in the United States by *C*.
    d. decrease the quantity consumed in the United States by *D*.

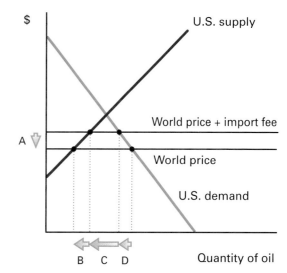

SELF TEST FIGURE 16-2

QUESTIONS AND PROBLEMS

1. *[imports and exports]* When the world price of a good is below the domestic price, will a country import or export the good? Will the country produce any of the good domestically? Explain, using a graph as part of your explanation.

2. *[imports and exports]* When the world price of a good is above the domestic price, will a country import or export the good? Will the country produce any of the good domestically? Explain, using a graph as part of your explanation.

3. *[the GATT]* What is the relationship between the World Trade Organization and the GATT?

4. *[NAFTA]* In your opinion, should the membership of NAFTA be expanded to include countries in Central America and South America? Why would other countries want to join NAFTA? What benefits might the United States receive if these countries joined? Why might there be opposition to expanding NAFTA?

5. *[tariffs]* Construct a supply and demand graph that illustrates the effects on price and quantity when a tariff is imposed on an imported good.

6. *[tariffs]* As stated in the chapter, most tariffs in the United States are 6 percent or less. Survey your family and friends to see what percentage they think tariff rates in the United States are at. Compute the average of the answers you obtain and compare it to the true figure. Did your family and friends overestimate or underestimate the actual average tariff in the United States? How far off were they? What factors could account for the inaccuracy in their answers?

7. *[tariffs]* Explain why a tariff can be viewed as a price support for domestic producers.

8. *[tariffs versus quotas]* Do consumers prefer tariffs or quotas, given that one or the other will be imposed on a particular import? Explain.

9. *[tariffs and quotas]* Use a supply and demand graph that illustrates the effects on price and quantity when a tariff is imposed on an imported good. Explain how the effects shown on your graph could alternatively be achieved through the imposition of a quota instead of the tariff.

10. *[voluntary export restraints]* From the perspective of producers in an exporting country, why is a voluntary export restraint preferable to a quota on imports of their product?

11. *[nontariff barriers]* List three examples other than quotas of nontariff barriers to trade discussed in the chapter. Then suppose that the United States wished to create a nontariff barrier to the imports of foreign-made televisions. Provide an example of a nontariff barrier not brought up in the text that could apply to television imports.

12. *[protectionism]* Select one of the arguments for protectionism presented in the text and write a short essay critical of the argument you select.

13. *[protectionism]* Suppose you are a member of Congress who wishes to protect tomato farmers, who have a lot of political clout in your area. Which of the arguments for protectionism would you apply to make your case to others in Congress? State your argument briefly and in writing, making sure to explicitly relate it to tomatoes.

14. *[national defense argument]* Name three products that might be able to persuasively use the national defense argument for protectionism. Name three other products where you could make a case, but not one you would support.

15. *[level playing field]* Do you think that nations should be put on a level playing field before being allowed to trade? Explain and defend your position.

 Visit **www.prenhall.com/ayers** for Exploring the Web exercises and additional self-test quizzes.

CHAPTER 17

ECONOMIC DEVELOPMENT

A LOOK AHEAD

The watershed events of history are often closely tied to economic forces. In 1989, the world witnessed a Wall come down in Berlin, shattering the symbol of a globe divided into two armed, hostile camps. Tearing down the Berlin Wall epitomized the failure of the centrally planned communist countries to keep up with either the freedom or the living standards in Western economies. The world witnessed communism being replaced with capitalism throughout the former Soviet empire. Yet only now, over a decade later, are the people of the former Soviet Union starting to experience the benefits of a market economy. The Explore & Apply section that concludes the chapter examines the economic forces that have caused this delay.

This chapter examines the transition of economies from poverty to wealth. We start by characterizing the countries of the developing world, noting the need to use development indicators to formulate a goal-oriented development agenda. We then turn to population growth, examining issues both old and new. We emphasize the importance of property rights as a foundation for development. To deal with these and other issues of development, countries can turn to the International Monetary Fund and World Bank for advice and financial help. Created by the wealthy nations to help the poorer ones, these institutions are evidence that in the global neighborhood, neighbors are committed to helping neighbors.

LEARNING OBJECTIVES

Understanding Chapter 17 will enable you to:
1. **Discuss the problems that are a priority for developing countries.**
2. **Describe the goals on the United Nations' development agenda.**
3. **Point out the incentives for population growth.**
4. **Explain the connection between economic development and property rights.**
5. **Identify the roles of the International Monetary Fund and the World Bank in economic development.**
6. **Describe how insecure property rights have hindered economic development in Russia.**

$\mathscr{E}$XPLORE
&
$\mathscr{A}$PPLY

In earlier chapters, you learned about key economic concepts such as scarcity and comparative advantage. You also saw how institutions such as the Federal Reserve impact the supply of money in an economy. Although our focus so far has been on developed countries, such as the United States, about 40 percent of the 207 countries in the world are less-developed countries where people struggle for basic necessities such as food and water. Economics helps us understand why some countries are rich while others are poor. It also helps us identify and implement solutions for poverty.

17.1 DEVELOPING ECONOMIES AND POVERTY

developed countries countries such as the United States, Japan, Germany, and the United Kingdom that rely on the free-market system.

less-developed countries (LDCs) nations that lag behind the wealthier countries; also known as developing countries.

transitional economies countries such as Russia, Hungary, and Poland that are moving away from central planning to the free-market system.

There are approximately 6.2 billion people in the world living in 207 countries. The International Monetary Fund (IMF) classifies these countries into three groups: developed, less developed, and transitional. **Developed countries** include the United States, Canada, Japan, Germany, France, Italy, and the United Kingdom. The economies in these countries rely on the free-market system. On average, a person working in the United States earns $34,000 a year. **Less-developed countries (LDCs),** also known as developing countries, include countries in Central and South America, many countries in Asia, and the countries of Africa. A person working in one of these areas may earn as little as $170 a year. **Transitional economies** refer to those countries that are moving away from the central planning of communism and toward the free market. Russia, Hungary, and the Czech Republic are examples of transitional economies. The map in Figure 17-1 highlights the developing countries and transitional

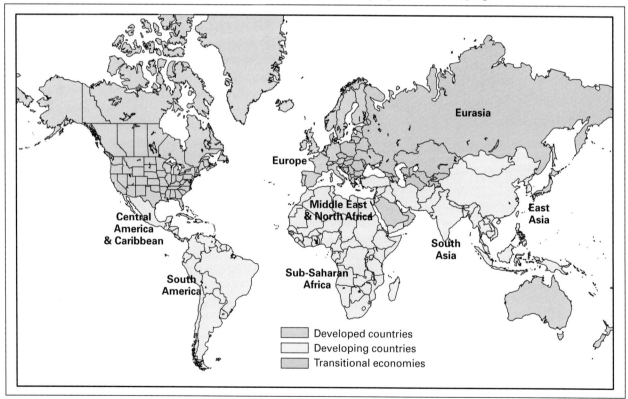

FIGURE 17-1

WORLD MAP Countries are grouped into three categories: developed countries (shown in blue), less-developed countries (shown in light green), and transitional economies (shown in purple). The U.S. Agency for International Development assists developing and transitional economies.

Source: Map available at http://www.usaid.gov/pubs/cbj2003/map.html.

economies served by the U.S. Agency for International Development (USAID), the primary government agency that assists LDCs. As you can see, these countries spread across the globe.

Economic development is a field within economics that studies why some countries remain mired deep in poverty, while other countries prosper. The data that describes a country's economic development are called *indicators*. A country is better off when its development indicators improve over time. The indicators examined in economic development studies vary. **Per capita income is probably the indicator referred to most frequently, but often a set of indicators is needed to assess the level of development in a country.** As we look at the developing countries in this chapter, you will see data on a wide variety of commonly used indicators.

economic development a field of economics that studies the poverty of nations.

PROBLEMS OF THE DEVELOPING ECONOMIES

The LDCs vary in their climate, natural resources, land area, population, and other characteristics. For this reason, there are significant differences in the problems they face. While the LDCs differ, they do share several problems:

- **Poverty.** Per capita income is low.
- **Deficiencies in infrastructure.** *Infrastructure* includes roads, bridges, dams, schools, airports, hospitals, water treatment facilities, sanitation facilities, and other capital that promotes prosperity and well-being.
- **Low life expectancy.** Disease and lack of medical care contribute to health problems and high death rates.
- **High population growth.** Overpopulation creates a lack of opportunity and strains scarce food and water. The result is sometimes malnutrition and even starvation.

The extreme poverty of the LDCs has enormous consequences for the people living in those countries, including the prospect of an early death. Annual life expectancies and per capita gross national income for selected developing countries are both quite low. For comparison, the life expectancy and per capita income in the United States, along with those less-developed countries, are both shown in Figure 17-2. Table 17-1 also shows the striking differences between development indicators in the poorest LDCs and the United States.

TABLE 17-1   LOW-INCOME COUNTRIES COMPARED TO THE UNITED STATES

DEVELOPMENT INDICATOR	LOW-INCOME COUNTRIES	UNITED STATES
Under-five mortality rate (per 1,000)	114.9	8.7
Infant mortality rate	76.1	7.1
Access to improved water source (% of population)	75.7	100.0
Access to improved sanitation (% of population)	45.1	100.0
Fixed line and mobile telephones (per 1,000 people)	28.7	1,097.6
Personal computers (per 1,000 people)	5.1	585.2
Gross national income per capita	$410	$34,100
Life expectancy at birth (years)	58.9	77.1

Source: World Bank, *World Development Indicators* database, April 2002.

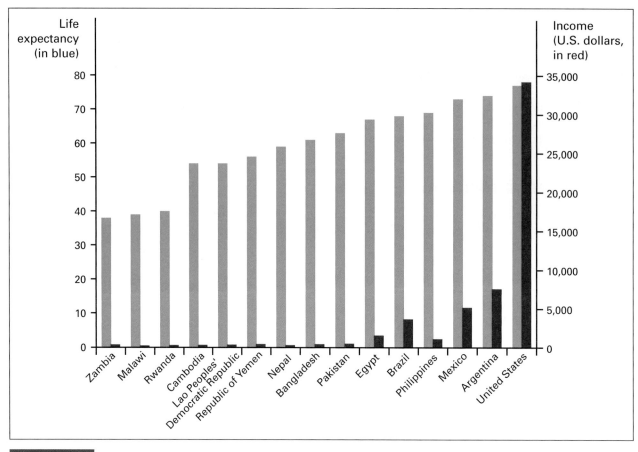

FIGURE 17-2

LIFE EXPECTANCY AND ANNUAL PER CAPITA GROSS NATIONAL INCOME There is a clear difference between the development indicators of life expectancy and annual per capita gross national income of developing countries such as Zambia and that of developed countries such as the United States. Economists can use these indicators to identify countries that need assistance.

Source: 2002 World Development Indicators database, World Bank, April 2002. Gross national income was previously called gross national product in World Bank publications.

STAGES OF DEVELOPMENT—FROM THE COUNTRYSIDE TO THE BIG CITY

To the impoverished worker who toils in the countryside without electricity, indoor plumbing, and safe drinking water, the hope of a better life often involves migrating to a big city. That would be the capital city of Nairobi to the more than 30 million people living in Kenya, the African country about twice the size of Nevada shown in Figure 17-3. Let's briefly consider life in Kenya in order to make several important points about development.

According to the U.S. Central Intelligence Agency (CIA), 75 percent of the population of Kenya can read and write, but 50 percent are unemployed. The chief occupation is farming, which provides a means to survive for 75 to 80 percent of the people. To put that number in perspective, about 2 percent of Americans earn a living from agriculture. Because of Kenya's bountiful wildlife, tourism is a major industry. Small-scale manufacturing is also important. A significant portion of Kenya's manufactured goods are exported to other countries.

Although the country's birth rate is high, so is its death rate, due to the prevalence of HIV/AIDS. The population is growing at better than 1 percent a year. Kenya's per capita GDP of

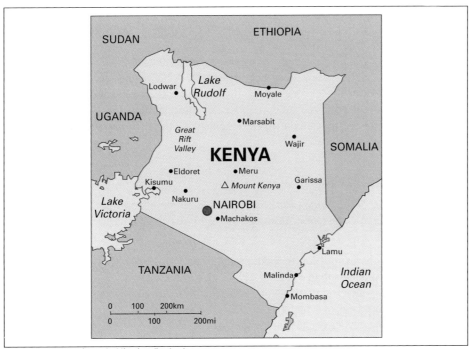

FIGURE 17-3

KENYA Kenya is a developing country on the east coast of Africa. While its population is mostly literate, about half of its people are unemployed.

Source: from www.cia.gov/publications/factbook

$1,500 is high for a country in Africa. You might be surprised that English is one of the country's two official languages, and that the Protestant and Roman Catholic faiths are professed by the majority of the population. Nairobi is a rapidly growing city of over 2,000,000 people, offering current movies, fine dining, and access to the Internet and other modern technologies.

Like other LDCs, Kenya mixes agriculture and urbanization. To understand this trait of LDCs, consider **Rostow's stages of economic development** model. In 1960, American economic historian Walter W. Rostow suggested that countries pass through five stages in their development.

Rostow's stages of economic development a model that says that countries begin as traditional societies, pass through the preconditions for takeoff, the takeoff, the drive to maturity, and conclude their development with the stage of high mass consumption.

- **Stage 1: Traditional society.** The first stage in Rostow's model, traditional society, describes a country where subsistence agriculture dominates economic activity.
- **Stage 2: Preconditions for takeoff.** In the second stage, agricultural production rises so as to permit people to trade excess production. Transportation is needed to take crops to distant markets, so that investment in transportation is a key in moving from stage 1 to stage 2.
- **Stage 3: Takeoff.** In the third stage, many farmers leave agriculture to take jobs in industry. Thus, the country begins the process of urbanization, but remains focused on agriculture and just a few manufacturing industries. Again, more investment is needed, this time to create a manufacturing sector.
- **Stage 4: Drive to maturity.** In the fourth stage, there is economic diversification, with many different goods and services produced.
- **Stage 5: High mass consumption.** In the final stage, the production of consumer goods and services dominates economic activity.

Clearly, stage 5 describes the United States and other high-income countries, but where lies Kenya? The answer is not clear. Kenya, like many LDCs, combines stages. It exhibits some qualities associated with traditional society, but has been able to increase its exports, which is consistent with stage 2. The growth of Nairobi suggests the third stage. What are we to make of this?

While Rostow's model can help us view economic development as occurring in a sequence of steps, development does not necessarily occur in the way specified by the model. Furthermore, the model does not identify the causes of movements from one stage to the next. The model is criticized by economists for these reasons, but it is still useful for emphasizing the role of investment in development. Let's turn now to efforts to move nations out of the earlier stages.

A DEVELOPMENT AGENDA

The stated mission of the *United Nations (UN)* is to promote world peace and prosperity through international cooperation. Consider the eight economic development goals set by the United Nations:

Goal 1. Eradicate extreme poverty and hunger. In 2001 it was estimated that 1.2 billion people lived on less than a dollar a day. Hunger is a problem for 826 million people.

Goal 2. Achieve universal primary education. One-third of children in the LDCs have less than five years of schooling.

Goal 3. Promote gender equality and empower women. Rates of school attendance and participation in the labor force are lower for women than men in LDCs.

Goal 4. Reduce child mortality. A global effort to vaccinate children was launched in early 2000, with the goal of eliminating polio, diphtheria, and other childhood diseases.

Goal 5. Improve maternal health.

Goal 6. Combat HIV/AIDS, malaria, and other diseases.

Goal 7. Ensure environmental sustainability.

Goal 8. Develop a global partnership for development.

The UN plans to achieve these goals by 2015. The goals are associated with *targets,* specific results that when achieved will mean each goal has been met. Table 17-2 restates the goals and shows a target for each goal.

TABLE 17-2   UNITED NATIONS GOALS AND SELECTED TARGETS FOR ECONOMIC DEVELOPMENT

GOAL	SELECTED TARGET
1. Eradicate extreme poverty and hunger.	Halve the proportion of people whose income is less than a dollar a day.
2. Achieve universal primary education.	Ensure that boys and girls have access to primary schooling.
3. Promote gender equality and empower women.	Eliminate gender disparity in all levels of education.
4. Reduce child mortality.	Reduce by two-thirds the under-five child mortality rate.
5. Improve maternal health.	Reduce by three-quarters the maternal mortality rate.
6. Combat HIV/AIDS, malaria, and other diseases.	Halt the spread of HIV/AIDS.
7. Ensure environmental sustainability.	Reverse the loss of environmental resources.
8. Develop a global partnership for development.	Deal with the debt problems of LDCs.

Source: United Nations.

Regarding the effort to combat HIV/AIDS, the sixth goal, the developing world is home to 95 percent of all HIV/AIDS sufferers. The World Health Organization (WHO) predicts that 70 million people will die in the next twenty years unless drastic action or a major breakthrough occurs in the treatment of HIV/AIDS. One estimate concludes that AIDS has killed more people than all wars and natural disasters throughout history and that 40 million children have already lost one or both parents to AIDS.

One reason that AIDS claims so many lives in the LDCs revolves around missing infrastructure. Without transportation facilities, life-prolonging medicines cannot reach those who need them. Without medical personnel, the sick cannot be properly cared for. Without education, AIDS is more likely to spread. In the LDCs, investments in infrastructure such as roads, hospitals, and schools will complement treatment with drugs in the fight against AIDS.

To track development progress, the UN refers to its world indicators, seen in Table 17-3. Grouping them, the indicators measure just two characteristics. One is infrastructure. The sanitation, water, computer, and telephone statistics shed light on access to capital, which makes people more productive. Note that the rural population has less access than the urban population. The second characteristic is health. The indicators that relate to infants and children's health reveal the effects of poverty.

TABLE 17-3   UNITED NATIONS DEVELOPMENT INDICATORS FOR THE WORLD

INDICATOR	VALUE
1. Sanitation, percentage of population with access to improved sanitation, rural	40%
2. Sanitation, percentage of population with access to improved sanitation, total	61%
3. Sanitation, percentage of population with access to improved sanitation, urban	85%
4. Water, percentage of population with access to improved drinking water sources, rural	71%
5. Water, percentage of population with access to improved drinking water sources, total	82%
6. Water, percentage of population with access to improved drinking water sources, urban	95%
7. Children one-year-old immunized against measles, percent	72%
8. Children under five mortality rate per 1,000 live births	83
9. Infant mortality rate (zero to one year) per 1,000 live births	57
10. Internet users	550 million
11. Internet users per 100 population	8.14
12. Personal computers	575 million
13. Personal computers per 100 population	9.37
14. Telephone main lines in use and cellular subscribers	2 billion
15. Telephone lines and cellular subscribers per 100 population	32.27

Source: United Nations *Millennium Indicators.* The values in the table are for 2000 or 2001.

QUICKCHECK

One of the UN goals is to reduce child mortality. The text mentions that the plan to reduce child mortality includes vaccinations against childhood diseases. Will progress in meeting any of the other goals also contribute to lower child mortality? Explain briefly.

Answer: Yes. For example, child mortality should also be reduced if hunger and poverty are reduced, since everyone's health partly depends on their diet. Meeting other goals could also reduce child mortality. Children should be healthier if maternal health is improved, and diseases such as AIDS and malaria are diminished.

S N A P S H O T   IT TAKES A HIGHWAY—ONE YOU CAN DRIVE AT NIGHT

Once crops are harvested, they must be transported to the cities before they spoil. Likewise, once goods are produced, they must be brought to buyers. It takes a highway to move the goods. Once the highway is built, other infrastructure is needed—gasoline stations, secondary roads, eating places, repair shops, rest areas, and government inspection stations to weigh and examine cargoes.

Even when all these have been built, the trucks may sit silently as nightfall comes. Trucks carry valuable cargo, which attracts hijackers who prefer the darkness as cover for their lawbreaking. For this reason you might find inspection stations in Africa crowded with trucks. The drivers must stop for inspection, but face long delays. Afterwards, they park overnight rather than venture into bandit-infested territory. Transportation first takes a highway, but then more. In this case, countries in a hurry to raise their living standards have been slowed down because of dangers that lurk in the night. ◄

17.2 POPULATION GROWTH

The world has seen its population grow rapidly, from just under 3 billion in 1960 to over 6 billion today. A longer perspective, as seen in Figure 17-4, shows that population has exploded over the last three-and-a-half centuries, and is projected to keep increasing. Part of the reason for this growth is that advances in medicine and hygiene have lowered death rates, thereby increasing longevity. Birth rates have also been high, however, especially among the segments of the population least able to afford raising children.

THE DISMAL SCIENCE

"the dismal science" a name given to economics because of Thomas Robert Malthus's nineteenth-century predictions of mass starvation.

Economics was once called "**the dismal science.**" The term dates to the early nineteenth century. At that time, Thomas Robert Malthus popularized the notion that economics could only hope to delay the day when the world's population finds itself at the brink of starvation.

According to this Malthusian view, starvation is the only force that can keep population in check. While economics can temporarily improve the world, the inevitability of population growth and the limits of the earth's capacity to produce must at some point reduce us all to no more than a subsistence existence. A dismal thought indeed!

Yet, the world has come a long way since the early 1800s, and both population and living standards have increased dramatically. For the most part, people of the world are much

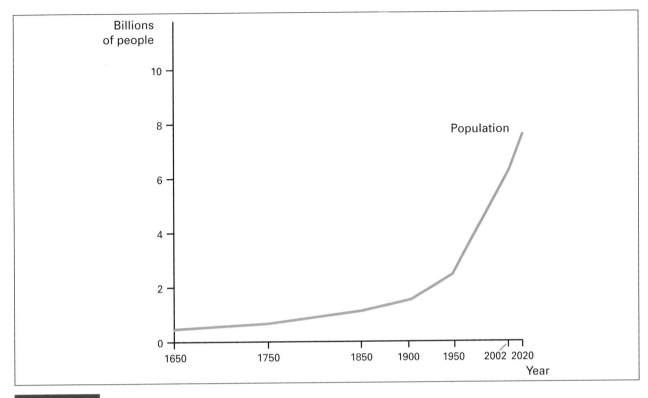

FIGURE 17-4

WORLD POPULATION GROWTH The world population has exploded over the centuries, which leads to concerns about when and how population growth will stop. A look at the data fails to reveal any obvious end in sight.

Source: Census Bureau, *Historical Estimates of World Population* and *Total Midyear Population for the World, 1950–2050.* The data through 1950 are estimates, while the data after 2002 are projections.

further removed from starvation now than then. Since the earth has not expanded, something else must have happened. That something is technology. Technological change has enabled the world to get much more output from its resources than ever imagined by Malthus.

There is still room for concern. If the world continues to experience the same population growth rate that it has over the course of the twentieth century, it must ultimately fill every nook and cranny with people. There would be no room to produce enough food to feed them. Since population grows geometrically, it doubles according to *the rule of seventy-two,* which states that doubling time equals seventy-two divided by the rate of growth. For example, at a growth rate of 1.5 percent, a country's population would double every forty-eight years.

Economic incentives can put a brake on population growth. Specifically, **as countries become wealthier, the opportunity cost of people's time rises.** Because children take time to nurture, people choose to have fewer of them. This is especially true in countries that provide reliable retirement benefits for the elderly. Otherwise, the cost of raising children is offset by the expectation that those children will provide for their parents' retirement. Figure 17-5 shows the fertility rate, meaning the number of children born per woman, in selected developing countries and in the United States. The fertility rate reflects both economic incentives and traditions such as attitudes toward family size.

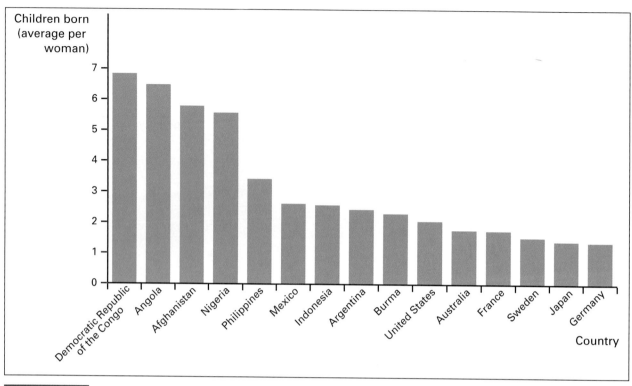

FIGURE 17-5

AVERAGE NUMBER OF CHILDREN BORN PER WOMAN, SELECTED COUNTRIES Generally, developing countries have higher fertility rates than do the developed nations.

Source: 2001 CIA World Factbook.

PROBLEMS WITH THE PRICE SIGNAL

Unless we face the full costs and benefits of our actions, we cannot be expected to make efficient choices. One group that frequently does not bear all the costs of its decisions is parents. For example, efficiency would suggest that parents should pay all costs of rearing children, including costs of food, shelter, and education. However, equity suggests that children should have comparable opportunities. A child born into poverty does not choose to be there, any more than does a child born in more comfortable circumstances. To promote equity, it makes sense for taxpayers to subsidize the infant formula, schooling, school lunches, and other elements necessary to bring up the less-fortunate child. The tradeoff is that those subsidies increase the number of children born into poverty.

To the extent that the costs of rearing children are paid by others, parents face a marginal cost of rearing children that does not reflect the full cost of those children to society. The effect is that those children are subsidized, as shown in Figure 17-6. Figure 17-6(a) shows that this government subsidy can influence parents to choose to have more children than they would were the marginal costs not subsidized. The lower the costs they face, the more rational it is for parents to choose a larger family size or to ignore the precautions that would keep family size down. The result is that government subsidies tend to increase population growth rates.

In some cases, such as that shown in Figure 17-6(b), couples may choose to have children they don't want—so-called *unwanted children*—in order to receive extra government

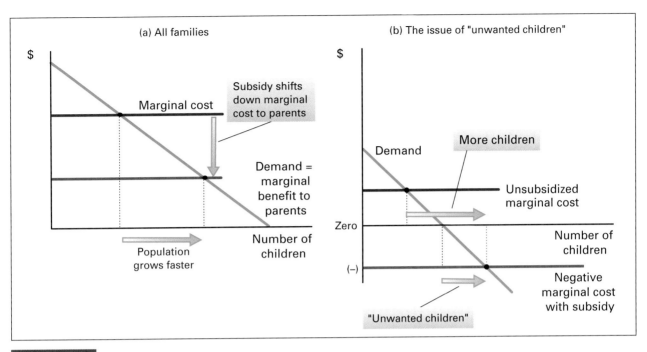

FIGURE 17-6

SUBSIDIZING POPULATION GROWTH Government spending intended to help children lowers the marginal cost to parents of raising children and increases population growth, as shown in (a). Occasionally, as shown in (b), parents choose to have additional children just to get aid that exceeds what the parents intend to spend, meaning that the parents' marginal cost inclusive of subsidy is negative. Some of those parents even choose to have so-called unwanted children, which occurs when the parents' demand lies below the horizontal axis but above the negative marginal cost.

aid or tax write-offs. These are children that the parents would prefer not to have, except for the extra income they cause. In other words, the parents' demand curves would be negative for these children. Public assistance intended to help children may in this way lead to more children who need help.

We know the world cannot sustain an ever-increasing population, nor wish to endure the other stresses of a crowded planet. For these reasons, government policy might seek to influence population growth rates by changing the incentives facing prospective families. Alternatively, countries can turn to command-and-control methods. For example and most notably, for more than two decades China has prohibited a family from having more than one child. Given a cultural preference for baby boys, and modern medical technology, the result has been a demographic nightmare. For example, in 2000, about 117 boys were born in China for every 100 baby girls. Historically, countries where young men could not find mates have soon become embroiled in violence or warfare.

In less-developed countries, people have many children for several reasons. One is because they lack access to birth control, or they may have customs or beliefs that do not accept its use. A second reason is due to ineffective or nonexistent government programs such as Social Security or other transfer payments. A couple in a less-developed country with several children can rely on them for assistance if they reach advanced ages. Education, medical care, and stable governments can help address population growth issues.

> ## *QUICKCHECK*
>
> **Would it be good public policy to ensure that prospective parents pay all of the costs of educating their children?**
>
> **Answer:** The question of good public policy is normative, meaning that economics cannot provide a definitive answer. Policymakers might weigh the often-conflicting goals of efficiency and equity for children. For example, the large majority of people think that it is equitable for all children to have equal access to education, even if that means publicly subsidizing that education. This policy leads to inefficiencies, because it gives parents less incentive to hold down family size.

17.3 PRICES AND PROPERTY RIGHTS

price signals the allocation of resources through the price system; prices guide consumption and investment.

For countries to develop, they need capital. Investments from private sources or government is the source of this capital. Consider private investment. In deciding which projects to fund, banks, private investors, and multinational firms look at market prices and the security of property rights. In other words, the investors follow **price signals** to guide them in the direction of the greatest profits. **Because of the central importance of prices in guiding consumption and investment spending throughout the world, the market economy is often called the price system.** Some LDCs have abundant natural resources, such as oil in the countries of the Middle East. Let's see how the price system responds to dwindling supplies of resources.

THE PRICE SYSTEM—FINDING NEW RESOURCES

Prices respond to scarcity. Other things equal, the scarcer are resources, the higher are their prices. Higher prices make it profitable to find or develop substitutes, which would not be economical at lower prices. Well before any resource is depleted, its increasing scarcity drives its price higher. When the price of a nonrenewable resource rises, the market is motivated to explore for additional supplies and to develop substitutes.

In the 1970s, the high price of oil resulted in major new finds in Mexico, Alaska, the North Sea, and elsewhere. Today, oil rigs can be found in many LDCs, as the search for oil has spread to the far corners of the globe. Substitutes for oil include technology to give motor vehicles more miles per gallon, insulation to reduce the energy costs of homes, and fuel alternatives such as coal and natural gas. However, oil prices have not remained high enough for most substitute fuels to be economical.

As price has risen, technology has responded to prevent shortages. At one time, for example, the world's copper supplies appeared to be running out. This shortage threatened growth because copper was needed for electricity and telephone connections. The rising price of copper spurred new technologies, such as fiber optics, that greatly reduced the world's need for copper. In the realm of food, too, technological advances have helped farmers increase yields per acre to meet the needs of growing populations. The hunger spots in the world today have much less to do with agricultural technology than with political instability that interrupt the production and distribution of food.

In the 1800s, an energy crisis was brought about by a scarcity of whale oil, which at the time was used in reading lamps. The scarcity was prompted by tight supplies and high prices, as whaling ships decimated the population of the world's whales in response to growing demand. The price system dangled the lure of profit to successful innovators who could find new energy sources. This incentive eventually brought about the age of petroleum. We can only speculate about whether the next energy age will be of solar power, new efficiencies in energy usage, or other possibilities that few of us currently envision.

Many developing countries' exports are heavily weighted toward natural resources. For example, countries in the Middle East export crude oil, countries with rainforests export tropical hardwoods, and so forth. The problem for these countries occurs when the prices of *commodities,* including natural resources such as copper, tin, and precious metals, and agricultural products such as rice, bananas, and cocoa, are not high enough to sustain development. The **Prebisch–Singer thesis,** which was advanced in the 1950s, states that developing countries will be trapped in poverty because the price of their exports will be driven down by increasing commodity supplies as the price system responds. This can lead to **immiserizing growth,** where increasing supplies of commodities exported by the LDCs causes prices to drop so far that these countries end up worse off because of trade. Although low commodity and agricultural prices are a problem for the LDCs that export these goods, the Prebisch–Singer thesis is not generally accepted by economists as an explanation for the ills of these countries. Thus, in the next section we turn our attention to the role of property rights in economic development.

Prebisch–Singer thesis a thesis that states that developing countries will remain in poverty because the prices of their exports of commodities are doomed to decrease.

immiserizing growth growth that leaves a country worse off; associated with the Prebisch–Singer thesis.

PROPERTY RIGHTS

A key ingredient of the market economy, one lacking in many less-developed countries, is the ingredient of secure **property rights,** meaning rights of ownership. Investors need to know that they will be able to retain the fruits of their investments, or they will not invest. They must not fear that government action in the future will prevent them from reaping the rewards that they envision when they make their investments in the present.

property rights clear rights of ownership.

For example, prospective investors would be deterred if they fear regulatory *takings,* in which government reduces the value of property by restricting how the investor can use it. In extreme cases, investors might fear government expropriation, such as the expropriation of oil wells that occurred in Colombia and other countries in the 1960s and 1970s. Investors must also be confident that government regulations will be enforced evenhandedly, and not skewed by bribery or favoritism. Civil unrest and terrorism are also problems that can drive investors away.

Table 17-4 presents the average annual growth rates, from 1990 to 2000, of selected high-growth countries, medium- to low-growth countries, and countries with negative growth. Most of the high-growth countries share a significant role for the price system and property rights. LDCs that can sustain a high-growth rate experience rising living standards. In general, the growth rates of the developed countries are 4 percent or less.

WATER WAR IN COCHABAMBA	*SNAPSHOT*

While people in the developed world may take clean, safe drinking water for granted, over a billion people around the world do not enjoy that resource. In Cochabamba, Bolivia's third-largest city, chronic water problems came to a head in 1999. The government chose to privatize the city's water system, selling it to Bechtel, an American-owned firm. The firm held out the hope that infrastructure investments, in the form of dams, pipelines, and purification facilities, would bring ample supplies of clean water to the populace.

Before investments could be made, the new owner said water rates had to rise. Considering that many Bolivians live on the country's $60-a-month minimum wage, the $20 and $30 monthly water bills that residents of Cochabamba began to receive generated outrage. Civil unrest in early 2000 put water back into the hands of the government. Since then, nothing has been done to solve the water problems, and many residents have water only a few hours a week, if at all. Meanwhile, the loss of property put a chill on foreign investment in Bolivia, leaving no winners from this Bolivian water war. ◄

TABLE 17-4   AVERAGE ANNUAL GROWTH RATES IN GDP, SELECTED COUNTRIES

HIGH-GROWTH COUNTRIES (IN PERCENT)		MEDIUM- TO LOW- GROWTH COUNTRIES		NEGATIVE-GROWTH COUNTRIES	
China	10.3	Australia	4.1	Moldova	− 9.7
Ireland	7.3	Guatemala	4.1	Ukraine	− 9.3
Malaysia	7.0	Panama	4.1	Russian Federation	− 4.8
Chile	6.8	Hong Kong, China	4.0		
Myanmar	6.6	Pakistan	3.7		
Lao Peoples' Democratic Republic	6.5	United States	3.5		
Mozambique	6.4	Philippines	3.3		
India	6.0	Mexico	3.1		
Lebanon	6.0	New Zealand	3.0		
South Korea	5.7	Japan	1.3		

Source: World Bank Development Indicators database. Growth rates cited are for 1990 to 2000.

WARRING OVER REAL ESTATE

Besides poverty, the LDCs have conflict in common. A study of the seventy-five countries that have USAID missions showed that between 1996 and 2001, two-thirds of them had major conflicts. There is nothing more destructive to standards of living than warfare. Property ownership is central to many of the world's conflicts. Conflict over property can range from boundary disputes to the control of entire countries. Borders between nations are often ill defined, with centuries of warfare shifting them back and forth. Disputes over property have triggered the wars among the countries of the former Yugoslavia and the many clashes between Palestinians and Israelis. Likewise, the Indians and Pakistanis have fought two wars over the Kashmir Province, where ethnic tensions are still running very high. Disputes sap vital energy that could be used to move countries ahead economically.

17.4 COUNTRIES HELPING COUNTRIES: FOREIGN AID, THE IMF, AND THE WORLD BANK

When one country helps another country, the mechanism is often *foreign aid*. Foreign aid consists of donated money or products. Countries provide foreign aid on their own and through membership in two of the most important organizations that channel resources to the poorer countries: the **World Bank** and the **International Monetary Fund,** commonly referred to by its initials (**IMF**).

FOREIGN AID—AN ANSWER TO SCARCITY OF CAPITAL?

Polls show that people in the developed countries support the principle of giving aid to the LDCs. The United States plays a major role in foreign aid. For example, as reported by the White House in 2002, the United States is:

World Bank institution that was created to loan money to developing countries.

International Monetary Fund (IMF) institution created in 1944 to promote a sound world financial system.

- The top importer of goods from developing countries, importing $450 billion in 2000, eight times greater than all Official Development Assistance (ODA) to developing countries from all donors.
- The top source of private capital to developing countries, averaging $36 billion annually between 1997 and 2000.
- The world leader in charitable donations to developing countries—$4 billion in 2000.
- One of the top two providers of Official Development Assistance (ODA). In 2000, the United States provided $10 billion in ODA. This ODA is expected to increase substantially from 2001 to 2003 in key sectors:
  - HIV/AIDS (54 percent)
  - Basic education (50 percent)
  - Trade and investment (38 percent)
  - Agriculture (38 percent)

The United States also contributes $1 billion per month for the war on terrorism and, in 2001, contributed $976 million to international peacekeeping efforts.

USAID's core Development Assistance account is expected to increase 22 percent overall from 2001 to 2003. Figure 17-7 shows the breakdown of this aid. As you can see, the greatest share goes to promote economic growth and agricultural development, since agriculture is especially important in LDCs that have difficulty raising enough food to feed themselves. Such aid might take the form of teaching farmers new technologies and techniques that promise to increase crop yields.

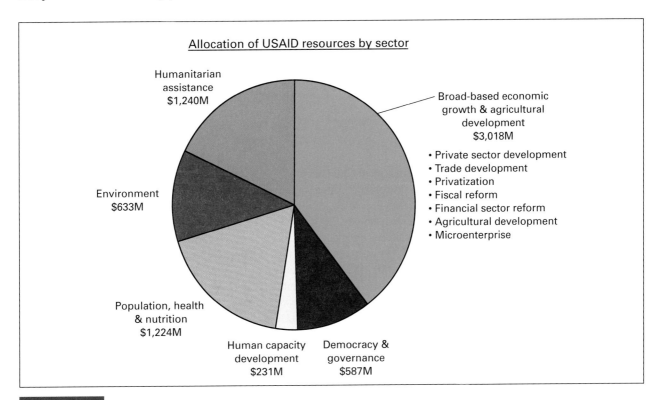

Allocation of USAID resources by sector

Humanitarian assistance $1,240M

Broad-based economic growth & agricultural development $3,018M
- Private sector development
- Trade development
- Privatization
- Fiscal reform
- Financial sector reform
- Agricultural development
- Microenterprise

Environment $633M

Population, health & nutrition $1,224M

Human capacity development $231M

Democracy & governance $587M

FIGURE 17-7

PURPOSES OF U.S. FOREIGN AID Foreign aid to developing countries by the USAID has a variety of purposes. Humanitarian assistance feeds the hungry and malnourished. Other aid is intended to protect the environment, improve health, develop skills and promote education, and encourage stable, responsive governments. The largest portion of aid goes toward promoting economic growth and agricultural development.

Source: U.S. Agency for International Development, *Broad-Based Economic Growth.* The breakdown in the chart represents budget requests for 2001.

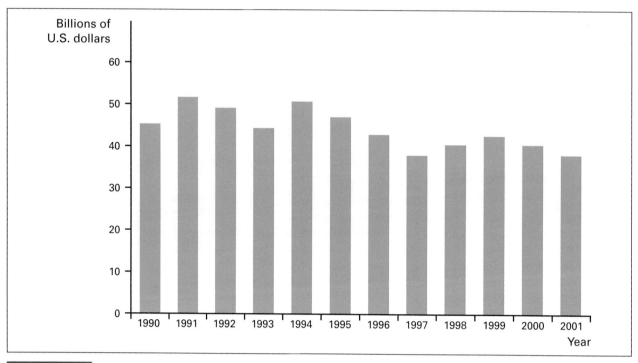

GOVERNMENT AID TO DEVELOPING COUNTRIES Foreign aid from governments drifted lower since 1990.
By 2001 it was $10 billion lower than in 1991. This drop in foreign aid probably reflects the public's
lack of support for foreign aid.

Source: World Bank, *World Bank Anticipates Global Upturn, Urges Increased Help to Poor Countries,* March 13,
2002.

Figure 17-8 tracks the total amount of aid from all countries during the 1990s. The value
of foreign aid is expressed in nominal terms, meaning the numbers have not been adjusted
for inflation. A striking feature of the figure is the more than $10 billion drop in aid in 2001
when compared to 1991.

Issues of aid and development received more than the usual media attention in the
spring of 2002, when an unlikely pair toured the world's poorest countries. The Irish singer,
Bono, of the group U2 was one. The other was Paul O'Neill, U.S. Secretary of the Treasury.
Their purpose was to assess opportunities for lifting up poor nations. One of the problems
poor nations face is a crushing debt load. Banks in the developed countries have loaned billions of dollars to the governments of LDCs to finance infrastructure. Unfortunately for many
LDCs, their economies do not generate enough tax dollars to repay the money owed.

Bono's opinion was that all debt should be forgiven. O'Neill argued for generosity in
ongoing aid, but that forgiveness of debt would be inappropriate. Their debate typifies the
differences of opinion on the issue of foreign aid. To provide debt relief to impoverished
countries, the United States and other countries help to pay for the debt initiative for Heavily
Indebted Poor Countries (HIPC). This program was established by the IMF and the World
Bank.

THE INTERNATIONAL MONETARY FUND (IMF)

As its name suggests, the IMF is a fund that can be drawn on by member countries needing
temporary financing to deal with monetary and financial problems. The IMF was established

in 1944 with the goal of ensuring a stable world monetary and financial system. According to its Articles of Agreement, the purposes of the IMF are to:

- Promote international monetary cooperation.
- Facilitate the expansion of international trade.
- Encourage exchange rate stability.
- Further the establishment of a *multilateral* (multicountry) payment system.
- Provide resources to member countries experiencing balance of payments problems.

Money to finance IMF operations comes from membership fees, called quotas, that are proportional to the size and economic strength of its 184 member countries. The United States has the largest quota, amounting to 17.6 percent of IMF funding. All member countries, rich and poor alike, have access to IMF resources.

The main activities of the IMF include:

1. **Surveillance.** This procedure involves a policy discussion between the IMF and a member country. An annual IMF appraisal of each member country's exchange rate policies is part of the process. Surveillance is intended to ensure that a country's economic policies furnish a strong foundation for stable exchange rates, which the IMF believes is a key to world prosperity. For example, the IMF urged Japan in 2000 to promote deregulation and competition in order to stimulate economic growth. Global surveillance is also carried out, such as in 2001 when the IMF pointed out in a *World Economic Outlook* report the need for countries to stimulate aggregate demand in the face of weakening global growth.

2. **Financial assistance.** As of February 2002, the IMF had about $77 billion in credits and loans outstanding to eighty-eight countries. This assistance is provided to countries that have balance of payments problems. The purpose of this assistance is to encourage reforms in the policies of countries receiving the assistance. Some of this assistance is in the form of debt relief provided through the HIPC initiative, mentioned earlier. IMF loans are intended to support reforms aimed at eliminating the root causes of a country's problems. For example, during the Asian financial crisis in 1998, the IMF's $21 billion loan to Korea was targeted toward reforming that country's financial and business sectors.

3. **Technical assistance.** Poor countries are often ill-equipped to develop their own fiscal and monetary policies because the human capital necessary to develop sound policies is not available domestically. Thus, the IMF provides help so that countries can design policies that strengthen their economies. For example, the IMF assisted Russia and other transition economies in setting up central banking and treasury systems. Part of the technical assistance offered is in the area of statistics. For a country to be able to implement and monitor effective policies, there must be statistics on unemployment, inflation, GDP, and other key macro variables. Countries that lack expertise in this area can tap into the IMF's expertise.

Through the provision of surveillance, financial assistance, and technical assistance, the IMF aims to tie member countries more closely into the world economy, and advise members on how to deal with problems that arise from their trade and financial interactions with other countries. Sometimes these problems call for IMF financial assistance, which the IMF offers under the condition that the countries undertake economic reforms that are in accord with IMF advice.

The reforms can be painful, which leads some countries to complain about IMF arm-twisting. They might even complain of IMF *imperialism*, saying that the IMF seeks to force the values of Western economies upon countries around the world. The IMF has responded to this criticism by reforms intended to make IMF loan conditions less burdensome.

The IMF is known for the massive loans that it extended to Mexico during the 1994 to 1995 peso crisis, to the countries of Asia during the 1997 to 1998 Asian financial crisis, and to Russia in 1998 as that country struggled through multiple economic and social crises. The purpose of these loans was to allow these countries to pay their debts to other countries, while reforming their economic and financial systems. Not surprisingly, when the IMF compiled a ranking of its largest borrowers between the years of 1947 and 2000, Mexico, Korea, and Russia were the top three recipients of IMF loans.

Critics of IMF lending practices term many IMF loans "bailouts" that will lead to more bailouts in the future, because countries' lenders will not be as careful when they realize the IMF will step in with money when the countries get into trouble. Careless lending practices can impede economic development and sound growth because money will go into projects that are unsound and should not be undertaken. The IMF has publicly recognized the *moral hazard* in making unlimited loans—that countries will be prompted to follow unsound policies that will lead to future crises, and that lenders will be encouraged to make unsound loans if they believe that the IMF will see that they are repaid in the event of default by borrowing countries.

THE WORLD BANK

The World Bank does what most people expect banks to do: loan money. **World Bank loans to less-developed member countries are intended to further their economic development.** Since its creation more than fifty years ago, the World Bank has loaned more than $400 billion. The similarities between the World Bank and the IMF include that they are both headquartered in Washington, D.C., they are both owned by the governments of member countries, virtually every country is a member of both institutions, and they were both started in July 1944.

Consider the World Bank's lending practices:

- World Bank loans, which only go to developing countries, must be repaid. Unlike aid programs, the World Bank does not provide grants, which are gifts of money. The money for the Bank's loans comes partly from government grants and partly from borrowings from the private sector and governments.
- Lending is of two types. The first is lending to countries that are able to pay near-market interest on the loans they receive. The second is lending to countries that cannot afford to pay interest. These loans are called *credits* and are provided through a World Bank affiliate, the International Development Association, for terms of thirty-five to forty years. Although interest is not charged, the credits must be repaid. Such credits only go to the very poorest countries and average about $6 billion per year.
- The World Bank can only lend to member governments or under a member government's guarantee.
- To ensure that money is well invested, the Bank evaluates projects and only lends when a project is expected to earn at least a 10-percent rate of economic return.

A top priority of the World Bank is to stimulate development of the private sector, although direct loans to the private sector are prohibited. The Bank seeks to encourage the private sector by promoting stable, honest government economic policies that focus on expanding the significance of markets. Although the Bank cannot make loans to the private sector, an affiliate called the International Finance Corporation exists for that purpose. It also aids governments in privatizing formerly government-owned businesses.

The World Bank's focus on the private sector is a relatively recent development. From its inception through the 1970s, the Bank tended toward policies that emphasized expanding

QUICKCHECK

What is the significance of the World Bank's requirement that a project have at least a 10-percent expected return? What problem is associated with this policy?

Answer: Projects with higher rates of return provide more benefits per dollar invested than do projects with lower rates of return. By seeking to finance only projects that offer the prospect of a relatively high rate of return, the World Bank stretches its budget further and helps more people. The problem is that it cannot know in advance whether a project will actually yield a 10-percent return after the project is completed.

the government sector in developing countries. It was thought that large-scale government projects were the key to bringing about prosperity, including promoting government-owned industries. However, the Bank changed its policies in response to the successes of the U.S. economy and the failure of central planning in the communist countries in the 1980s, along with the successes of market economies in Hong Kong, Malaysia, and elsewhere in the world.

THE BEST-LAID PLANS OF MICE AND GOVERNMENT

SNAPSHOT

To see why World Bank policies now emphasize markets, consider the outcome of government planning in Nigeria in the 1970s. To bring the nation up to modern standards required roads, bridges, airports, and other infrastructure. This modernization called for massive quantities of cement, much more than the nation could produce domestically. Thus, Nigeria's government planners ordered the needed cement, which was shipped in the holds of freighters from cement-producing nations around the world.

Oops! One slight oversight threw these best-laid plans into disarray. The Nigerian docks were incapable of handling such quantities of cement. In fact, at one point it would have taken nearly thirty years to unload the cement that lay in the holds of ships anchored off-shore. As time passed, the cement commenced to solidify within the ships, thereby providing a concrete example of the dangers inherent in centrally planned development. ◀

Explore & Apply

17.5 RUSSIA—A ROUGH TRANSITION TO THE PRICE SYSTEM

"If history could teach us anything, it would be that private property is inextricably linked with civilization."

—*Ludwig von Mises*

For much of the last century, Russia was part of the former Union of Soviet Socialist Republics (the Soviet Union), with an economy that rejected the price system of the free market. After the overthrow of communism in 1991, Russia embraced its new market economy, but only today is starting to realize its potential. Russia's had a rough transition, as demonstrated in Table 17-5, which shows the country's unemployment rate and output of goods and services (as a percentage of the previous year's output). During the

early years of the transition to a market-oriented system, output fell and unemployment increased. Russia had good reason to endure this process.

Unlike capitalist countries, the former communist countries of Eastern Europe and the Soviet Union had no competitive market prices to ensure an efficient allocation of resources. Prices were set to achieve equity and political expediency, not efficiency. Soviet planners tried to match resources to outputs and outputs to needs, but faced a difficult problem. To allocate efficiently, planners must know how much value consumers place on alternative outputs. They also must compute the opportunity costs of inputs. In contrast, free markets reveal this information automatically; it is implicit in market prices.

To acquire the information they need, the Soviet planners estimated *shadow prices,* which are what the market prices would have been if there had been a free market. This undertaking is something like trying to answer the old riddle, "How much wood would a woodchuck chuck, if a woodchuck could chuck wood?" Although the planners resorted to complex mathematical models, the estimated shadow prices were only rough approximations to true market prices. When planners imposed incorrectly estimated prices, people and businesses were led to many wrong decisions about what and how to produce. The result was both surpluses and shortages.

In response, we saw such strange occurrences as children using loaves of bread as footballs, even though the bread did not last long in that usage, and even though the cost of the ingredients to make the loaves far exceeded their value as footballs. The problem was that bread was priced very cheaply for political reasons, and customers bought it in much larger quantities than they would have if bread prices reflected the costs of the ingredients, labor, and other items used in producing that bread. Still, for political reasons, government attempted to turn out as much of this necessity as consumers would choose to buy.

Politically set prices had one interesting positive effect. They forced Soviet authorities to exercise monetary restraint. Too many rubles would just add more purchasing power, which consumers would spend on underpriced goods. The Soviet Union did not have the where-

TABLE 17-5   MACROECONOMIC INDICATORS FOR RUSSIA

YEAR	OUTPUT AS A PERCENTAGE OF THE PREVIOUS YEAR'S OUTPUT	UNEMPLOYMENT RATE
1994	87	7.8
1995	96	9.0
1996	96.6	10.0
1997	100.9	11.2
1998	95.1	13.3
1999	104.6	12.4
2000	110.2	9.9
2001	105.7	8.7

Source: The Central Bank of the Russian Federation. Prior to 1999, the output measure used was GDP; in 1999 an index of output replaced GDP. The 1998 unemployment rate is an authors' estimate. All other unemployment rates are from the source indicated.

withal to produce enough of these goods as it was. With the exception of bread and a few other items, shelves were often bare. The only way to prevent even greater shortages was to keep additional money from circulating in the economy. Thus, in the former Soviet Union, price inflation was kept low because government set the prices, and monetary growth was restrained in order to allow the policy of low prices to work. In contrast, when markets are free, the process is reversed. Monetary restraint must be exercised to keep inflation from taking hold in the marketplace.

It was small wonder that the Soviet economy spiraled downward over time. The arms buildup of the 1980s hastened that decline and prompted an overthrow of the central planners. First, there was Mikhail Gorbachev, would-be reformer of the communist system. Then came Boris Yeltsin, a free-market revolutionary who extricated Russia from the splinters of the Soviet Union. Many thought that, with markets freed from the central planners, living standards would quickly rise. The statistics said otherwise, and for good reason.

PROPERTY RIGHTS

Russia embraced capitalist ideas, but at first failed to impose a key ingredient necessary for the success of free markets: certainty over property rights. If individuals and businesses have no confidence that they will be able to keep the fruits of their labors and investments, the profit motive is lost. Few would seek profit in order to turn it over to the government. Unfortunately, in modern Russia, that has been a danger.

After the downfall of the Soviet Union, Russia had too many governments claiming jurisdiction over the same economic activity. For example, while it has been possible to buy land in Russia, it has also at times been nearly impossible to obtain a clear title to it. One government would grant the title, while another government would lie in wait to claim the land in the future. At least one U.S. entrepreneur saw this situation as a profit opportunity, and offered title insurance to remedy it.

Some Russian entrepreneurs have a different strategy. They specialize in having connections with both legitimate and illegitimate authorities. For example, Ben and Jerry's used these entrepreneurs to establish a network of Russian "scoop shops" to sell its ice cream. Even so, Ben and Jerry's ultimately abandoned its efforts to do business in Russia.

With all the governments came a host of taxes. To some extent, all taxes represent an expropriation of private property. Post-Soviet taxes sometimes carried this expropriation to an absurd extreme. Specifically, when taxes from the various jurisdictions were added together, they would often sum to over 100 percent. This means that, for every dollar of profit a business would make, it would owe more than a dollar to the government.

It seems unlikely that any business would voluntarily choose to operate under these conditions. Yet business did go on in Russia. The reason is at least threefold. First, many profits are hidden from the tax collector, either through bribery or techniques of accounting. Second, and related to the first, there has been and continues to be a thriving underground economy that is not reported to authorities. Third, business looked to the future, a future that is already unfolding in the form of greater clarification as to property ownership and taxation. The result of these early problems of transition is that Russia has since seen rapid economic growth.

Much of the underground economy in Russia is ruled by organized crime. Oftentimes, their leaders are former officials of the communist government, officials with connections to networks of "enforcers." In a way, these former officials are entrepreneurs whose skills are in demand. Those skills are the protection of property rights. For a price, the local crime boss will protect your property from other criminals. Through his connections, he can also offer some protection from excessive government regulation and taxation. It is thus not surprising to find that statistics from the Russian government show that the transition to free markets caused the Russian economy to shrink.

When economic activity is not reported, government cannot collect taxes on it directly. There is a way to collect taxes indirectly, however. That way is through inflation. Authorities in Russia's central bank printed money freely, allowing government to spend without collecting taxes. Instead, the tax was inflation that eroded purchasing power in the legitimate and underground economies alike.

Russia has undergone a dramatic upheaval, in which the old order of communism was thrown out to make way for the new order of capitalism. However, capitalistic free markets cannot function without the ownership of private property. There has been movement in this direction. For example, Russia now has in place a supply-side tax policy that attempts to secure property rights and avoid prohibitively high tax rates. The underground economy will diminish in importance because of those tax changes. But will the principles of private property that support free-market efficiency ever become firmly entrenched? We need only wait to see the answer, as the story unfolds before the Russian people and the world.

*𝒯*HINKING
*𝒞*RITICALLY

1. Consumers like low prices. Yet the transition from government-set prices to free-market prices leads to higher prices for many goods, such as bread and milk. How can it be in the consumer's interest to accept the transition from command-and-control pricing to free-market pricing? Do you think the typical consumer would recognize your reasoning?

2. Free markets rely on private property rights, but those rights are not absolute. In other words, it would not be in the social interest to allow private property to be put to any use whatsoever, without any restriction. What are some examples that in your opinion are legitimate government restrictions on the use of private property? Should government pay property owners to accept these restrictions?

Visit **www.prenhall.com/ayers** for updates and web exercises on this Explore & Apply topic.

SUMMARY AND LEARNING OBJECTIVES

1. **Discuss the problems that are a priority for developing countries.**
   - The poverty and low life expectancy in many less-developed countries provide the motivation for economic development efforts. Extreme poverty is associated with low per capita incomes in less-developed countries (LDCs).
   - Additional problems include lack of infrastructure and high population growth. LDCs need investments in roads, schools, and other infrastructure. They sometimes have trouble feeding their people, a problem compounded by high population growth.

2. **Describe the goals on the United Nations' development agenda.**
   - The eight goals are: (1) Eradicate extreme poverty and hunger. (2) Achieve universal primary education.

   (3) Promote gender equality and empower women. (4) Reduce child mortality. (5) Improve maternal health. (6) Combat HIV/AIDS, malaria, and other diseases. (7) Ensure environmental sustainability. (8) Develop a global partnership for development.
   - The UN's objective is to achieve the eight goals by 2015. Attached to each goal are specific targets.
   - Indicators are used to classify countries according to their level of economic development. A common set of fourteen world indicators are used by the UN to assess development. These indicators focus on infrastructure and health.

3. **Point out the incentives for population growth.**
   - Economics is sometimes referred to as "the dismal science" because of the predictions of Thomas Malthus. He forecast a future world in which popula-

tion growth would outstrip the ability to produce food. To this point, the world has escaped the Malthusian vision because technology has increased productivity in food production.

■ Population growth is a problem for many countries, especially the less-developed ones, as these countries must feed and provide jobs for their growing populations. A country's population growth varies according to a number of economic factors, including implicit government subsidies to larger families.

■ Government policies can change the price signals facing parents. One way is through subsidizing the expenses associated with raising children. A number of aspects of having and raising children can be subsidized, but the outcome is the same—an increase in the number of births.

4. **Explain the connection between economic development and property rights.**

■ Price signals guide investors in market economies. The price system has proven to be remarkably adept at responding to impending shortages of resources. As resources become more scarce, their prices rise. When resources become sufficiently costly because of scarcity, the price system has responded by offering new substitutes that can replace the older resources.

■ A good example of price signals from history is the transition from scarce whale oil to alternative energy sources, where higher whale oil prices increased the demand for substitute energy sources. That increase in demand in turn led to the development of petroleum resources.

■ Economic development is impeded by unclear property rights.

■ Market economies depend on clear property rights. Many less-developed nations lack this feature, which is a key ingredient in the economic success of nations. Regulatory takings and government expropriation of private property tend to deter investment.

■ The desire for territory has motivated many of the world's conflicts. Palestinians and Israelis have fought over the same land. Likewise, the Indians and Pakistanis have faced off over the Kashmir Province. Conflict impedes development.

5. **Identify the roles of the International Monetary Fund and the World Bank in economic development.**

■ The World Bank and the International Monetary Fund (IMF) were created by the industrialized countries to assist the less-developed countries. The World Bank provides loans to finance qualified development projects in poor countries. The mission of the IMF is to maintain a stable financial order that facilitates trade and development.

■ The IMF was founded in 1944 with the goal of promoting global prosperity through increased world trade and exchange rate stability. The IMF provides funds to its 184 member countries in the form of temporary loans to countries experiencing balance of payments problems. These funds are provided through fees assessed on member countries. The United States is the largest provider of funds to the IMF. Through surveillance, financial assistance, and technical assistance, the IMF helps countries achieve financial stability.

■ The World Bank was founded at the same time as the IMF. Its mission is to make loans to developing countries that finance projects that promise to provide benefits sufficient to earn a 10-percent return. World Bank policies favor the expansion of the market sector in countries receiving loans.

6. **Describe how insecure property rights have hindered economic development in Russia.**

■ Private property is an integral component of a market economy. Unclear ownership of property has hindered Russia's economic development during its transition from central planning to a market economy.

KEY TERMS

TEST YOURSELF

TRUE OR FALSE

1. The United States is an example of a country that lacks infrastructure.
2. The United Nations' development agenda does not address issues relating to the environment.
3. "The dismal science" is a term coined by Adam Smith.
4. When existing resources become more scarce, the price system responds through an increase in the demand for alternative resources.
5. The primary function of the World Bank is to provide grants to deserving poor countries.

MULTIPLE CHOICE

6. Life expectancy in the LDCs is generally
   a. about the same as in developed countries.
   b. higher than in developed countries because the people eat healthier foods.
   c. higher than in developed countries because the people eat less frequently.
   d. lower than in the developed countries.
7. The fourth stage in Rostow's stages model is
   a. traditional society.
   b. takeoff.
   c. drive to maturity.
   d. high mass consumption.
8. Which is not a specific goal of the United Nations' development agenda?
   a. Build mass transit systems.
   b. Universal primary education.
   c. Reduce child mortality.
   d. Combat disease.
9. The price system
   a. hinders economic development.
   b. has no effect on economic development.
   c. promotes economic development by offering people incentives to find and develop new resources.
   d. promotes economic development, but is clearly inferior to central planning in that role.
10. Which would NOT contribute to high population growth?
    a. Reliable retirement benefits to the elderly.
    b. Government subsidies to parents.
    c. Advances in medicine.
    d. Lower death rates.
11. Economics was called "the dismal science" because
    a. students often fell asleep in economics classes.
    b. of Matlthus's prediction that immigration would be so great as to destroy a country's unique culture through foreign influences.
    c. of its low level of scientific rigor.
    d. of Malthus's prediction that population growth would outstrip resources, leading to a subsistence standard of living for most people.
12. The downward shift in marginal cost shown in Self-Test Figure 17-1 is most likely caused by
    a. government subsidies to education.
    b. increased opportunities for women in the work force.
    c. Social Security.
    d. higher family income.

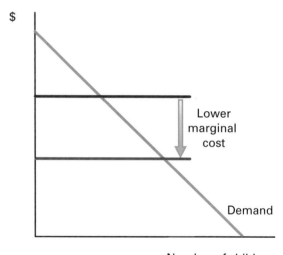

SELF-TEST FIGURE 17-1

13. In recent years annual foreign aid from all countries has totaled about
    a. $10 billion.
    b. $40 billion.
    c. $70 billion.
    d. $100 billion.
14. World Bank loans go only to countries
    a. that have never defaulted on their debts.
    b. that cannot get loans from any other source.
    c. that offer projects with at least a 10-percent expected return.
    d. that have achieved at least Rostow's stage-3 level of development.
15. The World Bank's loans are intended to promote
    a. central planning.
    b. economic development.
    c. policies that reduce world trade.
    d. population growth.

16. The primary role of the International Monetary Fund (IMF) is to
    a. promote central planning of economies.
    b. make sure that countries repay their loans to the World Bank.
    c. show farmers in LDCs how to produce enough food to avoid starvation.
    d. strengthen the world monetary and financial system.

17. Financing for the IMF comes from
    a. only the United States.
    b. only the United States and the countries of Western Europe.
    c. only the United States, Japan, and the countries of Western Europe.
    d. its members through the payment of membership fees that are proportional to the size and economic strength of each country.

18. The moral hazard associated with IMF actions is most closely associated with
    a. the way in which the IMF is financed.
    b. the stated mission of the IMF.
    c. the low life expectancy of citizens in less-developed countries.
    d. the idea that IMF bailouts would encourage countries to follow unsound policies.

19. Less-developed countries have sometimes accused the IMF of imperialism because
    a. the director of the IMF, who must by tradition be selected from the members of Britain's royal family, has often exhibited an imperial manner at public ceremonial events related to the IMF.
    b. the IMF encourages less-developed countries to become imperialists.
    c. of the conditions the IMF attaches to its help.
    d. the IMF offers money to countries but then offers no guidance on the best use of that money.

20. As Russia develops its market economy by reducing taxes and securing property rights, the underground economy in Russia will likely
    a. expand.
    b. diminish.
    c. remain the same.
    d. be legalized by the government.

QUESTIONS AND PROBLEMS

1. *[development indicators]* Why would per capita income be a good indicator of a country's level of development? What other indicators might be used to supplement per capita income in order to assess a country's level of development?

2. *[problems of LDCs]* List four common problems of developing nations. How do these problems affect everyday life in a developing country?

3. *[infrastructure]* Suppose you are a central planner in a less-developed country we shall call Poorlandia. Devise a policy statement that explains the significance of various items of infrastructure in helping Poorlandia grow and increase its standard of living.

4. *[development]* If you were to join the Peace Corps after graduating from college, and you were sent to a less-developed country, what single most important economic principle would you wish to share with the people of that country? Explain that principle in common-sense terms.

5. *[poverty and life expectancy]* Write a short essay that describes how poverty contributes to the short life expectancy of people in many less-developed countries.

6. *[Rostow model]* List Rostow's five stages of economic growth. Briefly describe each stage. Why is this model criticized by economists?

7. *[population]* Ecosystems have carrying capacities for the species within them. Do you think there is a comparable carrying capacity for humans within the world's ecosystem? If so, how far do you think we are from that capacity, and what would be the consequences of overshooting it?

8. *[population]* Explain why farmers in LDCs desire large numbers of children. Why might development slow down population growth?

9. *[population]* What roles do religious beliefs play in either promoting or hindering a solution to the world's population problems? Explain.

10. *[population]* What is your personal desire regarding how many children you would like to have? Explain how the costs and benefits of having children influences your choice.

11. *[price signals]* Explain how the price system responds to scarcity. Use the example in the text of the energy crisis involving whale oil. Is that example from history relevant to any modern energy crisis?

12. *[property rights]* How can clearly defined property rights assist in economic development? How does a country where property rights have been ambiguous go about establishing clearer property rights?

13. *[foreign aid]* Why do some people view foreign aid as a waste of tax dollars? What alternatives to government-provided aid exist? Explain.

14. *[World Bank]* In a series of bullet points, write a one-page policy statement for the World Bank that lists the criteria you would recommend be applied for approving development loans to poorer countries.

15. *[IMF]* In recent years there have been several large protests and demonstrations against the International Monetary Fund (IMF). Discuss the significance of the IMF in the context of economic development. In your discussion, comment on why you think the IMF has generated such hostility among the protestors.

 Visit **www.prenhall.com/ayers** for Exploring the Web exercises and additional self-test quizzes.

A

ability-to-pay principle states that those who can afford to pay more taxes than others should be required to do so.

absolute advantage the ability to produce a good with fewer resources than other producers.

action lag time between when the problem is recognized and when policies are enacted.

actual return the value an investment actually had, judged after the fact; expressed as a percentage.

adaptive expectations when people form expectations as to future prices according to what their experiences have been in the past.

aggregate demand relates how much real GDP consumers, businesses, and government will purchase at each price level; graphically, aggregate demand slopes downward.

aggregate expenditure function shows the economy's planned aggregate expenditures for each possible level of real GDP.

aggregate expenditures consumption + investment + government + net exports.

allocative efficiency involves choosing the most valuable mix of outputs to produce.

appreciation when a currency buys more of other currencies; makes imports cheaper and exports more expensive.

automatic stabilizers features embedded within existing fiscal policies that act as a stimulant when the economy is sluggish and act as a drag when it is in danger of inflation.

autonomous spending spending that would occur even if people had no incomes.

B

balance of payments accounts measure of a country's economic interactions with other countries.

balance of trade the monetary value of exported goods minus the monetary value of imported goods.

balanced budget occurs when government revenue equals government spending.

balanced-budget multiplier the effect on equilibrium GDP per dollar of additional government spending when that spending is paid for by additional taxation; this multiplier equals one.

bank reserves vault cash plus deposits held by the Fed.

barter the exchange of goods and services directly for one another, without the use of money.

benefit principle states that a fair tax is one that taxes people in proportion to the benefits they receive when government spends those tax revenues.

black market market in which goods are bought and sold illegally; associated with price controls.

bonds interest-paying investments; also called securities.

budget deficit occurs when government collects less revenue than it spends.

budget surplus occurs when government collects more revenue than it spends.

business cycle the uneven sequence of trough, expansion, peak, and recession that the economy follows over time.

C

capital anything that is produced in order to increase productivity in the future; includes human capital and physical capital.

capital account records the monetary value of capital inflows from other countries (foreign investment in the United States), and outflows to other countries (U.S. investment abroad).

capital formation the creation of new capital.

capital gains the difference between the current market value of an investment and its purchase price.

capital gains tax a tax on the capital gains from investments that are sold.

ceteris paribus holding all else constant.

circular flow a model of the economy that depicts how the flow of money facilitates a counterflow of resources, goods, and services in the input and output markets.

classical a macroeconomic school of thought that emphasizes the long run and reliance upon market forces to achieve full employment.

command and control government decrees that direct economic activity.

comparative advantage the ability to produce a good at a lower opportunity cost (other goods forgone) than others could do.

complements goods or services that go well with each other, such as cream with coffee.

comprehensive measure of income measures income by subtracting a person's wealth at the beginning of the year from that person's wealth at the end of the year, adding back consumption.

consumed-income tax an income tax that does not tax income that is saved.

consumer price index (CPI) measures prices of a market basket of purchases made by consumers living in urban areas.

consumer surplus consumers' total benefit minus cost; graphically, demand minus market price.

consumption function shows planned consumption spending for each possible level of real GDP.

consumption spending purchasing by households; makes up the majority of GDP spending.

consumption tax a tax on spending rather than on income.

contractionary fiscal policy (fiscal drag) occurs when the government reduces aggregate expenditures by increasing the amount of tax revenue it collects or reducing the amount of its spending.

contractionary monetary policy monetary policy intended to slow down the economy; also called a tighter monetary policy.

cost–push inflation occurs when an upward shift in short-run aggregate supply causes the economy to move up the aggregate demand curve to a higher price level and less output.

crowding-out effect when government borrowing attracts money that would otherwise have gone to private sector investment.

current account account that records the monetary value of imports and exports of goods and services, adjusted for international incomes and transfers.

cyclical unemployment unemployment from a downturn in the business cycle that affects workers simultaneously in many different industries.

D

deadweight loss reduction in social surplus caused by inefficient price; shown graphically as a triangular area.

demand relates the quantity of a good that consumers would purchase at each of various possible prices, over some period of time, *ceteris paribus*.

demand deposits checking account deposits at commercial banks.

demand for money quantities of money that people would like to hold at various nominal interest rates, *ceteris paribus;* the demand curve for money shows an inverse relationship between the quantity of money demanded and the interest rate, and thus slopes downward.

demand–pull inflation occurs when a rightward shift in aggregate demand moves the economy up short-run aggregate supply; associated with greater employment and output.

demand-side deflation occurs when aggregate demand shifts to the left. The result is a movement down the long-run aggregate supply curve to a lower price level, but no change in full-employment output.

demand-side inflation occurs when aggregate demand shifts to the right. The result is a movement up the long-run aggregate supply curve to a higher price level, but no change in full-employment output.

deposit multiplier upper bound on the value of the money multiplier; computed as 1 divided by the reserve requirement.

depreciation when a currency buys less of other currencies; makes imports more expensive and exports cheaper.

developed countries countries such as the United States, Japan, Germany, and the United Kingdom that rely on the free-market system.

development when technology is embodied into capital.

discount rate interest rate set by the Fed on loans it makes to banks.

discouraged workers people who would like to have a job, but have given up looking; not counted as unemployed because they are not included in the labor force.

discretionary policy public policy adjusted through explicit changes made by lawmakers.

dumping selling a good to another country for less than its cost of production.

E

economic development a field of economics that studies the poverty of nations.

economic growth the ability of the economy to produce more or better output; the change in real GDP over time.

efficiency means that resources are used in ways that provide the most value; implies that no one can be made better off without someone else becoming worse off.

entrepreneurship personal initiative to combine resources in productive ways; involves risk.

equation of exchange $M \times V = P \times Q;$ M represents the quantity of money, V is velocity, P is the price level, and Q is aggregate output.

equity fairness.

excess reserves the amount of bank reserves that exceed the amount needed to meet the reserve requirement.

exchange rate price of one currency in terms of another.

expansionary fiscal policy (fiscal stimulus) occurs when government adds to aggregate expenditures by lowering the amount of tax revenue it collects or increasing the amount of its spending.

expansionary monetary policy monetary policy designed to stimulate the economy; also called a looser monetary policy.

expected return the value of an investment if successful, multiplied by the probability of success; expressed as a percentage.

expenditure equilibrium the level of GDP that the economy tends toward in the short run, at a given price level.

expenditure multiplier $1/(1 - \text{mpc})$ or $1/\text{mps}$; when multiplied by a change in autonomous spending, gives the change in equilibrium GDP.

exports goods and services a country sells to other countries.

external benefit when some benefits are received by third parties who are not directly involved in the decision.

F

federal funds rate interest rate on loans that banks make to other banks.

Federal Reserve System U.S. central bank; conducts monetary policy, holds bank deposits, and performs several other functions.

fiat money money not backed by a commodity; money by decree of law.

fiscal policy government tax and spending policy.

floating exchange rates exchange rates that adjust according to the forces of supply and demand; called managed float or dirty float if the government attempts to influence these forces.

foreign exchange markets markets in which currencies are bought and sold.

free markets the collective decisions of individual buyers and sellers that, taken together, determine what outputs are produced, how those outputs are produced, and who receives the outputs; free markets depend on private property and free choice.

free trade international commerce unhindered by policy obstacles.

frictional unemployment unemployment associated with entering the labor market or switching jobs.

full employment 100 percent minus the natural rate of unemployment.

full-employment budget estimate of government revenue and spending were the economy to be at full employment.

full-employment equilibrium the long-run macroeconomic equilibrium that occurs at a full-employment output.

full-employment output the real GDP the economy produces when it fully employs its resources.

fully funded the ideal of having enough revenue in the Social Security trust fund to be able to pay off all obligations to current workers without recourse to taxing future workers.

G

GDP chained price index or GDP price index a price index used to compute real GDP by linking together successive years of data.

GDP implicit price deflator index of prices across the spectrum of GDP; ratio of nominal GDP to real GDP.

General Agreement on Tariffs and Trade (GATT) an agreement signed by most of the major trading countries of the world, which limits the use of protectionist policies; enforced by the World Trade Organization.

general human capital skills such as language and math that are easily transferred from job to job.

Gresham's law bad money drives good money out of circulation.

gross domestic product (GDP) the market value of the final goods and services produced in the economy within some time period, usually one quarter or one year.

gross investment the total amount of investment.

H

horizontal equity the idea that people with incomes that are equivalent after adjusting for individual circumstances should pay the same amount of tax.

housing vouchers government grants that recipients can spend only on housing.

human capital acquired skills and abilities embodied within a person.

I

immiserizing growth growth that leaves a country worse off; associated with the Prebisch-Singer thesis.

implementation lag time between when policies are enacted and when they take effect.

imports goods and services a country buys from other countries.

income–expenditure model shows planned and actual expenditures at each possible real GDP.

indexing automatically adjusting the terms of an agreement for inflation.

individual retirement accounts (IRAs) tax-free savings accounts earmarked for retirement income.

induced spending spending that depends upon income.

infant industries startup industries that might be unable to survive the rigors of competition in their formative years.

inferior goods demand for these goods varies inversely with income.

inflation persistent, widespread increases in the price level.

inflation rate the annual percentage increase in the price level.

inflationary expectations predictions about future inflation that people factor into their current behavior.

inflationary gap excess in the aggregate expenditure function above that necessary to achieve a full-employment equilibrium; this gap will be corrected by inflation.

inflationary spiral fluctuating output along with continually accelerating inflation.

in-kind benefits a government-provided good or service, as opposed to cash.

input market the market where resources are bought and sold.

interest payment made by a borrower to compensate a lender for the use of money.

interest rate the price of borrowed money; expressed as a percentage.

International Monetary Fund (IMF) institution created in 1944 to promote a sound world financial system.

investment spending now in order to increase output or productivity later; includes spending on capital, new housing, and changes in business inventories.

invisible hand the idea that self-interest and competition promotes to economic efficiency without any need for action by government.

K

Keynesian a macroeconomic school of thought that emphasizes the short run and the importance of fiscal policy.

L

labor the human capacity to work.

labor force individuals age 16 and over, excluding those in the military, who are either employed or actively looking for work.

labor force participation rate the ratio of the civilian labor force to the population age 16 and over.

labor productivity output per hour worked.

land natural resources in their natural states.

law of demand as price falls, the quantity demanded increases.

law of increasing cost the rise in the marginal opportunity cost of producing a good as more of that good is produced.

law of supply as price rises, the quantity supplied increases.

leading indicators statistics that are expected to change direction before the economy at large does, thereby indicating where the economy is headed.

less-developed countries (LDCs) nations that lag behind the wealthier countries.

liquidity how easily and quickly an item can be turned into a spendable form.

long run involves underlying economic forces that make themselves felt over time.

long-run aggregate supply the idea that, in the long run, the price level does not affect the amount of GDP the economy produces; graphically, long-run aggregate supply is vertical at full-employment GDP.

M

M1 most liquid measure of money; currency plus demand deposits, traveler's checks, and other checkable deposits.

M2 obtained by adding savings deposits, small time deposits, and money market fund balances to M1.

M3 expands M2 by adding large time deposits and several other near monies.

macroeconomics analyzes economic aggregates, such as aggregate employment, output, growth, and inflation.

the margin the cutoff point; decision making at the margin refers to deciding on one more or one less of something.

marginal benefit the incremental value of an additional unit of a good.

marginal propensity to consume (mpc) the fraction of additional income that people spend.

marginal propensity to save (mps) the fraction of additional income that people save.

marginal tax rate tax rate on additional income.

market equilibrium a situation in which there is no tendency for either price or quantity to change.

medium of exchange the purchasing function of money.

microeconomics analyzes the individual components of the economy, such as the choices made by people, firms, and industries.

minimum wage lowest wage legally allowed to be paid to workers.

mixed economies the mixture of free-market and command-and-control methods of resource allocation that characterize modern economies.

models simplified versions of reality that emphasize features central to answering the questions we ask of them.

monetarism school of thought that emphasizes the importance of the quantity of money in the economy and a rule for monetary policy; associated with economist Milton Friedman.

monetary base sum of currency in circulation plus bank reserves.

money a medium of exchange that removes the need for barter; also a measure of value and a way to store value over time; used to buy and sell things.

money market the market where the determination of the interest rate is by the demand and supply of money.

money multiplier the amount by which a new deposit is multiplied to arrive at the actual increase in the money supply; maximum value is given by the deposit multiplier.

multiplier effect sequence of spending that takes the economy from one equilibrium to another.

N

national debt how much money the government owes.

natural rate of unemployment the minimum sustainable level of unemployment; associated with zero cyclical unemployment.

net domestic product (NDP) gross domestic product minus depreciation.

net exports exports minus imports.

net investment gross investment minus depreciation.

new growth theory emphasizes the importance of new ideas in generating economic growth, and of intellectual property rights in providing the profit incentive to generate those ideas.

nominal GDP GDP that is stated without adjusting for inflation.

nominal value a value that is not adjusted for inflation.

nontariff barriers any of a variety of actions other than tariffs that make importing more expensive or difficult.

normal goods demand for these goods varies directly with income.

normative having to do with behavioral norms, which are judgments as to what is good or bad.

North American Free Trade Agreement (NAFTA) trading bloc that includes the United States, Canada, and Mexico.

O

open economy an economy with no restrictions on economic interactions with other countries.

open market operations buying and selling of Treasury bonds and Treasury bills by the Fed; tool of monetary policy.

opportunity costs the value of the best alternative opportunity forgone.

output gap the amount by which full-employment GDP exceeds actual GDP.

output market the market where goods and services are bought and sold.

P

pay-as-you-go referring to Social Security, meaning that current workers pay for current retirees.

Personal Security Accounts savings accounts individuals own, but that they are forced to contribute to by the government.

Phillips curve a graphical representation of data from the 1960s in the United States that shows a curvilinear tradeoff between low unemployment and low inflation.

positive having to do with what is, was, or will be.

Prebisch-Singer thesis a thesis that states that developing countries will remain in poverty because the prices of their exports of commodities are doomed to decrease.

precautionary motive holding money to cover unforeseen needs or wants.

price ceiling a maximum price that can legally be charged for a good.

price floor (price support) minimum price guaranteed to producers by the government.

price gouging price increases in response to increased demand related to emergencies.

price level prices of goods and services in the aggregate.

price rule conducting monetary policy in order to keep price increases in basic commodities within a low range.

price signals help consumers decide how much to buy and help producers decide how much to sell; critical component of the price system, which guides the allocation of resources in a market economy.

producer price index (PPI) measures wholesale prices, which are prices paid by firms.

producer surplus producers' revenue minus production cost; graphically, market price minus supply.

the production effect when a higher price level causes firms to increase output, employing workers who are willing to work extra hours to the extent that they do not correctly anticipate inflation.

production possibilities frontier a model that shows the various combinations of two goods the economy is capable of producing.

progressive tax a tax that collects a higher percentage of high incomes than of low incomes.

property rights rights of ownership.

proportional tax a tax that collects the same percentage of high incomes as of low incomes.

purchasing power effect the effect of the price level on consumers' ability to buy goods and services.

purchasing power parity theory that prices would be the same around the world for easily tradeable items.

Q

quantity demanded the quantity that consumers will purchase at a given price.

quantity supplied the quantity that will be offered for sale at a given price.

quantity theory of money a theory based upon the equation of exchange; shows that the effect of a change in the money supply is a proportional change in the price level; assumes velocity and aggregate output remain constant.

quota quantity limit on imports.

R

rational expectations when we base our expectations upon the best information available to us.

real business cycle when GDP rises or falls in response to major events that cannot be foreseen.

real GDP the value of GDP after nominal GDP is adjusted for inflation.

real value a value that results from adjusting a nominal value for inflation.

recession a sustained decrease in real GDP.

recessionary gap shortfall in the aggregate expenditure function below that necessary to achieve a full-employment equilibrium; this gap might persist in the short run unless the government takes action.

recognition lag time before policymakers recognize that a problem exists.

regressive tax a tax that collects a higher percentage of low incomes than of high incomes.

rent controls a price ceiling applied to the price of rental housing.

required reserves bank reserves held to meet the Fed's reserve requirement; expressed as a percentage of deposits.

research aimed at creating new products or otherwise expanding the frontiers of knowledge and technology.

Rostow's stages of economic development a model that says that countries begin as traditional societies, pass through the preconditions for takeoff, the takeoff, the drive to maturity, and conclude their development with the stage of high mass consumption.

S

saving putting aside income for later use.

scarcity a situation in which there are too few resources to meet all human wants.

search costs the costs of finding something; rent controls increase search costs for rental housing.

seasonal unemployment unemployment that can be predicted to recur periodically, according to the time of year.

shortage the excess of quantity demanded over quantity supplied, which occurs when price is below equilibrium.

short run a period of time during which the economy transitions to the long run.

short-run aggregate supply tells how much output the economy will offer in the short run at each possible price level.

short-run macroeconomic equilibrium where the economy tends in the short run, given by the intersection of aggregate demand and short-run aggregate supply.

Smoot-Hawley Act legislation passed by the U.S. Congress in 1930, the Act raised tariffs so high that imports nearly ceased.

Social Security trust fund the buildup of Social Security tax revenues above what is paid out in benefits; kept in the form of government bonds.

social surplus the sum of consumer surplus and producer surplus.

specific human capital human capital that is specific to a particular firm or kind of job.

speculative motive money held because current investment opportunities are unattractive.

stabilization policy general strategies of fiscal policy government can use to manage aggregate demand in order to reduce economic fluctuations.

stagflation the combination of high inflation and unemployment.

sticky prices prices that are slow to adjust, usually in a downward direction.

sticky wages wages that are slow to adjust, usually in a downward direction.

store of value the function of money related to holding wealth.

strategic dumping dumping with the intention of driving the competition out of business.

structural rigidities impediments within the economy that slow adjustment to a long-run equilibrium.

structural unemployment unemployment caused by a mismatch between a person's human capital and that needed in the workplace.

substitutes something that takes the place of something else, such as one brand of cola for another.

supply relates the quantity of a good that will be offered for sale at each of various possible prices, over some period of time, *ceteris paribus*.

supply shock an unexpected event that is major enough to affect the overall economy.

supply-side deflation occurs when long-run aggregate supply shifts to the right. The result is a movement down the aggregate demand curve to a lower price level and higher full-employment output.

supply-side economists (supply siders) economists who emphasize incentives for productivity and economic growth, such as lower marginal tax rates and less regulation.

supply-side inflation occurs when long-run aggregate supply shifts to the left. The result is a movement up the aggregate demand curve to a higher price level and lower full-employment output.

surplus the excess of quantity supplied over quantity demanded, which occurs when price is above equilibrium.

T

tariff tax on imports.

tax base that which is taxed.

tax expenditures exemptions, deductions, exclusions, and credits that reduce tax revenue.

tax incidence identifies those who eventually wind up paying a tax.

tax multiplier − mpc/(1 − mpc); when multiplied by a change in taxation, gives the change in equilibrium GDP.

technological efficiency the greatest quantity of output for given inputs; likewise, for any given output, requires the least-cost production technique.

technology possible techniques of production.

"the dismal science" a name given to economics because of Thomas Robert Malthus's nineteenth-century predictions of mass starvation.

trade creation effect trade that would otherwise not take place; adds to efficiency; caused by lower trade barriers among members of a trading bloc.

trade deficit a negative balance on the merchandise trade account, given when the dollar value of imported goods exceeds the dollar value of exported goods.

trade diversion effect trade among members of a trading bloc that would more efficiently be conducted with other countries outside of the bloc.

trading bloc agreement among a group of countries that provides for lower trade barriers among its members than with the rest of the world.

transactions motive holding money to make purchases.

transfer payments the redistribution of income from one group to another; the redistribution of social surplus from one party to another; rent controls create transfer payments from landlords to tenants.

transitional economies countries such as Russia, Hungary, and Poland that are moving away from central planning to the free-market system.

U

underground economy market transactions that go unreported to government.

unemployment equilibrium a short-run equilibrium GDP that is less than full-employment GDP.

unemployment rate the ratio of the number of unemployed persons to the number of persons in the labor force.

unit of account a use of money that occurs when the value of one item is compared with the value of another in terms of monetary units.

V

value added the difference between revenue and the cost of purchased inputs.

value added tax (VAT) a form of consumption tax that collects the difference between what companies earn in revenues and what they pay out in previously taxed costs.

velocity of money the number of times a dollar changes hands in a year.

vertical equity value judgment as to how much more someone with more ability to pay should in fact pay.

voluntary export restraints an alternative to import quotas in which exporting countries agree to voluntarily limit their exports to the target country; leads to higher price received by exporting countries.

W

wealth effect the change in the fraction of current income spent caused by a price-level change affecting the real value of savings.

World Bank institution that was created to loan money to developing countries.

World Trade Organization (WTO) international organization formed to administer the General Agreement on Tariffs and Trade.

ANSWERS TO TEST YOURSELF

CHAPTER 1

1. False
2. False
3. True
4. False
5. True
6. b
7. c
8. a
9. a
10. b
11. d
12. c
13. a
14. b
15. c
16. c
17. b
18. d
19. b
20. d

CHAPTER 2

1. True
2. False
3. True
4. False
5. False
6. b
7. c
8. a
9. d
10. c
11. c
12. a
13. a
14. a
15. a
16. c
17. a
18. c
19. b
20. a

CHAPTER 3

1. False
2. False

3. True
4. False
5. True
6. d
7. d
8. a
9. a
10. d
11. c
12. b
13. c
14. c
15. c
16. b
17. c
18. c
19. c
20. c

CHAPTER 4

1. False
2. False
3. True
4. False
5. False
6. c
7. c
8. a
9. c
10. c
11. b
12. c
13. c
14. c
15. d
16. c
17. b
18. b
19. a
20. b
21. d

CHAPTER 5

1. True
2. False
3. False
4. False
5. False

6. c
7. b
8. a
9. a
10. b
11. b
12. d
13. b
14. c
15. c
16. d
17. d
18. d
19. c
20. d

CHAPTER 6

1. False
2. True
3. False
4. False
5. True
6. a
7. a
8. b
9. b
10. c
11. a
12. c
13. d
14. c
15. c
16. c
17. b
18. b
19. b
20. b

CHAPTER 7

1. False
2. False
3. False
4. False
5. True
6. d
7. b
8. b
9. d

10. d
11. c
12. d
13. c
14. c
15. b
16. b
17. c
18. b
19. a
20. c

CHAPTER 8

1. False
2. True
3. False
4. True
5. False
6. d
7. b
8. a
9. a
10. c
11. d
12. d
13. b
14. b
15. c
16. b
17. c
18. d
19. a
20. c

CHAPTER 9

1. True
2. False
3. True
4. True
5. True
6. d
7. b
8. a
9. d
10. a
11. a
12. b
13. c

14. c
15. b
16. b
17. c
18. a
19. d
20. b

CHAPTER 10

1. False
2. True
3. True
4. False
5. False
6. b
7. a
8. a
9. d
10. b
11. d
12. d
13. b
14. c
15. a
16. d
17. b
18. b
19. b
20. c

CHAPTER 11

1. True
2. False
3. False
4. False
5. False
6. c
7. c
8. d
9. d
10. c
11. d
12. a
13. a
14. d
15. d
16. c
17. c

18. a
19. d
20. b

CHAPTER 12

1. False
2. True
3. False
4. True
5. False
6. a
7. b
8. d
9. d
10. d
11. a
12. d
13. b
14. d
15. c
16. a
17. d
18. d
19. b
20. a

CHAPTER 13

1. False
2. False
3. False
4. True
5. True
6. d
7. b
8. a
9. d
10. d
11. d
12. b
13. c
14. a
15. b
16. c
17. d
18. a
19. c
20. a

CHAPTER 14

1. False
2. False
3. False
4. False
5. False
6. c
7. c
8. d
9. d
10. c
11. c
12. b
13. b
14. b
15. c
16. c
17. c
18. b
19. b
20. d

CHAPTER 15

1. False
2. False
3. True
4. True
5. True
6. b
7. b
8. a
9. c
10. b
11. d
12. a
13. a
14. a
15. a
16. d
17. d
18. b
19. b
20. b

CHAPTER 16

1. False
2. False
3. False
4. False
5. False
6. a
7. a
8. d
9. a
10. d
11. a
12. a
13. c
14. c
15. c
16. d
17. d
18. b
19. a
20. d

CHAPTER 17

1. False
2. False
3. False
4. True
5. False
6. d
7. c
8. a
9. c
10. a
11. d
12. a
13. b
14. c
15. b
16. d
17. d
18. d
19. c
20. b

SOLUTIONS TO EVEN-NUMBERED QUESTIONS AND PROBLEMS

CHAPTER 1

2. Examples of decisions you might have made at the margin in the last twenty-four hours include when to get out of bed, how much cereal to put in the cereal bowl, how much water or juice to drink, how fast to walk to get to class, and how extensively to take notes in class.

4. **a.** Macroeconomics, since it pertains to the whole economy.
b. Microeconomics, since it pertains to a particular industry.
c. Macroeconomics, since it pertains to the whole economy.
d. Macroeconomics, to the extent that it pertains to the whole economy.
e. Microeconomics, since it pertains to a particular industry.

6. The three types of economic systems are free-market economies, command-and-control economies, and mixed economies. All modern economies are mixed, including those of Canada, the United States, and Western Europe. In these countries, the mix tends more toward the free-market end of the spectrum than toward command and control. In all mixed economies, free markets play a prominent role, but so too does government.

8. The tax system promotes equity to the extent that it redistributes income from the rich to the poor. This increase in equity comes at the cost of reduced efficiency, however, because it means there is less of an incentive to get the education and to do the hard work required for a high income.

10. Farmers grow food in order to sell it. If some of the farmers decide to quit, the result would be higher prices that would prompt the remaining farmers to produce more output.

12. Government policy greatly influences what occurs in a mixed economy. Since government policy is strongly influenced by politics, economics is sometimes known as political economy.

14. Saying that movies are too violent is expressing an opinion that is based on normative judgments. How much is too much? The statement about movies would become positive if it was restated as, "Movies are more violent today than they used to be." The statement is positive whether or not it is true. Its accuracy might be determined, however, by defining what kinds of acts involve violence and counting how often those acts of violence occur in a selection of recent movies relative to a selection of older ones of the same general type.

16. **a.** If classes are spread throughout the day and evening, the same number of students could get by with fewer parking places than if classes are bunched together, such as in the morning.
b. If there is good bus service to and from campus, students have less need to drive and thus less need for parking places.

c. If students have higher incomes, they're more likely to own cars, which would tend to increase the campus's need for parking places.

CHAPTER 2

2. Management skills can overlap with entrepreneurship, but the two are different. Entrepreneurship involves creativity, putting together resources in new and unique ways. While management might include entrepreneurship, it might also be merely carrying out directions from higher levels of management, or organizing activities according to someone else's direction. Those latter aspects are not entrepreneurship.

4. **a.** Ten baseball bats.
b. Six baseball bats.

6. The graph you draw should have a horizontal axis labeled with one good and a vertical axis labeled with another good. The production possibilities frontier itself should be increasingly downwardly sloping as you travel along it from the vertical axis to the horizontal axis. To show general growth, draw another production possibilities frontier that is everywhere outside the first one you drew. This means that, wherever the economy started on the first production possibilities frontier, it can increase its production of either good without decreasing the production of the other. In the production possibilities frontier in question 4, general growth would occur if each of the numbers in the list were increased.

8. When used as a medium of exchange, money allows goods and services to be traded for one another. Money's use as a medium of exchange means that barter does not need to take place. Money is part of the circular flow as it travels (flows) in the opposite direction of resources, goods, and services, so as to pay for those resources, goods, and services.

10. **a.** No, consumers in the United States like to make their own choices between California wine and French wine. Those who choose French wine would be worse off if they were not allowed that option. When consumers buy French wine in preference to California wine, they are in effect saying that the opportunity cost of California wine is more than it is worth to them. Therefore, even though Californian winemakers would prefer consumers to buy California wine, the resources producers would need to use to replace the French wine have more value elsewhere in the economy.
b. Either for variety or because they like it better, some French consumers presumably do drink imported U.S. wine.

12. Absolute advantage means being able to produce a good with fewer resources than it would take someone else to produce it. In reality, people specialize according to their comparative advantages, which means that each individual must compare the opportunity cost of the alternative things that particular person could do. Likewise, a country would also specialize according to comparative advantage. It would produce something, but exactly what it produces would depend on its own alternative opportunities. It would choose to produce goods for which its opportunity costs are relatively low.

14. **a.** A country cannot produce outside its production possibilities frontier unless it acquires new resources or new technology. That's why the production possibilities frontier is called a "frontier."

   b. The purpose of trade is to expand consumption possibilities beyond the confines of what the country can produce. For this reason, a country that trades with other countries can be expected to consume at a point outside of its production possibilities frontier. The country would consume at a point on its frontier only if it did not trade.

16. **a.** $1Y$.

   b. $1X$.

   c. $2Y$.

   d. $1/2X$.

   Tryhard will produce good X, and Trynot will produce good Y. The reason is that Tryhard can produce good X at a lower opportunity cost than can Trynot, and Trynot can produce good Y at a lower opportunity cost than can Tryhard.

CHAPTER 3

2. Draw a graph with the horizontal axis labeled "hot dogs" and the vertical axis labeled with "$" or "price." The demand curve that you label "individual's demand" should be a downwardly sloping line. The demand curve that you label "market demand" should start at the same point on the vertical axis as the other demand curve, but should slope downward less steeply, and reach the horizontal axis at the quantity that is twice as much as the quantity at which the first demand curve intersects the horizontal axis.

4. Insurance lowers the cost to you if your house is hit by a hurricane. Because the price is lower, in accordance with the law of demand, you're willing to accept the potential for more hurricanes and are therefore more willing to build a house in hurricane-prone areas. To graph the demand for the new houses in hurricane-prone areas, the horizontal axis would be labeled with "new houses" and the vertical axis would be labeled with "price" or "$." A lower price causes a movement along the demand curve to a greater quantity of new houses demanded.

6. Examples of complementary goods include: pencil and paper, baseball and bat, personal computer and printer, postage stamp and envelope, sugar and cereal, and butter and bread. In each case, if the price of the complement for the good were to increase, the demand for the good itself would decrease. Conversely, if the price of the complement for the good were to decrease, the demand for the good itself would increase.

8. In response to Mr. Johnson's income reduction, his demand for normal goods would decrease and his demand for inferior goods would increase. The following goods are likely to be normal goods for Mr. Johnson: restaurant food, Tommy Hilfiger clothing, fresh vegetables, antique furniture, and tickets to pro football games. The following goods are likely to be inferior goods for Mr. Johnson: generic paper towels, Spam, used cars, and Ramen noodles. Home-brewed coffee would be a normal good for Mr. Johnson if he most prefers the way he makes it himself. Home-brewed coffee would be an inferior good for Mr. Johnson if he prefers coffee from restaurants or coffee shops.

10. There is a difference between a change in demand and change in the quantity demanded. If there is a change in demand, the entire demand curve shifts, showing a new quantity demanded for each possible price. If there is a change in the quantity demanded, the reason might be simply that the price has fallen or risen, which would cause the consumer to move from one point to another along the same demand curve. For movements along demand in response to price changes, the demand curve itself does not shift.

12. For each of the following, you would draw a supply curve with the quantity supplied on the horizontal axis and price or $ on the vertical axis. The supply curve would slope upward to the right. If the supply curve increases, that means that the curve itself is shifted to the right. If the supply curve decreases, the curve is shifted to the left.

   a. Supply increases.

   b. Supply decreases.

   c. Supply decreases.

   d. Supply increases.

14. When the market clears, the quantity demanded just equals the quantity supplied. There is no surplus or shortage. This situation occurs when the market is in equilibrium. If there is a surplus or shortage, the price tends to change until it reaches that equilibrium. For example, if there is a shortage, there are not enough goods to go around to all of the consumers who want them, and sellers would be inclined to raise their prices. If there is a surplus, sellers have more than they can sell at the current price, and so lower their prices in order to sell more. At equilibrium, when quantity demanded equals quantity supplied, the market clears and price has no tendency to change.

16. A shortage results from a price that is below the equilibrium price. At that low price, consumers want to buy more than producers are willing to sell. In response, producers raise their prices.

18. If the market starts at equilibrium and demand increases, the market would experience a shortage if price does not rise. However, the market forces the price to rise to a new equilibrium.

20. You should have drawn two graphs, labeling the horizontal axis on each as "quantity" and the vertical axis on each as "price" or "$." Also, on each graph, you should have drawn a downward-sloping demand curve and an upward-sloping supply curve. On the first graph, draw another demand curve that has shifted only a little bit to the left and another supply curve that has shifted quite a bit to the right. If you compare the market equilibrium from the second set of supply and demand curves to the first set of curves you drew, you'll find that the equilibrium price and quantity have both increased. The reason is that the change in supply has dominated the change in demand. On the second graph, draw another demand curve that has shifted a large amount to the left and another supply curve that has shifted only a little bit to the right. In this case, you'll find that the equilibrium price and quantity have both fallen because the change in demand has dominated the change in supply.

CHAPTER 4

2. This answer is likely to vary from person to person. For example, it might have been a new car that you are very happy with, or a really great apartment that you rented at a low price. The difference between what you would have been willing to pay in the abstract and the price that you actually did pay would determine the amount of consumer surplus that you receive.

4. Yes, in the absence of market failures, which will be discussed later in the book, the market-equilibrium output is efficient. For each unit sold, the value to consumers equals or exceeds the price, which in turn equals or exceeds the cost of producing it. For any output above the market equilibrium, the cost of producing it would exceed its value to consumers, and so consumers would not buy it and firms would not choose to produce it.

6. A country will import a good when the world price of that good is less than the country's price would have been without trade. The result will be a lower price within the country after trade, which causes producers in the country to cut back on their output. The lower price moves them down their supply curve, but normally not so far down that they would produce nothing at all. The country as a whole will gain from trade because the trade increases consumer surplus more than it reduces producer surplus. To show this result graphically, label the horizontal axis with the quantity of some good and the vertical axis with its price, or with a $. Draw a downwardly sloping demand curve and an upwardly sloping supply curve to represent the domestic market. Then add a world price that is lower than what would have been the market-equilibrium price in the absence of imports.

The quantity actually consumed will be given by the point on the demand curve at the new lower price. The quantity produced in the domestic market will be given by the point on the supply curve at that same lower price. Producer surplus is given by the triangular area below the world price and above the domestic supply curve. Consumer surplus is given by the triangular area above the world price and below the market-demand curve. Note that the sum of these two areas is larger than the sum of the producer and consumer surplus that would occur at the higher price in the absence of trade.

8. For the price ceiling to have an effect, it must be set below the market-equilibrium price. In your first graph, you're instructed to show a ceiling price above the market-equilibrium price and interpret the result. The interpretation is that the ceiling price would be ignored. Anyone who tried to sell at that ceiling price would be undercut by other suppliers willing to sell at a lower price. The price would try to drop to the market equilibrium and there would be nothing to keep it from doing so. Therefore, the market would move to the market-equilibrium price. In your second graph, you're instructed to show a ceiling price that is below the market-equilibrium price and interpret that result. The interpretation is that the ceiling price would prevent price from rising to the market equilibrium, and for that reason would lead to a shortage in which the quantity demanded is greater than the quantity supplied.

10. Ticket scalping is efficient in that it makes sure the tickets go to those who are willing to pay the most for them. However, this may seem inequitable to people who get up early to stand in line for good seats, only to find them already gone because tickets for the best seats were purchased in bulk by the ticket scalpers.

12. Some inefficiencies of rent controls are: some people cannot find apartments who are willing to pay more than those who do find them, people waste time looking for apartments, apartments are not properly maintained, and too few apartments are offered for rent.

14. Price floors decrease consumer surplus because they increase the prices consumers pay and decrease the quantities that they purchase.

16. The minimum wage is a price floor, because it sets a lower bound on what wages employers are allowed to pay.

18. A black market is one that is illegal. When prices are held down, there'll be some consumers unable to buy at the controlled price. It is in the interest of these consumers and producers to break the law and make a deal at a higher price. Such deals are illegal and therefore would be part of the black market. In the case of price supports, however, producers are normally able to sell as much as they want to at the artificially high price, with the government being the buyer of what would otherwise be a surplus. For this reason, producers have no excess production and thus no incentive to undercut the support price by engaging in black market activities.

CHAPTER 5

2. The macro goals are not mentioned explicitly in the Constitution, but the phrase "life, liberty, and the pursuit of happiness" could be interpreted to include the prosperity implied by the achievement of the goals of price stability, high employment, and economic growth.

4. Excluding the value of intermediate goods is necessary to avoid counting the value of intermediate goods twice, which would inflate the value of GDP. Their value is included in the value of final goods.

6. Traczania's GDP = $150 + $55 + $75 + $20 − $25 = $275. Neither net investment nor government transfer payments should appear in the calculation of GDP.

8. No, household production is excluded from GDP since it does not have an explicit market value.

10. Since the value of scrap lumber is assumed to be zero, the market value of the birdhouses, $8,000, equals the value added produced by Mr. Jones.

12. The real value of GDP is computed in order to adjust the nominal value for price changes. Real GDP is a better measure of the change in the value of goods and services produced by the economy when there are price changes. If there were no price changes, real GDP and nominal GDP would be equal.

14. Your graph should label the horizontal axis "time" and the vertical axis "real GDP." The curve that shows the business cycle looks like a roller coaster tilted upward. The rising part shows the expansion, the top point shows the peak, the downward-sloping part shows the recession, and the bottom point shows the trough. The upward tilt reflects the upward trend in real GDP.

CHAPTER 6

2. Persons under age 16 are minors, discouraged from working because of the desire of society to have them finish their education. Few of them work, so excluding them from the labor force does not impair the accuracy of the data. Adults over age 65 may or may not be retired, and so many of them will be working. Excluding them from the labor force data would result in inaccuracies.

4. Labor force participation rate = (employed + unemployed)/Adult population; you should poll your classmates about their labor force participation in order to answer the second part of the question.

6. **a.** 9.7 percent in 1982.
   b. 4.0 percent in 2000.
   c. The data show a downward trend in the unemployment rate, interrupted by periodic upward movements, such as during the recession in the early 1990s and in 2001.

8. Worklandia's labor force participation rate equals 73 percent. The unemployment rate is 3 percent.

10. Human capital is a critical factor in employment. For example, to find a job as an airline pilot, a person must know how to fly an airplane. People without human capital or with obsolete human capital will have difficulty in finding and keeping a job.

12. A strong work ethic makes people less willing to stay unemployed. People will be more productive, other things equal. They will begin working earlier in life, and if they become unemployed, they will strive to minimize the period of time between jobs. Countries with weak work ethics are less productive. An argument could be made that too strong a work ethic focuses people too much on work, causing them to ignore other values. For example, some critics of the strong American work ethic maintain that children are harmed by parents spending too much time at work. Other arguments against the work ethic could be made, but they are always normative arguments calling for a value judgment.

14. Full employment occurs when the country achieves the natural rate of unemployment, which is currently thought to be 4 to 5 percent. Thus, an employment rate of 95 or 96 percent represents full employment. As the natural rate of unemployment has changed over time, so has the threshold for full employment. When the natural rate decreases, the full-employment percentage will become larger; when the natural rate increases, the full-employment percentage will become smaller.

CHAPTER 7

2. Inflation rates vary markedly from country to country. There is no reason for other countries' inflation rates to be the same as the inflation rate in the United States. For example, Japan has recently experienced mild deflation, while the United States experienced low inflation, and some other countries experienced high inflation.

4. The overall inflation rate is influenced by food and energy prices, while the core inflation rate excludes those prices. In this case, food and energy prices are rising more than other prices. The core inflation rate is often considered to be a more accurate reflection of inflation because food and energy prices are more volatile than prices in general.

6. Unanticipated inflation catches people by surprise, so they are less able to plan for unanticipated inflation. When inflation is planned for, people can make arrangements to adjust wage agreements, loan agreements, and other contracts for the effects of inflation.

8. The base period is the point of reference to which other time periods are compared. The index is set to 100 during the base period. Any particular value of the CPI can be compared to the base period by noting the difference between that value and the base period value of 100.

10. The value of the price index is 183: $(2 \times 8 + 1 \times 7 + 3 \times 3)/(1 \times 8 + .5 \times 7 + 2 \times 3) \times 100 = 32/17.5 \times 100 = 183$. The index says that prices are 83 percent higher than in the base year.

12. Johnson's nominal income is 25 percent higher than three years ago, computed as $(125 − 100)/100 = 25/100 = 25$

percent. The price index shows that prices have risen 16.7 percent, computed as $(175 - 150)/150 = 25/150 = 16.7$ percent. Since Johnson's nominal income has risen by more than the price index, his real income is higher than three years ago. Alternatively, we can compute Johnson's real income three years ago using the formula that says real income equals nominal income divided by the price index, computed as $100/150$ (multiplied by 100) = $66.67. Johnson's current real income equals $125/175 (multiplied by 100) = $71.43.

14. Real GDP = Nominal GDP/Price index × 100: $1,000/125 (multiplied by 100) = $800.

CHAPTER 8

2. According to the Phillips curve, inflation and unemployment are inversely related. When you draw the Phillips curve, place "unemployment" on the horizontal axis and "inflation" on the vertical axis. Then draw a downward-sloping line that is inwardly bowed. The Phillips curve fit the data nicely in the 1960s. Since then, however, there has been no obvious Phillips curve.

4. Actual GDP and full-employment GDP are not equal unless the economy is at a full-employment equilibrium.

6. Full employment equals 100 percent minus the natural rate of unemployment. The GDP that is produced when the economy is at full employment is termed full-employment GDP. Long-run aggregate supply is vertical at this amount of output.

8. In the long run, the price level does not matter. For example, there was once penny candy and stores that sold many items for nickels or dimes. Those prices have gone up, but so too have incomes, which means that people can still afford to buy the candy or the other items. The difference is just that the prices are higher to reflect higher incomes. In short, the amount of money people have in the aggregate doesn't affect the quantities they buy in the long run, only the prices that they pay.

10. Your graph should show real GDP on the horizontal axis and the price level on the vertical axis. The long-run aggregate supply curve should be vertical at the full-employment GDP. The aggregate demand curve should slope downward and intersect the long-run aggregate supply curve. The long-run macro equilibrium occurs at this point of intersection, which is characterized by no tendency for either price or aggregate output to change.

12. Use the same graph of aggregate demand and aggregate supply that you used in question 10 or question 11. To illustrate overheating, draw another aggregate demand curve that is to the right of the first one. That shift in aggregate demand might be caused by increased government spending, for example. The economy's response would be a higher price level as it moves from one point of macro equilibrium to the next.

14. On each of your graphs, the horizontal axis should be labeled as real GDP and the vertical axis labeled as the price level. On both graphs, start with the long-run macro equilibrium, given by the intersection of aggregate demand and long-run aggregate supply. To show demand-side deflation, draw a second aggregate demand curve that is to the left of the first one and intersects long-run aggregate supply at a lower price level. To show supply-side deflation, draw a second long-run aggregate supply curve that is to the right of the first one and intersects aggregate demand at a lower price level. Demand-side deflation and supply-side deflation might occur together if there is a technological advance and, simultaneously, less spending by consumers in response to concerns over the economy or levels of personal debt.

CHAPTER 9

2. Label the horizontal axis as "real GDP" and the vertical axis as the "price level." Draw a vertical long-run aggregate supply curve at full-employment GDP. Draw a short-run aggregate supply curve that curves upward across long-run aggregate supply and then becomes nearly vertical just past long-run aggregate supply. Draw a downwardly sloping aggregate demand curve that intersects the short-run aggregate supply curve prior to it intersecting the long-run aggregate supply curve. The intersection of aggregate demand and short-run aggregate supply is the unemployment equilibrium. An expansionary fiscal policy that shifts aggregate demand to the right can potentially eliminate the unemployment equilibrium. The unemployment equilibrium would be gone if aggregate demand were to intersect short-run aggregate supply at the same point short-run aggregate supply intersects long-run aggregate supply.

4. The three fiscal policy lags are the recognition lag, the action lag, and the implementation lag. The recognition lag is the time it takes for policymakers to recognize that the problem exists. The action lag is the amount of time it takes them to actually make a policy to address the problem. The implementation lag is the time it takes for the policy to be implemented, such as actually hiring the workers and beginning the project.

6. When the economy is at full employment, there is no reason for fiscal policy to be either expansionary or contractionary. For this reason, Keynesian economists suggest that the full-employment budget be balanced.

8. The national debt is the sum of the federal government's past budget deficits and surpluses. The result is a debt because the deficits have far exceeded the surpluses. This debt is mostly owed to the American public.

10. Structural rigidities represent features of the economy that prevent rapid adjustment of wages and prices. For example, if government were to increase spending in one segment of the economy, it might take awhile for the extra demand to diffuse to other sectors. In the meantime, wages and prices in the sector where the new spending occurs might be forced higher, even while there is unemployment in other sectors.

12. An actual price level below the expected price level occurs when aggregate demand intersects short-run aggregate supply somewhere to the left of long-run aggregate supply. This situation is known as an unemployment equilibrium. In the absence of government action, the unemployment equilibrium will persist until either the price level falls or workers revise their wage expectations downward. If fiscal policy shifts aggregate demand to the right, however, the economy will move up that short-run aggregate supply curve to a higher price level, perhaps one consistent with workers' expectations.

14. Cost–push inflation can reduce output to below the full-employment level, which might cause policymakers to want to take action to help out the economy. They might adopt an expansionary fiscal policy that shifts aggregate demand to the right, which would cause demand–pull inflation as it pulls the economy up the short-run aggregate supply curve. Workers might then adjust their own inflationary expectations upward, which would shift the short-run aggregate supply curve upward and cause cost–push inflation by pushing the economy up the aggregate demand curve. This process could continue in what is called an inflationary spiral. In the model of aggregate demand and aggregate supply, the spiral would appear as an increase in aggregate demand, followed by an increase in short-run aggregate supply, followed by an increase in aggregate demand, and so forth. The short-run equilibrium, representing the intersection of aggregate demand and short-run aggregate supply, would move upward in a zigzag pattern over time.

CHAPTER 10

2. In the aggregate, national income consists of what is paid for output. The value of aggregate output is thus equal to the value of the aggregate income.

4. Autonomous spending is only the spending that would occur in the absence of any income. The amount of autonomous spending is likely to vary from one family to another, depending on the amounts the families have saved. Actual spending is likely to vary even more, since this will depend on induced spending in addition to autonomous spending. Induced spending is based on income, which for this reason is likely to differ quite a bit from one household to another.

6. Use the income–expenditure graphs to answer this question. Place "real GDP" on a horizontal axis and "expenditure" on the vertical axis. Draw a 45-degree line that exactly splits the difference between the two axes. Starting at a point on the vertical axis, draw an upward-sloping line that crosses over the 45-degree line. Label this line as the aggregate expenditure function and label the point at which it crosses the 45-degree line as the unemployment equilibrium. To show that this point you have labeled unemployment equilibrium is indeed an unemployment equilibrium, draw a vertical line downward to the horizontal axis. Label

the point you reach on the horizontal axis as actual GDP. To the right of actual GDP, mark another point as full-employment GDP. Because full-employment GDP exceeds actual GDP, the point that you marked as the unemployment equilibrium is correctly labeled. To achieve full employment, fiscal policy would need to shift the aggregate expenditure function upward until it crosses the 45-degree line at a point directly above full-employment GDP. The amount of the required upward shift is the recessionary gap. It is the shortfall in aggregate expenditure below that which is necessary to achieve the full-employment GDP.

8. The sum of the marginal propensity to consume and the marginal propensity to save equals one to the extent that all income must either be spent or not spent. Money that is spent represents consumption and money that is not spent represents savings. Your own personal marginal propensity to consume can be found by imagining what you would do if you found some money, such as $100. If you would save $10 of it and spend $90, then your marginal propensity to consume would be 0.9.

10. **a.** The answer is found by multiplying $1 trillion by the expenditure multiplier, which equals 1/(1-mpc). In this example, the expenditure multiplier equals 1/0.4, or 2.5. The expenditure equilibrium for this economy is thus $2.5 trillion.

   b. To increase the expenditure equilibrium by $1 trillion, the change in autonomous spending multiplied by 2.5 must equal $1 trillion. To find this amount, divide 2.5 into $1 trillion. Doing so reveals the amount of autonomous spending necessary is $400 billion.

12. A decrease in the marginal propensity to save would increase the marginal propensity to consume and thus also increase the expenditure multiplier. Assuming unemployed resources and a constant price level, the higher multiplier would cause a larger equilibrium GDP as autonomous spending is multiplied by this multiplier.

14. The paradox of thrift occurs when people collectively save a larger fraction of their incomes, but see their total savings go down because their incomes fall. The result is less total spending at any given price level, and a shift to the left in aggregate demand. From the perspective of today, if the price level is downwardly sticky and we take a short-run perspective, we might not want to see people increase their marginal propensity to save. However, if we take a long-run perspective or if prices are not downwardly sticky, we do not need to worry about people increasing their propensity to save.

CHAPTER 11

2. Your pie chart showing sources of revenue for state and local governments should emphasize property taxes, sales taxes, and revenue sharing from the federal government. Many other taxes and charges are also used.

4. The average tax rate is simply the amount paid in taxes divided by the amount earned. In Sue's case, her average

tax rate equals $10,000 divided by $100,000, which is 10 percent.

6. What seems fair from one person's point of view might not seem fair from another's. There are many examples, and applying principles of tax equity will depend upon the example chosen. One example would be the personal income tax evaluated from the point of view of horizontal equity. The principle of horizontal equity is to tax people in equal circumstances an equal amount. Yet figuring out what equal circumstances actually are might be quite difficult. The couple with a family to support might think it is equitable to have deductions for the children that the couple must support. However, a childless couple might find it inequitable to be made to pay more in taxes than the couple with a family, merely because the childless couple could not have, or chose not to have, children.

8. A tax on football tickets would seem to satisfy the benefit principle of taxation, since those who go to football games benefit from the student athletics program. By associating the price of the program with the price of tickets, it might also promote efficient choice. Taxing football tickets would only be progressive, however, if college football attendance increased more than in proportion to increases in income. Taxing textbooks or vending machine drinks would not appear to satisfy any principle of tax equity, although such taxes might be relatively efficient in that they would be hard to escape. While taxing textbooks might be the hardest tax for a student to escape, taxing textbooks is also the most likely to be regressive, particularly if the tax is not covered by financial aid.

10. A payroll tax is a tax on paychecks workers receive for the jobs they do. In contrast, an income tax is levied on all income, although there are likely to be deductions allowed.

12. It is difficult to aid the poor without providing disincentives to work, so long as the aid depends upon a person having little or no income. To the extent that aid is reduced as income increases, the aid acts as a drag on that income and reduces the incentive to earn it. In addition, to pay for the many aid programs that make up the social safety net, government must resort to taxation. Taxes reduce the amount of income people get to keep for themselves, and so also reduce work incentives.

14. Horizontal equity means that people in equal circumstances should pay equal taxes. Vertical equity refers to how much more taxes a person should pay when that person has a greater ability to pay than do other taxpayers. Adjusting the tax system to account for horizontal equity is highly contentious. It wastes a lot of time and effort of those making laws. Probably more importantly, the resulting complicated tax system requires a large amount of paperwork and recordkeeping on the part of taxpayers. This waste of taxpayer time and effort, along with the associated expenses for tax lawyers and tax accountants, could be mostly eliminated and overall taxes reduced if the tax code were simplified and did not try to achieve hori-

zontal equity. Following the route of tax simplification might be considered to be tax reform by some, but would not be considered tax reform by those placing a greater emphasis on horizontal equity. Another possibility for tax reform would be to replace the personal income tax with a consumption tax, such as a sales tax or a value added tax. A consumption tax might be more efficient than the income tax, but would not allow the same possibilities for detailed fine-tuning in order to achieve either horizontal or vertical equity.

CHAPTER 12

2. When a recession first hits, firms reduce the production of goods, but are slow to lay off workers. The reason is that there are costs associated with layoffs and with rehiring workers when the economy improves. Many firms would prefer to retain their workers until it becomes clear that it is not economical to do so. As a result, with the reduction in output greater than the reduction in labor, output per worker falls. This effect is reversed when the economy begins to improve. Firms will be slow to increase their use of labor until they are sure that the economic rebound will continue. Output rises more than proportionally to the use of labor, and so labor productivity rises.

4. a. When Microsoft was started, the success of the firm would have required capital formation in computers and other office equipment.

   b. When Wal-Mart was started, store buildings, fixtures, and merchandise were examples of the capital formation that occurred.

   c. The start of Starbucks Coffee shops required store space, display cases, and coffee machines.

   d. When Motown Records started, various pieces of recording equipment, billing equipment, and office equipment would have been needed.

6. The supply of saving slopes upward because its slope represents a positive relationship between the quantity saved and the real interest rate. People save more when they get paid more to do so. Likewise, businesses invest more when it costs them less to obtain loans. For this reason, investment demand shows an inverse relationship between the real interest rate and the amount invested. When the quantity of saving supplied just equals the quantity of investment demanded, this market is at an equilibrium.

8. You should label the horizontal axis of your graph as "saving and investment." The vertical axis should be labeled as the "real interest rate." Draw a downward-sloping demand curve and an upward-sloping supply curve. The point of intersection is the initial equilibrium. To show an increase in investment demand, draw a second demand curve that's further out than the first. The new equilibrium will then occur at a higher real interest rate and a greater amount of saving and investment. If the supply of saving were to also shift to the right, it could potentially lower the

real interest rate back to what it was originally, or even to below what it was originally.

10. You should label the horizontal axis of your graph as "saving and investment." The vertical axis should be labeled as the "real interest rate." Draw a downward-sloping demand curve and an upward-sloping supply curve. The point of intersection is the initial equilibrium. To show the effect of taxing interest on saving, draw a second supply curve that is above and to the left of the first one. The supply curve has shifted because consumers now require a higher interest rate prior to the tax in order to pay the tax due on that interest. Observe that the equilibrium real interest rate has risen as a result of the tax, causing the equilibrium quantity of saving and investment to fall.

12. During the war, the economy reduced the production of civilian goods in favor of war goods. There were relatively few consumer goods available to purchase. At the same time, employment was high, as were incomes, as war production reduced unemployment. The combination of high incomes and few items to purchase led people to save more. Unless the war on terrorism results in shortages of consumer goods, an increase in the saving rate is unlikely.

14. Both focus on the causes of economic growth, but with different emphases. New growth theory emphasizes the role of technology in promoting growth, while supply-side economics emphasizes lower tax rates and less government regulation as the keys to growth. New growth theory also recognizes that technological improvements are encouraged when property rights (in the form of monopoly power) are granted to developers of new technologies.

16. The Laffer curve shows the dangers of setting tax rates too high. It might be the case that a tax would bring in more revenue if its rate was lower. For example, some argue that reductions in the capital gains tax rate might increase revenue from that tax. To graph this case, place the capital gains tax rate on the horizontal axis and note that it can go from zero to 100 percent. Place the amount of revenue collected on the vertical axis. Your curve should be hump-shaped, starting at zero on the horizontal axis, then rising to a maximum, before falling back to zero when you reach 100 percent on the horizontal axis. The argument that reducing the capital gains tax rate would lead to more revenue from the tax is equivalent to saying that we are on the downward-sloping portion of that Laffer curve.

CHAPTER 13

2. Once the inefficiencies of barter become apparent we might expect that people will spontaneously decide to adopt some commodity as money. The more people on the island the more likely the limitations of barter will be obvious because there will be more opportunities for exchange that would be facilitated by money. Barter might work for a group that expects to soon be rescued, but if they expect to remain on the island for a long time, money is likely to be adopted sooner. What form the money will take will depend on what is available. For example, if coconuts grow on the island, they might be used as money.

4. The balance sheet you create will depend on your personal circumstances. For example, if you own a car, computer, and television, and have a bank account balance, then these items would appear as assets. If you owe an unpaid balance on the car, that amount would appear as a liability, along with unpaid balances on your credit card, and other debts you owe. Decide which assets can easily be converted into consumption (liquid assets) and divide by your total assets. To see the value of liquidity, suppose you had $20,000 in cash in 2000, and your friend had $20,000 in the stock market. If those assets remain untouched, today you would still have $20,000 in assets, while your friend would have considerably less if the market value of your friend's stock declined.

6. Reserves can be kept as cash in the vault or as deposits at a Federal Reserve bank. Because of security concerns, banks must be concerned about keeping too much vault cash. However, vault cash is needed to satisfy customer withdrawals.

8. The Fed's functions and your interactions with the Fed would include:

   a. Banker's bank: Your bank's reserves might be deposited into an account at the Fed.

   b. Lender of last resort: Your bank might have outstanding discount loans from the Fed.

   c. Supervises banks: Your bank would have to be knowledgeable about and comply with Fed regulations.

   d. Issues currency: Your bank would obtain new currency supplies from your district Federal Reserve bank.

   e. Clears checks: Your bank might send checks deposited into the bank to the Fed for payment.

10. It is impossible for the Fed to control the money supply because the money supply depends not only on the Fed's actions, but also the behavior of the public and banks. The public controls how much money it wishes to hold as deposits and how much as currency. Banks control the amount of bank loans. Both of these affect the money multiplier, and hence the money supply.

12. The deposit multiplier assumes that all new deposits in the banking system are loaned out to the maximum extent. The result is that the deposit multiplier is used to compute the maximum expansion in the money supply. The money multiplier allows for banks to hold excess reserves, and the public to hold currency rather than bank deposits. This characteristic of the money multiplier means its value will be less than the value of the deposit multiplier.

14. The federal funds rate is the interest rate on overnight loans of bank reserves banks borrow from other banks. The discount rate is the interest rate on reserves that

banks borrow from the Fed. There is no reason for these interest rates to be equal since the first is determined by the demand and supply of federal funds, while the second is set by the Fed.

CHAPTER 14

2. Bringing down high inflation calls for slowing down the economy, which could lead to a recession. The two recessions in the early 1980s are believed to have occurred in response to Fed efforts to fight the high inflation of the late 1970s. Tradeoffs in monetary policy exist because in order to achieve one goal another goal may have to be sacrificed. For example, to promote high employment, an expansionary monetary policy may risk an increase in inflation.

4. The monetary policy instruments are the money supply and interest rates. The choice of instrument depends on the Fed's assessment of which instrument will most contribute to the achievement of the goals of monetary policy.

6. The interest rate is the opportunity cost of holding money, and is the "price" in that sense. When the interest rate is high, people will reduce their money holdings in order to buy assets that pay interest. When the interest rate is low, the opportunity cost of holding money is reduced, and so people will hold more money and less assets that pay interest.

8. A money market equilibrium occurs when the quantity demanded and the quantity supplied of money are equal. Label the horizontal axis "quantity of money" and the vertical axis "interest rate." Your graph should show a downward-sloping demand curve for money and a vertical money supply curve. The equilibrium occurs at the intersection of the two curves.

10. Both money and bonds are highly liquid assets. The difference is that money pays no interest, while bonds do. When the interest rate is high, people will economize on their holdings of money in order to own bonds.

12. The price level equals $4, found by substituting into the equation of exchange and solving for the price level. If the money supply were $600, then the price level would be $12.

14. Monetarism is a school of thought associated with economist Milton Friedman. Its foundation is the quantity theory of money, which is expressed through the equation of exchange: $M \times V = P \times Q$. A monetary policy that follows monetarism will expand the money supply at a steady rate of about 2 to 3 percent a year. This recommendation follows from the idea that the economy will, over the long run, show an increase in aggregate output of 2 to 3 percent a year, and so the money supply should grow to match the increased output.

16. Keynesians view an increase in the money supply as leading to a lower interest rate, which causes borrowing to increase. When people spend the borrowed money nominal GDP increases.

18. The federal funds rate is the interest rate on reserves that banks borrow from other banks. The Fed targets the federal funds rate primarily by conducting open market operations that affect the federal funds rate. A lower federal funds rate is associated with a looser monetary policy, while a higher rate is associated with a tighter policy.

CHAPTER 15

2. The capital account records the value of investment flows across international borders. In the capital account of the United States, capital inflows represent investment money that comes into the United States, such as to purchase land, factories, stock, or government securities. Capital outflows represent investment money that goes from the United States into other countries, such as to purchase land, factories, or foreign securities. The balance on the capital account is positive, which offsets the negative balance on the current account.

4. For the United States to run a trade deficit means that it imports more goods than it exports, where goods are measured in dollars according to their market values. The trade deficit is more limited than the current account deficit, which includes the value of not only goods, but also of services, incomes, and transfers.

6. If Middle-Eastern investors decide to sell their U.S. investments and use the proceeds to buy investments in other countries, they would be acquiring dollars from their sales that they would wish to convert to the currencies of other countries so that they could buy assets in those countries. Supposing these other countries are Middle-Eastern countries, then the dollar would depreciate relative to the Middle-Eastern currencies. Those Middle Easterners who did not sell their American assets would find that the value of those assets in terms of the Middle-Eastern currencies would be less after the depreciation of the dollar.

8. Depreciation of a currency occurs when there is less demand for it by holders of other currencies or when the holders of the currency increase the amount they offer for sale in exchange for other currencies. In terms of a supply and demand graph—measuring the quantity of the currency on the horizontal axis and the price of that currency in terms of other currencies on the vertical axis—depreciation would occur if demand were to shift to the left or supply were to shift to the right. If the currency depreciates, it will buy less in terms of foreign goods and services, which causes the quantity of goods and services imported to decrease. Likewise, goods and services that are priced in the country's currency will seem cheaper to holders of other countries' currencies. For this reason, exports would increase.

10. In considering the location of a new manufacturing plant, a company must consider the relative production costs in various countries, which will depend upon both exchange rates and the transportation costs from production facilities

to the products' markets. The market for the luxurious Mercedes-Benz M-class sport utility vehicle includes a large proportion of people with high incomes. The market for the smaller and less expensive Volkswagen Beetle would not be similarly skewed toward those with higher incomes. Since incomes in Mexico are lower than incomes in the United States, it is not surprising that the Beetle has been popular in Mexico, more so than the Mercedes-Benz SUV.

12. **a.** Specializing according to comparative advantage, country A would produce good *Y* and country B would produce good *X*. The reason is that good *Y* has a lower opportunity cost in country A (opportunity cost of 1*X*) than in B (opportunity cost of 2*X*). By the same token, good *X* has a lower opportunity cost in country B (opportunity cost of 1/2*Y*) than in country A (opportunity cost of 1*Y*).

     b. Whichever country you are trade minister for, you would help your country by recommending trading with the other country. By doing so, your country can consume more than it was previously able to consume.

14. Since the opportunity cost of a bottle of wine in Alpania is one yard of cloth, and since the opportunity cost of one bottle of wine in Betalia is two yards of cloth, Alphania has the comparative advantage in wine production. Conversely, the opportunity cost of a yard of cloth in Betalia is only ½ bottle of wine, compared to an opportunity cost of one bottle of wine in Alphania. So Betalia has the comparative advantage in cloth production.

CHAPTER 16

2. The country will export the good. Domestic producers will increase the price within the country to match the world price, which means that domestic consumers will not consume as much as they would without trade. Domestic producers will continue to produce the quantity that domestic consumers demand at this new, higher price. Your graph should show the quantity of the good on the horizontal axis and its price on the vertical axis, with a downward-sloping demand curve by domestic consumers and an upward-sloping supply curve by domestic producers. The world price should be above what would have been the domestic equilibrium price in the absence of trade. At the world price, the quantity demanded by consumers is less than the quantity supplied by producers, with the difference going to exports.

4. An advantage of expanding the membership of NAFTA would be the trade creation effect, and a disadvantage would be the trade diversion effect. Other countries might want to join NAFTA in order to capture the benefits of trade. Because trade can be beneficial for all those involved, the United States and other countries can be expected to gain. However, some individuals and groups within the countries would lose and therefore be expected to oppose the expansion of NAFTA.

6. You're likely to find in your survey that people have very little idea as to the tariff rates that importers face. The reason is most likely that people do not pay tariffs directly, and for this reason do not see them when they make their purchases. Because tariffs are hidden within product prices, consumers tend to be oblivious to their existence.

8. Because either tariffs or quotas can have an equivalent effect, consumers have no particular reason to prefer one to the other.

10. Producers in exporting countries would like to charge as high of a price as possible, which leads them to prefer the voluntary export restraint that is simultaneously agreed to by many different exporting countries. Otherwise, these exporting countries would be in competition with one another and would drive the price of their exports lower.

12. The chapter listed a number of possible reasons to restrict imports, and you could choose any one of these reasons to critique. For example, you might critique using tariffs to punish countries that engage in dumping, because you might argue that those countries are only hurting themselves in that they will never capture the world markets for the products they are dumping. The effect of dumping in that case is just to give consumers in the importing country lower prices at the expense of the other countries' exporters. A counterargument might emphasize the harm to the domestic industry and the people involved in that industry.

14. You're asked to evaluate the national defense argument in several examples of your own choosing. Following are a few possibilities. For reasons of national defense, it's hard to argue against favoring domestic industry in the production of weaponry, the use of a country's own citizens as troops and commanders, and favoring a country's own industries for high-tech research. More questionable is whether a country should restrict the export of its technology that might be used against it someday, since restricting technology exports might encourage new technology to be developed in other countries where no export barriers exist. Some might argue that food, clothing, and all other necessities be produced domestically for reasons of national defense. However, unless it seems likely that an enemy will control all sources of production and that domestic stockpiles cannot be effectively held, the advantages of trade might outweigh any perceived defense needs.

CHAPTER 17

2. Problems include poverty, little infrastructure, poor life expectancy, and high population growth. These and other problems in the LDCs make life a struggle to survive for many people.

4. Answers will vary from one student to another. For example, students might wish to explain how incentives affect population growth, how markets promote economic development, or the role of property rights in development.

6. Rostow's five stages are: traditional society, preconditions for takeoff, takeoff, drive to maturity, and high mass consumption. The first stage is characterized by subsistence agriculture, the second by excess production and the need for transportation, the third by urbanization and investment, the fourth by economic diversification, and the fifth by the dominance of production of consumer goods and services. The model is criticized for not fitting the way that development occurs in some cases, and for not explaining how economies move from one stage to the next.

8. A farmer can raise and harvest more crops with unpaid labor provided by the family's children. Development could slow down population growth as people move to the city where children become viewed as more of an expense and less of a source of labor.

10. Student answers will vary depending on family background, religious beliefs, and other influences on personal preferences regarding family size. Some students will emphasize the benefits from having more children, while others will emphasize the costs.

12. Without clearly defined property rights, the uncertainty about who owns resources will inhibit investment and business formation. Clear property rights must be established through the legal system.

14. There is no one right answer to this question, but policy statements should include items relating to the value of the projects that will be financed by the loans, the ability of the country to repay a loan, and the need for the World Bank to rank loan applications using a consistent set of criteria. Since loan funds are limited in amount, not all projects can receive loans, and thus choices must be made.

INDEX

PHOTO CREDITS

Smart Graphs are short interactive graph exercises and problems that allow you to manipulate variables and shift curves based on an economic scenario. Students can assess their understanding of a concept before moving on. Below is the list of Smart Graphs to accompany *MACROECONOMICS: Explore & Apply*.

SMART GRAPH	FIGURE	TITLE
SG1	Figure 1A.1, 1A.2	Understanding Graphs
SG2	Figure 2.2	Production Possibilities Frontier: Understanding Opportunity Cost
SG3	Figure 2.11	Production Possibilities Frontier: Understanding Growth
SG4	Figure 3.9	Supply and Demand: Understanding Equilibrium
SG5	Figure 3.10	Supply and Demand: Understanding Shifts (I)
SG6	Figure 3.10	Supply and Demand: Understanding Shifts (II)
SG7	Figure 3.10	Supply and Demand: Understanding Shifts (III)
SG8	Figure 3.10	Supply and Demand: Understanding Shifts (IV)
SG9	Figure 4.5	Market Efficiency
SG10	Figure 8.6	Aggregate Supply and Aggregate Demand: Demand Side Inflation and Deflation
SG11	Figure 8.7	Aggregate Supply and Aggregate Demand: Supply Side Inflation and Deflation
SG12	Figure 9.7	Short-run Instability: The Slope of the Aggregate Supply Curve
SG13	Figure 9.12	Short-run Instability: The Inflationary Spiral
SG14	Figure 10.7	Aggregate Expenditures
SG15	Figure 12.3	Savings and Investment: The Equilibrium Interest Rate
SG16	Figure 14.9	The Money Market and Monetary Policy
SG17	Figure 14.10	Monetary Policy: The Liquidity Trap

EXPLORING GRAPHS

In order to understand economic concepts, it is important to practice and develop your skills in reading and interpreting graphs. Prentice Hall has developed two levels of interactive graphing tools to help you achieve these goals: Active Graphs and Smart Graphs. Go to the text Web site, www.prenhall.com/ayers, for access to these valuable interactive tools along with other important Active Study Guide Web resources.

Active Graphs are comprehensive interactive graph exercises and problems that require you to consider several key concepts in sequence. Below is a list of Active Graphs to accompany *MACROECONOMICS: Explore & Apply*. See the preceding page for a list of Smart Graphs.

ACTIVE GRAPH	FIGURE	TITLE
AG 1	Figures 1A.1, 1A.2	Constructing and working with graphs
AG 2	Figure 1A.3	Nonlinear relationships
AG 3	Figure 1A.4	The marginal principle
AG 4	Figure 1A.5	Curves, which way do they shift?
AG 5	Figure 1A.5	Shifting a curve
AG 6	Figure 2.1	Opportunity costs
AG 7	Figure 2.4	Scarcity and the production possibilities curve
AG 8	Table 2.2	Comparative advantage and specialization
AG 9	Figure 3.1	The demand curve and the law of demand
AG 10	Figure 3.4	The supply curve and the law of supply
AG 11	Figure 3.7	The market demand curve
AG 12	Figure 3.8	The market supply curve
AG 13	Figure 3.9	Market equilibrium
AG 14	Figure 4.2	The demand curve and consumer surplus
AG 15	Figure 4.4	The supply curve and producer surplus
AG 16	Figure 4.5	Market efficiency
AG 17	Figures 4.7, 4.8	The effect of imports and exports on social surplus
AG 18	Figure 4.9	Rent control
AG 19	Figure 4.10	Agricultural price supports
AG 20	Figure 4.11	Supply and demand for labor
AG 21	Definitions in text	Real vs. nominal

ACTIVE GRAPH	FIGURE	TITLE
AG 22	Figure 8.1	Introduction to the Phillips curve
AG 23	Figures 8.6, 8.7	Aggregate demand, aggregate supply, and inflation
AG 24	Figure 9.2	Shifts of aggregate demand and the classical aggregate supply curve
AG 25	Figure 9.8	Shifts of aggregate demand and the Keynesian aggregate supply curve
AG 26	Figure 10.6	The multiplier
AG 27	Text	Government spending and taxation
AG 28	Figures 10.9, 10.10	From income-expenditure to aggregate demand
AG 29	Definition in text	Crowding out in the long run
AG 30	Text	The investment decision
AG 31	Text	How banks create money
AG 32	Figure 14.2	Monetary policy
AG 33	Figure 14.3	The demand for money
AG 34	Figure 14.4	Interest rate determination
AG 35	Figure 14.5	Long-run money neutrality
AG 36	Table 14.4	The practice of monetary policy: A model of the reserve market
AG 37	Figure 15.7	The determination of exchange rates
AG 38	Definition in text	Fixing the exchange rate
AG 39	Table 15.3	The relationship between net exports and exchange rates
AG 40	Figures 16.5, 16.6	Quotas, voluntary export restraints, and tariffs
AG 41	Definition in text	Protectionist policies
AG 42	Figure 17.6	Subsidizing population growth